The Essential Guide to Dreamweaver CS4 with CSS, Ajax, and PHP

David Powers

friendsof

DESIGNER TO DESIGNER™

an Apress® company

The Essential Guide to Dreamweaver CS4 with CSS, Ajax, and PHP

Credits

Lead Editor
Ben Renow-Clarke

Production Editor
Kelly Winquist

Technical Reviewer
Tom Muck

Compositor
Molly Sharp

Editorial Board
Clay Andres, Steve Anglin, Mark Beckner,
Ewan Buckingham, Tony Campbell, Gary Cornell,
Jonathan Gennick, Michelle Lowman, Matthew Moodie,
Jeffrey Pepper, Frank Pohlmann, Ben Renow-Clarke,
Dominic Shakeshaft, Matt Wade, Tom Welsh

Proofreader
Patrick Vincent

Indexer
Julie Grady

Project Manager
Beth Christmas

Artist
April Milne

Copy Editors
Kim Wimpsett, Marilyn Smith

Interior and Cover Designer
Kurt Krames

Associate Production Director
Kari Brooks-Copony

Manufacturing Director
Tom Debolski

CONTENTS AT A GLANCE

CONTENTS

Chapter 7: Using Spry Dynamic Effects and Components 257

Chapter 10: Introducing the Basics of PHP 425

Chapter 11: Using PHP to Process a Form 459

Chapter 12: Reducing Your Workload with PHP Includes 503

Chapter 13: Preserving Design Integrity with Templates and InContext Editing 539

Chapter 14: Storing User Records in a Database 583

ABOUT THE AUTHOR

 **David Powers** is an Adobe Community Expert and Adobe Certified Instructor for Dreamweaver and author of a series of highly successful books on PHP, including *PHP Solutions: Dynamic Web Design Made Easy* (friends of ED, ISBN: 978-1-59059-731-6) and *PHP Object-Oriented Solutions* (friends of ED, ISBN: 978-1-4302-1011-5), as well as the Dreamweaver CS3 edition of this book. As a professional writer, he has been involved in electronic media for more than 30 years, first with BBC radio and television and more recently with the Internet. His clear writing style is valued not only in the English-speaking world; several of his books have been translated into Spanish and Polish.

What started as a mild interest in computing was transformed almost overnight into a passion, when David was posted to Japan in 1987 as BBC correspondent in Tokyo. With no corporate IT department just down the hallway, he was forced to learn how to fix everything himself. When not tinkering with the innards of his computer, he was reporting for BBC TV and radio on the rise and collapse of the Japanese bubble economy.

David has also translated several plays from Japanese. To relax, he enjoys nothing better than visiting his favorite sushi restaurant.

About the Technical Reviewer

Tom Muck is the coauthor of nine Adobe/Macromedia-related books. Tom also writes extensions for Dreamweaver, available at his site http://www.tom-muck.com. Tom is also the lead PHP and ColdFusion programmer for Cartweaver, the online shopping cart software package; is a founding member of Community MX; and has written more than 150 articles on PHP, ColdFusion, SQL, and related topics. Tom has also been an Adobe Community Expert in its various incarnations since 1999.

Tom is an extensibility expert focused on the integration of Adobe/Macromedia products with ColdFusion, PHP, ASP, and other languages, applications, and technologies. Tom was recognized for this expertise in 2000 when he received Macromedia's Best UltraDev Extension Award. He has also written numerous articles for magazines, journals, and websites and speaks at conferences on related subjects.

ACKNOWLEDGMENTS

Many people contributed to this book in a variety of ways. Some—like the production staff at Apress/friends of ED—were involved directly. I'd like to pay particular thanks to my editor, Ben Renow-Clarke, who gave me free rein to shape the book the way I wanted but always maintained a critical eye from the reader's perspective. Thanks, too, to Beth Christmas and Kelly Winquist for keeping the project running smoothly and on time.

I was delighted when Tom Muck, an acknowledged Dreamweaver expert, agreed to act as my technical reviewer again. He saved me from several embarrassing mistakes (any that remain are my responsibility alone), and his deep knowledge of Dreamweaver and other web technologies added valuable perspective throughout the book.

I'm also grateful to Devin Fernandez and Scott Fegette of Adobe, who gave me unparalleled access to the Dreamweaver development team and endured my rants and complaints with good humor when I didn't like some of the changes being made to my favorite web development program. Thanks for restoring the colored icons, guys. Well, that and everything else—this version is a stunner.

Others are probably totally unaware of the role they played in shaping this book, but it was nonetheless significant. I'm referring to participants in the friends of ED and Adobe online forums, who asked how to do certain things with Dreamweaver, JavaScript, or PHP. Many of their ideas have been woven into this new edition.

Finally, thank you for choosing my book.

INTRODUCTION

Dreamweaver isn't a difficult program to use, but it's difficult to use well. I have been using Dreamweaver on a daily basis for about nine years, pushing it to the limit and finding out its good points—and its bad ones, too. The user interface has changed considerably in Dreamweaver CS4, and the introduction of new features, such as Related Files and Live view, is likely to have a big impact on the way even long-term Dreamweaver users create web pages.

The idea of this book is to help you get the best out of Dreamweaver CS4, with particular emphasis on building dynamic web pages using Cascading Style Sheets (CSS), Spry—the Adobe implementation of Ajax—and other JavaScript frameworks, and the open source server-side technology PHP. But how can you get the best out of this book?

Who this book is for

I like to credit my readers with intelligence, so this book isn't "Dreamweaver CS4 for the Clueless" or "Dreamweaver CS4 for Complete Beginners." You don't need to be an expert, but you do need to have an inquiring mind. It doesn't teach the basics of web design, nor does it attempt to list every single feature in Dreamweaver CS4. The emphasis is on building modern, standards-compliant websites. If you're at home with the basics of HTML and CSS, then this book is for you. If you have never built a website before and don't know the difference between an <a> tag and your Aunt Jemima, you might find this book a bit of a struggle.

> In this edition, I use HTML to refer equally to Hypertext Markup Language and Extensible Hypertext Markup Language (XHTML). HTML 4.01 and XHTML 1.0 are essentially the same. The only difference is that XHTML 1.0 applies stricter rules in the way it is written (see http://www.w3.org/TR/xhtml1/#diffs for the details). All the code examples adhere to the rules of XHTML 1.0, the default setting in Dreamweaver CS4.

I frequently dive into Code view and expect you to roll up your sleeves and get to grips with the code. It's not coding for coding's sake; the idea is to adapt the code generated by

Dreamweaver to create websites that really work. I explain everything as I go along and steer clear of impenetrable jargon. As for CSS, you don't need to be a candidate for inclusion in the CSS Zen Garden (http://www.csszengarden.com), but you should understand the basic principles behind creating a style sheet.

What about Ajax and PHP? I don't assume any prior knowledge in these fields. Ajax comes in many different guises; this book concentrates mainly on Spry, the Adobe Ajax framework (code library) that is integrated into Dreamweaver CS4. Most Spry features are accessed through intuitive dialog boxes. However, Chapter 8 gets inside the code, exploring not only Spry, but the improved support in Dreamweaver CS4 for other JavaScript libraries, such as jQuery (http://jquery.com/) and the Yahoo! User Interface (YUI) Library (http://developer.yahoo.net/yui).

Dreamweaver also takes care of a lot of the PHP coding, but it can't do everything, so I show you how to customize the code it generates. Chapter 10 serves as a crash course in PHP, and Chapter 11 puts that knowledge to immediate use by showing you how to send an email from an online form—one of the things that Dreamweaver doesn't automate. This book doesn't attempt to teach you how to become a PHP programmer, but by the time you reach the final chapter, you should have sufficient confidence to look a script in the eye without flinching.

"Do I need Dreamweaver CS4?"

Most definitely, yes. Although the PHP features remain basically unchanged since Dreamweaver 8.0.2, the changes to the Document window and Property inspector are so substantial that you would have considerable difficulty using this book with an earlier version of Dreamweaver. If you're still using Dreamweaver CS3, get a copy of the CS3 version of this book. If you want to use PHP in an earlier version of Dreamweaver, I suggest you read my *Foundation PHP for Dreamweaver 8* (friends of ED, ISBN: 978-1-59059-569-5) instead. Inevitably, some things have changed since those books were published, but all important corrections and updates are listed on the relevant errata pages at http://friendsofed.com/.

What's different from the CS3 edition?

I hate it when I buy a book and find myself reading familiar page after familiar page. This book is a revised edition of *The Essential Guide to Dreamweaver CS3 with CSS, Ajax, and PHP* (friends of ED, ISBN: 978-1-59059-859-7), updated to take account of the changes in Dreamweaver CS4. Most of the examples are inherited from the previous edition, but many of them have been reworked to take advantage of new features, such as Live view, Related Files, and the Code Navigator. I have also reorganized the exercises with the PHP server behaviors in what I hope you will agree is a more logical sequence. Chapter 14 offers a gentler introduction to interaction with a database before tackling the vital subject of server-side validation in Chapter 15.

I have also devoted more attention to working with Spry, as well as with other JavaScript libraries. Chapter 8 explores hand-coding with Spry and introduces web widgets that use jQuery and the YUI Library.

Every chapter has been completely revised and rewritten, and I have added a chapter on the basics of inserting content in a web page in Dreamweaver. This is mainly for the benefit of readers migrating from another web development program, such as Adobe GoLive, which has now been discontinued. It will also help newcomers to web development. However, as I mentioned earlier, you should already know the basics of HTML and CSS. Another new chapter deals with the mechanics of deploying a database-driven website on the Internet. You'll find details of all the major new features in Dreamweaver CS4 in the following chapters:

- Chapter 1 covers the changes to the user interface, Live Code, and screen sharing.
- Chapter 2 describes how to integrate your sites with Subversion version control.
- Chapter 3 shows you how to work with Photoshop Smart Objects.
- In Chapter 4 you'll begin working with the Related Files toolbar and Live view, and in Chapter 6 you're introduced to the Code Navigator—new tools that are used throughout the book.
- Chapter 8 covers the JavaScript Extractor and JavaScript web widgets.
- Chapter 13 describes in detail how to prepare pages for use with Adobe's new online service, InContext Editing.
- Chapter 19 shows you how to use the Spry Data Set wizard to create data sets from both HTML and XML data sources in a visually intuitive way.

Even though this book is about 200 pages longer than the previous edition, there are so many new features in Dreamweaver CS4 that I needed to drop some material. With reluctance, I decided the installation instructions for Apache, PHP, and MySQL in the Dreamweaver CS3 edition had to go. I did this for several reasons. Covering every combination of operating system and software was becoming too complicated. Separate instructions are needed for Windows XP and Vista, as well as for Mac OS X 10.4 and 10.5. With the release of MySQL 5.1, PHP 5.3, and Mac OS X 10.6 expected during the lifetime of this book, printed instructions rapidly go out of date. Perhaps most importantly, the all-in-one installation packages—XAMPP for Windows (http://www.apachefriends.org/en/xampp-windows.html) and MAMP for Mac OS X (http://www.mamp.info/en/mamp.html)—are reliable and easy to install.

Windows- and Mac-friendly

I have personally tested everything in this book in Windows and Mac OS X. The overwhelming majority of screenshots were taken on Windows Vista, but I have included separate screenshots from the Mac version where appropriate. I have also pointed out significant differences between the Windows and Mac versions of Dreamweaver, although there aren't many of them.

Keyboard shortcuts are given in the order Windows/Mac, and I point out when a particular shortcut is exclusive to Windows (some Dreamweaver shortcuts conflict with Exposé and

Spotlight in the Mac version). The only place where I haven't given the Mac equivalent is with regard to right-clicking. Since the advent of Mighty Mouse, right-clicking is now native to the Mac, but if you're an old-fashioned kind of guy or gal and still use a one-button mouse, Ctrl-click whenever I tell you to right-click (I'm sure you knew that anyway).

Some Mac keyboard shortcuts use the Option (Opt) key. If you're new to a Mac and can't find an Opt key on your keyboard, in some countries it's labeled Alt. The Command (Cmd) key has an apple and/or a cloverleaf symbol.

Using the download files

All the necessary files for in this book can be downloaded from http://www.friendsofed.com/downloads.html. The files are arranged in five top-level folders, as follows:

- examples: This contains the .html and .php files for all the examples and exercises, arranged by chapter. Use the File Compare feature in Dreamweaver (see Chapter 2) to check your own code against these files. Some exercises provide partially completed files for you to work with. Where indicated, copy the necessary files from this folder to the workfiles folder so you always have a backup if things go wrong. The easiest way to do this is to open the file in the examples folder and use File ➤ Save As to save the file to its new destination.

- extras: This contains a Dreamweaver extension that loads a suite of useful PHP code fragments into the Snippets panel, as well as a saved query for the Find and Replace panel, and SQL files to load data for the exercises into your database.

- images: This contains all the images used in the exercises and online gallery.

- SpryAssets: This contains the finished versions of Spry-related style sheets. With one exception, it does *not* contain the external JavaScript files needed to display Spry effects, widgets, or data sets. Dreamweaver should copy the JavaScript files and unedited style sheets to this folder automatically when you do the exercises as described in this book.

- workfiles: This is an empty folder, where you should build the pages used in the exercises.

Copy these folders to the top level of the site that you create for working with this book (see Chapter 2).

Support for this book

Every effort has been made to ensure accuracy, but mistakes do slip through. If you find what you think is an error—and it's not listed on the book's corrections page at http://www.friendsofed.com—please submit an error report to http://www.friendsofed.com/errataSubmission.html. When ED has finished with the thumbscrews and got me to admit I'm wrong, we'll post the details for everyone's benefit on the friends of ED site. I also plan to post details on my own website at http://foundationphp.com/dwcs4/updates.php of changes to Dreamweaver or other software that affect instructions in the book.

I want you to get the best out of this book and will try to help you if you run into difficulty. Before calling for assistance, though, start with a little self-help. Throughout the book, I have added "Troubleshooting" sections based heavily on frequently asked questions, together with my own experience of things that are likely to go wrong. Make use of the File Compare feature in Dreamweaver to check your code against the download files. If you're using a software firewall, try turning it off temporarily to see whether the problem goes away.

If none of these approaches solves your problem, scan the chapter subheadings in the "Contents" section, and try looking up a few related expressions in the index. Also try a quick search on the Internet: Google and the other large search engines are your friends. My apologies if all this sounds obvious, but an amazing number of people spend more time waiting for an answer in an online forum than it would take to go through these simple steps.

If you're still stuck, visit http://www.friendsofed.com/forums/. Use the following guidelines to help others help you:

- Always check the book's updates and corrections pages. The answer may already be there.

- Search the forum to see whether your question has already been answered.

- Give your message a meaningful subject line. It's likely to get a swifter response and may help others with a similar problem.

- Say which book you're using, and give a page reference to the point that's giving you difficulty.

- Give precise details of the problem. "It doesn't work" gives no clue as to the cause. "When I do so and so, x happens" is a lot more informative.

- If you get an error message, say what it contains.

- Be brief and to the point. Don't ask half a dozen questions at once.

- It's often helpful to know your operating system, and if it's a question about PHP, which version of PHP and which web server you're using.

- Don't post the same question simultaneously in several different forums. If you find the answer elsewhere, have the courtesy to close the forum thread and post a link to the answer.

The help I give in the friends of ED and Adobe forums is not limited to problems arising from my books, but please be realistic in your expectations when asking for help in a free online forum. Although the Internet never sleeps, the volunteers who answer questions certainly do. They're also busy people, who might not always be available. Don't post hundreds of lines of code and expect someone else to scour it for mistakes. And if you do get the help that you need, keep the community spirit alive by answering questions that you know the answer to.

Layout conventions

To keep this book as clear and easy to follow as possible, the following text conventions are used throughout.

Important words or concepts are normally highlighted on the first appearance in **bold type**.

Code is presented in `fixed-width` font.

New or changed code is normally presented in **`bold fixed-width font`**.

Pseudo-code and variable input are written in *`italic fixed-width font`*.

Menu commands are written in the form Menu ➤ Submenu ➤ Submenu.

Where I want to draw your attention to something, I've highlighted it like this:

> *Ahem, don't say I didn't warn you.*

Sometimes code won't fit on a single line in a book. Where this happens, I use an arrow like this: ➡.

```
This is a very, very long section of code that should be written all on ➡
the same line without a break.
```

Dreamweaver CS4 has a new look. At first glance, the changes might look superficial: a slightly different default layout of panels and a charcoal-gray livery. The program now shares the same user interface (UI) as other Creative Suite programs, making it easier for designers to create their basic design in Photoshop or Illustrator, and then prepare it for the Web in Dreamweaver.

Although the changes to the UI are important, it's the underlying functionality that really matters, and that's where Dreamweaver CS4 has changed dramatically. New features, such as Related Files, Live view, and the Code Navigator, make this the most significant release of Dreamweaver since Dreamweaver MX in 2002. The changes are aimed at helping designers and coders alike, and are likely to have a big impact on the workflow of existing users. Whether you're a newcomer to Dreamweaver or an old hand, to get the best out of the program, you need to find your way around the UI and new features.

In this chapter, you'll learn about the following:

- Using the OWL 2.0 UI
- Switching panels to iconic mode
- Converting the Insert panel into a tabbed Insert bar
- Using the Related Files feature to edit files linked to a web page
- Selecting options for Split view
- Previewing pages inside the Document window with Live view
- Navigating directly to style rules with the Code Navigator
- Editing HTML and Cascading Style Sheets (CSS) markup with the revamped Property inspector

Another important change with Dreamweaver CS4 is that Bridge and Device Central have become optional components. Bridge is a powerful file organizer (like Windows Explorer or Mac Finder on steroids). It has many features designed to appeal to designers and photographers, such as file previews, and keyword and metadata management. Device Central lets you see what your website will look like on a range of mobile devices. Both Bridge and Device Central are integrated with other Creative Suite programs, but many Dreamweaver users were unhappy that they had no choice whether to install them with the previous version. Adobe listened to the complaints, and has made many programs bundled with Dreamweaver CS4 optional. However, one optional program that you should install is Extension Manager, which is used to install extensions that add extra features and functionality to Dreamweaver. I'll show you how to use Extension Manager in Chapter 8, but the main emphasis throughout this book is, of course, on Dreamweaver CS4.

This chapter covers the nuts and bolts of the Dreamweaver interface. It's written with both newcomers and old hands in mind. If you're upgrading from a previous version of Dreamweaver, a lot of things will be instantly familiar; the UI is a subtle blend of old and new. However, even when things look the same, they often work slightly differently. For example, pressing F4 still hides most panels, but moving your mouse to the edge of the screen brings back anything hidden on that side (read "Temporarily hiding panels," if you want to disable that behavior). Because there are so many features in the UI, you might want to skim quickly through this chapter to see what it contains, and come back later when you need to find out how a particular feature works.

Let's begin with an overview of the Dreamweaver CS4 interface.

Exploring the UI

The common interface shared by all programs in Adobe Creative Suite 4 is officially known as OWL 2.0. OWL stands for OS (operating system) Widget Library. OWL not only gives a common feel and look to CS4 programs, but it also eliminates most differences in the way each program operates in Windows and Mac OS X. With only a few minor exceptions, the Mac version of Dreamweaver now looks and works identically to its Windows counterpart.

Inspecting the default workspace

The Dreamweaver CS4 workspace is infinitely configurable, and you can save your own layouts. Figures 1-1 and 1-2 show what greets you when you first open the program in Windows and Mac OS X, respectively.

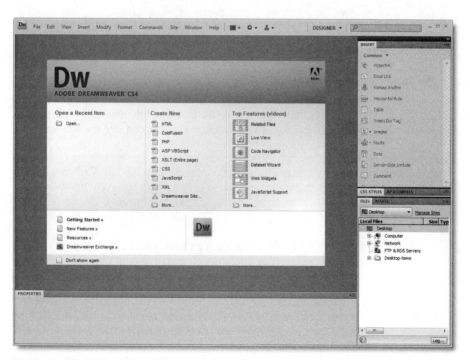

Figure 1-1. The default layout when you first open Dreamweaver CS4 in Windows

Figure 1-2. The Mac version of Dreamweaver CS4 is almost identical to the Windows one.

The only important differences between the two versions are that the Mac version retains the main Dreamweaver menus in the Mac menu bar, whereas they're integrated into the new Application bar in Windows; and the Windows version blocks out the Desktop, while the Mac version lets the Desktop show through when no document is loaded into the workspace.

> *The Mac version of some other programs in Creative Suite 4, such as Flash, emulates Windows behavior by adding a gray background to the whole program. However, this feature (known as the application frame) has not been implemented in Dreamweaver.*

The Welcome screen in the center of the workspace shows a list of the ten most recently opened pages, and provides shortcuts to opening new documents of the most commonly used file types. Of course, the list of recently opened pages is empty the first time you open the program.

The first thing most experienced Dreamweaver users do after installing a new version of the program is to select the Don't show again checkbox at the bottom left of the Welcome screen. Even if you're tempted to do so on this occasion, I suggest you follow the Top Features (videos) links on the right of the screen. These launch Adobe TV (http://tv.adobe.com/) videos explaining and demonstrating the main new features in Dreamweaver CS4. As they say, a picture is worth a thousand words, so the videos should give you a rapid introduction to the program's powerful new features. You need to be connected to the Internet to view the videos. If you have already hidden the Welcome screen, you can restore it by selecting Edit ➤ Preferences (Dreamweaver ➤ Preferences on a Mac), selecting the General category, and putting a check mark alongside Document options: Show Welcome Screen.

To activate all the panels, you need to open a document. If you're new to Dreamweaver, click HTML under the Create New heading in the Welcome screen. The default workspace layout is called Designer. Figure 1-3 labels all the main parts of the workspace, and Table 1-1 provides brief descriptions of these parts. (Because the UI in both Windows and Mac is almost identical, all screenshots in this book are taken from the Windows version, except where important differences exist).

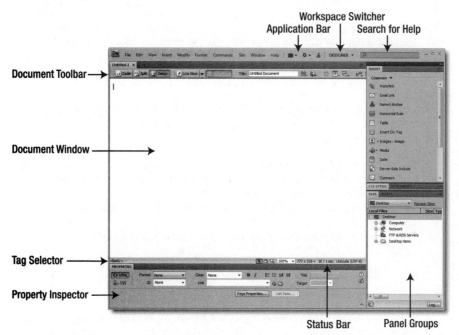

Figure 1-3.
The default Designer workspace in Dreamweaver CS4

Table 1-1. The main elements of the Dreamweaver workspace

Feature	Description
Application bar	On Windows, this contains all the main Dreamweaver menus plus four menus common to both Windows and Mac, and the Search for Help field. The common menus control layout of the Document window, Dreamweaver extensions, site management, and workspace layout. The Application bar can be closed on a Mac, but it is a permanent fixture in Windows.
Workspace switcher	This lets you choose from eight preset workspace layouts. It also has options to reset the current layout and manage custom layouts. This is hidden on a Mac if the Application bar is closed.

Continued

Table 1-1. *Continued*

Feature	Description
Search for help	In addition to the Help menu, you can now search for help directly through the UI. Enter a search term and press Enter/Return. If you are currently connected to the Internet, this launches the Adobe Community Help website, which displays results not only from Adobe's website, but also from selected blogs and community tutorial sites. If you're offline, the results come from Dreamweaver's local help files. This is hidden on a Mac if the Application bar is closed.
Document toolbar	This controls the display of the current document in the Document window, showing the page layout, underlying code, or a combination of the two. It also contains a number of tools for previewing the page, uploading it to the remote server, and checking the code for mistakes.
Document window	This is the main editing area. Each document is opened in a separate tab.
Tag selector	This displays where the current selection lies within the page's document tree structure. It can be used to select page elements and add attributes, such as an ID or class, to a tag.
Property inspector	This is Dreamweaver's main control center for working with the underlying code while viewing the web page in the Document window. It's a context-sensitive panel that displays all the main attributes of the current selection ready for editing. An important change from previous versions of Dreamweaver is the separation of the Property inspector into two views: HTML and CSS. Access to these views is controlled by two buttons at the top left of the Property inspector.
Status bar	This shows details of the Document window and current page, such as magnification, dimensions, size in kilobytes, and encoding.
Panel groups	Specialized panels control working with different aspects of web pages, such as styles, database connections (with a server-side language like PHP), and files in the current site (site definition is covered in Chapter 2). The most commonly used panels are displayed as a column on the right side of the screen, but they can be rearranged, minimized, or closed to suit your workflow, as described in this chapter.

This looks very familiar to long-term Dreamweaver users. The main difference lies in the large panel at the top right of the screen. This is the Insert panel, which was a much more compact toolbar in previous versions. It has been redesigned with labels alongside each icon to help newcomers to the program find tools easily. The other big change is that all the icons in the Insert panel are grayscale and display in color only when you mouse over them. The logic behind this is to reduce color noise—the theory being that colored icons distract you from the main design in the Document window. If you don't like either of these defaults, they can be changed.

I'll deal with the Insert panel (including restoring the tabbed Insert bar from previous versions) in the "Using and configuring the Insert panel" section later in this chapter, but switching to colored icons is something you might want to do immediately.

Switching between grayscale and colored icons

The idea of rendering all icons in grayscale makes a lot of sense in graphic design programs, such as Photoshop and Illustrator, because they have relatively few toolbars, and muting the icons lets you concentrate on the design with a minimum of distraction. Dreamweaver, on the other hand, has a lot of icons, many of which are very small. Without color to act as a visual clue, the grayscale versions can be difficult to distinguish, slowing down your workflow. However, in recognition of the way different people work, three of the preset workspace layouts (Classic, Coder, and Coder Plus) display colored icons by default, and you have the option to toggle colored icons on and off in all layouts. There are three ways of doing so, as follows:

- Select View ➤ Color Icons.
- Right-click the Insert panel and select Color Icons from the context menu (a page needs to be open in the Document window before you can do this).
- Click the View options button in the Document toolbar and select Color Icons (see the section "Exploring the Document toolbar" later in this chapter for a description of the Document toolbar's features).

Choosing a preset workspace layout

In addition to the default Designer workspace layout, Dreamweaver CS4 comes with seven other preset layouts. And if you don't like any of them, you can design and save your own personal layouts (as explained in the section "Managing workspaces" later in this chapter). You access the preset layouts and manage customized ones through the Workspace switcher (on Windows, it's at the right end of the Application bar; in the Mac version, it's much further to the left). Figure 1-4 shows the available options on the Workspace switcher.

Table 1-2 provides a brief description of the preset layouts, but the best way to understand them is to experiment by selecting each one in turn.

Figure 1-4. The Workspace switcher offers a wider choice of layouts than previous versions.

If you're an experienced user of Dreamweaver, and just want to get the UI back to its previous layout, select Classic from the Workspace switcher. However, the new options can do a lot to improve your workflow, so they're well worth exploring.

Table 1-2. Preset workspace layouts in Dreamweaver CS4

Layout	Panel groups	Description
App Developer	Databases, Bindings, Server Behaviors, Files, Assets, Snippets	The panel groups are displayed fully expanded in a column on the left. The Document window on the right is split horizontally to show Code view at the top and Design view below. The Property inspector is closed. Mainly suited to developing dynamic websites with a server-side technology.
App Developer Plus	Same as App Developer plus Insert, CSS Styles, AP Elements, Properties	Three extra design-related panels are added in iconic mode to the right of the Document window (the AP Elements panel displays details of elements that use absolute positioning). The Property inspector is displayed at the bottom of the Document window. Not suitable for a small monitor.
Classic	Insert, Properties, CSS Styles, AP Elements, Tag Inspector, Databases, Bindings, Server Behaviors, Files, Assets, Snippets	This is the same layout as Dreamweaver CS3. The Insert panel is converted to a toolbar at the top of the screen. The Property inspector is at the bottom of the Document window, and the panel groups are fully expanded on the right. Icons are displayed in color. An all-purpose layout suited to developers involved in both server-side development and page design.
Coder	Files, Assets, Snippets	This is a minimalist layout for developers who prefer to work in raw code. Just one panel group is displayed fully expanded on the left, with the Document window in Code view on the right. The Property inspector is closed. Icons are displayed in color.
Coder Plus	Same as Coder plus Insert, CSS Styles, AP Elements	This adds three design-related panels in iconic mode to the right of the Document window. Icons are displayed in color.
Designer	Insert, Properties, CSS Styles, AP Elements, Files, Assets	This is the layout shown in Figure 1-3. It provides the basic tools for designing static websites. A good choice for beginners.
Designer Compact	Same as Designer	The layout is the same as Designer, but the panels are displayed in iconic mode.
Dual Screen	Insert, CSS Styles, AP Elements, Databases, Bindings, Server Behaviors, Assets, Snippets, Files, Properties, Code Inspector	This blows the UI apart, displaying nearly every available panel ready for redistribution on a dual-monitor setup. The Property inspector is initially attached to the Document window, but like everything else, it can be detached. It's more of a starting point for a custom layout, rather than something you would use on a regular basis.

Expanding and collapsing panels vertically

As you can see in Figures 1-1 through 1-3, the Insert and Files panels are open in the default Designer workspace, but two panels in the middle (CSS Styles and AP Elements) are displayed as tabs only. All panels can be expanded vertically to give access to their contents, and collapsed to tabs to give you more room to see the contents of a different panel.

> The AP in AP Elements *stands for "absolutely positioned." The panel displays details of all page elements that have the CSS property* position: absolute.

The way you expand a panel that's currently displayed only as a tab depends on its position. If the tab is foremost in its group, you need to double-click it. Other tabs open with a single mouse click. To contract a panel to its tab, either double-click the tab or click once in the dark-gray area to the right of the last tab in the group. Panels that are grouped together expand and contract as a group. Clicking once in the dark-gray area also expands a closed group of panels.

Many panels also have keyboard shortcuts to expand and contract panels. Open the Window menu to see the shortcuts available for your operating system.

Resizing panels

Panels can be resized vertically and horizontally by clicking and dragging the top, bottom, or side of a panel or panel group. Dreamweaver remembers the new size until you change it again.

Using panels in iconic mode

Long-term users of Dreamweaver will begin to see the real differences in the UI by selecting one of the workspace layouts that use iconic mode, such as Designer Compact. The panel groups are identical to the Designer layout, but instead of the panel groups being fully expanded (as in Figure 1-3), they are collapsed to icons with labels alongside, as shown in Figure 1-5.

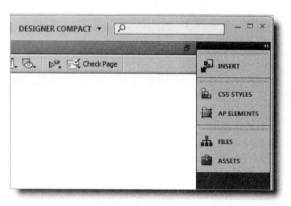

Figure 1-5. Dreamweaver panels can now be collapsed to icons.

Click the icon or its label, and the panel pops out, as shown in Figure 1-6. Once a panel is open, you can resize it by dragging its sides or corners. Dreamweaver remembers this size until you change it again. Only one panel can be opened at a time, and by default, the panel pops back in as soon as you click anywhere outside it. This means you can switch rapidly between panels by clicking the icon or label of the next panel you want to access. It also tidies the workspace by keeping the panel out of the way as soon as you start working in the Document window.

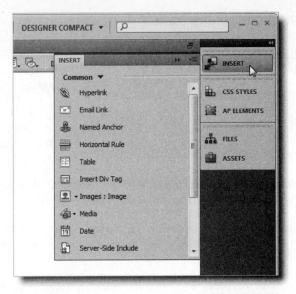

Figure 1-6. In iconic mode, panels pop out alongside their icons.

If this automatic disappearing act doesn't suit your way of working, you can disable it by right-clicking any of the panel icons and selecting Auto-Collapse Iconic Panels from the context menu. A check mark alongside this option indicates that auto-collapse is enabled. Clicking the option in the context menu toggles the behavior on and off.

Iconic mode is particularly useful on a small monitor, but Windows users might be annoyed by the large expanse of empty gray space beneath the icons (on a Mac, the Desktop shows through). There are two things you can do about that in both Windows and Mac:

- Minimize the icons to hide their labels.
- Float the icons.

Minimizing iconic panels

Once you're familiar with the panel icons, you can save space by positioning your cursor over the edge of a column of panels in iconic mode until it changes into a double-headed arrow. Hold down the left mouse button, and drag toward the opposite edge of the column until the labels disappear and the icons snap to their minimized shape, as shown in Figure 1-7.

The minimized icons work exactly the same as before. To help remind you what each icon represents, Dreamweaver displays a tooltip when you hover your cursor over one.

Although this saves space, you still get the gray column on Windows or the Desktop showing through on a Mac. If you don't like that, you can turn the panels into a floating vertical toolbar.

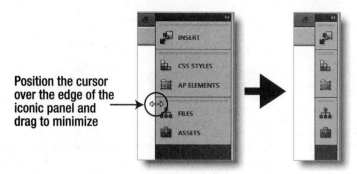

Position the cursor over the edge of the iconic panel and drag to minimize

Figure 1-7. The panels can be reduced to icons to save space.

Converting iconic panels into a floating toolbar

You can detach a column of iconic panels by clicking anywhere in the dark-gray strip at the top of the column, and then dragging it away from the edge of the screen. (Don't click the double-arrow at the top right—that expands all the panels in the column to their default width.) Once the panels have been detached from the edge of the screen, you can position them anywhere you want. While dragging them, they turn semitransparent to make it easier to decide where to locate them. As an independent toolbar, the icons occupy the minimum amount of space, and the gray column disappears on Windows. Figure 1-8 shows the minimized panels floating alongside part of a web page in the Document window.

Figure 1-8.
The minimized panels can be floated anywhere in the workspace.

Closing and restoring floating panels

Dreamweaver adds a close button to the dark-gray strip at the top of floating panels. Figure 1-9 shows the close buttons added to a floating toolbar of minimized icons on Windows and Mac. The close button follows the convention of the operating system, so it remains at the top right or top left when the icons are expanded to panels. Simply click the close button, and the panels are removed from the workspace.

11

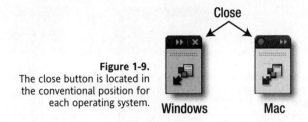

Figure 1-9.
The close button is located in the conventional position for each operating system.

To restore floating panels after closing them, open the Window menu and select the name of one of the panels in the group that has been closed. This opens the panel, along with all other panels (or icons) grouped with it. Many panels have keyboard shortcuts that toggle them open and closed. Using one of these shortcuts also restores a closed floating group. The keyboard shortcuts are listed on the Window menu.

Switching between panels and icons

A column of panels can be fully expanded or collapsed to icons by clicking the tiny pair of arrowheads at the top right of the column (see Figure 1-10). Dreamweaver remembers the width of both the expanded column and icons, so collapsing to icons displays them with labels or minimized, depending on your previous choice.

Figure 1-10. Click the pair of arrowheads to switch between icons and panels.

Temporarily hiding panels

When you want to clear the on-screen clutter to see your work in its full glory, just press F4. Most panels will disappear, leaving the Document window dominating the screen. You still have access to the Document toolbar, Tag selector, and Status bar, as they are integral parts of the Document window. The Application bar also remains visible at the top of the screen, as does the Insert panel if you have converted it to the Insert bar (see "Using and configuring the Insert panel" later in this chapter).

In Windows, the Document window expands to fill the entire workspace. On a Mac, the Document window doesn't change size. However, if you drag the resize handle at the bottom right of the Document window, you can get it to fill the whole screen. The panels return when you press F4 again, and on both Windows and Mac, the Document window shrinks back to fit inside the workspace. The next time you press F4 on a Mac, Dreamweaver remembers to fill the screen with the Document window.

1

Using Auto-Show

Pressing F4 to restore all the panels can get a bit tiresome if you want to spend most of your time in the Document window, so Dreamweaver CS4 has added a new feature that automatically shows hidden panels when you move your mouse pointer to the edge of the screen. If you move your mouse to the right edge of the screen, any panels hidden on that side automatically pop out. You can then work in the panels, and they automatically slide back out of view as soon as you move back into the document window. This is the default behavior.

If you want the panels to remain hidden, right-click any panel and select Auto-Show Hidden Panels. Like many options in context menus, a check mark alongside the item indicates that the option is enabled; no check mark indicates it's disabled. Clicking the option toggles it on and off.

> *Pressing F4 to hide the panels and using Auto-Show is a very convenient way of working. It gives you plenty of space to work in your document, but puts the panels quickly at your disposal. However, it can be difficult to control if you auto-hide the Taskbar on Windows or the Dock on a Mac. Moving your mouse pointer too far off the screen triggers the Taskbar or Dock, rather than the Dreamweaver panels.*

Hiding the Application bar (Mac only)

In the Windows version of Dreamweaver CS4, the Application bar (see Figure 1-3) contains all the main Dreamweaver menus, so it cannot be turned off.

In the Mac version, the main Dreamweaver menus remain part of the OS X interface, and the Application bar contains only a small number of shortcut menus to options that can also be accessed through the main menus. If the Application bar gets in the way on a Mac, you can hide it by selecting Window ➤ Application Bar. Select the same menu option to restore it.

Moving and regrouping panels

The preset workspace layouts organize panels in logical groups. For example, the CSS Styles and AP Elements panels are grouped together because they both deal with style rules. But these groups are only suggestions; you can reorganize the panels just about any way you want.

Moving a single panel

To move a single panel, click its tab and drag it away from its current position towards the Document window. When you release your mouse button, the panel floats independently. You can move the panel anywhere you like by grabbing the dark-gray bar at the top of the panel and dragging it to a new position. You can also collapse the panel to iconic mode (with or without a label), dock it in a different location, group it with one or more other panels, or close it.

Moving a panel to a different group

To change a panel grouping, grab the tab of a panel that you want to move and pull it away from its current position. As you drag it, it becomes semitransparent. Drag it over the target panel or panel group until a blue border appears around the target, as shown in Figure 1-11, and release the mouse button. Although Figure 1-11 shows the target as a single floating panel, the target can be an existing group; it doesn't matter whether it's floating or docked within a column of panels.

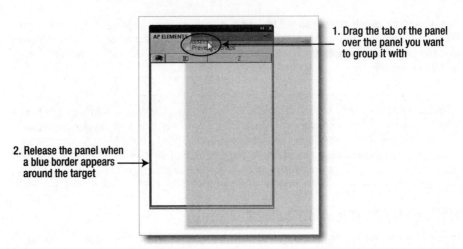

1. Drag the tab of the panel over the panel you want to group it with

2. Release the panel when a blue border appears around the target

Figure 1-11. It's easy to regroup panels.

Changing the order of panels within a group

If you prefer to display the panels in a different order, just drag one of the tabs to the left or right. Repeat this process until the tabs are in the order you want.

Moving a group of panels

Moving a group of panels is quite easy, but you need to take care where you click to drag the group as a single unit. Click anywhere between the last tab on the right and the tab group menu, as shown in Figure 1-12. With some groups, this leaves very little room in which to position your cursor. A simple way of getting around this problem is to make the panel column wider by dragging its open side. This opens up the clickable area. Once you have reorganized the panels the way you want, drag them back to the desired width.

Click in this area to drag the group

Figure 1-12.
Selecting the right place to drag a panel group can sometimes be tricky.

Tab group menu

Stacking and docking panels

In addition to grouping panels together, you can stack them together to form a new column, or dock them to the edge of the screen or another group of panels. As you drag a panel or group of panels, watch for a thick blue line to appear. This indicates a dockable target.

Using and configuring the Insert panel

As I mentioned earlier, by default, the Insert panel occupies a large amount of space because of the labels next to the icons. The Insert panel is also unusual in that it's really many panels in one.

As its name suggests, the Insert panel's role is to insert frequently used elements, such as images, tables, <div> tags, form elements, and Spry widgets, into a web page. They won't all fit conveniently into a single panel, so they're divided into categories, which can be accessed through a drop-down menu just below the tab, as shown in Figure 1-13. Dreamweaver is context-sensitive, so the menu sometimes displays more categories than shown in the figure (for example, the PHP category is accessible in a PHP page). Table 1-3 describes briefly what each category contains. For the benefit of readers upgrading from Dreamweaver CS3, I have indicated the main changes.

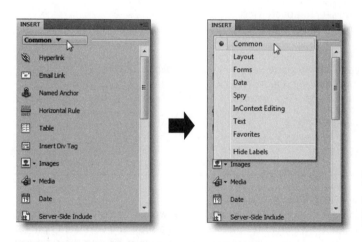

Figure 1-13.
The Insert panel contains several categories accessed through an internal menu.

Table 1-3. The main features of Insert panel categories

Category	Description	Changes from Dreamweaver CS3
Common	Inserts the most commonly used objects, such as tables, images, and <div> tags.	Horizontal Rule has been added. Flash Button and Flash Text have been removed from the Media submenu.
Layout	Offers various tools for layout, including table modification, frames, and Spry widgets, such as menu bar (see Chapter 6), and tabbed and collapsible panels (see Chapter 7).	No change.

Continued

15

Table 1-3. *Continued*

Category	Description	Changes from Dreamweaver CS3
Forms	Creates forms and inserts all form elements, including Spry validation widgets (forms and Spry validation are covered in Chapter 9).	Checkbox Group **and three new** Spry validation widgets (Password, Confirm, and Radio Group) **have been added.**
Data	Offers access to most dynamic features, including Spry data sets (see Chapter 19) and PHP server behaviors (see Chapter 14 onward). Also imports data from comma-separated value (CSV) files into a static web page.	Spry XML Data Set **and** Spry Table **have been removed and combined in a vastly improved** Spry Data Set **feature (see Chapter 19).**
Spry	Presents all Spry features gathered in a single category.	Spry Data Set **replaces** Spry XML Data Set **and** Spry Table. **New validation widgets and** Spry Tooltip **have been added.**
InContext Editing	Offers tools for Adobe's hosted online service that permits authorized users to update web pages through an ordinary browser (see Chapter 13).	**New category.**
Text	Provides an alternative to the Property inspector for common formatting options. It's also home to definition list and HTML entities.	**No change.**
Favorites	Provides a blank category for you to customize (see "Customizing the Favorites category" later in this section).	

Many icons on the Insert panel have a small downward facing arrow to the right, as shown alongside. This indicates that it contains a submenu of related options. The first time you click one of these icons, Dreamweaver displays the submenu showing all options (Figure 1-14 shows the options when you click the Images icon). Dreamweaver remembers your selection and always displays the most recently used option. If you want to use the same option again, click the icon itself. To select a different option, click the arrow to the right to reveal the menu again.

For many Dreamweaver users, the Insert panel is one of the heavily used parts of the UI. If you're happy working with just the icons, you can hide the labels. You can also convert the panel into a tabbed toolbar like the Insert bar in previous versions of Dreamweaver. Regardless of which layout you choose, you can populate the Favorites category with your own selection of frequently used items.

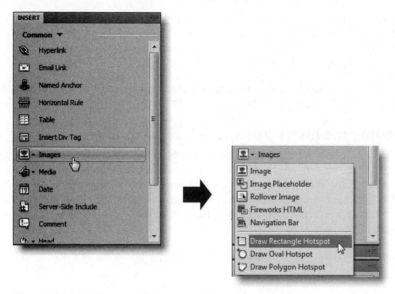

Figure 1-14. Many icons on the Insert panel conceal submenus.

Hiding the labels

If you want to save space by hiding the label alongside each icon, select Hide Labels from the bottom of the Insert panel's drop-down menu (shown on the right side of Figure 1-13). If you forget what an icon represents, just hover your mouse pointer over it to display a tooltip.

Hiding the labels leaves you with a vast expanse of unused panel. To reduce the height of the panel, click the bottom and drag it upwards, as shown in Figure 1-15.

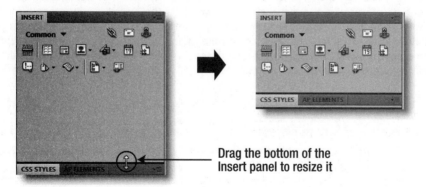

Drag the bottom of the
Insert panel to resize it

Figure 1-15. Hiding the labels on the Insert panel saves a lot of screen real estate.

If you do this with the Common category selected, you might notice that Dreamweaver prevents you from making the bottom of the panel fit snugly underneath the bottom row of icons. This is because other categories have more icons, so enough space if left to display the largest category without the need to resize the panel.

Although this saves space, you still need to activate the drop-down menu to switch categories. Converting the panel to a tabbed toolbar avoids this problem.

Converting the Insert panel to a tabbed toolbar

The easiest way to convert the Insert panel to a toolbar like the Insert bar in previous versions is to select Classic from the Workspace switcher. This moves the panel from its current location to the top of the screen and converts it into a tabbed toolbar. Each tab represents a category from the panel menu, giving you quick and easy access to all its tools. If the tabs aren't displayed, activate the drop-down menu on the left of the Insert bar and select Show as Tabs.

On Windows, the Insert bar is located beneath the Application bar and stretches the full width of the screen, as shown in Figure 1-16.

Figure 1-16. The only position for the Insert bar in Windows is directly beneath the Application bar.

Mac users have two options. The default Classic workspace layout in the Mac version of Dreamweaver attaches the Insert bar to the end of the Application bar, as shown at the top of Figure 1-17. The Mac version of the Application bar contains only a few items, so converting the Insert panel to a toolbar makes much better use of your screen real estate. As noted earlier, if you don't want the Application bar, you can turn it off in the Mac version by selecting Window ➤ Application Bar. This shifts the Insert bar left to occupy the space previously taken by the Application bar, as shown at the bottom of Figure 1-17. However, it doesn't offer any real benefit, as the full width of the screen is still reserved for the tabbed Insert bar. Unlike the Windows version, with the Mac, the Insert bar's background doesn't expand to fill the empty space on the right. Contrary to what you might expect, you cannot dock other panels to the right of the Insert bar. However, if you want to fill this empty space, you can float other panels over it.

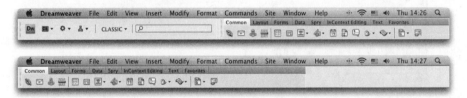

Figure 1-17. In the Mac version, the Insert bar can be displayed with or without the Application bar.

If you have already reorganized your workspace layout and don't want to use the Classic preset, you can detach the Insert panel from its current location by dragging its tab toward the top of the screen. Release the tab when you see a thick blue line indicating where it will be docked. On Windows, the only place you can dock the Insert panel and display the tabbed interface is directly beneath the Application bar. On a Mac, you can dock it to the right of the Application bar, underneath the Application bar, or if the Application bar is hidden, at the top of the screen.

The convenience of the tabbed Insert bar is somewhat marred by the fact that it's not resizable. Also, you cannot dock anything to the right of it on either Windows or Mac. On my 1680 × 1050 monitor, the icons in the Insert bar never stretch even halfway across the screen, so a lot of space is wasted. Apparently, this is because of constraints imposed by the common UI shared by all programs in Creative Suite 4. In testing Dreamweaver CS4, I have found the tabbed Insert bar to be the most efficient because I can afford the space on my large monitor. Unfortunately, if space is a consideration, undocking the tabbed Insert bar won't solve your problems. If you undock the Insert bar from the top of the screen by dragging the double column of dots on its left side, it automatically converts back into a panel, and the tabs are no longer accessible.

Switching between tabs and menu

If you prefer the drop-down menu to switch between categories, you can use it instead of the Insert bar's tabbed interface. Right-click anywhere in the dark-gray strip to the right of the last tab and select Show as Menu. This saves a few pixels of vertical space. To display the tabbed interface again, open the drop-down menu on the left of the Insert bar and select Show as Tabs.

Customizing the Favorites category

If switching among categories becomes too time-consuming, you can populate the Favorites category with your most frequently used items. This option is available regardless of how you have configured the Insert panel.

Right-click anywhere in the light-gray area of the Insert panel or Insert bar and select Customize Favorites from the context menu. The drop-down menu at the top left of the Customize Favorite Objects dialog box (shown in Figure 1-18) lets you choose from either a master list or individual categories. In the left panel, select one item at a time and click the button with the double chevron to add it to the Favorite objects panel on the right. To remove an item, select it in the right panel and click the trash can button at the top right. The up and down arrows next to the trash can can be used to change the position of the selected item. The Add separator button below the list inserts a separator after the current item.

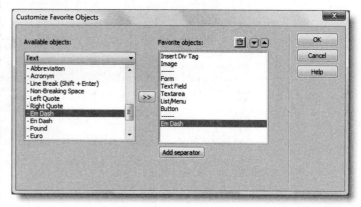

Figure 1-18. Customize the Favorites category of the Insert panel or Insert bar for quick access to frequently used options.

The Customize Favorite Objects dialog box gives access to all categories, including context-sensitive ones, such as PHP. Dreamweaver stores details of your Favorites category in your personal configuration folder, so different users on the same computer can have person-alized selections (as long as they use different user accounts). You can copy your Favorites category to another computer, as described in the "Migrating snippets and other personal settings" section later in this chapter.

Using the Property inspector

The Property inspector is the wide panel at the bottom of several preset workspace lay-outs, including the default Designer (see Figure 1-3). The tab actually reads Properties, so many people refer to it as the Properties panel, but the official name is Property inspector, and that's how I'll refer to it throughout this book.

The Property inspector is context-sensitive; it displays properties related to the current selection in the Document window. Figure 1-19 shows the contents of the Property inspec-tor when an image is selected. As you can see, it gives access to the main attributes of the <img> tag, including src, alt, width, height, and class. It also contains a small number of image editing tools.

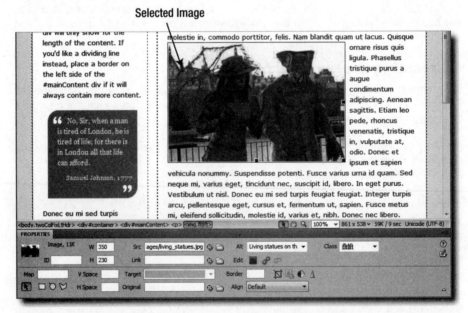

Figure 1-19. The Property inspector gives access to the main attributes of the <img> tag when an image is selected.

Selecting HTML and CSS view in the Property inspector

When the cursor is in an empty part of the Document window or text is selected, the Property inspector displays a completely different set of options. Figure 1-20 shows what it looks like when the pull quote on the left of the Document window is selected. The important thing to note is that there are two buttons on the left of the Property inspector: HTML and CSS. These are new to Dreamweaver CS4, and you need to check carefully which one is selected, as the options look very similar, but work in very different ways.

Selected Text

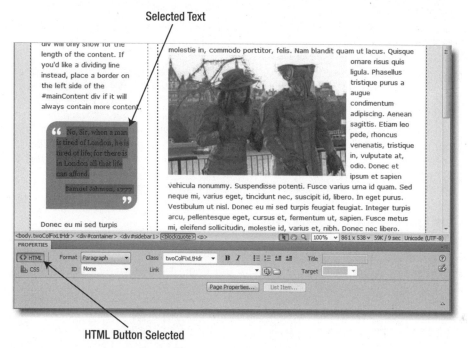

HTML Button Selected

Figure 1-20. When editing text, the Property inspector has separate options for HTML and CSS.

With the HTML button selected, you can format text by applying Hypertext Markup Language (HTML) tags such as paragraphs (<p>) and headings (<h1> through <h6>), bold (<strong>), italic (<em>), and bulleted and numbered lists (<ul> and <ol>), as well as applying hyperlinks (<a>). If you're upgrading from a previous version of Dreamweaver, selecting the HTML button in the Property inspector gives you most of the options that you're used to seeing. However, the options to select the font face, size, and color are missing. To access them, you need to select the CSS button.

Modern web standards advocate the separation of content and presentation by marking up the structure of the page with HTML, while leaving all stylistic elements, such as fonts, colors, and backgrounds, to CSS. In keeping with this approach, Dreamweaver CS4 has moved the tools for styling text and other elements to a separate view of the Property inspector. Figure 1-21 shows what the Property inspector looks like when you select the CSS button with the same pull quote selected as in Figure 1-20. As you can see, it has a drop-down menu on the left labeled Targeted Rule. This automatically selects what Dreamweaver judges to be the most appropriate rule to edit, but you can make your own selection or use it to create a new rule. Using the CSS features of the Property inspector is covered in Chapter 4.

Figure 1-21. Selecting the CSS button in the Property inspector reveals options for creating style rules for the current element.

"Where has my Link *field gone?" This was one of the most common cries for help during the public beta of Dreamweaver CS4. Regular users of Dreamweaver are used to always seeing the* Link *field in the same place in the Property inspector and panic when it's not there. It's still where it always used to be, but it's visible only when the* HTML *button is selected. Dreamweaver always remembers your most recent selection, so if you have been working with CSS, you need to switch back to access the* HTML *formatting options, including creating a hyperlink.*

Configuring the Property inspector

The Property inspector is not as versatile as the Insert panel when it comes to rearranging your workspace. You can cut its height in half by clicking the little upward-facing triangle at the bottom right of the Property inspector (see Figure 1-21). However, this conceals all the options in the lower half. There aren't many options for text in the lower half (see Figures 1-20 and 1-21), but as Figure 1-19 shows, there are many more for an image. To restore the Property inspector to its full height, click the triangle again (it points downward when the bottom half is concealed).

Unfortunately, the three icons on the right edge of the Property inspector have a nasty habit of disappearing on monitors smaller than 1280 × 1024 pixels (the minimum specification for Dreamweaver CS4 is 1024 × 768). The icons are hidden behind any panels to the right of the Property inspector. This is a known bug that makes collapsing the Property inspector a risky business and not recommended on small monitors. If you can't access the expand triangle, collapse any other panels to iconic mode. If that doesn't work, detach the Property inspector from the bottom of the screen by dragging its tab into the Document window. This should display the Property inspector full width, giving access to the expand triangle.

A better way to gain more room in the Document window is to click the dark-gray bar alongside the tab of the Property inspector. This collapses the panel containing the Property inspector to a narrow strip at the bottom of the screen. Click again, and the panel is restored to its normal size. You can also save space by automatically hiding all panels when not in use by pressing F4, as described earlier in the chapter.

A big complaint about the Property inspector is that it stretches horizontally to fill the available space at the bottom of the screen, but all the text fields remain the same size. On a large monitor, this results in a lot of wasted space. You can detach the Property inspector from the bottom of the screen and use it as a floating panel. Once floating, it can be collapsed to iconic mode with or without a label, as shown alongside. When you expand the Property inspector from iconic mode, it occupies 825 × 130 pixels and cannot be resized.

> *Detaching the Property inspector from its default position can be a frustrating experience. Even if you drag it some distance, it stubbornly snaps back to the bottom of the screen. The secret is to collapse other panels that are open, and then drag the Property inspector to the top half of the screen.*

Using the Results panel group

By default, the Results panel group remains hidden in all preset workspace layouts. It opens automatically at the bottom of the screen (below the Property inspector if that's already at the bottom) after performing certain operations, such as find and replace, validation, or link-checking. It also contains the Reference panel (Shift+F1), which has comprehensive guides to HTML, CSS, and other web technologies (unfortunately, the PHP material is rather out-of-date).

To minimize the Results panel group, press F7 or click the dark-gray bar to the right of the tabs. This leaves the tabs visible at the bottom of the screen. Pressing F7 or clicking the dark-gray bar toggles it open and closed. To get rid of this panel group completely, right-click the dark-gray bar and select Close Tab Group. However, it automatically reopens whenever prompted to do so by Dreamweaver. You cannot get rid of it permanently, nor should you want to; it contains useful information.

The problem with the Results panel group is that it cannot be resized in its default location, often making the contents difficult to read. The best way to use the Results panel group is to turn it into a floating panel by dragging the dark-gray bar to the right of the tabs into the Document window. Once it's floating, you can resize it by dragging either of the bottom two corners or any side except the top. Another benefit is that pressing F7 closes the panel group completely, rather than minimizing it. Alternatively, you can convert it into an iconic panel.

Managing workspaces

Being able to configure the workspace in such a variety of ways makes Dreamweaver CS4 extremely versatile, but what if you don't like the changes? Or what if you like the changes, but don't always want to work the same way? Adobe has provided for these cases by including options to reset the current workspace to its original settings and save customized ones.

At the bottom of the Workspace switcher (see Figure 1-4 earlier in the chapter) are the following three options:

- Reset '*Workspace*': This resets the current workspace to its original settings (*Workspace* is replaced by the actual name). It works with both the preset layouts that ship with Dreamweaver and your own customized layouts.

- New Workspace: This opens a dialog box that lets you save your own customized layout. Once you have configured the workspace to your own liking, just select this option, give the new workspace a name, and click OK. This adds the customized layout to the Workspace switcher, allowing you to switch to it at any time.

- Manage Workspaces: This displays a list of customized layouts stored in the current user's configuration folder with options to rename or delete them. Once you delete a customized layout, you cannot restore it.

The Workspace switcher is always visible in the Windows version of Dreamweaver CS4. If you have hidden the Application bar on Mac OS X, you can access the Workspace switcher options from the Workspace Layout submenu of the Window menu (the same options are available on Windows).

Dreamweaver stores details of customized workspace layouts as Extensible Markup Language (XML) files, a platform-neutral format, so you can share layouts with other users even if you're using different operating systems. For details, see the "Migrating snippets and other personal settings" section later in this chapter.

Exploring the Document window

Whether you're a designer, a coder, or a bit of both, the Document window is where you do most of your work in Dreamweaver. Like the UI, it has a lot of new features. Some, like Related Files and Live view, have a major impact on the Dreamweaver workflow. Others, like Vertical Split view and Split Code view, are simple improvements that both newcomers and old hands are likely to find welcome aids to productivity.

Figure 1-22 shows the main parts of the Document window (in Design view, showing a file used later in the book). The following sections describe briefly the various options available in the Document window. How they're used in the context of building a website is covered in the rest of the book.

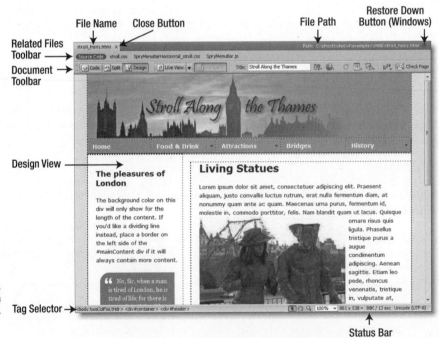

Figure 1-22.
A web page displayed in Design view.

Working with tabbed windows

By default, Dreamweaver displays web pages, JavaScript files, style sheets, and all other web documents in a tabbed interface. Tabs are created from left to right in the same order as the pages are opened, but you can drag and drop them into any order.

Viewing the file path

The physical file path of the currently selected document is displayed in the dark-gray bar alongside the tabs. Unfortunately, if you have a large number of tabs open, this conceals the file path. However, you can always see the file path by hovering your mouse pointer over the document's tab, where it is displayed as a tooltip. The Coding toolbar (described in the "Using the Coding toolbar" section later in this chapter) also displays a list showing the full path name of all open files.

Closing tabs

To close a document, click the close button on the right side of the tab. This is different from previous versions of Dreamweaver, and is particularly likely to confuse Windows users, who will need to get out of the habit of going to the top right of the Document window to close a document (where you're likely to hit the restore down button by mistake). Although this is different from previous versions, it brings Dreamweaver into line with the way that browsers work, so the change is quite logical. Mac users might also feel a little discomfort because the close button has moved from the left side of the tab to the right, so it's now on the opposite side from the Safari browser.

To close all tabs at once, right-click any tab and select Close All from the context menu. Alternatively, use File ➤ Close All on the main menu system, or the keyboard shortcut Ctrl+Shift+W/Shift+Cmd+W.

To close all documents except the selected tab, right-click the tab, and choose Close Other Files from the context menu. The tab context menu offers other options for opening, saving, and comparing documents (file comparison depends on setting up a third-party utility; see Chapter 2 for details).

Displaying documents outside the tabbed interface

If you decide you don't want your documents displayed in the tabbed interface, you can break them free. The method depends on your operating system.

On Windows, click the restore down button at the top right of the Document window to display the document in what looks like a normal window. It has minimize, maximize, and close buttons like any other window, but its movement is restricted to inside the Document window. If you open a new document, it opens in a similar window. Clicking the maximize button converts the window back to a Dreamweaver tab.

The Mac version works considerably differently. By default, the first document opens in an ordinary window. The tabbed interface appears only when you open two or more documents. If you prefer to open the first document in a tab as well, select Dreamweaver ➤ Preferences (Cmd+U), choose the General category, and enter a check mark in the Always show tabs checkbox. If you don't want tabs at all, make sure that both the Open documents in tabs and Always show tabs checkboxes are deselected. You can also move a document from its tab into a separate window by right-clicking the tab and selecting Move to New Window from the context menu.

Getting quick access to related files

Dreamweaver CS4 has two powerful new tools that give you instant access to style sheets, external JavaScript files, and other documents linked to a web page. The Related Files feature supports all linked files, whereas the Code Navigator is dedicated to working with style sheets.

Using the Related Files toolbar

If you work regularly with external style sheets, JavaScript files, or server-side includes, be prepared for one of the biggest improvements to your workflow. The Related Files feature automatically detects whether the current document has links to external files and lists them in the Related Files toolbar just above the Document toolbar (see Figure 1-22). Dreamweaver loads the code of each file into memory, giving you instant access just by clicking the file name in the Related Files list. This means that you no longer need to search in the Files panel to locate a style sheet or JavaScript file for editing; it's there at the click of your mouse.

The Related Files toolbar doesn't list images, SWF files, or other visual assets, so it doesn't get cluttered with irrelevant files. Normally, Dreamweaver goes only one level deep, so just the files that are directly linked to the page are listed. For example, if the main document uses a server-side include called menu.inc.php, it's listed, but any files included directly by menu.inc.php are not listed. Style sheets are the only exception. All style sheets that affect the main document are listed however deep they are in the site hierarchy. For example, if styles.css uses @import to link to more_styles.css, both are listed, even though the main document doesn't have a direct link to more_styles.css.

If the main document has so many related files that the names won't all fit in the Related Files toolbar, a double chevron appears at the end of the list. Click it to reveal a list of the remaining files. Files are listed in the order they are linked to the main document. You cannot change the order in the Related Files toolbar. Files added to a page after it has been opened in the Document window are added automatically to the Related Files toolbar. If a file fails to appear in the toolbar, press F5. This is a keyboard shortcut for refreshing Design view, which also has the effect of updating the Related Files toolbar.

When you click a file name in the Related Files toolbar, Dreamweaver opens Split view, displaying the code of the related file in one half of the Document window, while leaving the main document in Design view in the other half, as shown in Figure 1-23 (see the "Switching between Code, Design, and Split views" section later in the chapter for details on how to change the layout). The related file is editable, and you can see the results of changes immediately by pressing F5 or clicking in the Design view half of the Document window. There's no need to save the related file first, so if you don't like the result, you can continue editing the file until you achieve the desired result. Dreamweaver puts an asterisk (*) alongside the name of the file you have edited to indicate that the changes haven't been saved. To save the changes, make sure the focus is in Code view and press

Ctrl+S/Cmd+S or select File ➤ Save. To reject the changes, click No when prompted to save them when you close the main document.

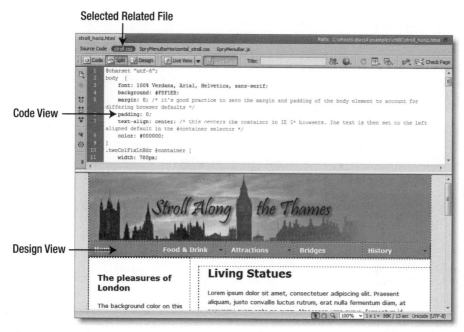

Figure 1-23. The Related Files feature lets you edit style sheets in Code view and see the results instantly in Design view.

> When upgrading to Dreamweaver CS4, you might find the Related Files feature disorienting to begin with, as there's no longer any need to open style sheets and external JavaScript files in separate tabs. If you open a related file in a tab of its own, Dreamweaver keeps both versions in sync with each other, but keeping track of where you're working can be confusing. If you find the Related Files feature doesn't fit into your workflow, you can disable it by selecting Edit ➤ Preferences (Dreamweaver ➤ Preferences on a Mac), choosing the General category, and deselecting Enable Related Files. You need to restart Dreamweaver for the change to take effect. The Related Files feature cannot be turned on and off on the fly.

Using the Code Navigator to edit style sheets

If the current page has style rules, either in an external style sheet or in the <head> of the document, leave your cursor in the Document window for a few seconds without any other activity, and a little icon like a ship's wheel (as shown alongside) pops up. It doesn't matter whether you're in Code view or Design view; it keeps on making an appearance. If you don't know what it is, it will probably drive you insane after a short while. Even if you do know what it is, its persistence can be just as maddening.

The icon has been put there for discoverability (if it doesn't appear, don't worry, because I'm going to recommend that you disable it and use a keyboard and mouse shortcut instead). The idea is to get you to discover the wonders of the Code Navigator.

Figure 1-24 shows what happened when I placed my cursor inside the pull quote to the left of the image, waited for the icon to pop up, and then clicked it. The Code Navigator displayed a list of style rules affecting the pull quote, showing the details of each one in a pop-up window as I moused over the name of the rule. As if that isn't impressive enough, each style rule is a hyperlink. Just click, and Dreamweaver opens the style sheet as a related file in Split view, with your cursor inside the selected rule ready for editing.

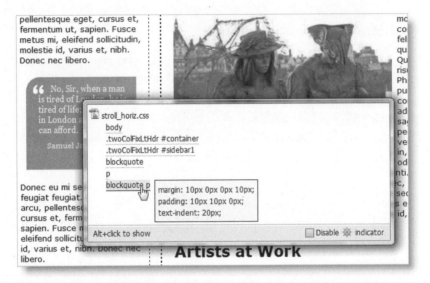

Figure 1-24. The Code Navigator is a powerful tool for inspecting and editing CSS.

If your web page is created from a Dreamweaver template or contains a library item, the Code Navigator also provides a link to the master template or library file (templates are covered in Chapter 13; library items are not covered in this book, as PHP includes—covered in Chapter 12—are more efficient). Similarly, if the page contains an <iframe>, the Code Navigator provides a link to the source document. When you click one of these links, the file opens in a new tab, ready for editing.

Once you have discovered the Code Navigator, I recommend that you get rid of the annoying icon popping up every few seconds. Just put a check mark in the Disable indicator checkbox at the bottom right of the Code Navigator (see Figure 1-24). After disabling the icon, you can display the Code Navigator by holding down the Alt key (Opt+Cmd on a Mac) while clicking anywhere in the Document window.

Although you can resize the Code Navigator, you can't move it to a different position. If you find that it's blocking your view of the page, keep in mind that where you click while holding down Alt or Opt+Cmd key doesn't change the current selection or position of the cursor in Design view. It simply determines the location of the top-left corner of the Code Navigator (if there's insufficient space, it goes for the nearest position).

If you prefer to use a keyboard shortcut to invoke the Code Navigator, it's Ctrl+Alt+N on Windows and Opt+Cmd+N on a Mac. The Code Navigator is also accessible through the View menu, the context menu in any view, and the Coding toolbar (see Figure 1-31, later in the chapter). There are so many ways to access the Code Navigator, something tells me Adobe doesn't want you to miss it!

To dismiss the Code Navigator, just click anywhere else on the screen.

Exploring the Document toolbar

Running across the top of the Document window is the Document toolbar, which is mainly concerned with controlling how your main work environment looks (see Figure 1-25). The first three buttons on the left let you switch quickly between Code view, Design view, and a combination of both called Split view, as shown earlier in Figure 1-23. The next button, labeled Live View, toggles on and off another major innovation in Dreamweaver CS4, which renders the page as it will look in a standards-compliant browser without the need to leave Design view.

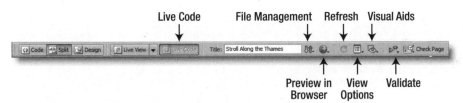

Figure 1-25. The Document toolbar mainly controls the look of the Document window

The following sections describe each of these features briefly.

Switching between Code, Design, and Split views

Some web designers, particularly those from a graphic design background, never want to see the HTML, CSS, or JavaScript code that lies behind Design view. This is a recipe for disaster with Dreamweaver. Although it's a visual design environment, you can't treat it like a word processor or desktop publishing program. You need to have a good understanding of where you're inserting elements into a page—something that's particularly important when you mix dynamic elements into a page using a server-side technology like PHP or JavaScript widgets. You don't need to know every tag and property, but you do need to have a good understanding of the technologies that lie behind the creation of a standards-compliant web page. Dreamweaver helps you by making it easy to switch quickly between the Code view and Design view, as well as displaying both in Split view.

The labels on the three buttons at the left end of the Document toolbar are fairly self-explanatory:

- Code: This displays the raw code. When the document is a static web page, it gives access to the code as you might see it in a browser's source view. If the page uses a server-side technology, such as PHP, it displays the server-side code before it has been processed. Pages that contain only code, such as JavaScript files and style sheets, are always displayed in Code view.

- Split: This displays Code view in one half of the screen and Design view in the other half.

- Design: This is Dreamweaver's visual environment for creating and editing web pages. It displays a very close approximation of what the page should look like in a browser.

The default setting for Split view is to split the page horizontally with Code view on top, as shown earlier in Figure 1-23. You can reverse the layout by displaying Design view at the top and Code view at the bottom. Even better, you can now split the screen vertically, as shown in Figure 1-26. This layout works best on a large monitor (the screenshot was taken in the Classic workspace layout with Dreamweaver maximized on a 1680 × 1050 monitor and all the panels hidden). The default is to show Design view on the right, but you can reverse this.

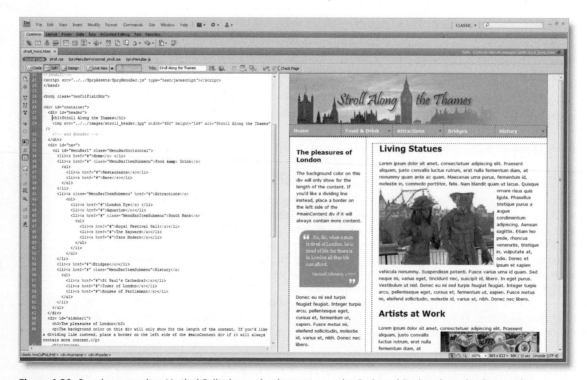

Figure 1-26. On a large monitor, Vertical Split view makes it easy to see the Code and Design views simultaneously.

Vertical Split view has long been requested by regular Dreamweaver users. Another of their requests has also been granted: Split Code view, which enables you to see different sections of code from the same document. Split Code view can be displayed with the screen split horizontally or vertically. Each section of screen scrolls independently. You can cut and paste from one section to the other, but you cannot drag and drop.

Access to all these Split view options is either through the View menu or the Layout control on the Application bar, as shown in Figure 1-27. Unless you have hidden the Application bar on the Mac version, using the Layout control is easier because there are fewer options to choose from. If the Split Vertically and Design View on Left options are grayed out, switch to Split view by selecting Code and Design. (When the screen is split horizontally, Design View on Left changes to Design View on Top.)

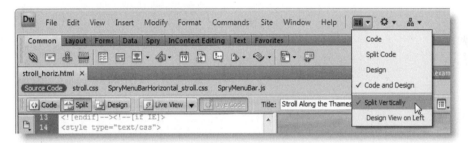

Figure 1-27. You can use the Layout control on the Application bar to switch to Vertical Split view.

If you have more than one document open, the Split view options are specific to each tab. To set your preferred Split view layout as a default, close all documents except one. Set your desired options, and then close the document. Dreamweaver remembers your preferences and applies them to all future documents, but you can switch to a different layout at any time.

Using Live view to test pages

Yet another major change in Dreamweaver CS4 is the introduction of Live view. This uses the open source WebKit browser engine (http://webkit.org/) to display the current document exactly as it will look in a standards-compliant browser. Dreamweaver uses essentially the same version of WebKit as Safari 3, but with certain modifications to provide extra functionality within Design view. Dynamic features, such as rollovers, JavaScript menus, and server-side code, work as you would expect in a browser. Although this is no substitute for testing the page in all your target browsers, used in combination with the Related Files feature, it makes editing dynamic features a breeze. Figures 1-28 and 1-29 show Live view in action.

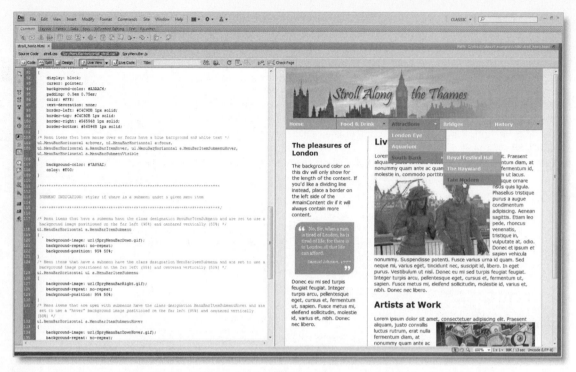

Figure 1-28. Using Live view makes it possible to view the effect of changes to style rules for dynamic features.

Live view makes a huge difference when working with Ajax or Spry (Adobe's implementation of Ajax). The screenshot in Figure 1-28 shows how you can test the rollover effect in a Spry menu bar (see Chapter 6) without needing to leave the Document window. I turned on Live view, activated the menu bar in Design view, invoked the Code Navigator, and then selected the :hover style rule for menu items. This opened the style sheet as a related file in Split view, ready for me to edit. After changing the color property, I pressed F5 to refresh Design view and moused over the menu bar to see the results of the change. I didn't like the result, so I clicked No when prompted to save the changes when closing the document.

> *Ajax stands for Asynchronous JavaScript and XML (see* http://en.wikipedia.org/ wiki/AJAX). *Originally, Ajax referred to using JavaScript to communicate with the web server and redraw parts of the page without the need to reload the whole page. Since then, its meaning has broadened to encompass just about any technique that uses one of the popular JavaScript libraries such as Prototype (*http://www.prototypejs.org*), script.aculo.us (*http://script.aculo.us/*), and jQuery (*http://jquery.com/*). Spry is Adobe's JavaScript library that powers the Spry menu bar (Chapter 6), various effects and widgets (Chapters 7, 8, and 9), and Spry data sets (Chapter 19).*

Figure 1-29. Working with Ajax and Spry data sets is transformed by Live view.

The top screenshot in Figure 1-29 shows what an image gallery built with a Spry data set looks like in Design view. In Dreamweaver CS3, you needed to load the page into an external browser every time you wanted to see the finished page. Live view makes that a thing of the past (the data must come from a static source; Spry data sets that use dynamically generated data still need to be viewed in a browser). The bottom screenshot in Figure 1-29 shows the same page with Live view turned on. Not only do you see the page as it will look in a browser, but also the main image changes when you click one of the thumbnails.

Live view also works with server-side pages, such as PHP, as long as you have defined a testing server in the site definition (see Chapter 2). If you're upgrading from a previous version of Dreamweaver, this effectively replaces Live Data view (the next section explains the difference). Even if you don't have a testing server, Live view still displays the static HTML parts of the page.

The down arrow to the right of the Live View button opens a menu controlling the following options:

- Freeze JavaScript: The menu option is mainly a reminder of the keyboard shortcut (F6) to freeze dynamic effects controlled by JavaScript. For example, rollovers depend on the position of your mouse. If you press F6, the rollover remains frozen even when you move the mouse away to work on a related file.

- Disable JavaScript: This option lets you see what the page looks like in a browser that doesn't support JavaScript or where JavaScript has been turned off.

- Disable Plugins: This disables plugins, such as Flash Player, so you can see the effect in a browser that doesn't have the plugin.

- Use Testing Server For Document Source: This applies only to pages that use a server-side technology, such as PHP. A testing server needs to be set up in the site definition (see Chapter 2) for server-side code to be processed. When you click the Live View button in a PHP page, Dreamweaver automatically asks if you want to update the page on the testing server. You must click Yes for the dynamic code to be processed. If you click No, it asks if you want to use the local source files instead. Using the local source files results in only the static HTML elements being displayed.

- Use Local Files For Document Links: This does *not* mean that you can use hyperlinks in Live view to navigate to other pages in your site. It refers to using local versions of style sheets and external JavaScript files, rather than using those on the testing server.

- HTTP Request Settings: This opens a dialog box that lets you set POST and GET variables to be passed to the page when displayed in Live view.

With the exception of HTTP Request Settings, all Live view menu options are toggled on and off by clicking them. A check mark alongside an option indicates that it has been turned on.

What happened to Live Data and how does Live view differ?

If you're upgrading from a previous version of Dreamweaver, you might be confused by the difference between Live view and Live Data view.

In previous versions, Live Data made it easy to envisage the output of pages using server-side code, such as PHP and Active Server Pages (ASP), by processing the code through a testing server and displaying it in Design view. Live view, on the other hand, works for all web pages, not just ones that use server-side technology; and it uses a real browser engine to display the content of your page. You still need a testing server to display dynamic output from server-side code, but Live view renders the page far more accurately than Live Data. For most purposes, Live view replaces Live Data view.

Although Live view is much more accurate, a potential drawback is that you cannot edit directly in Design view when Live view is turned on. You must either switch off Live view or edit the source code in the Code view section of Split view. However, there are times when it can be useful to edit the HTML elements of a page while viewing the output of server-side code. For example, you might want to edit the static header cells of a dynamically generated table. For this reason, Live Data view has been retained in Dreamweaver CS4. However, it's no longer accessible from the Document toolbar. To activate Live Data, use the menu option View ➤ Live Data or the keyboard shortcut Ctrl+Shift+R/Shift+Cmd+R (the menu option is visible only when the current document is a dynamic page).

> *Only static HTML can be edited in Live Data view. Output generated by server-side code cannot be altered except by editing the underlying code directly in Code view.*

Inspecting dynamically generated code with Live Code

The resurgence of interest in JavaScript stemming from the popularity of Ajax and libraries such as jQuery and Spry has undoubtedly brought benefits. JavaScript sees a web page in terms of a hierarchical structure known as the Document Object Model (DOM), which can be manipulated to produce dynamic effects, including rollovers and sliding panels, and to rearrange the content of the page. The difficulty, from the developer's perspective, is that JavaScript manipulates the DOM behind the scenes inside the browser, so it can be very difficult to troubleshoot if anything goes wrong. If only you could see the HTML code generated by the JavaScript . . . Well, now you can, thanks to the Live Code button on the Document toolbar.

The Live Code feature lets you inspect the HTML generated not only by JavaScript, but also by server-side languages such as PHP (as long as you have defined a testing server). It relies on Live view, so the Live Code button remains grayed out on the Document toolbar until Live view is invoked. When you click the Live Code button, Dreamweaver opens Split view (if it's not already open) and displays the generated code in Split view. As a visual reminder that you're viewing the generated code rather than the original, the background color of Split view turns yellow. Figure 1-30 shows part of the script from the Spry image gallery in Figure 1-29 as seen in Code view normally (top screenshot) and with Live Code turned on (bottom screenshot). The JavaScript commands highlighted in gray in the top screenshot are interpreted by the Live Code engine to generate two <option> tags with values drawn from a Spry data set.

Figure 1-30. Live Code lets you see the HTML generated by JavaScript and server-side languages.

If you find the bright-yellow background color of Live Code too much to bear, you need to dive into the bowels of your computer to change it.

On Windows, you need to modify the Windows Registry. This is not difficult, but it could affect the operation of your computer if you're not careful. On Windows Vista, click the Start *button and type* regedit *in the search field. This should display* regedit.exe *at the top of the result list. Click it to open the Registry Editor. On Windows XP, launch the Registry Editor by clicking* Start ➤ Run, *typing* regedit *in the* Run *dialog box, and click-ing* OK. *In the Registry Editor, select this entry in the left pane:* HKEY_CURRENT_USER\ Software\Adobe\Dreamweaver CS4\Tag Colors. *In the right pane, select* Background Color – Live Code, *right-click, and choose* Modify *from the context menu. Type a new color in hexadecimal notation (e.g.,* #FFC *for a lighter yellow) into the* Value data *field and click* OK. *Close the Registry Editor and restart Dreamweaver.*

On a Mac, open Macintosh HD:Users:<username>:Library:Preferences:Adobe Dreamweaver 10 Prefs *in a text editor such as BBEdit or TextWrangler (both from* http://www.barebones.com). *Locate this line:* background color – live code=#FF7. *Change the* #FF7 *to a new color in hexadecimal notation. Then save the file and restart Dreamweaver.*

Live Code is a useful addition to a developer's arsenal of debugging tools. However, don't confuse it with a real debugger like the FireBug plugin for the Firefox browser (http://www.joehewitt.com/software/firebug/). It won't tell you about syntax errors in your code. But by showing you exactly what is being output by the JavaScript or server-side code, Live Code provides confirmation (or otherwise) that your script is doing what you intended. Live Code displays generated content, so you cannot edit Code view when it's turned on.

Other options on the Document toolbar

The following list briefly describes the other options on the Document toolbar:

- Title: This is where you enter the document title that is displayed in the browser title bar.

- File management: This offers a quick way of uploading and downloading the current file to and from your remote server. Setting the connection details is covered in Chapter 2.

- Preview in browser: This displays the current page in an external browser or Device Central. Dreamweaver automatically detects the browsers installed on your computer and lists them in a drop-down menu. Device Central is an emulator that lets you see what your web page will look like in a mobile device. It's a separate program automatically installed with Dreamweaver, unless you deselect it during the installation process.

- Refresh: This refreshes Design view. It's used only when you're working in the underlying code in Split view. Otherwise, Design view refreshes automatically. You can also use F5.

- View options: This turns rulers and guides on and off in Design view. It also controls Code view features, such as line numbering and word wrap.

- Visual aids: This controls the CSS visual aids described in Chapter 4.

- Validate: This option checks your document, selected files, or the entire site against World Wide Web Consortium (W3C) standards. However, it doesn't work on PHP pages, and Dreamweaver's validator misses some errors, particularly when checking against a Strict Document Type Definition (DTD). Double-check against the official W3C Markup Validation Service at http://validator.w3.org.

- Check page: This runs checks on the current page for browser compatibility and accessibility. The results are shown in the Results panel group. It checks only static code, so it might not always produce meaningful results on pages that generate output dynamically with Spry or PHP. The browser-compatibility check provides links to more detailed explanations and suggested solutions on the Adobe website. You can also access the CSS Advisor website (http://www.adobe.com/go/bccdw) directly from the Check page menu.

Getting the best out of Code view

Code view is not just for inspecting the underlying code. It's a great editing environment with many features, such as code hinting, syntax coloring, and automatic code completion, designed to make coding a pleasure rather than a chore. In fact, some regular Dreamweaver users confess to spending 100 percent of their time here. Regardless of whether you're a coder or a designer, it's useful to know your way around Code view.

Two new features that will be of particular interest to readers upgrading from a previous version of Dreamweaver are code introspection for JavaScript and the ability to print code in color.

Using the Coding toolbar

The Coding toolbar is displayed on the left side of Code view by default. It's also available in the Code Inspector (F10/Opt+F10), which allows you to view the underlying code of a page in a separate window. The Coding toolbar can't be undocked, but you can hide it in Code view by deselecting it from the View ➤ Toolbars menu (or from the context menu of any toolbar). In the Code Inspector, it's controlled independently by the View Options menu at the top of the inspector.

> Don't confuse the Code Inspector with the Code Navigator, which is new to Dreamweaver CS4 and was described earlier in the chapter. The Code Navigator is dedicated to working with CSS, whereas the Code Inspector displays the underlying code of the current document in a separate panel. It's normally used only in a dual-monitor workspace layout, effectively letting you see Code view and Design view full screen on separate monitors. To launch the Code Inspector, press F10/Opt+F10 or select Window ➤ Code Inspector.

Figure 1-31 shows the purpose of each button on the Coding toolbar; the same information is displayed as a tooltip whenever you hover your mouse pointer over one of these buttons. If there's not enough room to display all the buttons, a double chevron appears after the last button that can fit into the available space. Click it to display the rest of the toolbar along the bottom of Code view.

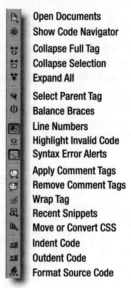

	Open Documents
	Show Code Navigator
	Collapse Full Tag
	Collapse Selection
	Expand All
	Select Parent Tag
	Balance Braces
	Line Numbers
	Highlight Invalid Code
	Syntax Error Alerts
	Apply Comment Tags
	Remove Comment Tags
	Wrap Tag
	Recent Snippets
	Move or Convert CSS
	Indent Code
	Outdent Code
	Format Source Code

Figure 1-31.
The Coding toolbar

Two buttons have been added since Dreamweaver CS3: Show Code Navigator and Syntax Error Alerts in Info Bar. Also, the icon of Move or Convert CSS has been changed to match the CSS Styles panel in iconic mode.

Let's take a quick look at what each button does:

- Open Documents: This displays a list of currently open documents together with the full pathname of each file. This is very useful if you have several pages open, all with the same name (such as index.php from different folders or sites). Click the name of a file, and it comes to the front—no more guessing whether you have the correct file open.

- Show Code Navigator: This displays the Code Navigator, which was described earlier in this chapter. The style rules displayed by the Code Navigator depend on the current location of the cursor. The ability to identify the appropriate style rules seems to be less accurate in Code view. When working in Split view, it is advisable to select elements in the Design view half of the Document window before clicking this button.

- Collapse Full Tag: This selects the code block in which your cursor is currently located and collapses everything inside, including the opening and closing tags. Unfortunately, it cannot be used to select a PHP code block. To collapse everything *outside* a full tag, hold down the Alt/Opt key while clicking the Collapse Full Tag button. This is useful for isolating a block of code and hiding the rest of the page.

- Collapse Selection: This collapses the currently selected code. To collapse all code *outside* the selection, hold down Alt/Opt while clicking the Collapse Selection button.

- Expand All: Click this to expand all collapsed sections.

- Select Parent Tag: This selects the parent tag of the current selection or wherever the insertion point is currently located. For example, if your cursor is inside a paragraph, it selects the entire paragraph and the enclosing <p> tags. Clicking again moves up the document hierarchy, always selecting the parent element of the current selection.

- Balance Braces: This selects all code between matching curly braces, brackets, or parentheses. *This button will help maintain your sanity when working with JavaScript and PHP code.*

- Line Numbers: This toggles on and off the display of line numbers in Code view.

- Highlight Invalid Code: Dreamweaver highlights incorrectly nested tags in yellow. This can be distracting in Code view, particularly when working with PHP, where conditional structures might result in code that Dreamweaver incorrectly interprets as invalid. This button toggles the yellow highlighting on and off in Code view. The default is off.

- Syntax Error Alerts in Info Bar: This pops up a yellow bar at the top of Code view whenever Dreamweaver discovers what it thinks is a syntax error in JavaScript. As you can see in Figure 1-32, Dreamweaver treats any incomplete statement as an error. It doesn't remove the warning until you type the closing brace of the function block. If you write your own JavaScript, you'll find the constant nagging extremely annoying. Turn off the alerts by clicking this button, and just use it to check your script when you have finished. Clicking the button toggles it on and off, and Dreamweaver remembers your last selection.

Figure 1-32.
The JavaScript syntax checker tends to be overzealous in what it regards as errors.

- Apply Comment Tags: This lets you apply different types of comment tags to the current line or selection. PHP comments are covered in Chapter 10.

- Remove Comment Tags: This removes comment tags from the current line or selection.

- Wrap Tag: This provides a quick way to wrap the current selection in an HTML tag. Dreamweaver lets you select any tag, even if it's inappropriate in the current context. This is based on the principle that, if you're working in Code view, you should know what you're doing. When mixed with PHP conditional logic, apparently invalid code is often perfectly OK, so Dreamweaver makes no attempt to intervene.

- Recent Snippets: This displays a list of the most recently used items from the Snippets panel, providing quick access to frequently used code snippets.
- Move or Convert CSS: This provides a quick way to move style rules, as described in Chapter 4.
- Indent Code: This moves the opening tag of the current selection to the right. If nothing is selected, Dreamweaver automatically selects the parent tag and moves it. The Tab key performs the same function.
- Outdent Code: This moves the opening tag to the left. You can also use Shift+Tab.
- Format Source Code: This reveals a menu that lets you apply default formatting to the entire page or the current selection. It also provides quick access to the Code Format category of the Preferences panel and to the Tag Library Editor. The Tag Library Editor gives you control over how every single HTML tag is formatted in your underlying code. It's mainly of interest to advanced users, but the interface is intuitive and easy to use.

In addition to using the Coding toolbar to collapse sections of code, you can use the keyboard shortcuts listed in Table 1-4. When you collapse a section of code, it affects only what you see in Code view; the contents remain fully expanded in Design view. Dreamweaver remembers which sections of code are collapsed when a page is saved, so the same layout is visible in Code view the next time you open a document.

Table 1-4. Keyboard shortcuts for collapsing code

Action	Windows shortcut	Mac shortcut
Collapse full tag	Ctrl+Shift+J	Shift+Cmd+J
Collapse outside tag	Ctrl+Alt+J	Opt+Cmd+J
Collapse selection	Ctri+Shift+C	Shift+Cmd+C
Collapse outside selection	Ctrl+Alt+C	Opt+Cmd+C
Expand all	Ctrl+Alt+E	Opt+Cmd+E

To inspect a collapsed section, highlight it and use the plus button in the left margin (it's a triangle in the Mac version) to expand it, or hover your mouse pointer over it and view the content as a tooltip.

To select sections of code in Code view, use the Select Parent Tag or Balance Braces buttons. Alternatively, use your mouse or keyboard in the same way as with any text editor. Double-clicking selects the current word. Triple-clicking selects the parent tag. (The GoLive selection shortcuts *do not work* in Dreamweaver.)

Setting Code view options

Code view has a number of options that you can set by accessing View ➤ Code View Options or from the View Options menu on the Document toolbar (see Figure 1-25 and the screenshot alongside). You toggle the options on and off by clicking them. A check mark alongside an option indicates that it's active. These options work as follows:

- Word Wrap: The way Dreamweaver wraps text in Code view confuses many people. There are two options: soft and hard wrapping. Soft wrapping is *on* by default and works like a word processor. When code would normally extend beyond the right edge of Code view, Dreamweaver automatically wraps it to the next line. If you resize the Code view window, the code reorganizes itself to fit the viewport. No new line characters are inserted into the code until you hit Enter/Return. If you prefer your code to be in a single line and don't mind scrolling horizontally, deselect Word Wrap. Hard wrapping is *off* by default. When turned on, it automatically inserts a new line character a preset distance from the left margin. Although this makes code look tidy, it causes serious problems with JavaScript and is *not* recommended. It's controlled by the Automatic wrapping option in the Code Format category of the Preferences panel (Edit ➤ Preferences or Dreamweaver ➤ Preferences). If you have turned this option on, I strongly recommend that you turn it off and rely on soft wrapping instead.

- Line Numbers: Dreamweaver displays line numbers in the left margin of Code view. They are generated automatically and don't become part of your code. The line numbers are particularly useful for locating problems with PHP code. You can also toggle them on and off from the Coding toolbar. Lines that are soft-wrapped have only one line number, even if they span several lines on the screen.

- Hidden Characters: This option reveals characters that aren't normally visible in your code. It should normally be turned off, but can be useful for debugging problems caused by unwanted newline characters in PHP or JavaScript.

- Highlight Invalid Code: This menu option does the same as the button on the Coding toolbar described in the preceding section.

- Syntax Coloring: Dreamweaver highlights HTML, PHP, and other code in preset colors according to the role it fulfils, making it easy to identify key sections of code quickly. Forgetting to close a pair of quotes results in the subsequent code being displayed in the wrong color, alerting you to the mistake. In normal circumstances, this option should always be on. You can adjust the colors to your liking by going to Edit ➤ Preferences (Dreamweaver ➤ Preferences on a Mac) and selecting Code Coloring. Choose the appropriate Document type, and click Edit Coloring Scheme.

- Auto Indent: With this option selected, Dreamweaver automatically indents your code according to the settings in the Code Format category of the Preferences panel and the Tag Library Editor.

- Syntax Error Alerts in Info Bar: This option does the same as the button on the Coding toolbar described in the preceding section.

- Design View on Left: This option is available only in Vertical Split view; in the default Split view, it changes to Design View on Top. In both cases, it controls on which side Design view is displayed in Split view.

- Color Icons: This toggles icons between grayscale and color.

Using code hints and auto completion

By default, Dreamweaver displays context-sensitive code hints in Code view. For example, if you type an opening angle bracket after the <body> tag of an HTML page, a context menu pops up, displaying all valid HTML tags, as shown in the screenshot alongside. You can scroll down to find the tag you want and double-click to insert it, or just continue typing. As soon as you type di, the context menu highlights <>div. Press Enter/Return, and Dreamweaver completes the tag name.

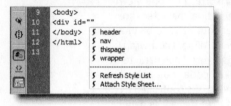

When you press the spacebar, another context menu springs up, this time showing you all the valid attributes for the tag. Again, scroll down to select the one you want or continue typing. If you type id and press Enter/Return, Dreamweaver enters id="" and positions the insertion point between the quotes, ready for you to insert the ID value. Even better, if your page already has a style sheet attached to it, Dreamweaver populates a list of defined IDs, as shown in the screenshot alongside. Use your keyboard arrow keys and Enter/Return to insert your choice. Alternatively, select it with your mouse pointer and double-click.

These context menus continue to appear until you type the closing angle bracket of the tag. If you lose the context menu, just press Ctrl+spacebar anywhere between the opening and closing brackets of a tag.

> *The keyboard shortcut for code hints on the Mac version is the same as Windows (Ctrl+spacebar) to avoid a conflict with Spotlight, which uses Cmd+spacebar.*

Dreamweaver is smart enough to keep track of which tags are open. As soon as you type </ in Code view, it automatically inserts the correct closing tag. For example, let's say you have the following code in a page:

```
<p>This text is <strong>bold and <em>italicized
```

If you type </ three times, Dreamweaver automatically completes the open tags in the correct order like this:

```
<p>This text is <strong>bold and <em>italicized</em></strong></p>
```

> *The only exception to this automatic completion of the closing tag is with <script>. This is to prevent Dreamweaver from closing the <script> tag incorrectly inside a block of JavaScript.*

For compatibility with older versions, you can get Dreamweaver to insert the matching closing tag as soon as you type the closing angle bracket of an opening tag. So, if you enter <p>, Dreamweaver inserts </p> and places the insertion point between the opening and closing tags. This setting can be useful when working with PHP because Dreamweaver sometimes gets confused as to which tag should be completed if dynamic code lies in between. You can also tell Dreamweaver never to complete tags. To change the default settings, select Edit ➤ Preferences (Dreamweaver ➤ Preferences on a Mac) and choose the Code Hints category.

Most people find code hints invaluable, but if they annoy you or get in your way, you can delay their appearance by up to five seconds or turn them off altogether. However, Dreamweaver is much more responsive if you leave the delay at its default setting of zero. The Menus option in the Code Hints category of the Preferences panel lets you turn off code hints for individual categories. For example, you may decide that you want code hints only for HTML tags and CSS properties. All categories are enabled by default.

Introducing improved support for JavaScript code hints

Previous versions of Dreamweaver have offered only limited support for JavaScript code hints. Not only were the code hints incomplete, they were also available only in external JavaScript files. JavaScript code hints are now also available in `<script>` blocks in web pages. Moreover, the range of code hints now means serious JavaScript programmers can continue working inside Dreamweaver CS4 without needing to switch to a different program.

Dreamweaver now has code hints for properties and methods of the following primitive data types: `Object`, `Array`, `Boolean`, `Date`, `Number`, `RegExp`, and `String`. It also has support for the main built-in DOM object. The code hints are triggered as soon as you type a period after a variable or object.

The most welcome news of all for programmers is that Dreamweaver CS4 is also capable of **code introspection**. This means that Dreamweaver scans your own functions, classes, and JavaScript Object Notation (JSON) objects and provides code hints for them, too. Your custom definitions can be either in the same document or in an external file (as long as it's linked to the document you're working in). Figure 1-33 shows an example of a code hint being displayed for a custom function defined in the `<head>` of a web page.

```
6   <script type="text/javascript">
7   function annoyingScript(message) {
8       alert('Hi, there! ' + message);
9   }
10  </script>
11  </head>
12
13  <body onload="annoyingScript(">
```

annoyingScript(**message**)

Figure 1-33. Dreamweaver CS4 now provides code hints for your own JavaScript functions, classes, and JSON.

Printing code in color

This is something that has been requested for many years: Dreamweaver CS4 finally prints code in color. To print the code of the current document, select File ➤ Print Code, right-click in Code view and select Print Code from the context menu, or press Ctrl+P/Cmd+P.

Dreamweaver uses the same colors as in Code view. However, it does not print the background color, even if you have changed it from the default white; any parts of code that are white or nearly white are converted to black. To print code in black and white, deselect Syntax Coloring in View ➤ Code View Options or the View Options menu of the Document toolbar.

Line numbers are included in the printout. To turn them off, deselect Line Numbers in View ➤ Code View Options or the View options menu of the Document toolbar.

> *Using the keyboard shortcut Ctrl+P/Cmd+P prints the underlying code even if you invoke it while in Design view. It does not print the page layout. To print what the page looks like, you need to launch the web page in a browser and print it from there.*

A quick look at other changes in Dreamweaver CS4

The main focus of this chapter has been an in-depth tour of the UI for both newcomers and old hands. But so much has changed in Dreamweaver CS4, it has also been a guide to what's new. So I think it's worth spending a little time looking at the remaining new features, most of which are covered in greater depth in later chapters. It's also important to note that some features have been removed from Dreamweaver, so I'll also cover what's gone.

Screen sharing

It's often a lot quicker and more effective to show a client or colleague how to do something than try to explain the procedure in words. Thanks to a new feature called Creative Suites Extended Services (CSXS), you can do that with Dreamweaver and most other CS4 applications, even if the other person is on the other side of the world. In fact, you can invite up to three others to participate in the demonstration. All you need is an Adobe ID, which involves registering a few basic details on the Adobe website (http://www.adobe.com). If you don't already have an ID, you can apply for one the first time you access CSXS.

At the time of Dreamweaver CS4's initial release, only two services were available: the Search for help feature (see Figure 1-3 and Table 1-1) and Share My Screen, which provides instant desktop sharing through an Internet connection. There is currently no charge for the screen-sharing service, so why not give it a try?

> *Why is screen sharing free? No doubt because Adobe hopes the experience of using this type of desktop conferencing will encourage businesses to subscribe to the paid-for version, which can host up to 15, 500, or 1,500 participants, depending on the level of subscription (http://www.adobe.com/products/acrobatconnect/).*

Setting up a screen-sharing session

The following instructions guide you through the basic process of sharing your screen with up to three other people. The screen-sharing service is hosted through Adobe ConnectNow, so you need to be connected to the Internet to use it.

1. Inside Dreamweaver CS4, select File ➤ Share My Screen.

2. Dreamweaver communicates with the ConnectNow server, and when it establishes a connection, you should see the login panel shown in Figure 1-34.

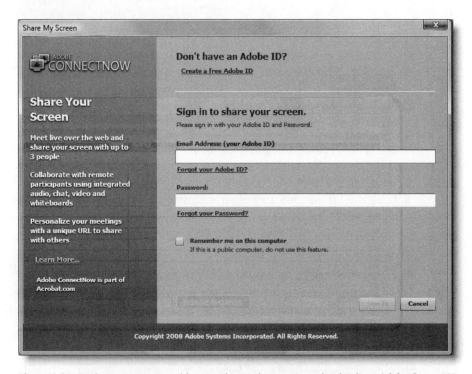

Figure 1-34. To share your screen with up to three others, you need to log in to Adobe ConnectNow.

If you don't have an Adobe ID, click the Create a free Adobe ID link, and follow the on-screen instructions.

If you already have an Adobe ID, enter your email address and Adobe password in the appropriate fields.

If you select the checkbox labeled Remember me on this computer, the next time you access File ➤ Share My Screen, the login panel disappears as soon as Dreamweaver has connected with the Adobe server.

If this is the first time you are logging in, or if you prefer not to be logged in automatically, click the Sign In button (it's grayed out in Figure 1-34 because the required fields haven't been filled in yet).

3. Once you have logged in, you will be presented with the exclusive URL that enables others to view your screen, as shown in Figure 1-35. Adobe ConnectNow automatically assigns the URL based on your name. If you want to change it, click the Customize Your Meeting URL link. There's also a link that creates email invitations to send to the people you want to join the session.

Figure 1-35.
Adobe ConnectNow gives you a
personalized URL for your screen-
sharing sessions.

4. When you click the Close button, ConnectNow launches your browser. If this is the first time you have participated in a session using ConnectNow or the paid-for version, Connect, you might be prompted to install a special plugin. This is necessary for screen sharing to work. It should normally be a very quick process.

5. Once the browser has connected successfully to ConnectNow, it launches the screen shown in Figure 1-36. This is your online meeting room, which is actually a desktop application that runs in the Adobe Integrated Runtime (AIR).

Figure 1-36. The ConnectNow meeting room lets you control what others see.

At this stage, no one can see your screen. The ConnectNow window has a chat panel that works just like instant messaging. In the center is a button labeled Share My Computer Screen. Before clicking this, you should be aware that once you start sharing, other participants will be able to see *everything* on your desktop, not just Dreamweaver. So make sure there's nothing there that you wouldn't want your mother or the taxman to see. You can minimize the ConnectNow window to tidy things up, if necessary.

6. When your guests access your personal URL, they will be asked to sign in either as a guest, or using their Adobe ID. Once they sign in, they will be presented with a screen telling them that the meeting is private, and that a message has been sent to the host.

As the host, a pop-up window will appear at the bottom of your screen, informing you that Mickey Mouse, Bill Gates, or whoever you invited would like permission to join. When you accept, the other person gets to see the same ConnectNow window as in Figure 1-36. Again, it might be necessary to install a plugin if it's the first time the guest has accessed a Connect or ConnectNow session.

7. When you're ready to share, click Share My Computer Screen. You will be asked to confirm that you're ready to start sharing. Click Share (or Cancel, if you're not ready). You'll then be presented with the short message shown in Figure 1-37, telling you the difference between what you see as host and what others see.

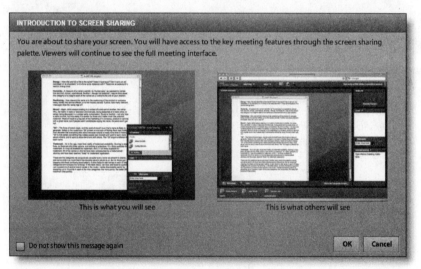

Figure 1-37. The host of the meeting sees a different screen layout from other participants.

8. Click OK to start sharing. As soon as you do so, the ConnectNow window shrinks to show just a list of attendees and the chat window, exposing the rest of your desktop, as shown in Figure 1-38. Everyone else sees your desktop framed in the Screen Sharing section of the maximized ConnectNow window. The only thing the others can't see is your small version of the ConnectNow window. Unless you want to keep an eye on the chat window, it's probably a good idea to minimize the ConnectNow window while sharing your screen.

Figure 1-38. Once you start sharing, your whole desktop is exposed.

9. To stop sharing, click the x button at the top right of the host's ConnectNow window, as shown in Figure 1-39.

Figure 1-39.
While sharing, the host's
ConnectNow window
shows attendees, a chat
window, and tools to
control the session.

10. To end a meeting, select Meeting ➤ End Meeting in the maximized ConnectNow window. You cannot end a meeting while still sharing your screen. You will be presented with a suggested farewell message, which you can edit or simply send as is to all participants. Once the meeting is over, close the ConnectNow window.

This has been only a brief overview of screen sharing. The best way to find out more is to try it out for yourself, and launch the Help menu inside the ConnectNow window. As you'll discover, the service supports the use of webcams, speech through Voice over Internet Protocol (VoIP), and telephone conferencing. Although the ConnectNow service is free, telephone conferencing is charged at long-distance rates.

> *The screen-sharing service lets others take over control of your screen—as long as you give them permission first. This is both very useful and potentially dangerous. Make sure you know who the other person is before handing over control of your computer.*

Managing CSXS

Other hosted services will become available after the release of Dreamweaver CS4. To prepare for them, there is a new Connections panel, shown in Figure 1-40. To open it, select Window ➤ Extensions ➤ Connections.

> *The Extensions item on the Window menu is confusingly named. It has nothing to do with extensions to the program's functionality that have been a major feature of Dreamweaver ever since the first version. To install Dreamweaver extensions, launch Extension Manager 2 directly from the Start menu on Windows or Finder on a Mac. Alternatively, use Manage Extensions on the Commands or Help menus.*

Figure 1-40. The Connections panel is intended to provide access to future hosted services.

If you log into the Connections panel with your Adobe ID, Dreamweaver will automatically check the server for updates to CSXS and install them. If you want to disable this default behavior, click the panel options menu button at the top right of the panel, as shown in Figure 1-40. The Update preferences menu item lets you choose whether Dreamweaver automatically checks for updates and installs them. The Offline options menu item lets you choose to be kept offline. Selecting this option disables the Share My Screen feature described in the preceding section.

Other new features

In addition to the CSXS features already described, the following features have been added or significantly changed:

- **JavaScript extractor**: This identifies most or all of the JavaScript in a web page and moves it to an external file. Its use is described in Chapter 8.

- **Spry data sets**: The interface for creating Spry data sets has been completely redesigned. It now generates data sets from HTML sources as well as XML. Its use is covered in Chapter 19.

- **New Spry widgets**: Four new Spry widgets have been added. Three of them handle the validation of form elements (radio button groups, password fields, and password confirmation fields). These are covered in Chapter 9. The other widget creates tooltips and disjointed rollovers, and is covered in Chapter 7.

- **JavaScript widgets galore**: You're no longer restricted to using Spry widgets in Dreamweaver CS4. Adobe has sought the cooperation of leading developers of JavaScript widgets, including members of the Yahoo! User Interface (YUI) and jQuery teams, to create versions of their widgets that can be directly integrated into Dreamweaver. See Chapter 8 for details.

- **Subversion integration**: Subversion (http://subversion.tigris.org/) is one of the most popular open source version control systems. Dreamweaver now provides direct access to a Subversion repository through the Files panel. This feature is described in the next chapter.

- **Cloaking of individual files**: Cloaking excludes certain files from being uploaded to your remote server. In previous versions of Dreamweaver, cloaking was restricted to all files with specified file name extensions and whole directories (folders). You can now cloak individual files as well. Cloaking is covered in the next chapter.

  A related improvement excludes cloaked files from reports on orphaned files (files that have no incoming links). To run a check for orphaned files, select Site ➤ Check Links Sitewide. When the Link Checker tab opens in the Results panel group, choose Orphaned Files from the Show drop-down menu at the top left of the panel.

- **Photoshop Smart Objects**: Photoshop integration has been improved by the addition of support for Smart Objects (images that are directly linked to the original Photoshop file). This is covered in Chapter 3. Dreamweaver does *not* support Smart Objects imported from other Creative Suite programs, such as Illustrator.

- **Inserting Flash and Flex movies**: The way that Flash and Flex movies are embedded in a web page has changed. Pages created in Dreamweaver CS4 use the new method, which includes an express installer that updates the version of Flash Player

1

if necessary. Pages created in previous versions of Dreamweaver are not updated, but can be edited without problems. See Chapter 3 for details.

- **InContext Editing**: This is an Adobe online hosted service that permits authorized users to edit web pages through a web browser. What can and cannot be changed is determined by the developer creating editable regions and setting rules through Dreamweaver CS4. InContext Editing is covered in Chapter 13.

- **Online help**: Most of Dreamweaver's help files are now hosted online. When you access Dreamweaver Help from the Help menu (or press F1), Dreamweaver detects whether you are online and launches the help system in your default browser. Adobe says it has adopted this system so that the content can be updated more easily and corrected if necessary. A limited set of help files is included in the program for use when you are offline.

  The new Search for help field in the Application bar also brings up online help from relevant community sites. The search is powered by Google, but Adobe monitors the content to make sure only reliable articles are referenced.

Considerable disappointment was voiced by many people at the lack of new features for PHP and other server-side technologies when the public beta of Dreamweaver CS4 was released in May 2008. This disappointment is understandable, as the server behaviors have remained essentially unchanged since Dreamweaver MX came out in 2002. Speaking personally, my disappointment is more than compensated for by the other changes in Dreamweaver CS4. As I said at the beginning of this chapter, I consider this to be the most significant upgrade to the program since Dreamweaver MX. Making significant changes to the server-side features would have involved either dropping other features or risking more buggy implementation.

However, it's not true to say that nothing has changed with regard to support for PHP. The PHP code hints have been cleaned up by adding many new PHP 5 functions and removing incorrect and deprecated items. Changes have also been made to some of the server behavior code to ensure it doesn't break in PHP 6. The changes might seem small, but they're important; they have also been done in a way that remains compatible with pages developed in earlier versions of Dreamweaver.

What is no longer there

Adobe took the unusual step of announcing more than a year before the release of Dreamweaver CS4 that certain features would be removed. If you missed that announcement and can't find some of your favorite features, here's a list of what has been removed:

- Layout mode
- Timelines
- Flash elements, Flash buttons, and Flash text
- Site map
- ASP.NET and JavaServer Pages (JSP) server behaviors and recordsets
- JavaBeans
- Web Services panel

The removal of some of these items is likely to upset some people, but the first three have been removed in the interests of creating more standards-compliant web pages. Layout mode and timelines generated horrendously complex code that has no place in a modern website. Also, the Flash elements created by Dreamweaver were rather crudely built and made websites inaccessible. Their removal doesn't mean you can't use Flash elements in Dreamweaver any longer—just that you need to build them in Flash; Dreamweaver won't create them for you.

The decision to remove support for ASP.NET and JSP is more controversial, but it appears to be due to Adobe's recognition that it was fighting a losing battle trying to support five server-side technologies. It will be interesting to see what approach it takes to server-side support in future versions.

Changing default settings

In addition to the features already described, Dreamweaver has many other preferences that can be configured to suit your workflow. The default settings are fine for most people, but if you want to change the way Dreamweaver looks or works—and it hasn't already been covered in this chapter—the first place to look is in the Preferences panel (see Figure 1-41), which you access from the Edit menu in the Windows version and the Dreamweaver menu on a Mac. The keyboard shortcut is Ctrl+U/Cmd+U.

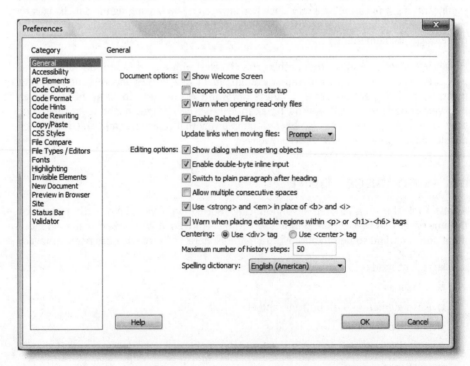

Figure 1-41. The Preferences panel controls most other aspects of how Dreamweaver looks and works.

As you can see from Figure 1-41, the Preferences panel contains 19 categories, the names of which are mostly self-explanatory. AP Elements controls the look of absolutely positioned <div> elements, which older versions of Dreamweaver refer to as *layers*. Although CSS absolute positioning can be useful, many inexperienced users misunderstood the interaction between Dreamweaver layers and other page elements, so their use is now generally discouraged.

I'll describe the most important categories at the appropriate point in later chapters. Here, I'll just touch on other important categories that don't fit in naturally elsewhere.

- Code Coloring: This lets you edit the syntax coloring scheme for different types of documents and code.
- Code Format: One of the most important settings in this category lets you choose whether to indent code for ease of reading and whether to use spaces or tabs for indentation. If you find your web pages display with unusual spacing, check that Line break type is set to LF (Unix). This is the most reliable setting even if you're working in Windows or on a Mac.
- Fonts: This controls the default size and style of fonts in Design and Code views. By default, Dreamweaver uses Unicode (utf-8). If you use a different encoding for your pages, you need to select the appropriate one from the Font settings list. Dreamweaver calls Latin-1 (iso-8859-1) encoding Western European on Windows and Western on a Mac.

Migrating snippets and other personal settings

Moving your collection of snippets, workspace layouts, or favorites simply involves copying and pasting a file or folder from your Dreamweaver configuration files.

Locating the Dreamweaver configuration files

The Dreamweaver configuration files are hidden on Windows, so you need to enable the option to view hidden files and folders in order to locate them, as follows.

- In Windows Vista, select Start ➤ Computer ➤ Organize ➤ Folder and Search Options ➤ View. In Advanced settings, choose Show hidden files and folders.
- In Windows XP, select Start ➤ My Computer ➤ Tools ➤ Folder Options ➤ View. In Advanced settings, choose Show hidden files and folders.

Once you turn on this option, hidden folders are displayed as dimmed icons to remind you to treat them with care.

Dreamweaver CS4 creates at least three configuration folders on your computer. Two of them control how the program works for everyone on the computer. In Windows, they're located in Program Files; on a Mac, they're in Applications. You should not attempt to touch them unless you know what you're doing. If you make a mistake, Dreamweaver could stop working completely.

Each time it starts up, Dreamweaver looks for another configuration folder that stores the personal settings for the current user. Editing this folder is relatively harmless. Because a separate folder is created for each user account on the computer, changing your own settings doesn't affect anyone else and vice versa. Even if you make a complete mess of things, all that's necessary is to delete the folder and all its contents. If Dreamweaver can't find your personal settings, it creates a new configuration folder loaded with all the default settings.

The location of the personal configuration folder depends on your operating system and version of Dreamweaver. For Dreamweaver CS4, it's as follows:

- **Windows Vista**: C:\Users\<*username*>\AppData\Roaming\Adobe\Dreamweaver CS4\<*language*>\Configuration
- **Windows XP**: C:\Documents and Settings\<*username*>\Application Data\ Adobe\Dreamweaver CS4\<*language*>\Configuration
- **Mac OS X**: Macintosh HD:<*username*>:Library:Application Support:Adobe: Dreamweaver CS4:<*language*>:Configuration

In all cases, <*username*> is the name of your user account on the computer and <*language*> indicates the language of your operating system. The language is usually represented by two pairs of characters separated by an underscore, as in en_US (English), es_ES (Spanish), or fr_FR (French).

Earlier versions of Dreamweaver located the personal configuration folder in a slightly different location. This is where it can be found in Dreamweaver CS3:

- **Windows Vista**: C:\Users\<*username*>\AppData\Roaming\Adobe\Dreamweaver 9\Configuration
- **Windows XP**: C:\Documents and Settings\<*username*>\Application Data\ Adobe\Dreamweaver 9\Configuration
- **Mac OS X**: Macintosh HD:Users:<*username*>:Library:Application Support: Adobe:Dreamweaver 9:Configuration

Migrating snippets

Dreamweaver does a very good job of migrating site definitions from an existing version of Dreamweaver to a new one located on the same computer (migrating them to another computer is covered in the next chapter), but it leaves behind any snippets that you have installed. (As the name suggests, snippets are short sections of useful or frequently used code ready to drop directly into a page.)

To migrate your snippets from one version of Dreamweaver to another, close Dreamweaver, and open your personal configuration folder in the version that contains the snippets. Inside, you should find a folder named Snippets. Just copy it and all its contents, and paste it into your personal configuration folder in the new version of Dreamweaver. When you start the program, your snippets should be ready for use.

Transferring workspace layouts

As mentioned earlier, you can transfer your workspace layouts from one computer to another. Dreamweaver CS3 workspace layouts are different from CS4, so you shouldn't try to mix them.

Your workspace layouts are stored in your personal configuration folder in a folder called, logically enough, Workspace. The files have the same name that you used to save the layout. Simply copy them to the Workspace folder in the other version, and restart Dreamweaver. Since the files are written in XML, you can share them among Windows and Mac users.

Moving favorites

As with workspace layout migration, changes between Dreamweaver CS3 and CS4 mean you shouldn't attempt to migrate your Insert bar favorites from one version to another. However, if you want to move your Favorites category from Dreamweaver CS4 on one computer to another, copy insertbar.xml from the Objects folder of your personal configuration folder to the same location on the other computer. If the target computer doesn't have an Objects folder inside your personal configuration folder, create one.

Troubleshooting mysterious Dreamweaver errors

The previous section described how to find your personal configuration folder, for the purpose of migrating personal settings. Another file in this folder happens to be the source of some unexplained Dreamweaver errors.

To speed up its operation, Dreamweaver creates a file called WinFileCache-********.dat on Windows and MacFileCache-********.dat on Mac OS X (the ******** represents a series of numbers and letters). Occasionally, this file gets corrupted, causing Dreamweaver to act in an unpredictable way. The most common problem is for Dreamweaver to display alerts about JavaScript errors or about "translators not found." If this happens, close Dreamweaver, delete WinFileCache-********.dat or its Mac equivalent from your personal configuration folder, and restart the program.

Deleting the cache file is normally sufficient. However, sometimes the cause lies with a third-party extension that you have installed in Dreamweaver. If you have installed any extensions, the only solution is to disable all of them and reinstall them one by one until you can identify the culprit (extensions are covered in Chapter 8).

Chapter review

This has been a marathon tour of the Dreamweaver CS4 UI and new features. Familiarity with the UI and features of any program is essential to using it successfully. Most of us are creatures of habit, so readers who have upgraded from a previous version of Dreamweaver or migrated from a different program might find the new environment difficult to get used to. Dreamweaver has a very rich feature set, but not everyone needs the same ones, and very few people are likely to need all of them. Experiment with the different aspects of the UI and find those that suit you best.

In the next chapter, I'll cover everything you need to know about setting up a website in Dreamweaver. If you're an experienced Dreamweaver user, most of it will be familiar to you, although there are some new features. If you're new to Dreamweaver, it's essential reading. Without an understanding of the role of site definition, you'll run into a lot of avoidable problems.

Dreamweaver is not just a tool for creating web pages; it's for creating websites. You create an exact copy of the website on your local computer, tell Dreamweaver how to connect with the remote web server, and upload it. When pages need updating, you download the latest version from the remote server (unless you work on your own and know the remote version hasn't changed), make any amendments, and upload it again. Even if you don't yet have a remote server, Dreamweaver expects you to organize your files exactly as they would be in a real site. This is necessary because Dreamweaver needs to keep track of the images and other assets, such as style sheets and JavaScript files that make up each page. If you decide to move files to a different location, Dreamweaver automatically updates internal links, but it can't do so unless it knows certain basic details about the site. So, defining your site within Dreamweaver is an essential first step before you even think about creating a web page.

In this chapter, you'll learn about the following:

- Choosing the best location for your files
- Understanding the difference between document- and root-relative links
- Creating virtual hosts on Windows and Mac OS X
- Setting up and testing a Dreamweaver site definition
- Integrating a site with a Subversion repository
- Backing up and migrating your site definitions

This is quite a long chapter, but many parts of it are relevant only to some readers. For instance, you can skip the entire section on virtual hosts if you decide not to use them. Also, in many cases, there are separate sets of instructions for Windows and Mac. However, don't be in a rush to get through this chapter. Site definition in Dreamweaver is not difficult, but you need to get it right, particularly when working with a server-side technology like PHP—the focus of the second half of this book.

Dreamweaver supports three popular server-side technologies: ASP (sometimes referred to as classic ASP), ColdFusion, and PHP. In this book, I cover only PHP, but setting up a site for any server-side technology involves the same process. Server-side pages need to be processed (or **parsed**) before you can see the dynamically generated output. This affects how you set up your site in Dreamweaver. So, let's begin with the considerations for site organization.

Deciding how to organize your site

Site definition in Dreamweaver involves the following three basic steps:

1. Telling Dreamweaver where to find the version of the site on your local computer.
2. Registering details of the remote server. This is the live version of the site on the Internet.
3. Registering details of the server that will process server-side code (in the case of this book, PHP) while testing pages locally.

If you don't yet have a remote server, you can skip step 2 and register the details later. Likewise, if you don't plan to use any server-side code in the site, you can omit step 3. Even if you don't have any immediate plans to use PHP, I suggest that you read through the next few pages so that you don't make any decisions you might later regret. Planning ahead saves time later.

Deciding where to test your pages

Building PHP pages involves a lot of testing—much more than you might normally do with a static website. It's not only a question of what your pages look like; you also need to check that the dynamic code is working as expected. Dreamweaver doesn't care where your testing server is, as long as it knows where to find it, there's an available connection, and, of course, the server is capable of handling PHP pages. This means that you can test on your local machine, another computer on a local network, or a remote host.

These are the advantages of creating a local test environment:

- **Security**: Dreamweaver installs files on the testing server to communicate with your database. If you use your remote server for testing, a malicious attacker might be able to use these files to gain access to your data. As long as your computer is protected by a firewall, this danger is eliminated by testing locally.

- **Stability**: If an error in your code causes the server to slow down or even crash, the only person affected is you. Keep your mistakes to yourself; don't inflict them on others. You're likely to make a lot of mistakes until you gain a level of competence in PHP (don't let that put you off—it's an important part of the learning process).

- **Ease of organization**: You can build the website offline, test it, and upload it directly to the live site when it's ready. If you use your remote server for testing, the test site is visible to everyone on the Internet unless you build it in a separate testing folder or password protect it. The first option involves changing all internal links as soon as the site goes live. Password protection also affects you, so neither option is optimal.

- **Speed**: There's no waiting. Even with a broadband connection, the response is usually slower from a remote server.

- **Convenience**: You can continue work even if there is a disruption to your Internet service.

There are also disadvantages to creating a local test environment:

- **Setup time**: Each piece of software requires a multimegabyte download, which then must be set up and configured.

- **Complexity**: Some people find configuring the software daunting. However, if setting up a testing environment is beyond your capabilities, you should perhaps reconsider whether you're ready to work with a server-side technology. PHP is not difficult, but it does require clear thought and concentration.

> *In previous books, I have given detailed instructions about how to set up a local testing environment with a web server, PHP, the MySQL database, and a graphical interface to MySQL called phpMyAdmin. However, new versions of PHP, MySQL, and phpMyAdmin are expected to be released around the time this book is published, so anything I write risks being out of date by the time you read it.*

If you don't already have a PHP testing environment on your local computer, I suggest that you get XAMPP for Windows (http://www.apachefriends.org/en/xampp-windows.html) or MAMP for Mac OS X (http://www.mamp.info/en/mamp.html). Both give you a fully working PHP/MySQL testing environment on your local computer. They're easy to install, and should have you up and running in a few minutes. Both XAMPP and MAMP have online forums, where you should be able to get help if you run into problems.

If you already have Microsoft Internet Information Services (IIS) installed for development with ASP or ASP.NET, you can also install PHP to run with IIS. The official IIS website gives instructions for installing PHP on Vista: http://learn.iis.net/page.aspx/246/using-fastcgi-to-host-php-applications-on-iis7/. Windows XP uses a different version of IIS, but a web search for "install PHP on IIS 6" should provide some helpful guides. However, don't use IIS unless you also need ASP or ASP.NET, as some parts of PHP are not supported on IIS.

Although Chapters 3 through 9 of this book don't require PHP, I recommend that you set up a PHP testing environment at this stage rather than wait till later.

> *Chapter 9 covers the creation of an online form. The form is built entirely with HTML, but processing an online form requires server-side scripting. Chapter 11 shows you how to do this with PHP. However, you can use any other mail-processing script with the form from Chapter 9.*

Before setting up a site in Dreamweaver, you need to make a number of decisions. Figure 2-1 summarizes the process, which is described in detail in the following sections.

Choosing the appropriate file name extension

Web servers use the three- or four-letter extension at the end of a web page's file name to decide how to display it. Generally speaking, files that end in .html or .htm can contain only static HTML, JavaScript, and CSS. For PHP server-side code to be processed, you need to give the file names a .php extension.

> *You may be wondering what the difference is between .html and .htm. There isn't any. The use of .htm dates back to the days when Windows file names were limited to an 8.3 format (a maximum of eight characters followed by a period and a three-character file name extension). All operating systems now support .html, which is the default file name extension that Dreamweaver uses for static web pages.*

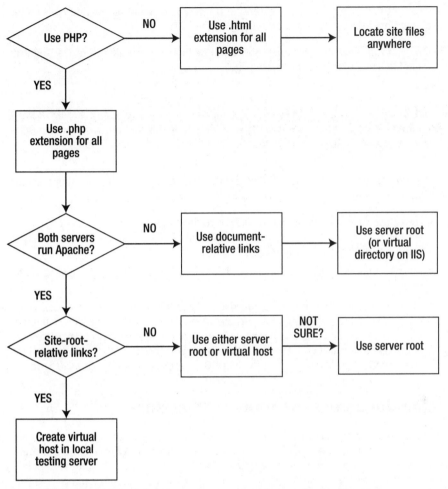

Figure 2-1. Deciding where to locate your Dreamweaver site on a local testing server

As with all rules, there are exceptions. It is possible to configure a server to process PHP even if it's in an .html or .htm file. However, it's not recommended, and it makes working with PHP in Dreamweaver more difficult. You might also come across alternative file name extensions for PHP, such as .php4 or .php5. Although Dreamweaver recognizes both of these alternatives, you need to edit the file name extension manually when creating files, so use .php exclusively unless you have a pressing reason to do otherwise.

It's perfectly acceptable to mix .html, .htm, and .php files in the same website. However, when planning a new website, it's a good idea to use the same file name extension for all pages. That means that if you plan to use PHP anywhere in your site, all pages should have a .php file name extension, even if some pages don't contain any PHP code. Technically speaking, the web server sends every page that has a .php file name extension to the PHP engine for processing, so it's a wasted journey if the page contains only static HTML. In practice, the difference in the time it takes to serve the page is infinitesimal. The advantage of using a `.php` file name extension is that you can add server-side code to the page at any time in the future without changing the URL.

In summary, if the server where your website will be hosted is capable of processing PHP, use a `.php` file name extension for every page.

> In spite of my recommendation to use a `.php` file name extension for all pages, all the examples in Chapters 3 through 8 use `.html`. I have done this so that readers who don't have access to a PHP server can use the files that are available for download.

While on the subject of file names, let's lay down some basic rules for naming files and folders on a website:

- Never use spaces in the names of files or folders. Replace spaces in existing names with an underscore (_) or hyphen (-). Spaces in file names and folders are likely to cause broken links on many servers.

- Most web servers are case-sensitive. Avoid problems by using all lowercase for names.

- Many web browsers can handle Internationalized Resource Identifiers (IRIs), which accept file and folder names that use accented characters and different writing systems, such as Chinese and Japanese (see `http://www.w3.org/International/articles/idn-and-iri/`). However, to be safe, you should stick to unaccented letters, numbers, underscores, and hyphens. Do not use symbols, such as ?, #, or /.

Choosing document- or root-relative links

By default, Dreamweaver creates internal links that are relative to the current document, but it also offers the option to use links relative to the site root. With a static website, it doesn't matter which you choose, but with a PHP site, the decision isn't quite so simple. If you're not sure what the difference is, the following explanation should help.

Understanding the difference

Let's say you have a simple website structure like that shown in Figure 2-2.

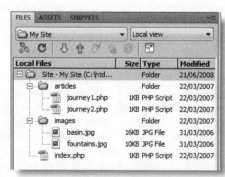

Figure 2-2.
A simple website structure displayed in the Dreamweaver Files panel

If index.php contains a link to journey1.php, Dreamweaver creates code that looks like this:

```
<a href="articles/journey1.php">Read more</a>
```

And a link back to index.php inside journey1.php looks like this:

```
<a href="../index.php">Back to main page</a>
```

Similarly, if index.php contains the image called fountains.jpg, the <img> tag looks like this (I have omitted all attributes other than src, because that's the only one we're interested in at the moment):

```
<img src="images/fountains.jpg" . . . />
```

A reference to the same image in journey1.php, however, looks like this:

```
<img src="../images/fountains.jpg" . . . />
```

The ../ before index.php and the images folder name tells the web server that it needs to look one level higher in the website hierarchy to find the correct folder. If you change the structure of the website using the Files panel, Dreamweaver automatically updates all links, adding or removing the requisite number of ../ to ensure that everything works as intended.

However, many developers prefer to make the links relative to the site root, rather than the document. With root-relative links, the two links look like this:

```
<a href="/articles/journey1.php">Read more</a>
<a href="/index.php">Back to main page</a>
```

The <img> tag in *both* index.php and journey1.php looks like this:

```
<img src="/images/fountains.jpg" . . . />
```

The difference is that the pathname always begins with a leading forward slash, which indicates the top level of the site—in other words, the site root.

Which should you choose?

You might wonder why the document-relative vs. root-relative issue matters. After all, both achieve the same thing. When building static sites with .html pages, it doesn't make any difference which you choose.

However, root-relative links can be extremely useful with PHP. The advantage is that the link to the image is identical in index.php and journey1.php, even though the pages are at different levels of the site hierarchy. This means that you can put some of your code, such as a navigation menu, in an external file and the links will always work. As you'll see in Chapter 12, your site navigation menu can be included in multiple pages using a simple PHP command, and changes to the external file are automatically propagated to all of them—a great time-saver.

Because root-relative links are so useful, you may think that they're the best choice for a PHP site. Unfortunately, life is not quite so simple. Although links relative to the site root are essential *inside* external files, PHP expects you to include the external file using a document-relative link. Moreover, if your hosting company runs PHP on a Windows server using IIS, choosing root-relative links in Dreamweaver generates PHP code that results in errors galore and a site that doesn't work.

If you're new to PHP, all this might sound confusing. Don't worry about the details for the moment (if you're curious, the explanation is in Chapter 12). For development with PHP, I recommend the following:

- In the vast majority of cases, choose the Dreamweaver default: links relative to the document. When creating external files that will be included in other pages, you can easily override this and create individual links relative to the site root.
- Choose links relative to the site root only if both your testing environment and remote server run on the Apache web server. If you choose root-relative links, you need to set up a virtual host for each site in your local testing environment.

Choosing where to store your files

With a static website consisting of .html pages, it doesn't matter where you locate files on your local computer. You simply tell Dreamweaver which folder is the site root, and that's it. With a PHP site, though, Dreamweaver needs to send the files to the testing server before it can display the output. This leaves you with the following options:

- Store the files with your ordinary documents and set up the testing server in a different location. Unless the testing server is on a different computer, this is a waste of disk space, as you end up with two copies of every file.
- Store the files in a subfolder of the server root of your testing server. This is the best way to set up a site that uses document-relative links.
- Create a virtual host on your testing server and store the files there. You must do this if you use site-root-relative links. This setup is also suitable for document-relative links.
- If you don't want to set up a local testing environment, it doesn't matter where you store your files locally. However, I cannot emphasize strongly enough that using a remote server as the testing server is *not* recommended.

Finding the testing server root

The location of your testing server root depends on your operating system and how you installed the testing environment.

Apache on Windows

The Apache server root is a folder called htdocs. If you installed Apache 2.2 as a separate program, the server root is at the following location:

```
C:\Program Files\Apache Software Foundation\Apache2.2\htdocs
```

I don't think it's a good idea to store your web files in among all your program files, so I suggest that you move the server root to a different location, as follows:

1. Create a new folder called htdocs. The actual location is not important, but I find it best to put it at the top level of my C drive.

2. You need to edit the Apache configuration file, httpd.conf, which is located at C:\Program Files\Apache Software Foundation\Apache2.2\conf\httpd.conf.

   ● In Windows XP, you can open the file directly in Notepad or any other text editor by double-clicking its icon in Windows Explorer.

   ● In Vista, you need to select Run as administrator even if you are logged in to an administrator account. For Notepad, go to Start ➤ All Programs ➤ Accessories, right-click Notepad, and select Run as administrator from the context menu. Enter your administrator password when prompted. Inside Notepad, select File ➤ Open and navigate to httpd.conf. The Open dialog box in Notepad shows only .txt files, so you need to select All Files (*.*) from the drop-down menu at the bottom right of the dialog box.

3. Locate the following section in httpd.conf:

```
144  #
145  # DocumentRoot: The directory out of which you will serve your
146  # documents. By default, all requests are taken from this directory, but
147  # symbolic links and aliases may be used to point to other locations.
148  #
149  DocumentRoot "C:/Program Files/Apache Software Foundation/Apache2.2/htdocs"
150
```

4. Change the pathname shown on line 149 of the preceding screenshot to the same as your new folder. (Use the line numbers simply as a guide; they are not part of the file and may be different in a later version of Apache). In my case, I change it to this:

DocumentRoot **"C:/htdocs"**

> *Make sure that you use forward slashes in the pathname in steps 4 and 5, instead of using the Windows convention of backward slashes.*

5. Scroll down about 30 lines until you find this section:

```
174  #
175  # This should be changed to whatever you set DocumentRoot to.
176  #
177  <Directory "C:/Program Files/Apache Software Foundation/Apache2.2/htdocs">
```

The instruction shown on line 175 is pretty straightforward: change the pathname to match the previous change. In my case, I end up with this:

<Directory **"C:/htdocs"**>

6. Save httpd.conf and restart Apache for the changes to take effect.

XAMPP on Windows

The server root should be at the following location:

```
C:\xampp\htdocs
```

This location is fine; you don't need to move it.

IIS on Windows

The Default Web Site server root on both Windows Vista and XP is located at this location:

```
C:\Inetpub\wwwroot
```

On Windows Vista, you can define as many websites as you like in the Internet Information Services (IIS) Manager. Right-click Sites in the Connections panel on the left, and select Add Web Site from the context menu. The server root is the location specified in the Physical path field of Content Directory.

Apache on Mac OS X

If you are using the version of Apache that comes preinstalled in Mac OS X, you have two choices of server root. The main one is located here:

```
Macintosh HD:Library:WebServer:Documents
```

Every user account on a Mac also has its own dedicated server root, located here:

```
Macintosh HD:Users:username:Sites
```

Any site within this folder can be viewed in a browser using the address http://localhost/~username/ followed by the name of the site's subfolder, where username is the name of your home folder. The address for the main server root is simply http://localhost/, so it is probably the most convenient to use, unless you share the computer with others and want to keep things separate.

MAMP on Mac OS X

The server root is at the following location:

```
Macintosh HD:Users:username:Applications:MAMP:htdocs
```

MAMP installs Apache, PHP, MySQL, and phpMyAdmin as a complete package. This poses a potential conflict, because Mac OS X comes with a preinstalled version of Apache, and you can't normally run both of them simultaneously. To get around this, MAMP uses nonstandard settings to serve web pages and communicate with the MySQL database. Everything in MAMP is configured to work together smoothly. So, if you're using MAMP, use the MAMP version of everything. To avoid problems when you deploy your site on your remote server, turn off any conflicting programs and change the MAMP settings as follows:

1. Make sure that the preinstalled version of Apache is not running by opening System Preferences ➤ Internet & Network ➤ Sharing. Select Web Sharing from the list of Services and make sure there is no check mark in the checkbox alongside. The panel on the right should display Web Sharing: Off.

2. If you have ever installed MySQL on your computer, stop the MySQL server and change any system preferences that start it automatically whenever your computer starts up. MySQL is not preinstalled on Mac OS X, so there's nothing to worry about if you have never installed it.

3. Click the Preferences button on the MAMP control panel. In the dialog box that opens, select Ports, and click the button labeled Set to default Apache and MySQL ports. The values in Apache Port and MySQL Port should be the same as those shown in Figure 2-3.

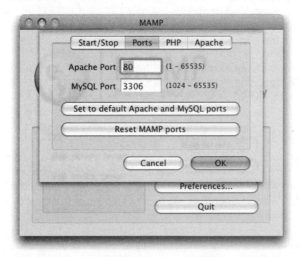

Figure 2-3. The default MAMP settings need to be changed.

4. Click OK. Enter your Mac password when prompted. MAMP should restart both Apache and MySQL with the standard settings for Apache and MySQL.

Creating virtual hosts on Apache

When it's first installed, Apache is capable of hosting only one website, which is identified in a local testing environment by the URL http://localhost/. To get around this restriction, it's common practice to develop websites in subfolders of the Apache server root. For example, if you have two sites called site1 and site2 and create separate subfolders for them in the server root, you access them in your testing environment as http://localhost/site1/ and http://localhost/site2/. This works perfectly well as long as you use document-relative links all the time. However, if you want to use links relative to the site root, you need to create virtual hosts for each site.

Virtual hosting is a technique that web servers use to host more than one website on the same machine. If you have bought a web-hosting package from a hosting company, it's almost certainly on a shared server that uses virtual hosts. Continuing with the previous example, once you create virtual hosts for site1 and site2 in Apache, you can test them locally using http://site1/ and http://site2/. This is essential for testing sites that use links relative to the site root. If you're serious about web development, you should learn sooner or later how to set up virtual hosts in your testing environment. Once you have mastered the technique, it takes only a few minutes to set up each one.

The rest of this section is entirely optional. If you don't want to set up virtual hosts, you can skip it. You can come back and set up virtual hosts at any time.

You can call your virtual hosts whatever you like, as long as you don't use any spaces or characters that would be illegal in a domain name. I always use the same name as the actual website, *without* the top-level domain. For example, for my own site, http://foundationphp.com/, I have created a virtual host called foundationphp in my local testing setup. This means that I access it as http://foundationphp/. It's then a simple matter of clicking in the browser address bar and adding the .com to see the live site. Whatever you do, *don't* use the top-level domain as the name of a virtual host in your testing setup. If you do, your computer will always point to the local version of the site and never access the real one on the Internet.

Apache allows you to create as many virtual hosts as you want. It's a two-stage process. First, you tell the operating system the names of the virtual hosts, and then you tell Apache where the files will be located. There are separate instructions for Windows and Mac OS X.

Registering virtual hosts on Windows

Although you can locate your virtual hosts anywhere on your hard drive system, it's a good idea to keep them in a single top-level folder, as this makes it easier to set the correct permissions in Apache. The following instructions assume that all your virtual hosts are kept in a folder called C:\vhosts and show you how to create a virtual host called dwcs4 within that folder.

> *To edit the necessary files in Vista, you need to select* Run as administrator *even if you are logged in to an administrator account. For Notepad, go to* Start ➤ All Programs ➤ Accessories, *right-click* Notepad, *and select* Run as administrator *from the context menu. Enter your administrator password when prompted. Inside Notepad, select* File ➤ Open *and navigate to the relevant file. The* Open *dialog box in Notepad shows only* .txt *files, so you need to select* All Files (*.*) *from the drop-down menu at the bottom right of the dialog box.*

1. Create a folder called C:\vhosts and a subfolder inside it called dwcs4.

2. Open C:\WINDOWS\system32\drivers\etc\hosts in Notepad or a script editor and look for the following line at the bottom of the file:

   127.0.0.1 localhost

   127.0.0.1 is the IP address that every computer uses to refer to itself.

3. On a separate line, enter 127.0.0.1, followed by some space and the name of the virtual host. For instance, to set up a virtual host for this book, enter the following:

   127.0.0.1 dwcs4

4. If you want to register any further virtual hosts, add each one on a separate line and point to the same IP address. Save the hosts file and close it.

5. Open the Apache configuration file, httpd.conf. The default location is C:\
   Program Files\Apache Software Foundation\Apache2.2\conf\httpd.conf. If you
   installed XAMPP, it should be at C:\xampp\apache\conf\httpd.conf.

6. Scroll down to the Supplemental configuration section at the end of httpd.conf,
   and locate the following section:

```
462  # Virtual hosts
463  #Include conf/extra/httpd-vhosts.conf
```

7. Apache uses the hash sign (#) to indicate comments in its configuration files.
   Uncomment the command shown on line 463 in the preceding screenshot by
   removing the #, like this:

   Include conf/extra/httpd-vhosts.conf

   This tells Apache to include the virtual host configuration file, which you must
   now edit.

8. Save httpd.conf, and close it.

9. Open httpd-vhosts.conf. The default location is C:\Program Files\Apache
   Software Foundation\Apache2.2\conf\extra\httpd-vhosts.conf. If you installed
   XAMPP, it should be at C:\xampp\apache\conf\extra\httpd-vhosts.conf. The
   main part of the file looks like this:

```
13  # You may use the command line option '-S' to verify your virtual host
14  # configuration.
15
16  #
17  # Use name-based virtual hosting.
18  #
19  NameVirtualHost *:80
20
21  #
22  # VirtualHost example:
23  # Almost any Apache directive may go into a VirtualHost container.
24  # The first VirtualHost section is used for all requests that do not
25  # match a ServerName or ServerAlias in any <VirtualHost> block.
26  #
27  <VirtualHost *:80>
28      ServerAdmin webmaster@dummy-host.home
29      DocumentRoot /www/docs/dummy-host.home
30      ServerName dummy-host.home
31      ServerAlias www.dummy-host.home
32      ErrorLog logs/dummy-host.home-error_log
33      CustomLog logs/dummy-host.home-access_log common
34  </VirtualHost>
35
36  <VirtualHost *:80>
37      ServerAdmin webmaster@dummy-host2.home
38      DocumentRoot /www/docs/dummy-host2.home
39      ServerName dummy-host2.home
40      ErrorLog logs/dummy-host2.home-error_log
41      CustomLog logs/dummy-host2.home-access_log common
42  </VirtualHost>
```

10. Position your cursor in the blank space shown on line 15 in the preceding screen-shot, and insert the following four lines of code:

```
<Directory C:/vhosts>
  Order Deny,Allow
  Allow from all
</Directory>
```

This sets the correct permissions for the folder that contains the sites you want to treat as virtual hosts. If you chose a location other than C:\vhosts as the top-level folder, replace the pathname in the first line. Remember to use forward slashes in place of backward slashes. Also surround the pathname in quotes if it contains any spaces.

11. Lines 27–42 in the preceding screenshot are examples of virtual host definitions. They show all the commands that can be used, but only DocumentRoot and ServerName are required. When you enable virtual hosting, Apache disables the main server root, so the first definition needs to reproduce the original server root. You then add each new virtual host within a pair of <VirtualHost> tags, using the location of the site's web files as the value for DocumentRoot and the name of the virtual host for ServerName. If the path contains any spaces, enclose the whole path in quotes. If your server root is located, like mine, at C:\htdocs, and you are adding dwcs4 as a virtual host in C:\vhosts, change the code shown on lines 27–42 so they look like this:

```
<VirtualHost *:80>
  DocumentRoot c:/htdocs
  ServerName localhost
</VirtualHost>
<VirtualHost *:80>
  DocumentRoot c:/vhosts/dwcs4
  ServerName dwcs4
</VirtualHost>
```

For XAMPP, use C:/xampp/htdocs instead of C:/htdocs.

12. Save httpd-vhosts.conf, and restart Apache.

All sites in the server root will continue to be accessible through http://localhost/sitename/. Anything in a virtual host will be accessible through a direct address, such as http://dwcs4/.

Registering virtual hosts on Mac OS X

The following instructions apply *only* to the preinstalled version of Apache on Mac OS X. To enable virtual hosts with MAMP, I recommend that you invest in MAMP PRO (http://www.mamp.info/en/mamp-pro/index.html). It's not free, but it automates the configura-tion of virtual hosts and other aspects of your development environment.

You need to edit hidden files. The simplest way to do this is to use a specialized script editor. I recommend using either BBEdit (http://www.barebones.com) or TextWrangler (a free, cut-down version of BBEdit available from the same location).

The following instructions assume that all your virtual hosts are kept in the Sites folder in your Mac home folder, and show how to create a virtual host called dwcs4 within that folder. Setting up virtual hosts on a Mac changed substantially between OS X 10.4 and 10.5, so there are separate instructions for each version. First, Mac OS X 10.5:

1. Open BBEdit or TextWrangler and select File ➤ Open Hidden. In the Open dialog box, select All Files from the Enable drop-down menu. Then navigate to Macintosh HD:private:etc:hosts and click Open.

2. This opens a system file, so you need to unlock it by clicking the icon of a pencil with a line through it on the left side of the toolbar, as shown in the following screenshot:

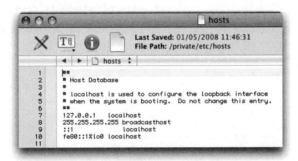

3. You will be told that the document is owned by "root" and asked to confirm that you want to unlock it. Click Unlock. This removes the line through the pencil and readies the file for editing.

4. Place your cursor on a new line at the end of the file, and type 127.0.0.1, followed by a space and the name of the virtual host you want to create. To create a virtual host for this book called dwcs4, it should look like this:

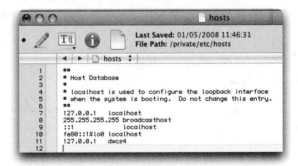

5. Save the file. Because it's owned by root, you will be prompted to enter your Mac password. You now need to tell Apache about the virtual host.

6. Use BBEdit or TextWrangler to open the main Apache configuration file, httpd.conf. It's a system file, so you need to open and unlock it in the same way as the hosts file. It's located at Macintosh HD:private:etc:apache2:httpd.conf.

7. Scroll down to around line 460 and locate the following lines:

```
# Virtual hosts
#Include /private/etc/apache2/extra/httpd-vhosts.conf
```

8. Remove the hash sign (#) from the beginning of the second of these two lines so it looks like this:

```
Include /private/etc/apache2/extra/httpd-vhosts.conf
```

This enables the configuration file for virtual hosts, which now needs to be edited.

9. Use BBEdit or TextWrangler to open httpd-vhosts.conf. Again, it's a system file, so it needs to be handled the same way as the previous two files. The file is located at Macintosh HD:private:etc:apache2:extra:httpd-vhosts.conf.

10. The section of the file that you're interested in is shown in the following screenshot:

```
17    # Use name-based virtual hosting.
18    #
19    NameVirtualHost *:80
20
21    #
22    # VirtualHost example:
23    # Almost any Apache directive may go into a VirtualHost container.
24    # The first VirtualHost section is used for all requests that do not
25    # match a ServerName or ServerAlias in any <VirtualHost> block.
26    #
27    <VirtualHost *:80>
28        ServerAdmin webmaster@dummy-host.example.com
29        DocumentRoot "/usr/docs/dummy-host.example.com"
30        ServerName dummy-host.example.com
31        ServerAlias www.dummy-host.example.com
32        ErrorLog "/private/var/log/apache2/dummy-host.example.com-error_log"
33        CustomLog "/private/var/log/apache2/dummy-host.example.com-access_log" common
34    </VirtualHost>
35
36    <VirtualHost *:80>
37        ServerAdmin webmaster@dummy-host2.example.com
38        DocumentRoot "/usr/docs/dummy-host2.example.com"
39        ServerName dummy-host2.example.com
40        ErrorLog "/private/var/log/apache2/dummy-host2.example.com-error_log"
41        CustomLog "/private/var/log/apache2/dummy-host2.example.com-access_log" common
42    </VirtualHost>
```

Lines 27–42 are examples of virtual host definitions. You need to replace these with your own definitions. When you enable virtual hosting, Apache disables the main server root, so the first definition needs to reproduce it.

You don't need all the options shown in the examples, so replace the code shown on lines 27–42 of the preceding screenshot with the following:

```
<VirtualHost *:80>
  DocumentRoot "/Library/WebServer/Documents"
  ServerName localhost
</VirtualHost>
<VirtualHost *:80>
  DocumentRoot "/Users/username/Sites/dwcs4"
  ServerName dwcs4
</VirtualHost>
```

Replace *username* in the second definition with your own Mac username.

11. Save all the files you have edited, and restart Apache by going to Sharing in System Preferences ➤ Internet & Network, deselecting Web Sharing, and selecting it again. You should now be able to access the virtual host with the URL http://dwcs4/.

Follow these instructions for Mac OS X 10.4:

1. Open NetInfo Manager, which is in the Utilities subfolder of Applications.

2. Click the lock at the bottom left of the dialog box that opens, and enter your administrator's password when prompted.

3. Select machines, then localhost, and click the Duplicate icon. When prompted, confirm that you want to make a copy.

4. Highlight the copy, and double-click the name in the lower pane, as shown in the following screenshot.

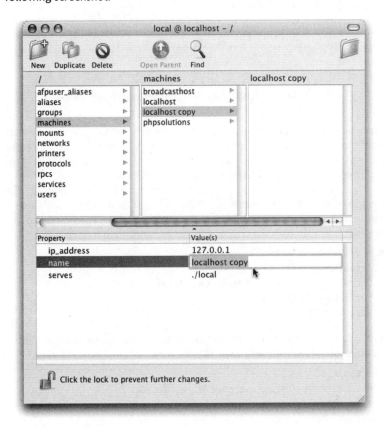

5. Change localhost copy to whatever you want to call the virtual host. For example, to create a virtual host for this book, enter dwcs4.

6. Click any of the other entries in the left column of the top pane. The operating system will ask you twice if you really want to make the changes. You do. This registers the name of the virtual host with your computer.

7. Repeat steps 3–6 for any other virtual hosts you want to create. When you have finished, click the lock icon in the bottom-left corner of the NetInfo Manager, and close it.

8. Open BBEdit or TextWrangler, and select File ➤ Open Hidden. In the Open dialog box, select All Files from the Enable drop-down menu, and open Macintosh HD:etc:httpd:httpd.conf.

9. Scroll almost to the bottom of httpd.conf, and locate the following section:

```
1073  #
1074  # Use name-based virtual hosting.
1075  #
1076  #NameVirtualHost *:80
1077
1078  #
1079  # VirtualHost example:
1080  # Almost any Apache directive may go into a VirtualHost container.
1081  # The first VirtualHost section is used for requests without a known
1082  # server name.
1083  #
1084  #<VirtualHost *:80>
1085  #    ServerAdmin webmaster@dummy-host.example.com
1086  #    DocumentRoot /www/docs/dummy-host.example.com
1087  #    ServerName dummy-host.example.com
1088  #    ErrorLog logs/dummy-host.example.com-error_log
1089  #    CustomLog logs/dummy-host.example.com-access_log common
1090  #</VirtualHost>
```

10. Click the pencil icon at the top left of the editor window, and confirm that you want to unlock the document, entering your administrator password when prompted. Uncomment the command shown on line 1076 in the screenshot by removing the hash sign (#). This enables virtual hosting but disables the main server root, so the first virtual host needs to reproduce the Mac's server root. The example (on lines 1084–1090) is there to show you how to define a virtual host. The only required commands are DocumentRoot and ServerName. After uncommenting the NameVirtualHost command, your first definition should look like this:

```
NameVirtualHost *:80
<VirtualHost *:80>
  DocumentRoot /Library/WebServer/Documents
  ServerName localhost
</VirtualHost>
```

11. Add any further definitions for virtual hosts. To create one for this book, use this (replace *username* with your own Mac username):

```
<VirtualHost *:80>
  DocumentRoot /Users/username/Sites/dwcs4
  ServerName dwcs4
</VirtualHost>
```

12. Save httpd.conf, and restart Apache. All sites in Macintosh HD:Library:WebServer:Documents can still be accessed using http://localhost/ and those in your Sites folder using http://localhost/~username/sitename/, but named virtual hosts can be accessed directly, such as http://dwcs4/. Of course, a site must exist in the location you defined before you can actually use a virtual host.

Registering virtual directories on IIS

Windows Vista uses IIS 7, which lets you set up separate websites, each with its own server root, just like Apache virtual hosts. However, the version of IIS that runs in Windows XP does not support virtual hosts. Instead, you can set up virtual directories, but localhost always remains the basic address of the web server, so you cannot use root-relative links. The main advantage of using virtual directories is that they avoid the need to locate all web files in the default IIS server root at `C:\Inetput\wwwroot`.

To set up a virtual directory in IIS 6 on Windows XP, **open the** Internet Information Services **panel (Start ➤** Control Panel ➤ Administrative Tools ➤ Internet Information Services**), highlight** Default Web Server, **right-click, and select** New ➤ Virtual Directory. **A wizard will walk you through the process. If you create a virtual directory called** dwcs4, **the URL becomes** `http://localhost/dwcs4/`.

Creating the site definition

By this stage, you should have decided where you are going to store your local files. The setup process in Dreamweaver is basically the same whether you test your PHP files locally or on your remote server.

There are several ways to open the Site Definition dialog box. If the Dreamweaver Welcome screen is open, you can choose Dreamweaver Site from the bottom of the Create New column. However, it's probably more convenient to choose New Site from the Site menu or from the Site icon on the Application bar (see alongside). Another convenient way is to select Manage Sites from the bottom of the site list at the top left of the Files panel.

Dreamweaver has been designed with both beginners and more advanced users in mind, so you may see either the basic dialog box shown on the left of Figure 2-4 or the advanced one on the right.

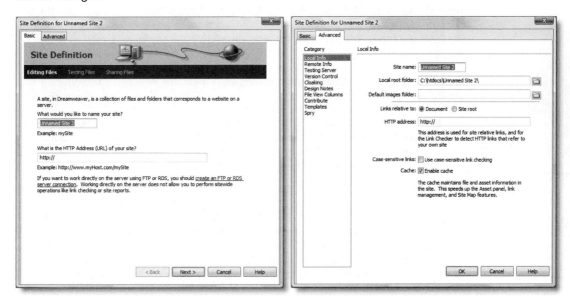

Figure 2-4. The Site Definition dialog box has two interfaces: Basic (left) and Advanced (right).

The Basic dialog box sets up only the bare essentials, so it's better to use the Advanced one. If you see the screen on the left of Figure 2-4, click the Advanced tab at the top left (it's in the center of the Mac version).

If you select Manage Sites from the Files panel, you will be presented with the dialog box shown in Figure 2-5. This lists the sites that you have already defined in Dreamweaver. The buttons on the right let you perform a variety of management functions, as described in the "Managing Dreamweaver sites" section later in the chapter. To create a new site, click the New button at the top right and select Site from the menu that appears.

Figure 2-5.
The Manage Sites dialog box lets you
create a new site or edit an existing one.

Telling Dreamweaver where to find local files

The first stage of site definition involves defining the basic details of the site. Open the Site Definition dialog box, and make sure the Advanced tab is selected. If necessary, select Local Info from the Category column on the left. You should see the same screen as shown on the right side of Figure 2-4.

Let's take a look at what each option means, with particular reference to defining a PHP site for use with this book.

- Site name: This identifies the site within Dreamweaver. The name appears in the drop-down menu at the top of the Files panel and in the Manage Sites dialog box (Figure 2-5), so it needs to be reasonably short. It's used only within Dreamweaver, so spaces are OK. I used Dreamweaver CS4.

- Local root folder: This is the top-level folder of the site. Everything should be stored in this folder in exactly the same hierarchy as you want to appear on the live website. For a static site using .html pages only or when using a remote server to test PHP, this folder can be anywhere on your computer. When testing a PHP site locally, this folder should be inside your server root (see the "Finding the testing server root" section earlier in this chapter), a virtual host, or a virtual directory (IIS only). Click the folder icon to the right of the Local root folder field and navigate to the appropriate location on your hard disk. If the folder doesn't exist, navigate to the parent folder, and then click Create New Folder in the Choose local root folder dialog box.

> *With large sites, it's sometimes convenient to create a site definition in Dreamweaver for just part of the site. If the local root folder is already in another defined site, Dreamweaver warns you that some functions, such as site synchronization, won't work. However, it won't prevent you from creating the subsite.*

- Default images folder: This field is optional, but is very useful if you plan to use images that are on other parts of your file system or even in other Dreamweaver sites. Whenever you insert an image in a web page, Dreamweaver automatically copies it to this folder and creates the correct link in the `<img>` tag's `src` attribute. To set this option, click the folder icon to the right of the Default images folder field, navigate to the local root folder that you selected for the previous option, and select the images folder. If the folder doesn't exist, click the Create New Folder button to create it.

- Links relative to: This option lets you select the default style of links used in the site (see the "Choosing document- or root-relative links" section earlier in the chapter). Unless your testing server and remote server both run on Apache, I strongly advise you to accept the default Document.

- HTTP address: This field should contain the URL of the final site on the Internet. If you are using the site only for local testing, you can leave this field empty. If you have selected root-relative links, Dreamweaver will display the following warning:

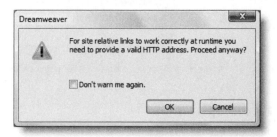

You can safely ignore this warning for local testing, and click OK. However, it is important to get the URL correct for remote testing or a site that you plan to deploy on the Internet.

- Case-sensitive links: The vast majority of PHP websites are hosted on Linux servers, which treat `products.php` and `Products.php` as completely different file names. If you select this option, Dreamweaver checks that internal links match the case of

file names when you run Site ➤ Check Links Sitewide. I recommend selecting this
option to maintain the internal integrity of your site.

■ Cache: As the Site Definition dialog box explains, this speeds up various aspects of
site management in Dreamweaver. Very large sites (with several hundred pages)
tend to slow down dramatically if the site cache is enabled. However, with a PHP
site, you should draw content from a database into a dynamically generated page,
rather than create a new page every time. I suggest that you leave this option
selected, and disable it only if you run into performance problems.

The Local Info category is the only one you need to complete in order to get to work with
static pages (in other words, ones that don't use a server-side technology) on your local
computer. If you're not ready to upload files to your live website or work with PHP, just
click OK in the Site Definition dialog box, and then click Done to close the Manage Sites dialog box. Otherwise, continue with the next sections.

Telling Dreamweaver how to access your remote server

When you first open the Remote Info category in the Site Definition dialog box, you're presented with a single drop-down menu labeled Access. It has six options, as shown in the
following screenshot (the final option—Microsoft Visual SourceSafe—is not available in the
Mac version).

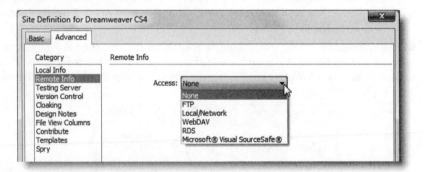

Choosing an access option

First, let's take a look at the Access options:

■ None: Choose this if you don't plan to deploy the site on the Internet, or if you
don't want to set up your remote server immediately. If you choose this option,
you can skip ahead to the "Defining the testing server" section.

■ FTP: This is the most common choice. It sets up Dreamweaver's built-in File
Transfer Protocol (FTP) program to communicate with your remote server.

■ Local/Network: This allows you to deploy your live website to another folder on
your local computer or network. This is normally done only by organizations that
run their own live web servers.

- WebDAV: This uses the Web-based Distributed Authoring and Versioning (WebDAV) protocol to communicate with the remote server. It requires a remote server that supports the WebDAV protocol.

- RDS: This uses Remote Development Services (RDS), which is supported only by ColdFusion servers. You cannot use it with a PHP site unless the server also supports ColdFusion.

- Microsoft Visual SourceSafe: This requires access to a Microsoft Visual SourceSafe database. It is not appropriate for the Dreamweaver PHP MySQL server model.

Since FTP is the most common method of connecting to a remote server, that's the only one I'll describe. Click the Help button at the bottom of the Remote Info category of the Site Definition dialog box for detailed descriptions of the options for the other methods.

Using FTP

When you select the FTP option from the Access drop-down menu, the Remote Info category of the Site Definition dialog box presents you with the options shown in Figure 2-6. Most of them are straightforward, but I'll describe each one briefly.

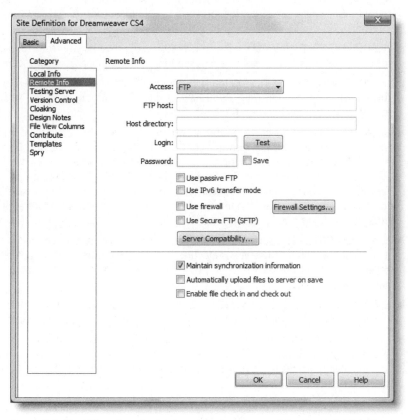

Figure 2-6. The FTP options for the Remote Info category of the Site Definition dialog box

- FTP host: Enter your remote server's FTP address in this field. You should normally get this from your hosting company. It usually takes either of the following forms: ftp.example.com or www.example.com.

- Host directory: This is the pathname of the top level of your website. The important thing to realize is that the directory (folder) that you enter in this field should contain only those files that will be accessible to the public through your site's URL. Often it will be named htdocs, public_html, or www. If in doubt, ask your hosting company or server administrator.

- Login: This is the username given to you by your hosting company or server administrator.

- Password: Enter your remote server password in this field. Dreamweaver displays your password as a series of dots. It also automatically saves your password, so deselect the Save checkbox if you want to be prompted for the password each time you connect to the remote server. Click the Test button to make sure that Dreamweaver can connect successfully. If the test fails, make sure Caps Lock isn't turned on, as passwords are normally case-sensitive. Other reasons for failure include being behind a firewall, so check the remaining options before trying again. Many antivirus programs include a software firewall, as does Windows Vista, so you should also check whether it's preventing Dreamweaver from accessing the Internet.

- Use passive FTP: Try this option if a software firewall prevents you from connecting to the remote server. For more details, see http://www.adobe.com/go/15220.

- Use IPv6 transfer mode: This option is designed to prepare Dreamweaver for the future. Select this option only if you have been told that your remote FTP server uses Internet Protocol version 6 (IPv6).

- Use firewall: You can normally ignore this option unless you are behind a corporate firewall. The Firewall Settings button opens the Site Preferences dialog box. Enter the firewall host and firewall port (if it's different from 21) in the appropriate fields, and click OK to return to the Site Definition dialog box. If you are using a software firewall, such as Norton Internet Security or ZoneAlarm, you need to set permission for Dreamweaver to access the Internet in the software firewall's configuration settings rather than here.

- Use Secure FTP (SFTP): Secure FTP (SFTP) gives you a more secure connection, but it is not supported by all servers. Selecting this option automatically disables these other options: Use passive FTP, Use IPv6 transfer mode, Use firewall, Firewall Settings, and Server Compatibility.

- Server Compatibility: Click this button if you are still having problems connecting through FTP. The two options in the dialog box that opens are self-explanatory.

- Maintain synchronization information: This is selected by default and enables you to synchronize your remote and local files through the Files panel. However, it's not very reliable, particularly if you live in a part of the world that observes daylight saving time.

- Automatically upload files to server on save: Do *not* select this option. You should always test files locally before uploading them to your remote server. Otherwise, all your mistakes will go public. It overwrites your original files, so you can no longer use them as backup.

- Enable file check in and check out: Select this option only if you are working in a team and want to use Dreamweaver's Check In/Check Out system. For more information, launch Dreamweaver Help (press F1) and select Check In/Check Out from the Index, or go to http://www.adobe.com/go/15447. *All* team members must have this option enabled and must always use Dreamweaver to edit files. Failure to do so results in chaos. This option should be used with extreme caution.

After you have completed the Remote Info category, select Testing Server from the Category list on the left of the Site Definition dialog box.

Defining the testing server

When you first open the Testing Server category of the Site Definition dialog box, it looks similar to the Remote Info category in its initial state, but with two drop-down menus instead of one, as shown in the following screenshot.

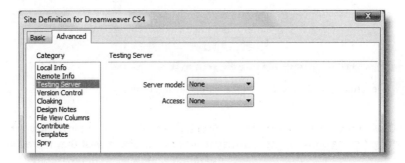

This is probably the most important dialog box when building dynamic sites in Dreamweaver. It's quite easy to fill in, but if you get the details wrong, Dreamweaver cannot communicate with any of your databases.

Activate the Server model drop-down menu, and select PHP MySQL. What you choose for Access depends on whether you want to test your PHP pages locally or by using your remote server. The options are different, so I'll cover them separately.

Selecting options for local testing

The Access drop-down menu determines how you communicate with the testing server. If you have a local test environment on your computer or another computer on a local area network (LAN), choose Local/Network. This reveals two options that Dreamweaver attempts to fill in automatically. Figure 2-7 shows what happened when I had defined the local root folder in the Local Info category as a virtual host on Windows.

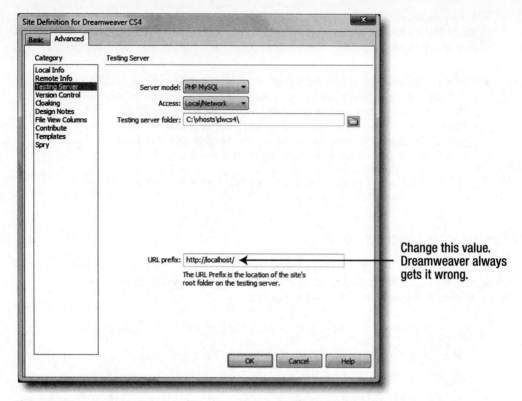

Figure 2-7. Dreamweaver attempts to fill in the testing server details automatically.

Dreamweaver usually gets the value for Testing server folder correct, but invariably gets URL prefix wrong. Getting both correct is crucial, so let's take a look at what they represent.

Testing server folder and URL prefix must both point to the same location. The value you enter in Testing server folder is the physical path to your site root (where you keep the home page). The URL prefix is the address you would enter in a browser address bar to get to the same page (minus the page name).

The value for Testing server folder should normally be the same folder that you selected as the Local root folder in the Local Info category. The only exception is if you want to use a testing server elsewhere on your local network. In this case, click the folder icon to the right of the field to browse to the correct location.

The value for URL prefix depends on how you have set up your testing environment. If your testing server folder is in the server root or a virtual directory, it will be http://localhost/*sitename*/. If you are using a virtual host, it will simply be http://*sitename*/. If the testing server is on another computer on a local network, replace localhost with the correct IP address.

It's critical that URL prefix is set correctly, as it controls all dynamic aspects of Dreamweaver. Because so many people seem to get this wrong, Table 2-1 shows the values for Testing server folder and URL prefix for the various scenarios described earlier.

Table 2-1. Testing server folder and URL prefix values for various scenarios

Scenario	Testing server folder	URL prefix
Site in a subfolder of the Apache server root of the same machine on Windows	`C:\htdocs\dwcs4\` or `C:\xampp\htdocs\dwcs4\`	`http://localhost/dwcs4/`
Site in a virtual host called dwcs4 on Windows	`C:\vhosts\dwcs4\`	`http://dwcs4/`
Site in an IIS virtual directory on Windows	Can be anywhere	`http://localhost/dwcs4/`
Site in a subfolder of the main server root of the same machine on a Mac	`Macintosh HD:Library:WebServer:Documents:dwcs4`	`http://localhost/dwcs4/`
Site in a subfolder of your Sites folder of the same machine on a Mac	`Macintosh HD:Users:username:Sites:dwcs4`	`http://localhost/~username/dwcs4/`
Site in a virtual host called dwcs4 on a Mac	`Macintosh HD:Users:username:Sites:dwcs4`	`http://dwcs4/`
Using MAMP on a Mac with the default Apache and MySQL ports	`Macintosh HD:Users:username:Applications:MAMP:htdocs:dwcs4:`	`http://localhost/dwcs4/`
Using MAMP on a Mac with the MAMP default ports	`Macintosh HD:Users:username:Applications:MAMP:htdocs:dwcs4:`	`http://localhost:8888/dwcs4/`

Selecting options for remote testing

I strongly advise against using a remote server for testing PHP pages. In addition to the advantages of a local testing server mentioned at the beginning of this chapter, you should also take into consideration the fact that using a remote server for testing overwrites existing files. You can get around this problem by using temporary files for previewing (see the "Setting options for Preview in Browser" section at the end of this chapter), but you can't use temporary files to test links or work with a database. Of course, you may still decide to use your remote server as the Dreamweaver testing server, and this section describes the necessary settings.

The Access drop-down menu in the Testing Server category offers fewer options than the Remote Info category, because RDS and Microsoft SourceSafe are not appropriate for working with the Dreamweaver PHP MySQL server model. The most common choice is FTP. Dreamweaver is intelligent enough to copy across the main details from the Remote Info category, and it presents you with the dialog box shown in Figure 2-8. Although most details should be correct, the URL prefix is almost certain to need editing.

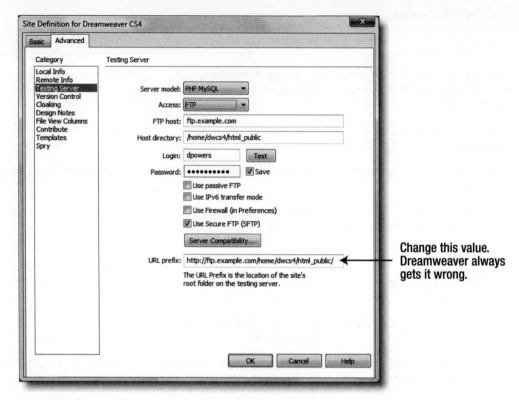

Figure 2-8. When you select a remote server for testing, Dreamweaver copies details from the Remote Info category, but you normally need to change at least the URL prefix.

As you can see from Figure 2-8, Dreamweaver incorrectly combines the values in the FTP host and Host directory fields. This won't work, and the URL prefix value must be changed.

It's vital that the URL prefix and Host directory fields point to the same place. However, this does *not* mean that the values should be the same. The distinction is as follows:

- Host directory: This is the pathname that the FTP program uses for the top level of your site.

- URL prefix: This is the address that anyone surfing the Internet uses to reach the top level of your site. In other words, it's normally http:// followed by the domain name and a trailing slash.

So, if /home/dwcs4/html_public/index.php is your home page, and users access it by typing http://www.example.com/index.php in their browser address bar, the correct value for URL prefix should look like this:

```
http://www.example.com/
```

## 2

> *In Figure 2-8, notice that even though the* Use Secure FTP (SFTP) *checkbox is selected, the three checkboxes above and the* Server Compatibility *button are not grayed out, as in the* Remote Info *category. This is a known bug in Dreamweaver. Make sure you don't accidentally select them if you're using SFTP. The settings should be the same as in the* Remote Info *category.*

Setting other site options

The basic site definition is now complete. To save the site definition, click OK in the Site Definition dialog box, and then click Done to close the Manage Sites dialog box. However, there are seven more categories in the Site Definition dialog box. Most of the time, you can leave these at their default values.

- Version control: Dreamweaver CS4 now offers integration with Subversion (http://subversion.tigris.org/), one of the most popular open source version control systems. See the next section for details on using this option for your site.

- Cloaking: Some developers like to keep source files, such as .fla files for Flash movies or .psd files for Photoshop, in the same folder as their site. To prevent them from being uploaded to your remote server when uploading or synchronizing a complete site, you can use Dreamweaver's cloaking feature. The Cloaking category of the Site Definition dialog box lets you automatically cloak all files with specific file name extensions. There are just two options. The first one, Enable cloaking, is selected by default. To cloak specific types of files automatically, select the Cloak files ending with checkbox and enter the file name extensions as a space-delimited list. In new sites created in Dreamweaver CS4, the field is prepopulated with .fla .psd (in sites migrated from older versions of Dreamweaver, it's prepopulated with .png .fla).

> *To cloak individual files or folders, select them in the* Files *panel, right-click, and select* Cloaking ➤ Cloak *from the context menu. The ability to cloak individual files is new to Dreamweaver CS4.*

- Design Notes: Design notes serve a number of different purposes. One is to store notes about individual files. This is mainly of use in a team environment, where different members can add notes regarding the status of the file (draft, first revision, things remaining to be done, and so on). Dreamweaver also creates design notes automatically to store information about related files, file synchronization, and locally created variables. For instance, if you create an image in Fireworks and import it into Dreamweaver, the location of the original .png file is stored in a design note, enabling you to open it directly from the Document window if you want to edit the original image. By default, Dreamweaver enables design notes and creates them in a hidden folder called _notes inside most folders within your site. If you don't want design notes, you can turn them off in the Design Notes category of the Site Definition dialog box. If you're working in a team environment, there's an option to upload design notes to the remote server.

- File View Columns: This lets you customize the look of the Files panel.

- Contribute: This allows you to use rollback and event logging when developing the site to be updated with Contribute (http://www.adobe.com/products/contribute/).

- Templates: This is for backward compatibility with older versions of Dreamweaver templates. It should be left at its default setting (enabled).

- Spry: Adobe's Ajax framework, Spry, relies on code libraries that need to be uploaded to your remote server. By default, Dreamweaver inserts these files in a folder called SpryAssets at the top level of your site root. For most people, this is ideal. However, if you want to locate the code libraries elsewhere, specify the folder name in the Spry category of the Site Definition dialog box. This allows Dreamweaver to update or remove the files when you make changes to elements that use Spry.

Using version control with Subversion

Some form of **version control** is standard in team environments, but it's something that individual developers either don't know about or tend to treat like regular backups of hard disks—you know you ought to do it, but never quite get around to it. If you have ever made changes to a file and wished you could roll back to the original, you need version control. In one respect, version control acts as a database, storing project files at different stages of development. Instead of overwriting the original file each time, it stores a snapshot of each stage. It also allows different people to work simultaneously on separate versions of the same document, review each other's changes, and merge them.

Although this is a typical team development scenario, it can also be useful for individual developers. Say you normally work on a desktop computer, but occasionally use a laptop when you're on the move. By storing your files in a repository, you can always have access to the most current version, regardless of which computer you're using. You can also keep different versions of projects. And if you commit files to the repository on a regular basis, you can experiment with a file and roll back to a previous version if you don't like the changes. Once you get into the habit of using version control, you'll wonder how you ever did without it.

As mentioned in the previous section, Dreamweaver CS4 lets you integrate with Subversion. Note that Dreamweaver is not a full Subversion client. It offers a limited range of version control functions. Nevertheless, these functions are extremely useful for keeping track of changes in a site's files, whether you're working on your own or in a team.

> *At the time of this writing, Dreamweaver CS4 supports only Subversion 1.4. For details, see the Adobe TechNote at http://www.adobe.com/go/kb406661.*

Subversion is preinstalled on Mac OS X 10.5, and Windows users can install a very user-friendly tool called TortoiseSVN (http://tortoisesvn.tigris.org/), which makes it easy to set up a Subversion repository. If you don't want to go to the trouble of configuring everything yourself, there are hosted Subversion repositories (some of them free); for example, see http://beanstalkapp.com/ and http://cvsdude.com/product.pl. You can also download a free book called *Version Control with Subversion* from http://svnbook.red-bean.com/.

Registering a site with a Subversion repository

Once you have set up a Subversion repository, adding a Dreamweaver website to it is easy. The following instructions describe the process (refer to Figure 2-9 to see the settings in the dialog box):

1. In the Advanced tab of the Site Definition dialog box, select Version Control from the Category list on the left.

2. In the Access field, select Subversion from the drop-down menu (there are only two options: None and Subversion).

3. In the Protocol field, select the method of connection to the repository from the drop-down menu. There are four options: HTTP, HTTPS, SVN, and SVN+SSH. The choice depends on how the repository has been set up.

4. Enter the domain name where the repository resides in the Server address field. If it's on the same computer, enter localhost. Do *not* prefix this with http://.

5. In the Repository path field, enter the path to the project in which you want to store the site. The project doesn't need to exist in the repository. As you can see in Figure 2-9, I have put a forward slash at the beginning of the path. This is optional; Dreamweaver accepts the path with or without a leading slash.

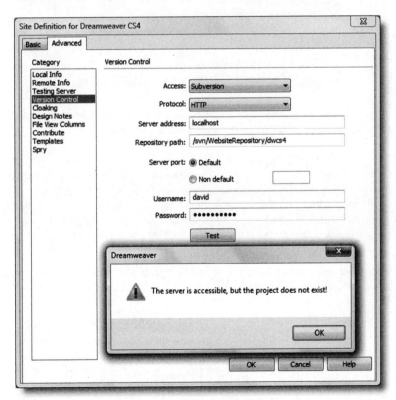

Figure 2-9. As long as Dreamweaver can access the server, you can add a new project to the repository.

6. If the Subversion repository uses a nonstandard port, select the Non default radio button and enter the port number in the field alongside. Otherwise, leave Server port set to Default. This uses the standard Subversion port (3690).

7. Enter the repository username and password in the appropriate fields. If the repository doesn't have user accounts, leave both fields blank.

8. Click Test to make sure Dreamweaver can access the repository. If Dreamweaver connects successfully and the project already exists, you should see an alert with the following message: Server and project are accessible! If the project hasn't yet been created, you should see the message shown in Figure 2-9.

9. Click OK to dismiss the alert.

10. If you need to make changes to any other categories of the Site Definition dialog box, do so, and then click OK to save the changes, and then click Done to dismiss the Manage Sites dialog box.

11. If you entered the name of a new project in step 5, you should see the following alert:

If you click Yes, Dreamweaver should connect to the repository, create the new project, and install the necessary Subversion files in your site.

> *Subversion treats your site as the working version and keeps track of your files by creating* .svn *folders in every folder of the site. These folders are normally hidden in the Dreamweaver* Files *panel, but you can see them in Windows Explorer or Finder on a Mac. Do* not *delete them unless you no longer want to keep track of the project in Subversion.*

If the folder where you defined the site already contains files and folders, Dreamweaver adds a plus (+) icon to the left of each name in the Files panel, as shown in Figure 2-10.

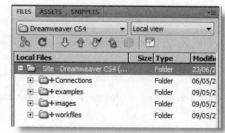

Figure 2-10.
Items that haven't yet been added to the repository are marked with a plus icon in the Files panel.

If you're creating a new site in an empty folder, the same icon will be added to each new file or folder that you create. This indicates that it hasn't yet been added to the repository. The next section describes how to commit new files and changes to the repository.

If the site already exists in the Subversion repository, select the Site folder at the top of the Files panel, right-click, and select Version Control ➤ Get Latest Versions from the context menu. Dreamweaver connects to the repository and downloads the most up-to-date version of each file as your working copy.

Committing new files and changes to the repository

New files and folders that haven't yet been added to the repository are marked with a plus icon in the Files panel. Files in your working copy that have been edited since they were retrieved from the repository are indicated by a check mark alongside the file name, as shown in Figure 2-11. The following instructions explain how to commit new files and changes to the repository.

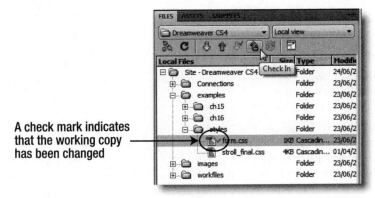

A check mark indicates that the working copy has been changed

Figure 2-11. The Files panel marks files that have been edited since being checked out of the repository.

1. When you're ready to add new or edited files to the repository, select them in the Files panel. You can select multiple files with Shift-click or Ctrl/Cmd-click. A quick way to select the entire site is to click the Site folder at the top of the panel, as shown in Figure 2-10. With the files selected, click the Check In icon at the top of the Files panel, as shown in Figure 2-11. The icon is an up arrow with a gold padlock.

> *Don't confuse the* Check In *icon with the* Put File(s) *icon two icons further left. Both look very similar. The up arrow* without *a padlock is used for uploading files to your remote server.*

2. The CheckIn dialog box opens, as shown in Figure 2-12. This displays a list of files that will be added to the repository. You can exclude any files by selecting them in the top pane and clicking the red circle with the horizontal slash. This changes the

Action to Ignore. If you change your mind, you can restore the item to the list by clicking the up arrow alongside. Before committing the files to the Subversion repository, you should enter a brief description of the changes in the Commit Message field. This makes it easier to identify stored versions later.

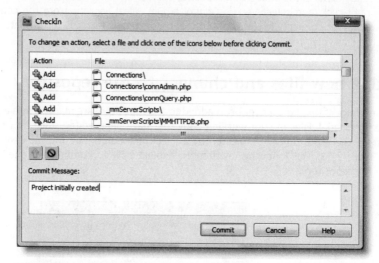

Figure 2-12. When committing files to the repository, it's a good idea to add a message summarizing the changes.

3. Click Commit to upload the files to the Subversion repository. If there are no problems, the icons alongside the file and folder names in the Files panel disappear, indicating that all local files have been committed to the repository. If any changes in a working copy conflict with the latest copy stored in the repository, Dreamweaver displays the following alert:

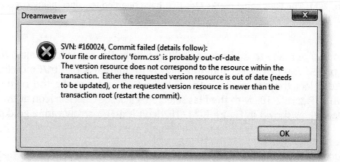

You need to resolve any conflicts, as described in the next section, before you can commit the edited file to the repository.

Viewing revisions and resolving conflicts

Subversion doesn't simply upload your new version of a file to the repository. It compares it with the latest version held in the repository and merges the changes. This is vital when more than one person is working on the same file. If two people check out a file and edit it, you don't want any changes made by one of them to be overwritten by the other. If there's no conflict, both sets of edits are merged into the latest version. However, if both people make incompatible changes (for example, one changes the color in a style rule to red and the other changes it to green), you need to view the revisions and resolve the conflict manually.

To view the revisions made to a file, select it in the Files panel, right-click, and select Version Control ➤ Show Revisions from the context menu. This brings up the Revision History panel, as shown in Figure 2-13.

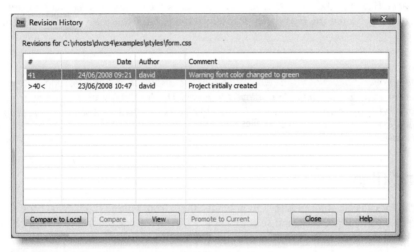

Figure 2-13. The Revision History panel lets you inspect different versions of the file in the repository.

The Revision History panel lists all versions of the selected file in reverse order, with the most recent at the top. When you select a file in the list, the buttons at the bottom of the panel perform the following actions:

- Compare to Local: This launches a third-party file-comparison utility to compare the selected version in the repository with your local working copy. See the "Using a file-comparison utility" section later in this chapter.

- Compare: This uses a third-party comparison utility to compare different versions in the repository. It is grayed out when only one version is selected in the panel.

- View: This opens the selected revision in the Document window. Dreamweaver gives the file a name based on its original file name and revision number. For example, revision 41 of form.css is opened as form_rev41.css.

- Promote to Current: This is how you roll back to an older version: by promoting the selected version to the most recent.

If Dreamweaver fails to commit your changes to the repository because of a conflict, you need to use this panel to get a copy of the latest version and resolve the conflict manually before committing the file back to the repository.

Keeping your working copies up-to-date

When using more than one computer or working in a team environment, you must always check out the latest version from the repository before making any changes to a file. You can do this by selecting the file in the Files panel and clicking the Check Out File(s) icon (see alongside) or by right-clicking and selecting Version Control ➤ Get Latest Versions from the context menu.

If a new file has been created by another member of the team, you can retrieve it from the repository by selecting Repository view from the drop-down menu at the top right of the Files panel. Highlight the file(s) that you want and click the Check Out File(s) icon or use the context menu. Switch the Files panel drop-down menu back to Local view when you have finished.

> *Color provides a useful visual clue as to what is displayed in the* Files *panel. When in Local view, folder icons are displayed in green. They're displayed in yellow when in Remote view or Repository view, and in red when you select* Testing server *from the drop-down menu.*

Locking files

You can lock files in the repository to prevent others from editing them. Select the file(s) in the Files panel, right-click, and select Version Control ➤ Lock from the context menu. To unlock a file, select Unlock from the context menu.

Subversion also uses working copy locks (see "The three meanings of 'lock'" in *Version Control with Subversion* at http://svnbook.red-bean.com/ for an explanation). If you get error messages about working copy locks, select the file in the Files panel, right-click, and select Version Control ➤ Clean Up from the context menu.

Managing Dreamweaver sites

To change any settings in your site definition, select Manage Sites from the Site menu to open the Manage Sites dialog box (see Figure 2-14). Select the name of the site that you want to change and click Edit. This reopens the Site Definition dialog box, ready for you to update the settings. If you're feeling really impatient, though, the quickest way of opening the Site Definition dialog box is to double-click the site's name in the drop-down menu at the top left of the Files panel.

Figure 2-14.
The Manage Sites dialog box helps you
organize the sites on your computer.

The other buttons on the right side of the Manage Sites dialog box are fairly self-explanatory. However, the following is a quick guide to each one:

- New: This offers two options: Site and FTP & RDS Server. The first opens the Site Definition dialog box. The second option is rarely used, but lets you create a direct FTP connection to a remote site (RDS is for ColdFusion only). You might want to use this to upload a single file without defining a local site in Dreamweaver.

- Duplicate: This creates an exact copy of the site definition for whichever site is highlighted in the left panel. You might find this useful if a new site shares common settings with an existing one. It's important to understand that creating a new site definition doesn't make a mirror version of the common files and folders. Editing or deleting a shared file in one site affects both sites, as there is only one set of files.

- Remove: This removes only the site definition from Dreamweaver. The actual files and folders remain untouched.

- Export: This exports your site definition as an XML file (Dreamweaver gives it an .ste file name extension). You can export multiple site definitions by using Shift-click or Ctrl/Cmd-click to select several sites in the left panel. If any of the site definitions contain login details for a remote server, Dreamweaver asks if you want to back up your settings with details of your username and password. If you select Share settings with other users, the login details are omitted. The export option you choose applies to all sites being exported at the same time. Dreamweaver then asks where to save the file. Just browse to the folder where you want to store the .ste files and accept the default value for File name. Definitions for all selected sites are exported in a single operation.

- Import: This imports site definitions from .ste files. If the .ste files are in the same folder, you can import multiple sites simultaneously. If a site of the same name already exists, Dreamweaver creates a duplicate site definition with a number after the name, rather than overwriting the existing definition.

Dreamweaver occasionally loses all your site definitions. It doesn't happen very often, but once is enough. Use the Export button to create a backup each time you add a new site or amend a site's definition. It could save you a lot of agony.

Setting options that apply to all sites

The options set in the Site Definition dialog box are specific to each individual site. Any edits that you make to the settings apply immediately to that site, but not to any other. Before concluding this chapter, let's take a look at Dreamweaver preferences that affect all sites. All are accessed through the Preferences panel, which is on the Edit menu in Windows and the Dreamweaver menu on a Mac. Alternatively, use the keyboard shortcut, Ctrl+U/Cmd+U.

Setting new document preferences

The New Document category of the Preferences panel, shown in Figure 2-15, sets global preferences for all web pages created in Dreamweaver.

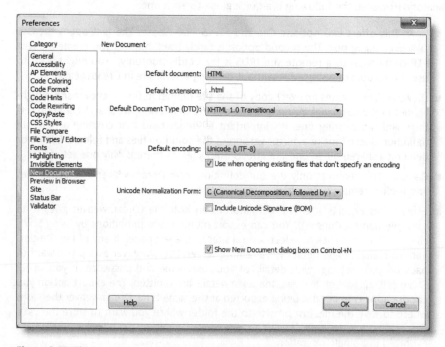

Figure 2-15. The New Document category of the Preferences panel

Let's take a look at what each of the options means:

- Default document: This lets you to choose the type of document that will be created when you use the keyboard shortcut for a new document (Ctrl+N/Cmd+N). For this to work, you must deselect the option at the bottom labeled Show New Document dialog box on Control+N/Cmd+N. Otherwise, the dialog box shown in Figure 3-2 will appear.

- Default extension: This affects only HTML files. Change the value only if you want to use .htm to maintain unity with the naming convention of older sites.

- Default Document Type (DTD): This sets the default DOCTYPE declaration for all new web pages. You cannot set one value for, say, .html and another for .php pages. See the next section for more information about choosing a default document type.

- Default encoding: This lets you choose the character set to be used in all web pages. The Dreamweaver default is Unicode (UTF-8). In the Mac version, this is listed as Unicode 5.0 UTF-8. The checkbox below this option tells Dreamweaver to use the same character set to display existing pages that don't specify a particular encoding. It doesn't insert any extra coding in such pages.

- Unicode Normalization Form: This is required only when using UTF-8 for encoding. It should normally be set to C (Canonical Decomposition, followed by Canonical Composition), and the Include Unicode Signature (BOM) checkbox should be deselected. If you use any other encoding, set Unicode Normalization Form to None.

Choosing the default document type

Many people misunderstand the purpose of the DTD (the DOCTYPE declaration before the opening <html> tag). It simply tells the browser how you have coded your page and is intended to speed up the correct rendering of your design. It's not a badge of honor or magic spell that somehow renders your web pages future-proof, although omitting the DOCTYPE altogether or using the wrong one switches most browsers into quirks mode, which could result in your page not looking the way you expect. The default setting is XHTML 1.0 Transitional, and this is the appropriate choice for most people when creating a new web page *as long as you understand the stricter rules imposed by Extensible Hypertext Markup Language (XHTML)*.

> *Visit* http://www.w3.org/TR/xhtml1/#diffs *to learn about the differences between HTML and XHTML.*

The full range of options is as follows:

- None: Don't use this. All pages should have a DOCTYPE declaration.

- HTML 4.01 Transitional: Choose this if you don't want to use XHTML.

- HTML 4.01 Strict: This excludes deprecated elements (those destined for eventual elimination). Use this only if you have a good knowledge of HTML and have made a conscious decision not to use XHTML.

- XHTML 1.0 Transitional: This offers the same flexibility as HTML 4.01 Transitional by permitting the use of deprecated elements but applies the stricter rules of XML.

- XHTML 1.0 Strict: This excludes all deprecated elements. Use this only if you are competent with XHTML.

- XHTML 1.1: This DTD should not be used on pages delivered using the text/html MIME type, the current standard for web servers.

- XHTML Mobile 1.0: This is a subset of XHTML Basic for mobile devices. You can find the full specification at http://www.openmobilealliance.org/tech/affiliates/wap/wap-277-xhtmlmp-20011029-a.pdf.

If you choose an HTML document type, Dreamweaver automatically creates code according to the HTML specification. Similarly, if you choose XHTML, your code automatically follows the stricter rules, using lowercase for tag names and event handlers and inserting a closing slash in empty tags such as <img>. You need to be careful when copying and pasting code from other sources. If you're not sure about the quality of the code, run Commands ➤ Clean Up XHTML, which should correct most, if not all, problems.

If you select a Strict DTD, it's important to realize that Dreamweaver does *not* prevent you from using deprecated elements or attributes. Dreamweaver expects you to understand the difference yourself.

Setting options for Preview in Browser

Live view, which was described in the previous chapter, is very useful for getting a quick view of what your page is likely to look like in a standards-compliant browser, but it's no substitute for viewing it in your main target browsers. Pressing F12/Opt+F12 or using the menu option File ➤ Preview in Browser automatically launches your default browser and displays the page currently open in the Document window.

Dreamweaver normally detects your default browser the first time that you use this option, but you can also designate other browsers in the Preview in Browser category of the Preferences panel. If Dreamweaver has detected other browsers on your system, they are listed in the Browsers field. You can designate one of them as your secondary browser, which can be launched using Ctrl+F12/Cmd+F12 as a shortcut.

Add other browsers by clicking the plus (+) button. Type the browser's name in the Name field, click the Browse button to locate its executable file, and then click OK to register it. The Edit button lets you change the details of the selected browser. Click the minus (–) button to remove the selected browser from the list. Although default keyboard shortcuts exist for only two browsers, you can launch the current page in one of the other browsers by using File ➤ Preview in Browser or clicking the Preview/Debug in browser icon on the Document toolbar, as shown in the following screenshot.

The Preferences panel offers the option of previewing pages using a temporary file. By default, this option is disabled. Opinions differ on whether to enable it. The advantage of using a temporary file for previewing is that you don't need to save the file beforehand, so you can test various things without needing to overwrite the existing file. On the other hand, you cannot test server behaviors that insert, update, or delete database records with a temporary file. So, in a local testing environment, my preference is to leave the option disabled. However, if you have defined your remote server as the testing server, the opposite advice is true. You should enable preview with a temporary file for the following reasons:

- Even if you haven't entered any details in the Remote Info category of the Site Definition dialog box, Dreamweaver uploads the file to the remote server and permanently overwrites the existing file on the remote server.

- Dependent files, such as images, style sheets, and external JavaScript files, must also be uploaded to the remote server unless you preview using a temporary file.

Using a file-comparison utility

Dreamweaver lets you specify a third-party application to compare files. It can be used with files in your local site, on the remote server, or in a Subversion repository.

Setting up the File Compare feature

If you already have a file-comparison utility installed on your computer, all that's necessary is to register the program inside the Dreamweaver Preferences panel. If you don't yet have one, here are some suggestions:

- For Windows, consider WinMerge (http://winmerge.sourceforge.net/) or Beyond Compare (http://www.scootersoftware.com). WinMerge is free. Beyond Compare is moderately priced, but you can try it free for 30 days.

- For Mac OS X, you might use TextWrangler or BBEdit (both from http://www.barebones.com). TextWrangler is not just a file-comparison utility; it's an excellent script editor, and it's free. BBEdit is expensive if you only need it for file comparison, but it is widely recognized as the Rolls Royce of Mac script editors.

Once you have installed a file-comparison utility, select File Compare in the Preferences panel, click the Browse button, and navigate to the executable file for the program. Windows users should have little difficulty recognizing the correct file to select; it will normally be in a subfolder of Program Files.

On a Mac, the location is somewhere you may never even have known existed:

- **TextWrangler**: Macintosh HD:usr:bin:twdiff

- **BBEdit**: Macintosh HD:usr:bin:bbdiff (this is the BBEdit file-comparison utility— make sure you choose bbdiff and not bbedit, which is listed just below it)

Even though the usr:bin directory is normally hidden on a Mac, the Dreamweaver Select External Editor dialog box will display it by default. All you need to do is select the correct file name and click Open. If you can't find twdiff or bbdiff, open Preferences from the TextWrangler or BBEdit menu, select Tools, and click the Install Command Line Tools button.

Comparing files

To compare two files in the same site, highlight both in the Files panel, right-click, and select Compare Local Files.

If you select just one file in the Files panel and right-click, the context menu will display either Compare with Remote or Compare with Local, depending on the location of the selected file. For this type of comparison, Dreamweaver will select only a file of the same name and in the same location on the other computer. So you can compare the local or remote equivalent of myfile.php in myfolder in the same Dreamweaver site but not myotherfile.php or the same file in a different folder or different site.

Beyond Compare produces a false negative when comparing the remote and local versions of a file. This is easily remedied by opening the main Beyond Compare window and selecting Tools ➤ Options ➤ Startup. Set Show dialog with quick comparison results to Rules-based quick compare.

> *You cannot use the merge or copy feature of your file-comparison program to make changes to a remote file, because Dreamweaver works with a temporary copy of the remote file rather than the original. Local files can be changed, because you always work with the original.*
>
> *On Windows, you can merge local and remote versions of a file by launching Beyond Compare outside Dreamweaver. Select New from the Beyond Compare Session menu, and choose Synchronize with FTP site. Alternatively, make a copy of the local file in the Files panel and give it a different name. You can then download the remote file and compare both of them locally.*

Chapter review

This chapter has covered a lot of ground. If you're an experienced developer, you'll probably need to implement most of the features. If you're just setting out and learning how to use Dreamweaver, the most important sections were "Deciding where to test your pages" and "Creating the site definition."

As long as you have defined your site correctly in Dreamweaver, you should be on solid ground. But if you run into problems later with internal links not pointing to the right location or updating correctly, the answer almost certainly lies in this chapter. You can change the settings for a site any time by opening the Site Definition dialog box as described in the "Managing Dreamweaver sites" section. Site definition is the key to success in Dreamweaver. Leave the more advanced options, such as Subversion integration, until after you have gained more experience.

In the next chapter, you'll get down to creating web pages with the main focus on creating modern, standards-compliant layouts using CSS.

When you create a new web page in Dreamweaver, it presents you with a blank canvas. Although it shares a common interface with graphical design programs in the Adobe Creative Suite, it doesn't work like a desktop publishing program. If you attempt to drag and drop elements onto the page and move them round without understanding what's happening to the underlying code, you'll end up banging your head against the keyboard with frustration. To create a web page, you need to know the basics of inserting and organizing elements on the Dreamweaver page.

In this chapter, you'll learn about the following:

- Inserting text, images, and Flash and Flex movies
- Using Photoshop Smart Objects as images
- Adding structure to text with headings, paragraphs, and lists
- Creating tables to display data
- Importing and exporting table data
- Inserting <div> tags to organize content in a logical structure
- Creating links with text and images
- Creating an image map

This chapter is aimed mainly at newcomers to Dreamweaver. It concentrates on the mechanics of adding content in the Document window. If you're upgrading from a previous version of Dreamweaver, most of this material should be familiar. However, you will want to learn about the important changes to the way Flash and Flex movies are inserted, as well as the redesign of the Property inspector to separate HTML structural elements from the creation of CSS style rules.

This chapter doesn't contain any formal exercises, but you can use the files in the examples/ch03 and images folders (available for download) to practice the techniques described. Most of the techniques covered in this chapter will form the basis of hands-on exercises in the next chapters, which show you how to style your raw content with CSS.

> *As explained in Chapter 1, Dreamweaver CS4's UI is highly configurable. For consistency, all screenshots in this and the remaining chapters have been taken using the preset* Classic *Workspace layout and the tabbed interface of the* Insert *bar. To avoid repetition, references to a particular tab on the* Insert *bar apply to the menu category of the same name on the* Insert *panel.*

Creating a new document

Dreamweaver can create a wide variety of document types, and you have several ways to start your new document.

Starting from the Welcome screen

The easiest way to create a new document is to select the type of page you want from the Create New list in the center of the Dreamweaver Welcome screen (see Figure 3-1). This list includes the most frequently used types of documents.

If you choose one of the first four types (HTML, ColdFusion, PHP, or ASP VBScript), Dreamweaver uses the default DOCTYPE declaration set in the Preferences panel (see Chapter 2). If you haven't changed it, the Dreamweaver default is to use XHTML 1.0 Transitional.

3

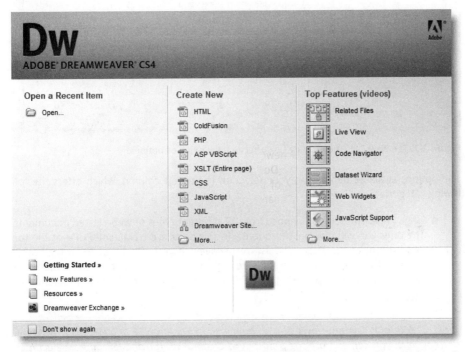

Figure 3-1. The Dreamweaver Welcome screen offers a quick shortcut to create the most frequently used documents.

The disadvantage of using the Welcome screen is that it disappears as soon as you open a document. Unless you never have more than one document open at a time, you need an alternative way of creating a new document.

Using the New Document dialog box

The document-creation method that offers the most choices is through the New Document dialog box (see Figure 3-2). Select File ➤ New to open this dialog box.

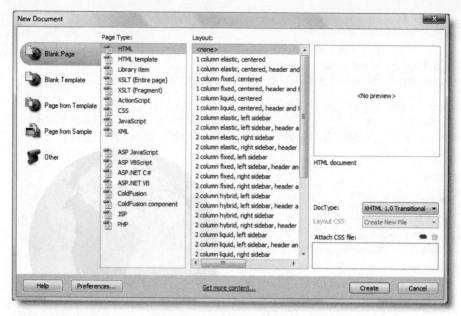

Figure 3-2. The New Document dialog box offers a huge range of options.

The options available depend on your selection in the left column, which offers the following categories:

- Blank Page: This lets you choose from 17 different types of web-related documents. The ones you will use most frequently in this book are HTML and PHP—at the top and bottom of the Page Type list, respectively. If you select <none> in the Layout column, Dreamweaver creates a page with no content other than the basic HTML skeleton used by every web page. The choices offered by the Layout column are discussed in Chapter 5.

> Although Dreamweaver CS4 no longer supports ASP.NET and JSP server behaviors, you can still use the program to create ASP.NET and JSP pages. Selecting one of these page types inserts processing instructions that tell the web server how to treat the page, and gives the page the appropriate file name extension.

- Blank Template: This lets you create a Dreamweaver template from scratch. Templates are covered in Chapter 13.

- Page from Template: This lists all the sites you have defined in Dreamweaver, along with templates associated with each one. Use this option to create a child page from an existing template.

- Page from Sample: This contains a selection of sample style sheets that can be used as a starting point for creating your own. It also offers a range of framesets. Frames, although very popular in the late 1990s, are now widely frowned upon because they cause usability problems (see http://apptools.com/rants/framesevil.php). The use of frames is not covered in this book.

> *Previous versions of Dreamweaver included a range of common layouts in the* Page from Sample *category. These have been removed from Dreamweaver CS4 because they used table layout with deprecated HTML styling. Whether you like it or not, Dreamweaver CS4 is pushing you more and more to adopt CSS in place of old-school habits.*

3

- Other: This creates other web-related documents, including plain text files.

In addition to the range of page types, the New Document dialog box lets you select a different DOCTYPE from the default and attach one or more external style sheets to the new page.

Other ways of opening a new document

You can create a new document in three other ways:

- Click the New icon on the Standard toolbar. In spite of its name, the Standard toolbar is not displayed by default. To display it, select View ➤ Toolbars ➤ Standard. The Standard toolbar contains icons for common file operations, such as open, save, cut, copy, and paste.

- Press Ctrl+N/Cmd+N. Depending on how you have set up the New Document category in Preferences (see Chapter 2), this either opens the New Document dialog box or creates a blank page of the current site's default page type.

- Right-click in the Files panel and select New File from the context menu. This creates a blank page of the current site's default page type. The file name is automatically placed in editable mode, ready for you to change it.

When you use either of the last two methods, the default page type is determined by whether you have defined a testing server for the site. If the testing server uses PHP MySQL as its server model, the default page type is created with a .php file name extension. If no testing server has been defined, the page is created with an .html extension.

> *The first time you open a new document in Dreamweaver, it's displayed in Split view. Thereafter Dreamweaver remembers your latest setting. If the current document is in Code view, a new document or an existing one will also open in Code view. If the current document is in Design view, that's how the next document will open. When you close Dreamweaver, the state of the last document to be closed determines how the first document will open when you next launch the program. Some documents, such as style sheets and JavaScript files, can be opened only in Code view, so this also affects how the next document is displayed.*

Inserting text

When you create a new web page, such as one with an `.html` or a `.php` file name extension, Dreamweaver automatically inserts all the necessary HTML tags for a basic page. In Design view, you're presented with what looks like a completely blank page, but if you look in Code view or Split view, you'll see the basic skeleton tags with the insertion point (or cursor) between the opening and closing <body> tags, as shown in Figure 3-3.

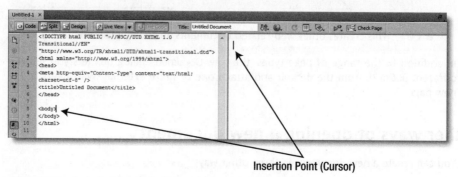

Insertion Point (Cursor)

Figure 3-3. In the underlying code, the insertion point is automatically placed between the <body> tags.

Inserting text directly

If you start typing in Design view, your text will appear, just as it would in a word processor. The same text will also appear in Code view, as shown in Figure 3-4. There is usually a slight delay between typing in Design view and the appearance of the text in Code view. The length of the delay depends on your computer specifications and any other programs running at the same time.

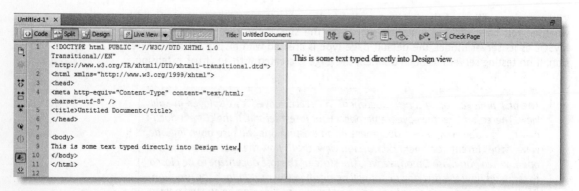

Figure 3-4. Anything entered in Design view is replicated in Code view.

Notice that the text in the Code view half of the page in Figure 3-4 is inserted directly between the `<body>` tags. As soon as you press Enter/Return, Dreamweaver automatically wraps the existing text in `<p>` tags and creates a new pair of `<p>` tags with a nonbreaking space (` `) in between, as shown on lines 9 and 10 in Figure 3-5.

Figure 3-5. Dreamweaver automatically formats text as paragraphs when you press Enter/Return.

As soon as you start typing in the new paragraph, Dreamweaver removes the nonbreaking space (` `) from the underlying code and replaces it with the new text. Text is automatically aligned left and wraps when it reaches the edge of the Document window. In this and many other respects, entering text is like working with a word processor. However, you need to press Enter/Return only once between paragraphs. As you can see in Figure 3-6, a space roughly equivalent to one line is left between each block of text. Pressing Enter/Return twice results in an empty paragraph (`<p> </p>`) being inserted in the underlying code.

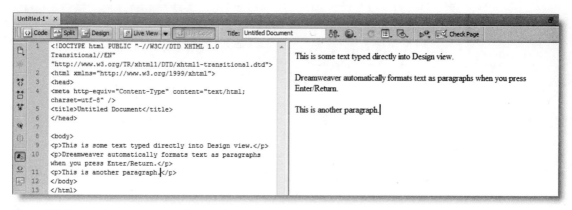

Figure 3-6. Paragraphs are automatically spaced apart in Design view, just as they would be in a browser.

Newcomers frequently ask how to prevent Dreamweaver from inserting a space between lines. This usually indicates a fundamental misunderstanding of how HTML works. HTML tags such as <p> (paragraph) and <h1> (level 1 heading) are intended to represent the structure of the document not primarily in the sense of how it looks on the screen, but according to its meaning. Control over how a page looks is the role of CSS, not HTML.

If you want to eliminate or reduce the space between lines, you should begin by considering the meaning of the text. Do you want paragraphs, or should you be creating a list? If it's the latter, use the appropriate HTML element, such as <ul> (unordered list) or <ol> (ordered list). The bullets can easily be removed from an unordered list with CSS. If you simply want to break a line within a text element, press Shift+Return/Enter to insert a line break (<br />). If you do want paragraphs, but don't like the default space between them, the correct way to deal with it is to create a CSS style rule to adjust the margins of all paragraphs. You'll start working with CSS in the next chapter.

Copying and pasting text

If you're building a website for a client, you're likely to get the text in the form of a word-processed document. To paste text from other applications, place your cursor in Design view and select Edit ➤ Paste, press Ctrl+V/Cmd+V, or right-click and select Paste from the context menu. (You can practice this with the Stroll.doc and Stroll.docx files in the examples/ch03 folder of the accompanying download files.) Dreamweaver does a pretty good job preserving most, if not all, of the formatting. It also offers you a choice of how much formatting to keep, if any.

Dreamweaver uses the paste options set in the Preferences panel. To set the default paste behavior, open the Preferences panel from the Edit menu (Dreamweaver menu on a Mac) or press Ctrl+U/Cmd+U, and select the Copy/Paste category. This presents you with the dialog box shown in Figure 3-7.

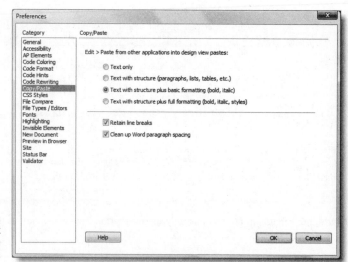

Figure 3-7.
You can set the default paste options in the Preferences panel.

The following options are available:

- Text only: This means exactly what it says. You get the plain text and nothing else. All formatting and line breaks are stripped out.

- Text with structure: This preserves headings, paragraphs, lists, tables, and other structural formatting.

- Text with structure plus basic formatting: This also preserves bold and italic text.

- Text with structure plus full formatting: This converts fonts, colors, and other styles into CSS. The result in Design view is very impressive, but the CSS is a nightmare. *Do not use this option*. It's much better to choose Text with structure plus basic formatting and create your own CSS.

- Retain line breaks: This checkbox cannot be selected independently. It merely indicates whether line breaks will be preserved by the selected option (all do, except Text only).

- Clean up Word paragraph spacing: This removes the extra line between paragraphs in text pasted from Microsoft Word.

If you want to choose a different option without changing the default settings, choose Edit ➤ Paste Special, press Ctrl+Shift+V/Shift+Cmd+V, or right-click and choose Paste Special from the context menu. This brings up a dialog box with the same options as shown in Figure 3-7. Choose the options you want, and then click OK. The new options apply only to the current paste operation.

> *When pasting from Microsoft Word, Dreamweaver expects a blank line between paragraphs. If new paragraphs begin on the next line, Dreamweaver treats the text as a single paragraph and inserts a `<br />` tag between each one. To format paragraphs correctly on a large amount of text, it's usually quicker to use Find and Replace in Word to replace single paragraph marks (^p) with two (^p^p).*

Importing Microsoft Word documents (Windows only)

Microsoft Word has become a de facto standard for word-processed documents, so Dreamweaver has the option to import entire Word documents directly into the Document window. It works in a very similar way to copying and pasting.

To import a Word document, select File ➤ Import ➤ Word Document. In the dialog box that opens, navigate to the document you want to import. Dreamweaver CS4 supports both older Word files that use the `.doc` file name extension and the newer `.docx` standard created by Word 2007 and Word 2008 for Mac. As shown in Figure 3-8, the Formatting drop-down menu at the bottom of the dialog box offers the same choices as are available for pasting. (The `Stroll.doc` and `Stroll.docx` files are available with the downloadable files, in the `examples/ch03` folder.)

Figure 3-8. The Import Word Document dialog box offers the same formatting choices as are available when pasting.

Importing a Word document like this produces exactly the same result as copying and pasting, but it has the advantage that you don't need to open the Word document to bring its contents into a web page. The disadvantage is that it's an all-or-nothing option: you get the whole document. If you know what the document contains—and you want it in its entirety—this is a useful alternative to copying and pasting. It's also important to remember that the results are only as good as the original formatting of the document. Sometimes it's better to select Text only and format the content yourself inside Dreamweaver.

Inserting images

Images are inserted into HTML with the `<img>` tag, which takes attributes describing the source of the image file, its height and width, and alternate text for nonvisual browsers. When you insert an image in either Design view or Code view, Dreamweaver takes care of generating the necessary code. All you need to do is decide where the image should go.

Inserting images stored on your computer

There are several ways of inserting an image. Perhaps the simplest way, assuming the image is already stored within your site, is to drag the image from either the Files or Assets panel. You can also drag and drop images into the Document window (but not into the Files panel) from Adobe Bridge, Windows Explorer, or Finder on a Mac.

Dragging and dropping images

Dreamweaver inserts the image wherever you drop it. The Files panel is fine if you know the file name of the image you want, but if you want to see a thumbnail preview, open the Assets panel (it's grouped with the Files panel in all preset workspace layouts or can be opened from the Window menu).

As Figure 3-9 shows, the Assets panel sorts site assets into nine categories accessed by clicking one of the icons in the left margin. In addition to showing a thumbnail preview of an image, the panel displays its dimensions and size. If you decide to change the image before inserting it, click the Edit button at the bottom right of the panel to launch your default graphic design program.

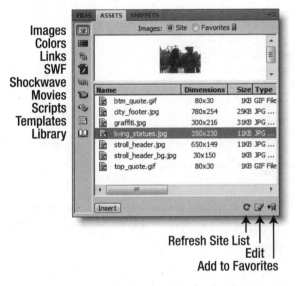

Figure 3-9. The Assets panel gives a quick preview of assets such as images and colors.

If you have a lot of images or other assets, you can add them to your favorites by clicking the Add to Favorites button at the bottom right of the panel or by right-clicking and selecting Add to Favorites from the context menu. Toggle between your favorites and the full set by clicking the radio buttons at the top of the Assets panel.

As well as dragging and dropping an image from the Assets panel, you can click the Insert button at the bottom left of the panel to insert the image wherever your cursor is located in the Document window.

Selecting an image through the file system

The other way to insert images is through the Select Image Source dialog box (see Figure 3-10). To open this dialog box, select Insert ➤ Image, click the Image icon on the Common tab of the Insert bar, or press Ctrl+Alt+I/Opt+Cmd+I. The Select Image Source dialog box also displays a thumbnail preview of the image (on Windows, there's a checkbox at the bottom of the dialog box that lets you turn this off), as well as its dimensions and file size.

Figure 3-10. The Select Image Source dialog box also lets you see a preview of the image before inserting it.

If you're using the default setting of document-relative links (see Chapter 2), Dreamweaver displays the following alert when you try to insert an image in a page that hasn't yet been saved.

This is simply a gentle reminder that Dreamweaver is a site-based program. It needs to know where the page is located in your site before it can insert the correct value in the `<img>` tag's `src` attribute. When you click OK, Dreamweaver still inserts the image in the page, but creates a tag that looks like this:

```
<img src="file:///C|/vhosts/dwcs4/images/graffiti.jpg" width="300" ➡
height="216" />
```

As soon as you save the page in a defined site, Dreamweaver changes the src attribute to a valid relative link, like this:

```
<img src="../../images/graffiti.jpg" width="300" height="216" />
```

Provided that you always create web pages within a defined site, you can safely ignore this alert. The alert is displayed only for links relative to the current document; it doesn't apply to site-root-relative links.

3

A common question in the Dreamweaver forum (http://www.adobe.com/support/forums/) is "Why don't my images display when I upload the page to my website? They look fine in Design view." In the vast majority of cases, it's because the src attribute begins with file:///. In other words, it's still pointing to the location of the image on the designer's local computer. This usually happens because the designer has failed to define a site in Dreamweaver, and then uploaded the pages independently. Site definition is the key to maintaining your sanity with Dreamweaver.

Adding alternate text

Before Dreamweaver inserts the image into the page, it displays the Image Tag Accessibility Attributes dialog box, as shown in Figure 3-11. This prompts you to add alternate text to describe the image. This text is inserted into the <img> tag's alt attribute for the benefit of visually impaired people using assistive technology to surf the Web, as well as those who prefer to turn off images or use text browsers.

Figure 3-11. Dreamweaver automatically prompts you to insert alternate text for images.

According to the W3C specifications, the alt attribute is required (not optional). However, alternate text should be used only for images that convey meaning. Don't use it for purely decorative images or transparent images designed to space apart page elements (**spacers**). Imagine the frustration of a blind person visiting your page with a screen reader listening to an endless recitation of "spacer gif"! To comply with the W3C specifications without driving others mad, activate the drop-down menu for Alternate text and select <empty>. This inserts an empty alt attribute (alt="") in the <img> tag.

The Long description field is for the URL to a more detailed description of the image. This is optional, and it is normally used only for complex images, such as bar charts or graphs.

After filling in the Alternate text field (and the Long description field, if necessary), click OK to insert the image. If you click Cancel, the image is still inserted, but the alternate text and long description are ignored.

A link at the bottom of the Image Tag Accessibility Attributes dialog box takes you to the Accessibility category of the Preferences panel, where you can turn off this and other accessibility prompts. I don't recommend doing so, as most industrialized countries now impose a legal obligation on website designers to make their sites accessible to people with disabilities.

Text and image alignment

When you insert an image on a page that already contains text, the text does not automatically flow around the image. Instead, the text is aligned with the bottom of the image, as shown in Figure 3-12. This should come as no surprise if you're familiar with HTML. In the past, it was common practice to use the align, hspace, and vspace attributes in the <img> tag to solve this problem. Dreamweaver CS4 still lets you insert these attributes, but CSS offers a much more versatile solution, as you'll see in Chapter 4.

Figure 3-12. Text does not flow automatically around images.

Inserting remote images

As well as using images stored in your own site, the src attribute of the <img> tag accepts the URL of an image on another website. To insert a remote image, select the Image button on the Insert bar, use Insert ➤ Image, or press Ctrl+Alt+I/Opt/Cmd+I. In the Select Image Source dialog box, delete any content in the URL field and replace it with the URL of the remote file, as shown in the following screenshot (use the full URL beginning with http://).

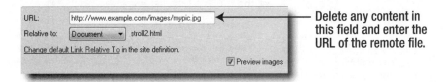

Delete any content in this field and enter the URL of the remote file.

When you click OK, Dreamweaver presents you with the Image Tag Accessibility Attributes dialog box, and then inserts the <img> tag for the remote image. By default, if you are connected to the Internet, Dreamweaver accesses the remote image, inserts the correct height and width dimensions in the <img> tag, and displays the image in Design view. Obviously, this doesn't happen if Dreamweaver can't access the remote file for any reason. In that case, it creates the <img> tag without the height and width attributes, and displays a broken-image icon in Design view.

On a slow connection or a page that uses a large number of remote files, this can slow Dreamweaver to a crawl. If you experience performance problems, turn off Display External Files on the View menu. Like many options on Dreamweaver menus, a check mark alongside the menu item indicates that the option is enabled. Clicking the menu item toggles the option on and off.

> *Including remote images in a web page is a practice known as **inline linking** or **hotlinking** (see http://en.wikipedia.org/wiki/Inline_linking). You should do it only with the permission of the site whose image you're using. Linking to an image without permission could land you in legal hot water over breach of copyright. It could also leave you with egg on your face. When the owner of a site discovers images are being linked to without permission, it's quite common to replace them with one that reads "This image was stolen from . . ."*

Inserting placeholder images

Sometimes, you don't have the images available when laying out a page. In this case, use a placeholder. Using an image placeholder has the advantage that you can specify its size and other attributes in a single operation. It also prevents Dreamweaver from displaying a broken-image icon, as happens if you use the name of a nonexistent image, Position your cursor in the Document window where you want the image to be inserted and select Image Placeholder from the Common tab of the Insert bar, as shown in Figure 3-13 (click the down arrow to the right of the Image icon to open the submenu). Alternatively, select Insert ➤ Image Objects ➤ Image Placeholder.

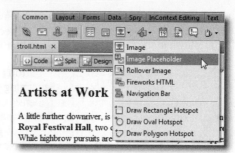

Figure 3-13.
Using an image placeholder is convenient when you don't have access to the original.

This presents you with a dialog box with the following fields:

- Name: This is simply a name to identify the placeholder. If you enter a name here, it's used as both the name and id attributes of the <img> tag, so the name must begin with a letter and it cannot contain any spaces or special characters. If you leave this field blank, Dreamweaver inserts name="", but no id attribute.

- Width: The width of the placeholder in pixels. The default is 32.

- Height: The height of the placeholder in pixels. The default is 32.

- Color: This inserts an inline CSS style attribute for background-color. Its main purpose is to make the placeholder stand out or blend in with the rest of your page. You can use either the color picker in the dialog box or enter a hexadecimal number in the text field. If you don't choose a color, Dreamweaver doesn't insert a style attribute, but displays the placeholder as light gray in Design view.

- Alternate text: This is for the alt attribute. If you leave this blank, Dreamweaver inserts alt="" in the <img> tag.

When you click OK, a solid block of color is placed in Design view, displaying the name and dimensions of the placeholder, as shown in Figure 3-14.

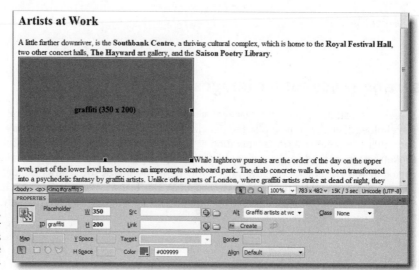

Figure 3-14.
The Property inspector for an image placeholder has options to create a new image or link to an existing one.

When you're ready to replace the placeholder with a real image, click the placeholder in Design view to reveal its details in the Property inspector (see Figure 3-14). You can then either create a new image or replace the placeholder with an existing one, as follows:

- **Create a new image**: Click the Create button in the center of the Property inspector. This launches Adobe Fireworks (assuming you have it installed) with the canvas automatically sized to the same dimensions as the placeholder. Click the Done button at the top left of the Fireworks workspace when you have finished, and follow the instructions to save the image. This is a Fireworks-only operation. It won't launch Photoshop, even if Photoshop is your primary image editor. However, Photoshop users get their day in the sun with Smart Objects, which are covered in the next section.

- **Replace the placeholder with an existing image**: Type the path to the image in the Src field of the Property inspector. Alternatively, click the folder icon to the right of the Src field, and navigate to the image in the file system. You can also use the Point to File tool just to the left of the folder icon. As shown in Figure 3-15, you drag the icon shaped like a crosshair sight to the name of the image file in the Files panel. Release the mouse button when the correct file is highlighted, and Dreamweaver inserts the correct path to the image in the Src field of the Property inspector.

Figure 3-15. The Point to File tool offers a quick way of linking to a file in the Files panel.

Whichever method you choose to select the image, Dreamweaver replaces the placeholder with the new image and automatically updates the height and width attributes to the correct values.

> *The inline* style *attribute for* background-color *is not removed from the* <img> *tag when you replace the placeholder. In most circumstances, this makes no difference, but it could affect style rules embedded in the head of the document or an external style sheet. To avoid any problems, delete the value in the* Color *field of the Property inspector before setting the* Src *field. This leaves an empty style attribute in the* <img> *tag. It's redundant, but won't do any harm.*

Using Photoshop Smart Objects as images

A **Smart Object** is a web image, such as a .jpg or .gif file, that retains a link to the original source file from which it was created. This makes it easy to edit and reoptimize the web image. When working with a Smart Object, changes are made only to the web image, leaving the original untouched. However, if you do make any changes to the original Photoshop file, the Smart Object link simplifies updating the web image.

The concept of Smart Objects will be very familiar to designers migrating from Adobe GoLive, which has now been discontinued. However, Smart Objects have been integrated into Dreamweaver in a slightly different way from their treatment in GoLive. Moreover, you can use Smart Objects only in conjunction with Photoshop. They do not work with any other Creative Suite program or with PDF files.

Inserting a Photoshop Smart Object

There's no need to open Photoshop to insert a Smart Object. You don't even need Photoshop installed. All that's needed is the original image stored as a Photoshop .psd file. Dreamweaver CS4 has all the necessary functionality to generate a .gif, .jpg, or .png file from the Photoshop original. As Figure 3-16 shows, you can even make some adjustments to the image that's generated. However, don't be fooled into thinking you get a free cut-down version of Photoshop with Dreamweaver. You can't edit the .psd file; that requires a full version of Photoshop.

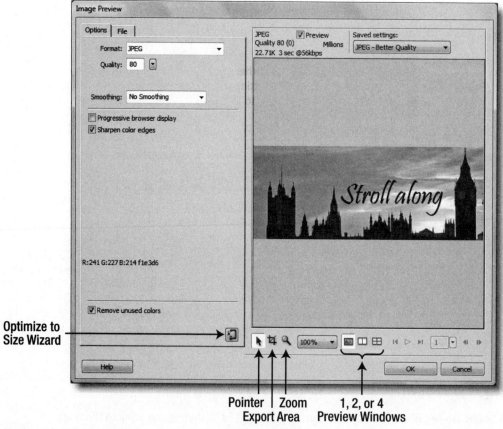

Figure 3-16. The Image Preview dialog box lets you optimize and preview the web image before inserting it into the page.

You insert a Smart Object in the same way as an ordinary image: by opening the Select Image Source dialog box (click the Image icon on the Common tab of the Insert bar, select Insert ➤ Image, or press Ctrl+Alt+I/Opt+Cmd+I). Navigate to the Photoshop .psd file that you want to use as the original. If you want to practice using Smart Objects, use the stroll_header.psd file in the examples/ch03 folder of the accompanying download files.

It can be anywhere on your file system; it doesn't need to be in your site. However, the location of the Photoshop original needs to remain constant for the Smart Object link to work. You can also drag and drop a Photoshop .psd file from the Files panel if it's stored within your site.

When you have selected the Photoshop file, click OK (or Choose on a Mac). This opens the Image Preview dialog box (see Figure 3-16). This is where you optimize the web image before inserting it in the page. The dialog box has a large number of options, all of which are described in detail if you click the Help button at the bottom left.

The preview window on the right side of the dialog box displays a flattened version of the whole Photoshop file. Depending on the size of the original, you need to use the Pointer and/or Zoom tools to view the entire image. The Zoom tool and magnification drop-down menu alongside it work only in fixed steps. You can't drag the Zoom tool around a specific area to display it.

What looks like the Crop tool in Photoshop and other image editors determines the area that will be exported from the .psd file. Like all settings in the Image Preview dialog box, it affects only the web image. No changes are made to the Photoshop original.

The Optimize to size wizard is a rather crude device that sets a target size for the web image in kilobytes. Figure 3-17 shows the result of selecting a target size of 10KB. What I actually got was a 2.6KB image with heavy **banding**, or **posterization** (unacceptably abrupt changes of color), and a severe loss of definition.

Figure 3-17. Using the Optimize to size wizard can produce very unsatisfactory results.

You get much better results by using one of the options in the Saved settings drop-down menu, or by selecting your own values for Format, Quality, and Smoothing. You can compare different settings by selecting one, two, or four preview windows.

Once you have made your decision, click OK. Dreamweaver presents you with a dialog box in which you specify the name of the web image and where you want to save it. After saving the image, Dreamweaver prompts you to set alternate text for the image, and finally inserts it into the page.

If you are upgrading from Dreamweaver CS3, this process is very similar to copying the whole or part of a Photoshop file and pasting it into Dreamweaver. Copying and pasting still works in Dreamweaver CS4, and opens the same Image Preview *dialog box. However, copying and pasting from Photoshop does* not *create a Smart Object. To create a Smart Object, you must import the* .psd *file through the* Select Image Source *dialog box or drag and drop it from the* Files *panel.*

Updating a Smart Object

As an image file, a Photoshop Smart Object is no different from any other .jpg, .gif, or .png file. What makes it special is the link that Dreamweaver preserves with the original .psd file. This link is indicated in Design view by a Smart Object icon in the top-left corner of the image, as shown in Figure 3-18.

Figure 3-18. The status of a Smart Object is indicated by the icon in the top-left corner of the image.

Resizing a Smart Object

If you resize the image in Design view, the icon is superimposed with an exclamation mark inside a yellow triangle, as shown alongside. If you hover your mouse pointer over the icon, a tooltip explains that the dimensions of the image are different from the HTML width and height attributes. Right-click the image and select Update From Original from the context menu. Alternatively, select the image, and choose Modify ➤ Image ➤ Optimize.

Dreamweaver re-creates the web image from the Photoshop original, resampling it to get the same optimization settings as before. This all takes place in the background, and when the process is complete, the Smart Object icon reverts to the synchronized state shown in Figure 3-18.

Reverting to the Smart Object's original size

If you decide you don't like the new size, right-click the Smart Object in Design view, and select Reset Size To Original from the context menu. This resets the size, but does *not* resample the image. Right-click again, and select Update From Original from the context menu.

The context menu also has a Reset Size option. This reverts the image to the previous size. In other words, it acts like an undo command. The same options are available through the Modify ➤ Image submenu.

Changing the optimization settings of a Smart Object

You can change the quality and other optimization settings of a Smart Object image at any time by right-clicking and selecting Optimize from the context menu. This reopens the Image Preview dialog box shown in Figure 3-16. Any changes to the image are applied immediately. Even if you change the export area, you don't get the opportunity to assign it a different name. As always, the changes are made only to the web image, not to the Photoshop original.

Alternative ways to reopen the Image Preview dialog box are through the Modify ➤ Image ➤ Optimize menu option, or by clicking the Edit Image Settings button in the Property inspector, as shown in the following screenshot.

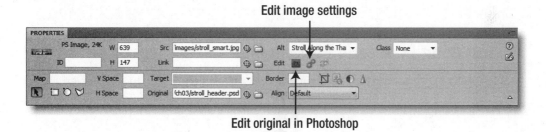

Edit image settings

Edit original in Photoshop

Editing the original image

If you decide to make changes to the Photoshop original (for example, to capitalize the initial letter of *along* in the example I have been using), select the Smart Object in Dreamweaver and click the Edit button in the Property inspector as shown in the preceding screenshot. Alternatively, select Modify ➤ Image ➤ Edit With ➤ Photoshop. Of course, you can also just open the .psd file directly in Photoshop.

> *If you don't have Photoshop installed, Dreamweaver displays a message saying it can't find a valid editor. When you click OK to dismiss the message, you're taken to the File Types/Editors category of the Preferences panel, where you can select another graphics editor to handle .psd files. However, editing a .psd file in another program could result in losing Photoshop-specific data.*

After you have made the changes, save the .psd file. The Smart Object icon in Dreamweaver changes to indicate that the Smart Object is out of sync with the original. The changed icon is shown in the screenshot alongside, but the difference might be difficult to make out in the black-and-white image. Like the regular Smart Object icon, it consists of two arrows in a circle, but instead of both arrows being green, the bottom one is deep red.

Changing the Photoshop original does *not* automatically update Smart Objects in Dreamweaver. This gives you ultimate control over whether to update the web image. To bring the web image into sync with the Photoshop original, right-click and choose Update From Original or use the main menu option: Modify ➤ Image ➤ Update From Original.

Updating Smart Objects from the Assets panel

If you use a Smart Object in more than one page in a site, you can update all instances simultaneously by selecting the image in the Assets panel and updating it there. The menu options are the same as described in the previous sections.

> *Smart Objects rely on Design Notes that Dreamweaver creates in the folder where you save the web image. Design Notes are stored in a subfolder called _notes, which is normally hidden in the* Files *panel, but which can be seen in Windows Explorer or Finder on a Mac. If you delete the _notes folder or its contents, the Smart Object link with the Photoshop original is destroyed.*

Inserting Flash and Flex movies

Inserting a Flash or Flex movie into a web page is very similar to inserting an image. However, the underlying code is very different. There are also important differences from the way previous versions of Dreamweaver handled these files.

The first change is relatively minor. The Media submenus of the Insert menu and Common tab of the Insert bar no longer refer to Flash, but to SWF. This is because movies made in Flash (http://www.adobe.com/products/flash/) and Flex (http://www.adobe.com/products/flex/) both use the SWF format and run in the Flash Player browser plugin.

> *Historically, SWF stands for both Shockwave Flash and Small Web Format. It's normally pronounced "swiff."*

The other changes reflect developments on the Web. In 2006, a dispute over patents between Microsoft and a company called Eolas resulted in changes to Internet Explorer that forced users to click embedded objects, including Flash movies, to activate them. Dreamweaver CS3 got around this problem by using a JavaScript file to load Flash. Since Microsoft and Eolas have settled their dispute, this is no longer necessary. However, instead of reverting to the old method of embedding SWF files, Dreamweaver CS4 adopts a new approach for the following reasons:

- It avoids using the <embed> tag, which is not part of the HTML standard.
- It prompts users to upgrade their version of Flash Player if it's too old to support features used by the SWF file. This is particularly important for movies created in Flex, which require a minimum of Flash Player 9.

To insert a SWF, position your cursor in the Document window where you want the movie to be, and select SWF from the Media submenu of the Insert menu or the Common tab of the Insert bar. For keyboard shortcut enthusiasts, the secret code is Ctrl+Alt+F/ Opt+Cmd+F. Navigate to the SWF file in the Select File dialog box and click OK. (The images folder of the download files contains a Flash movie called fireworks.swf, which you can use for practice.) This presents you with the Object Tag Accessibility Attributes dialog box, where you can enter a title, access key, and tab index for the movie. All items are optional, but it's a good idea to give the movie at least a title attribute. As with images, clicking Cancel doesn't stop the movie from being inserted into the page; all it does is ignore the accessibility attributes.

By default, Dreamweaver displays a placeholder for the SWF, as shown in Figure 3-19. To see what the movie looks like in the context of the page, select the placeholder in Design view and click the Play button at the bottom right of the Property inspector. This consumes processor power, so click the button again (its label now reads Stop) to return to the placeholder when you no longer need to view the movie.

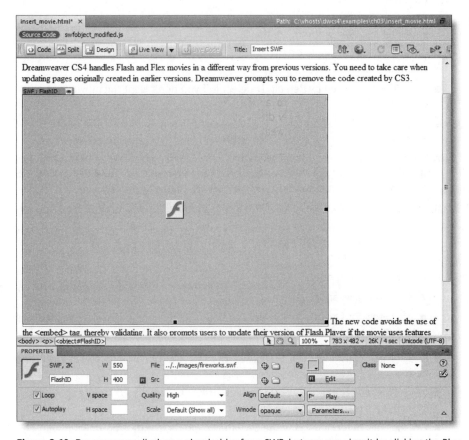

Figure 3-19. Dreamweaver displays a placeholder for a SWF, but you can view it by clicking the Play button in the Property inspector.

As you can see in Figure 3-19, the Property inspector has a lot of options for controlling the settings of Flash and Flex movies. At the top left, it displays the file type and size.

Immediately below is an unlabeled field that displays the id attribute of the <object> tag. Dreamweaver automatically assigns FlashID as the value for the first SWF object. Subsequent SWF movies inserted in the same page are numbered FlashID2, FlashID3, and so on. The field is editable, so you can enter your own choice of id instead. Most of the other options are self-explanatory, but I'll describe each one briefly.

- W and H: The movie's width and height in pixels. These are filled in automatically when you insert the SWF object.
- File: The pathname of the SWF. The Point to File tool and folder icons work the same way as for images.
- Src: This field is for you to enter the location of the FLA file from which a Flash movie was created.
- Bg: This inserts a parameter in the <object> tag to set the background color for the SWF.
- Edit: This opens the movie's FLA file for editing. To use this option, you must first enter the location of the file in the Src field.
- Class: This lets you apply a CSS class to the <object> tag. This is covered in the next chapter.
- Loop: This is selected by default. Deselect it if you don't want the movie to run as a continuous loop.
- Autoplay: This is selected by default. Deselect it if you don't want the movie to run automatically when the page is first loaded.
- V space and H space: These insert the deprecated vspace and hspace attributes into the <object> tag to add vertical and horizontal space around the movie. CSS offers a more versatile solution, as you'll see in Chapter 4.
- Quality: This controls the look of the movie during playback. Choose from the following settings:
  - High: This is the default setting. It gives the best quality, but requires a lot of processor power.
  - Low: Select this option if speed is more important than quality.
  - Auto Low: This prioritizes speed, but improves quality when possible.
  - Auto High: This gives equal priority to both speed and appearance, but sacrifices quality if more speed is required.
- Scale: This determines how the movie fits into the dimensions set in width and height.
- Align: This inserts the deprecated align attribute in the <object> tag. Use CSS instead, as explained in the next chapter.
- Wmode: This determines how the SWF movie interacts with drop-down menus and other elements controlled by JavaScript. Choose from the following options:
  - Opaque: This is the default. It allows drop-down menus to display correctly over the movie. It gives the movie an opaque background so that elements with a lower z-index are hidden behind. (z-index is a CSS property that controls the stacking order of positioned elements.)

- Transparent: If the SWF movie has transparent elements, this allows elements with a lower z-index to show through behind it.

- Window: This removes the wmode parameter from the <object> tag. Select this option if the movie is not affected by dynamic elements, such as drop-down menus. It is more efficient and user-friendly to screen readers for the visually impaired.

- Parameters: This opens a dialog box to set extra parameters expected by the movie.

Dreamweaver places a bright blue tab with an open-eye icon at the top left of the SWF placeholder. Click the icon to display the alternate content that will appear when a user accesses the page with a browser using an old version of Flash Player, as shown in Figure 3-20. You can edit or delete this content however you like.

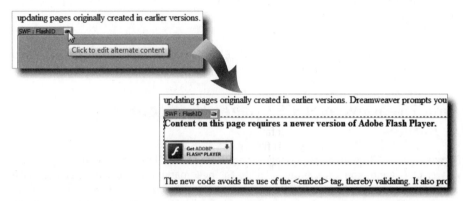

Figure 3-20. Dreamweaver inserts a customizable message to be displayed when an old version of Flash Player is detected.

Notice that the image linking to the Flash Player download page is surrounded by a blue border because it is used as a link. Older versions of Dreamweaver eliminated the border by inserting border="0" in the <img> tag, but this is deprecated, and you are now expected to create a CSS rule to eliminate it yourself. I'll describe how to do this in the "Using images as links" section later in the chapter.

To close the alternate content and restore the SWF placeholder in Design view, click the eye icon again. If you can't see the blue tab and icon, move your mouse pointer inside the area containing the alternate content. As soon as the mouse pointer passes over the dotted line surrounding the alternate content in Design view, it triggers the reappearance of the tab and a blue border around the alternate content. If the tab and blue border fail to reappear, make sure there's a check mark alongside Invisible Elements in the View ➤ Visual Aids submenu.

The first time you save a page containing a SWF, you should see an alert telling you that expressInstall.swf and swfobject_modified.js have been copied to the Scripts folder in your site. Dreamweaver creates the Scripts folder if it doesn't already exist. These files are shared by all pages that include SWF files, so this happens only once in each site.

> When uploading your site to the remote server, don't forget to upload expressInstall.swf and swfobject_modified.js. SWF movies won't be displayed correctly without them.

To delete a SWF movie from a page, select the blue tab at the top left of the placeholder and press Delete. This removes all the associated code cleanly from the page.

If your page generates JavaScript errors after removing a SWF, open Code view and see if you can locate a block of JavaScript like this at the bottom of the page:

```
<script type="text/javascript">
<!--
swfobject.registerObject("FlashID");
//-->
</script>
```

If you changed the id attribute of the SWF, FlashID will be replaced by the value you used. Remove the entire <script> block, and the errors should be eliminated.

Editing Dreamweaver CS3 pages that contain SWF movies

Dreamweaver CS3 created completely different code for Flash or Flex movies. Dreamweaver CS4 cannot convert the old script to the new markup. If you don't need to make any changes to the Flash movie's settings, you can leave the code as it is. However, to make any changes to the settings of a movie embedded using the old method, you *must* delete the movie from the page and insert it again. Failure to do so results in the code being only partially updated.

To remove a Flash movie embedded in a previous version of Dreamweaver, select the movie placeholder in Design view and press Delete. Dreamweaver should remove the code cleanly, ready for you to reinsert the movie. You should also remove the following line of code from the <head> of the page, as it's no longer needed:

```
<script src="../../Scripts/AC_RunActiveContent.js" type="text/ ➡
javascript"></script>
```

Adding structure to your page content

In the past, adding structure to a web page meant creating a grid using tables and fitting the content into table cells. Tables have the advantage of being easy to visualize. They're flexible, too, because table rows and columns stretch and contract to accommodate the content placed inside them. However, these advantages are heavily outweighed by the problems created by table-based design.

Using tables, anything but the simplest of designs normally involves nesting tables inside one another, making the page impossible for disabled people to navigate with assistive technology. Equally important, from the design point of view, complex table structures are very fragile. Adding a new element to the page can bring the structure tumbling down like a house of cards. Previous versions of Dreamweaver attempted to solve this problem with Layout mode, which let you lay out your page in Design view rather like a desktop publisher. Although Layout mode usually produced visually pleasing results, the underlying HTML code it generated was a horrendous tangle that was impossible to edit and a serious barrier to accessibility.

> *If you are upgrading from a previous version of Dreamweaver and can't find Layout mode, stop looking. It has been permanently removed from Dreamweaver CS4. Rather than attempt to edit pages originally created with Layout mode, you should redesign them from scratch.*

Another layout tool that attracted a lot of excitement was what Dreamweaver called *layers*. The term *layer* was dropped in Dreamweaver CS3 and replaced by **AP Div**. *AP* stands for absolutely positioned, and is a much more accurate description because AP Divs use CSS absolute positioning. The instant appeal of absolute positioning is that it makes web design feel like desktop publishing. You can place elements on a page exactly where you want them to be. Your page looks wonderful in Dreamweaver Design view. It might even look good in a browser. But it all starts to fall apart if the browser window or text is resized. A common question is "Why does my AP Div (layer) move when the window is resized?" The answer is "It doesn't." What you see is an optical illusion. The absolutely positioned element stays exactly where you put it in relation to its parent element (usually the browser window). All other elements of the web page move with the flow of the document. Although AP Divs have a useful role to play in website design, I strongly recommend that you avoid them until you have a solid understanding of CSS and the rules of positioning.

So what's left if tables and AP Divs are to be avoided? Thanks to CSS, the possibilities are endless. In Chapter 5, I'll show you how to adapt one of Dreamweaver's built-in CSS layouts. The layouts are a good starting point for a new page, but to be able to use them successfully, it's important to understand the basics of page structure. If your page is structured logically, it's easier to maintain and style with CSS.

As you saw earlier in the chapter, Dreamweaver automatically encloses text typed into Design view with <p> (paragraph) tags when you press Enter/Return. You can also import text from Microsoft Word or paste text from other applications, and Dreamweaver will attempt to preserve the structure and formatting.

Text is normally structured using one or more of the following elements:

- Paragraphs (<p>)
- Headings (<h1> through <h6>)
- Preformatted text (<pre>)

- Inline tags (for example, `<strong>`, `<em>`, `<code>`, etc.)
- Lists (`<ul>`, `<ol>`, or `<dl>`)
- Block quotes (`<blockquote>`)
- Tables (`<table>`)

There are five basic ways of adding these structural elements:

- Through the HTML view of the Property inspector
- Through the Text tab of the Insert bar (tables use the Common and Layout tabs)
- Through the Format menu (tables use the Insert and Modify menus)
- By using keyboard shortcuts (not available for all elements)
- By typing the code directly into Code view

Typing the code directly needs no explanation. Refer to Chapter 1 for details of code hints and auto-completion. You can also look up keyboard shortcuts on the relevant menus. The following sections concentrate on using the Property inspector, the Insert bar, and menus. Let's begin by looking at changes to the Property inspector that might confuse newcomers and experienced users alike.

Selecting the HTML view of the Property inspector

The Property inspector has two buttons labeled HTML and CSS on the left side. The top screenshot in Figure 3-21 shows the HTML view, and the bottom screenshot shows the CSS view. They look very similar, but their functions are completely different.

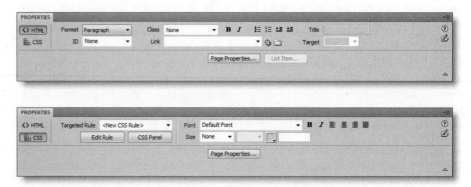

Figure 3-21. The HTML and CSS views of the Property inspector are easily confused.

The HTML view is primarily concerned with HTML markup, although the Class drop-down menu and Page Properties button give some access to CSS. The CSS view is exclusively devoted to CSS. The Bold and Italic buttons that are common to both views work in very different ways. If you click the Bold button in the HTML view, Dreamweaver inserts `<strong>` tags in the underlying code. Clicking the same button in the CSS view launches the New Style Rule dialog box or opens an existing style rule for editing, depending on the value displayed in the Targeted Rule drop-down menu.

Here, we'll concentrate on using the HTML view to add structural elements.

The first time you launch Dreamweaver CS4, the HTML *view of the Property inspector is displayed by default. Thereafter, Dreamweaver always remembers your most recent selection, so it's important to be aware which view is displayed. The current selection is indicated by its label on the left of the Property inspector being inset. Another visual clue is that the* CSS *view does not have a* Link *field.*

Creating paragraphs, headings, and preformatted text

The Format drop-down menu at the top left of the HTML view of the Property inspector (see Figure 3-21) adds structure to text by wrapping it in paragraph (<p>), heading (<h1> through <h6>), or preformatted text (<pre>) tags. It also removes those tags when you select None as the option.

To understand how the Format drop-down menu works, it's a good idea to open Split view and watch where tags are inserted or removed. It's important to understand that *the structure is not applied to selected text, but to the entire block where your cursor is currently located.* If your cursor is located inside a paragraph and you select Heading 2 from the Format drop-down menu, the <p> tags are replaced by <h2> tags. If you select None, the nearest pair of <p>, <h1> through <h6>, or <pre> tags is removed. No other tags are affected.

The Text tab of the Insert bar (see Figure 3-22) and the Paragraph Format submenu of the Format menu work basically the same way. The Paragraph button on the Text tab of the Insert bar is the fifth icon from the left. Note that the Insert bar offers only the first three levels of headings (<h1> through <h3>), and has no option for removing tags once they have been inserted (after all, it is the Insert bar).

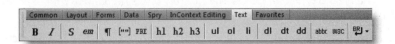

Figure 3-22. The Text tab of the Insert bar adds structure to text elements.

When choosing headings, you should consider the meaning of the heading within the structure of the page. Normally, pages should have only one main heading (<h1>). Subsequent headings should be the next level down (<h2>). Less important subheads after an <h2> should use <h3>. Don't worry about the size of the heading when you first structure the page. The size, color, and alignment can be fixed with CSS. Search engines give more weight to well-structured documents, so don't fall into the old-school habit of using <h6> just because you want small text. You should rarely need more than <h1>, <h2>, and <h3>.

Adding inline tags

Strictly speaking, making text bold or italic doesn't alter the structure of the text, but I'm covering it here because the HTML view of the Property inspector has buttons that insert <strong> and <em> tags. They're the first two of the group of icons immediately to the right of the Class drop-down menu, as shown in the following screenshot.

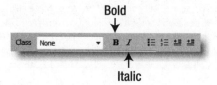

Using the Bold and Italic buttons

The Bold and Italic buttons in the HTML view of the Property inspector work the same way as in a word processor. If you click one of the buttons, nothing happens in Code view, but as soon as you start typing, Dreamweaver inserts <strong> or <em> tags. Click the button again. The insertion point doesn't move in Code view, but as soon as you start typing again, it jumps outside the closing tag and reverts to normal text. You can also highlight a selection of text and wrap it in <strong> or <em> tags.

The Bold and Italic buttons appear inset when inside bold or italic text. Selecting all or part of the formatted text and clicking the button again removes the formatting from the selection. Using these buttons is very versatile and intuitive.

The equivalent buttons on the Text tab of the Insert bar are much less versatile. They insert <strong> and <em> tags, but cannot be used to remove bold or italic formatting.

> *Immediately to the right of the* Bold *and* Italic *icons on the* Insert *bar are two others labeled* S *and* em, *which also boldface and italicize text, respectively. The Dreamweaver default is to use* <strong> *and* <em> *tags in place of the presentational tags* <b> *and* <i>. *If you change the default in the* General *category of the Dreamweaver* Preferences *panel, the* Bold *and* Italic *buttons insert* <b> *and* <i> *tags.*
>
> *Current best practice advocates the use of* <strong> *and* <em> *because it's more meaningful to assistive technology for the visually impaired. However, this is a controversial subject. Sometimes, you want to make text bold or italic simply to distinguish text from its surrounding context. In such cases, it might be more meaningful to create a style rule that sets the* font-weight *property to bold or* font-style *to italic. In other cases, you can use special HTML tags, such as* <cite> *for book and magazine titles. Most browsers render the* <cite> *tag as italic text.*

Using the Format ➤ Style menu

The Style submenu of the Format menu offers a much wider range of inline tags, many of which are designed to add structure to your document. As you can see in Figure 3-23, in addition to Bold and Italic, this submenu offers less frequently used, but important tags such as Code (<code>), Keyboard (<kbd>), and Citation (<cite>).

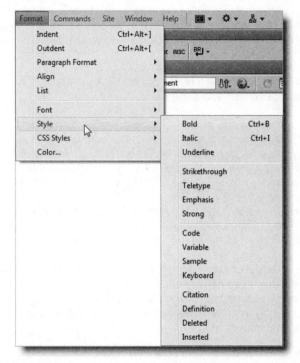

Figure 3-23. The Style submenu of the Format menu inserts both structural and presentational tags.

The Style submenu works in the same way as the Bold and Italic buttons in the HTML view of the Property inspector. You can select an option, start typing, and select the option again to insert the closing tag. Alternatively, you select an option to wrap highlighted text in the inline tags, or remove the tags from a selection. The same submenu is accessible from the context menu when you right-click in Design view.

Using Wrap Tag and Remove Tag

Yet another way to add inline tags is to highlight a section of text, right-click, and select Wrap Tag from the context menu. This opens a mini window with the cursor inside an empty tag and a pop-up menu of inline tags, as shown in the following screenshot.

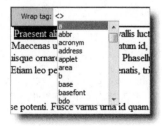

You can either start typing or scroll down to find the tag you want to wrap around the selected text. As you type, the pop-up menu automatically scrolls to the closest matching tag. Once you reach the tag you want, double-click the name in the pop-up menu or press Enter/Return to insert the name inside the empty tag. If you want to add any attributes inside the tag, press the spacebar, and a list of appropriate attributes appears. Once you have finished, press Enter/Return again to close the Wrap tag mini window and insert the tag in the underlying code.

If you select a tag that would create invalid HTML code in the current context, Dreamweaver displays an alert and discards any changes.

> *If you are upgrading from a previous version of Dreamweaver,* Wrap Tag *is the new name context menus use for the* Quick Tag Editor *when you make a partial selection in the Document window. If you select a complete tag in the Tag selector at the bottom of the Document window, the context menu still refers to the* Quick Tag Editor. *Both work exactly the same way. The reason for the different names is because* Wrap Tag *adds a new tag around the current selection, while the* Quick Tag Editor *edits an existing tag; for example, by adding a new attribute.*

To remove a tag, insert your cursor anywhere inside a block of text in Design view and right-click to bring up the context menu. The Remove Tag option on the context menu identifies the closest pair of tags surrounding the position of your cursor. Select the option, and the tags are removed cleanly from the underlying code. For example, take the following text as it appears in Code view:

```
<p>Lorem ipsum <code>dolor</code> sit amet.</p>
```

If you place your cursor anywhere inside dolor in Design view, the context menu displays Remove Tag <code>, and removes the <code> tags from the underlying code if you select it. However, if your cursor is anywhere else in that sentence, the context menu displays Remove Tag <p>, and removes the <p> tags if you select the option.

> *The* Remove Tag *option is available only in Design view and the Tag selector. In Design view, it always selects the closest pair of tags surrounding the current position of the cursor. When used in the Tag selector, it removes the selected tag, but leaves its content intact. It's a very useful tool if you understand the underlying structure of the HTML code in your page.*

Creating lists

HTML creates three types of lists:

- **Unordered list**: By default, browsers display each item as a bullet point. The list is surrounded by <ul> tags, and each item is wrapped in <li> tags. You can change the bullet style or remove it completely with CSS.

- **Ordered list**: By default, browsers prefix each item with a number, starting from 1. The list is surrounded by <ol> tags and each item is wrapped in <li> tags. The style and starting point of the numbering can be controlled by CSS.

- **Definition list**: This type of list is designed for a glossary, list of terms, or collection of name/value pairs. The list is surrounded by <dl> tags; each term to be defined is wrapped in <dt> tags; and the definitions are wrapped in <dd> tags. Most browsers display the definitions indented one line below the preceding term. As always, this can be changed by CSS.

Creating bullet points and numbered lists

The icons to the right of the Class drop-down menu in the HTML view of the Property inspector create unordered and ordered lists—in other words, bullet points and numbered lists—as shown in the following screenshot.

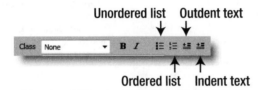

The Unordered List and Ordered List buttons in the HTML view of the Property inspector work just like the corresponding buttons in a word processor. Click the appropriate button, start typing, and your text appears as a bulleted or numbered list with a new item added each time you press Enter/Return. When you have finished the list, press Enter/Return, and click the list button again to exit the list. Alternatively, you can select several paragraphs and convert them to a bulleted or numbered list by clicking the appropriate button.

To nest a list inside another, press Enter/Return to create the first item of the nested list, and then click the Indent Text button (see the preceding screenshot). You can nest numbered lists inside bulleted lists and vice versa. Just click the Unordered List or Ordered List button inside the first item of the nested list. To return to the main list, press Enter/Return after the last item in the nested list, and click the Outdent Text button.

Creating unordered and ordered lists with the Text tag of the Insert bar or the List submenu of the Format menu and Design view context menu works in the same way. The only difference is that you cannot use the Insert bar to nest lists.

> *List items in <li> tags can contain paragraphs and other HTML block elements. Unfortunately, if you press Enter/Return inside a list, Dreamweaver automatically assumes that you want to create the next <li> item, even if you are inside a paragraph. This is a known bug. The only way around it is to fix the code manually in Code view.*

Creating a definition list

To create a definition list, you need to use the Text tab of the Insert bar or one of the menu options. Click the Definition List button on the Text tab of the Insert bar—it's the sixth from the right and labeled dl (see Figure 3-22 earlier in the chapter). When you start typing, Dreamweaver wraps the text in the first <dt> tag. Press Enter/Return, and Dreamweaver creates a <dd> tag in the underlying code and indents the next block of text. Each time you press Enter/Return, Dreamweaver alternates between <dt> and <dd> tags, creating a list that looks like the following screenshot in Split view (it's in definition_list.html in the exercises/ch03 folder of the download files):

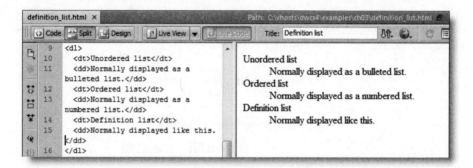

To end a definition list, press Enter/Return after the last item. Then click the Outdent Text button in the HTML view of the Property inspector. Alternatively, select Format ➤ Outdent, or right-click in Design view and select List ➤ Outdent from the context menu.

> *The* Text *tab of the* Insert *bar also has buttons for* <li>, <dt>, *and* <dd> *tags. Do* not *use these in Design view, as they simply insert tags in the underlying code. They do not convert a* <dt> *element, for example, to a* <dd> *one. To do that, you need to use the* Remove Tag *option from the Design view context menu, as described earlier. Then select the text you want to wrap in* <dd> *tags and click the button in the* Insert *bar. These three buttons are designed primarily for use in Code view.*

Creating block quotes

The HTML specification (http://www.w3.org/TR/html401/struct/text.html#h-9.2.2) describes the <blockquote> tag as being "for long quotations (block-level content)." However, to distinguish long quotations from regular text, browsers have always indented text inside <blockquote> tags. As a consequence, this has become one of the most abused HTML elements, with <blockquote> tags sometimes nested several times within one another simply to shift content from the left margin. In the days before CSS, this was understandable. Now it's both lazy and inefficient (adjusting margins with CSS is covered in the next two chapters).

The reason for this mini history lesson is the confusing way Dreamweaver has implemented the creation of block quotes. Everything is based on the now outdated assumption that the <blockquote> tag should be used to indent text. When not used in connection with a list, the Indent Text button in the HTML view of the Property inspector inserts a pair of <blockquote> tags in the underlying code. If your cursor is inside text wrapped in <blockquote> tags, the Outdent Text button removes the <blockquote> tags. The same applies to the Indent and Outdent options on the Format menu.

Now here's where it gets really confusing. The sixth icon from the left on the Text tab of the Insert bar (shown alongside) displays a tooltip labeled Block Quote. However, if your cursor in the underlying code is inside any sort of list, instead of inserting <blockquote> tags, it creates a nested list.

The moral of this tale is to avoid using <blockquote> unless the structure of your text justifies it, and check in Code view or Split view that the intended code has been inserted. This mess really needs to be cleaned up in the next version of Dreamweaver.

Using tables

How tables should be used in web pages is the subject of endless acrimonious debate, often of a quasi religious nature. This is what the HTML specification (http://www.w3.org/TR/html401/struct/tables.html) says (in part): "The HTML table model allows authors to arrange data—text, preformatted text, images, links, forms, form fields, other tables, etc.—into rows and columns of cells. . . . Tables should not be used purely as a means to layout document content as this may present problems when rendering to non-visual media. Additionally, when used with graphics, these tables may force users to scroll horizontally to view a table designed on a system with a larger display. To minimize these problems, authors should use style sheets to control layout rather than tables."

These days, it's considered best practice to use tables purely to present data that needs to be laid out in rows and columns. There are other circumstances where the grid pattern created by a table is useful—for example, the display of thumbnail images. Regardless of what you use tables for, they're easy to insert and edit in Dreamweaver.

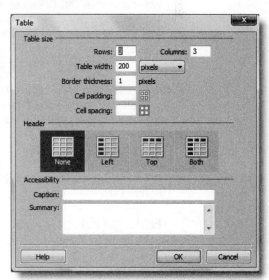

Inserting tables

To insert a table in a page, position your cursor where you want the table to begin and click the Table icon (shown alongside) in either the Common or Layout tab of the Insert bar. Alternatively, select Insert ➤ Table or press Ctrl+Alt+T/Opt+Cmd+T. This opens the Table dialog box, as shown in Figure 3-24.

Figure 3-24. The Table dialog box lets you specify the basic dimensions of a table.

The dialog box offers the following options:

- Rows and Columns: Enter the number of rows and columns you want in the table. You can add more columns or rows or remove them later.

- Table width: You can set the width either in pixels or as a percentage. If you don't want to specify a width, delete the value in this field and leave it blank.

- Border thickness: This sets the border attribute in the opening `<table>` tag and applies the same border thickness to both the table and all table cells. CSS gives you greater control over table and cell borders. Leave this field blank to remove all borders or if you want to use CSS.

- Cell padding: This sets the cellpadding attribute in the opening `<table>` tag and applies the same amount of internal padding around all sides of every cell. For finer control, leave this field blank and use CSS instead.

- Cell spacing: This sets the cellspacing attribute in the opening `<table>` tag and applies the same amount of spacing on all sides between table cells.

- Header: This controls the use of table header `<th>` cells and the scope attribute to indicate whether the header applies to a table row or column. Visual browsers normally display text in `<th>` cells bold and centered. The scope attribute makes it easier for visually impaired people to navigate the table with a screen reader. Choose one of the four options: None, Left, Top, or Both.

- Caption: If you want to give the table a caption, enter the text in this field. By default, the caption is displayed above the table, but you can use CSS to move it to the bottom.

- Summary: This is for the benefit of screen readers for the visually impaired. Any text entered here is read by the screen reader, but does not appear on the screen.

When you click OK, Dreamweaver creates the table skeleton and inserts a nonbreaking space ( ) in each cell in the underlying code. This prevents empty cells from looking odd in a browser. As soon as you insert content into the cell, Dreamweaver normally deletes the . However, if you find text misaligned in a table cell, it's a good idea to check the underlying code and remove the   manually, if necessary.

If you left Table width blank in the Table dialog box and find it difficult to position your cursor inside table cells, select the Expanded button on the left of the Layout tab of the Insert bar. Alternatively, select View ➤ Table Mode ➤ Expanded Tables Mode or press Alt+F6/Opt+F6. This expands the table cells in Design view to make them easier to edit; it doesn't affect the underlying code or how the table will be rendered in a browser. Once you have inserted content into the table, click the exit link at the top of the Document window or select the Standard button on the Layout tab of the Insert bar to collapse the table to its normal shape and size.

Editing tables

Once you have inserted a table, you can change its basic properties by selecting the table in Design view and using the Property inspector. To select the table, click one of its edges in Design view. If you find this difficult, the surefire way of selecting a table is to click inside any cell, and then select `<table>` from the Tag selector at the bottom of the

Document window. Figure 3-25 shows the options available in the Property inspector when a table has been selected.

Figure 3-25. You can change the basic structure of a table in the Property inspector.

Most of the options are the same as in the Table dialog box. The blank field on the left of the Property inspector is where you can enter an id attribute for the table. If style rules have been created, a list of unused IDs can be accessed as a drop-down menu in this field (IDs must be unique, so IDs that have been assigned to other elements are not listed).

If you increase the number of rows or columns in the Property inspector, they are added to the bottom and right of the table, respectively. If you reduce the number, they are removed from the bottom and right, and any content in them is deleted.

The Align drop-down menu at the top right inserts the deprecated align attribute in the opening <table> tag to align the table left, right, or center of its parent element. Best practice is to leave this at Default (left aligned) and use CSS to position the table.

The four icons at the bottom left of the Property inspector remove the height and width attributes from all table cells and convert widths between pixels and percentages. You can identify their roles from the tooltips displayed when you hover your mouse pointer over each one.

> The Fireworks icon and Src field grayed out at the bottom center in Figure 3-25 are ghosts from the past. Several deprecated table attributes have been removed from the Property inspector since the last version. This icon and field somehow got left behind, but both are disabled and serve no purpose.

The Property inspector changes when you put your cursor inside a table cell or select just part of a table. As Figure 3-26 shows, the top half of the Property inspector displays the CSS or HTML view, depending on which button is selected on the left, and the bottom half contains options related to table cells.

Figure 3-26. The Property inspector for table cells has both HTML and CSS views.

The top half applies to content inside the cell; the bottom half applies to the selected cell(s). Most of the options in the bottom half insert deprecated attributes (horizontal and vertical alignment, width, height, no text wrap, and background color). These values should normally be set through CSS, rather than using the Property inspector.

The useful options in the Property inspector for table cells are the Header checkbox, which toggles the selected cell(s) between using <th> and <td> tags, and the two icons at the bottom left, which merge and split cells. In Figure 3-26, the icon that merges cells using rowspan and colspan attributes is grayed out because it is active only when more than one cell is selected in Design view. Conversely, the split icon is active only when a single cell is selected. When you click it, the Split Cell dialog box appears, asking whether you want to split the cell into columns or rows and how many to create.

> *Menu options for merging and splitting cells also exist on the* Table *submenus of the* Modify *menu and the Design view context menu. They are labeled* Decrease *and* Increase Column/Row Span. *However, they merge or split only one row or column at a time and are quite difficult to master. It's much simpler to select the target cells in Design view and use the Property inspector. Table-based layout relies heavily on merging and splitting cells, which can lead to a complex and unstable structure. When tables are used for displaying data, the need for merging and splitting cells is greatly reduced.*

Inserting and deleting rows and columns accurately

Using the Rows and Cols fields of the Property inspector to increase or decrease the number of rows and columns is a very crude measure, as you get no choice where the rows or columns are added or deleted.

A quick way to add a single row or column is to use the Layout tab of the Insert bar. As shown in Figure 3-27, the Layout tab has four buttons to insert a row or column on a specific side of the current insertion point.

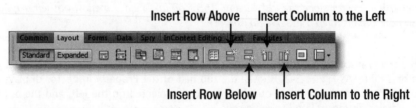

Figure 3-27. The Layout tab of the Insert bar has options for inserting rows and columns.

Position your cursor inside a table cell and select the appropriate button. And that's it— you're done.

If you prefer working with menu options, you can also insert a single row or column using the Table submenu of the Modify menu and Design view context menu. Insert Row adds a new row below the current one. Insert Column adds a new column to the left of the current one.

To add more than one row or column in a single operation, select Modify ➤ Table ➤ Insert Rows or Columns (the same option is available on the Table submenu of the Design view context menu). This opens the Insert Rows or Columns dialog box, which lets you specify whether to insert rows or columns, how many, and on which side in relation to the current cell.

Selecting table cells, rows, and columns

The ability to select cells, rows, and columns is important for several reasons. You may need to select these areas when you're applying styles, editing tables, and applying PHP server behaviors, such as Repeat Region.

To select a single cell, position your cursor inside the cell and select <td> (or <th> if it's a header cell) from the Tag selector at the bottom of the Document window. Dreamweaver displays a thick border around the cell to indicate that it's selected.

To select one or more cells at the same time, hold down the Ctrl/Cmd key and click inside each cell. Cells selected this way can be in any part of the table; they do not need to be contiguous (you might want to do this to apply the same class to individual cells). To select a block of contiguous cells, you can also hold down the mouse button and drag across the cells.

To select a single row, the quickest and most accurate way to do it is to position your cursor inside a cell in the target row, and then select <tr> from the Tag selector at the bottom of the Document window. An alternative way to select a row is to position your mouse pointer over the left of the target row until it changes to an arrow, as shown in the left screenshot of Figure 3-28. Click once to select the whole row. To select more than one row, hold down the Ctrl/Cmd key while selecting each subsequent row.

Figure 3-28. The mouse pointer changes to an arrow indicating that you can select the complete row or column.

You select columns the same way, by positioning your mouse pointer at the top of the target column until it changes into an arrow, as shown in the right screenshot of Figure 3-28. Use the Ctrl/Cmd key to select more than one column.

> *Selecting rows accurately is very important when applying the Repeat Region server behavior. A common mistake is to drag to select all the cells in the row. This selects only the cells (the* <td> *or* <th> *tags) and not the row (the surrounding* <tr> *tags), producing unexpected results. Even if you spend most of your time in Design view, you should always be aware of what's happening in the underlying HTML code. Otherwise, your pages are likely to be difficult to maintain.*

Importing data tables from Microsoft Excel (Windows only)

In the Windows version of Dreamweaver, you can import data tables directly from Microsoft Excel spreadsheets by selecting File ➤ Import ➤ Excel Document. Dreamweaver CS4 handles both .xlsx and .xls formats (you can experiment with weather.xslx and weather.xsl in the examples/ch03 folder of the download files). The options in the Import Excel Document dialog box are the same as for importing a Microsoft Word document (see Figure 3-8 earlier in the chapter). However, Dreamweaver doesn't preserve any formatting other than the table structure (if you select Text only, you just get the raw data).

The problem with importing data directly using this method is that Dreamweaver is incapable of handling multiple worksheets. You get only the data from the worksheet that was selected when the Excel document was last closed. Also, Dreamweaver has a habit of adding a large number of empty rows at the bottom of the table. You get much better results by copying and pasting from a spreadsheet. You get exactly the data you want, and Dreamweaver preserves the table structure.

Importing data from a CSV file

A common way of exporting data from spreadsheets and databases is as comma-separated values in a .csv file. The examples/ch03 folder of the download files contains celsius.csv and fahrenheit.csv, which contain average weather data for London and the southeast of England, formatted like this:

```
Month,Max Temp °C,Min Temp °C,Sun (hours),Days of Rainfall >= 1mm
Jan,7.2,1.5,54.6,12.8
Feb,7.5,1.2,73.0,9.7
Mar,10.1,2.8,111.0,11.0
```

You can import this sort of data and create a table from it by clicking the Import Tabular Data icon (shown alongside) on the Data tab of the Insert bar (it's the first icon on the left). Alternatively, select File ➤ Import ➤ Tabular Data or Insert ➤ Table Objects ➤ Import Tabular Data. This opens a dialog box that asks you to select the data file and delimiter (the character used to separate each item of data). It also has basic formatting options for the table that will be built from the data.

> You can also export data from an HTML table to a CSV file. Insert your cursor in any table cell, and select File ➤ Export ➤ Table. Dreamweaver prompts you to select the character you want to use as a delimiter and the type of line breaks (Windows, Mac, or Unix). Click Export and then choose a name for the CSV file and where to save it. This can be very useful for transferring data from a web page to a database.

Organizing content into a logical structure

The reason tables became the standard way of laying out web pages is because they create a grid that helps you organize your page in a logical structure. The following illustration shows a very simple, yet typical, layout for a web page. In terms of a table, it consists of four rows and two columns. The cells in the first two rows and the final row are merged so they spread across the full width of the page.

The problem with table-based layout is that designers frequently want another grid within each section, and that's when things start to become really complicated. You either need to nest tables within individual cells or build one large table with a complex pattern of merged rows and columns. Before long, it becomes a rat's nest of tags that only the original designer has any hope of understanding. Often, it defeats even the person who built it in the first place.

In spite of the problems, tables were the only option for a long time. CSS first made an appearance in 1996, but browser support was very poor. Although browser support is still not perfect, CSS is now considered the standard way to construct and style pages. Instead of using table cells as a grid, your page content needs to be organized into logical blocks. The main tool for this is the <div> tag.

Grouping related content with <div> tags

A lot of misunderstanding surrounds <div> tags as a result of what earlier versions of Dreamweaver called *layers*. A layer was an absolutely positioned <div>. So, while it's true that every layer was a <div>, the converse is not true: a <div> is not a layer.

So what is a <div>? The HTML specification (http://www.w3.org/TR/html401/struct/global.html#edef-DIV) says that a <div> is "a generic mechanism for adding structure to documents" that defines content to be block-level, but imposes "no other presentational idioms." Translating that into language that's more friendly to ordinary human beings, a <div> is a simple tool for grouping elements of a page that you want to keep together. Moreover, it doesn't have any default styles.

HTML treats every element on a page as being one of the following types:

- **Block-level**: By default, a block-level element is always displayed on a new line, and occupies the full width of available horizontal space. Examples of block-level elements are headings, paragraphs, and tables. Unless you use CSS to change the default behavior, two block-level elements cannot appear side by side.

- **Inline**: As long as there is enough room, an inline element appears alongside whatever precedes it. Examples of inline elements are `<strong>` and `<em>` tags. Images are also treated as inline elements.

Many block-level elements have default styles. For example, most browsers display `<h1>` elements in a bold font and twice the size of ordinary text. They also add a deep bottom margin to separate the heading from the following content.

A `<div>`, on the other hand, has no styles whatsoever. It's a blank canvas for you to style however you like. In combination with the `id` attribute, it's also a powerful way of applying consistent styles to everything within the same `<div>`. Once you have organized your content into a logical structure using `<div>` tags and other block-level elements, you can use CSS to style them visually, adding background images and colors, and altering their position and relationship with other elements by adjusting margins and padding. CSS styling offers a much more powerful tool set than tables, but of course, learning how to master that tool set is something that comes only through experience.

> The main focus of this book is on using the tools in Dreamweaver CS4. It's not a complete guide to web design and CSS. To learn more about CSS best practice, read Beginning CSS Web Development: From Novice to Professional by Simon Collison (Apress, ISBN: 978-1-59059-689-0) or CSS Mastery: Advanced Web Standards Solutions by Andy Budd et al. (friends of ED, ISBN: 978-1-59059-614-2). Also, any book by Eric Meyer will give you a solid grounding in CSS.

Inexperienced web designers or those just making the transition to CSS layout tend to use `<div>` tags to excess, wrapping a `<div>` around everything that would have been in a table cell before (a phenomenon known as *divitis*). This isn't necessary if the element is self-contained. For example, a paragraph on its own doesn't need to be wrapped in a `<div>` because it's already a block-level element and can be styled independently. However, a group of paragraphs does need to be wrapped in a `<div>` for them to be treated as a single unit.

The HTML specification also defines the `<span>` tag as "a generic mechanism for adding structure to documents." The difference between `<span>` and `<div>` confuses a lot of people, but it's very simple. Browsers automatically put a line break before and after a `<div>`. A `<span>` is an inline device typically used to add style to several words in the middle of a paragraph. No line breaks are inserted around a `<span>`, nor should a `<span>` contain block-level elements. You can put a `<span>` inside a paragraph or heading, but not the other way round. You can put anything inside a `<div>`.

To insert a `<div>` tag, select the Insert Div Tag button on the Common tab of the Insert bar, as shown in the following screenshot. Alternatively, use the Insert Div Tag button on the Layout tab of the Insert bar, or select Insert ➤ Layout Objects ➤ Div Tag.

This opens the Insert Div Tag dialog box, as shown in Figure 3-29. In spite of its simple looks, this dialog box is quite versatile and can be used to wrap the current selection in a <div> or to insert a new <div> with considerable precision. And because the <div> tag plays such an important role in CSS, you can define associated style rules directly from the dialog box.

Figure 3-29. The Insert Div Tag dialog box makes it easy to group page elements and apply style rules.

You'll get a better idea of how to use this dialog box in exercises throughout this book, but here are brief descriptions of the options it offers:

- Insert: This drop-down menu is context-sensitive. If content is selected in the Document window, it displays Wrap around selection, as shown in Figure 3-29. If nothing is selected, the default value is At insertion point. Both of these options are self-explanatory.

  Selecting one of the other options in the Insert menu activates the drop-down menu alongside (it's grayed out in Figure 3-29). Both menus work in conjunction and insert a <div> with placeholder text as follows:

  - Before tag: This option is available only when elements on the page have id attributes. It inserts the <div> immediately before the element selected in the right drop-down menu.

  - After start of tag: This inserts the <div> immediately after the opening tag of the element selected in the right drop-down menu. In addition to elements with id attributes, the right menu lists the <body> tag.

  - Before end of tag: This inserts the <div> immediately before the closing tag of the element selected in the right drop-down menu. In addition to elements with id attributes, the right menu lists the <body> tag.

  - After tag: This option is available only when elements on the page have id attributes. It inserts the <div> immediately after the closing tag of the element selected in the right drop-down menu.

- Class: Enter the name of the CSS class you want to apply to the <div>. Existing classes are listed as a drop-down menu.

- ID: Enter the name of the id attribute you want to assign to the <div>. Existing IDs defined in style sheets associated with the page are listed as a drop-down menu.

Since an ID can be used only once on a page, the list displays only those IDs that have not yet been assigned to another element.

- New CSS Rule: This lets you define a new style rule that will be applied to the <div>.

Inserting a horizontal rule

A simple HTML device for adding structure to your web page is the horizontal rule (<hr />). This is a block-level element that acts as a separator by drawing a line across the width of its parent element. In a revamp of the Insert bar in Dreamweaver CS3, it was accidentally left out. Fans of the horizontal rule will be pleased to know that it has been given a reprieve. It's the fourth button from the left in the Common tab of the Insert bar (see alongside). Alternatively, select Insert ➤ HTML ➤ Horizontal Rule. You can also insert a horizontal rule by selecting Insert HTML from the Design view context menu. Type hr and press Enter/Return.

Creating links

I'll never forget my first experience of the Internet. It was in the very early days using a 300 bit/second modem. There were no images; just text. Although it was fantastic to be reading something I had just downloaded from a computer on the other side of the world, what really amazed me was clicking a link and being transported to a completely different article on a different computer in another part of the world. Forget the eye candy for a moment. What made the Internet the success it is today is the ability to dig down to the information you're after by following hyperlinks. And it's all done with the humble <a> tag.

Links can take you to other pages in the same site, jump to specific locations in a page, or transfer you to a different site. You can also use links to send email. In addition to text links, you can use images, or parts of them, as links. The following sections describe each in turn.

Using text to link to other pages

Creating a text link is very easy. Just select the text that you want to use as the link, and use one of the following methods:

- Select the HTML view in the Property inspector. In the Link field, type the address of the page you want to link to.
- If the page is in the current site, select the HTML view in the Property inspector and use the Point to File tool to choose the target page in the Files panel (the Point to File tool was described in the "Inserting placeholder images" section earlier in this chapter; see Figure 3-15).
- If the page is in the current site, hold down the Shift key and drag from the selected text to the target page in the Files panel.
- If the page is in the current site, select the HTML view in the Property inspector and click the folder icon to the right of the Link field. Navigate to the target file in the Select File dialog box (see Figure 3-30).

- Click the Hyperlink button in the Common tab of the Insert bar (shown alongside). This opens the Hyperlink dialog box (see Figure 3-31).

- Select Hyperlink from the Insert menu. This opens the Hyperlink dialog box (see Figure 3-31).

- Right-click and select Make Link from the context menu. This option is available only in Design view; it opens the Select File dialog box (see Figure 3-30).

With seven different ways of creating a link, you might wonder which to use. Although most methods do exactly the same thing, there are some differences that might influence your choice. When linking to an external web page, you need to type the URL manually in the Link field of the Property inspector or Hyperlink dialog box. The Select File dialog box has a URL field that you could use instead, but if you don't want to use the Property inspector, the Hyperlink dialog box has options that are more appropriate to an external link.

> When creating a link to a page on an external website, don't forget to add http:// or https:// at the beginning of the URL. If you omit this, browsers attempt to link to a page on your own site.

Using the Select File dialog box

The Select File dialog box has two options that tend to make it the best choice for creating internal links. The dialog box always remembers the last folder you navigated to. Although this is useful, it sometimes means a tortuous route to find the file you want this time. That's when the Site Root button is a huge time-saver. It's at the top of the dialog box in Windows (see Figure 3-30) and at the bottom right in the Mac version. Click it, and Dreamweaver takes you directly to the root of the current site.

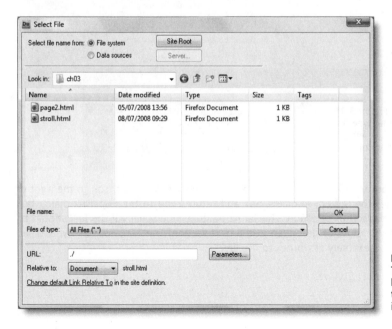

Figure 3-30.
The Select File dialog box lets you override the default type of internal link.

The other great advantage of the Select File dialog box is the Relative to drop-down menu just below the URL field. This defaults to the choice you made in your site definition regarding links relative to the current document or to the site root (see Chapter 2). The drop-down menu lets you override the default choice manually. This is particularly useful when working with PHP sites. PHP commands that include other files into the current web page or script expect links relative to the current document, but links *inside include files* need to be relative to the site root.

If you decide to change the default setting for your site, there's a link that takes you directly to the relevant section of the site definition. Changing the setting in the site definition does *not* affect existing links; the new default applies only to links created after the change.

Using the Hyperlink dialog box

The Hyperlink dialog box (shown in Figure 3-31) is useful if you want to set more options for the link. It also takes a slightly different approach from other methods of creating a link, in that you don't need to select text beforehand. You can use the Text field in any of the following ways:

- If you haven't selected any text, whatever you type directly into the Text field is inserted into the page and used as the link.
- If you selected text before launching the Hyperlink dialog box, you can edit it in the Text field. The revised text is used as the link.
- If you leave the Text field blank, Dreamweaver uses the value entered in the Link field as the hyperlink. This is useful if you just want to display the URL of an external site, as it saves you the effort of typing it twice.

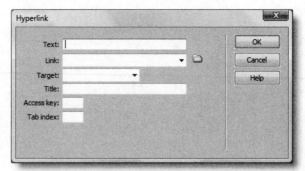

Figure 3-31.
The Hyperlink dialog box lets you set extra options.

The page you want to link to goes in the Link field. Clicking the folder icon to the right of the field launches the Select File dialog box and returns you to the Hyperlink dialog box once you have made your selection. The Target field lets you specify if the link should be opened in a new window, as described in the next section. The Title, Access key, and Tab index fields add accessibility attributes to the link.

Opening a link in a new window

Normally, clicking a hyperlink opens the new page in the same browser window. Sometimes, though, it's desirable to open a new window. To do so, set the Target drop-down menu alongside the Link field in the Property inspector to _blank, as shown in the following screenshot (the same option is available in the Hyperlink dialog box).

There are three other options in the drop-down menu (_parent, _self, and _top). These are used only with framesets, which are considered bad practice and not covered in this book.

Some web designers use this technique on every external link in the mistaken belief that opening the other website in a new window will prevent the user from leaving the current site. Usually what happens is that the visitor's screen gets filled with so many new windows or browser tabs that the likelihood of returning is greatly reduced. It also annoys many users so intensely they refuse to visit your site again anyway. Use this technique only when it serves a useful purpose, such as opening a set of instructions to help the user fill in an application form, or when the link leads to a large PDF file. In the latter case, tell visitors how big the file is and that it will open in a new window. Alternatively, add a note alongside the link suggesting that visitors right-click and save the file rather than opening it in a browser.

Linking to a specific part of a page

When you have a page with a lot of content, it's useful to be able to link directly to a specific part of a page, either from within the same page or from elsewhere. Originally, the only way to do this was to create what's known as a *named anchor*. This is an <a> tag with a name attribute instead of an href one. Dreamweaver CS4 still allows you to insert named anchors (using the icon shaped like a ship's anchor on the Common tab of the Insert bar or Insert ➤ Named Anchor). However, this is an old-fashioned technique that adds unnecessary code to your page. Instead, use IDs.

Simply insert your cursor in the element that you want to link to (usually a heading or a paragraph), select the HTML view of the Property inspector, and enter a unique identifier in the ID field (it mustn't begin with a number or contain any spaces or special characters).

To link to that element from the same page, create a link, and enter the hash symbol (#) followed by the ID. To link from another page, add the hash symbol and ID to the end of the file name. For example, you might want to link to a section called "What We Do" that begins with an <h2> heading. If you enter services in the ID field, the underlying code will look like this:

```
<h2 id="services">What We Do</h2>
```

To link to that section from within the same page, enter #services in the Link field. To link from another page, add #services to the end of the file name in the Link field like this: aboutus.html#services.

IDs are often used for CSS, so they serve a dual purpose. Remember, though, that the same ID cannot be used more than once on a page. IDs identify, so they must be unique.

Using images as links

Links don't always need to be text. You can use an image as a link, too. Just select the image in Design view, and add the link in exactly the same way as you would add a text link. However, don't use any of the options that open the Hyperlink dialog box, because it automatically creates a text link if the Text field is left blank. Consequently, you end up with both an image and a text link.

Removing the link border

Using an image as a link wraps the <img> tag in a pair of <a> tags. By default, browsers add a blue line under text links and a blue border around images used as links. Older versions of Dreamweaver got rid of this blue border by adding border="0" to the <img> tag. However, it no longer does so, because the border attribute for images is deprecated. To get rid of the border, you can type 0 manually into the Border field of the Property inspector for each image used as a link. You *can*, but it's a huge waste of effort. The far more efficient way is to add the following style rule to your CSS:

```
a img {border:none;}
```

This tiny snippet of code removes the blue border from every single image used as a link in your site (of course, a style sheet containing this rule needs to be linked to each page. Creating style rules and attaching a style sheet are covered in the next chapter.

Creating an image map

Not only can you turn an entire image into a link, you can also add multiple links to an image by creating invisible **hotspots** over different parts of the image and adding a link to each one. Figure 3-32 shows the search page of an online guide to Japanese gardens in the U.K. and Ireland that I created several years ago (http://japan-interface.co.uk/gardens/search.php). The map of the British Isles is a single image, but each region has a hotspot that links to details of gardens in that area. Using an image like this is known as an **image map**, not because this particular example uses a geographical map, but because the details of the hotspots are wrapped in the HTML <map> tag and associated with the image by the usemap attribute.

The underlying code for the South West region highlighted in Figure 3-32 looks like this:

```
<area shape="poly" coords="85,261,107,256,118,261,120,252,129,248, ➥
143,251,146,239,149,230,134,228,109,241" href="results.php? ➥
searchCrit=SWest" alt="South West" title="South West" />
```

Figure 3-32.
Invisible hotspots allow you to add multiple links to different parts of an image.

The code looks pretty horrendous, but Dreamweaver takes care of it all, making the creation of hotspots a breeze. This is what you do:

1. Insert the image you want to use as an image map in the normal way, and leave it selected in Design view.

2. Enter a name for the map in the Map field at the bottom right of the Property inspector (see Figure 3-33). The name must not begin with a number or contain any spaces or special characters. If you forget to enter a name, Dreamweaver automatically uses Map, Map2, Map3, and so on.

3. Depending on the shape of the hotspot you want to draw, select one of the hotspot tools in the Property inspector (see Figure 3-33). To create a rectangular or circular hotspot, click and drag across the area of the image that you want to use as a link. The area of the hotspot is displayed as an aqua-colored mesh on top of the image. Dreamweaver displays an alert reminding you to create alternative text for the hotspot.

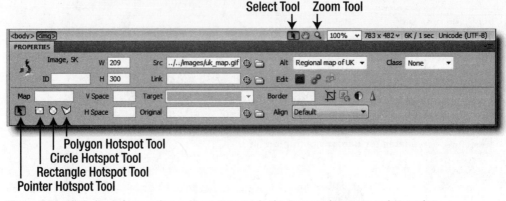

Figure 3-33. All the tools for creating an image map are in the Property inspector and Status bar.

To create an irregularly shaped hotspot, choose the Polygon hotspot tool, and click once at the edge of the shape you want to turn into a link. Dismiss the alert reminding you to create alternative text, and click at another point around the edge of the shape. Continue clicking around the edge of the shape. As soon as you have three points, the hotspot area is displayed as an aqua-colored mesh on top of the image.

4. If you need to adjust the shape, size, or position of the hotspot, select the Pointer hotspot tool in the Property inspector. To move the hotspot, click in the center of the mesh and drag it to the new position. To alter the shape or size, click one of the square handles around the edge of the hotspot and drag.

5. As soon as you create a hotspot, the Property inspector changes to display options related to it. Enter the details of the link in the Link field and set Target, if required. Also enter some alternative text in the Alt field.

6. If you want the hotspot to display a tooltip in all browsers, as illustrated in Figure 3-32, open the Tag Inspector panel, select the Attributes button, and enter the tooltip text in the title field.

To edit a hotspot, select it in Design view and make any adjustments. To delete a hotspot, select it in Design view and press Delete. All the related code is automatically removed.

You can practice creating image maps with the map in Figure 3-32, which is provided as uk_map.gif *in the* images *folder of the download files. Creating irregular-shaped hotspots on a small image can be tricky. To get a better view, select the* Zoom *tool in the Status bar (see Figure 3-33) and drag it across the area of the image that you want to work with. After changing the magnification, be sure to click the* Select *tool button in the Status bar. To restore the magnification to normal, select* 100% *from the drop-down menu alongside the* Zoom *tool. A version of the image map is in* image_map.html *in* examples/ch03.

Chapter review

This chapter has covered all the main techniques for getting content into a web page and creating links in Dreamweaver, but the results in both Design view and a browser look rough and unpolished. That's the role of CSS, which we'll begin to explore in the next chapter. However, successful design with CSS depends on building a solid underlying structure with HTML. The quality of your HTML code is also vital to working with Spry and other JavaScript libraries, as well as to the successful integration of PHP server-side code. Even if you're principally a graphic designer, it's important to understand the code Dreamweaver is generating on your behalf. Remember that Dreamweaver is a tool. If you use it correctly, it will create clean, valid code. If you try to treat it like a drag-and-drop desktop publisher, you're likely to end up with a mess.

3

Stroll Along the Thames

Living Statues

Take a walk near the **London Eye** on the South bank of the Thames statues—and no wonder, because they are alive. Covered from hea motionless; but if anyone drops a coin into container at their feet uttering a word, before resuming their pose. To do it for hours on

great dea

Lorem ips
adipiscing
convallis l
diam, at c
Maecenas
in, comm
ut lacus. (
Phasellus
adipiscing
rhoncus v
odio.

Donec et ipsum et sapien vehicula nonummy. Suspendisse potenti neque mi, varius eget, tincidunt nec, suscipit id, libero. In eget p sed turpis feugiat feugiat. Integer turpis arcu, pellentesque eget, Fusce metus mi, eleifend sollicitudin, molestie id, varius et, nibh.

Artists at Work

A little further downriver, is the **Southbank Centre**, a thriving cultural complex, which is home to the **Royal Festival Hall**, two other concert halls, **The Hayward** art gallery, and the **Saison Poetry Library**.

While highbrow pursuits are the order of the day on the upper level, part of the lower level has become an impromptu skateboard park. The drab concrete walls have been transformed into a psychedelic fantasy by graffiti artists. Unlike other parts of London, where graffiti artists strike at dead of night, they can be found at work in broad daylight underneath the Southbank Centre.

Lorem ipsum dolor sit amet, consectetuer adipiscing elit. Praesent aliquam, justo convallis luctus rutrum, erat nulla fermentum diam, at nonummy quam arcu ac quam. Maecenas urna purus, fermentum id, molestie in, commodo porttitor, felis. Nam blandit quam at lacus. Quisque ornare risus quis ligula. Phasellus tristique purus a augue condimentum adipiscing.

The previous chapter showed you how to get content into a web page, but quite frankly, the results look abysmal. Content may be king, but without a touch of style, it's unlikely to be able to compete for attention with the millions of other web pages out there.

Judging by the runaway success of books such as *CSS Mastery* by Andy Budd with Simon Collison and Cameron Moll (friends of ED, ISBN: 978-1-59059-614-2), web designers have finally got the message that using CSS is *the* way to design a website. Getting the message is the easy part, but many designers rapidly find their initial enthusiasm takes a severe dent when they run into the reality of creating a CSS-driven site. Creating a style rule is simple enough, and most CSS properties have intuitive names. The difficulty lies in the infinite number of ways in which style rules can be combined. And *that's* what makes it so powerful and worthwhile. You need only visit the CSS Zen Garden at http://www.csszengarden.com to see why—the underlying HTML of every page is identical; what makes each one so different is the CSS.

Whether you're capable of designing a masterpiece worthy of the CSS Zen Garden or just a beginner, the embedded WebKit browser engine in Dreamweaver CS4's Live view should make life easier by showing you the impact of your style rules inside the Document window. Another welcome change is the way Dreamweaver no longer generates meaningless class names, such as style1, style2, style45, and so on. Not only has the Property inspector been split into HTML and CSS views, but also the New Style Rule dialog box has been redesigned to help you create CSS selectors with meaningful names.

This chapter puts into practice the theory from the previous chapter, and shows you how to give basic styles to your unadorned content. It also looks at the main CSS management tools in Dreamweaver CS4. In particular, it examines the CSS Styles panel. This extremely powerful tool takes a little getting used to, but once you know how it works, it speeds up the design process immensely.

In this chapter, you'll learn about the following:

- Using page properties to create basic style rules
- Centering page content with a wrapper <div>
- Exploring the CSS Styles panel in All mode
- Exporting style rules to an external style sheet
- Attaching an external style sheet to a page
- Using drag and drop to move style rules
- Converting inline styles to style rules
- Setting Dreamweaver preferences for CSS
- Checking how your styles will look in other media

This chapter is much more hands-on than the other chapters so far, so get ready to roll up your sleeves and dive into the program. All the necessary files can be found in the examples/ch04 and images folders of the download files.

As mentioned in the previous chapter, the main focus of this book is on using the tools in Dreamweaver CS4. To learn about CSS, refer to one of the books I recommended earlier.

Creating basic style rules

Dreamweaver is designed to suit many different workflows. Experienced designers will often have a core set of style rules that is applied to every site, so they just need to link the core style sheet to their pages, and they're ready to go. Alternatively, they just open a new CSS document and start creating style rules from scratch.

If you're new to CSS, the Page Properties dialog box offers a simple interface to create basic styles that are automatically applied to the entire page. It's not capable of anything sophisticated, but it does provide a gentle starting point. In addition to setting basic CSS style rules, the Page Properties dialog box lets you change settings such as the HTML DOCTYPE and encoding for the current page. So let's take a quick look at the features it offers.

Modifying page properties

The quickest way to open the Page Properties dialog box is to click the Page Properties button in the Property inspector whenever your cursor is inside text or an empty page. Alternatively, select Modify ➤ Page Properties or press Ctrl+J/Cmd+J. As you can see in Figure 4-1, six categories are listed in the column on the left side of the dialog box.

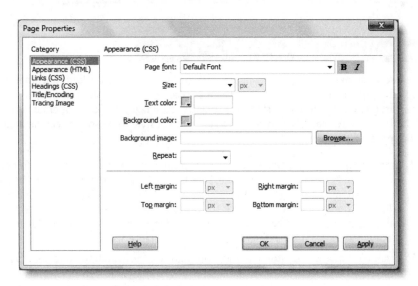

Figure 4-1. The Page Properties dialog box can be used to control the basic look of a page.

4

The focus of this chapter is CSS, so we'll focus on the three categories labeled CSS. But first let's take a quick look at the other three categories that are *not* related to CSS.

- Appearance (HTML): This sets the look of the page background, link styles, and margins using deprecated HTML attributes. It lets you alter the values on legacy pages, but should not be used for new pages, unless there is a specific reason for using HTML attributes instead of CSS (for example, creating an email newsletter).

- Title/Encoding: This lets you change the page title, DOCTYPE, and encoding. Since the page title is easily accessible through the Document toolbar, the only reason you would ever want to use this option is to change the DOCTYPE or page encoding.

- Tracing Image: Some designers like to use an image as a guide for laying out a page. This option lets you add such an image to the page and control its transparency. It's important to realize that the image does *not* become part of the page. It's purely a layout guide and has nothing to do with CSS. If you want the image to appear in the page, use the CSS background or background-image property. I'll show you how to add background images to page elements in the next chapter.

The best way to describe the CSS categories in the Page Properties dialog box is through a hands-on exercise.

> For all the exercises, I suggest that you create a folder called workfiles *at the top level of the site you are using with this book. Create a separate folder for each chapter inside the* workfiles *folder, naming them* ch04, ch05, *and so on. If you encounter any problems, use the File Compare feature described in Chapter 2 to check your own files against those in the equivalent subfolder of the* examples *folder in the download files.*

Using page properties to create basic styles for a page

This exercise shows you how to import text from a Microsoft Word document (as described in the previous chapter) and create a basic set of style rules for a page. As this chapter progresses, you'll build on this exercise to add images and other elements to the page, and eventually export the style rules to an external style sheet so they can be applied to other pages.

1. Create a new HTML file and save it as stroll.html in the workfiles/ch04 folder. If you use File ➤ New to create the file, select Blank Page on the left side of the New Document dialog box, HTML as the Page Type, and <none> as the Layout. If anything is listed in the Attach CSS file field at the bottom right of the dialog box, select each item and click the trash can icon to remove the style sheets listed there (the use of the Attach CSS file field is described in the next chapter).

2. If you have a large monitor, you might find it useful to switch to Split view to keep an eye on the code Dreamweaver creates. If you find Split view uncomfortable to work in, select Design view. Whichever you choose, click inside the Design view section of the Document window to ensure that it has focus.

3. In Windows, select File ➤ Import ➤ Word Document, and navigate to examples/ch04 in the Import Word Document dialog box. Select either stroll.doc or stroll.docx (they both contain the same content), set Formatting to Text, structure, basic formatting (bold, italic), and make sure that the Clean up Word paragraph spacing checkbox is selected. Click Open to import the Word document.

If you're using the Mac version, use Finder to navigate to examples/ch04, and open either stroll.doc or stroll.docx. Select all the text and press Cmd+C to copy it to your clipboard. Return to Dreamweaver, click in Design view to give it focus, and paste the contents of the clipboard into stroll.html. If you have set Text with structure plus basic formatting (bold, italic) for Copy/Paste in the Dreamweaver Preferences panel (see Figure 3-7 in the previous chapter), just press Cmd+V (or select Edit ➤ Paste) to paste the content with its basic structure and formatting. Otherwise, press Shift+Cmd+V (or select Edit ➤ Paste Special) to bring up the Paste Special dialog box, and select Text with structure plus basic formatting (bold, italic) and Clean up Word paragraph spacing before clicking OK.

Your Document window should now look like Figure 4-2. The page has basic formatting, but lacks real style.

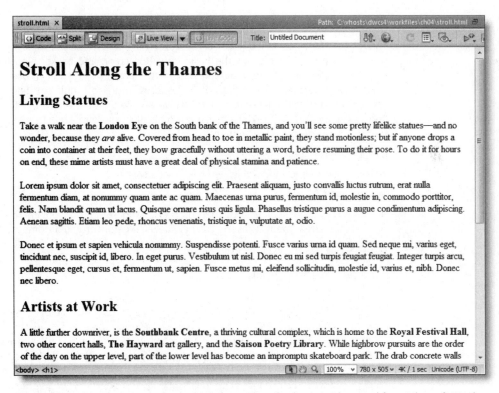

Figure 4-2. Dreamweaver preserves the basic formatting of a document imported from Microsoft Word.

> *If your page looks completely different, check it against* stroll_01.html *in* examples/ch04. *Also, if you can't open the Word document, copy* stroll_01.html *to* workfiles/ch04, *and rename the file* stroll.html.

4. All web pages should have a title, so delete Untitled Document from the Title field in the Document toolbar at the top of the Document window, and replace it with a title of your choice. I used Creating basic styles.

5. Click the Page Properties button in the Property inspector as shown in the following screenshot. It doesn't matter whether you're in the HTML or CSS view of the Property inspector. If you can't see the button, click the expander triangle at the bottom right of the Property inspector.

Alternatively, select Modify ➤ Page Properties (Ctrl+J/Cmd+J).

6. This opens the Appearance (CSS) category of the Page Properties dialog box, as shown in Figure 4-1. This sets the basic font, text color, and background for the page. It's a good idea to set a default font for the page, which you can override in special cases, such as for headings or pull quotes. You also should set default colors for the text and page background. However, you shouldn't set the font size here, even if you think the default size is too big. It's usually much better to control font size for different page elements.

Use the following settings:

- Page font: Trebuchet MS, Arial, Helvetica, sans-serif
- Size: leave blank
- Text color: #000 (if you click the color well, and select black from the color swatches, Dreamweaver inserts the hexadecimal color for you automatically)
- Background color: #FFF (white)

Leave the other fields blank.

> *Dreamweaver CS4 uses shorthand hexadecimal numbers for colors wherever possible. HTML and CSS normally specify colors using six-digit hexadecimal notation, with each pair of digits representing the red, green, and blue elements of the color. However, when both digits of each pair are identical, you can use just one. So, #FFFFFF can be shortened to #FFF. To use the shorthand, all three color elements must consist of an identical pair. So #006633 (dark green) can be shortened to #063, but #006634 has no shorthand equivalent.*

7. Select the Links (CSS) category from the column on the left. The Links (CSS) category lets you set the font and colors for hyperlinks. The color options are the equivalent of the following CSS pseudo-classes:

- Link color: `a:link`
- Visited links: `a:visited`
- Rollover links: `a:hover`
- Active links: `a:active`

The Underline style option lets you choose whether your links are always under-lined, never underlined, show an underline on hover, or hide the underline on hover. If you decide not to underline links, it's a good idea to choose a distinctive color and select the Bold icon alongside Link font.

Use the settings shown in the following screenshot:

8. Select the Headings (CSS) category from the column on the left. This lets you choose a different font for headings (the same choice applies to all six levels). You can also set the size and color separately for each level. Using percentage sizes or ems gives visitors more freedom to adjust your page to their visual needs and pref-erences, so these choices are better from the accessibility point of view, but you can use pixels if you prefer.

> An em is a typographical measure based on the width of the letter m. In CSS, it means the height of the specified font. So, 1em is the default height, and .8em is 80 percent of the default height.

I used the following settings:

9. When you have finished, click OK to close the Page Properties dialog box. Your styles are immediately applied to the page in Design view. What's more, they're applied automatically.

10. Position your cursor anywhere inside the first paragraph, and select Heading 3 from the Format menu in the HTML view of the Property inspector. The paragraph is transformed into a large, brown Verdana. Select Paragraph again from the Format menu, and it switches back to normal black Trebuchet MS or Arial. This is because the Format menu changes the surrounding tags from <p> to <h3> and back again. Everything is controlled by the CSS **type selectors** that Dreamweaver has embedded into the <head> of the page. Type selectors change the default style of HTML tags.

11. Select some text in one of the paragraphs, and type # in the Link field of the HTML view of the Property inspector to create a dummy link. The text is automatically styled as a link. If you have been used to the old-school way of selecting everything and applying colors and fonts, this should be an exciting revelation that convinces you of the power of CSS.

12. Click the Live View button in the Document toolbar. You won't notice much difference, if any at all. Now mouse over the dummy link you created in the previous step. The color should change, and a line appears under the text, indicating that it's a clickable link.

13. Press F12/Opt+F12 to view the page in your primary browser. It should look similar to Figure 4-3. It's a little more stylish than before, but the text spreads across the full page. It also needs livening up with some images.

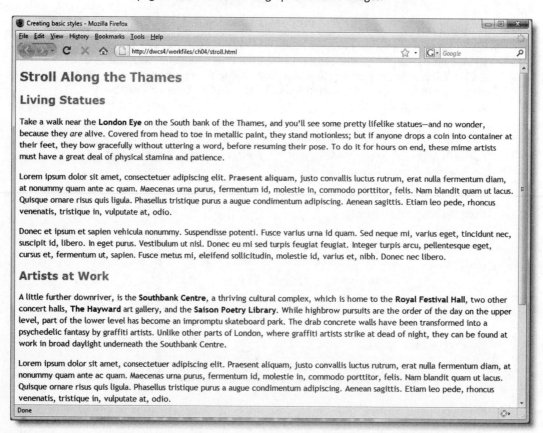

Figure 4-3. The style rules created by the Page Properties dialog box make only a small improvement.

14. Save `stroll.html`. You'll continue improving it throughout the chapter. If you want to compare your code with the download files, check it against `stroll_02.php` in `examples/ch04`.

Unfortunately, the Page Properties dialog box creates only the most basic rules. To improve the look of the page, you need to add some structure with a `<div>` tag and create other style rules with the CSS view of the Property inspector.

Before doing that, however, let's take a look at where the Page Properties dialog box has created the CSS for the page.

Inspecting the rules created by Page Properties

If you switch to Code view or Split view and scroll to the top of the underlying code, you'll see that the Page Properties dialog box has created a `<style>` block in the `<head>` of the document, as shown in Figure 4-4. All the style rule definitions use type selectors. In other words, they redefine the look of HTML tags. Consequently, they apply to any new element that uses one of those tags.

```
1   <!DOCTYPE html PUBLIC "-//W3C//DTD XHTML 1.0 Transitional//EN"
    "http://www.w3.org/TR/xhtml1/DTD/xhtml1-transitional.dtd">
2   <html xmlns="http://www.w3.org/1999/xhtml">
3   <head>
4   <meta http-equiv="Content-Type" content="text/html; charset=utf-8" />
5   <title>Creating basic styles</title>
6   <style type="text/css">
7   <!--
8   body,td,th {
9       font-family: Trebuchet MS, Arial, Helvetica, sans-serif;
10      color: #000;
11  }
12  body {
13      background-color: #FFF;
14  }
15  a:link {
16      color: #066;
17      font-weight: bold;
18      text-decoration: none;
19  }
20  a:visited {
21      text-decoration: none;
22      color: #096;

35  h.
36      font-size: 150%;
37      color: #B67E4D;
38  }
39  h2 {
40      font-size: 130%;
41      color: #B67E4D;
42  }
43  h3 {
44      font-size: 115%;
45      color: #B67E4D;
46  }
47  -->
48  </style></head>
```

Figure 4-4. The Page Properties dialog box embeds the style rules in the head of the page.

This is extremely useful, but putting the rules in the <head> of the page like this means that the styles apply only to the current page. The real value of CSS comes from using an external style sheet that can be attached to every page in the site, instantly changing its look. As you'll see later in the chapter, Dreamweaver makes it very easy to export style rules into an external style sheet. Before that, let's continue exploring the tools for creating CSS.

Inserting and styling a <div>

Text that spreads across the browser window is difficult to read. You could constrain the width by adding the width property to the rules for paragraphs and headings. However, a more common technique is to wrap the entire content in a <div> and apply a width to the <div>. This has the advantage of letting you center the page within the browser. You can also apply other styles, such as a background and border, to the <div>.

Creating a wrapper <div>

In this exercise, you'll wrap the content of the page from the previous exercise in a wrapper <div>, and create a style rule to constrain its width and center it. You'll also use Dreamweaver's visual aids to examine the CSS box model. (If you're not familiar with the CSS box model, there's a comprehensive and well-written explanation at http://www.brainjar.com/css/positioning/default.asp.)

Continue working with stroll.html from the previous exercise. Alternatively, use stroll_02.html from exercises/ch04 as your starting point.

1. Click <body> in the Tag selector at the bottom left of the Document window, as shown in the following screenshot, to select the entire content of the page.

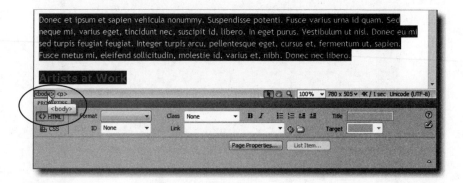

2. Click the Insert Div Tag button in the Common or Layout tab of the Insert bar (or choose Insert ➤ Layout Objects ➤ Div Tag). In the dialog box that opens, Insert

should automatically have been set to Wrap around selection. Type wrapper into the ID field, and click the New CSS Rule button at the bottom of the dialog box as shown in the following screenshot.

3. This opens the New CSS Rule dialog box shown in Figure 4-5. This is where you define the type of CSS selector you want, its name, and where the rule will be defined. I'll explain this dialog box in the next section. For the moment, just check that the settings are the same as in Figure 4-5. Then click OK.

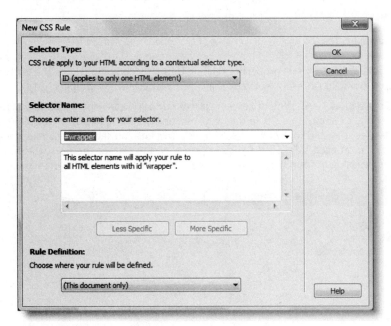

Figure 4-5. The New CSS Rule dialog box is where you define the type of selector you want to use.

4. The CSS Rule definition dialog box now opens. As shown in Figure 4-6, this is another multiple category dialog box. As with the New CSS Rule dialog box, I'll go over how it works in the next section. For the moment, select the Box category in the list on the left side of the dialog box.

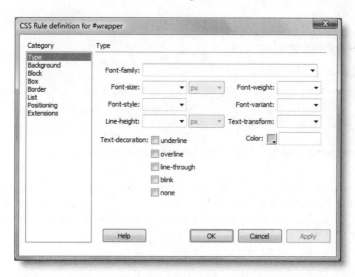

Figure 4-6. The CSS Rule definition dialog box supports CSS 1 properties.

5. The Box category sets properties relating to the CSS box model. Set the Width field to 720 px. No prizes for guessing that sets the width of the wrapper <div>.

Once a block-level element has a declared width, you can center it by setting its left and right margins to auto. In the Margin section on the right side of the dialog box, deselect the checkbox labeled Same for all. This lets you set different values for the margin on each side. Click the down arrow to the side of the field labeled Right, and select auto from the drop-down menu, as shown in the following screenshot.

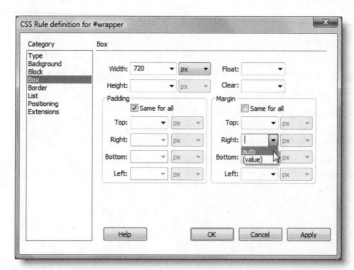

6. Do the same with the field labeled Left. So the values you have changed in the Box category should be as follows:

- Width: 720 px
- Margin Same for all: unchecked
- Margin Right: auto
- Margin Left: auto

Leave the other fields blank.

7. Click OK to close the CSS Rule Definition dialog box. This returns you to the Insert Div Tag dialog box. Click OK to close it.

8. Switch to Design view, if necessary. You should see the page content surrounded by a dotted line and centered in the Document window. If you have a small monitor, press F4 to hide the panels and see the effect more clearly. If you can't see a dotted line around the content, open the Visual Aids menu on the Document toolbar (or select View ➤ Visual Aids), and check that you have the default settings as shown in the following screenshot.

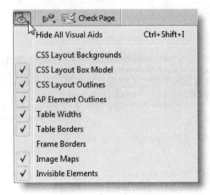

Each setting is toggled on and off by clicking it. A checkmark indicates that the option is turned on. All visual aids should be turned on except CSS Layout Backgrounds and Frame Borders.

The dotted line surrounding the content is purely a visual aid; it won't appear in the page when displayed in a browser. It indicates the extent and position of the wrapper <div> you have just created. As the screenshot of the Visual Aids menu shows, you can hide all visual aids through the menu or by pressing Ctrl+Shift+I/ Shift+Cmd+I. Try it, and then restore the visual aids.

9. Move your cursor until it touches the dotted line surrounding the wrapper <div>. When the line turns solid red, click once. This triggers the CSS Layout Box Model visual aid, surrounding the wrapper <div> in a thick blue line, and displaying its margins as a crosshatched pattern, as shown in Figure 4-7.

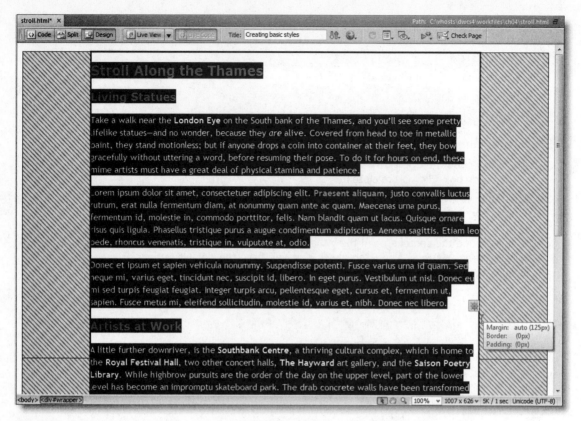

Figure 4-7. Dreamweaver's visual aids let you inspect CSS style rules.

As you move your cursor around, different tooltips should appear, displaying details of the CSS rule applied to that area. In Figure 4-7, my cursor was just to the right of the wrapper <div>. The tooltip shows that the margin is set to auto; the figure in parentheses is the calculated value (125px). It also shows that the border and padding of the <div> are set to 0px. Again, these are calculated values, as indicated by the parentheses. Neither value was set explicitly in the style rule you just created.

When you move your cursor inside the <div>, you should see a more detailed tooltip with details of its style properties. Most values are blank because they haven't been set. Sometimes the tooltips seem to have a shy gene, so you might need to move your cursor around a bit to trigger their appearance.

Notice that the Tag selector at the bottom left of the Document window shows the ID you gave the <div> like this: <div#wrapper>. The tag is inset in the Tag selector, indicating that this is the current selection. If you find it difficult to trigger the visual aids by clicking the edge of a <div>, use the Tag selector instead.

10. To dismiss the visual aids, click anywhere inside the Document window.

11. Save stroll.html and press F12/Opt+F12 to preview it in your main browser. The content should now be constrained to 720 pixels in width and centered in the browser window. If you need to check your code, compare it with stroll_03.html in examples/ch04.

This exercise introduced you to the New CSS Rule and CSS Rule definition dialog boxes. These are important parts of the Dreamweaver tool set for creating style rules. The next section describes their roles in greater detail.

Creating new style rules

Creating a style rule involves two steps: first define the selector, and then add property/value pairs to the style block. The selector determines which parts of the page the rule applies to.

The main types of CSS selectors are as follows:

- **Type**: A type selector uses the name of the HTML tag that you want to style. For instance, using h1 as the selector for a style rule applies the rule to all <h1> tags. Dreamweaver calls this a **tag selector**.

- **Class**: A class can be applied to many different elements in a page. The selector name always begins with a period, for example, .warning.

- **ID**: An ID selector applies the rule to an element identified by its id attribute. If the element, such as a list, has child elements, the rule also applies to the children. The name of an ID selector always begins with the hash sign (#), as in #wrapper.

- **Pseudo-classes and pseudo-elements**: These selectors style elements according to their positions or roles in a document, such as a link when the mouse passes over it or the first line of a paragraph. They consist of a type selector followed by a colon and the name of the pseudo-class or pseudo-element, for example, a:hover or p:first-line.

- **Descendant**: A descendant selector combines two or more of the previous types to target elements more precisely. For instance, you may want to apply a different style to links inside a <div> with the id attribute footer. Descendant selectors are separated by a space between the individual parts of the selector, like this: #footer a.

- **Group**: When you want to apply the same set of rules to several selectors, you can group them together as a comma-separated list, as in h1,h2,h3,h4,h5,h6.

Dreamweaver refers to the last three types as **compound selectors**.

Defining a selector

You define the selector in the New CSS Rule dialog box (see Figures 4-5 and 4-8). There are several ways to open this dialog box:

- Select Format ➤ CSS Styles ➤ New from the main menus.

- Click the New CSS Rule button in the Insert Div Tag dialog box (this is the method you used in the previous exercise).

- Click the New CSS Rule icon (shown alongside) at the bottom right of the CSS Styles panel.

- Right-click inside the CSS Styles panel and select New from the context menu.

- Select the CSS view of the Property inspector, set the Targeted Rule **drop-down menu to** <New CSS Rule>, **and click the** Edit Rule **button directly below, as shown in the following screenshot.**

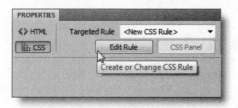

Previous versions of Dreamweaver automatically assigned meaningless class names, such as style1, style2, and so on, when you used the Property inspector to style text. Dreamweaver CS4 no longer does that. The New CSS Rule dialog box has been redesigned in Dreamweaver CS4 to make it easier to choose the appropriate selector. Depending on where your cursor is when you launch the dialog box, Dreamweaver tries to make a helpful suggestion. When I took the screenshot in Figure 4-8, the cursor was inside a paragraph nested in the wrapper <div>. Consequently, Dreamweaver suggested creating a Compound selector called #wrapper p. This is a much more useful selector, as it will be applied automatically to every paragraph inside the wrapper <div>.

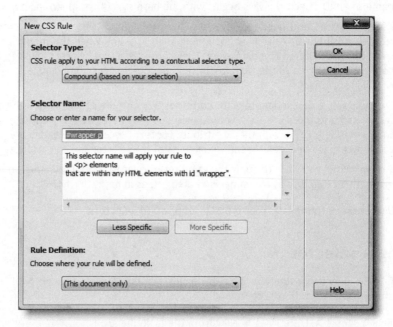

Figure 4-8. When creating a new style rule, you must specify its type, selector name, and location.

Let's take a look at the various options in the New CSS Rule dialog box.

- Selector Type: This determines the type of CSS selector. You can choose from four options:

    - Class (can apply to any HTML element): This creates a CSS class.

    - ID (applies to only one HTML element): This creates an ID selector.

    - Tag (redefines an HTML element): This creates a CSS type selector.

    - Compound (based on your selection): This is used for pseudo-classes, pseudo-elements, and descendant and group selectors.

    As you can see, the options are labeled in a helpful way to assist newcomers to CSS by reminding them of the purpose of each type of selector.

- Selector Name: This is where you enter the name for the CSS selector. When creating a class or an ID selector, it doesn't matter whether you prefix the name with a period (for a class) or a hash sign (for an ID selector); Dreamweaver automatically adds the correct symbol if necessary. When creating a tag (or type) selector, the field turns into a drop-down menu listing all valid HTML tags. You can either type in the tag name (without any angle brackets) or select it from the menu.

    The text area below the Selector Name field describes which elements will be affected by the new style rule.

- Less Specific: Dreamweaver automatically suggests a selector based on your current insert position. If a descendant selector, such as #wrapper p, is suggested, clicking this button creates a less specific selector by removing the leftmost element. In the example shown in Figure 4-8, this removes #wrapper, leaving just p. In a more deeply nested descendant selector, you can continue clicking to remove one element at a time. The effect of the changes is described in the text area above the button.

- More Specific: This is grayed out by default, but is made active as soon as you edit the suggested descendant selector by clicking the Less Specific button as just described. It reverses the edits by restoring one element at a time. So, after removing #wrapper by clicking Less Specific, you can restore it by clicking the More Specific button.

- Rule Definition: This option lets you choose where to put the new rule. The drop-down menu lists all style sheets currently attached to the page and contains an option to create a new external file. If you choose (This document only), the style rule is embedded within <style> tags in the <head> of the document.

When you click OK in the New CSS Rule dialog box, Dreamweaver opens the CSS Rule definition dialog box, unless you decide to create the rule in a new style sheet. In that case, you're first asked to specify the name of the new file and where it is to be located. Attaching style sheets is covered later in this chapter, in the "Attaching a new style sheet" section.

4

Defining the rule's properties

As you discovered in the preceding exercise, the CSS Rule definition dialog box (see Figure 4-6) is a multiple-category panel. Table 4-1 describes what each category contains. Most are obvious; others less so.

Table 4-1. Properties that can be set in the CSS Rule definition dialog box

Category	Properties covered
Type	All font-related properties, plus color, line-height, and text-decoration
Background	All background properties, including background-color and background-image
Block	word-spacing, letter-spacing, vertical-align, text-align, text-indent, white-space, and display
Box	width, height, float, clear, padding, and margin
Border	All border properties
List	list-style-type, list-style-image, and list-style-position
Positioning	CSS positioning, including visibility, z-index, overflow, and clip
Extensions	page-break-before, page-break-after, cursor, and nonstandard filters

The CSS Rule definition dialog box is intended to make life easier for beginners, but the need to hunt around in the different categories can be very frustrating and time-consuming. It also lists only CSS1 properties, so you may end up looking for something that's not there.

> *CSS is constantly evolving. The current version is CSS2.1, which adds a small number of new properties, such as cursor and outline, to the core properties defined in CSS1. Work is in progress on CSS3, and although it won't be completed for many years, Firefox, Safari, and Opera already support some of its features.*

Fortunately, Dreamweaver CS4 now lets you create the new style rule without setting any properties. Of course, a rule with no properties won't have any effect on the way your page looks, but you can add new properties to the empty style block through the CSS Styles panel or by editing the style sheet directly in Code view.

Before exploring the CSS Styles panel, let's add some extra style rules to the stroll.html example from earlier exercises.

Adding paragraph margins and images

This exercise continues to improve the look of `stroll.html` by adjusting the line height, text size, and margins of paragraphs. This demonstrates the use of the Targeted Rule field in the CSS view of the Property inspector. You'll also add images and wrap text around them with simple CSS style rules.

Continue working with `stroll.html` from the preceding exercise. Alternatively, if you want to jump in at this stage, use `stroll_03.html` from examples/ch04.

1. With `stroll.html` open in Design view, position your cursor inside one of the paragraphs, and then click the CSS button on the left side of the Property inspector to select the CSS view. The Property inspector should look like the following screenshot.

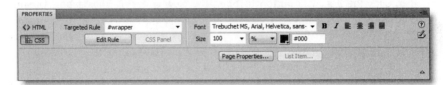

The Targeted Rule field indicates which rules will be affected by any changes you make in the CSS view of the Property inspector. It also controls which rule is edited when you click the Edit Rule button. Make sure that the Targeted Rule field is set to #wrapper.

When you created the #wrapper style rule in the previous exercise, the only properties you set controlled the width and the left and right margins. However, the Property inspector shows the font family, color, and size. This is because the wrapper `<div>` inherits the rules set in the Page Properties dialog box in the first exercise.

2. Change the Size setting to 85, and then press Enter/Return to apply the new value. This reduces the size of not only the text in the paragraphs, but also of the headings (if you get giant text instead, make sure that the drop-down menu alongside the Size field is set to %). The headings are affected because the Targeted Rule is #wrapper.

3. Switch to Code view and scroll up to find the `<style>` block. The #wrapper rule looks like this:

```
#wrapper {
  width: 720px;
  margin-right: auto;
  margin-left: auto;
  font-size: 85%;
}
```

Changing the Size value in the Property inspector with #wrapper selected as Targeted Rule has added the font-size property to the style rule. CSS inheritance will apply this rule to everything in the wrapper `<div>`, causing potential difficulties, so delete the line highlighted in bold.

4. Switch back to Design view, and position your cursor inside one of the paragraphs again. The values in the CSS view of the Property inspector should look like the screenshot in step 1 again.

5. Click the down arrow to the right of the Targeted Rule field, and select <New CSS Rule> from the menu as shown in the following screenshot.

6. Click the Edit Rule button to open the New CSS Rule dialog box. Dreamweaver automatically suggests a Compound (descendant) selector called #wrapper p (see Figure 4-8, shown earlier).

7. Click OK to open the CSS Rule definition dialog box. In the Type category, set Size to 85, and select % from the drop-down menu alongside.

Also set Line height to 1.4, and select multiple from the drop-down menu alongside. This adds vertical space between the lines of the paragraph to make the text easier to read. You can use pixels or percent to set the line-height property, but I find that choosing multiple gives the most reliable results.

8. Select the Box category from the column on the left side of the CSS Rule definition dialog box. This category lets you define such properties as width, padding, and margin. Both Padding and Margin have a checkbox labeled Same for all, which is selected by default. This applies to all sides whatever value you enter in the Top field. Let's put a wide margin on both sides of each paragraph, but not on the top and bottom. Deselect the checkbox for Margin, and enter the following values:

- Top: 0 px
- Right: 20 px
- Bottom: 8 px
- Left: 40 px

By setting the top margin to 0 and the bottom one to 8 pixels, you'll get good spacing between paragraphs. Setting the left margin to 40 pixels indents the text nicely in comparison with the headings.

9. Click Apply to view the effect of the new style rule for paragraphs. If you need to get a better view of the Document window, move the CSS Rule definition dialog box to one side. If you want to make any changes to the settings, do so, and then click OK to close the CSS Rule definition dialog box.

10. Let's liven the page up with a couple of images. Insert living_statues.jpg anywhere inside the first paragraph and graffiti.jpg inside the paragraph following the Artists at Work heading. Both images are in the images folder of the download files. (Refer to Chapter 3 if you need a refresher on how to insert images.)

11. To wrap text around images, you need to float the image either left or right and add a margin on the opposite side to leave some breathing space between them. You'll now create two classes that can be applied to any image.

If an image is selected in Design view, the CSS view of the Property inspector is not visible. Deselect the image and repeat step 5 to select <New CSS Rule> in the Targeted Rule field, and then click Edit Rule to open the CSS Rule definition dialog box. Alternatively, use any of the other methods listed in the "Defining a selector" section earlier in the chapter.

12. In the New CSS Rule dialog box, select Class (can apply to any HTML element) in the Selector Type drop-down menu. This clears any suggested value from the Selector Name field. Type floatleft in the empty field. Make sure that Rule Definition is set to (This document only), and then click OK.

> *When typing the name of a class in the* New CSS Rule *dialog box, you can omit the leading period. This is a change from previous versions of Dreamweaver.*

13. In the CSS Rule definition dialog box, select the Box category, and set Float to left. Deselect the Same for all checkbox for Margin, and set Right to 10 px. Leave all other settings blank. This aligns any element that uses the floatleft class to the left of its parent element and puts a 10-pixel margin on the right side. This is much more flexible than using the HTML hspace attribute, which puts the same amount of space on both sides. The advantage of CSS is that you can put a different margin on each side. Click OK to save the new class rule.

14. Select one of the images in Design view, and open the Class drop-down menu on the right side of the Property inspector. This lists all classes defined in your styles. Select floatleft, as shown in Figure 4-9.

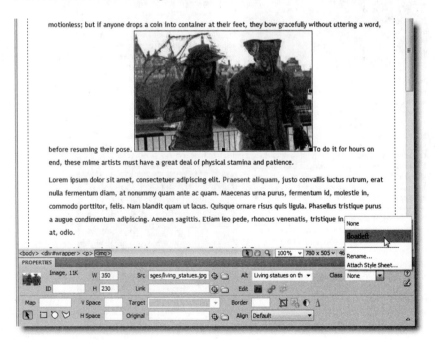

Figure 4-9. To apply a class to the current element, select the class from the Class field in the Property inspector.

The image should now be flush with the left margin of the paragraph. The text flows naturally around the image, with a comfortable 10-pixel margin.

15. Repeat steps 11–14 to create another class called floatright. For this class, set the value of Float to right, and create the margin on the left. Apply the new class to the other image.

16. Save stroll.html and press F12/Opt+F12 to view it in your main browser. It should now look like Figure 4-10. It's still relatively plain, but it looks a lot more stylish than the original version. If you want to check your version, compare it with stroll_04.html in exercises/ch04.

Figure 4-10. With the help of basic style rules, the page is beginning to look much better.

If you found hopping around in the CSS Rule definition dialog box tedious and repetitive, you'll be pleased to know that Dreamweaver CS4 makes it easy to work directly with style rules through the CSS Styles panel and the Code Navigator. The Code Navigator, which is new to Dreamweaver CS4, was described in Chapter 1. The next section introduces you to the powerful CSS Styles panel.

Introducing the CSS Styles panel

To get the most out of the CSS Styles panel, you need a solid understanding of CSS. Although that statement is likely to provoke sighs of despair—or even anger—from readers expecting Dreamweaver to do everything for them, it's true of any tool or piece of software. The greater your understanding of the tools you're working with, the easier the job becomes. Also, with a little persistence, using the CSS Styles panel should help beginners improve their skills, because it shows you exactly which rules affect a particular part of the page. And even if the theory behind CSS taxes your brain, you can quickly check how your page will look in a standards-compliant browser by switching on Live view.

Over the next few pages, I'll explain the key features of the CSS Styles panel in preparation for using it to style one of Dreamweaver's preinstalled CSS layouts in the next chapter.

Opening the CSS Styles panel

To open the CSS Styles panel, double-click the CSS Styles tab at the top right of the screen in the Classic workspace, or click the CSS Styles icon (shown alongside) if you're using iconic mode. Alternatively, select Window ➤ CSS Styles. On Windows, there's also the keyboard shortcut Shift+F11. (Mac keyboard shortcut enthusiasts are out of luck, because the same combination runs Exposé in slow motion on OS X.)

Viewing All and Current modes

The CSS Styles panel has two modes, All and Current, which are toggled by clicking the button at the top of the panel. Figure 4-11 shows both modes with an explanation of the icons at the bottom of the panel and in the middle pane of Current mode. Current mode (on the right of Figure 4-11) is more powerful, but it's also more complex, so beginners should try to get used to working in All mode first.

A good way of regarding All mode is as a window into all CSS rules available to the page, regardless of whether they are embedded in the <head> of the document or in multiple external style sheets. The top pane (labeled All Rules) displays the hierarchy of style rules as a tree menu. If the rules are embedded in the <head> of the document, the root of the tree (at the top) is displayed as a <style> tag, as in Figure 4-11. If they're in an external style sheet, the file name appears at the root. The tree menus are collapsible to make it easier to work when multiple style sheets are attached to the page. The only style rules that you cannot inspect or edit in All mode are inline styles, although you can see them in Current mode.

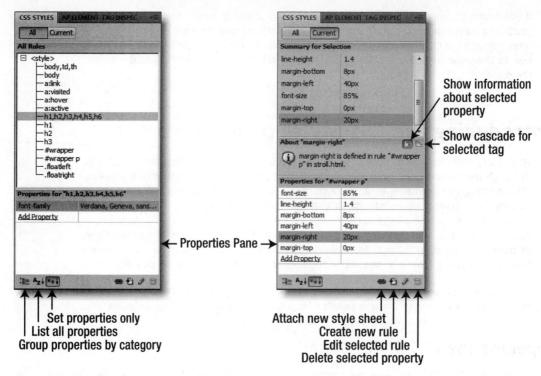

Figure 4-11. The CSS Styles panel crams a lot of tools and information into a small space.

The Properties pane at the bottom of the CSS Styles panel is common to both modes. It displays details of the currently selected style rule and lets you edit or delete properties and add new ones.

> *Don't confuse the* Properties *pane of the* CSS Styles *panel with the Property inspector, which is normally docked at the bottom of the Document window. If you're not familiar with Dreamweaver, the names are easy to mix up, because the title bar of the Property inspector says* Properties. *When working with CSS, any reference to the* Properties *pane means the pane at the bottom of the* CSS Styles *panel as shown in Figure 4-11.*

Use All mode when you need to do any of the following:

- View the overall structure of the styles attached to a page.
- Change the order of rules.
- Inspect or edit the contents of a style rule identified by its selector.
- Add a new style rule (you can do this in both modes).
- Attach a style sheet to the current page (this is one of several places you can do this).

I'll describe the features of Current mode in the next chapter. For the moment, let's take a look at the seven icons at the bottom of the CSS Styles panel, as they apply to both modes.

Exploring the Properties pane of the CSS Styles panel

The default setting of the Properties pane is to display only those CSS properties that have been set in a particular style rule, as shown in Figure 4-11. However, the two leftmost icons let you display properties grouped by category or alphabetically.

Displaying CSS properties by category

If you select the leftmost icon (see alongside) at the bottom of the CSS Styles panel, the Properties pane lists all available CSS properties grouped together in easily identifiable categories, as shown in Figure 4-12. If you're new to CSS and find it difficult to remember the names of the various properties, I recommend that you use this display until you gain sufficient confidence to use the less cluttered default view.

Click the plus (+) and minus (–) symbols (triangles in the Mac version) to expand or close each category, and click in the right column alongside the property name to edit it. If a fixed range of options is available, a drop-down menu appears. Similarly, a folder icon or color picker appears if the property requires a pathname or color. To remove a property, highlight it and click the trash can icon at the far right. Unlike the default display, the property remains listed, but the value is deleted.

Figure 4-12.
Displaying all available CSS properties organized by category makes life easier for beginners.

Displaying CSS properties alphabetically

Clicking the middle icon (shown alongside) at the bottom left of the CSS Styles panel lists virtually all available CSS properties in alphabetical order, as shown in Figure 4-13. Properties that have already been set move to the top of the list. To set a new one, you need to scroll down to find it, making this view the least user-friendly.

This alphabetical list omits a small number of poorly supported CSS properties, such as counter-increment and counter-reset, but as you can see from Figure 4-13, nonstandard properties beginning with -moz are also listed. These are supported mainly by Firefox and Mozilla, but are expected to become part of CSS3. Dreamweaver also lists some Microsoft-only properties, such as layout-grid, and properties that were dropped from the CSS2.1 specification, such as font-stretch. This wide choice is useful if you are a CSS expert, but could lead you astray if you're a novice. Use the alphabetical display with care.

Figure 4-13.
You can also display all available CSS properties in alphabetical order.

Displaying only CSS properties that have been set

To restore the Properties pane to its default display of only those properties that have been set (see Figure 4-11), click the third icon from the left at the bottom of the CSS Styles panel (shown alongside).

Attaching a new style sheet

The chain icon (shown alongside) at the bottom right of the CSS Styles panel opens the Attach External Style Sheet dialog box (see Figure 4-14). This lets you attach the file using either <link> or @import and set the media type.

The File/URL field lists recently used style sheets in a drop-down menu. Click the Browse button to navigate to a new style sheet. If you type the file name of a nonexistent style sheet in the File/URL field, Dreamweaver displays a warning, and asks if you want to create the link/import statement anyway. If you click Yes, you can create the necessary style sheet afterward, and it becomes immediately available inside your page.

Normally, you can leave the Media field empty. If you do so, browsers apply your styles to all media. However, if you want to create separate style sheets for different purposes, such as mobile devices and print, select a media type from the drop-down menu in the Media field, or enter a comma-separated list of any of the following media types: all, aural, braille, handheld, print, projection, screen, tty, and tv. Use screen for visual browsers, or all to apply your styles to all types of media.

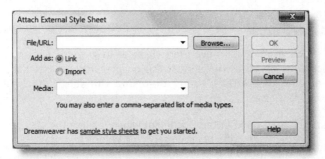

Figure 4-14. You can attach an external style sheet using <link> or @import.

If you choose a media type other than screen or all, use the Style Rendering **toolbar**, which is described later in this chapter, to see the effect of your styles in **Design** view.

> *There are several other ways of attaching external style sheets. As you'll see in the next chapter, you can attach style sheets in the* New Document *dialog box when first creating a page. There is also an option to attach a new style sheet at the bottom of the* Class *drop-down menu in the* HTML *view of the Property inspector and in the* New CSS Style *dialog box (see Figure 4-8).*

Adding, editing, and deleting style rules

The final three icons at the bottom right of the CSS Styles panel let you add new rules, edit existing rules, and delete existing rules and properties. Most editing and deletion is done directly in the CSS Styles panel, and I'll show you how to do that in the next chapter.

Moving style rules

All the rules you have created in the exercises so far are in the <head> of the document, so they apply only to the current page. The real value of CSS lies in the ability to apply the same styles to an entire website by storing the rules in one or more external style sheets. That way, any change to the external style sheet is propagated throughout the site. It also reduces page size because the browser caches the style sheet the first time it loads. Moving style rules is a breeze, because Dreamweaver automates the process for you.

Exporting rules to a new style sheet

If you have CSS style rules defined in a document, you can easily move them into an external style sheet. The best way to show you how this works is with a hands-on exercise.

Moving embedded styles

This exercise shows you how to move the style rules from the <head> of the page that has been used in the exercises throughout this chapter into an external style sheet. If you have been doing the exercises, continue working with stroll.html. Otherwise, use stroll_04.html from examples/ch04.

1. With stroll.html open in the Document window, open the CSS Styles panel and select All mode, as described in the preceding section.

2. If necessary click the plus (+) icon (disclosure triangle on a Mac) alongside <style> to expand its contents. Use Shift-click to select all the style rules, as shown in the following screenshot.

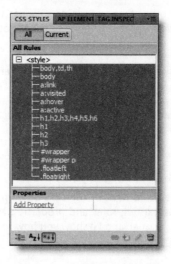

3. Right-click and select Move CSS Rules from the context menu. This brings up the following dialog box.

4. In the Move To External Style Sheet dialog box, select the radio button labeled A new style sheet, and then click OK.

5. In the next dialog box, navigate to the workfiles/ch04 folder, and save the new style sheet as stroll.css.

6. Check the CSS Styles panel. The styles should now be listed below stroll.css, as shown in the following screenshot.

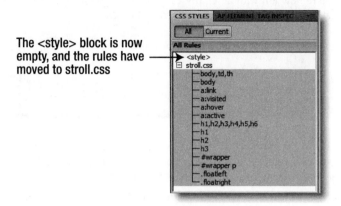

The <style> block is now empty, and the rules have moved to stroll.css

7. Check the Document window. The Related Files toolbar has been added between the document tab and Document toolbar, as shown in the following screenshot.

The external style sheet is now listed as a related file

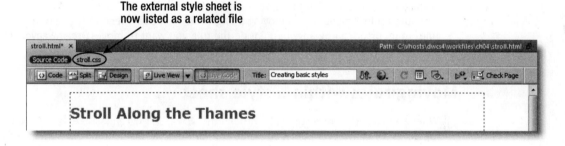

8. Click stroll.css in the Related Files toolbar. Dreamweaver switches to Split view, with the external style sheet in the Code view section and the main page in the Design view section, as shown in the following screenshot.

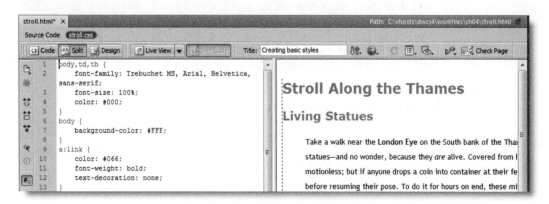

9. Click Source Code in the Related Files toolbar. This displays the source code of stroll.html in Code view. Scroll to the top of the document. In the <head> section, you're now left with an empty <style> block followed by a <link> tag to the external style sheet, as the following screenshot shows.

```
5   <title>Creating basic styles</title>
6   <style type="text/css">
7   <!--
8   -->
9   </style>
10  <link href="stroll.css" rel="stylesheet" type="text/css" />
11  </head>
```

10. To get rid of the empty <style> block shown on lines 6–9 in the preceding screenshot, you can delete it manually in Code view. Alternatively, select <style> in the CSS Styles panel in All mode, and then press Delete.

   If you want to examine the finished files, they're stroll_05.html and stroll.css in examples/ch04.

The preceding exercise demonstrated how to move all rules from the <head> of a page using the CSS Styles panel. You can also use the Move CSS Rules command in Code view. Highlight the rules you want to move, right-click, and select CSS Styles ➤ Move CSS Rules from the context menu. When moving a single rule, you don't need to highlight the whole rule. Your cursor can be anywhere inside the rule you want to move. Dreamweaver treats partial selection of a rule as affecting the whole rule.

Moving rules within a style sheet

Whenever you add a new style rule through the New CSS Rule and CSS Rule Definition dialog boxes, Dreamweaver puts it at the bottom of the style sheet. To take advantage of the cascade order, or simply to group your rules in a more logical way, you need to be able to move them. Nothing could be easier.

Simply highlight the rules you want to move (use the Shift or Ctrl/Cmd key to select multiple rules), and drag and drop them within the top pane of the CSS Styles panel in All mode. As the following screenshot shows, the mouse pointer turns into a document icon while dragging. The thick blue line indicates where the rule(s) will be located when you release the mouse button.

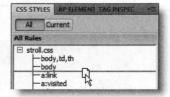

Moving rules between external style sheets

The ability to drag and drop style rules doesn't apply only to rules within the same style sheet or <style> block. If more than one style sheet is attached to a page, you can move them at will from one to another.

Changing the look of the page by moving style rules

The following exercise demonstrates the power of this feature. Not only are the style rules moved, any change in the cascade is immediately reflected in Design view.

1. Open `move_styles.html` in examples/ch04. Open the CSS Styles panel in All mode, and expand the tree menus for both style sheets. The page should look like this:

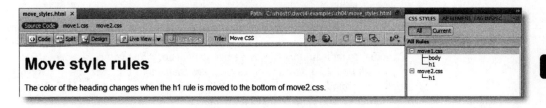

In All mode, the CSS Styles panel displays CSS selectors in the same order that they are applied to the page. As you can see from the preceding screenshot, the first style sheet contains two rules (for body and h1), and the second one contains only a rule for h1. If you inspect the properties for h1 in the Properties pane, you will see that the first style sheet sets the color to maroon, but the second one sets it to deep blue. Because the second rule is lower in the cascade, it takes precedence. That's why the page heading in Design view is deep blue.

2. Drag the h1 selector from the first style sheet to immediately below the h1 selector in the second style sheet. Dreamweaver detects a conflict and displays the following dialog box so that you can compare both versions of the rule.

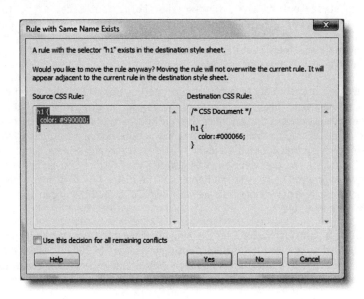

When a rule with the same name exists in the target style sheet, the rule being moved is displayed in the left panel, and the rule in the target style sheet is shown on the right. If you click Yes, Dreamweaver preserves the rule in the target style sheet and inserts the rule being moved alongside it.

Selecting No instructs Dreamweaver not to move the rule currently displayed but to carry on with the rest of the operation. Cancel tells Dreamweaver to abandon the operation, and no rules are moved. If you select the checkbox labeled Use this decision for all remaining conflicts, the Yes and No buttons are treated as Yes to All and No to All.

3. Click Yes. The page heading should immediately turn maroon in Design view. An asterisk is inserted alongside the names of the two style sheets in the Related Files toolbar to indicate that they have been changed. When you close move_styles.html, you will be asked if you want to save the changes to the style sheets. Dreamweaver always reminds you if changes have been made to related files, but it's up to you whether to make the changes permanent.

The ability to move and edit style rules without ever needing to leave Design view makes Dreamweaver a very powerful tool for creating websites with CSS.

Moving inline styles to a style sheet

Unless you need to create HTML email, inline styles are the most inflexible way of applying CSS. As the name suggests, an **inline style** is a style rule embedded in the target element's opening tag. For example, the following paragraph has an inline style that displays its content as 12-pixel, bold, red Arial, Helvetica, or sans-serif:

```
<p style="color: #F00; font-weight: bold; font-size: 12px; font-family:
Arial, Helvetica, sans-serif;">The styles affect only this para.</p>
```

Using inline styles is inefficient because only one element is affected, and the properties in an inline style always override any other rules.

Dreamweaver makes it easy to extract the properties from inline styles and convert them into an ordinary style rule in the <head> of the page or an external style sheet. Use the Tag selector to select the tag that contains the rule you want to convert, right-click, and select Convert Inline CSS to Rule from the context menu. Alternatively, position your cursor anywhere inside a tag that contains an inline style, right-click, and select CSS Styles ➤ Convert Inline CSS to Rule. In Code view, you can also use the Move or Convert CSS button on the Coding toolbar (see Figure 1-31 in Chapter 1). The dialog box that opens lets you choose whether to create a new class or define your own CSS selector. You can also choose where to create the new rule.

This feature is particularly useful for cleaning up pages that have absolutely positioned elements defined using inline styles (layers in Dreamweaver MX 2004 or earlier). You can convert only one layer at a time, but it's a much quicker and more accurate way of tidying up legacy pages than attempting to cut and paste everything manually. It doesn't matter whether you're in Code view or Design view; as long as your cursor is anywhere inside the absolutely positioned element, just right-click and select CSS Styles ➤ Convert Inline CSS to Rule from the context menu. Dreamweaver presents you with the Convert Inline CSS dialog box, as shown in Figure 4-15.

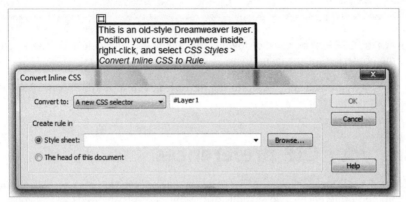

Figure 4-15. As long as your cursor is inside a layer, Dreamweaver can move the inline styles to an external style sheet or the head of the document.

Dreamweaver automatically chooses the ID as the name of the selector for the new rule. Although you can change the name in the dialog box, this affects only the new style rule. It doesn't change the ID of the <div>. The Convert to drop-down menu at the top left of the dialog box has two other options: to create a class based on the inline styles or to apply the styles to all <div> elements. They are for converting other inline styles and should not be used when converting old-style absolutely positioned elements. You can test this feature using layers.html in examples/ch04.

Creating inline styles for HTML email

Not all email programs are capable of displaying CSS correctly, so it's a common practice to revert to <font> tags and other old-style formatting techniques to create the content for HTML email. In previous versions of Dreamweaver, switching back temporarily to HTML formatting was easy: you just deselected the option in the General category of the Preferences panel to use CSS instead of HTML tags. When you had finished creating the content for HTML email, you turned the option back on, and continued working with CSS. However, that option has been removed from the Preferences panel in Dreamweaver CS4, leaving no easy way of creating <font> tags apart from hand-coding them in Code view. The solution is to use inline CSS, which most, if not all, email programs support.

To create inline CSS, select the element you want to style. Then, in the CSS view of the Property inspector select <New Inline Style> in the Targeted Rule drop-down menu, and click the Edit Rule button, as shown in the following screenshot.

This opens the CSS Rule definition dialog box (see Figure 4-6 and Table 4-1), where you can define the properties for the inline style.

Inline styles are automatically copied to the next paragraph when you press Enter/Return to create a new paragraph.

Setting your CSS preferences

Developers have individual ways of working, and Dreamweaver tries to accommodate most common preferences. Two sections of the Preferences panel (Edit ➤ Preferences, or Dreamweaver ➤ Preferences on a Mac) control the way Dreamweaver handles CSS:

- The CSS Styles category of the Preferences panel (see Figure 4-16) controls the creation and editing of style rules.

- The Code Format category of the Preferences panel also lets you determine how style rules are laid out.

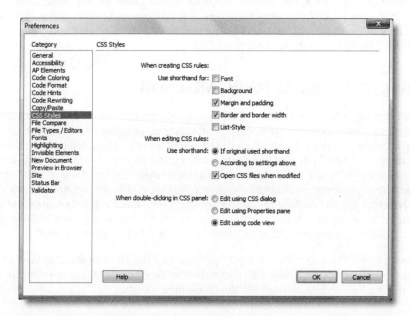

Figure 4-16. My personal preferences for the way style rules are created and edited

First, let's take a look at the options in the CSS Styles category.

Creating and editing style rules

There are two ways of writing style rules for font, background, margin, padding, border, and list-style: the long way and shorthand. For example, the following style rules both have the same meaning:

```
/* long way of declaring font and margin properties */
p {
    font-family: Arial, Helvetica, sans-serif;
    font-size: 85%;
    line-height: 1.4;
    margin-top: 0;
    margin-right: 5px;
    margin-bottom: 5px;
    margin-left: 15px;
}
/* shorthand version of preceding example */
p {
    font: 85%/1.4 Arial, Helvetica, sans-serif;
    margin: 0 5px 5px 15px;
}
```

The advantage of the long way of declaring these properties is that the meaning is crystal clear. The disadvantage is that it makes your style sheets much longer. The shorthand version is more compact, but it comes at a price: you need to remember the correct order of the property values. For margin and padding, it's easy: they start at the top and go in a clockwise direction—top, right, bottom, and left. The shorthand for border is also easy: the width, style, and color properties can go in any order. As shown in Figure 4-16, the CSS Styles category of the Preferences panel lets you choose the default way of writing these rules. My preference is to use shorthand for margin, padding, and border only.

The next set of options lets you specify whether to use shorthand when editing existing style rules. If you're working as part of a team, the first option (If original used shorthand) prevents Dreamweaver from messing up the styles used by your colleagues. If you're on your own, choose the second option so that Dreamweaver converts style rules to your own preferred format.

The checkbox labeled Open CSS files when modified makes a critical difference to the way Dreamweaver handles changes to an external style sheet. What happens depends on whether Related Files is enabled or disabled.

With Related Files enabled, if you select Open CSS files when modified, Dreamweaver tracks changes in external style sheets and marks the file in the Related Files toolbar as having changed. You can undo the last change by selecting the style sheet's name in the Related Files toolbar and pressing Ctrl+Z/Cmd+Z or selecting Edit ➤ Undo. To undo all changes, close the main file, and click No when prompted to save the changes to the style sheet. If you deselect Open CSS files when modified, Dreamweaver automatically saves any changes to external style sheets. *There is no way to undo them.* However, if you open the external style sheet in Split view by selecting its name in the Related Files toolbar, all subsequent changes are tracked and undoable.

4

With Related Files disabled, if you select Open CSS files when modified, Dreamweaver opens the external style sheet in a new tab, but leaves the focus in the main page. You can undo any changes by selecting the tab that contains the style sheet. If you deselect Open CSS files when modified, changes are made silently to the external style sheet and automatically saved. *There is no way to undo them.*

> *In previous versions of Dreamweaver, I preferred Dreamweaver not to open CSS files when modified, because I found it a nuisance to save the style sheet every time I wanted to preview my page in a browser. However, Dreamweaver CS4 lets you preview the effects of changes in Live view without saving the style sheet. So, selecting the option to open CSS files when modified makes it much easier to undo the changes if you don't like the effect.*

The final section lets you choose what happens when you double-click inside the CSS Styles panel. The first option, Edit using CSS dialog, opens the CSS Rule definition dialog box (see Figure 4-6) described earlier in the chapter. This dialog box can be helpful, but I don't recommend its use on a regular basis. The most useful option is the last one, Edit using code view. This opens the style sheet in the Document window and positions your cursor inside the selected rule, ready to edit it.

Setting the default format of style rules

To control the way your style rules are laid out, select the Code Format category in the Preferences panel, and click the CSS button in the Advanced Formatting section. This opens the CSS Source Format Options dialog box (see Figure 4-17).

Figure 4-17. The CSS Source Format Options dialog box controls how style rules are formatted.

190

The options are self-explanatory, and the Preview panel at the bottom of the dialog box shows you what your selections will look like. Click OK to close the dialog box, and click OK to save your new preferences. All new style rules will use the new settings.

To apply your format preferences to existing style sheets, open the style sheet, and select Apply Source Formatting from the Commands menu. This is an all-or-nothing option: you can't apply the formatting to a selection. Dreamweaver is smart enough to apply the CSS format options to <style> tags in the <head> of a page, but it ignores styles inside conditional comments (covered in the next chapter).

Checking how styles will look in other media

Many people think of style sheets in terms of "one size fits all"—in other words, they create one set of style rules and hope that the site will look just as good in every medium. However, you can specify different style sheets for a variety of media. Style sheets for ordinary browsers (screen), print, and handheld devices have the best support. By default, Dreamweaver Design view and Live view show your page as it will look in a visual browser, but the Style Rendering toolbar and Device Central let you check what your page will look like with style sheets designed for other media.

Using the Style Rendering toolbar

One of Dreamweaver's best-kept secrets—because it isn't enabled by default—is the Style Rendering toolbar (see Figure 4-18). It's indispensable if you work with style sheets for different types of media. To enable it, select View ➤ Toolbars and choose Style Rendering.

The Style Rendering toolbar lets you see the effect of each media style sheet in Design view. It also allows you to disable CSS entirely, so that you can see the logical flow of your web page in the same way that it would be presented to a search engine or a visually disabled person using a screen reader.

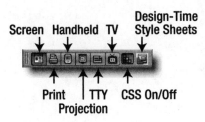

Figure 4-18.
The Style Rendering toolbar displays the effect of different style sheets without leaving Design view.

The Design-time Style Sheets button gives direct access to the Design-time Style Sheets dialog box, giving you control over which style sheets are applied or hidden while working in Design view. This allows you to view two or more style sheets in combination, whereas the Style Rendering toolbar selects only one at a time. Design-time style sheets are covered in Chapter 12.

If you prefer working with menus, you can access the Style Rendering submenu from the View menu. You can also access the Design-time Style Sheets dialog box by selecting Format ➤ CSS Styles ➤ Design-time.

Using Device Central CS4

In addition to Live view and launching a variety of browsers from within Dreamweaver to preview your website, you can see how it will look in a mobile device by launching Adobe Device Central CS4. This is a separate program shared by most programs in the Adobe Creative Suite, which is installed at the same time as Dreamweaver unless you deselected it during the installation setup. Figure 4-19 shows how Device Central emulates the display of stroll.html in a generic mobile device, but you can choose skins from all the main mobile phone manufacturers from the Device Central online library.

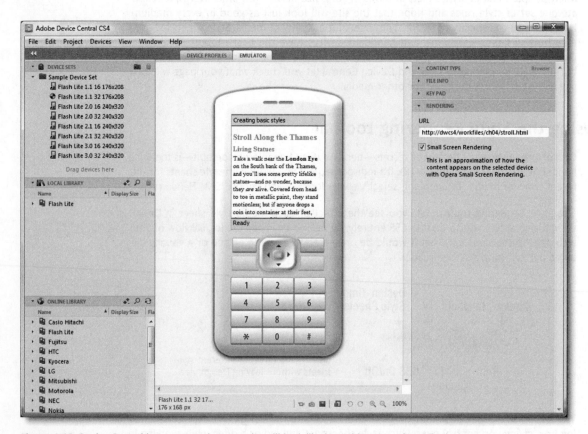

Figure 4-19. Device Central lets you see what your site will look like in a wide range of mobile devices.

You access Device Central by selecting File ➤ Preview in Browser ➤ Device Central. The keyboard shortcut (Ctrl+Alt+F12/Ctrl+Opt+F12) is easy to remember because it's so similar to the shortcut for previewing in your default browser (F12/Opt+F12). The display in Device Central is interactive, so you can use the mobile keypad and click links to navigate to other pages. Although Device Central is intended to be used as an emulator in a development environment, you can also view live pages on the Internet. Just type the website address into the URL field in the right panel and press Enter/Return.

Chapter review

This chapter has shown you how to create basic style rules in Dreamweaver and covered the main CSS tools in Dreamweaver. The next chapter builds on that knowledge by adapting one of the 32 built-in CSS layouts in Dreamweaver. You'll also learn about using the CSS Styles panel in Current mode, a powerful tool for analyzing the effect of the cascade within your style sheets.

4

5 CREATING A CSS SITE STRAIGHT OUT OF THE BOX

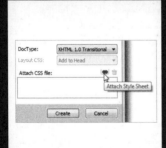

In this chapter, I'll lead you through the process of creating a page using one of the 32 built-in CSS layouts in Dreamweaver CS4, showing you how to get the most out of the CSS Styles panel in Current mode. The CSS layouts were originally introduced in Dreamweaver CS3 and provide a very solid foundation for creating a standards-compliant website consisting of header, sidebar, main content area, and footer. For a sneak preview of where this chapter ends up, load `stroll_final.html` from examples/ch05 into a browser, or take a look at Figure 5-7 later in this chapter. If you're new to CSS, you may find some parts of this chapter daunting, but come along for the ride. Even if you don't understand how all the style rules fit together, you'll pick up some cool techniques that will give your own sites that extra lift.

In this chapter, you'll learn about the following:

- Attaching external style sheets when creating a new page
- Making sure conditional comments are applied correctly
- Adapting a Dreamweaver CSS layout
- Getting the most out of the CSS Styles panel in Current mode
- Understanding the impact of the CSS cascade
- Refining selectors in the New CSS Rule dialog box
- Using Dreamweaver's Find and Replace feature

Using a built-in CSS layout

If you click HTML or PHP in the Create New section of the welcome screen, Dreamweaver opens a blank page using your default settings (see "Setting new document preferences" in Chapter 2). You get a much bigger choice with File ➤ New, which opens the New Document dialog box (see Figure 5-1).

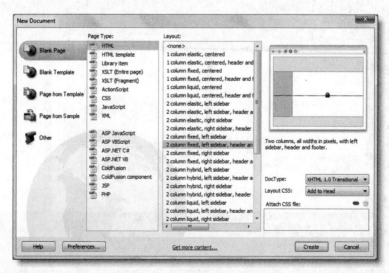

Figure 5-1. Open the New Document dialog box to select one of the built-in CSS layouts.

In both the Blank Page and Blank Template categories, the Layout column offers you a choice of 32 CSS layouts when the Page Type is suitable for a complete web page, such as HTML or PHP. You can also choose just a blank page by selecting <none> from the top of the Layout column. The dialog box remembers your choices the next time you open it.

Choosing a layout

The layouts cover the most commonly used conventions of web page design: one-, two-, and three-column pages, with and without a header and footer. They have been tested in all the main browsers and provide a rock-solid basis for building a site.

> *The minimum versions required for the CSS layouts are Firefox 1.0, Opera 8, Safari 2.0 (Windows and Mac), and Internet Explorer 5.5 (Windows).*

5

You can choose four different types of column widths, identified by simple diagrams, as follows:

- **Fixed**: The width is defined in pixels.

- **Elastic**: The width is defined in ems.

- **Liquid**: The width is defined as a percentage.

- **Hybrid**: The main column width is defined as a percentage; other columns are defined in ems.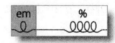

As you select each layout, a diagram appears on the right of the New Document dialog box showing the style together with a brief description, as shown in Figure 5-1.

Deciding where to locate your style rules

When you select a layout, the Layout CSS menu at the bottom right of the New Document dialog box is activated (it's grayed out when <none> is selected). The menu has three options, as follows:

- Add to Head: This embeds the style rules in the <head> of the document.
- Create New File: This puts all the style rules in an external style sheet.
- Link to Existing File: This discards all style rules associated with the layout and links to an existing style sheet.

Linking to existing style sheets

The third option is typically for subsequent pages based on the same layout. Before clicking Create, you must specify the style sheet by clicking the chain icon alongside Attach CSS file, as shown here:

This opens the Attach External Style Sheet dialog box, which was described in the previous chapter. After selecting the style sheet, click OK, and you will be returned to the New Document dialog box. You can add as many style sheets as you want. The text area below the chain icon displays a list of the selected style sheet(s).

When you're satisfied, click Create to load the new layout page into the Document window. When you first save the page, Dreamweaver automatically adjusts any document-relative paths to style sheets.

In many dialog boxes, Dreamweaver remembers your last set of options—and this includes the list of attached style sheets at the foot of the New Document dialog box. That's very helpful if you want to link the same style sheets to your next document, but it may give you a nasty surprise if you forget. To remove style sheets from the list, highlight them, and click the trash can icon alongside the chain icon.

Making sure conditional comments are applied

To make the style sheets easier to edit, as well as to ensure standards compliance, the layouts don't use any weird and wonderful CSS hacks to overcome bugs in Internet Explorer. Instead, special rules to correct these bugs are embedded in conditional comments just before the closing `</head>` tag of the layout page. Conditional comments are a Microsoft extension of HTML comments and look like this:

```
<!--[if IE 5]>
<style type="text/css">
.twoColFixLtHdr #sidebar1 { width: 230px; }
</style>
<![endif]-->
```

Only the Windows version of Internet Explorer takes any notice of the style rules embedded in them. All other browsers treat them as ordinary comments and ignore them. It's a perfect, standards-compliant way of tackling Internet Explorer bugs. However, for them to be effective, they *must* come after all other style rules. If your style rules are in external style sheets, the conditional comments must come after the `<link>` or `@import` commands that attach them to the page. Although you can put special rules for Internet Explorer in an external style sheet and use a conditional comment to attach the style sheet, the comments themselves cannot go in an external style sheet. They must be in your web page.

> *Visit* http://msdn.microsoft.com/workshop/author/dhtml/overview/ccomment_ovw.asp *to learn more about Microsoft conditional comments.*

This has important implications if you attach further style sheets. When you click the Attach Style Sheet icon at the bottom of the CSS Styles panel, as described in Chapter 4, Dreamweaver attaches external style sheets immediately before the closing </head> tag—in other words, after any conditional comments. This means you must always move the code that attaches your style sheet to before the conditional comments. Even if you're sure there's no conflict of style rules, it's safer to do so because Dreamweaver ignores the conditional comments in the same way as a non-Microsoft browser, so you won't notice any difference in Design view if you forget to move the link to the new style sheet. However, it will be immediately apparent to anyone using a version of Internet Explorer with bugs that the conditional comments are meant to correct.

You must move the link to the external style sheet manually in Code view. Dragging and dropping the style rules in the CSS Styles panel in All mode has no effect.

Styling a page

The layout I have chosen for this chapter is 2 column fixed, left sidebar, header and footer. It creates a 780-pixel wide page centered horizontally in the browser. This is designed to fit in an 800 × 600 monitor. You can change the width to suit your own needs, but I'm going to leave it as it is.

Preparing the basic layout

The following exercise shows how to start transforming the basic layout. Of course, I didn't just pluck the settings out of thin air; it took some experimentation. But the way I did it was exactly the same—using the CSS Styles panel to edit each property and watching the gradual transformation of the page in Design view. The page you'll build uses some of the same materials as the previous chapter but results in a much more sophisticated design.

These instructions assume you have already familiarized yourself with using the CSS Styles panel in All mode, as described in Chapter 4.

1. Open Dreamweaver, and select File ➤ New. In the New Document dialog box, select the Blank Page category, and use the following settings:

   - Page Type: HTML
   - Layout: 2 column fixed, left sidebar, header and footer
   - DocType: XHTML 1.0 Transitional
   - Layout CSS: Create New File

   Make sure there are no style sheets listed under Attach CSS file, and click Create.

2. Dreamweaver prompts you to save the style sheet. Navigate to the workfiles folder, create a new subfolder called ch05, and save the style sheet in the new folder as stroll.css. When you click Save, the CSS layout loads into the Document window as an unnamed and untitled document. Save it in workfiles/ch05 as stroll.html. The style sheet is added to the Related Files toolbar at the top of the Document window.

Your first reaction may be "Ugh, what an ugly duckling!" But this ugly duckling has the right genes, or infrastructure, to turn it into a beautiful swan. The first task is to analyze the structure. Do this with the help of the CSS visual aids by moving your mouse around the Document window and clicking any solid lines that indicate the presence of a <div> as described in the previous chapter. Also click in each part of the document to see the structure revealed in the Tag selector.

To assist you, Figure 5-2 shows how the page is divided. The whole page is wrapped in a <div> called container, which centers the content in the browser. The rest of the page consists of four sections, each within a <div> named header, sidebar1, mainContent, and footer. The sidebar and main content are both floated left.

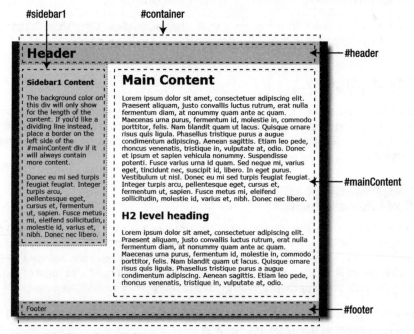

Figure 5-2. The main underlying structure of the two-column fixed layout with header and footer

3. Select stroll.css in the Related Files toolbar to display the contents of the style sheet in Split view. As Figure 5-3 shows, the style sheet begins with an @charset rule. This is not strictly necessary when working with English, but it tells Dreamweaver and the web server which encoding you're using. It must come before any CSS selectors.

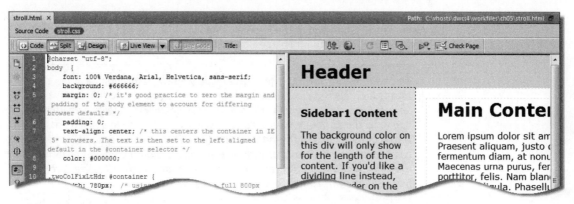

Figure 5-3. The style rules are liberally commented to make it easy to understand the role they play in the layout.

The rules are copiously sprinkled with CSS comments that explain their purpose. The styles applied to the body selector control the fonts and give the page a dark gray background color. The white background is common to all elements in the container <div>, but the header, sidebar1, and footer override this with various shades of gray.

Most of the content on the page is dummy text, but the first paragraph in the left sidebar contains the important information that the background color stretches only as far as the content. It also advises adding a border to the left side of the mainContent <div> if it will always contain more content. So let's start by fixing that.

4. You can edit the style rules directly in stroll.css in Split view and see the effects reflected in the Design view section of the Document window. However, I want to show you how to use the CSS Styles panel in Current mode to identify which style rules affect a particular part of the page when you don't know the name of the selector.

In Design view, click in the text beneath the Main Content headline, select <div#mainContent> in the Tag selector at the bottom of the Document window, and then click the Current button at the top of the CSS Styles panel. The panel should now look similar to the screenshot alongside.

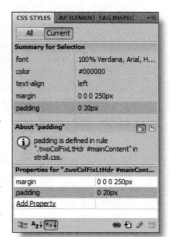

In Current mode, the CSS Styles panel consists of three sections, which you may need to resize to see everything (the width of the columns is also resizable by dragging horizontally). The top pane (Summary for Selection) shows the rules that apply to the current selection both through its own selector and through the rest of the cascade, whereas the bottom pane (Properties) shows you the style rules for the currently highlighted selector. By default, the middle pane tells you where the property selected in either pane is defined in the style sheet.

201

Although it looks confusing at first glance, Current mode presents you with a lot of useful information and is an extremely effective place to edit CSS. Using it in practice makes it easier to understand, so just follow along for the time being.

> *The built-in CSS layouts use a technique known as giving the page a **CSS signature**. This is a class added to the <body> tag of the page, identifying the layout. Each style rule uses a descendant selector that begins with the class name. So the style rule for the* mainContent <div> *is called* .twoColFixLtHdr #mainContent. *Adding the class makes the style rules more specific, so you can combine one of these layouts with an existing site that already has its own style rules. If you add new rules yourself, remember that CSS selectors are case sensitive. Use the same camel-case spelling.*

5. Click Add Property at the bottom of the Properties pane. This opens a blank drop-down menu. This is where you specify the CSS property you want to add to the rule. To create a left border, you need the border-left property. The drop-down menu is editable, so either you can click the down arrow on the right of the menu to reveal all the options or you can start typing the name of a CSS property. If you don't want to type the full name, type just bor, and press the down arrow key (or click the menu's down arrow). The border property should already be highlighted. Scroll down to border-left, as shown alongside.

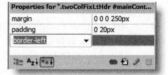

Press Tab or click border-left, and Dreamweaver opens the right side of the pane for you to type the value you want to assign to the CSS property. If it doesn't open automatically, click to the right of border-left. Type 1px dashed #000, and press Enter/Return.

Click anywhere in the mainContent <div> to deselect it, and you should see a dotted black border on the left side of the text.

> *The drop-down menu that contains the CSS properties remains editable only when you first open it. Once you have selected a property, you cannot change it; only the value field to the right of the property name remains editable. If you choose the wrong property, highlight it, and press Delete or click the trash can icon at the bottom right of the* CSS Styles *panel. Then click* Add Property *again to choose the correct property.*

6. Now let's deal with the sidebar background. Click anywhere in the sidebar. If you look at the Properties pane of the CSS Styles panel, you'll see that it refers to .twoColFixLtHdr #container and not the sidebar. Because nothing is actually selected, Dreamweaver shows you the rules for the parent <div> for the whole page. Although this seems counterintuitive, it's actually quite useful.

As you can see from the screenshot alongside, background, border, margin, and width are all struck through with a horizontal line. This indicates that a more specific rule is overriding these properties in the sidebar. The useful piece of information here is that the background property for the container <div> is white (#FFFFFF). If you remove the background for the sidebar, it will inherit the color of its parent.

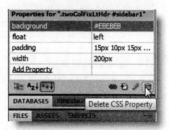

7. Click <div#sidebar1> in the Tag selector at the bottom of the Document window. The Properties pane now shows the rules for .twoColFixLtHdr #sidebar1, which set the background color of the sidebar to light gray (#EBEBEB). Highlight background, and press Delete or click the trash can icon at the bottom of the CSS Styles panel, as shown here.

> *If you delete the wrong property, you cannot undo it by pressing Ctrl+Z/Cmd+Z or selecting* Edit ➤ Undo *because the change has been made to an external style sheet. Select the style sheet's name in the Related Files toolbar to undo the change.*

8. The sidebar should now have the same white background as the mainContent <div>. Let's do the same to the footer, which has a slightly different gray background color (#DDDDDD). Position your cursor anywhere in the footer <div>, select <div#footer> in the Tag selector, and then delete background from the Properties pane of the CSS Styles panel.

9. If you look at stroll.html in Design view or Live view, the gray background should be gone from the sidebar and footer, and there should be a dashed border down the left side of the main content. The only gray background remaining is behind the header. However, if you press F12/Opt+F12 to preview the page in your main browser, the gray backgrounds are still all there. Why? The answer lies in the Related Files toolbar.

10. Switch back to Dreamweaver. You should see an asterisk alongside stroll.css in the Related Files toolbar, as shown in the following screenshot:

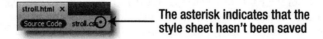

The asterisk indicates that the style sheet hasn't been saved

Changes made to the style sheet are not automatically saved when working with the Related Files toolbar. This allows you to roll back any changes, but it also means you need to remember to save them if you want to keep them. To save a related file that has been edited, select the file name in the Related Files toolbar, and select File ➤ Save or press Ctrl+S/Cmd+S.

Selecting a file name in the Related Files toolbar always opens the related file in Split view. If you don't want to open it, select File ➤ Save All, or right-click the main document's tab and select Save All from the context menu.

> It's important to note that you cannot normally undo changes to an external style sheet if the option Open CSS files when modified has been deselected in the CSS Styles category of the Preferences panel (see Chapter 4). If you set your preferences not to open CSS files and are wondering why your changes haven't been automatically saved, it's because selecting stroll.css in the Related Files toolbar in step 3 has the effect of opening it, making all changes undoable.

11. Save stroll.css, and test stroll.html in a browser. The sidebar and footer backgrounds should now have disappeared.

Check your files, if necessary, against stroll_border.html and stroll_border.css in examples/ch05.

Getting rid of the background colors doesn't make a dramatic difference to the look of the page. The real transformation begins with adding background images. By using the CSS Styles panel, the changes are reflected immediately in Design view.

Adding background images

In this exercise, you'll add a background image and banner to the header <div>, and you'll position a background image at the bottom of the container <div>. Continue working with the same files as in the preceding exercise.

1. Instead of white or gray, I've chosen a shade of cornflower blue as the background color for the header. This is because I'm going to use a background image but want a similar color to be displayed if the image fails to load.

Click in the header <div>, select <div#header> in the Tag selector, and delete background from the Properties pane of the CSS Styles panel. Although you're going to use a different color, I've suggested deleting the shortcut property because it's easier to use the separate background-color and background-image properties.

2. With the header <div> still selected, click Add Property, and select background-image using either the arrow keys or the drop-down menu. Dreamweaver not only opens the right side of the pane for you to type the name of the image but also displays two icons that should be familiar from the main Property inspector, as shown here.

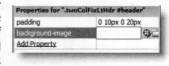

You can click the Point to File icon on the left to point to the image in the Files panel, or you can click the folder icon to navigate to the file. It's often easier to close the Files panel when working in the CSS Styles panel, so the latter tends to be more useful. Use either method to select images/stroll_header_bg.jpg.

3. Click Add Property, select background-repeat, and select repeat-x from the drop-down menu that appears alongside. This tiles the background image only horizontally.

4. Click Add Property again, and select background-color from the drop-down menu. This time, Dreamweaver inserts the color picker alongside the property, as shown alongside.

5. Click the color picker, and use the Eyedropper tool to get the color of the background image in the header <div>. It has a slight pattern, so the precise color isn't important. I told you that it was a lot easier not using shortcuts for the background property.

Properties for ".twoColFixLtHdr #header"	
padding	0 10px 0 20px
background-image	url(../../images/s...
background-repeat	repeat-x
background-color	
Add Property	
	Color picker

6. Remove all padding from the header <div> by clicking the value alongside padding, and change it from 0 10px 0 20px to 0. Sizes in CSS must always be accompanied by a unit of measurement, such as em or px, with no gap between the number and unit. The only exception is 0, which doesn't require a unit of measurement. Although 0px is valid, the px isn't necessary—and leaving it out saves typing.

7. Select the word Header, and replace it with Stroll Along the Thames. Then select the <h1> tag in the Tag selector, and press the right arrow key on your keyboard. If you open Split view, you'll see that this positions the cursor between the closing </h1> tag and the closing </div> tag in the underlying code.

> When opening Split view with Related Files enabled, Dreamweaver remembers which file was opened most recently in Split view. To make sure you open the right file, always use the Related Files toolbar, rather than clicking the Split View button on the Document toolbar. To inspect the HTML code of the main document, click Source Code in the Related Files toolbar.

8. Insert the header image by selecting the Insert Image button in the Common category of the Insert bar or by selecting Insert ➤ Image. Browse to images/stroll_header.jpg. In the Image Tag Accessibility Attributes dialog box, set Alternate text to Stroll Along the Thames, and click OK.

9. Change the Document title to Stroll Along the Thames by replacing Untitled Document in the Document toolbar. The top of the page should now look like this in Design view:

The text heading in the <h1> tags is for the benefit of search engines and browsers that can't cope with CSS, but you need to hide the text for visual browsers. Once it's out of the way, you can tuck the header image neatly into the top of the page.

10. Position your cursor in the text heading, and select the <h1> tag in the Tag selector. Highlight the padding property in the Properties pane of the CSS Styles panel, and delete it. Then add the following two properties and values:

- position: absolute

- top: −500px

Using absolute positioning removes the heading from the flow of the document, and giving it a top position of −500 pixels moves it conveniently out of the way.

> *When entering a value like −500px, you can either type the unit of measurement immediately after the number or select it from the drop-down menu that Dreamweaver places alongside. Since you're already at the keyboard, it's quicker to type it yourself.*

11. Now let's add a bit of interest to the bottom of the page. Click anywhere in Design view, and select <div#container> in the Tag selector. Highlight background in the Properties pane of the CSS Styles panel, and delete it. The whole of Design view will turn a dark gray, but fear not. You can restore the light right away by clicking Add Property, selecting background-color, and setting its value to #FFF.

12. Next add the background-image property, and navigate to images/city_footer.jpg. It tiles throughout the page, so you need to set the following properties and values:

- background-repeat: no-repeat

- background-position: left bottom

The first of these properties accepts only one value, so Dreamweaver lists valid options as a drop-down menu. The second accepts combined values, so no drop-down menu is available. Nevertheless, Dreamweaver still comes to your rescue by displaying code hints when you hover your mouse pointer over the field where the values need to be entered.

13. Click the Live View button in the Document toolbar. If your monitor is large enough, the page should look similar to Figure 5-4.

If you want to check the page in a browser, remember to save stroll.css first.

14. The page is beginning to look pretty good, but the margins on both sides look drab. Their color is controlled by the body selector; and after some experimentation, I decided to make them a light pink to match the winter sunset sky behind Saint Paul's Cathedral. The color I chose was #F8F1EB. Select <body.twoColFixLtHdr> in the Tag selector, and click the value of background in the Properties pane of the CSS Styles panel. Replace #666666 with #F8F1EB.

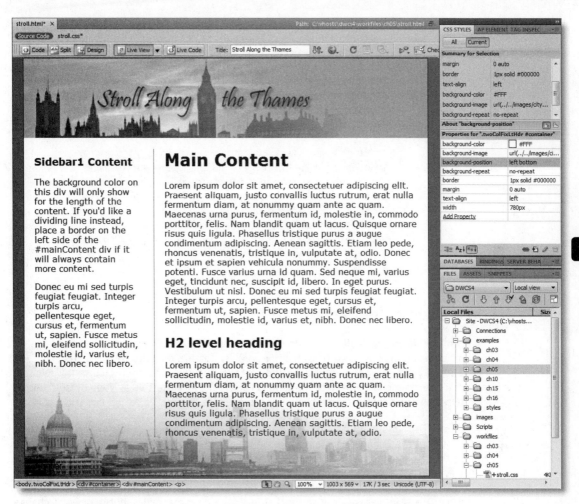

Figure 5-4. The built-in CSS layout looks very different after changing some background settings.

15. The border around the container `<div>` is now a little too dark, so select `<div#container>` in the Tag selector. The Properties pane of the CSS Styles panel shows that border has been set to 1px solid #000000—in other words, a solid, black border all around. Although I have set my preferences to use shorthand styles for the border property, you can use shorthand only when all sides have the same value. I want no border at the top and bottom, but a deep russet on either side.

Highlight the existing border property, and delete it. Then click Add Property to create two separate rules for border-left and border-right with the value 1px solid #C99466.

16. Save `stroll.html` and `stroll.css`, and preview the page in a browser. It's now looking quite respectable. If you want to check your progress, compare your files with `stroll_bg.html` and `stroll_bg.css` in examples/ch05.

Making these changes to the background has already transformed the basic CSS layout, but to make further changes, you need to exploit the Current mode of the CSS Styles panel to its full potential by using it to analyze the way style rules interact with each other—in other words, the cascade.

> *Cascading style sheets are so called because of the way rules inherit properties from each other, rather like the increased flow of water cascading down a waterfall. Not only do rules inherit from one another, a more powerful influence further down the cascade can override everything that has gone before. Understanding how the cascade works is the key to successful implementation of CSS.*

Inspecting the cascade in Current mode

Halfway down the right side of the CSS Styles panel in Current mode are two insignificant-looking icons (shown alongside). By default, the left one is selected, but the right one holds the key to the cascade of rules affecting the currently selected tag. I recommend you select the icon on the right and use this as your default setting (Dreamweaver always remembers your most recent choice).

Study Figure 5-5 carefully. The title bar of the Properties pane is identical in both screenshots, but the Summary for Selection is different, and all the properties are struck through in the left screenshot. No, it's not a bug; Dreamweaver isn't broken. The left screenshot was taken with the insertion point in the text of one of the paragraphs in the mainContent `<div>`. The properties are struck through because they don't affect the paragraph directly. What Dreamweaver is telling you is that you can edit these values, but they won't change the look of the current selection in Design view. The screenshot on the right was taken with the whole of mainContent `<div>` selected. As a result, the properties are no longer struck through; they apply directly to the current selection. They're also listed in the Summary for Selection.

The Rules pane in the middle shows the full cascade of all style rules that affect the current selection. As you hover your mouse pointer over each one, Dreamweaver displays the rule's specificity as four comma-separated numbers (see "Calculating specificity").

The real power of Current mode comes in the ability to select any of the properties listed in the Summary for Selection or any of the selectors in the Rules pane. Doing so immediately displays the relevant style rule in the Properties pane. For example, selecting font in the top pane displays the body style rules ready for editing in the bottom pane (see Figure 5-6).

It takes a while to get used to working with the CSS Styles panel in Current mode, but once you do, you'll wonder how you ever did without it.

Figure 5-5.
In Current mode, the CSS Styles panel shows the different impact of the cascade on text in the mainContent <div> (left) and on the <div> itself.

5

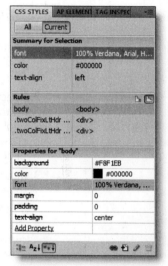

Calculating specificity

Specificity determines which rule "wins" when there's a conflict—the higher the numbers, the greater the precedence that's given to a particular rule. Specificity is calculated in a rather unusual way using a series of comma-separated values like this:

- For every ID attribute in the selector, add 0, 1, 0, 0.
- For every class, attribute selector, and pseudo-class (such as a:link), add 0, 0, 1, 0.
- For every HTML element or pseudo-element, add 0, 0, 0, 1.

Figure 5-6. The 100-percent font size in the body selector needs to be overridden further down the cascade.

Precedence is given to numbers on the left. So a CSS selector with a specificity of 0, 1, 0, 0 overrides one that has a specificity of 0, 0, 0, 2. If you find this confusing, a simple rule of thumb is that ID attributes have the highest precedence, followed by classes. Type (tag) selectors have the lowest precedence of all.

You might be wondering why there's a fourth digit in specificity calculations since the first one doesn't seem to be used at all. Actually, an inline style has a specificity of 1, 0, 0, 0, and overrides all other style rules. Inline styles are very inflexible and are rarely justified, except perhaps for creating HTML email because of poor support for CSS in some email programs.

For more details about specificity, see www.w3.org/TR/REC-CSS2/cascade.html#specificity.

Finishing the layout

Let's return to stroll.html and smarten it up a little more by adding some images, changing the font size, and adding a pull quote.

Inserting images and adjusting fonts

Continue working with stroll.html and stroll.css. Alternatively, copy stroll_bg.html and stroll_bg.css from examples/ch05 to your workfiles/ch05 folder. If Dreamweaver asks you whether you want to update links, click Update.

1. Position your cursor near the top of the first paragraph in mainContent <div>, say at the beginning of the third sentence, and insert images/living_statues.jpg. Give the image some alternate text, such as Living statues on the South Bank.

2. Select the image in Design view, and click the arrow to the right of the Class drop-down menu in the Property inspector. This lists all classes defined in the style sheet. Adobe has anticipated the need to wrap text around images and provided two classes, .fltlft and .fltrt, which float elements left and right, respectively. Choose fltlft from the Class drop-down menu to float the image to the left.

3. Insert images/graffiti.jpg into the text beneath the second heading, give it some alternate text, and select fltrt from the Class menu to float the image to the right.

4. The size of the text is a bit too large for my liking, so let's adjust it. Position your cursor anywhere in the text in the mainContent <div>, and open the CSS Styles panel in Current mode. It should look like the left screenshot in Figure 5-5.

   Select font in the Summary for Selection pane. This reveals that all the font properties for the page are defined in the <body> tag, as shown in Figure 5-6. Although you could edit the font size here, it would affect fonts throughout the rest of the page, and using a percentage other than 100 percent on the body selector makes it difficult to calculate font sizes further down the cascade. So let's create a new rule.

5. Click the New CSS Rule icon (see alongside) at the bottom of the CSS Styles panel.

   Dreamweaver makes an intelligent guess and suggests .twoColFixLtHdr #container #mainContent p as the name of the new selector, as shown here:

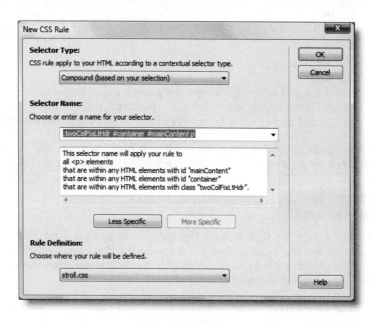

This isn't what you want, because it would apply only to paragraphs in the mainContent <div>. To apply it to all paragraphs, you want a simple type (tag) selector.

6. You can do this in two ways. First, you could change Selector Type to Tag (redefines an HTML element), and then type p in the Selector Name field.

The other way is to use the Less Specific button. The first time you click the Less Specific button, .twoColFixLtHdr is removed from the Selector Name field. Click twice more, and you're left with just p. Although Selector Type still says Compound (based on your selection), Dreamweaver creates the correct style rule.

Use either method to create a new style rule for all paragraphs, and click OK.

7. This opens the CSS Rule Definition dialog box. As I explained in Chapter 4, I find this a rather clumsy way of defining a new rule because you need to wade through the different categories to find what you want. But if you're new to CSS, it may help fix the available properties in your mind. Anyway, it opens automatically at the Type category, which is what you want.

Enter 85% in the Size field, set Line-height to 1.3, and select multiple from the drop-down menu alongside the Line-height field. Click Apply to view the result in Design view (move the CSS Rule Definition dialog box if necessary). Make any adjustments you want, and then click OK to create the rule.

8. The footer text is obscured by the background image, so let's adjust that too. Click anywhere in the footer <div>, and switch to Current mode in the CSS Styles panel. The Dreamweaver CSS layout has already defined a selector called .twoColFixLtHdr #footer p with values for margin and padding.

Click Add Property, and use the following settings:

- color: #8A5B31
- text-align: right

Moving the text across to the right and giving it a dark brown color makes it stand out against the lighter part of the background image. Select File ➤ Save All to save stroll.html and stroll.css, but keep them open for the next exercise.

Since it's a page about London, there's just one final touch I'd like to add: Samuel Johnson's famous assertion that when a man is tired of London, he's tired of life.

Adding a pull quote

In the bad old days, the <blockquote> tag was misused by all and sundry to indent text. Well, let's be honest, it still is, but you know better, don't you? You're going to use <blockquote> for its real purpose—to highlight a quotation—and then style it with CSS to turn it into a distinctive pull quote.

1. Place your cursor at the end of the first paragraph in the sidebar, and press Enter/Return to create a new paragraph. Type: No, Sir, when a man is tired of London, he is tired of life; for there is in London all that life can afford. **Press Enter/Return again,** and type the attribution: Samuel Johnson, 1777.

2. Select both paragraphs in Design view, and click the Text Indent button in the HTML view of the Property inspector, as shown here (make sure you're in HTML view; the icons in the CSS view look very similar but perform different functions):

This wraps the paragraphs in a pair of <blockquote> tags.

> *The names of the* Text Indent *button and the one to its left (*Text Outdent*) still reflect the old presentational type of markup that you should avoid in a standards-compliant site. When applied to ordinary text, think of them as the "blockquote" and "remove blockquote" buttons. When used in an ordered or unordered list, they create or remove a nested list, as explained in Chapter 3.*

3. Switch to the CSS view of the Property inspector, and select <New CSS Rule> from the Targeted Rule menu, as shown in the following screenshot:

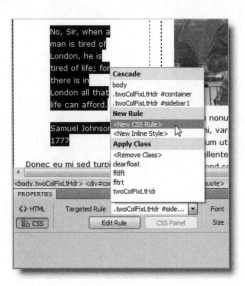

5

Click the Edit Rule button to open the New CSS Rule dialog box.

4. Dreamweaver suggests using the following selector: .twoColFixLtHdr #container #sidebar1 blockquote p. That's too precise for what you want to do at the moment, so choose Tag (redefines an HTML element) for Selector Type. Because you have a <blockquote> selected in Design view, Dreamweaver should automatically enter blockquote in the Selector Name field. If for any reason it doesn't, choose blockquote from the Selector Name drop-down menu, and click OK.

5. In the CSS Rule Definition dialog box, select the Type category, and set Font to Georgia, Times New Roman, Times, serif and Color to white (#FFF). Next, select the Background category, and set Background color to #999 (medium gray). You need to add a few more properties, but it's much easier to do the rest in the CSS Styles panel, because you can see exactly how they affect the look of the pull quote in Design view.

Click OK to save the current rules. The pull quote should now look like the one shown alongside.

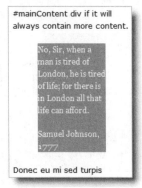

6. The default margin around the <blockquote> is too wide, so position your cursor anywhere in the quote, and select <blockquote> in the Tag selector. With the CSS Styles panel in Current mode, click Add Property to add the following settings:

- margin: 10px
- padding: 0

7. The text in the pull quote now needs to be pulled in from the edges. Click anywhere in the <blockquote> element in Design view. This deselects <blockquote> in the Tag selector but puts the insertion point in a paragraph nested in the <blockquote>. You'll see why this is important when you open the New CSS Rule dialog box.

213

8. Open the New CSS Rule dialog box in the same way as in step 3. Alternatively, click the New CSS Rule icon at the bottom right of the CSS Styles panel. Dreamweaver suggests the same selector as in step 4 (.twoColFixLtHdr #container #sidebar1 blockquote p). This time, it's appropriate, but you don't really need it to be so specific. Click the Less Specific button three times to change the contents of the Selector Name field to blockquote p.

9. The descendant selector blockquote p restricts the rule to paragraphs in a <blockquote>. Click OK, select the Box category in the CSS Rule Definition dialog box, and use the following settings for Padding and Margin:

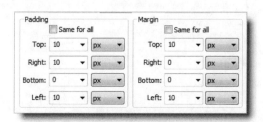

10. When you click OK to save the settings for the blockquote p rule, you'll see that the bottom line is flush with the gray background. Everything comes right in a moment.

    Select <blockquote> in the Tag selector again, and click Add Property in the Properties pane of the CSS Styles panel. Select background-image, and navigate to images/top_quote.gif. The image tiles horrendously, so add two further properties as follows:

    - background-repeat: no-repeat

    - background-position: left top

11. Just a couple more tweaks and you're there. The beginning of the pull quote overlaps the quotation marks of the background image, so click in the first paragraph of the quote, and add the following property to the blockquote p style rule:

    - text-indent: 20px

12. CSS doesn't let you apply two background images in the same rule (you'll have to wait for CSS3 to do that), so you need to create a new rule for the quote attribution within the <blockquote>. Position your cursor in the paragraph that reads Samuel Johnson, 1777, and switch to the HTML view of the Property inspector. Enter quote_attrib in the ID field, and press Enter/Return to register the change.

13. Use the ID selector #quote_attrib to create a new CSS rule. With your cursor still in the same paragraph, open the New CSS Rule dialog box. This time, Dreamweaver suggests .twoColFixLtHdr #container #sidebar1 blockquote #quote_attrib as the selector. Click the Less Specific button four times until you're left with #quote_attrib in the Selector Name field. Then click OK to open the CSS Rule Definition dialog box.

14. Select the Background category, and set Background image to images/btm_quote.gif, Repeat to no-repeat, Background-position (X) to right, and Background-position (Y) to bottom.

Then use either the CSS Rule Definition dialog box or the CSS Styles panel to set the remaining properties:

- font-size: 70%
- margin-top: 0
- padding-bottom: 30px
- text-align: right
- text-indent: 0

15. Select File ➤ Save All to save both stroll.html and stroll.css, and press F12/Opt+F12 to preview the page in a browser. It should look similar to Figure 5-7 (I've changed the headings to give the page a more authentic look). The ugly duckling in Figure 5-2 is now an elegant swan. You can compare your files with stroll_final.html and stroll_final.css in examples/ch05.

5

Figure 5-7. With a little imagination and work, you can transform the basic CSS layouts into attractive pages.

Creating a new page with the same styles

All the hard work of creating an external style sheet is repaid by the fact that you can apply the same styles instantly to any other page in the site. To round out this series of exercises in adapting one of Dreamweaver's CSS layouts, I want to show you quickly how to create another page using the same style sheet.

Creating a subsequent page

This exercise shows you how to reuse the stroll.css style sheet with a new page. It also shows you how to turn off the display of styles temporarily to make it easier to add content.

1. Open the New Document dialog box by selecting File ➤ New or pressing Ctrl+N/Cmd+N.

2. In the Blank Page category, select HTML as Page Type and 2 column fixed, left sidebar, header and footer as Layout (these are the same options as before).

3. At the bottom right of the New Document dialog box, set the value of Layout CSS to Link to Existing File.

4. Click the chain icon to attach the existing style sheet, as shown here:

5. In the Attach External Style Sheet dialog box, click the Browse button, navigate to workfiles/ch05/stroll.css, and then click OK (Choose on a Mac) to select it.

6. Click OK to close the Attach External Style Sheet dialog box and return to the New Document dialog box. The settings at the bottom right should now look like this:

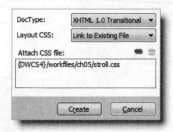

7. Click Create to create the new page with the attached style sheet. Dreamweaver might display a warning about document-relative paths. This is nothing to worry about. Just dismiss the warning by clicking OK.

8. Save the new page as page2.html in workfiles/ch05. If your monitor is large enough, it should look like Figure 5-8. It has picked up all the styles from stroll.css, but what has happened to the header?

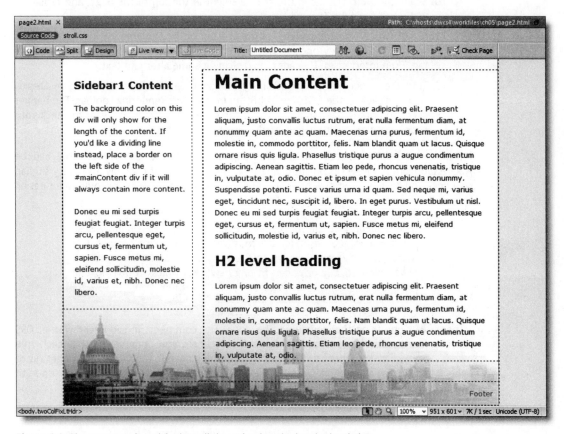

Figure 5-8. The new page has picked up all the styles, but the header is missing.

You can't see the header because the style rule for the <h1> heading was set to an absolute position of –500px from the top. You need to disable that rule temporarily to change the value of the header and insert the banner image.

> *If you're wondering why the background image doesn't make the header visible, it's because the <div> doesn't have a height. Absolute positioning removes the <h1> content from the flow of the document, and backgrounds don't show if an element doesn't have a height. Of course, a simple solution would be to add the height of stroll_header.jpg to the style rule for the header <div>, but I want to show you another technique.*

9. Select View ➤ Style Rendering ➤ Display Styles. Alternatively, if you have enabled the Style Rendering toolbar (see Figure 4-18) as described in the previous chapter, click the CSS On/Off button. This temporarily disables CSS in Design view.

10. Select the word Header in the <h1> element at the top of the page, and replace it with Stroll Along the Thames.

11. Select <h1> in the Tag selector at the bottom of the Document window, and press your right arrow key once to move the insertion point outside the closing </h1> tag. Then insert stroll_header.jpg, giving it some alternate text.

12. Turn the display of CSS back on by selecting View ➤ Style Rendering ➤ Display Styles or clicking the CSS On/Off button in the Style Rendering toolbar. The banner at the top of the page should now be correctly displayed. If you want to check your code, compare it with page2.html in examples/ch05.

That concludes this exercise in transforming one of the 32 CSS layouts that can be accessed from the New Document dialog box. The structure of each layout is very similar, so once you have learned how to adapt one, working with the others becomes a lot easier.

> As I mentioned at the beginning of this chapter, Dreamweaver remembers your last choice in most dialog boxes. Don't forget that stroll.css is now listed in the New Document dialog box and will be automatically attached to any new page unless you remove it from the Attach CSS file field.

There's just one thing that remains to be done. The comments in the Dreamweaver CSS layouts are deliberately verbose—they're there to help you understand what each rule does. Although commenting style sheets is a good idea, you'll probably want to get rid of the Dreamweaver comments once you're familiar with the layouts. It's easy to do with Dreamweaver's Find and Replace feature.

Using Find and Replace

Dreamweaver's Find and Replace feature is very powerful, so it's useful to get to know how it works. In many ways, it's similar to the Find and Replace feature in word processing programs such as Microsoft Word, but it has dedicated features designed for working with HTML and other web-related languages. It not only searches code and text, but you can get it to search for specific attributes in tags or for tags that have a missing attribute. And if that's not enough for you, it will perform the same search on multiple files or even through the whole current site.

To launch Find and Replace, select Edit ➤ Find and Replace, or press Ctrl+F/Cmd+F. This opens the dialog box shown in Figure 5-9.

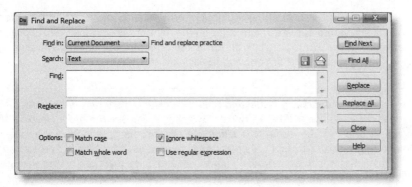

Figure 5-9. The Find and Replace dialog box enables you to perform sophisticated searches.

The basic dialog box has the following options:

- Find in: This determines the broad scope of the search. The options are as follows:

    - Current Document: This is limited to the document that currently has focus in the Document window. It does not include files listed in the Related Files toolbar.

    - Selected Text: This limits the scope to highlighted text or code.

    - Open Documents: This applies not only to documents currently open in the Document window but also to files listed in the Related Files toolbar.

    - Folder: When you select this option, a field opens alongside for you to enter the name of the folder you want to search. A folder icon alongside the field opens the Choose Search Folder dialog box for you to navigate to the folder.

    - Selected Files in Site: This searches within files that have been selected in the Files panel. Related files are not included.

    - Entire Current Local Site: Use this to search the entire site.

- Search: This narrows the scope of the search. The options are as follows:

    - Text: This limits the search to text that can be seen in Design view. In other words, tags and attributes are excluded.

    - Source Code: This searches everything, including text, tags, attributes, comments, JavaScript, and server-side code.

    - Text (Advanced): This allows you to narrow your search for text to specific parts of a page. For example, you can search for a word or phrase that appears in an `<h3>` tag but ignore all other instances.

    - Specific Tag: This looks for specific tags with or without specified attributes.

- Find: This is what you want to search for.

- Replace: This is what you want to replace the search term with. You don't need to enter anything in this field if you're just doing a search.

- Options: Most of these are self-explanatory. The Use regular expression checkbox lets you perform complex searches using Perl-compatible regular expressions (regex), a powerful pattern-matching language. You'll see how this works in an exercise later in this chapter.

5

The two icons at the top right of the text area where you enter the search term are for saving and loading stored queries. The buttons on the right of the Find and Replace dialog box are self-explanatory. The dialog box performs the dual purpose of simply finding something or finding specific text or code and replacing it.

> *Dreamweaver is capable of conducting Find and Replace operations in documents that are not currently open in the Document window. If you set the broad scope of the search in the* Find in *menu to include closed documents and click* Replace All, *Dreamweaver warns you that the operation cannot be undone. This is a very powerful but potentially dangerous feature. It's a good idea to make a backup of your site before altering a large number of documents without first checking the effect such changes will have. There isn't a simple undo command for changes to open documents. However, if you save them before running Find and Replace, you can either close the documents without saving the changes or select* File ➤ Revert. *This discards all changes to a document and restores it to its last saved state.*

As you can see, there are many options. Let's start by looking at how to perform a basic search.

Searching for text

Searching for text is quite simple. The Find and Replace feature works just like it does in most word processors. Since this option is limited to Design view, it's not available if the current document contains only code (for example, a style sheet or JavaScript file). The basic procedure is as follows:

1. Launch Find and Replace (Edit ➤ Find and Replace or Ctrl+F/Cmd+F).

2. Set the broad scope of the search with the Find in menu, as described in the preceding section.

3. Set the Search menu to Text.

4. Type the text you're searching for in the Find field.

5. Enter the replacement text (if any) in the Replace field.

6. Select any options by putting a check mark in the appropriate checkbox. Make sure that Use regular expression is *unchecked*.

7. Choose the appropriate button on the right to perform the operation you want.

You can step through the Find and Replace process one instance at a time by using the Find Next and Replace buttons. This gives you the opportunity to inspect each instance before replacing it. Alternatively, if you just want to find all instances, click Find All. If you're happy to do a global replace operation without checking, click Replace All.

As soon as you click one of the buttons (except for Close and Help), the Results panel springs open and lists the items found or replaced. Some people find this intensely annoying, particularly on a small monitor, but you cannot disable this behavior. To minimize the Results panel, click the dark gray bar anywhere to the right of the tabs, or press F7.

Searching source code

Searching the source code is identical to searching for text, except for step 3, where you should choose Source Code from the Search menu. The important thing to remember about selecting this option is that it searches everything, regardless of whether it's part of code or text. Also, searching the source code of any document that's currently open includes the code in all files listed in the Related Files toolbar.

Searching text and source code

If you're not careful, a Find and Replace operation can alter your HTML in unintended ways. The following exercise demonstrates the difference between searching text and source code, and it demonstrates the danger of choosing the wrong one. The download files in examples/ch05 contain two files called search_me.html and search_me.css, which are copies of the finished exercise file from Chapter 4. You'll discard the changes to the files at the end of the exercise, so you can work on them in their current location.

1. Open search_me.html in the Document window, and launch Find and Replace by selecting Find ➤ Find and Replace or pressing Ctrl+F/Cmd+F.

2. Use the following settings:

   - Find in: Current Document
   - Search: Text
   - Find: graffiti
   - Replace: doodle

3. Click Replace All.

4. The Results panel opens at the bottom of the Workspace, as shown in Figure 5-10.

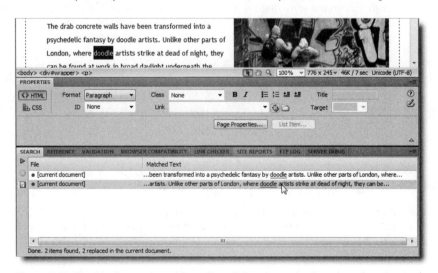

Figure 5-10. The Results panel provides a direct link to items that have been found and replaced.

At the bottom of the panel, it reports how many items have been found and replaced (if you're searching multiple files, it also reports how many documents it searched). In the body of the panel, it shows the replaced text in context and underlined in red. Double-click one of the results, and Dreamweaver selects the text in the Document window, as shown in Figure 5-10.

5. To discard the changes, select File ➤ Revert. When prompted, confirm that you want to revert to the previously saved version and lose the changes.

6. Open the Find and Replace dialog box again by clicking the right-facing green arrow on the left of the Results panel, just below the Search tab.

7. Use the same settings as in step 2, except change the Search menu from Text to Source Code.

8. Click Replace All.

9. This time, Split view opens because the search has been conducted in the underlying code, and four items are listed in the Results panel. Double-click the first one, and you'll see that the name of graffiti.jpg has been changed to doodle.jpg. The word graffiti has also been changed in the image's alt attribute.

   The two remaining instances are the same as before, confirming that Source Code means *both* code and text.

10. Discard the changes by selecting File ➤ Revert.

11. Open the Find and Replace dialog box again. Leave Find in and Search at Current Document and Source Code, respectively. Enter h1 in the Find field. It doesn't matter what's in the Replace field.

12. Click Find All. The Results panel should show two items: the opening and closing <h1> tags around Stroll Along the Thames.

13. Change Find in to Open Documents, and click Find All again.

14. This time the Results panel reports four items; two of them are in search_me.css. Even though the style sheet is not open in a tab of its own, it's listed in the Related Files toolbar so is considered to be an open document. Of course, this won't happen if you have disabled the Related Files feature in the Preferences panel.

> *In addition to providing a direct link to items that have been found and replaced, the* Results *panel lets you upload the amended files directly to your remote server. Just select the file in the* Results *panel, right-click, and select* Put *from the context menu.*

Performing advanced text searches

The options in the Find and Replace dialog box change when you select Text (Advanced) or Specific Tag in the Search menu. The following screenshot shows what the dialog box looks like when you first select Text (Advanced):

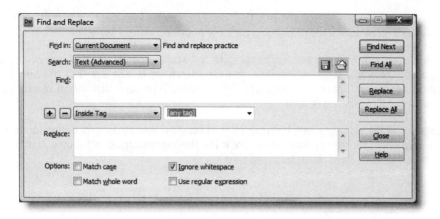

The new menu inserted between the Find and Replace fields has two options: Inside Tag and Not Inside Tag. The drop-down menu alongside lists all valid tags. So, for example, you could select Inside Tag and table, and the search would be confined to text in a table. Alternatively, Not Inside Tag and table would ignore any matching text in a table but would search for matches elsewhere.

If you click the plus (+) button alongside the menu between the Find and Replace fields, a new set of options is added, as shown in the next screenshot:

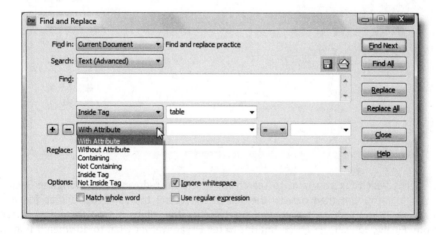

The related fields depend on which option you choose, as follows:

- With/Without Attribute: This lets you choose an attribute, a comparison operator, and a value. The comparison operator can be set to equal to, greater than, less than, or not equal to.

- Containing/Not Containing: This offers two choices: Text or Specific Tag. If you choose Text, you enter the text in the adjacent field. If you choose Specific Tag, the adjacent field turns into a drop-down menu listing valid tags.

- Inside/Not Inside Tag: The adjacent field turns into a drop-down menu listing valid tags.

You can continue adding refinements to your search by clicking the plus button again. If you decide to remove a set of options, click the minus (–) button alongside.

Using the options, you can build quite complex text search operations. However, you need to specify individual tags. For instance, you can search for text in any <h1> heading, but you cannot search for text in a range of heading levels. To perform that sort of search, you need to use a regular expression.

Although all the settings relate to tags and attributes, the Text (Advanced) option looks for text only within those tags. You cannot use it for altering the tags or attributes. That's the job of the Specific Tag option described next.

Performing complex replacements with specific tags

The Specific Tag option in the Search menu lets you drill down into your code to look for a particular tag and perform a replace operation on it. For example, you might want to search your code to insert an empty alt attribute in <img> tags that don't have one.

Selecting the Specific Tag option changes the Find and Replace dialog box like this:

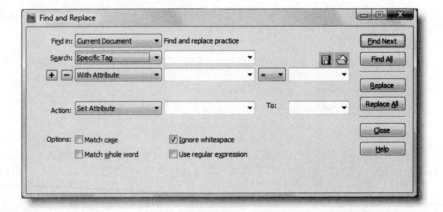

You specify which tag you want to search for in the drop-down menu alongside Search Specific Tag. You can then narrow the search by setting the same options as for Text (Advanced). If you just want a general search, click the minus button to remove those options. Finally, you set the Action options to tell Dreamweaver what to do when it finds a matching tag.

The options offered by the Action menu differ according to your previous selections, but they include the following:

- Replace Tag & Contents
- Replace Contents Only
- Remove Tag & Contents

- Strip Tag: This removes the tag but leaves the contents.
- Change Tag: For example, you could change <h1> tags to <h2>.
- Set Attribute
- Remove Attribute
- Add Before/After Start Tag: This inserts text or code immediately preceding or after the opening tag.
- Add Before/After End Tag: This inserts text or code immediately preceding or after the closing tag.

Specific tag Find and Replace operations are particularly powerful when used in combination with regular expressions, which you'll look into in more detail now.

Using regular expressions in searches

Regular expressions (often shortened to **regexes**) describe patterns of text and other characters. They are like wildcard characters but much more powerful. Regular expressions use character sequences known as **metacharacters** to represent different types of characters that you want to match in a pattern. Table 5-1 lists the most commonly used.

Table 5-1. Commonly used character sequences in regular expressions

Sequence	Meaning	Sequence	Meaning
\n	Newline character	*	Match zero or more times
\r	Carriage return	+	Match at least once
\w	Alphanumeric character or underscore	?	Match zero or one time
\d	Number	{n}	Match exactly *n* times
\s	Whitespace	{n,}	Match at least *n* times
.	Any character, except new line	{x,y}	Match at least *x* times, but no more than *y* times
\.	Period (dot)	*?	Match zero or more times but as few as possible
^	Beginning of a string	+?	Match one or more times but as few as possible
$	End of a string		

Learning how to use regular expressions is not easy, but it's a skill worth acquiring, because regexes are widely used in programming languages such as JavaScript and PHP. There are two types of regex: Perl-compatible regular expressions (PCRE) and Portable Operating System Interface (POSIX). Dreamweaver uses the Perl-compatible type, which is more efficient and also the preferred type in PHP. To learn more about regexes, see *Regular Expression Recipes: A Problem-Solution Approach* by Nathan A. Good (Apress, ISBN: 978-1-59059-441-4). The standard work (not for faint hearts) is *Mastering Regular Expressions, Third Edition* by Jeffrey Friedl (O'Reilly, ISBN: 978-0-59652-812-6). You can also learn about regexes online at `www.regular-expressions.info`, and there's a repository of regexes (some good, some not so good) at `http://regexlib.com/`.

> *There are a couple of important differences about the way Dreamweaver uses regular expressions in the* Find and Replace *dialog box. Perl-compatible regular expressions are normally enclosed in a pair of characters known as **delimiters** (forward slashes are used the most frequently, but you can use any nonalphanumeric character). You omit the delimiters when using a regex in Dreamweaver. This also means you cannot use any of the modifiers that follow the closing delimiter.*

In spite of the difficulty of regular expressions, as you'll see from the following exercise, they can do some amazing things.

Automatically adding a title attribute to images

Many designers like to display the alternate text of an image as a tooltip when the user moves the mouse pointer over the image. Internet Explorer does this automatically with the alt attribute, but this is actually incorrect behavior. Other browsers use the title attribute instead. So, if the title attribute is missing, no tooltip appears. This exercise shows you how to use regular expressions to copy the content of every image's alt attribute to its title attribute.

1. Open search_me.html from the previous exercise in the Document window (it's in examples/ch05).

2. Select one of the images in Design view, and click the Split View button to inspect the underlying code. You should be able to see that it contains an alt attribute but not a title one. Do the same with the other image.

3. Launch the Find and Replace dialog box (Edit ➤ Find and Replace or Ctrl+F/Cmd+F).

4. Use the following settings:

   - Find in: Current Document
   - Search: Specific Tag

5. Activate the drop-down menu alongside Specific Tag, and select img.

6. Set the option immediately below to With Attribute (if there's no option available between Search and Action, click the plus button, and select With Attribute from the menu that appears).

7. Select alt from the menu alongside With Attribute, set the comparison operator to the equal sign (=), and enter (.+) in the next field. The opening parenthesis, period, plus symbol, and closing parenthesis is a regex that copies any value as long as it contains at least one character.

8. Select Set Attribute from the Action menu, select title from the drop-down menu alongside, and enter $1 in the To field. $1 is a regular expression that contains the value captured by the first regex.

9. Select the Use regular expression checkbox. The settings in the Find and Replace dialog box should now look like this:

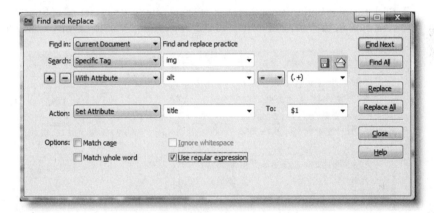

10. Click Replace All. The Results panel should open and report that two replacements have been made. Double-click one of them to confirm that the content of the alt attribute has been copied to a new title attribute.

11. You'll use the same file in the next exercise, so restore the page to its original state by selecting File ➤ Revert and confirming that you want to abandon the changes.

Preventing an existing title from being overwritten

Being able to copy the value of a tag's alt attribute into its title attribute is pretty impressive, but you probably don't want to overwrite any existing title values. This exercise improves on the settings used in the previous exercise to skip images that already have a title attribute, thereby preserving the original value.

1. Continue working with search_me.html from the previous exercise. Let's begin by making sure that empty alt attributes aren't copied.

2. Select one of the images in Design view, click the little arrow in the Alt field in the Property inspector to open the drop-down menu, and select <empty>. This sets the alt attribute to alt="".

3. Open the Find and Replace dialog box. Dreamweaver should have remembered the previous settings, so click Replace All. If it hasn't remembered the settings, use those shown in step 9 of the previous exercise.

This time, the Results panel should report only one replacement. The image with the empty alt attribute was ignored. That's good but still not perfect. You need to make sure that existing title attributes are not overwritten.

4. Restore the page to its original state by selecting File ➤ Revert.

5. Select one of the images. The Property inspector doesn't have a field to set the title attribute. You could use the Tag Inspector panel, but it's probably quicker to dive into Code view and add a title attribute to one of the images. It doesn't matter what value you give it, as long as it's different from the alt attribute.

6. Open the Find and Replace dialog box. It should still have the previous settings.

7. Click the plus button alongside With Attribute to add a new set of options. Set the new options to Without Attribute and title. The settings should now look like this:

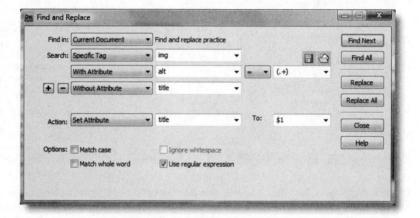

8. Click Replace All. This time, the Results panel should report just one replacement: the image that you didn't add a title attribute to. Check the other image to make sure its original title is still intact.

9. You can close search_me.html without saving the changes, but don't make any changes to the settings in the Find and Replace dialog box just yet.

If you think that's useful, it gets even better. You can store Find and Replace operations for future use, as described in the next section.

Saving queries for future use

The two icons at the top right of the Find and Replace dialog box (see alongside) are for working with stored queries. The icon that looks like a floppy disk (remember them?) launches the Save Query dialog box. When you have a query you want to store for future use, click this icon, navigate to a folder where you want to store the query (it doesn't need to be in a Dreamweaver site), and give the query a name that will help you remember what its purpose is. Dreamweaver automatically gives it a .dwr file name extension. I have saved the query in step 7 of the previous exercise as add_title.dwr in examples/ch05.

Crafting a regular expression to perform a complex query requires a lot of patience and experimentation. Saving the query to a .dwr file can save a lot of heartache if you accidentally delete the regex in the Find and Replace dialog box. Save early, and save often.

Once you have saved a query, all you need to do is click the icon that looks like a folder with a sheet of paper protruding from it. This opens the Load Query dialog box. Navigate to the folder where you keep your stored queries, select the one you want, and click Open. Dreamweaver loads the query into the Find and Replace dialog box ready to run. That's all there is to it.

Using a stored query to remove CSS comments

Now that you know all about Find and Replace, regular expressions, and stored queries, you can strip the verbose comments from the style sheet created by the Dreamweaver CSS layout in the exercises in the first half of this chapter.

The regex to describe a CSS comment looks like this:

```
/\*[\s\S]+?(?=\*/)\*/
```

Because this regex is so useful—and easy to mistype—I have created a stored query to automate the process. It's called css_comment_remover_v3.dwr and is in the examples/ ch05 folder. Simply load it as described in the previous section. To remove all the CSS comments in a single operation, click Replace All. This removes *all* comments, including any CSS hacks that look like comments. If you're in any way uncertain, remove the comments selectively by clicking Find Next to highlight the first one. Then click Replace to remove it or Find Next to move to the next one.

Dreamweaver always remembers your last Find and Replace operation, so these settings will be displayed the next time you open the Find and Replace dialog box. Delete the regular expression from the Find field, and *deselect* the Use regular expression checkbox (unless you plan to use another regex). This final point is very important. When a Find operation fails for no obvious reason, it's usually because you have selected the Use regular expression checkbox by accident.

Chapter review

Depending on your knowledge of CSS, this chapter is likely to have been relatively easy or something of a nightmare. If you fall into the latter category, I encourage you to persevere. It can take a long time for CSS to sink in. If you find it difficult to understand how to build your own style sheets, download a page from a site you admire, complete with images and style sheets. Then use the CSS Styles panel to change or delete individual properties. Watch the effect of each change. Also select different parts of the page to analyze the cascade of styles.

Mastering the CSS Styles panel takes time and patience, but it will reward you in the end. Remember that Current mode shows the cascade as it affects the current insertion point or selection. Use the Tag selector at the bottom of the Document window to highlight specific elements, and then use the Summary for Selection and Rules panes to drill down to the CSS rules you want to inspect or edit.

You'll get some more practice with the CSS Styles panel in the next chapter when you integrate a Spry menu bar into the page layout. The menu bar and other Spry widgets come with their own predefined style sheets, so you need to know how to adapt them to blend in with your own design.

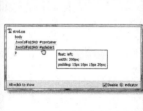

Efficient and attractive navigation is an important element in every website. The Spry menu bar combines CSS and JavaScript (using Spry, Adobe's implementation of Ajax) to create a flexible menu with flyout submenus that remains accessible even if JavaScript is turned off. In essence, it's an unordered list with optional nested lists for submenus. It comes in two versions: horizontal and vertical. Figure 6-1 shows what the horizontal version of the Spry menu bar looks like when integrated into the page built in the previous chapter.

Figure 6-1. You can easily integrate the Spry menu bar into a page by making a few adjustments to the CSS.

Although you can insert a Spry menu bar in seconds, the downside is that styling it requires a good understanding of CSS. Knowing which style rules to change—and which to leave alone—presents more of a challenge. This process has been made considerably easier in Dreamweaver CS4 by the introduction of Live view and Code Navigator.

In this chapter, you'll learn about the following:

- The structure of the Spry menu bar
- How to insert and remove a Spry menu bar
- The style rules that control a Spry menu bar
- How to customize a Spry menu bar using Live view and Code Navigator

By the end of the chapter, you'll be able to transform the rather bland default design of a menu bar into something much more elegant like the menu in Figure 6-1. Because the Spry menu bar is styled with CSS, this chapter assumes you're familiar with the CSS Styles panel, which was described in detail in Chapter 4.

Examining the structure of a Spry menu bar

The Spry menu bar relies on external files to control the way it looks and works, so you must always save your page in a Dreamweaver site (see Chapter 2 for how to define a site) before attempting to insert a menu bar. If you forget, Dreamweaver tells you to save your page and opens the Save As dialog box.

The best way to understand how a Spry menu bar works is to launch Dreamweaver and start experimenting.

Inserting a horizontal menu bar

This brief exercise takes you through the steps of inserting a horizontal Spry menu bar in a new page.

1. Create a blank HTML page in Dreamweaver by selecting File ➤ New. In the New Document dialog box, select Blank Page, HTML for Page Type, and <none> for Layout. Make sure that no style sheets are listed under Attach CSS file before clicking Create. Alternatively, just select New ➤ HTML from the welcome screen. Save the file as horiz.html in workfiles/ch06.

2. Select the Spry tab on the Insert bar, and click the Spry Menu Bar button (it's the fifth from the right), as shown in the following screenshot:

3. This opens the Spry Menu Bar dialog box. There are just two options: Horizontal and Vertical. Select Horizontal, and click OK.

4. Dreamweaver inserts a horizontal Spry menu bar at the top of the page, as shown in Figure 6-2. Like all Spry widgets, the menu bar is surrounded in Design view by a turquoise border and a tab at the top-left corner. The tab tells you what type of widget it is, followed by the widget's id attribute. Dreamweaver calls the first menu bar on a page MenuBar1. The next one is MenuBar2, and so on. This means you can have as many menu bars on a page as you want (don't go mad—think of usability).

Figure 6-2. The Spry menu bar is given basic styling ready for you to customize.

5. Notice that the Related Files toolbar lists two files: `SpryMenuBar.js` and `SpryMenuBarHorizontal.css`. Until you save the page, these are temporary files. You can verify this by switching to Code view and inspecting the code in the <head> of the page, as in Figure 6-3.

```
5  <title>Untitled Document</title>
6  <script src="file:///C|/Users/Work/AppData/Roaming/Adobe/Dreamweaver
   CS4/en_US/Configuration/Temp/Assets/eam8AB9.tmp/SpryMenuBar.js" type="text/javascript"></script>
7  <link href="file:///C|/Users/Work/AppData/Roaming/Adobe/Dreamweaver
   CS4/en_US/Configuration/Temp/Assets/eam8AB9.tmp/SpryMenuBarHorizontal.css" rel="stylesheet" type=
   "text/css" />
8  </head>
```

Figure 6-3. Dreamweaver uses temporary files for the style sheet and JavaScript until you save the page.

As you can see on lines 6 and 7 in Figure 6-3, the links to the external JavaScript file and style sheet point to a temporary folder on my local hard disk. Therefore, it's essential to save the file before doing anything else. Otherwise, any changes you make to the style sheet are likely to be lost. Moreover, the menu won't work unless the files are saved to your Dreamweaver site.

6. Save `horiz.html`. If this is the first time you have inserted a Spry menu bar in the current site, you are prompted to save the dependent files (see Figure 6-4).

Figure 6-4. The Spry files need to be copied to your site the first time you insert a menu bar.

As you can see in Figure 6-4, four images are also copied to your site. These are the navigation arrows that appear on submenus. When you click OK, Dreamweaver locates the files in the Spry assets folder. By default, this is called `SpryAssets`, but you can specify a different location in your site definition (see "Setting other site options" in Chapter 2). Once the files have been copied to the Spry assets folder, they are shared with further instances of the menu bar in the same site.

7. Click the Live View button in the Document toolbar, and run your mouse pointer over the menu bar. As you can see in Figure 6-5, you already have a menu bar ready to customize.

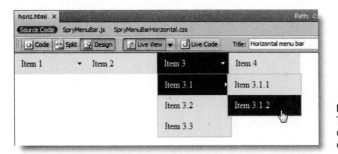

Figure 6-5.
The structure and styling of the default menu bar are fully customizable.

Inserting a vertical menu bar is the same. The only differences are that you select the Vertical radio button in step 3 and Dreamweaver inserts SpryMenuBarVertical.css instead of the style sheet for the horizontal menu bar. The menu items in the vertical menu bar are stacked vertically, and the first-level submenus fly out to the right rather than beneath the main menu, as shown in the screenshot alongside.

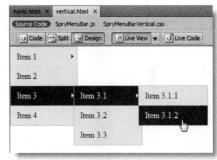

Looking at the menu bar's structure

The Spry menu bar is a series of nested unordered lists (<ul>) styled with CSS to look like a series of buttons. The submenu flyouts are controlled by JavaScript. You can see the underlying structure of the menu either by switching to Code view or by toggling the Turn Styles Off/On button in the Property inspector. (If you can't see the button, click the Spry Menu Bar tab at the top left of the menu bar.) Figure 6-6 shows the horizontal menu bar in horiz.html, but the structure is identical in a vertical menu. The different look and functionality are controlled entirely by JavaScript and CSS.

Click this tab to display the menu bar details in the Property inspector

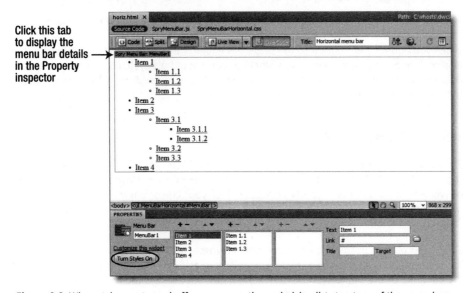

Figure 6-6. When styles are turned off, you can see the underlying list structure of the menu bar.

6

Figure 6-7 shows the same menu in Code view. The code on lines 6 and 7 link the external JavaScript file and style sheet to the page. The unordered list that contains the menu bar is on lines 11–33. The block of JavaScript at the foot of the page on lines 34–38 initializes the JavaScript object that controls the menu.

```
 5   <title>Horizontal menu bar</title>
 6   <script src="../../SpryAssets/SpryMenuBar.js" type="text/javascript"></script>
 7   <link href="../../SpryAssets/SpryMenuBarHorizontal_stroll.css" rel="stylesheet" type="text/css" />
 8   </head>
 9
10   <body>
11   <ul id="MenuBar1" class="MenuBarHorizontal">
12     <li><a class="MenuBarItemSubmenu" href="#">Item 1</a>
13        <ul>
14          <li><a href="#">Item 1.1</a></li>
15          <li><a href="#">Item 1.2</a></li>
16          <li><a href="#">Item 1.3</a></li>
17        </ul>
18     </li>
19     <li><a href="#">Item 2</a></li>
20     <li><a class="MenuBarItemSubmenu" href="#">Item 3</a>
21        <ul>
22          <li><a class="MenuBarItemSubmenu" href="#">Item 3.1</a>
23             <ul>
24               <li><a href="#">Item 3.1.1</a></li>
25               <li><a href="#">Item 3.1.2</a></li>
26             </ul>
27          </li>
28          <li><a href="#">Item 3.2</a></li>
29          <li><a href="#">Item 3.3</a></li>
30        </ul>
31     </li>
32     <li><a href="#">Item 4</a></li>
33   </ul>
34   <script type="text/javascript">
35   <!--
36   var MenuBar1 = new Spry.Widget.MenuBar("MenuBar1", {imgDown:"../../SpryAssets/SpryMenuBarDownHover.gif",
     imgRight:"../../SpryAssets/SpryMenuBarRightHover.gif"});
37   //-->
38   </script>
39   </body>
40   </html>
```

Figure 6-7. The scripts at the top and bottom of the page control the menu's look and action.

When you add further content to the page, this initialization script remains just before the closing </body> tag. If a menu stops working, you should always check that you haven't deleted the initialization script by mistake. If you have, you need to go back and reinsert the menu from scratch.

Editing a menu bar

Since the menu bar is just a series of nested unordered lists, you can turn off the styles, as shown in Figure 6-6, and edit the menu directly in Design view. However, it's much more convenient to do it in the Property inspector. Place your cursor anywhere inside the menu bar, and click the Spry Menu Bar tab at the top left to display the menu bar details in the Property inspector.

The three columns in the center of the Property inspector show the menu hierarchy, with the top level on the left. When you select an item in this column, the middle one displays the contents of the related submenu. The right column displays the next level down from whatever is selected in the middle one.

To edit a menu item, highlight it, and fill in the fields on the right of the Property inspector as follows:

- Text: This is the label you want to appear on the menu button.
- Link: This is the page to which you want to link. Either type the file name directly into the field or click the folder icon to the right of the field to browse to the target page.
- Title: This adds a `title` attribute to the link. Most browsers display this as a tooltip. It can also improve accessibility for visually impaired people using a screen reader by describing the link's destination more fully.
- Target: This adds a `target` attribute to the link. This was originally designed for use with frames. A value of _blank opens the linked page in a new browser window. Although there are sometimes legitimate reasons for opening a new window, it's rarely justified to do so from a site's navigation menu. The practice of using `target="_blank"` provokes a lot of heated debate, so use with care.

To add an item, click the plus (+) button at the top of the relevant column. To delete an item, select it and click the minus (–) button. You can also change the order of items by highlighting them and using the up and down arrows at the top of each column.

As Figure 6-6 shows, the Property inspector lets you work on two levels of submenus. To create a submenu at a deeper level, insert another nested list either by turning off styles as shown in Figure 6-6 or editing directly in Code view. Two levels of submenus should be sufficient for most purposes. If your menus require more levels, it's probably time to rethink the structure of your site.

After editing a menu bar, select one of the items in the left column before moving to another part of the page. If you forget to do this, the submenus remain exposed in Design view, preventing you from working on the underlying part of the page.

If this happens, position your cursor inside any part of the menu bar, and select the Spry Menu Bar tab at the top left. This populates the Property inspector with the menu bar details again. You can then select an item in the left column to hide the submenus.

Maintaining accessibility with the Spry menu bar

The Spry menu bar is much more accessible than the JavaScript pop-up menus in old versions of Dreamweaver, because the underlying structure and links are written in HTML, rather than being obscured in JavaScript that search engines can't follow. However, it's important to realize that JavaScript still controls the submenu flyouts. If someone visits your site with JavaScript disabled or an ancient browser that can't understand the Spry code, the only parts of the menu that remain accessible are the top-level items.

This means you should always link the top-level items to a real page and not just use dummy links to act as triggers for the submenus. So, for instance, if anyone clicks Attractions in the menu shown in Figure 6-1, it should link to an introductory page leading to that section. Unless you do so, some visitors may never be able to get to the pages about London Eye and so on.

6

Customizing the styles

Although the color scheme of the default style sheets isn't exactly inspiring, the structural layout has been carefully thought out, so you don't need to change many properties to achieve a rapid transformation of the menu bar. Select SpryMenuBarHorizontal.css in the Related Files toolbar, and take a look at how the style rules are divided into the following sections:

- **Layout Information**: This controls the structure, such as font size and menu widths.
- **Design Information**: This styles the color scheme and borders.
- **Submenu Indication**: The rules in this section control the display of the arrows that indicate the existence of a submenu. Change these only if you need to adjust the submenu arrows.
- **Browser Hacks**: These rules deal with bugs in Internet Explorer. You should leave them alone.

The style sheet for a vertical menu (SpryMenuBarVertical.css) is laid out in the same way. In fact, both style sheets contain almost identical rules, although the names of the CSS selectors reflect the orientation of the menu. The horizontal bar uses the class MenuBarHorizontal, and the vertical one uses MenuBarVertical.

Customizing the CSS rules requires a good understanding of the hierarchy within the menu bar's nested lists. The entire menu is contained in an unordered list, so all selectors begin with either ul.MenuBarHorizontal or ul.MenuBarVertical. Submenus are also unordered lists nested within the main one, so rules that apply to submenus all use ul.MenuBarHorizontal ul or ul.MenuBarVertical ul. However, the same rules apply to links in both the main menu and the submenu, so they use ul.MenuBarHorizontal a or ul.MenuBarVertical a.

There are a few other things to note:

- All the measurements use relative units (ems and percentages).
- The width of the horizontal menu is set to auto, but the vertical menu has a fixed width of 8em.
- The width of the menu items in both versions is fixed at 8em; submenus are 8.2em.

Changing the menu width

The use of ems for the width of the menu and submenu items makes the menu bar very fluid. As explained in Chapter 4, an em is a typographical term that has been borrowed by CSS to mean the height of the specified font. So, the width expands and contracts depending on the size chosen for the font. For a fixed layout, such as that used in stroll.html in the previous chapter, you need to change all instances of 8em and 8.2em in the Layout Information section to a fixed width in pixels.

Changing colors

All colors are defined in the Design Information section of the style sheet. Changing them is simply a matter of substituting the existing hexadecimal numbers for background-color and color in the relevant style rules. The default colors are light gray (#EEE) for the background and dark gray (#333) for the text of menu items in their normal state, and navy blue (#33C) for the background and white (#FFF) for the text of items in a rollover state.

The menu bar uses JavaScript to assign a class dynamically to the links when the mouse pointer moves over them. For some reason, Adobe has put the selectors for this dynamic class in a separate style rule, which duplicates the a:hover and a:focus rules like this:

```
ul.MenuBarHorizontal a:hover, ul.MenuBarHorizontal a:focus
{
  background-color: #33C;
  color: #FFF;
}
ul.MenuBarHorizontal a.MenuBarItemHover, ul.MenuBarHorizontal
a.MenuBarItemSubmenuHover, ul.MenuBarHorizontal a.MenuBarSubmenuVisible
{
  background-color: #33C;
  color: #FFF;
}
```

Since both rules contain the same properties and values, it's simpler to combine the selectors like this:

```
ul.MenuBarHorizontal a:hover, ul.MenuBarHorizontal a:focus,
ul.MenuBarHorizontal a.MenuBarItemHover, ul.MenuBarHorizontal
a.MenuBarItemSubmenuHover, ul.MenuBarHorizontal a.MenuBarSubmenuVisible
{
  background-color: #33C;
  color: #FFF;
}
```

Don't forget to add a comma after a:focus in the first line of the selector. Otherwise, it won't work. The equivalent rules for the vertical menu bar are identical, except for the class name MenuBarVertical.

Adding borders

By default, a light gray border is added to the outer edge of the submenu containers in both the horizontal and vertical menu bars. In addition, the vertical menu bar has the same border around the entire menu. Change the following rules to alter the menu and submenu borders:

```
ul.MenuBarHorizontal ul
ul.MenuBarVertical
ul.MenuBarVertical ul
```

6

Individual menu items don't have any borders, so the menu looks seamless. If you want to give your menu a more button-like feel, apply a border to the following rules:

```
ul.MenuBarHorizontal a
ul.MenuBarVertical a
```

The links in the menu bar are styled to display as a block and have no fixed width. Consequently, applying a border to the link style has the advantage of surrounding the individual menu items without affecting either height or width. You'll see how this is done when inserting a menu bar into stroll.html.

Changing the font

The font-size property is set to 100% in two separate rules: ul.MenuBarHorizontal and ul.MenuBarHorizontal li (ul.MenuBarVertical and ul.MenuBarVertical li). Change the wrong one and you get the mysterious shrinking text shown in Figure 6-8.

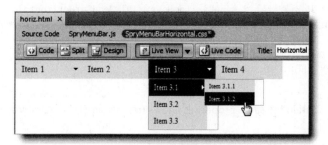

Figure 6-8. The text gets progressively smaller if you change font-size in the li selector.

The style rules that affect the size of the text in the horizontal menu bar are ul.MenuBarHorizontal and ul.MenuBarHorizontal li. Both of them set font-size to 100%. The shrinking text in Figure 6-8 was caused by changing font-size in ul.MenuBarHorizontal li to 85%.

Although this reduces the text in the main menu items to 85 percent of its original size, the nesting of the submenus results in the first-level submenu being displayed at 85 percent × 85 percent—in other words, 72.25 percent. The second-level submenu is further reduced by another 85 percent—resulting in 61.4 percent.

To prevent this happening, leave the ul.MenuBar Horizontal li selector at 100%, and change only the first one. The following rules produce a consistent text size:

```
ul.MenuBarHorizontal
{
  font-size: 85%;
}
ul.MenuBarHorizontal li
{
  font-size: 100%;
}
```

The rules for the vertical menu bar are identical, except for the class name MenuBarVertical.

If you decide to use pixels instead of percentages, it doesn't matter which rule you change. You should be aware, however, that using pixels for fonts can cause accessibility problems for people with poor eyesight. Many designers mistakenly believe that using pixels for font sizes "locks" their design. It doesn't, because all browsers—apart from Internet Explorer for Windows—permit users to adjust font sizes by default, and Internet Explorer's accessibility features have an option to ignore font sizes. If a change in font size causes your page to fall apart, you need to rethink your design criteria—fast.

Styling a Spry menu bar

If you're completely at home editing style sheets in Code view, the preceding sections tell you all you need to know about customizing the CSS for a Spry menu bar. With the Related Files feature enabled, you can edit the style rules in the Code view section of Split view and monitor the changes by refreshing the Design view section of the Document window. I'm going to devote the rest of the chapter to showing you how to add a horizontal menu bar to stroll.html, the CSS layout that you styled in the previous chapter. You can see the finished menu in Figure 6-1 at the beginning of this chapter.

To wrap or not to wrap, that is the question . . .

When I started working with Spry, my first instinct was to use the horizontal Spry menu bar without a <div>. After all, it's an unordered list, which is a block element, and it has its own ID, so it should be possible to drop one into a page without the need for a wrapper. After much experimentation, though, I discovered that a horizontal menu bar in a fixed-width design like stroll.html behaves unpredictably in some older browsers unless you wrap it in a <div> with both a specified width and height. The height is needed because all the menu items are floated.

Inserting the horizontal menu bar

Continue working with your files from the previous chapter. Alternatively, copy stroll_horiz_start.html and stroll_horiz_start.css from examples/ch06 to workfiles/ch06. Rename the files stroll_horiz.html and stroll_horiz.css, and update any links when prompted.

1. With stroll_horiz.html open in the Document window, select the Common or Layout tab of the Insert bar, and click the Insert Div Tag button.

2. You're going to insert the <div> to accommodate the Spry menu beneath the header <div>, so use the following settings in the Insert Div Tag dialog box (refer to Chapter 3 if you need to refresh your memory about inserting a <div>):

3. Click the New CSS Rule button at the bottom of the Insert Div Tag dialog box.

4. The New CSS Rule dialog box should automatically be populated with the correct values for Selector Type and Selector Name, but you should make sure that Rule Definition is set to the existing style sheet (stroll.css). Check that your values are the same as in Figure 6-9, and then click OK to accept.

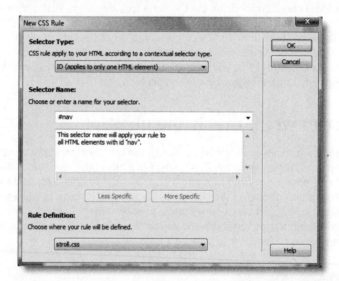

Figure 6-9. The settings for creating the style rule for the nav <div>

5. In the CSS Rule Definition dialog box, select the Box category, where you need to set the width and height for the nav <div>. The width is easy; it needs to be the same as the container <div> that wraps the page content: 780px. This ensures the menu bar will remain snugly in the <div>, even if the user increases the font size. I calculated the height by adding together the top and bottom padding (0.5em each) for the links in the menu bar. The font-size property is set to 100%, which is the same as 1em. That makes 2em. After testing, I decided to add an extra .2em to make sure everything fits. Using relative units for the height ensures that the <div> expands vertically to accommodate enlarged text.

Set Width to 780px and Height to 2.2em. Click OK to save the rule. This returns you to the Insert Div Tag dialog box. Click OK again to close it. You should now have a <div> with some placeholder text in it just beneath the header, as shown here:

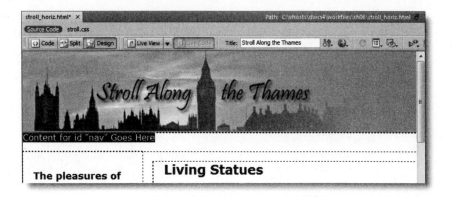

> When using a vertical menu bar, you can simply drop it into a sidebar, which provides the necessary wrapper. Unless the sidebar is particularly wide, there is no need for a separate `<div>` for the menu itself.

6. You need to get rid of the placeholder text for the nav `<div>`. Normally, pressing Delete when the text is highlighted is sufficient. However, it's a good idea to open Split view to make sure that it's only the text between the `<div>` tags that is selected.

If necessary, go into Code view to adjust the selection, and press Delete. Make sure your cursor is between the empty `<div>` tags.

7. Click the Spry Menu Bar button on the Spry tab of the Insert bar (it's also on the Layout tab), and insert a horizontal menu bar.

8. Save `stroll_horiz.html`. If you did the other exercises earlier in this chapter, Dreamweaver won't prompt you to save dependent files this time, because they have already been copied to the Spry assets folder. The top of your page should now look like Figure 6-10.

Figure 6-10. The Spry menu bar needs to be restyled to fit into the rest of the page.

9. Select the Spry Menu Bar tab, and edit the menu items as described in "Editing a menu bar" earlier in the chapter. If you want to follow my structure, here it is:

```
Home
Food & Drink
    Restaurants
    Bars
Attractions
    London Eye
    Aquarium
    South Bank
        Royal Festival Hall
        Hayward Gallery
        Tate Modern
Bridges
History
    St Paul's Cathedral
    Tower of London
    Houses of Parliament
```

In a live website, you need to create links to real pages, but for the purposes of the example page, I have left the value of each link as # so the menu bar displays correctly, even though it doesn't link to other pages.

10. If you have used the same menu structure as me, you'll see that a long item, such as Food & Drink, wraps onto a second line. This pushes the sidebar across to the right, as shown in Figure 6-11.

Figure 6-11. Long menu items prevent subsequent floated elements from moving to the left of the viewport.

To rectify this, you need to add clear: left to the sidebar's style block. This is necessary because both the menu buttons and the sidebar are floated, so the sidebar tries to move into the nearest available space. By adding clear: left, the sidebar is instructed to move below any previously floated elements and go to the left side of its parent, the container <div>.

Hold down the Alt key on Windows or Opt+Cmd on a Mac, and click anywhere inside the sidebar to launch the Code Navigator.

The Code Navigator displays the names of all CSS selectors that apply to the section of the page that you clicked. Each selector displayed in the Code Navigator is a link that shows the existing properties and values. Click the link for the .twoColFixLtHdr #sidebar1 selector, as shown here:

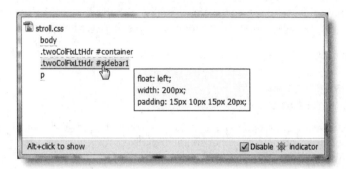

11. This opens the style sheet in Split view, with your cursor in the selected rule ready to edit it. Add clear: left; to the .twoColFixLtHdr #sidebar1 rule, and press F5 to refresh Design view. You should see the sidebar move to its correct position, as shown in Figure 6-12.

Figure 6-12. Pressing F5 after editing a style rule in Split view lets you see the effect instantly.

12. Select File ➤ Save All to save the changes to both stroll_horiz.html and stroll.css.

Customizing the design

If you test the page in Live view or a browser, you have a navigation bar, but it looks pretty ugly. The challenge is to customize the CSS to fit the rest of the page. This involves two basic stages, namely:

- Adjusting the width of the menu items so that the navigation bar stretches the full width of the page. The submenus have a separate width so that needs to be adjusted too.

- Changing the colors so they blend in harmoniously with the rest of the page. At the same time, you can add borders to the items to make them look more like buttons.

First, though, you need to do a little housekeeping with the menu's style sheet.

Editing the default selectors

All style rules exclusive to the menu bar are in SpryMenuBarHorizontal.css in the Spry assets folder. Since this is common to all horizontal menu bars, it's a good idea to give it a different name. Also, as I mentioned earlier, the rollover colors for the submenus are declared in a separate style rule. Unless you want them to be different from the main menu items, it makes life a little easier to combine them into a single rule.

1. Select SpryMenuBarHorizontal.css in the SpryAssets folder in the Files panel, and gently click the file name once to open its name for editing (alternatively, press F2, or right-click and select Edit ➤ Rename from the context menu). Change the style sheet's name to SpryMenuBarHorizontal_stroll.css, and press Enter/Return.

   Accept the option to update links when prompted. This updates the link to the external style sheet in both horiz.html and stroll_horiz.html. Since horiz.html was only a test page, it doesn't matter on this occasion, but in a working project, you need to check which links are being updated.

2. Open stroll_horiz.html in Code view. As explained in the previous chapter, Dreamweaver adds new style sheets immediately before the closing </head> tag. This puts the styles in SpryMenuBarHorizontal_stroll.css lower in the cascade than the style rules in the conditional comments. Although nothing is likely to clash, it's good practice to cut and paste the link above the conditional comments. Place it immediately after the link to stroll_horiz.css.

3. Select SpryMenuBarHorizontal_stroll.css in the Related Files toolbar, and locate the following section:

```
98    /* Menu items that have mouse over or focus have a blue background and white text */
99    ul.MenuBarHorizontal a:hover, ul.MenuBarHorizontal a:focus
100   {
101        background-color: #33C;
102        color: #FFF;
103   }
104   /* Menu items that are open with submenus are set to MenuBarItemHover with a blue background and
      white text */
105   ul.MenuBarHorizontal a.MenuBarItemHover, ul.MenuBarHorizontal a.MenuBarItemSubmenuHover,
      ul.MenuBarHorizontal a.MenuBarSubmenuVisible
106   {
107        background-color: #33C;
108        color: #FFF;
109   }
```

4. Insert a comma after a:focus at the end of line 99 in the preceding screenshot, and delete lines 100–104 (use the line numbers in the screenshot only as a guide; it's the code that matters). You should end up with this:

```
98   /* Menu items that have mouse over or focus have a blue background and white text */
99   ul.MenuBarHorizontal a:hover, ul.MenuBarHorizontal a:focus,
100  ul.MenuBarHorizontal a.MenuBarItemHover, ul.MenuBarHorizontal a.MenuBarItemSubmenuHover,
     ul.MenuBarHorizontal a.MenuBarSubmenuVisible
101  {
102      background-color: #33C;
103      color: #FFF;
104  }
```

Save SpryMenuBarHorizontal_stroll.css, and switch back to Design view.

Customizing the menu bar: setting widths

The default width of the menu items is 8em, but this is a fixed width design, so you need to adjust the menu bar to fit. There are five top-level items, and the width of the container <div> is 780 pixels. A quick calculation reveals that dividing 780 by 5 equals 156. So that's the width each item needs to be.

1. The menu bar is a styled unordered list, so the width of each item is controlled by the <li> element. Hold down the Alt key (Opt+Cmd on a Mac), and click anywhere in the menu bar to open the Code Navigator. Move the mouse pointer over the link for the ul.MenuBarHorizontal li rule, as shown in the following screenshot:

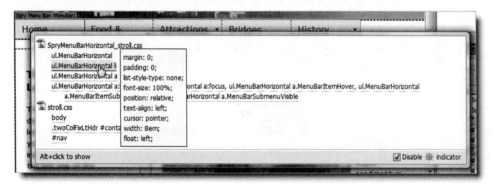

As you can see, the width property is set to 8em. Click the link for the ul.MenuBarHorizontal li rule to open the style sheet in Split view.

2. Dreamweaver should position your cursor at the beginning of the ul.MenuBarHorizontal li rule. Change the value of the width property to 156px, and press F5 to refresh Design view. You should now see the menu fits neatly across the page, as shown in Figure 6-13 (you might need to switch back to Design view if your monitor isn't wide enough to see the effect in Split view).

Figure 6-13. Giving the <li> elements a fixed pixel width matches the width of the container <div>.

3. Click the Live View button, and move your mouse pointer over the menu bar until you trigger one of the submenus. As you can see from the screenshot alongside, the submenus are now narrower than the main menu items.

The width of the submenus is controlled independently. Some of my submenu items are long, so let's make the submenus 20px wider than the main items, in other words, 176px. With your mouse still over one of the submenu items, hold down the Alt key (or Opt+Cmd), and click to activate the Code Navigator. This is where Live view and the Code Navigator really shine. This time, the Code Navigator also detects the style rules that affect the submenus in their hover state. As you mouse over each selector in the Code Navigator, the properties and values of each style rule are displayed as a tooltip.

Go down each one in turn until you find the rule that sets the width for the submenus. It's `ul.MenuBarHorizontal ul`, as shown in Figure 6-14. Click it to edit the rule in Split view.

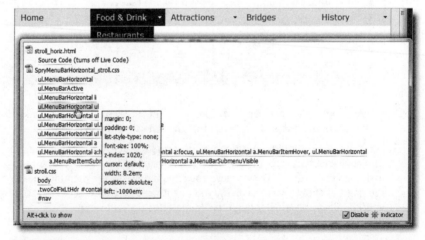

Figure 6-14. In Live view, the Code Navigator detects style rules that affect dynamically generated elements.

4. Change the width property of ul.MenuBarHorizontal ul to 176px.

5. Press F5 to refresh Design view, and move the mouse pointer over the menu to trigger one of the submenus again. Contrary to what you might expect, the submenu items are still too narrow. If you look closely, you'll see that there's a thin gray border surrounding the whole submenu (I have deliberately exaggerated the border in the screenshot alongside to make it stand out more on the printed page). It's the correct width, but the individual submenu items are still their original width.

6. Open the Code Navigator again, and inspect the style rules until you find one that defines the width property as 8.2em (it's ul.MenuBarHorizontal ul li). Click the link to edit the style rule, and change the value of width to 176px.

7. Press F5 to refresh Design view, and test the submenu again. The individual items should now be the correct width.

8. I'm going to add a border to each menu item, so let's get rid of the default border around the submenus. Trigger one of the submenus in Design view, and open the Code Navigator again. The border is defined in the ul.MenuBarHorizontal ul selector. As explained earlier in this chapter, the rules in the style sheet are divided into sections covering colors, layout, and so on. Consequently, there are two rules for ul.MenuBarHorizontal ul. Click the second one, which contains the border property, and change the value in the style sheet to border: **none;**.

Keep stroll_horiz.html open, because I'll show you how to adjust the colors next.

Customizing the menu bar: changing colors and fonts

The main colors of the Spry menu bar are controlled in style rules applied to the links. These instructions assume you have edited the menu bar style sheet as described in "Editing the default selectors."

1. Make sure Live view is still active, hold down the Alt key (or Opt+Cmd), and click any menu item that *doesn't* lead to a submenu. In stroll_horiz.html, this means Home or Bridges. The colors of the menu items are defined in the ul.MenuBarHorizontal a rule. This is a descendant selector that applies to all links in the menu bar. Click the selector in the Code Navigator so you can edit the rule's properties in Split view.

2. Change background-color from #EEE to #A3AAC6 (mauve) and color from #333 to #FFF (white). Press F5 to see the colors updated in Design view.

3. Things are beginning to look better, but let's add a border around the links to make them look like buttons. Add the following properties and values to the ul.MenuBarHorizontal a rule (I'll explain how I arrived at these values later in the chapter):

```
border-left: #C4C9DB 1px solid;
border-top: #C4C9DB 1px solid;
border-right: #565968 1px solid;
border-bottom: #565968 1px solid;
```

4. Press F5 to refresh Design view. The menu links should now look more button-like, but when you pass your mouse over them, the rollover colors need fixing.

   Although you could use the Code Navigator to find the rollover selector, it's a lot quicker to just scroll down in the style rules in Split view, because it's the next rule down (it begins with ul.MenuBarHorizontal a:hover).

   Change background-color from #33C to #7A85AD (dark mauve) and color from #FFF to #333 (very dark gray). Press F5, and mouse over the menu to see the changes in Design view.

5. There's just one final change: the font would look better if it were bold and slightly smaller. As I explained in "Customizing the styles" earlier in the chapter, the place to change font properties is in the ul.MenuBarHorizontal rule. The quickest way to find it in the style sheet is with the Code Navigator, so hold down Alt/Opt+Cmd, and click the menu in Design view. Then click the ul.MenuBarHorizontal selector in the Code Navigator.

6. Change the value of font-size to 90%, and add font-weight: bold; to the rule.

7. Select File ➤ Save All to save the page and style sheet. Test the page in a browser. You should now have an attractive menu bar as shown in Figure 6-1 at the beginning of this chapter.

   You can check your files against stroll_horiz.html in examples/ch06 and SpryMenuBarHorizontal_stroll.css in the SpryAssets folder.

Even if the text size is enlarged, the page structure is preserved, and the dark gray rollover text ensures that spillover text remains reasonably legible. Enlarging the text does disrupt the original design of the page, but certain trade-offs are inevitable in web design. The purpose here has been to show you how to customize a Spry menu bar, rather than seek a definitive answer to accessibility issues.

These instructions have concentrated on customizing a horizontal menu bar, but the process is the same for a vertical one. The main difference is that you don't need to wrap a vertical menu bar in a <div> of its own. However, if you do decide to use a separate <div>, it shouldn't have a fixed height. Otherwise, you may run into display problems if the user enlarges the text in the browser.

Choosing border colors

In the past, it was common to use images to create menu buttons, but that's no longer necessary with CSS. Styling links to display as a block makes the background color fill the full width and height of each link. To give the link a raised effect like a button, all you need to do is put a border around them, using a lighter color for the top and left borders and a darker one for the right and bottom borders.

A neat way of finding the right colors is to create a rectangle in a graphics program like Fireworks, give the rectangle the same color as your buttons, and then apply an inner bevel effect. Figure 6-15 shows how it's done in Fireworks CS4.

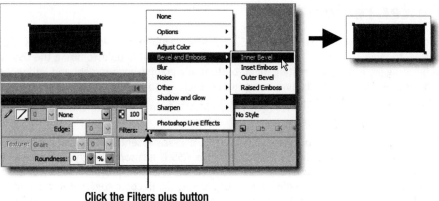

**Click the Filters plus button
to apply an inner bevel**

Figure 6-15. Use a graphics program to add a bevel to a block of solid color to find the best colors for CSS borders.

Use an eyedropper tool to find the appropriate colors for the lighter and darker borders, and make a note of the hexadecimal number. In this case, it's probably easier to use the eyedropper tool in your graphics program, but there's a useful trick if you want to copy the color of an object outside Dreamweaver. Adjust the size of the Dreamweaver workspace so that you can see the object, click the color picker, and hold down the mouse button. You can then drag the eyedropper outside Dreamweaver. The color picker in Dreamweaver constantly updates to show the color currently being sampled by the eyedropper. Release the mouse button when you find the color you want.

Removing a menu bar

Removing a menu bar is quite simple: click the Spry Menu Bar tab at the top left of the menu (see Figure 6-6), and press Delete. That's it—not only is the HTML code removed but so too are the links to the external JavaScript file and style sheet, as well as the initialization script at the bottom of the page. However, the dependent files in the Spry assets folder are *not* removed. This ensures they remain accessible to other pages that may rely on them.

Moreover, the links to the external JavaScript file and style sheet are not removed if another instance of the same type of menu exists on the page.

> *It's important to remove menu bars cleanly by selecting the* Spry Menu Bar *tab and pressing Delete. Otherwise, the initialization script shown on lines 34–38 of Figure 6-7 remains in the underlying code and might trigger errors when the page is loaded into a browser.*

Chapter review

Because it's built with HTML and CSS, the Spry menu bar is accessible and search engine–friendly. However, I'm sure that many noncoders will find customizing the CSS an uphill struggle. Instead of creating menu buttons in a graphic environment and letting the software take care of the coding, much more is left up to the designer's individual skill. However, Live view and the Code Navigator make the job considerably easier than it was in Dreamweaver CS3.

The CSS skills required to customize a menu bar are essential for building modern standards-compliant sites. In my own experience, CSS is not something you can pick up overnight, but once the various pieces begin to fall together, progress becomes much more rapid. So if you're struggling, keep at it, and it will all come together in the end. In Chapter 12, I'll show you how to adapt the menu bar and move it to an external file that can be included in all pages on a site, greatly reducing the amount of maintenance required.

The menu bar is just one of many Spry widgets and effects in Dreamweaver. In the next chapter, we'll look at Spry effects, tabbed panels, the accordion, and collapsible panels.

7 USING SPRY DYNAMIC EFFECTS AND COMPONENTS

Dreamweaver was first released in 1997 at the height of the "browser wars" between Microsoft and Netscape. Both companies fought for dominance of the market by introducing new features that were frequently incompatible with those of their rivals. This presented a major headache for anyone trying to use JavaScript to add dynamic features, such as image replacement, rollovers, and validation of user input. What worked in Internet Explorer didn't work in Netscape, and vice versa. Dreamweaver came to the rescue of many web designers by creating prepackaged scripts called **behaviors** that resolved the inconsistencies and incompatibilities. Even though the browser wars are now part of Internet history, their legacy still lingers on. The version of JavaScript used by Microsoft Internet Explorer (JScript) still doesn't fully comply with standards laid down by the World Wide Web Consortium (W3C). So, designers and developers still need help with scripts that will work cross-browser.

Behaviors are still part of the Dreamweaver toolset, but they're showing their age. Designed to overcome problems caused by ancient browsers, such as Netscape 4, they lack the features offered by recently developed JavaScript **frameworks** (code libraries), such as Prototype (http://www.prototypejs.org/), script.aculo.us (http://script.aculo.us/), or jQuery (http://jquery.com/). Adobe's answer has been to develop Spry, an extensive JavaScript code library that you can download free of charge from http://labs.adobe.com/technologies/spry/home.html. You don't actually need Dreamweaver to use Spry; it's completely tool-independent. As with any JavaScript framework, there's a learning curve involved if you want to integrate Spry features into your web pages. However, the Spry learning curve is considerably shortened—or even eliminated—by Dreamweaver. As you saw in the previous chapter, you can insert a Spry menu bar into a page in seconds. What takes the time is customizing the CSS, not building the JavaScript to control the submenu flyouts—all that is generated automatically. In this chapter, we'll continue our exploration of Spry by using Spry effects and components.

A common dilemma with website design is too little space to display all the content that needs to be on a particular page. In common with other Ajax frameworks, Spry makes it easy to build components—such as accordions and tabbed and collapsible panels—that slot into a web page and give it a much more dynamic feel. The Spry tabbed panels and accordion (see Figure 7-1) are a series of interlinked panels, in which just one panel is open at a time. Tabbed panels use the intuitive metaphor of tabs like a card index, while the panels of an accordion slide up and down to reveal their contents. Spry collapsible panels look the same as an accordion, except that each panel is independent so they can be opened and closed in any combination.

From the user's point of view, all three are intuitive metaphors that shouldn't need any explanation. Equally important, from the developer's point of view, they are easy to insert and customize. All you have to do is supply the content and skin the components with CSS. If you struggled with the Spry menu bar in the previous chapter, you'll be pleased to know that the style sheets of these Spry widgets are a lot simpler to edit. Dreamweaver CS4 adds another space-saving widget, the Spry Tooltip, which displays hidden content when the user mouses over an image or other element.

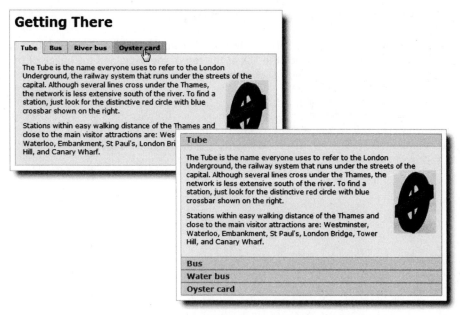

Figure 7-1. Tabbed panels and accordions are familiar website interfaces that users find easy to use.

In this chapter, you'll learn about the following:

- Applying Spry effects to different page elements
- Saving space with tabbed panels, accordions, and collapsible panels
- Selecting harmonious colors
- Styling user interface components
- Using the Spry Tooltip widget
- Removing Spry components cleanly from a page

Before diving into the user interface components, I will cover Spry effects. This is a series of dynamic effects, such as making page elements fade in and out, shrink, grow, and slide.

Animating page elements with Spry effects

Spry effects alter the look of a page element—or of the whole page itself—when a particular event occurs, such as the page loading, clicking a link, or mousing over an image. From a technical point of view, they manipulate the **Document Object Model (DOM)** of a web page. You don't need to know the intricate details of the DOM to use Spry effects, but it is important to understand the basic principle that underlies it.

DOM 101—why clean code matters

Figure 7-2 shows fade.html in examples/ch07, which contains a simple demonstration of the Spry Appear/Fade effect. Click the link at the top of the page, and the image of the Golden Pavilion in Kyoto fades out. Click it again, and the image fades back in.

Figure 7-2. The dynamic effect depends on JavaScript being able to identify the correct element to fade in and out.

Before adding the Spry effect to the page, the HTML looked like this:

```
<!DOCTYPE html PUBLIC "-//W3C//DTD XHTML 1.0 Transitional//EN" ➥
"http://www.w3.org/TR/xhtml1/DTD/xhtml1-transitional.dtd">
<html xmlns="http://www.w3.org/1999/xhtml">
<head>
<meta http-equiv="Content-Type" content="text/html; charset=utf-8" />
<title>Spry effects - fade in/out</title>
</head>
<body>
<p><a href="javascript:;">Fade image out/in</a></p>
<p><img src="../../images/kinkakuji.jpg" alt="Golden Pavilion" ➥
name="goldenpav" width="270" height="346" id="goldenpav" /></p>
</body>
</html>
```

The DOM sees this code in terms of the family tree shown in Figure 7-3.

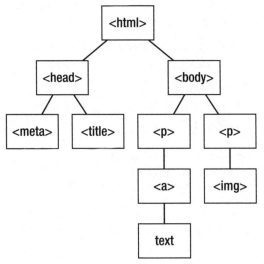

Figure 7-3. The contents of fade.html as seen by the DOM

For the Spry effect to fade the image in and out, it needs to pass the message from the text in the <a> tag in the first paragraph to the image in the second paragraph. The DOM acts as a sort of road map to make sure the message reaches the right destination. Either it can do it the hard way by following the hierarchy all the way up to the <body> tag and then drilling down to the <img> tag or it can do it the easy way with an id attribute. As you can see from the code listing, I have given the <img> tag an id attribute of goldenpav. Following the road map analogy, this acts as a signpost guiding Spry to the correct destination.

For all this to work smoothly, the road map needs to be clear. Tags need to be properly nested, and you should give id attributes to elements that you want the DOM and/or CSS to handle in a particular way. Dreamweaver makes this task a lot easier by warning you when tags are incorrectly nested (a message usually appears in the Property inspector, and the invalid code is highlighted in yellow). But remember: Dreamweaver is only a tool. It will do what you tell it. Even if Dreamweaver keeps your code perfectly valid, you should be aware of what's going on in Code view. If you clutter up your page with unnecessary <span> and <div> tags, the DOM road map becomes harder to navigate, resulting in pages that are sluggish and not user-friendly.

The other thing to remember is that an id attribute cannot be used more than once on the same page. Inexperienced web designers sometimes think, "I want all these elements to work the same way, so I'll give them all the same ID." It might work with CSS, but it won't work with Spry or any other JavaScript that relies on DOM manipulation.

An ID should be a unique identifier. Never use the same ID for more than one element on a page.

Dreamweaver CS4 makes it a lot easier to assign an ID to page elements through the Property inspector. Most elements now have an ID field on the left of the Property inspector (for text elements, it's in the HTML view of the Property inspector). When assigning an ID, you should also bear the following rules in mind:

- Use only alphanumeric characters, hyphens, or underscores.
- Do not use spaces or punctuation.
- Never begin with a number.

Applying a Spry effect

Spry effects are event-driven, so you need to decide which event to use and which element to trigger it. For example, you could attach a Spry effect to the <body> element of a page and use the onload event to trigger it as soon as the page finishes loading. Other common choices are using a text link that triggers the effect when it's clicked, or using an image to trigger an effect when the mouse passes over it. The other decision you need to make is which element to apply the effect to. Dreamweaver refers to this as the **target** element.

All Spry effects are grouped with the original Dreamweaver behaviors, which are in a slightly different location from previous versions. The Behaviors panel has been combined with the Tag Inspector panel, and you access its features by clicking the Behaviors button, as shown in Figure 7-4.

Figure 7-4.
Dreamweaver behaviors and Spry effects are now in the Tag Inspector panel.

Like the Property inspector, the Tag Inspector panel is context-sensitive. Its options depend on where the insertion point is currently located in the Document window. Click in an element or select it in the Document window before using the Tag Inspector panel. To open the panel, double-click its tab or, if you're using iconic mode, click its icon. You can also use Window ➤ Tag Inspector or press F9/Shift+Opt+F9. There are also menu and keyboard shortcuts that take you directly to the Tag Inspector panel in Behaviors mode: Window ➤ Behaviors or Shift+F4 (the keyboard shortcut is the same on both Windows and Mac).

> Don't confuse the Tag Inspector *panel in* Behaviors *mode with the* Server Behaviors *panel. Dreamweaver uses* behaviors *to mean JavaScript-driven features. Server behaviors use server-side code, such as PHP. You'll work with the* Server Behaviors *panel a lot in the second half of this book.*

To apply a Spry effect, select the element that will be used to trigger the effect, open the Tag Inspector panel in Behaviors mode, click the plus (+) button, and select the effect from the Effects submenu, as shown in Figure 7-5.

Figure 7-5.
The Spry effects are grouped with the original Dreamweaver JavaScript behaviors.

7

Fading an image

This brief exercise shows how to apply the Spry Appear/Fade effect to an image. The basic procedure for applying all Spry effects is identical, so once you understand the technique, you can quickly apply any effect.

1. Create a new subfolder called ch07 in the workfiles folder.
2. Create a new HTML document called fade.html, and save it in workfiles/ch07.

3. Type some text to act as a trigger, and press Enter/Return. This wraps the text in paragraph tags and creates a new paragraph.

4. Insert an image in the new paragraph. I used `kinkakuji.jpg`, but you can use any image in the images folder. It's not necessary for this exercise to give the image alternate text, but you should get in the habit of doing so.

5. With the image selected in the Document window, give it a unique identity by entering a name in the ID field of the Property inspector. Press Enter/Return to register the change. Your page should now look similar to this:

Give the image an ID

6. Select the text in the first paragraph, and convert it into a dummy link by entering javascript:; in the Link field of the HTML view of the Property inspector, as shown here:

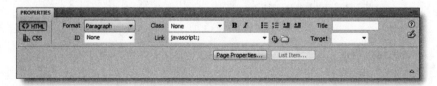

Using `javascript:;` rather than # for a dummy link prevents the page from jumping to the top if you have a lot of content on the page.

7. Press Enter/Return or Tab to ensure that the link is created. This is important, because you can't apply the Spry effect until the trigger element exists.

> *Values entered in the Property inspector and other panels are not added to the underlying code until the focus moves to another part of the UI. Pressing Enter/Return registers the new value in the underlying code. Pressing the Tab key or clicking elsewhere in the Document window has the same effect.*

8. Open the Tag Inspector panel in Behaviors mode, click the plus button to activate the Behaviors menu, as shown in Figure 7-5, and select Effects ➤ Appear/Fade.

9. The dialog box that opens sets the options for the effect. The Target Element drop-down menu lists all elements that can be used as targets (usually elements that have an ID). The other options are self-explanatory. The Toggle effect checkbox at the bottom of the dialog box lets you run the effect in reverse when the trigger event is repeated. So, in the case of this effect, it makes the target element fade back into view when the event is triggered again.

Choose the image as the target element, and select the option to toggle the effect. Check your settings with the following screenshot, and click OK:

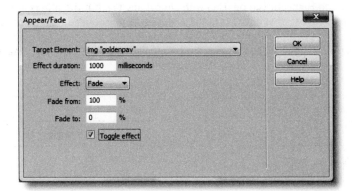

10. The effect is now listed in the Tag Inspector panel, as shown here:

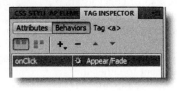

The event that will be used to trigger the effect is displayed on the left. You can change this value by clicking it to open a menu of the available events. However, the default value, onClick, is fine in this case (although Dreamweaver displays the event with an uppercase *C*, the underlying code inserts onclick all in lowercase if you have selected an XHTML document type).

To change any of the effect's settings, make sure the trigger element is selected in the Document window, and double-click the listing shown in the preceding screenshot (or right-click, and select Edit Behavior from the context menu).

11. Save fade.html. If this is the first time you have used a Spry effect in the current site, Dreamweaver displays a message telling you that it has copied SpryEffects.js to your Spry assets folder (the default name is SpryAssets). Click OK.

12. Click the Live View button in the Document toolbar, and then click the text link in fade.html. The image should fade out over one second. Click the link again, and the image should fade back in.

If necessary, you can check your code against fade.html in examples/ch07.

The basic procedure for applying the original Dreamweaver JavaScript behaviors is the same. Since many of them are rather old, I don't plan to cover them in this book. You can find a description of each one in Dreamweaver Help (F1 or Help ➤ Dreamweaver Help) ➤ Applying JavaScript behaviors ➤ Applying built-in Dreamweaver behaviors.

Exploring the available effects

Table 7-1 summarizes what each Spry effect does and which target elements it can be used with. Appear/Fade and Highlight can be used with almost any tag, but the others are more restricted. The complete list of supported target elements is reproduced mainly for reference. Most effects can be applied only to a block element, such as a heading, paragraph, or <div>. Appear/Fade, Highlight, and Shake can be applied directly to an <img> tag. If in doubt, wrap the target element in a <div>, and assign it an ID.

Table 7-1. Spry effects and supported target elements

Effect	Action	Supported targets	Not supported
Appear/Fade	Fades an element in or out	Most tags	applet, body, iframe, object, tbody, th, tr
Blind	Reveals or conceals an element, like pulling a window blind up or down	address, applet, center, dir, dd, div, dl, dt, form, h1–6, li, menu, p, pre, ol, ul	Any other tag
Grow/Shrink	Grows or shrinks an element to either the center or top left	address, applet, center, dd, dir, div, dl, dt, form, img, menu, p, pre, ol, ul	Any other tag
Highlight	Applies a color transition to the element's background	Most tags	applet, body, frame, frameset, noframes

Effect	Action	Supported targets	Not supported
Shake	Shakes an element horizontally for half a second	address, applet, blockquote, dd, dir, div, dl, dt, fieldset, form, h1–6, hr, iframe, img, li, menu, object, p, pre, ol, table, ul	Any other tag
Slide	Slides an element up or down to conceal or reveal it	blockquote, center, dd, div, form, img	Any other tag
Squish	Collapses or expands an element to or from its upper-left corner	address, applet, center, dd, dir, div, dl, dt, form, img, menu, p, pre, ol, ul	Any other tag

The dialog box for each effect is very similar, and all share the following common settings:

- Target Element: Dreamweaver automatically identifies every element on the page that the effect can be applied to. Select the element from the drop-down list. Unless the effect is being applied to the trigger element, the target must have an ID. In the case of the Shake and Squish effects, this is the only setting.

- Effect duration: This is the length of the effect, measured in milliseconds. The default setting is 1000—in other words, one second.

- Effect: The available options depend on the effect but normally specify the direction in which the target element will move.

- Toggle effect: Selecting this option reverses the effect the next time the event is triggered.

The best way to learn how to use Spry effects is to experiment with them. However, the hints in the following sections should help you.

Appear/Fade

This effect can be applied to just about any element on a page, and it affects everything inside the target element. Making an element fade to nothing does not alter the layout of the page. An empty space remains where the element originally was.

The <body> tag cannot be used as the target element of this effect. To get the whole page to fade in after it finishes loading, wrap the entire contents of the page in a <div>. Use the <body> tag as the trigger, set the <div> as the target element, and set the event to onLoad. You can see this in fade_in.html in examples/ch07. A <div> called container has been selected as the target element, the effect duration set to 3000 (3 seconds), and the effect set to Appear.

Blind

This is very similar to Slide, except that Blind acts like a mask scrolling up or down in front of the target element, whereas Slide moves the whole target element. Blind up results in the target element disappearing from the bottom; with Blind down, the target element is normally hidden, and the mask moves down to reveal it. Content below the target element moves up and down in time with the effect.

Images need to be wrapped in a block element such as a paragraph or <div> to use Blind. Use the block element as the target. For an example, see blind.html in examples/ch07.

Grow/Shrink

This effect works with a wide range of block elements and images, but it can have unexpected results (see Figure 7-6), so you need to test your pages and CSS carefully when using it.

There are two options for the direction of movement: to and from the center of the target element (see Figures 7-6A and 7-6B) or to and from its top-left corner (see Figures 7-6C and 7-6D). Grow/Shrink can be applied directly to an image or its containing element. Each screenshot shows what happens when the target element is shrunk to 50 percent of its original size but in a variety of circumstances. (You can test the results in shrinkA.html, shrinkB.html, shrinkC.html, and shrinkD.html in examples/ch07.)

- Figure 7-6A shows what happens when the image itself is selected as the target element and shrunk to its center. Any content below the target element moves up, but the image moves down, resulting in an overlap. The same happens if the effect is applied to a surrounding element with the same width and height as the image.

- Figure 7-6B shows what happens if the effect is applied to a surrounding block element with no fixed height and is shrunk to its center: the parent element and its contents shrink together but move to the center of the page.

- Figure 7-6C shows what happens if the effect is set to move to the top left and is applied to the surrounding <div>, regardless of whether the <div> has fixed dimensions. The same happens if the image is selected as the target but *only* if the surrounding <div> has no height.

- Figure 7-6D shows the gap created by applying the effect directly to the image and shrinking it to its top-left corner when the surrounding <div> has a fixed height. The text remains in its original position, much further down the page.

Test your layout carefully if you use this effect.

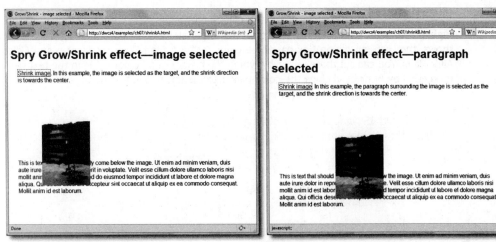

A: Image shrunk to center

B: Container with no height shrunk to center

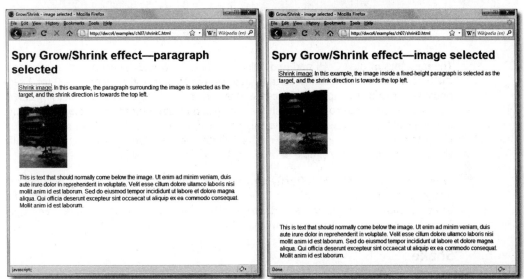

C: Image or container shrunk to top left

D: Image shrunk to top left; container has height

Figure 7-6. The Grow/Shrink Spry effect can produce unexpected changes to your layout (see text for details).

Highlight

Highlight changes the background color of the target element. As the following screenshot shows, the Highlight dialog box has three color settings: Start Color, End Color, and Color After Effect. You can set these either by typing the hexadecimal color value in the text field (preceded by #) or by clicking the color picker to the left of the text field.

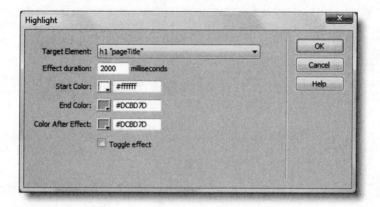

The meanings of Start Color and End Color are what you would expect. Effect duration sets the time taken (in milliseconds) to transition from one color to the other—2000 (or 2 seconds) seems to be the optimal choice—and the transition follows a visually pleasing curve. Color After Effect is the color to which the background is set after the transition, and it cuts in immediately. You need to choose this color carefully. I find it's best to set this value either to the same as Start Color or End Color. Otherwise, the transition appears unnaturally abrupt. You can see an example in highlight_text.html in examples/ch07.

When Highlight is applied directly to an image, there must be padding around the image for the background color to be visible. Adding only margins to the image has no effect, because background color does not affect the margin of an element. See highlight_padding.html and highlight_margin.html in examples/ch07.

Shake

This is my least favorite effect. It has only one option: the target element, which it shakes horizontally for half a second. It might be appropriate in advanced Ajax contexts to indicate that an element has been updated asynchronously, but it would be more useful if you could set the speed and duration of the movement. The danger is that it will become the modern equivalent of the <blink> tag—mercilessly abused because it looks "cool." Use with care. Depending on your layout, this effect sometimes spawns a horizontal scrollbar in the browser. There's an example in shake.html in examples/ch07.

Slide

Slide is similar to Blind, but rather than a mask moving over the target element, the element itself moves. As Table 7-1 shows, this effect can be applied to only a small range of block elements or images. You cannot apply the Slide effect directly to the element you want to slide in and out of view. Instead, the target element must be a <div> wrapped around it. Although that's straightforward, what makes matters slightly complicated is that the Slide effect is very picky about the elements it accepts immediately inside the wrapper. The child element of the wrapper <div> *must* be one of the following: <blockquote>, the deprecated <center> element, <dd>, <form>, <img>, or another <div>. If the child element is anything else, you get this warning:

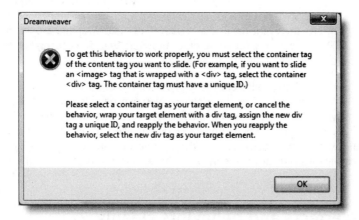

The image of the Golden Pavilion in slide.html in examples/ch07 is wrapped in a <div>, not a paragraph. If you want to use a paragraph with the Slide effect, you must wrap the paragraph in two <div> tags and use the outer one as the target element.

Squish

Squish collapses the target element from the bottom-right corner toward the top left until it disappears completely and is very easy to apply. The Squish dialog box has only one setting: the target element. Any content below the target element moves up to fill the gap, as demonstrated in squish.html in examples/ch07. Unlike other Spry effects, there's no toggle option in the Dreamweaver dialog box, and you can't specify the start and end sizes of the target element.

Applying multiple events to a trigger element

You're not limited to applying a single event to the trigger element for a Spry effect or behavior. In the examples of the Highlight effect, I have applied the onmouseover and onmouseout events to the image. The first event applies the Highlight effect when you

mouse over the image. The second event applies the same effect in reverse. To apply multiple events to the same trigger, just apply the effect again, and select a different event from the drop-down menu in the Tag Inspector panel, as shown here.

> *Dreamweaver often seems reluctant to let you change the trigger event from* onClick. *I usually find it accepts the change the second time you select the new event.*

When you select an image, the drop-down menu contains a duplicate set of events preceded by <A>, as shown in the screenshot alongside. This option inserts the event handler in a pair of <a> tags wrapped around the image. This is necessary for some older browsers that don't recognize event handlers attached directly to an image.

If you choose different event handlers, the order that behaviors or effects are listed doesn't matter. However, you may need to change the order when you use the same event handler for more than one behavior. This sometimes happens when adding several behaviors to the <body> tag to be executed when the page first loads. You do this by selecting an event in the Tag Inspector panel and moving it up or down the list with the up and down arrows at the top of the panel.

Removing effects and behaviors cleanly

A question I often see in online forums is "Why does my browser report errors on the page?" Frequently, the answer is that an effect or behavior has been removed, but the event handler that triggers it has been left behind. Another cause is the removal of a page element, such as an image or a <div>, that an effect or behavior is attempting to find. If you treat Dreamweaver purely as a WYSIWYG tool, you're likely to end up with similar problems. If you remove an element that triggers an effect or behavior or is the target of one, you must do it in the correct manner.

Removing an effect or behavior involves three simple steps, as follows:

1. Select the page element that the effect or behavior is applied to.

2. Select the effect or behavior in the Tag Inspector panel.

3. Click the minus (–) button, as shown in the following screenshot:

Instead of clicking the minus button, you can right-click and select Delete Behavior. You can even just press Delete (but make sure the behavior is selected in the Behaviors panel first).

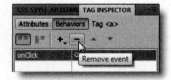

Everything is removed cleanly, preventing errors from popping up later in your page. However, SpryEffects.js is *not* deleted from the SpryAssets folder, in case it's needed by other pages. The link to the external JavaScript file is also preserved if it's required by other effects in the page.

Restoring a deleted effect or behavior

If you delete a behavior by mistake, you can restore it by pressing Ctrl+Z/Cmd+Z or by selecting Edit ➤ Undo Remove Behavior (Edit ➤ Undo on a Mac). This always undoes the last action. By default, Dreamweaver remembers your last 50 steps. So, you can continue pressing Ctrl+Z/Cmd+Z to restore a deleted effect or behavior if you change your mind after doing something else (although you lose those changes too).

An alternative way to undo several steps is to use the History panel. The History panel is not displayed by default but is automatically added to the bottom of the panel groups the first time you open it (Window ➤ History). The keyboard shortcut (Shift+F10) is available on Windows only. To learn more about the History panel, open Help (F1), and select Adding content to pages ➤ Automating tasks ➤ Use the history panel.

You can change the number of steps that can be undone by altering Maximum number of history steps in the General category of the Preferences panel (Edit/Dreamweaver ➤ Preferences). Resist the temptation to increase this number by a significant amount, because it is memory intensive. The default 50 is the optimal level.

Another useful way of retracing your steps is the Revert command on the File menu. This undoes all changes in a document and restores it to the last saved state.

Conserving space with Spry UI components

Dreamweaver CS4 comes with four Spry user interface components or widgets designed to solve the problem of putting a lot of information at the user's fingertips without creating interminably long pages: tabbed panels, accordion panels, collapsible panels, and—new to this version—tooltips. Several features are common to working with all Spry widgets. If you worked through the previous chapter about the Spry menu bar, they should be familiar to you, but it's worth repeating them here:

- Always save your page in a Dreamweaver site before inserting a Spry widget. Dreamweaver prompts you if you forget.

- After inserting a widget, save the page to link the external JavaScript file and style sheet, and copy them to the site's Spry assets folder (see "Setting other site options" in Chapter 2). All instances of a widget in a site share the same files, so they are copied only when inserting the first instance. *You must upload these files to your remote server when deploying your site on the Internet. The Spry widgets won't work without them.*

7

Dreamweaver attaches the widget's style sheet immediately above the closing </head> tag. If your page has style rules embedded in conditional comments, move the link to the style sheet above the conditional comments.

- Dreamweaver inserts a block of JavaScript at the bottom of the page to initialize the widget when the page loads.

- To see the widget's details in the Property inspector, hover your mouse pointer over the widget in Design view, and click the tab at the top left of the surrounding border.

Although the Spry UI components are great space savers, the contents of hidden panels are loaded at the same time as the rest of the page. Don't put lots of heavy graphics in these widgets or overuse them on any individual page. The external JavaScript file and style sheet for each widget add about 20KB to a page but are stored in the browser's cache after loading the first time.

Building a tabbed interface

Tabbed panels use the common metaphor of tabs at the top of folders in a filing cabinet. Click the tab, and the associated content is displayed in the panel beneath. It's a clean, intuitive way of storing a lot of content in a relatively small space. The example in Figure 7-7 has four tabs, so the total space required to display the information is one fourth of what it would normally be.

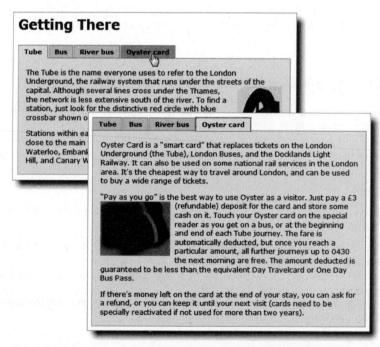

Figure 7-7. Tabbed panels are a great way of presenting related information in a confined space.

The Spry tabbed panels widget takes only the click of a button to insert, and it degrades gracefully in old browsers or if JavaScript is turned off. The panels expand to display their contents if the browser cannot handle the JavaScript. The accordion, collapsible panels, and tooltip expand in a similar way, making all four user interface widgets accessible.

Let's take a look at the anatomy of a tabbed panels widget.

Examining the structure of the tabbed panels widget

You can insert a Spry tabbed panels widget in three ways: from the Spry tab of the Insert bar, from the Layout tab of the Insert bar, or by choosing Insert ➤ Spry ➤ Spry Tabbed Panels. This creates a default two-tab widget (see Figure 7-8) at the current insertion point in the page.

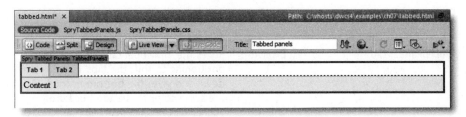

Figure 7-8. The default tabbed panels widget contains two tabs styled with a neutral gray interface.

As you can see in Figure 7-8, the Related Files toolbar displays the names of two dependent files (SpryTabbedPanels.js and SpryTabbedPanels.css). Until you save the page, these are stored in a temporary folder, so you should always save the page immediately after inserting a Spry widget for Dreamweaver to update the links and copy the dependent files to the site's Spry assets folder.

The tabbed panels are controlled by JavaScript and CSS, but unlike the Spry menu bar, there's no option on the Property inspector to toggle the CSS on and off. However, if you switch to Code view, the underlying HTML looks like this:

```
<div id="TabbedPanels1" class="TabbedPanels">
  <ul class="TabbedPanelsTabGroup">
    <li class="TabbedPanelsTab" tabindex="0">Tab 1</li>
    <li class="TabbedPanelsTab" tabindex="0">Tab 2</li>
  </ul>
  <div class="TabbedPanelsContentGroup">
    <div class="TabbedPanelsContent">Content 1</div>
    <div class="TabbedPanelsContent">Content 2</div>
  </div>
</div>
```

The whole widget is wrapped in a <div>; the tabs are an unordered list, and the panels are in a nested <div>. Each individual panel is also a <div>, nested one level further down. The only element that has an ID is the overall wrapper <div>. Dreamweaver automatically calls the first tabbed panels widget on a page TabbedPanels1 and numbers subsequent instances TabbedPanels2, and so on. Everything else is controlled by classes. Although each element has a class assigned to it explicitly in the underlying code, other classes are generated dynamically by the external JavaScript file. Table 7-2 explains what each class is for. In common with all user interface widgets, the class names are long but descriptive.

Table 7-2. The classes used to style the tabbed panels widget

Class	Type	Purpose
TabbedPanels	Explicit	Eliminates margin and padding surrounding the widget and clears any preceding floats. *This class must always have an explicit width.* The default value is 100% to fill all available space.
TabbedPanelsTabGroup	Explicit	Removes margin and padding from the tabs as a group.
TabbedPanelsTab	Explicit	Styles the individual tabs. Uses relative positioning to shift the tabs 1 pixel down and gives the bottom border the same color as the top border of TabbedPanelsContentGroup. This creates the illusion that the tabs are being drawn behind the content panel. Two non-standard properties (-moz-user-select and -khtml-user-select) are set to none to prevent users from selecting the text in Firefox, Mozilla, and Konqueror.
TabbedPanelsTabHover	Dynamic	Controls the rollover look of the tabs.
TabbedPanelsTabSelected	Dynamic	Sets the background color and bottom border of the currently selected tab to the same as the TabbedPanelsContentGroup to create the illusion that the tab is part of the panel.
TabbedPanelsContentGroup	Explicit	Ensures that the panels sit beneath the tabs. Sets the background and border colors for the panels.
TabbedPanelsContent	Explicit	Styles the content of an individual panel. By default, only adds 4px padding.
TabbedPanelsContentVisible	Dynamic	Empty style rule that can be used to give a different style to the currently visible panel.

The `<li>` tags contain the `tabindex` attribute, which makes the code invalid according to the W3C specifications. Although Spry generates classes dynamically, Internet Explorer doesn't support setting `tabindex` through JavaScript, so this was the compromise adopted to make it possible to navigate the panels with the Tab key. If W3C validation is vital to you, remove the `tabindex` attributes. However, this will make your page less accessible to assistive technology for the disabled and keyboard users. Occasionally bending the rules like this makes sense and has no adverse effect in any browser.

Editing a tabbed panels widget

The Property inspector has only three settings for the tabbed panels widget (see Figure 7-9): ID, number and order of panels, and the default panel. The Customize this widget link opens Dreamweaver Help at the page listing the style settings.

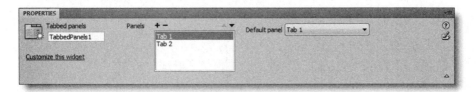

Figure 7-9. The Property inspector for the tabbed panels widget is very simple.

Use the plus (+) and minus (–) buttons to add or remove panels, and use the up and down arrows to reorder them. The name of each panel changes when you edit the tabs in Design view. The Default panel drop-down menu on the right determines which panel is open when the page first loads.

You can open a tab or panel for editing in Design view in two ways, as follows:

- Bring up the details of the widget in the Property inspector, and select the panel name in the Panels list.
- Position your mouse pointer over the right side of the tab until an eye icon appears, as shown in Figure 7-10, and click.

Figure 7-10. Click the eye icon at the right side of a tab to reveal its associated panel for editing.

Each panel is a `<div>`, so you can insert anything you like: text, images, and so on.

Inserting and editing a tabbed panels widget

Roll up your sleeves, and insert a tabbed panels widget into stroll.html. To make it easier to dip into individual chapters, the files in examples/ch07 use the version of stroll.html from Chapter 5 without the Spry menu bar, because it involves fewer dependent files.

1. Copy stroll.html and stroll.css from examples/ch07 to workfiles/ch07. Update links if prompted by Dreamweaver. Save a copy of stroll.html as stroll_tabbed.html.

   Note that in Dreamweaver CS4, using File ➤ Save As (Ctrl+Shift+S/Shift+Cmd+S) opens the renamed version in a separate tab and gives it focus in the Document window. In previous versions, Dreamweaver closed the original document and displayed the new one in the same tab. Later in the chapter, you'll make fresh copies of stroll.html to experiment with other widgets, but you don't need it at the moment, so you can close it if you prefer to keep as few documents open as necessary.

   > *If you make any changes to a file before using* File ➤ Save As, *the changes are saved* only *in the renamed file, and the original file is restored to its last saved state.*

2. Scroll down to the end of the first block of text in the mainContent <div> (just above the Artists at Work heading). Press Enter/Return to insert a new paragraph. Type Getting There, and convert it to a heading by selecting Heading 2 from the Format drop-down menu on the left of the Property inspector.

3. With your cursor at the end of the new heading, click the Spry Tabbed Panels button on the Spry tab of the Insert bar (or use the Layout tab or Insert menu as described earlier). You should now have a tabbed panels widget in the middle of the page, as shown in Figure 7-11.

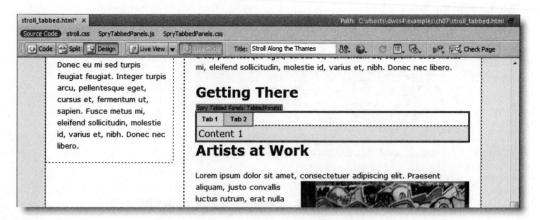

Figure 7-11. By default, the tabbed panels widget fills the available horizontal space.

> As long as your cursor is at the beginning or end of an existing element when you insert a widget, Dreamweaver correctly places the widget outside the existing element. If your cursor is anywhere else, Dreamweaver splits the existing element by creating closing and opening tags and inserting the widget between them.

4. Save `stroll_tabbed.html`, and click OK if prompted to copy the dependent files (this happens only the first time you create a tabbed panel widget in a site).

5. Rename `SpryTabbedPanel.css` in the Spry assets folder as `SpryTabbedPanel_stroll.css`, and update the links when prompted. Move the link to `SpryTabbedPanel_stroll.css` above the conditional comments in the <head> of the page. There won't be any conflicts of style rules, but this is a good habit to adopt.

6. Place your cursor inside the first tab, delete Tab 1, and type Tube.

7. Open `getting_there.doc` in examples/ch07, and copy the paragraphs labeled Tube to your clipboard. If you can't open a Word document, the text is in `getting_there.txt`, but Dreamweaver won't do the automatic formatting in the next step.

8. Highlight Content 1 in the tabbed panels widget, and paste the contents of your clipboard into the panel. If you set the Copy/Paste options in the Preferences panel using the settings shown in Figure 3-7 in Chapter 3, Dreamweaver should automatically preserve the paragraph structure from the Word document. Otherwise, press Ctrl+Shift+V/Shift+Cmd+V or select Edit ➤ Paste Special, and select Text with structure plus basic formatting (bold, italic) and Clean up Word paragraph spacing (Paste Special is described in Chapter 3).

If you used the plain text in `getting_there.txt`, you need to format it manually as paragraphs with the Format drop-down menu in the HTML view of the Property inspector. Dreamweaver places a <br /> tag between the paragraphs, so you need to split them by pressing Enter/Return and then remove the extra line created by the <br /> tag.

9. Position your cursor inside the second tab, and rename it Bus.

10. Open the second panel for editing by selecting it in the Property inspector (click the turquoise tab at the top left of the widget, if necessary) or clicking the eye icon as shown earlier in Figure 7-10. Copy the Bus paragraphs from `getting_there.doc`, and paste them in place of the placeholder text in the second panel.

11. Click the turquoise Spry Tabbed Panels tab at the top left of the widget to bring up its details in the Property inspector, and click the plus button in the Property inspector to add two more panels. Rename them Water bus and Oyster Card, and replace the placeholder text in each panel with the copy from `getting_there.doc`.

12. With the Oyster Card panel open, insert `oystercard.jpg` from the images folder at or near the beginning of the second paragraph. Enter Oyster Card as the Alternate text when prompted.

13. To make the text wrap around the image, with the image still highlighted, select fltlft from the Class drop-down menu in the HTML view of the Property inspector.

7

14. Open the first panel (Tube) for editing, and insert underground.jpg at the beginning of the first paragraph. Set Alternate text to Underground station sign and Class to fltrt.

15. Click the Live View button in the Document toolbar. The bottom half of the page should look like Figure 7-12. Click the various tabs to display the other panels. You'll see that the height of the panels expands and contracts depending on the amount of content. All content below the tabbed panels is repositioned according to the height of the selected panel, so you need to be careful when incorporating this widget in a design where the layout needs to be pixel perfect.

Check your code if necessary with stroll_tabbed.html in examples/ch07.

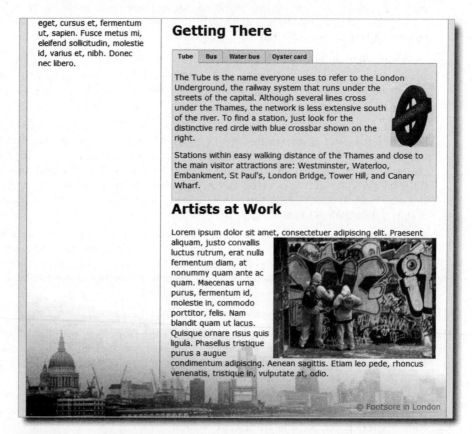

Figure 7-12. Even without customizing the styles, Spry tabbed panels look at home in most pages.

The neutral gray styling fits in easily with many designs, so you could leave it as it is. However, I don't imagine that you'll let me get away with that, so let's restyle the panels. The bottom of the panels is too close to the following headline, so that needs fixing, too.

Selecting harmonious colors

The tabbed panels style sheet uses four shades of gray, ranging from light (#EEE) to dark (#999). I decided to use as my base colors the pink (#F8F1EB) from the page background and the russet (#C99466) border down both sides of the container `<div>`. Table 7-3 lists the colors that I finally decided on.

Table 7-3. Conversion chart for Dreamweaver defaults and substituted colors

Default color	Replacement	Applies to
Pale gray (#EEE)	Light pink (#FAF3ED)	Panel background color and selected tab
Light gray (#DDD)	Darker pink (#F2E1D2)	Nonselected tabs
Medium gray (#CCC)	Light brown (#DFBD9F)	Tabs on rollover and lighter borders
Dark gray (#999)	Russet (#C99466)	Darker borders

To simplify customization of a Spry widget, make a similar chart of the default colors and your chosen replacements. You can then go through the style rules quite quickly to make the substitutions.

7

Styling a tabbed panels widget

Let's style the tabbed panels using the color scheme outlined in Table 7-3. Continue working with `stroll_tabbed.html` from the previous exercise.

1. Select SpryTabbedPanels_stroll.css in the Related Files toolbar, and take a quick look at the rules it contains. In addition to copious comments describing the role of each selector, there are a lot of properties. Editing this style sheet with either the CSS Styles panel or the Code Navigator is a lot of work. Surely there's a simpler way? There most certainly is: the Find and Replace dialog box (see Chapter 5 for a detailed description of how to use it).

2. With SpryTabbedPanels_stroll.css still selected in the Related Files toolbar and the style sheet open in Split view, launch the Find and Replace dialog box (Edit ➤ Find and Replace or Ctrl+F/Cmd+F).

3. In the Find and Replace dialog box, set Find in to Current Document. The Search option will be grayed out because Source Code is the only option inside a style sheet. Enter #EEE in the Find field, and enter #FAF3ED in the Replace field. Make

sure all the options at the bottom of the dialog box are deselected. Your settings should look like this:

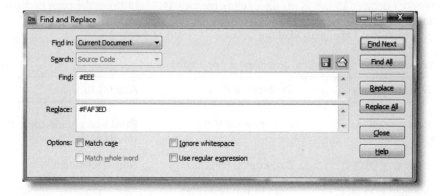

4. Click Replace All. The Results panel should open and report that it has made five substitutions, as shown in the next screenshot:

Click this arrow to relaunch Find and Replace →

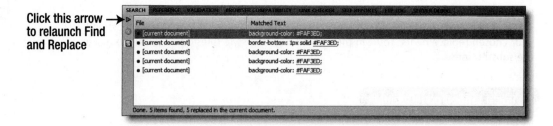

5. You now need to substitute the other colors. Use the right-facing green arrow at the top left of the Results panel, as indicated in the preceding screenshot, to relaunch the Find and Replace dialog box (the Search menu becomes selectable when you open the dialog box this way, but it should remain set to Source Code). Repeat steps 3 and 4 three times using the following values taken from Table 7-3:

- Find: #DDD   Replace: #F2E1D2
- Find: #CCC   Replace: #DFBD9F
- Find: #999   Replace: #C99466

6. Close the Results panel, and test the tabbed panels in Live view. They now look more in harmony with the page, but some fine-tuning still needs to be done to margins and padding.

7. The TabbedPanels class controls the horizontal and vertical space around the tabbed panels, as well as their overall width. As Figure 7-12 shows, there's no gap between the bottom of the panel and the following heading. So, you need to adjust the margin property.

Hold down the Alt key (or Opt+Cmd on a Mac), and click anywhere inside the tabbed panels to bring up the Code Navigator. Click the link for the .TabbedPanels selector, as shown here:

8. Change the margin property from 0px to 0 0 15px 0. This adds a 15-pixel margin on the bottom but leaves the other sides with a 0-pixel margin.

   If you want to constrain the width of the panels, this is where you should edit the width property. However, do *not* delete the width property, because it's required for the widget to display correctly in Internet Explorer.

9. Press F5 to refresh Design view. There should now be a nice offset between the bottom of the tabbed panels and the following heading.

10. Now let's improve the look of the text. Turn off Live view if it's still active, and bring up the Code Navigator by holding down Alt/Opt+Cmd and clicking in one of the tabs. Click the link for the third selector (.TabbedPanelsTab).

   The font property uses the shorthand version like this:

   `font: bold 0.7em sans-serif`

   Change it to this:

   font: bold 0.7em **Verdana, Geneva,** sans-serif;

   A neat way of doing this is to high-light sans-serif and press Ctrl+space (the combination is the same on Windows and Mac). This brings up code hints with a list of suggested font families, as shown here:

Use your down arrow key to select the fonts you want, and press Enter/Return to insert them. You can also double-click your choice, but this is trickier and often results in part of the original selection remaining in the code.

11. The one final improvement is to reduce the size of the text and add some horizontal padding to the paragraphs. Position your cursor anywhere in one of the paragraphs in the tabbed panels widget, and launch the New CSS Rule dialog box. If you use the icon at the bottom right of the CSS Styles panel or the CSS view of the Property inspector, the New CSS Rule dialog box suggests this horrendous dependent selector:

```
.twoColFixLtHdr #container #mainContent #TabbedPanels1 ➡
.TabbedPanelsContentGroup ➡
.TabbedPanelsContent.TabbedPanelsContentVisible p
```

Click the Less Specific button five times to reduce the selector to this:

```
.TabbedPanelsContent.TabbedPanelsContentVisible p
```

Then edit the Selector Name field manually to this:

```
.TabbedPanelsContent p
```

12. Set Rule Definition to SpryTabbedPanels_stroll.css, and click OK.

13. In the Type category of the CSS Rule Definition dialog box, set Size to 75%. Then select the Box category, deselect Same for all in the Padding section, set Right and Left to 10px, and click OK.

14. Test the page in Live view and a browser. The contents of the tabbed panels should now look more compact but with more breathing space on either side. If necessary, compare your style sheet with SpryTabbedPanels_stroll_horiz.css in the SpryAssets folder.

Converting to vertical tabs

The tabbed panels style sheet also contains a default set of rules that let you change the orientation of the tabs. Instead of running across the top, you can have them running down the left side of the panel. Table 7-4 describes the purpose of each selector.

Table 7-4. Style rules for vertical tabs

Selector	Type	Notes
.VTabbedPanels .TabbedPanelsTabGroup	Explicit	Vertical tabs are displayed in a column. This selector sets the background color, border, height, and width of the column. The height (default 20em) needs to be the same as in .VTabbedPanels .TabbedPanelsTabGroup. Don't use a pixel height unless the panels contain elements of fixed dimensions, such as images.

Selector	Type	Notes
.VTabbedPanels .TabbedPanelsTab	Explicit	Works in combination with .TabbedPanelsTab. Overrides top, left, and right borders, float, and margin. All other rules, such as background color and font, are preserved from the .TabbedPanelsTab class.
.VTabbedPanels .TabbedPanelsTabSelected	Dynamic	Overrides the background and bottom border colors of the selected tab. With horizontal tabs, the bottom border is set to the same color as the panel to create the illusion that the tab is part of the panel, but with vertical tabs, a solid bottom border is needed.
.VTabbedPanels .TabbedPanelsTabGroup	Explicit	Sets the height and width of the panels but inherits the background color and borders from the .TabbedPanelsTabGroup class.

7

These descendant selectors work in conjunction with the classes listed in Table 7-2, which control the basic colors. So, you need to perform steps 2–5 of the previous exercise to set the colors for vertical tabbed panels. The main problem with vertical tabs is the need to set a height, which must be sufficient to accommodate the content of the biggest panel. It should be specified in ems so that the panels can expand if the user increases the size of text in the browser. It is possible to omit the height to create a flexible layout, but the result doesn't look as good, as you'll see shortly.

Switching the orientation of tabbed panels

Let's convert the tabbed panels widget in stroll_tabbed.html to use vertical tabs. This time, I think it's easier to use the CSS Styles panel in All mode to change the style rules (using All mode was described in Chapter 4). Continue working with the same files as in the previous exercise.

1. Click anywhere in the tabbed panels widget in Design view, and select <div.TabbedPanels#TabbedPanels1> in the Tag selector at the bottom of the Document window. This is the main <div> that wraps around the tabbed panels widget. Right-click, and choose Set Class ➤ VTabbedPanels from the context menu, as shown in Figure 7-13.

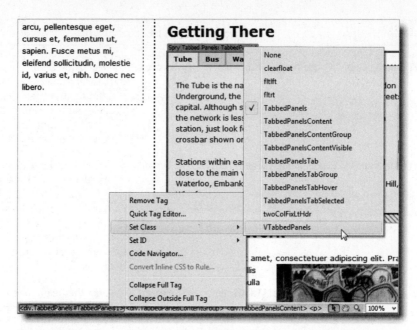

Figure 7-13. The first step in converting to vertical tabs is to change the class of the surrounding <div>.

This changes the class of the <div> from TabbedPanels to VTabbedPanels, and the widget immediately inherits the default rules for vertical tabs. Because the default widths (10em + 30em) are too great, the design falls apart completely in Design view.

2. Open the CSS Styles panel in All mode, and highlight the first vertical tab selector (.VTabbedPanels .TabbedPanelsTabGroup). Change the width property from 10em to 20%, as shown here:

3. Next highlight the final selector that controls vertical tabs (.VTabbedPanels .TabbedPanelsContentGroup), and change the width property from 30em to 78%. The widget springs back into shape. Choosing figures that add up to less than 100 percent avoids rounding errors. To display a web page, the browser needs to convert percentages to whole pixels. If it rounds up, floated content no longer fits and is pushed down the page, breaking your design.

4. Activate Live view, and test the tabbed panels. You'll probably notice two things: the fixed height makes the first panel (Tube) look rather bare, and there's hardly any gap between the bottom of the panel and the following headline. Click the fourth tab (Oyster Card), and you'll see that the contents of the panel spill out, as shown in Figure 7-14.

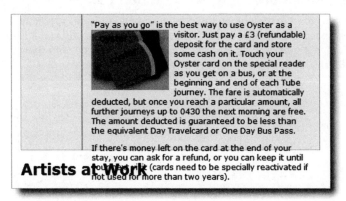

Figure 7-14. The danger with a fixed height is that text might spill out of the panel.

5. Fixing the gap between the tabbed panel widget and the next headline is easy. Add the margin-bottom property to the .VTabbedPanels .TabbedPanelsContentGroup selector, and set its value to 15px.

6. Dealing with the text overspill problem is not so easy. One solution is to change the height property of the .VTabbedPanels .TabbedPanelsTabGroup and .VTabbedPanels .TabbedPanelsContentGroup selectors to 23.5em. The problem with this is that the panels with less content begin to look decidedly empty.

7. The alternative is to remove the height property from both selectors. This causes each panel to expand or contract according to its contents. However, the background color of the column of tabs stretches down only as far as the last tab, as shown in Figure 7-15. You can't give a background color to the surrounding <div>, because both the tabs and panels are floated inside, so the <div> itself has no height.

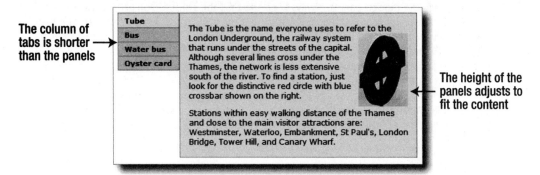

Figure 7-15. Varying amounts of content result in an uneasy compromise.

7

287

8. To revert to horizontal tabs, repeat step 1, changing the class back to TabbedPanels. Compare your style sheet with SpryTabbedPanels_stroll_both.css in the SpryAssets folder, if you need to check your own code. It contains the styles for both horizontal and vertical tabs.

Avoiding design problems with tabbed panels

As the previous exercise demonstrates, content overspill creates problems with the panels. You also need to take care with the tabs, because on a horizontal layout, they are floated left. If you make the labels too long, you might end up with the effect shown in Figure 7-16.

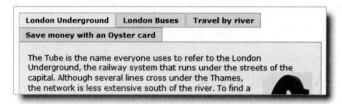

Figure 7-16. Too much content in the tabs breaks the design.

The result can look even more disastrous if you attempt to constrain the width of the tabs by setting a width property in the .TabbedPanelsTab class, as Figure 7-17 shows.

Figure 7-17. Setting a fixed width on the tabs leads to even more unpredictable results.

When using Spry tabbed panels, always keep the tab labels short. Don't try to get them to fit exactly across the top of the panels, because some visitors are likely to increase the text size, forcing one or more tabs to drop down in the same way as too much content does in Figure 7-16. In this sense, Spry tabbed panels aren't 100-percent bulletproof, but the original short labels (Tube, Bus, Water bus, and Oyster Card) don't cause any problem even when the largest font size is chosen in Internet Explorer. In Firefox, you need to increase the text size four times before the last tab slips down. Somebody who needs to make the text so large is unlikely to be concerned about design aesthetics. Still, if you are worried about overflow, you might consider adding the following properties to the .TabbedPanelsTab class:

```
max-width: /* less than total width divided by number of tabs */
white-space: nowrap;
overflow: hidden;
```

This keeps all the tabs on one line, regardless of how much the text is enlarged. The disadvantage is that the end of the label may be hidden if it's too long. Web pages cannot be controlled as rigidly as print, so you need to take into account the need for flexible design. Alternatively, avoid using design elements such as tabbed panels if you need to maintain pixel-perfect accuracy in your layout.

Using the accordion widget

The Spry accordion is another convenient way of storing a lot of information in a compact space. Figure 7-18 shows the same set of travel information as in the tabbed panels displayed in a Spry accordion. Instead of a tab, each panel has an individual title bar. When the user clicks the title bar of a closed panel, it glides open and simultaneously closes the panel that was previously open. By default, the panels are a fixed height and automatically display scrollbars if the content is too big. However, it's quite simple to change this so that the panels expand and contract in line with the content.

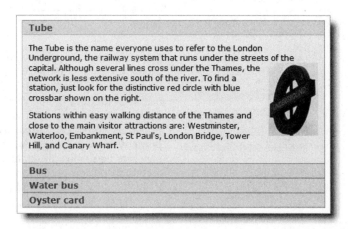

Figure 7-18. The accordion widget displays a series of interlinked panels one at a time.

Examining the structure of an accordion

To insert an accordion widget, click the Spry Accordion button on the Spry or Layout tab of the Insert bar. Alternatively, use the main menu: Insert ➤ Spry ➤ Spry Accordion.

Dreamweaver inserts a default two-panel accordion. The layout in Design view is very similar to the tabbed panels widget, and you access closed panels for editing in exactly the same way, by moving your mouse pointer over the right edge of the panel's title bar and clicking the eye icon.

The underlying HTML looks like this:

```
<div id="Accordion1" class="Accordion" tabindex="0">
  <div class="AccordionPanel">
    <div class="AccordionPanelTab">Label 1</div>
    <div class="AccordionPanelContent">Content 1</div>
  </div>
```

```
<div class="AccordionPanel">
  <div class="AccordionPanelTab">Label 2</div>
  <div class="AccordionPanelContent">Content 2</div>
</div>
</div>
```

It's a simple structure consisting of a wrapper <div>, inside which each panel is a <div> with two more nested inside: one each for the title bar and the content panel. Like the tabbed panels widget, the use of tabindex makes the code technically invalid. Remove it from the opening <div> tag if W3C validation is a requirement, but doing so will disable keyboard navigation of the accordion.

All the styles are controlled by classes and descendant selectors, which are described in Table 7-5. As with Spry tabbed panels, some classes are declared explicitly in the HTML; others are generated dynamically by JavaScript.

Table 7-5. Style rules for the accordion widget

Selector	Type	Notes
.Accordion	Explicit	Sets all borders for the accordion, except for the top border, which is taken from the first title bar. Also sets overflow to hidden to prevent the content of hidden panels from being displayed. Add the background-color property to this rule if you want the panels to be shaded. By default, accordion widgets expand horizontally to fill all available space. Add the width property to this selector to constrain the space it occupies.
.AccordionPanel	Explicit	Eliminates padding and margin for each panel so the accordion displays as a single unit.
.AccordionPanelTab	Explicit	Sets the default background color and border of the title bar of each panel. The top border of the first title bar becomes the top border of the whole widget. Change this rule to style the text in the title bar. The nonstandard properties -moz-user-select and -khtml-user-select prevent users from selecting the title bar label in Mozilla, Firefox, and Konqueror browsers.

Selector	Type	Notes
`.AccordionPanelContent`	Explicit	Sets the height and overflow properties of the open panel. Change these properties if you want a different or flexible height. Do *not* change or delete the padding property, which is set to 0. Always add padding or margins to elements inside the accordion panel, rather than to the `<div>` itself.
`.AccordionPanelOpen` `.AccordionPanelTab`	Dynamic	Sets the background color of the title bar for the currently open tab. However, this is overridden by later dynamic rules if the accordion has focus.
`.AccordionPanelTabHover`	Dynamic	Sets the background color of the title bar in rollover state.
`.AccordionPanelOpen` `.AccordionPanelTabHover`	Dynamic	Sets the background color of the title bar of the currently opened panel when the mouse rolls over the title bar.
`.AccordionFocused` `.AccordionPanelTab`	Dynamic	Sets the background color of the title bar of all panels when the accordion has focus.

`.AccordionFocused`
`.AccordionPanelOpen`
`.AccordionPanelTab`
	Dynamic	Sets the background color of the title bar of the currently open panel when the accordion has focus.

Editing and styling a Spry accordion

Although the structure of the accordion makes it relatively easy to style, the proliferation of dynamic classes and selectors can be confusing. It's easier to understand how they work through hands-on experimentation. So let's get to work.

Inserting the accordion and adding content

The following exercise is based on stroll.html, which you should have copied to your workfiles/ch07 folder for the Spry tabbed panels exercises earlier in the chapter. If you don't have the file, copy stroll.html and stroll.css from examples/ch07 to workfiles/ch07. Update links if prompted by Dreamweaver.

1. Open stroll.html in the Document window, and save it as stroll_accordion.html.

2. Create the new level 2 heading Getting There just above the Artists at Work heading.

3. With your cursor at the end of the new heading, click the Spry Accordion button on the Spry or Layout tab of the Insert bar. The page should look like this:

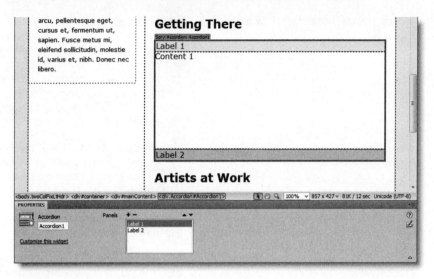

The Property inspector for a Spry accordion has very few options (hover your mouse pointer over the accordion in Design view, and click the Spry Accordion tab at the top left, if the Property inspector is showing something else). Dreamweaver automatically assigns Accordion1 as the ID of the first accordion in a page and numbers subsequent instances Accordion2 and so on. The Property inspector displays the ID in the field on the left, where you can change it if you want. The only other options are to add, remove, and reorder panels using the plus, minus, and arrow buttons. Clicking Customize this widget opens Dreamweaver Help at the page with details of the style rules that control an accordion.

4. Save stroll_accordion.html, and click OK to copy the dependent files.

5. Rename SpryAccordion.css in the Spry assets folder as SpryAccordion_stroll.css, and update the links when prompted. Since the web page contains style rules embedded in conditional comments, move the link to SpryAccordion_stroll.css from just before the closing </head> tag to above the conditional comments.

6. You edit an accordion in the same way as a tabbed panels widget. The only difference is that instead of Tab 1, and so on, the accordion uses Label 1, and so on. Follow steps 6 through 11 of "Inserting and editing a tabbed panels widget" to populate the accordion with four panels labeled Tube, Bus, Water bus, and Oyster Card. Because the title bar of each panel stretches the full width of the accordion, the eye icon that opens closed panels is much further to the right than in the tabbed panels.

7. When you paste the text into some panels, the end appears to be cut off. This is because the default styles set a height of 200 pixels and hide the overflow. To display the accordion content for editing when this happens, double-click inside one of the panels that have an overflow (sometimes you need to double-click twice). Alternatively, right-click, and select Element View ➤ Full from the context menu. This expands the whole accordion in Design view.

   With the accordion fully expanded, insert underground.jpg in the first panel and oystercard.jpg in the fourth panel, and apply the fltrt and fltlft classes to them, respectively (see steps 12 through 14 of "Inserting and editing a tabbed panels widget").

8. To collapse the accordion after editing, press F5, or right-click and select Element View ➤ Hidden from the context menu.

9. Activate Live view, and test the accordion panels. You'll notice that the panels are all the same height, and a vertical scrollbar appears inside each one. The colors are the same neutral grays as in the tabbed panels widget.

10. Save stroll_accordion.html, and press F12/Opt+F12 to preview the page in a browser. Use the Tab key to shift focus to the accordion. As soon as it has focus, the color of the title bars changes from neutral grays to rather ghastly shades of blue. This is the effect of the last two selectors listed in Table 7-5.

   We'll sort out the colors next, but first press the down arrow on your keyboard. As long as you haven't removed the tabindex, the next panel should glide open, closing the previous one behind it. While the accordion has focus, you can navigate through the panels in sequence with the up and down keyboard arrows. Alternatively, you can click any title bar to open a particular panel. Click anywhere outside the accordion and the colors revert to gray.

7

> *The different colors should serve as an important reminder that you should always test your pages in a browser—and preferably all the main browsers—before deploying a site on the Internet. Live view speeds up the process of development, but it's no substitute for the real thing when it comes to judging what your site will really look like.*

Changing the default colors of an accordion

The following instructions show you how to change the colors of stroll_accordion.html from the preceding exercise, but they apply equally to any accordion. Just use your own colors in place of those suggested here. The color scheme I have used is essentially the same as for the tabbed panels. Table 7-6 summarizes the default background colors and my replacements. The default style sheet uses keywords rather than hexadecimal notation for some colors.

Table 7-6. Background colors used in the accordion widget

Default color	Replacement	Applies to
Gray (gray)	Light brown (#DFBD9F)	Lighter borders
Black (black)	Russet (#C99466)	Darker borders
Medium gray (#CCCCCC)	Dark pink (#F2E1D2)	Closed title bar
Pale gray (#EEEEEE)	Dark pink (#F2E1D2)	Open title bar
Royal blue (#3399FF)	None	Closed title bar with focus
Sky blue (#33CCFF)	None	Open title bar with focus

1. Select SpryAccordion_stroll.css in the Related Files toolbar, and launch the Find and Replace dialog box (Edit ➤ Find and Replace or Ctrl+F/Cmd+F). Replace the first four colors listed in Table 7-6 in the same way as you did with the tabbed panels widget earlier in this chapter.

2. Close the Results panel, scroll down to the bottom of SpryAccordion_stroll.css, and locate the following section:

```
108  .AccordionFocused .AccordionPanelTab {
109      background-color: #3399FF;
110  }
111
112  /* This is an example of how to change the appearance of
     the panel tab that is
113   * currently open when the Accordion has focus.
114   */
115  .AccordionFocused .AccordionPanelOpen .AccordionPanelTab
     {
116      background-color: #33CCFF;
117  }
```

3. Delete the background-color properties and values shown on lines 109 and 116 of the preceding screenshot. This leaves both style rules empty. I have left them like this in case you decide you want to add different colors to indicate when the accordion has focus. Of course, if you don't want a visual indication that the accordion has focus, you can delete these two rules in their entirety.

4. Save the style sheet, and load stroll_accordion.html into a browser. When you test the accordion, the colors no longer clash with the rest of the page, but the styles could still do with some improvement.

   Currently, the panels have no background color, and the text in the title bars needs to look a bit more substantial.

5. I'll leave it up to you whether to make the remaining changes directly in the style sheet or in the CSS Styles panel in All mode. The important thing here is to understand which rules you're changing and why.

To give the panels a background color, add the background-color property to the .Accordion selector, and set it to #FAF3ED (light pink).

6. The .AccordionPanelTab selector styles the tab or title bar of each panel, so this is where you can make changes to the text in the title bars. Add the following properties and values:

```
font-family: Verdana, Geneva, sans-serif;
font-size: 90%;
font-weight: bold;
color: #555;
```

7. The text could also do with a bit of horizontal space, so change the value of the padding property in the .AccordionPanelTab selector from 2px to 2px **10px**. This gives 2 pixels of padding top and bottom and 10 pixels on either side.

8. The .AccordionPanelTabHover selector controls the rollover state of the title bars, but only when the accordion doesn't have focus. Change the color property to a slightly darker gray (#333). Also add the background-color property, and set it to #ECD3BD (dusky pink). This keeps the rollover color in harmony with the rest of the accordion when the focus is elsewhere in the page.

9. Give the next selector (.AccordionPanelOpen .AccordionPanelTabHover) the same values as in step 8. This makes the rollover colors the same, regardless of whether the accordion has focus.

10. One final change: because you cannot add padding to the AccordionPanelTab class, it's a good idea to create a new rule for .AccordionPanelContent p. By this stage, I expect you should have sufficient experience of creating new style rules. Define it in SpryAccordion_stroll.css using the following properties and values:

```
font-size: 75%;
padding-left: 10px;
padding-right: 10px;
```

This makes the text slightly smaller than in the rest of the page and gives 10 pixels breathing space on either side of the paragraphs inside the accordion. You can check your code against SpryAccordion_stroll_done.css in the SpryAssets folder.

The smaller font size created by the final change to the default styles removes the vertical scrollbar from all except the last panel. In the next chapter, I'll show you how to tweak the settings of an accordion so that the panels expand and contract to fit the content in the same way as the tabbed panels. You can't do it with CSS alone; you need to get your hands dirty (not very) with the Spry JavaScript code.

Using collapsible panels

Collapsible panels are very similar to the accordion. In fact, they look identical to an accordion if you use several of them in succession. The difference is that each panel is separately controlled, so they can be all open, all closed, or any combination in between.

7

Examining the structure of a collapsible panel

To insert a collapsible panel, click the Spry Collapsible Panel button in the Spry or Layout tab of the Insert bar. Alternatively, use the menu option: Insert ➤ Spry ➤ Spry Collapsible Panel. This inserts a default collapsible panel (see Figure 7-19) at the current insertion point of the page.

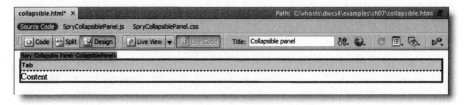

Figure 7-19. A collapsible panel consists of a single tab and content area.

The underlying HTML is extremely simple: a <div> for the tab and another for the content, both nested in a wrapper <div> like this:

```
<div id="CollapsiblePanel1" class="CollapsiblePanel">
  <div class="CollapsiblePanelTab" tabindex="0">Tab</div>
  <div class="CollapsiblePanelContent">Content</div>
</div>
```

This simple structure makes for equally simple CSS styling. Table 7-7 lists the default selectors. As with the tabbed panels and accordion widgets, the use of tabindex is technically invalid but is a compromise to make the panels accessible through keyboard navigation.

Table 7-7. Style rules for the collapsible panel widget

Selector	Type	Notes
.CollapsiblePanel	Explicit	This zeros margin and padding on the widget and sets a light-colored border on the left and bottom and a darker-colored on the right and top. By default, collapsible panels expand horizontally to fill the available space, so set a width here if required. Set a background color for the panel here.
.CollapsiblePanelTab	Explicit	This styles the tab. Only the bottom border is set, as the top, left, and right border styles come from the preceding selector. Change this rule to style the text in the title bar. The nonstandard properties -moz-user-select and -khtml-user-select prevent users from selecting the title bar label in Mozilla, Firefox, and Konqueror browsers.
.CollapsiblePanelContent	Explicit	This zeros padding and margins. Do *not* change or delete the padding property. Always add padding or margins to elements inside the panel, rather than to the <div> itself.

Selector	Type	Notes
`.CollapsiblePanelTab a`	Explicit	This doesn't actively affect the widget in its default state. If you put a dummy link around the text in a tab, this style rule limits the focus lines around the text, rather than around the entire tab.
`.CollapsiblePanelOpen` `.CollapsiblePanelTab`	Dynamic	Sets the background color of the tab when the panel is open.
`.CollapsiblePanelTabHover,` `.CollapsiblePanelOpen,` `.CollapsiblePanelTabHover`	Dynamic	Sets the background color of the tab in rollover state.
`.CollapsiblePanelFocused` `.CollapsiblePanelTab`	Dynamic	Sets the background color of the tab when the panel has focus.

Editing and styling collapsible panels

When you insert a collapsible panel widget, it's open by default, ready for editing. However, since you can have collapsible panels open and closed in any combination, the options in the Property inspector need a little explanation. As you can see in Figure 7-20, there are two drop-down menus that are set to Open by default. The first one—labeled Display—controls whether the content of the collapsible panel is visible in Design view. The second—labeled Default state—controls whether the panel is open or closed when the web page first loads.

Figure 7-20. Two settings control the state of a collapsible panel—one for Design view, the other for the web page.

The Display setting is purely for your convenience when editing the page in Dreamweaver. If you set Default state to Closed, the panel is closed when the page first loads into a browser window.

The Enable animation option at the bottom of the Property inspector is checked by default. If you deselect it, the collapsible panel snaps open and closed, rather than gliding.

If you have more than one collapsible panel on a page, Dreamweaver initializes each one independently, so you need to set the options individually for each panel. There is no way of setting global options for all panels on a page.

7

Since collapsible panels are so similar to the Spry accordion, I won't give step-by-step instructions for inserting and editing them. Table 7-8 lists the default colors used in SpryCollapsiblePanel.css together with the substitutes I used to fit the color scheme in the exercise file that we have been using throughout this chapter.

Table 7-8. Background colors used in collapsible panels

Default color	Replacement	Applies to
Pale gray (#EEE)	Light pink (#FAF3ED)	Open tab
Light gray (#DDD)	Dark pink (#F2E1D2)	Tab
Medium gray (#CCC)	Light brown (#DFBD9F)	Tab on rollover and light borders
Dark gray (#999)	Russet (#C99466)	Dark borders
Royal blue (#3399FF)	Dusky pink (#ECD3BD)	Tab on focus

All the other changes follow the same pattern as for an accordion. To give the panels a background color, add a background-color property to the .CollapsiblePanel selector. I used #FAF3ED (light pink).

To make the text in the tabs look more substantial, I added the same rules to .CollapsiblePanelTab as I did with the accordion tabs, namely:

```
color: #555;
font-family: Verdana, Geneva, sans-serif;
font-size: 90%;
font-weight: bold;
```

To ensure the text in the tabs stands out on rollover, add a color property to .CollapsiblePanelTabHover, .CollapsiblePanelOpen .CollapsiblePanelTabHover. I used #333.

Finally. because you cannot add padding to the CollapsiblePanelTab class, it's a good idea to create a new rule for .CollapsiblePanelContent p in the same way as for the accordion. I used the following properties and values:

```
font-size: 75%;
padding: 5px 10px;
margin: 0;
```

You can see the finished result in stroll_collapsible.html. The amended style sheet is in SpryCollapsiblePanel_stroll.css in the SpryAssets folder.

Creating tooltips with Spry

The Spry Tooltip widget is new to Dreamweaver CS4. It makes it very easy to add an extended tooltip to a page element. Figure 7-21 shows a Spry Tooltip attached to one of the images in stroll.html, but any page element can be used as a trigger.

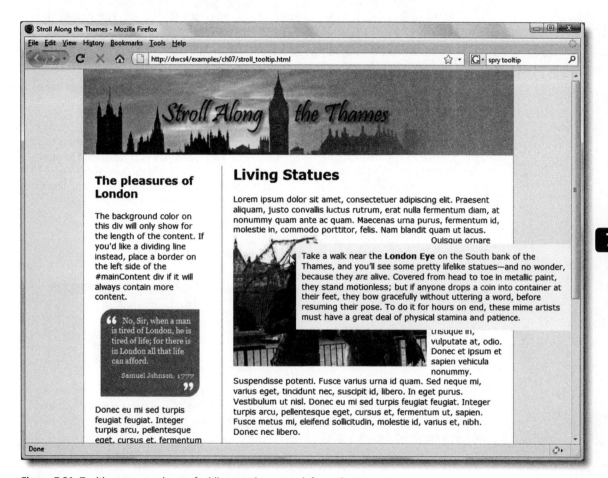

Figure 7-21. Tooltips are a good way of adding supplementary information to a page.

Examining the structure of a Spry tooltip

To insert a Spry Tooltip, click the Spry Tooltip icon on the Spry tab of the Insert bar or use the menu option: Insert ➤ Spry ➤ Spry Tooltip.

A Spry Tooltip consists of two parts: the trigger element and the tooltip. The tooltip is always a <div>, which Dreamweaver places at the end of the document, just before the closing `</body>` tag (although you can move this later). The trigger depends on what, if anything, is selected in the page, as follows:

- If nothing is selected, the trigger consists of placeholder text wrapped in a `<span>` and inserted at the current insertion point.
- If an HTML element, such as an image, paragraph, or `<div>`, is selected, Dreamweaver adds an `id` attribute to the element's tag to associate it with the tooltip.
- If the element already has an `id` attribute, the existing ID is preserved and used to associate the element with the tooltip.
- If only part of a text element is selected, the selected portion is wrapped in a `<span>`, and an `id` attribute is added to the `<span>` tag.

Like all Spry widgets, the Spry Tooltip relies on an external JavaScript file (`SpryTooltip.js`) and a style sheet (`SpryTooltip.css`). In contrast with the other UI components, the style sheet is extremely simple. It contains just two selectors: `.iframeTooltip` and `.tooltipContent`. The first selector is a hack that overcomes a problem with Internet Explorer and shouldn't be altered. The `.tooltipContent` selector contains just a single property: the background color of the tooltip, which is set to light yellow (#FFFFCC).

Inserting and styling tooltips

The following screenshot shows the Property inspector for a Spry Tooltip:

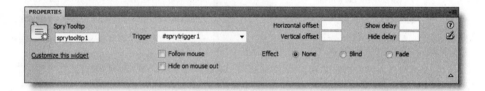

The field on the left of the Property inspector displays the ID of the selected tooltip `<div>`. Dreamweaver automatically assigns this value, incrementing the number for each tooltip added to the page. You can change this value, but you must ensure that the same ID is not used elsewhere on the same page.

The other options are as follows:

- Trigger: This displays the ID of the trigger element. You can change the trigger element by clicking the arrow on the right of the field to reveal a list of all IDs on the current page, except that of the tooltip `<div>`.
- Follow mouse: Selecting this checkbox makes the tooltip follow the mouse within the bounds of the trigger element.
- Hide on mouse out: By default, tooltips are hidden when the mouse moves off the trigger element. Selecting this option keeps the tooltip open as long as the mouse remains over the tooltip, even if it's no longer over the trigger element. See the following exercise for a practical example.

- Horizontal/Vertical offset: By default, the top-left corner of the tooltip is displayed 20 pixels to the right and below the cursor. To set a different offset, enter the desired values (use only numbers without px) in these fields. Negative numbers move the tooltip above and to the left of the cursor. Positive numbers move it below and to the right. The new offset is calculated from the current position of the cursor, not from the default top left of the tooltip.

- Show/Hide delay: These fields let you delay the appearance or disappearance of the tooltip by a specified number of milliseconds (1000 = 1 second).

- Effect: This determines how the tooltip is displayed. There are three options:

  - None: The whole tooltip appears or is hidden immediately.

  - Blind: The tooltip is revealed from the top. When being hidden, it disappears from the bottom. This effect sometimes results in the background being drawn too big or too small. Test it thoroughly in your target browsers.

  - Fade: This fades the tooltip in or out.

Applying tooltips to text and images

This exercise shows you how to add tooltips to various elements in the page that has been used throughout this chapter. It also examines how the tooltips are dynamically generated.

1. Save stroll.html as stroll_tooltip.html in exercises/ch07.

2. Click anywhere in the sidebar. Then select <div#sidebar1> in the Tag selector at the bottom of the Document window. This selects the whole <div>.

3. Insert a Spry Tooltip using either the Insert bar or the Insert menu. Although it looks as though nothing happened, scroll down to the bottom of the page, and you should see that the tooltip <div> has been inserted below the footer, as shown in Figure 7-22. Notice that the value of the Trigger field is #sidebar1, indicating that Dreamweaver has used the existing id attribute of the selected element.

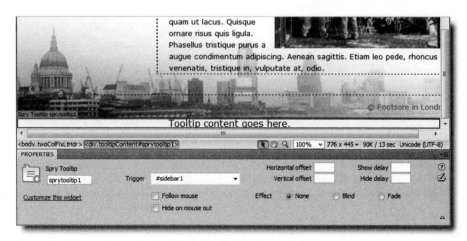

Figure 7-22. The tooltip <div> is always placed at the foot of the page.

4. Save `stroll_tooltip.html` to copy the dependent files to the site's Spry assets folder.

5. Rename `SpryTooltip.css` to `SpryTooltip_stroll.css`, and update the link to `stroll_tooltip.html` when prompted.

6. As you can see in Figure 7-22, the placeholder text in the tooltip is centered. To understand why, hold down the Alt key (or Opt+Cmd), and click inside the tooltip `<div>`. The Code Navigator displays two CSS selectors: .tooltipContent and body. Mouse over them to inspect the style rules they define. You'll see that the .tooltipContent selector specifies only a background color. It's the body selector that's centering the text, as the following screenshot shows:

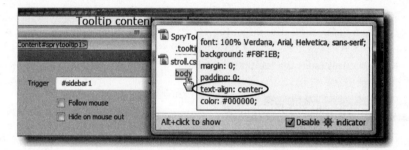

If you read the comments in `stroll.css`, you'll see that it's to center the container `<div>` in Internet Explorer 5. The text in the container `<div>` is realigned in a separate rule. However, as I explained before, Dreamweaver inserts the tooltip `<div>` just before the closing `</body>` tag, so it's outside the container `<div>` and not affected by its style rules. Although Internet Explorer 5 is becoming increasingly rare, rather than risk problems, it's better to change the text alignment for the tooltip.

7. Select `SpryTooltip_stroll.css` in the Related Files toolbar. and amend the .tooltipContent style rule by adding the text-align and padding properties like this:

```
.tooltipContent
{
  background-color: #FFFFCC;
  text-align: left;
  padding: 0 10px;
}
```

8. Replace the placeholder text with something relatively short like This is the sidebar.

9. Select `living_statues.jpg` in Design view, and apply a Spry Tooltip. Scroll down to the bottom of the page. You'll see that the new tooltip `<div>` has been inserted below the footer but above the previous tooltip `<div>`. Check the value of Trigger in the Property inspector. The image didn't have an ID, so Dreamweaver has automatically assigned #sprytrigger1.

10. Replace the placeholder text in the new tooltip <div> with a paragraph containing several sentences. You can use the text in tooltip.doc or tooltip.docx in examples/ch07. The bottom of the page should now look like this in Design view (the size of the text in the second tooltip is smaller because it's in a paragraph):

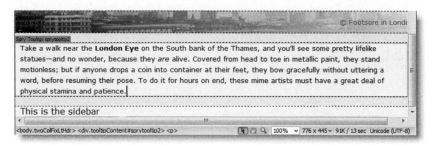

11. Save both stroll_tooltip.html and its style sheet. Then preview the page in a browser. As you move your mouse over the sidebar, the first tooltip should appear and disappear again when you move your mouse away.

12. Now, mouse over the image of the living statues. Move your mouse from the top left of the image down toward the bottom right. As the mouse reaches the top left corner of the tooltip, the tooltip jumps to maintain its distance and keeps on doing so until you're no longer over the image.

13. Return to Dreamweaver, and select the second tooltip (click the turquoise tab at the top left to bring up its details in the Property inspector). Select the Hide on mouse out option.

14. Save the page, and view it again in the browser. Mouse over the image from the top left again. This time, the tooltip remains in its original position until your mouse leaves both the image and the tooltip.

15. I'll leave you to experiment with other options, but finally let's examine how the browser displays the tooltip. Back in Dreamweaver, switch to Split view, and select Source Code in the Related Files toolbar. Press F4 to hide the panels if you need more room to see both the underlying HTML and part of the page in Design view. You don't need to see the whole page, but just enough to be able to mouse over the image of the living statues.

16. Activate Live view, and mouse over the image to display the tooltip. Now press F6 to freeze the JavaScript. This lets you move your mouse off the image to click the Live Code button in the Document toolbar (or select View ➤ Live Code). The Code view section of the Document window turns yellow, indicating that it's showing the dynamically generated code.

17. Scroll down the Code view section of the Document window until you find the beginning of the tooltip <div>. It should look like this:

```
49   <div class="tooltipContent" id="sprytooltip2" style="
     position: absolute; z-index: 9999; display: block; left:
     289px; top: 127px; visibility: visible; ">
50     <p>Take a walk near the <strong>London Eye</strong> on
     the South bank of the Thames, and you'll see some pretty
```

Notice that it has an inline `style` attribute that converts the `<div>` into an absolutely positioned element. This is dynamically generated by the Spry Tooltip's external JavaScript file.

When the page first loads, the JavaScript sets the `visibility` property to `none`, hiding it from view. Passing the mouse over the image triggers a JavaScript event that manipulates the DOM. Live Code shows you the information being passed to the browser to display the tooltip.

18. Turn off Live Code by clicking the Live Code button or selecting View ➤ Live Code. The same section of code should now look like this:

```
53   <div class="tooltipContent" id="sprytooltip2">
54       <p>Take a walk near the <strong>London Eye</strong> on
     the South bank of the Thames, and you'll see some pretty
```

The inline `style` attribute has gone. Also, the line numbers have changed. This reflects the fact that the DOM is no longer being manipulated by JavaScript.

Like all Spry widgets, the tooltip degrades gracefully when JavaScript is turned off. The content of each tooltip `<div>` is displayed as ordinary text. Dreamweaver locates them at the bottom of the page, but you can put them anywhere in the page as long as it's a valid place to locate a `<div>`. After all, as far as HTML is concerned, a tooltip `<div>` is no different from any other. It's the JavaScript that converts it temporarily into an absolutely positioned element.

To preserve the logical flow of the page for search engines and anyone browsing without JavaScript enabled, it's a good idea to move each tooltip `<div>` to the section of the page to which it refers. However, you should always do this in Code view.

> *Do not use Design view to move a tooltip `<div>` to a different part of the page. When you cut the `<div>`, it also removes a vital part of the JavaScript code, which is not restored when you paste the `<div>` in its new location.*

Removing a Spry widget

Removing a Spry widget is very easy: just click the turquoise tab at the top left of the widget, and press Delete. Dreamweaver removes both the widget and its associated JavaScript. However, if you have renamed the style sheet (as in the exercises in this chapter), the link to the style sheet *isn't* removed. Dreamweaver removes only style sheets that retain the default name.

Although this sounds simple and convenient, it comes with a big downside: *removing a widget also removes all its contents*. So, think carefully before pressing Delete. Do you need to display the contents in some other format? If so, make sure you have a copy before blasting everything to cyberoblivion.

Chapter review

In this chapter, I've given you an in-depth look at Spry effects and user interface components. The effects are easy to use: just a couple of clicks, and you're done. The user interface components are also easy to insert into a page. The difficulty comes with styling them to fit in with the rest of your design. However, once you have worked out a set of colors to replace the defaults, you can customize them fairly quickly.

As I said at the beginning of the chapter, you don't even need Dreamweaver to use Spry. You could, in fact, implement everything in this chapter by downloading the external JavaScript files of the Spry framework and hand-coding a few lines to embed the effects and widgets in your page. There's no doubt that Dreamweaver lightens the load when using these features, but it can't automate everything. For example, you can't create a link to open an accordion or tabbed panel without learning about the Spry application programming interface (API) and diving into Code view. Dreamweaver code hints for Spry, as well as improved support for the DOM and other JavaScript libraries, make this easier. So, in the next chapter, I invite you to roll up your sleeves and get closer to the code.

7

The Spry effects and widgets described in the previous chapter owe their existence to a fundamental shift that has taken place in the past few years in the way that JavaScript is used to generate dynamic effects in the browser. Traditionally, JavaScript has been used to tackle specific tasks. For example, if you wanted to change an image on rollover, you would write a script designed simply for that purpose or use an existing one (Dreamweaver automates the process for you with Insert ➤ Image Objects ➤ Rollover Image). This has the advantage of producing lightweight dedicated scripts. For example, Dreamweaver's image rollover script is fewer than 20 lines of code. However, improvements in browser capabilities and better support for the DOM (see Chapter 7) spurred developers to see how far they could push JavaScript. The Spry effects might look quite simple, but they all involve changing the state of the target element (its position, transparency, or color) over a specified period. The amount of scripting required for each effect is considerable. Yet each effect shares common tasks: the need to identify the target element, a timer to control the transition, ways of dynamically manipulating the element's style rules, and so on. Rather than reinvent the wheel for each new script, it became more efficient to develop a framework or library of common functions.

The sudden explosion of JavaScript frameworks in recent years is a mixed blessing for web developers. In one respect, using a framework reduces the amount of code the developer needs to write because most complex tasks are handled by the framework. On the other hand, it involves a considerable learning curve. Books about the most popular frameworks, Prototype, script.aculo.us, jQuery, and Mootools, run to hundreds of pages. Dreamweaver has tried to reduce the Spry learning curve by automating the insertion and configuration of a large number of widgets and effects. All the JavaScript coding is handled for you seamlessly behind the scenes (it might come as a surprise that `SpryEffects.js` contains nearly 2,500 lines of code).

If you don't want to get your hands dirty with JavaScript, you can skip this chapter. On the other hand, if you do, you might find yourself frustrated at not being able to use Spry to its full extent. Because Spry is a fully fledged JavaScript framework, it's capable of doing much more than you can achieve through the Property inspector or dialog boxes. Doing things such as opening a panel from a link or making the height of accordion panels expand and contract depending on the amount of content in them involves diving under the hood and hand-coding JavaScript. Spry code hints make this a relatively painless process.

In this chapter, you'll learn about the following:

- Passing additional arguments to Spry effects and widgets
- Creating an accordion with flexible-height panels
- Opening Spry panels from links
- Combining Spry effects
- Using the Spry selector to manipulate styles on the fly
- Saving bandwidth with minified Spry files
- Creating unobtrusive JavaScript with the JavaScript Extractor
- Using other JavaScript libraries with Dreamweaver CS4
- Installing Dreamweaver extensions
- Experimenting with jQuery and YUI Library web widgets

If you have worked previously with JavaScript, you should have little difficulty customizing Spry effects and widgets. However, for the benefit of readers taking their first steps with programming, the following section explains some of the basic concepts.

> *In spite of the similarity of names, JavaScript is wholly unrelated to Java. They are different programming languages, and "Java" should never be used as an abbreviation for JavaScript.*

Programming terminology 101

Programming languages like JavaScript and PHP (which you'll use in the second half of this book) change the output displayed in a web page in response to events or user input. Since the developer has no way of knowing in advance how users will interact with a page, programming languages use a variety of mechanisms to produce the required output. The following are some of the most important.

A **variable** acts as a placeholder for an unknown or changeable value, which may come from user input, a database, the result of a calculation, and so on. Although this sounds abstract, we use variables all the time in everyday life. My name is David, and my editor's name is Ben. In this case, "name" plays the same role as a variable—the word "name" always remains the same, but the *value assigned* to it can change.

Functions can be regarded as the verbs of programming languages; they do things. Many functions are built into the language, but you can also build your own functions by combining a series of commands. In both JavaScript and PHP, function names are always followed by a pair of parentheses. Often, the parentheses contain variables, known as **parameters** or **arguments**. Passing a value as an argument tells the function to do something with it, such as perform a calculation or format text.

JavaScript is triggered by **events**, such as when the page has finished loading or the user clicks a link. You tell the browser to run a function by assigning it (plus any arguments, if necessary) to an **event handler** such as onclick, onmouseover, or onmouseout. To give a trivial example, the following code pops up an annoying message when the link is clicked:

```
<a href="#" onclick="alert('You clicked!')">Click me quick</a>
```

A **string** is the name that programming languages give to text. A string is always enclosed in quotes (single or double). By contrast, numbers should not normally be enclosed in quotes, unless they're part of a string.

An **array** is a variable that can hold multiple values, rather like a shopping list.

An **object** is like a super variable, which can have variables (called **properties**) and functions (called **methods**) of its own. New instances of an object are created using the new keyword followed by a constructor function, which looks and works very much like any other function.

8

> *Both JavaScript and PHP are case-sensitive. You must use the right combination of uppercase and lowercase when typing JavaScript and PHP code. Dreamweaver code hints are invaluable in helping get the spelling right.*

Understanding Spry objects

In common with other JavaScript frameworks, Spry uses JavaScript objects. The idea of using objects is that all the complex coding remains locked away in the object definition, so you need concern yourself only with parts exposed through the object's methods and properties. Methods are functions that can be used to get the object to perform particular actions. Properties define the state of an object. All Spry effects and widgets are objects. So, for example, the properties of an accordion determine whether a panel is open or whether the panels have a fixed height; and to open the panel of a tabbed panels object, you use its showPanel() method.

> *The object definitions aren't literally locked away. You can study them by opening the external JavaScript files that Dreamweaver copies to the Spry assets folder. However, you should never edit the JavaScript in those files unless you really know what you're doing. And if you do know what you're doing, you would probably create your own methods and properties without touching the original files.*

Initializing a Spry object

When you insert a Spry tabbed panels widget, Dreamweaver initializes the JavaScript object at the bottom of the page just before the closing </body> tag like this:

```
<script type="text/javascript">
<!--
var TabbedPanels1 = new Spry.Widget.TabbedPanels("TabbedPanels1");
//-->
</script>
</body>
```

The line of JavaScript highlighted in bold creates a new tabbed panels object and stores a reference to it in a JavaScript variable with the same name as the ID of the <div> that contains the panels. The ID and the JavaScript variable don't need to be the same, but Dreamweaver adopts this convention to make it easy to use Spry properties and methods.

Dreamweaver normally handles all the coding for you, but if you want to get more adventurous with Spry widgets, you need to understand what the code means. So, let's analyze it piece by piece:

- var: This is a JavaScript keyword used to declare a new variable. Variable names in JavaScript cannot begin with a number and should not contain any spaces or punctuation, except for the underscore (_).

- TabbedPanels1: This is the name of the new variable, which can be used elsewhere in the script to represent whatever value is assigned to it.

- The assignment operator (=): This assigns the value on the right to the variable on the left. Try not to think of it as an equal sign, because both JavaScript and PHP use *two* equal signs to indicate equality.

- new: This is a JavaScript keyword that creates an instance of an object.

- Spry.Widget: This is the object of which a new instance is being created.

- TabbedPanels("TabbedPanels1"): This is the constructor method of the object. In this case, it creates a tabbed panels widget. The value in quotes between the parentheses is an argument being passed to the new object. Arguments set the values of specific properties. In the case of Spry objects, the first argument is always the ID of the target element.

If you change the value of the Default panel in the Property inspector to Tab2, Dreamweaver changes the initialization code like this:

```
var TabbedPanels1 = new Spry.Widget.TabbedPanels("TabbedPanels1", ➥
{defaultTab:1});
```

The format of the second argument is important. Unlike the first argument, it's not enclosed in quotes but in a pair of curly braces. In JavaScript, this is called an **object literal**. An object literal is simply a shorthand way of creating a new object. It consists of name/value pairs surrounded by curly braces. Each name/value pair defines a property, with a colon separating the value from the property name. This object literal contains a single name/value pair: defaultTab, which is a property of a tabbed panels widget, and 1, which is the value assigned to that property. No, it's not a mistake. Like most programming languages, JavaScript counts from zero, so the number of the second tab is 1, not 2.

The second argument in most Spry constructor methods sets various options. Since an object literal can accept multiple name/value pairs as a comma-separated list, using an object literal as the second argument makes it easy to pass multiple options to the Spry effect or widget like this:

```
var TabbedPanels1 = new Spry.Widget.TabbedPanels("TabbedPanels1", ➥
{property1:value1, property2:value2, property3:value3});
```

You can put whitespace around the colons and insert new lines after the commas for ease of reading. Don't worry if all this terminology sounds intimidating. As you'll see in the following exercises, hand-coding Spry is relatively painless.

Changing accordion defaults

As explained in Chapter 7, the Property inspector for an accordion lets you change only the ID and the number and order of panels. Unlike Spry tabbed panels, there's no option to select a panel to be displayed by default when the page first loads. What's more, changing

8

the default behavior of using fixed-height panels isn't just a question of tweaking the style sheet. To make both changes, you need to pass options to the accordion object constructor.

Changing an accordion's default open panel

By default, an accordion is always displayed with the first panel open. This exercise shows how to display a different panel when the page first loads. This technique always displays the same panel. It cannot be used to open a specific panel from a link in a different page.

1. Create a new folder called ch08 in your workfiles folder, copy accordion_start.html from examples/ch08, and save it in the new folder as accordion.html. Update the links when prompted. The page should look like this in Design view:

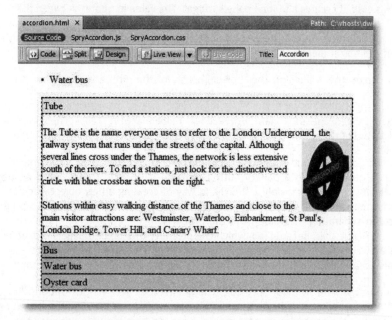

The accordion contains the same material as used in Chapter 7. However, I have left the accordion unstyled apart from constraining its width.

2. To change the default open panel, open the page in Code view, and scroll down to the bottom. Locate the following line of code, which initializes the accordion object:

```
var Accordion1 = new Spry.Widget.Accordion("Accordion1");
```

3. Insert your cursor just before the closing parenthesis, and type a comma. Dreamweaver displays the following code hint:

```
61  <script type="text/javascript">
62  <!--
63  var Accordion1 = new Spry.Widget.Accordion("Accordion1",);
64  //-->
65  </script>
```

Accordion(element, {options})

This tells you that Spry expects the constructor method to take two arguments: element (the ID of the <div> that houses the accordion) and options. Because options is highlighted in bold, that's what Dreamweaver now expects you to enter. The curly braces remind you that options must be a JavaScript object literal.

4. Type an opening curly brace. This pops up a second code hint, as shown here:

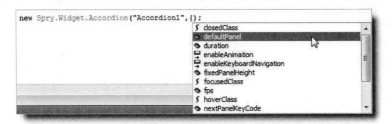

This shows you some of the available options. Double-click defaultPanel, or use the down arrow key to select it and press Enter/Return. Dreamweaver inserts the defaultPanel property followed by a colon ready for you to insert the value. JavaScript numbers the panels from 0, so to open the third panel, type 2 followed by a closing curly brace. The code should now look like this:

```
var Accordion1 = new Spry.Widget.Accordion("Accordion1", ➥
{defaultPanel:2});
```

5. Save accordion.html, and load it in a browser (or activate Live view). The third panel (Water bus) should open instead of the first one.

Check your code, if necessary, with accordion_default.html in examples/ch08.

8

Converting an accordion to flexible height

Using a fixed height for an accordion is very useful when you need to keep different parts of a page in alignment, but the scrollbars tend to look unsightly (only Internet Explorer for Windows supports the nonstandard CSS properties for styling scrollbars).

Converting an accordion to flexible height involves two stages: editing the CSS and passing an option to the accordion object's constructor method. Continue using accordion.html from the preceding exercise.

1. With accordion.html open in the Document window, select SpryAccordion.css in the Related Files toolbar. Then select File ➤ Save As, and save the style sheet as SpryAccordion_flexible.css. This opens the style sheet in a new tab. Close the new tab straightaway, because you'll work with it as a related file.

2. Although you have saved the style sheet with a different name, the original style sheet is still attached to accordion.html. The quickest way to attach the new style sheet is to select Source Code in the Related Files toolbar to reveal the HTML code of accordion.html. Change SpryAccordion.css to SpryAccordion_flexible.css in the

<link> tag in the <head> of the document, save the page, and press F5 to update the Related Files toolbar, as shown here:

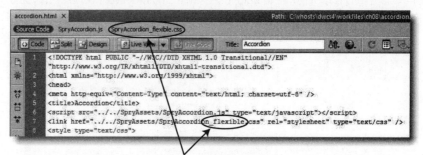

**Change the name of the style sheet in the code.
Then press F5 to update the Related Files toolbar.**

3. You need to change the properties in the `.AccordionPanelContent` selector of the style sheet. There are several ways you can do it, but a quick way to find the right section of code to edit is to switch to Design view, hold down the Alt key (or Opt+Cmd on a Mac), and click anywhere inside the accordion. Click the link for the `.AccordionPanelContent` selector in the Code Navigator, as shown in the following screenshot:

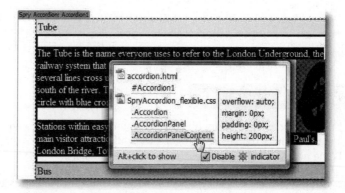

4. Change the value of `overflow` from `auto` to `hidden`. If you leave the `overflow` property set to `auto`, some longer panels still spawn a scrollbar. You need to set it to `hidden` so that only the currently open panel is visible. Also delete the `height` property from the rule, which should now look like this:

```
.AccordionPanelContent {
  overflow: hidden;
  margin: 0px;
  padding: 0px;
}
```

That takes care of the CSS. Now you need to tell the Accordion object to use flexible height.

5. Select Source Code in the Related Files toolbar to return to the HTML code for accordion.html, and then scroll right to the bottom of the page and locate the code that initializes the Accordion object (see step 2 in the preceding exercise).

6. If you changed the default open panel in the preceding exercise, amend the constructor function like this (new code is in bold):

    var Accordion1 = new Spry.Widget.Accordion("Accordion1", ➥
    {defaultPanel:2, **useFixedPanelHeights:false**});

    If you just want to remove the fixed panel heights, amend the code like this:

    var Accordion1 = new Spry.Widget.Accordion("Accordion1", ➥
    {useFixedPanelHeights:false});

    Make sure you don't omit the comma after "Accordion1".

7. Select File ➤ Save All to save the changes to both accordion.html and the style sheet, and test the page in your browser. You now have a flexible-height accordion and no ugly scrollbars.

    Check your code, if necessary, with accordion_flexible.html in examples/ch08. The style sheet, SpryAccordion_flexible.css, is in the SpryAssets folder.

Using an object's methods

Once you have created an object, you can use its methods. You do this by adding a period to the end of the variable that contains the object, followed by the method name and any arguments. So, to open the second panel of a tabbed panels widget stored in TabbedPanels1, you use its showPanel() method like this:

    TabbedPanels1.showPanel(1)

Opening panels from a link on the same page

The technique for opening a specific panel differs not only for each type of Spry widget but also depending on whether the link is located in the same page. This section contains instructions for opening a panel from links within the same page as the widget. There are separate instructions for tabbed panels, accordions, and collapsible panels.

Opening a tabbed panel from a link on the same page

This exercise shows you how to open a specific panel in a tabbed panels widget from a link in the same page.

1. Copy tabbed_start.html from examples/ch08 to workfiles/ch08, and save the file as tabbed.html. Update the links when Dreamweaver prompts you to do so.

8

As with the accordion in the previous exercises, the panels are unstyled apart from a rule that constrains their width.

2. In Design view, select the tab named Bus in the Property inspector, or click its eye icon to reveal the panel content.

3. Select the words Oyster Card in the final sentence, and type javascript:; in the Link field of the HTML view of the Property inspector to create a dummy link.

4. With the words Oyster Card still highlighted, open Split view to reveal the underlying code, and position your cursor just before the closing angle bracket of the <a> tag.

5. Press the spacebar. Code hints should pop up. Type onc, and press Enter/Return when onclick is highlighted. The link surrounding Oyster Card should now look like this (with the cursor between the quotes following onclick):

```
<a href="javascript:;" onclick="">Oyster Card</a>
```

6. To call one of the Spry methods (functions) on a widget, type the ID of the widget followed by a period and the name of the method. The ID of this widget is TabbedPanels1. As soon as you type the period after the ID, Dreamweaver pops up code hints for the selected widget, showing the available methods (see Figure 8-1).

Figure 8-1. Code hints recognize Spry widgets and display available methods.

Use your mouse or keyboard arrow keys to select showPanel(elementOrIndex), and double-click or press Enter/Return. This inserts showPanel followed by an opening parenthesis. Type 3 followed by a closing parenthesis.

Following JavaScript convention, Spry counts the panels from 0, so 3 represents the fourth panel (Oyster Card). The Oyster Card link code should now look like this:

```
<a href="javascript:;" onclick="TabbedPanels1.showPanel(3)">Oyster ➡
Card</a>
```

7. Activate Live view. Select the Bus tab, and click the Oyster Card link within the displayed panel. The fourth panel should open.

8. The link to open another panel doesn't need to be inside the widget; it can be anywhere in the page. You can also identify the panel you want to open with an ID rather than counting its number from zero. This is particularly useful if the order of the panels is likely to change.

Switch off Live view, and select the Water bus tab. With your cursor anywhere inside the content of the third panel, select <div.TabbedPanelsContent> in the Tag selector at the bottom of the Document window. This selects the <div> that contains the third panel.

9. Enter waterbus in the Div ID field of the Property inspector, and press Tab or Enter/Return. The ID of the <div> should be added to the selected tag in the Tag selector, as shown here:

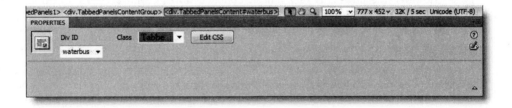

10. You can now use this to open the panel from a link. Select the text in the bullet point at the top of the page, and create a dummy link by entering javascript:; in the Link field of the HTML view of the Property inspector.

11. Open Split view, and insert an onclick event handler inside the link as you did in steps 5 and 6. However, this time, use the ID of the panel. The link should look like this:

```
<a href="javascript:;" onclick="TabbedPanels1.showPanel('waterbus')"> ➡
Water bus</a>
```

Note that the ID of the panel must be in single quotes. Do *not* use double quotes. In programming languages, quotes must always be in matching pairs. The onclick attribute uses double quotes, so any quotes used inside must be single. Otherwise, the code won't work.

> *Understanding the use of quotes is vital when working with languages like JavaScript and PHP. In many circumstances, it doesn't matter whether you use single or double quotes, as long as they're a matching pair. For example, onclick could use single quotes, but in that case, the ID nested inside would need to use double quotes. When a programming language sees an opening quote, it grabs the next matching one as the closing quote. So, you always need to make sure you don't accidentally end a command prematurely by using the wrong type of quotation mark.*

12. Activate Live view, and click the Water bus link. The Water bus panel should open.

13. Turn off Live view, select the tabbed panels widget by clicking the turquoise tab at the top left, and use the up and down arrows in the Property inspector to move the Water bus and Oyster card panels to different positions.

14. Test the page in Live view again. The Water bus panel should still open correctly. However, the link that you created in the Bus panel will no longer open the Oyster card panel. Instead, it opens whatever has been moved to the fourth position.

Check your code, if necessary, against tabbed_link.html in examples/ch08.

Opening an accordion panel from a link on the same page

Unlike a tabbed panels widget, an accordion doesn't have a showPanel() method. However, the process is very similar. Continue working with accordion.html from the exercises earlier in the chapter. Alternatively, copy accordion_flexible.html from examples/ch08, and save it as accordion.html in workfiles/ch08. Update the links when Dreamweaver prompts you to do so.

1. If you did the exercises with the accordion earlier in this chapter, remove the defaultPanel argument from the options used to initialize the accordion constructor. Open Code view, and make sure the code at the bottom of the page looks like this:

```
var Accordion1 = new Spry.Widget.Accordion("Accordion1", ➡
  {useFixedPanelHeights:false});
```

2. Back in Design view, highlight the text in the bullet point at the top of accordion.html, and type javascript:; into the Link field of the HTML view of the Property inspector to create a dummy link. Open Split view, and add an onclick attribute to the <a> tag in the same way as in step 5 in the preceding exercise.

3. With your cursor between the quotes of the onclick attribute, type Accordion1 followed by a period. As soon as you type the period, Dreamweaver pops up code hints of the available methods. Scroll down to the bottom of the list, as shown in the following screenshot:

Note that showPanel() is not listed, but there are four methods that target specific panels: openFirstPanel(), openLastPanel(), openNextPanel(), and openPreviousPanel(). Because they target specific panels, you don't need to add anything between the parentheses. However, Water bus is the third panel, so none of these will work. Select openPanel(elementOrIndex).

4. Since Water bus is the third panel, JavaScript counts its position (or index) as 2. So, add 2, and close the parentheses. The link should look like this:

```
<a href="javascript:;" onclick="Accordion1.openPanel(2)">Water bus</a>
```

5. Save accordion.html, and load the page into a browser. Click the link at the top of the page. The Water bus panel slides open. This is a considerable improvement over the version of Spry in Dreamweaver CS3, which forced you to go through two steps to open a panel using its index.

6. As you saw in the previous exercise, using a number to identify a panel is risky because you need to recode everything if the panel's position changes. Giving the panel an ID and passing it as an argument to the openPanel() method is more reliable. However, you need to make sure you apply the ID to the correct element.

Open the Water bus panel in Design view. Select all or part of it to make it easy to identify in Split view. Notice that the tab and the panel content are each in a separate <div> nested inside another <div> that holds tab and content together like this:

```
<div class="AccordionPanel">
  <div class="AccordionPanelTab">Water bus</div>
  <div class="AccordionPanelContent">
   <p>For many years, Londoners . . .</p>
  </div>
  </div>
</div>
```

7. The ID *must* be applied to the outer <div>. Applying it to the <div> that contains the tab or panel content won't work. To make sure you get the correct <div>, either work in Code view or click inside the content of the panel in Design view and select <div.AccordionPanel> from the Tag selector, as shown in the following screenshot:

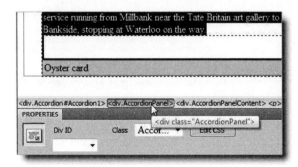

After selecting the correct tag, enter the ID in the Div ID field of the Property inspector. For this exercise, enter waterbus.

8

8. Amend the argument passed to the openPanel() method in step 3 like this (using single quotes around the ID):

```
<a href="javascript:;" onclick="Accordion1.openPanel('waterbus')"> ➥
Water bus</a>
```

9. Select the turquoise tab at the top left of the accordion widget to open its details in the Property inspector, and use the up or down arrow to move the Water bus panel to a different position.

10. Save the page, and test it in a browser. When you click the Water bus link, the correct panel should still open.

   You can check your code, if necessary, against accordion_link.html in examples/ch08.

Opening a collapsible panel from a link in the same page

Since collapsible panels work independently, opening one from a link is simply a matter of applying the open() method to the JavaScript variable that identifies the target panel. By default, Dreamweaver names the first panel on a page CollapsiblePanel1 and increments the number by one for each subsequent panel.

This exercise shows how to open collapsible panels from a link on the same page.

1. Copy collapsible_start.html from examples/ch08, and save it in workfiles/ch08 as collapsible.html. Update the links when Dreamweaver prompts you to do so.

   The page contains four collapsible panels with the same content as before. The first panel is set to display open, while the others remain closed. Again, the only styling on the page limits the width of the panels.

2. Select Water bus at the top of the page, and create a dummy link as you have done in all previous exercises.

3. Switch to Code view, and scroll to the bottom of the page. The code that initializes the collapsible panel objects looks like this:

```
58  <script type="text/javascript">
59  <!--
60  var CollapsiblePanel1 = new Spry.Widget.CollapsiblePanel("CollapsiblePanel1");
61  var CollapsiblePanel2 = new Spry.Widget.CollapsiblePanel("CollapsiblePanel2", {contentIsOpen:false});
62  var CollapsiblePanel3 = new Spry.Widget.CollapsiblePanel("CollapsiblePanel3", {contentIsOpen:false});
63  var CollapsiblePanel4 = new Spry.Widget.CollapsiblePanel("CollapsiblePanel4", {contentIsOpen:false});
64  //-->
65  </script>
66  </body>
```

   As you can see, there are four separate objects. The first argument passed to the constructor method of a Spry object is always the ID of the target element, so CollapsiblePanel3 is a unique identifier for the Water bus panel. Even if you move the panels about on the page, each one retains its original ID.

4. Scroll back up to the dummy link, and add an onclick attribute to the <a> tag.

5. With your cursor between the quotes of the onclick attribute, type CollapsiblePanel3 followed by a period. As soon as you type the period, Dreamweaver pops

up code hints of the available methods. Scroll down until you locate open(), as shown here:

```
<p><a href="javascript:;" onclick="CollapsiblePanel3.">Water bus</a></p>
<p>Open all | Close all</p>                              ○ hasFocus          Spry...CollapsiblePanel   SpryCollapsiblePanel.js
<div id="CollapsiblePanel1" class="CollapsiblePanel">    ○ hoverClass        Spry...CollapsiblePanel   SpryCollapsiblePanel.js
    <div class="CollapsiblePanelTab" tabindex="0">Tube   ■ isOpen()          Spry...CollapsiblePanel
    <div class="CollapsiblePanelContent">                ■ onBlur(e)          Spry...CollapsiblePanel   SpryCollapsiblePanel.js
      <p>The Tube is the name everyone uses to refer to  ■ onFocus(e)         Spry...CollapsiblePanel   SpryCollapsiblePanel.js
"Underground station sign" width="80" height="114" cl   ■ onKeyDown(e)       Spry...CollapsiblePanel   SpryCollapsiblePanel.js
capital. Although several lines cross under the Thame    ■ onTabClick(e)      Spry...CollapsiblePanel   SpryCollapsiblePanel.js
look for the distinctive red circle with blue crossba   ■ onTabMouseOut(e)   Spry...CollapsiblePanel   SpryCollapsiblePanel.js
        <p>Stations within easy walking distance of the ■ onTabMouseOver(e)  Spry...CollapsiblePanel   SpryCollapsiblePanel.js
                                                         ■ open()            Spry...CollapsiblePanel
```

6. Double-click open(), or press Enter/Return. That's it.

7. Save the page, and test it in a browser. When you click the Water bus link at the top of the page, the Water bus panel opens. Because collapsible panels are independent of each other, this has no effect on any other panels that are open.

You can check your code with `collapsible_link.html` in examples/ch08.

Although it's useful to open a collapsible panel from a link, wouldn't it be nice to be able to close it as well? As you scrolled down the list of code hints in step 5 of the previous exercise, you probably noticed that there's a close() method, too. Although you can use that with a different link, how about toggling a panel open and closed from the same link?

Toggling a collapsible panel open and closed from a remote link

This next exercise shows you how to build a custom function to toggle any collapsible panel open and closed from a link on the same page. Continue working with `collapsible.html` from the preceding exercise.

The instructions in this exercise are deliberately verbose to help readers who are new to JavaScript. If you already have experience writing your own JavaScript, you might prefer to skim over most of the explanations and study the finished (very simple) script in `collapsible_toggle.html`.

1. As you have already learned, a collapsible panel object has both an open() method and a close() method. To toggle a panel open and closed, you need a way of finding out its current state. Take a closer look at the screenshot in step 5 of the preceding exercise. Among the code hints is another method called isOpen() (it's the third one down in the screenshot). There isn't an equivalent method that tells you whether a panel is closed, but that's not important. If a panel's not open, it must be closed.

2. Open Code view, and scroll up to the closing </head> tag (it should be around line 24). Create some space before the closing </head> tag, and insert a <script> block like this (the new code is shown in bold):

```
</style>
<script type="text/javascript">
</script>
</head>
```

8

321

3. To create a custom function, you type the keyword function followed by the name you want to use for the function. The name is followed by a pair of parentheses. The body of the function goes between a pair of curly braces. So, amend the code like this:

```
<script type="text/javascript">
function togglePanel()
{
}
</script>
```

4. Since we have been working with the Water bus panel (CollapsiblePanel3), let's continue doing so. Decisions in programming languages are made by determining whether a condition is true or false. The isOpen() method produces a **Boolean value** (true or false). So, CollapsiblePanel3.isOpen() will equate to true if it's open. Otherwise, it equates to false. In programming terms, a function or method is said to **return** a value. So, what we're interested in is whether it returns true or false.

Conditional decisions are handled by using the keyword if followed by the condition in parentheses. Any code you want to run only if the condition is true goes inside a pair of curly braces.

If the panel is open, you want to close it, but if it's closed, you want to open it. To run different code when a condition is false, you use the else keyword and put the code in another pair of curly braces.

Put everything together, and it looks like this:

```
<script type="text/javascript">
function togglePanel()
{
  if (CollapsiblePanel3.isOpen()) {
    CollapsiblePanel3.close();
  } else {
    CollapsiblePanel3.open();
  }
}
</script>
```

5. To use this function, you now need to change the code in the dummy link. It currently looks like this:

```
<a href="javascript:;" onclick="CollapsiblePanel3.open()">Water bus</a>
```

Change it to this:

```
<a href="javascript:;" onclick="togglePanel()">Water bus</a>
```

6. Save collapsible.html, and test the page in a browser. When you click the Water bus link, the panel should now open or close depending on its current state.

Check your code, if necessary, with collapsible_toggle_waterbus.html in examples/ch08. JavaScript is intolerant of mistakes, so use the File Compare feature, as described in Chapter 2, if you're having problems. A missing period, quotation mark, parenthesis, or curly brace will prevent the function from working.

7. This works fine, but it's very inflexible, because it works only with CollapsiblePanel3. This is where passing an argument to a function makes it far more useful. The argument is a variable that goes between the parentheses at the end of the function name. You then use that variable inside the function to represent the actual value that's passed when the function is used. We're toggling the open and closed states of a panel, so let's call the variable panel.

   Change the function like this (the changes are in bold):

   ```
   function togglePanel(panel)
   {
     if (panel.isOpen()) {
       panel.close();
     } else {
       panel.open();
     }
   }
   ```

8. Finally, you need to pass the ID of the panel you want to open as an argument to togglePanel() like this:

   ```
   <a href="javascript:;" onclick="togglePanel(CollapsiblePanel3)">Water ➡
   bus</a>
   ```

   Note that the ID is *not* in quotes because you're passing the object, and not a string.

9. Save collapsible.html, and test the page in a browser again. It should toggle the Water bus panel open and closed as before.

10. Now, the *real* test. Copy and paste the Water bus link, and change it like this:

    ```
    <p><a href="javascript:;" onclick="togglePanel(CollapsiblePanel3)"> ➡
    Water bus</a></p>
    <p><a href="javascript:;" onclick="togglePanel(CollapsiblePanel4)"> ➡
    Oyster card</a></p>
    ```

11. Save the page, and test the new link, which should toggle the Oyster card panel open and closed.

    Check your code, if necessary, against collapsible_toggle.html in examples/ch08.

That solves the problem of toggling a single panel open and closed. How about opening and closing all panels with a single click? Actually, this feature is already built into the external JavaScript file that controls collapsible panels, but you need to implement it manually. It's very easy, as the next exercise shows.

8

Opening and closing all collapsible panels simultaneously

This exercise shows you how to group collapsible panels so they can be opened or closed as a single unit. Each panel, however, can be opened or closed independently.

1. Continue working with the file from the preceding exercise. Alternatively, copy collapsible_toggle.html from examples/ch08, and save it as collapsible.html in workfiles/ch08.

2. To open and close all panels simultaneously, you need to wrap them in an outer <div>. Selecting multiple elements in Design view can be tricky, so the safest way to do this is in Code view. Insert a new <div> tag just before the first collapsible panel. It needs both an ID and a class. The ID can be anything you like, as long as it's unique on the page (I used panelgroup). The class must be CollapsiblePanelGroup. The amended code looks like this (it should be around line 40):

```
<p>Open all | Close all</p>
<div id="panelgroup" class="CollapsiblePanelGroup">
<div id="CollapsiblePanel1" class="CollapsiblePanel">
```

> You can combine CollapsiblePanelGroup *with other classes in the same* class *attribute, but you need to do this in Code view or the* Tag Inspector *panel, because Dreamweaver doesn't support assigning multiple classes through the Property inspector.*

3. Scroll to the end of the last panel, and insert a closing </div> tag. It should go immediately above the <script> block around line 70, like this:

```
more than two years).</p>
    </div>
  </div>
</div>
<script type="text/javascript">
```

4. When you create a collapsible panel group like this, it's no longer necessary to initialize each panel individually. You just need to create an instance of the CollapsiblePanelGroup object.

The <script> block at the bottom of the page currently looks like this:

```
71  <script type="text/javascript">
72  <!--
73  var CollapsiblePanel1 = new Spry.Widget.CollapsiblePanel("CollapsiblePanel1");
74  var CollapsiblePanel2 = new Spry.Widget.CollapsiblePanel("CollapsiblePanel2", {contentIsOpen:false});
75  var CollapsiblePanel3 = new Spry.Widget.CollapsiblePanel("CollapsiblePanel3", {contentIsOpen:false});
76  var CollapsiblePanel4 = new Spry.Widget.CollapsiblePanel("CollapsiblePanel4", {contentIsOpen:false});
77  //-->
78  </script>
```

5. Delete the code shown on lines 73–76 of the preceding screenshot, and replace it with this single line of code:

```
var panelgroup = new Spry.Widget.CollapsiblePanelGroup("panelgroup");
```

6. Save `collapsible.html`, and test the page in Live view or in a browser. The first thing you should notice is that all the panels are open when the page loads, but you can open and close them independently.

7. You probably don't want all of them open when the page loads, so amend the code at the bottom of the page like this:

```
var panelgroup = new Spry.Widget.CollapsiblePanelGroup("panelgroup", ➥
{contentIsOpen: false});
```

This passes the `contentIsOpen` property to the constructor and makes sure that all panels are closed when the page first loads.

8. What's that? You don't want them all closed? No problem. Remember that the code at the bottom of the page initializes Spry widgets when the page loads, so all you need to do is open one of the closed panels.

Insert a new line after the one you entered in the last step, and type panelgroup followed by a period. Since panelgroup is the variable to which you assigned the CollapsiblePanelGroup object, Dreamweaver displays code hints for the available properties and methods. Scroll down until you find openPanel(panelIndex), as shown here:

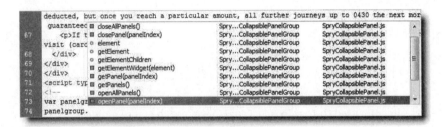

9. Double-click the code hint, or press Enter/Return to insert it. Then type the number of the panel you want to open (counting from zero), followed by a closing parenthesis and a semicolon. To open the first panel, the code looks like this:

```
panelgroup.openPanel(0);
```

10. Save `collapsible.html`, and test it again. This time, the first panel should slide open as the page loads (it might not render correctly in Live view, so test it in a browser).

11. As you can see in the preceding screenshot, the code hints for a CollapsiblePanelGroup object show that it has a closeAllPanels() method and an openAllPanels() one, too. So, to wire up the links to open and close all panels, all you need to do is create a dummy link on each one and add an onclick attribute to call the appropriate method on the panelgroup object. You have done this plenty of times before, so I'll just show the final code, which looks like this:

```
<p><a href="javascript:;" onclick="panelgroup.openAllPanels()">Open ➥
all</a> | <a href="javascript:;" onclick="panelgroup. ➥
closeAllPanels()">Close all</a></p>
```

12. Save the page, and test it. The panels now work both individually and as a group. There's just one problem: the togglePanel() function created in the preceding exercise no longer works because the individual objects identifying each panel no longer exist. Let's fix that.

13. To be able to toggle an individual panel open and closed, you need to know which panel group it belongs to and its position within the group. So, I have renamed the function toggleGroupPanel(), and the function will now take two arguments: group and num.

To find the individual panel, you first need to use the getPanels() method of the CollapsiblePanelsGroup object. This gets an array of all panels within the group. However, you can't just use the array index to get the panel. You need to pass the array element to the getElementWidget() method. Once you have identified the panel, the rest of the function remains the same. Here's the rewritten function with the amended parts highlighted in bold:

```
function toggleGroupPanel(group, num)
{
  var allPanels = group.getPanels();
  var panel = group.getElementWidget(allPanels[num-1]);
  if (panel.isOpen()) {
    panel.close();
  } else {
    panel.open();
  }
}
```

In the fourth line, I have subtracted 1 from the value of num, so the second argument passed to toggleGroupPanel() can use the more intuitive practice of counting the panels from one rather than zero.

14. Finally, amend the links that toggle the Water bus and Oyster card panels like this:

```
<p><a href="javascript:;" onclick="toggleGroupPanel(panelgroup, 3)"> ➥
Water bus</a></p>
<p><a href="javascript:;" onclick="toggleGroupPanel(panelgroup, 4)"> ➥
Oyster card</a></p>
```

Check your code, if necessary, against collapsible_all.html in examples/ch08.

> A restriction with the CollapsiblePanelsGroup object in Spry 1.6.1 appears to be that nothing else should be inside the outer <div> that's wrapped around the panels. Although everything works correctly to start with, the code rapidly gets confused and behaves erratically.

So far, all the methods of opening panels have been confined to links on the same page. While that's useful, it's arguably more useful to be able to target a particular tab or panel to open when linked to from a different page. It can be done, but it requires part of the

Spry framework that's not included with Dreamweaver. I'll come back to that later in the chapter, but before that I'll show you how to combine different Spry effects to make custom effects of your own.

Using the Cluster object to combine effects

Spry effects bring together several complex actions to create a smooth transition onscreen. The secret weapon that makes this possible is the Spry.Effect.Cluster object, which determines whether to run each part of the effect simultaneously or in sequence. Since the built-in effects rely on the Cluster object, it's automatically at your disposal.

The Cluster object has many methods, but the following four are the ones that interest us:

- call(): This initiates the object. It expects two arguments: the effect's target element and an object literal containing any options.
- addNextEffect(): This chains effects in sequence. It takes an effect object as its sole argument.
- addParallelEffect(): This runs an effect in parallel with other effects. It takes an effect object as its sole argument.
- start(): This runs the effect. It takes no arguments.

To create a new effect, you need to extend the Spry.Effect.Cluster object. You do this by defining a function with the name of the new effect. Then you define a new JavaScript class using the same name and assigning its prototype object as Spry.Effect.Cluster. Finally, you assign the function as the constructor of the new class. It sounds more complicated than it really is. The basic syntax looks like this:

```
NewEffect = function(element, {options})
{
  Spry.Effect.Cluster.call(this, options);
  // details of effect go here
};
NewEffect.prototype = new Spry.Effect.Cluster();
NewEffect.prototype.constructor = NewEffect;
```

The best way to show you how to use the Cluster object is through a couple of practical examples. The next two exercises create a dissolve effect that can be used to fade one image into another, and an extension of the Spry highlight effect that makes a smooth transition to the final color.

Dissolving one image into another

This exercise demonstrates the use of the addParallelEffect() method of the Cluster object to fade out one image at the same time as another is faded in. Although images are used in this exercise, the effect could be applied to any elements on a page.

8

1. Copy `dissolve_start.html` from examples/ch08, and save it in workfiles/ch08 as `dissolve.html`. The page contains a dummy link at the top and two images along-side each other inside a paragraph, as shown in the following screenshot:

The two images will eventually be superimposed on each other. The image on the left has an ID called pond, and the other has an ID called duck. If you have a small monitor and the second image is pushed down below the first one, use two smaller images of your own.

2. Click the Live View button. The image of the duck should disappear.

3. Turn off Live view, and look in Code view to see why the duck vanished. The following <style> block embedded in the <head> of the page reduces the opacity of the duck image to zero when the page is displayed. In other words, whatever is behind it shows through.

```
<style type="text/css">
#duck {
  opacity: 0;
  filter: alpha(opacity=0);
}
</style>
```

The `filter` property is nonstandard CSS but is required by Internet Explorer.

4. Create an external JavaScript file by selecting File ➤ New. In the Blank Page section of the New Document dialog box, select JavaScript as Page Type, and click Create. Save the new page as `clusters.js` in workfiles/ch08.

5. Following the basic syntax outlined earlier, let's call the new effect Dissolve. Add the following code to `clusters.js`:

```
Dissolve = function(elem1, elem2, duration)
{
  Spry.Effect.Cluster.call(this, {duration: duration});
};
Dissolve.prototype = new Spry.Effect.Cluster();
Dissolve.prototype.constructor = Dissolve;
```

Notice that I am using three arguments to be passed to the Dissolve effect: the first two are the IDs of the elements to be cross-faded, and the last one is for the duration in milliseconds. This is the only option, so it is passed to Spry.Effect.Cluster.call() as an object literal.

6. The Dissolve() function needs to instantiate two effects: one to reduce the opacity of the first element to zero and the other to increase the opacity of the second element from zero to fully opaque. The Spry effects library contains an object for precisely this purpose: Opacity. Amend the Dissolve() function definition like this:

```
Dissolve = function(elem1, elem2, duration)
{
  Spry.Effect.Cluster.call(this, {duration: duration});
  var fadeOut = new Spry.Effect.Opacity(elem1, 1, 0, {duration: ➥
duration, toggle: true});
  var fadeIn = new Spry.Effect.Opacity(elem2, 0, 1, {duration: ➥
duration, toggle: true});
};
Dissolve.prototype = new Spry.Effect.Cluster();
Dissolve.prototype.constructor = Dissolve;
```

The Opacity object takes four arguments: the target element, the starting opacity (1 is fully opaque, 0 is fully transparent), the ending opacity, and an object specifying any options. So, the Opacity object stored as fadeOut fades the first element from total opacity to total transparency, while fadeIn does the reverse to the second element. The same options are passed to both: they take the value of the duration property from the third argument passed to Dissolve() and set the toggle property to true. This last option reverses the effect the next time it is triggered.

7. With both effects stored as variables, you can now use the addParallelEffect() method to attach them to the target element (identified by this) as follows:

```
Dissolve = function(elem1, elem2, duration)
{
  Spry.Effect.Cluster.call(this, {duration: duration});
  var fadeOut = new Spry.Effect.Opacity(elem1, 1, 0, {duration: ➥
duration, toggle: true});
  var fadeIn = new Spry.Effect.Opacity(elem2, 0, 1, {duration: ➥
duration, toggle: true});
  this.addParallelEffect(fadeOut);
  this.addParallelEffect(fadeIn);
};
Dissolve.prototype = new Spry.Effect.Cluster();
Dissolve.prototype.constructor = Dissolve;
```

8

8. Save clusters.js, and switch back to dissolve.html in the Document window. The code you have just created is dependent on the SpryEffects.js external file, so both JavaScript files need to be attached to the HTML page.

9. A quick way to add external JavaScript files to a page is to display a representation of the page's <head> content in Design view. Select View ➤ Head Content, or press Ctrl+Shift+H/Shift+Cmd+H. This opens a section at the top of the Document window with icons representing HTML elements in the <head> of the page, as shown in Figure 8-2.

Figure 8-2.
The <head> isn't visible in Design view, but you can inspect its contents by displaying them as icons.

Head content ➞

The icons are displayed in the same order as in the <head>, and you can drag them to the left or right to reposition them. You can also inspect and edit most elements by selecting an icon and viewing its contents in the Property inspector.

10. Click to the right of the last icon in the Head Content bar (it represents the embedded <style> block that you inspected in step 3). The Head Content bar should turn white to indicate that it has focus. Click the Script button in the Insert bar, or select Insert ➤ HTML ➤ Script Objects ➤ Script.

In the Script dialog box, click the folder icon alongside the Source field, navigate to SpryAssets/SpryEffects.js, and select it. Dreamweaver automatically selects text/javascript as the value for Type. Leave the Content and No script fields empty (these are for embedding JavaScript directly into the body of a page). The values should look like the following screenshot:

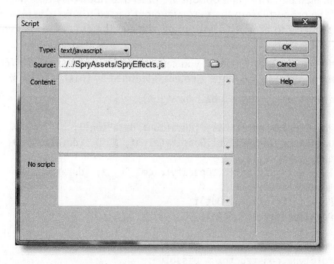

11. Click OK to close the Script dialog box. Dreamweaver will display the following message:

Like the Content and No script fields, this applies only when you are embedding JavaScript directly into a page. You can safely ignore the message.

12. Repeat steps 10 and 11 to attach clusters.js to the page. There should now be two script icons in the Head Content bar, and both external files should be listed in the Related Files toolbar, as shown here:

The scripts are listed in the Related Files toolbar and represented as icons in the Head Content bar

13. Close the separate tab that contains clusters.js. You'll work with it through the Related Files feature from now on, so having two versions open in the Document window is likely to lead to confusion. You can also close the Head Content bar by selecting Head Content in the View menu or by pressing Ctrl+Shift+H/Shift+Cmd+H.

14. Switch to Code view, and create a <script> block at the foot of the page, just before the closing </body> tag. Create a Dissolve object like this:

```
var myDissolve = new Dissolve('pond', 'duck', 2000);
```

As soon as you type the opening parenthesis after Dissolve, Dreamweaver should display code hints for your newly defined effect like this:

```
      pond" name="duck" width="400" height="300" id="duck" /></p>
19    <script type="text/javascript" Dissolve(elem1, elem2, duration)
20    var myDissolve = new Dissolve(
21    </script>
22    </body>
23    </html>
```

This is Dreamweaver CS4's new code introspection at work.

15. Add an onclick event to the dummy link at the top of the page, and set it to apply the start() method to the effect you have just created like this (you refer to it through the variable in which it is stored):

```
<a href="javascript:;" onclick="myDissolve.start()">Dissolve images</a>
```

8

16. Save the page, and activate Live view. Click the Dissolve images link at the top of the page, and the two images should begin a simultaneous transition: the pond fading out and the duck fading in, as shown in Figure 8-3.

Figure 8-3. The new Dissolve effect switches the transparency of both images simultaneously.

17. If the effect doesn't work, load the page into a browser, such as Firefox, and use Tools ➤ Error Console (or a debugging extension, such as Firebug) to troubleshoot any JavaScript errors. You can also compare your files with dissolve_01.html and clusters_01.js in examples/ch08.

18. Amend the style rule for the duck image like this:

```
#duck {
  opacity: 0;
  filter: alpha(opacity=0);
  position: relative;
  left: -400px;
}
```

Both images are 400 pixels wide, so this simply moves the duck image the same distance to the left so that both images are superimposed. Note that this won't work if the browser window is less than 800 pixels wide, because the second image will drop down and be pushed too far left. If this happens, you might need to use absolute positioning instead.

If you test the page now, the images should dissolve from one to the other.

19. There's just one refinement that needs to be made to clusters.js. It's a good idea to set a default duration property. Then, the effect can be instantiated with just two arguments: the IDs of the elements you want to dissolve. Amend the code in clusters.js like this:

```
Dissolve = function(elem1, elem2, duration)
{
  var dur = 2000;
  if (duration != null) dur = duration;
  Spry.Effect.Cluster.call(this, {duration: dur});
  var fadeOut = new Spry.Effect.Opacity(elem1, 1, 0, {duration: dur, ➡
toggle: true});
  var fadeIn = new Spry.Effect.Opacity(elem2, 0, 1, {duration: dur, ➡
toggle: true});
  this.addParallelEffect(fadeOut);
  this.addParallelEffect(fadeIn);
};
Dissolve.prototype = new Spry.Effect.Cluster();
Dissolve.prototype.constructor = Dissolve;
```

The two new lines added at the top of the function create a variable, dur, with a default value of 2000. If the third variable passed to the Dissolve() constructor is omitted, it uses the default value. Note that the variable, dur, is now used as the value for the duration property in all the option objects.

20. Remove the duration from the code that instantiates the Dissolve object at the bottom of dissolve.html like this:

```
var myDissolve = new Dissolve('pond', 'duck');
```

21. Save both dissolve.html and clusters.js, and test them. The effect should now use the default duration of 2000 milliseconds. If you add a different value, it will use that instead.

Check your code, if necessary, against dissolve.html and clusters_dissolve.js in examples/ch08.

The next exercise shows how to create a custom effect that chains effects one after another. Rather than go through everything step by step, I'll just explain the main points, because the principles are the same as when running effects in parallel.

Creating a smooth highlight transition

The default Spry highlight effect uses three colors: a start color, the end color, and the color to which the background reverts at the end of the transition. I find this sudden switch at the end rather jarring, so this exercise creates a new effect that runs two color transitions in sequence.

1. Add the following code to clusters.js from the preceding exercise:

```
HighlightTransition = function(element, options)
{
  Spry.Effect.Cluster.call(this, options);
  var col1 = '#FFFFFF';
```

8

```
        var col2 = '#DCBD7D';
        var col3 = '#FFFFFF';
        var dur1 = 2000;
        var dur2 = 2000;
        if (options.col1 != null) col1 = options.col1;
        if (options.col2 != null) col2 = options.col2;
        if (options.col3 != null) col3 = options.col3;
        if (options.dur1 != null) dur1 = options.dur1;
        if (options.dur2 != null) dur2 = options.dur2;
        var transition1 = new Spry.Effect.Color(element, col1, col2, ➡
{duration: dur1, transition: Spry.sinusoidalTransition});
        var transition2 = new Spry.Effect.Color(element, col2, col3, ➡
{duration: dur2, transition: Spry.sinusoidalTransition});
    this.addNextEffect(transition1);
    this.addNextEffect(transition2);
};
HighlightTransition.prototype = new Spry.Effect.Cluster();
HighlightTransition.prototype.constructor = HighlightTransition;
```

This defines a new HighlightTransition object using the same syntax as before to extend the Spry.Effect.Cluster object. The important lines are highlighted in bold. They create two Spry Color objects and then add them to the current object using the addNextEffect() method. This runs the effects in sequence one after the other, instead of running them in parallel like the Dissolve effect.

The Spry Color object is another basic effect in the Spry effects library. It takes four arguments: the target element, the starting color, the end color, and an object literal with any options. I have used two options: the duration of the effect and the type of transition. The Spry.sinusoidalTransition starts slowly, speeds up in the middle, and then slows down again at the end. Table 8-1 lists the available transition options for Spry effects.

The first effect, stored as transition1, changes the background color of the target element from col1 to col2, and the second effect (transition2) changes the background color from col2 to col3.

The rest of the code sets defaults for all the colors and durations. This means you need set only those options that you want to change from the default, although you must set at least one option for the effect to work.

Table 8-1. Transition options for Spry effects

Transition	Description
Spry.linearTransition	Progresses evenly throughout
Spry.circleTransition	Rapid start followed by a long easing
Spry.fifthTransition	Similar to Spry.linearTransition but eases toward the end
Spry.growSpecificTransition	Starts gently, then dips back before rapid finish

Transition	Description
Spry.pulsateTransition	Rapid pulsation between start and finish values, ending with finish value
Spry.sinusoidalTransition	Starts slowly, speeds up, then eases toward the end
Spry.squareTransition	Starts slowly and gradually speeds up
Spry.squarerootTransition	Starts quickly and gradually eases

2. Copy highlight_transition_start.html from examples/ch08, and save it as highlight_transition.html in workfiles/ch08.

3. Link SpryEffects.js and clusters.js to highlight_transition.html in the same way as in steps 10–12 of the preceding exercise.

4. The image has 20 pixels of padding that can be used as a test for the new highlight effect. The image's ID is goldenpav, so add the following code to the bottom of the page to initialize a HighlightTransition object:

```
<script type="text/javascript">
var myHighlight = new HighlightTransition('goldenpav', {dur2: 1000});
</script>
```

The options must be passed to the constructor method as an object literal, using the same names as in HighlightTransition definition in step 1 (col1, col2, col3, dur1, and dur2). You must pass at least one option to the constructor in this way. This example changes the duration of the second color change from the default 2000 milliseconds to 1000.

5. Add an onclick attribute to the dummy link at the top of the page to trigger the effect like this:

```
<p><a href="javascript:;" onclick="myHighlight.start()">Highlight ➥
image</a></p>
```

6. Test the page. The image should be surrounded by a golden brown border that fades in and out smoothly. Experiment with other colors and durations.

Check your code, if necessary, with highlight_transition.html and clusters.js in examples/ch08.

Using Spry utilities

As I explained in Chapter 7, Spry is software neutral. You can download the latest copy of the Spry framework from Adobe Labs at http://labs.adobe.com/technologies/spry/home.html and use it with any script editor. At the time of this writing, the current version is 1.6.1, which is the same as Dreamweaver CS4, although newer versions will be posted when available. In addition to the same external JavaScript files that Dreamweaver uses,

8

the Spry framework contains a lot of documentation and samples. If you're interested in getting the most out of Spry, it's well worth downloading. The drawback for inexperienced developers is that most examples assume a good understanding of JavaScript. Often the explanation of how something works is lurking in comments in the source code.

The full Spry framework also includes several useful files that are missing from Dreamweaver. Two of the most useful are SpryDOMUtils.js, which makes it easy to manipulate the DOM (see Chapter 7), and SpryURLUtils.js, which lets you pass options to Spry objects through a URL—essential for opening a specific panel from a link on a different page.

To continue with the exercises in this section, you need to download the most recent version of the Spry framework from http://labs.adobe.com/technologies/spry/home.html and unzip the compressed file. The Readme.html and docs.html files contain links to all the documentation and samples. I'll leave you to explore them at your leisure. The files you need for the following exercises are in the includes folder. Copy SpryDOMUtils.js and SpryURLUtils.js to the SpryAssets folder in the site you're using for this book.

Passing information to a Spry widget through a URL

When you link from one page to another, you can pass information to the target page by adding parameters to the end of the URL. There are two ways of doing this:

- A query string: This is a series of name/value pairs following a question mark, like this: ?variable1=value1&variable2=value2. Each name is separated from its value by an equal sign, and each pair is separated by an ampersand (in XHTML, the ampersand needs to be embedded in the link as &).

- A fragment identifier: This is the hash (or pound) symbol followed by the name of an ID or anchor tag, indicating the section of the page you want the browser to go to, for example, #thisSection.

The SpryURLUtils.js file contains a method called getLocationParamsAsObject(), which extracts this information from a URL. You can then pass this information to the code that initializes the Spry widget when the page loads.

Opening a tab or accordion panel from another page

To open a specific tab or panel in a Spry widget on a different page, you need to pass the information as a query string. For example, to open the second accordion panel, you would add this to the end of the URL: ?panel=1. If the panel is identified by an ID, you pass the ID as the value instead, for example, ?panel=waterbus.

To open a specific tab or panel—and go straight to it—you need to combine both methods like this: ?panel=waterbus#waterbus.

> It's important to get the order right. The query string must come before the fragment identifier. If you put them the other way round, both sets of information will be ignored.

In the page that contains the Spry widget, you use the getLocationParamsAsObject() method in SpryURLUtils.js like this:

```
var params = Spry.Utils.getLocationParamsAsObject();
```

This stores the query string as an object called params, enabling you to pass the values it contains to the widget's constructor method. Since the page might be accessed directly, the values passed to the constructor need to use the JavaScript conditional (or ternary) operator like this:

```
{defaultTab: params.tab ? params.tab : 0}
```

If the URL used to access the page has a query string that contains a variable called tab, its value will be held in params.tab. This rather cryptic piece of code means "If params.tab exists, assign its value to defaultTab; but if params.tab doesn't exist, use 0 instead."

That's the theory. Now, let's get coding.

Preparing the target page

This exercise demonstrates how to open a specific tab of a tabbed panels widget from a link in another page. The same technique applies to an accordion.

1. Copy tabbed_start.html from examples/ch08 to workfiles/ch08, and rename it tabbed_other.html.

2. Attach SpryURLUtils.js by adding it to the <head> of tabbed_other.html. If you're not sure how to do this, use the same technique as described in steps 10 and 11 of the "Dissolving one image into another" exercise earlier in the chapter.

3. Switch to Code view, and add the following code block inside the <head> section. It doesn't matter where it goes, but it must come after the <script> tag that attaches SpryURLUtils.js to the page. Spry code hints should help you get the spelling and combination of uppercase and lowercase correct.

```
<script type="text/javascript">
var params = Spry.Utils.getLocationParamsAsObject();
</script>
```

This calls the getLocationParamsAsObject() method from SpryURLUtils.js, which converts all the information passed to the page through the URL into a JavaScript object called params. You can now use params to retrieve the values from the URL.

4. Scroll down to the bottom of the page until you come to the code that initializes the tabbed panels. It currently looks like this:

```
var TabbedPanels1 = new Spry.Widget.TabbedPanels("TabbedPanels1");
```

5. To open a specific panel, you need to pass a second argument to the constructor method. As explained in "Initializing a Spry object" earlier in this chapter, this needs to be in the form of an object literal. For a tabbed panels widget, the

8

property that controls the default panel is called defaultTab. For an accordion, it's defaultPanel.

If the value of the tab or panel you want to open is passed through the URL, it will be a property of the params object you created in step 3. You can call the properties sent through the URL anything you like, but it makes sense to use tab for a tabbed panels widget and panel for an accordion. So, the selected value will be params.tab or params.panel.

However, you need to take into account the likelihood that nothing is passed through the URL (for example, when a user accesses the page directly). So, change the code in step 4 like this:

```
var TabbedPanels1 = new Spry.Widget.TabbedPanels("TabbedPanels1",
{defaultTab: params.tab ? params.tab : 0});
```

If you're using an accordion, the code should look like this:

```
var Accordion1 = new Spry.Widget.Accordion("Accordion1",
{defaultPanel: params.panel ? params.panel : 0});
```

This uses the conditional (ternary) operator, which is the same in both JavaScript and PHP, to determine the value assigned to defaultTab or defaultPanel. When used like this with an object literal, the conditional operator can seem confusing because it also uses a colon. The first colon is part of the object literal syntax and separates the object property from its value. The second colon is part of the conditional operator, which comprises a question mark and a colon.

If the expression to the left of the question mark equates to true, the value immediately to the right of the question mark is used. However, if the expression equates to false, the value following the colon is used instead.

So if params.tab or params.panel has a value, it will equate to true, and its value will be assigned to the defaultTab or defaultPanel property. If params.tab or params.panel doesn't have a value, 0 is used instead, making the first tab or panel the default.

6. Tabs and panels can be identified either by their index (position within the widget counted from zero) or by an ID. When linking from another page, it's safer to use an ID in case the order of tabs/panels changes. Instructions on how to add an ID were given in the exercises on creating links from the same page earlier in this chapter.

   For the purposes of this exercise, give the third panel an ID of waterbus.

7. Save tabbed_other.html, and test it in a browser. The first tab should be displayed when the page loads.

   You can check your code, if necessary, against tabbed_other.html in examples/ch08.

That finishes the changes to the target page. There is no need to create named anchors for the tabbed panels or accordion, because you can use the ID Dreamweaver automatically assigns to each set of tabbed panels or accordion.

Creating the link from the other page

All that's necessary now is to create a link to the target page using a query string, as described at the beginning of this section.

1. Create a new HTML page, and save it as `link_to_tab.html` in `workfiles/ch08`.

2. Type some text in the page to use as a link to the Water bus tab of `tabbed_other.html`.

3. Highlight the text you plan to use as a link, and select the HTML view of the Property inspector. You can type the link and query string directly into the Link field. However, if you prefer to let Dreamweaver create the correct syntax for you, click the folder icon to the right of the Link field.

4. In the Select File dialog box, select `tabbed_other.html`, and click the Parameters button, as shown in the following screenshot:

5. In the Parameters dialog box, enter tab in the Name field. Then use the Tab key or mouse to open the Value field, and enter waterbus, as shown here:

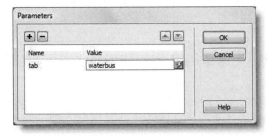

On this occasion, the query string consists of a single name/value pair, but a query string can contain several pairs. Use the plus and minus keys to add or remove name/value pairs. You can also change their order with the up and down arrows.

6. Click OK to close the Parameters dialog box, and then click OK again (Choose on a Mac) to close the Select File dialog box.

The value in the Link field of the Property inspector should now look like this:

```
tabbed_other.html?tab=waterbus
```

7. Save link_to_tab.html, and load it in a browser. Click the link. This time, when tabbed_other.html loads, the Water bus tab should be displayed instead of the first tab.

Check your code, if necessary, against link_to_tab.html and tabbed_other.html in examples/ch08.

Opening a collapsible panel from another page

The principle behind opening a collapsible panel through a URL is identical to opening a tab or accordion panel. The main difference is that each panel is independent. Its open or closed state is determined by the contentIsOpen option. Consequently, the ID is not important when sending a query string. All you need is a name to identify the panel and to give it a value of true or false.

You can see a working example of this in collapsible_other.html and link_to_collapsible.html in examples/ch08. The query string in link_to_collapsible.html looks like this:

```
<a href="collapsible_other.html?oyster=true">Oyster Card</a>
```

The code that initializes the fourth collapsible panel in collapsible_other.html looks like this:

```
var CollapsiblePanel4 = new Spry.Widget.CollapsiblePanel( ➡
"CollapsiblePanel4", {contentIsOpen: params.oyster ? ➡
params.oyster : false});
```

This means that if the URL contains a variable called oyster, its value will be used for the contentIsOpen option. Otherwise, contentIsOpen is set to false.

You could, in fact, dispense with a value for oyster and use this instead:

```
var CollapsiblePanel4 = new Spry.Widget.CollapsiblePanel( ➡
"CollapsiblePanel4", {contentIsOpen: params.oyster ? ➡
true : false});
```

Selecting and manipulating page elements with Spry.$$

If you thought Spry was just about widgets and effects, think again. In common with other JavaScript frameworks like Prototype and jQuery, Spry uses CSS selectors to manipulate the DOM and change the look or behavior of targeted page elements. Table 8-2 describes the selectors supported by Spry 1.6.1. If you're familiar with either Prototype or jQuery, you'll immediately recognize them. They're based on the proposed selectors for CSS3 (http://www.w3.org/TR/css3-selectors). Although CSS3 is still a long way from becoming a reality, the selectors have basically been agreed upon, so learning them for use with a JavaScript framework serves a dual purpose.

While the Spry selector utility matches Prototype and jQuery in its ability to select elements on a page, it currently has only ten methods (listed in Table 8-3) that manipulate the DOM. They're mainly useful for changing the CSS styles of an element in response to a JavaScript event.

The Spry selector utility uses the Prototype convention of two dollar signs to select elements but avoids conflict with other frameworks by prefixing them with Spry. The following code selects all elements that use a class called optional:

```
Spry.$$('.optional')
```

As a simple example of how you can use the selector utility, you can create a function to toggle the display of selected elements on and off by creating a class called hideMe with the property display: none like this:

```
function toggleOpts()
{
  Spry.$$('.optional').toggleClassName('hideMe');
}
```

Table 8-2. CSS selectors supported by Spry.$$, as of Spry 1.6.1

Pattern	Meaning	Example
*	Any element.	Spry.$$(*)
E	An element of type E, e.g., an HTML tag.	Spry.$$('div')
E.class	An E element with a specified class (the element is optional).	Spry.$$('img.floatleft') Spry.$$('.floatleft')
E#id	An E element with a specified ID (the element is optional).	Spry.$$('div#nav') Spry.$$('#nav')
E F	An F element descendant of an E element, e.g., all links in unordered lists.	Spry.$$('ul a')
E > F	An F element that is a direct child of an E element.	Spry.$$('p > a')
E + F	An F element immediately preceded by an E element (an adjacent sibling), e.g., the first paragraph after a level 1 heading.	Spry.$$('h1 + p')

Continued

8

Table 8-2. Continued

Pattern	Meaning	Example
E ~ F	All F elements preceded by having the same parent as an E element, e.g., all paragraphs at the same level as a level 1 heading that precedes them. Other elements may intervene.	Spry.$$('h1 ~ p')
E[foo]	An E element with a foo attribute, e.g., all links with a title attribute. Do not use E[class] as a bug in Internet Explorer adds a class attribute to every element.	Spry.$$('a[title]')
E[foo="bar"]	An E element with a foo attribute exactly equal to "bar".	Spry.$$('img[width="50"]')
E[foo^="bar"]	An E element with a foo attribute that begins with the string "bar".	Spry.$$('img[title^="Art"]')
E[foo$="bar"]	An E element with a foo attribute that ends with the string "bar".	Spry.$$('a[href$=".pdf"]')
E[foo*="bar"]	An E element with a foo attribute that contains the substring "bar".	Spry.$$('p[class*="left"]')
E[foo~="bar"]	An E element with a foo attribute that comprises a list of space-separated values, one of which is exactly equal to "bar".	Spry.$$('p[class~="warn"]')
E:first-child	An E element that is the first child of its parent, e.g., the first row in a table.	Spry.$$('tr:first-child')
E:last-child	An E element that is the last child of its parent.	Spry.$$('tr:last-child')
E:only-child	An E element that is the only child of its parent, e.g., an image wrapped in a <div>.	Spry.$$('img:only-child')
E:first-of-type	An E element that is the first sibling of its type, e.g., the first cell in a table row.	Spry.$$('td:first-of-type')
E:last-of-type	An E element that is the last sibling of its type, e.g., the last cell in a table row.	Spry.$$('td:last-of-type')
E:only-of-type	An E element that is the only sibling of its type.	Spry.$$('img:only-of-type')
E:nth-child(n)	An E element that is the nth child of its parent (see main text for an explanation).	

Pattern	Meaning	Example
`E:nth-last-child(n)`	An E element that is the nth child of its parent, counting from the last one.	
`E:nth-of-type(n)`	An E element that is the nth sibling of its type.	
`E:nth-last-of-type(n)`	An E element that is the nth sibling of its type, counting from the last one.	
`E:empty`	An E element that has no children (including text nodes).	`Spry.$$('td:empty')`
`E:not(s)`	An E element that does not match simple selector s, e.g., everything except a paragraph.	`Spry.$$('*:not(p)')`
`E:checked`	An E element that is checked (radio buttons or checkboxes).	`Spry.$$('input:checked')`
`E:disabled`	A form E element that is disabled.	`Spry.$$('input:disabled')`
`E:enabled`	Form elements that are not explicitly disabled.	`Spry.$$('input:enabled')`
`E[hreflang|="en"]`	An E element with an hreflang attribute that has a hyphen-separated list of values beginning with "en".	`Spry.$$('link[hreflang|="en"]')`

8

Attribute selectors do not permit spaces around the operators. For example, the following is incorrect:

```
Spry.$$('a[href $= ".pdf"]') // WRONG
```

It must be like this:

```
Spry.$$('a[href$=".pdf"]')   // RIGHT
```

The nth-child selectors are designed to select elements in a repeating pattern. The simplest way to use them is for odd and even elements like this:

```
tr:nth-child(odd)   // picks odd rows
tr:nth-child(even)  // picks even rows
```

The following function (in odd_even.html in examples/ch08) adds class names to odd and even table rows:

```
function init() {
    Spry.$$('tr:nth-child(odd)').addClassName('odd');
    Spry.$$('tr:nth-child(even)').addClassName('even');
    Spry.$$('tr:first-child').removeClassName('odd'). ➡
addClassName('headerRow');
}
```

The function runs when the page loads and produces striped table rows, as shown in Figure 8-4. The final line uses the first-child selector to remove the odd class from the first row and apply a different class. Spry selector utility methods can be chained in the same way as with other JavaScript libraries.

Average Monthly Climate for South-East England

Month	Max Temp °C	Min Temp °C	Sun (hours)	Days of Rainfall >= 1mm
Jan	7.2	1.5	54.6	12.8
Feb	7.5	1.2	73.0	9.7
Mar	10.1	2.8	111.0	11.0
Apr	12.5	3.9	159.4	9.4
May	16.3	6.9	201.4	9.2
Jun	19.1	9.7	194.4	8.8
Jul	21.7	11.9	210.4	7.2
Aug	21.6	11.8	205.0	7.9
Sep	18.5	9.8	147.3	9.4
Oct	14.5	7.0	112.5	11.0
Nov	10.3	3.8	72.1	11.4
Dec	8.1	2.4	47.9	12.2

Figure 8-4. The alternating background colors are applied automatically to odd and even rows.

You can achieve even more ambitious effects with nth-child by using the formula $an+b$, where a and b are both numbers. The first number represents how many elements are in the repeat sequence. The second number identifies the element that you want to select within the sequence. So if you want a repeating pattern of three, the formula works like this:

```
tr:nth-child(3n+1)  // picks rows 1, 4, 7, etc
tr:nth-child(3n+2)  // picks rows 2, 5, 8, etc
tr:nth-child(3n+3)  // picks rows 3, 6, 9, etc
```

You can see the effect in Figure 8-5 and nth-child.html in examples/ch08.

Average Monthly Climate for South-East England

Month	Max Temp °C	Min Temp °C	Sun (hours)	Days of Rainfall >= 1mm
Jan	7.2	1.5	54.6	12.8
Feb	7.5	1.2	73.0	9.7
Mar	10.1	2.8	111.0	11.0
Apr	12.5	3.9	159.4	9.4
May	16.3	6.9	201.4	9.2
Jun	19.1	9.7	194.4	8.8
Jul	21.7	11.9	210.4	7.2
Aug	21.6	11.8	205.0	7.9
Sep	18.5	9.8	147.3	9.4
Oct	14.5	7.0	112.5	11.0
Nov	10.3	3.8	72.1	11.4
Dec	8.1	2.4	47.9	12.2

Figure 8-5. Using the nth-child selector targets repeating elements in a user-defined sequence.

Table 8-3. Methods used by the Spry selector utility

Method	Argument(s)	Description
addClassName()	class	Adds the specified class to all selected elements. The argument should be in quotes.
addEventListener()	event, handler, capture	Adds a listener for the specified event. The first argument should be a string consisting of the event name (without "on"). The second argument is the name of the function to be used as the event handler. The final argument is a Boolean (true or false) that specifies whether the handler should respond in the capture phase. Internet Explorer does not support the capture phase, so you should normally use false.
forEach()	function	Runs the specified function on each selected element.
removeAttribute()	attribute	Removes the specified attribute from the selected elements. The name of the attribute should be in quotes.
removeEventListener()	event, handler, capture	Removes the specified event listener. The arguments are the same as for addEventListener().
removeClassName()	class	Removes the specified class. The class name should be in quotes.

Continued

8

Table 8-3. Continued

Method	Argument(s)	Description
setAttribute()	attribute, value	Adds the attribute and value to all selected elements. Both arguments should be in quotes.
setProperty()	property, value	Sets a property on the selected object(s). Both arguments should be in quotes.
setStyle()	style	Sets the specified styles on the selected elements. The argument should be a string consisting of CSS property/value pairs separated by semicolons.
toggleClassName()	class	Removes the specified class if it already exists on the selected elements. Otherwise, adds it. The class name should be in quotes.

I have included Tables 8-2 and 8-3 to whet the appetite of readers who already have some experience with JavaScript and encourage them to delve deeper into the Spry application programming interface (API). If you're new to JavaScript, all this might seem like impenetrable gobbledygook, but you should have little difficulty implementing the code in the following exercise.

> *To get up to speed on JavaScript, I suggest you read an up-to-date introductory text, such as* Beginning JavaScript with DOM Scripting and Ajax: From Novice to Professional *by Christian Heilmann (Apress, ISBN: 978-1-59059-680-7). Do not read anything published before, say, 2005. The whole approach to JavaScript has changed radically since the early days of the Web. It's important not to get stuck with outdated concepts and techniques.*

Styling on the fly with the Spry selector

This exercise uses the Spry.$$ selector to style alternate items in an ordered list with a different background color. It also uses a class selector to toggle on and off the display of certain items. The page also gracefully degrades in a browser that has JavaScript disabled.

1. Copy spry_selector_start.html from examples/ch08, and save it in workfiles/ch08 as spry_selector.html. The page looks like the following screenshot.

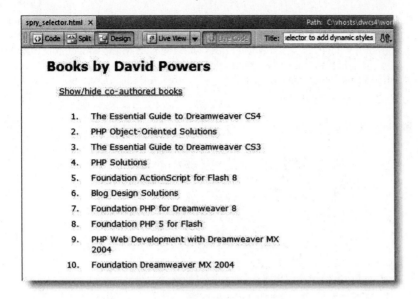

It contains an ordered list of books that I have written for friends of ED and Apress over the past few years. Some of the books were coauthored with other writers. The dummy link at the top of the page will be used to hide and display those books.

2. Open Code view. You'll see that, in addition to a few style rules to improve the look of the text, there are three classes embedded in the <head> of the page: odd, even, and hideMe.

The only class that's added to any of the HTML tags is coauthored, but there are no style rules for the coauthored class. That's because you're going to use that class to identify the books that will be hidden or displayed when the link is clicked at the top of the page.

3. To use the Spry.$$ selector, you need to attach SpryDOMUtils.js to the page <head>. You should be familiar with doing this by now, but refer to steps 9–11 of the "Dissolving one image into another" exercise if you're still unsure.

4. Let's start off by giving the list items an alternating background color. Add the following <script> block to the <head> anywhere after the <script> tag that links SpryDOMUtils.js to the page (code hints will help you a lot with the typing):

```
<script type="text/javascript">
function init()
{
  Spry.$$('li:nth-child(odd)').addClassName('odd');
  Spry.$$('li:nth-child(even)').addClassName('even');
}
</script>
```

This uses the nth-child structural pseudo-selector to select odd and even <li> tags and adds the appropriate class to each one.

8

5. What you have just created is a function, so you need to trigger it to run when the page loads. Either you can put a call to the function in a <script> block at the bottom of the page, as Dreamweaver does with the calls to the widget constructors, or you can add it to the <body> tag as an onload event. Let's take the latter course, so amend the <body> tag like this:

```
<body onload="init()">
```

6. Switch to Design view, and activate Live view. The list should now look like this:

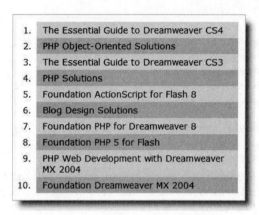

1.	The Essential Guide to Dreamweaver CS4
2.	PHP Object-Oriented Solutions
3.	The Essential Guide to Dreamweaver CS3
4.	PHP Solutions
5.	Foundation ActionScript for Flash 8
6.	Blog Design Solutions
7.	Foundation PHP for Dreamweaver 8
8.	Foundation PHP 5 for Flash
9.	PHP Web Development with Dreamweaver MX 2004
10.	Foundation Dreamweaver MX 2004

The list items now have alternating background colors—certainly a lot easier than adding the odd and even classes manually to each item, because the same code works however many items are in the list. In fact, it works for any list on a page. Also, by changing the selector from li to tr, you could easily apply this to a table with many rows.

7. Now let's wire up the link that toggles the display of coauthored books. Switch back to Code view, and add the following function definition inside the same <script> block as in step 4:

```
function showCoauthored()
{
  Spry.$$('li.coauthored').toggleClassName('hideMe');
}
```

This selects all <li> elements with the class coauthored and toggles the hideMe class on and off. As described in Table 8-3, the toggleClassName() method adds a class if it's absent and removes it if it's already applied to an element. So, this will have the effect of adding or removing a style rule that sets the element's display property to none.

8. Add it to the dummy link at the top of the page with the onclick attribute like this:

```
<p><a href="javascript:;" onclick="showCoauthored()">Show/hide
co-authored books</a></p>
```

9. Switch to Design view, and activate Live view. Click the link at the top of the page. The list of books should display only those books I wrote on my own, as shown in Figure 8-6.

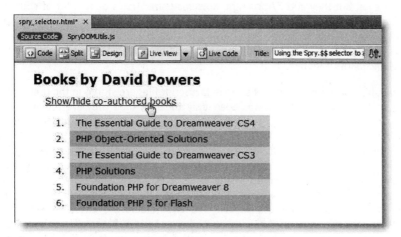

Figure 8-6. The contents of the list have been dynamically altered without needing to reload the page.

Click the link again, and the full list is restored.

10. There's one final improvement: the link should be visible only when JavaScript is enabled. Switch off Live view, and position your cursor inside the link at the top of the page. Select the <p> tag in the Tag inspector at the bottom of the Document window, and choose hideMe from the Class drop-down menu in the HTML view of the Property inspector. The link will disappear.

11. You want the link to be visible when JavaScript is enabled, so you can use the Spry.$$ selector to remove the hideMe class. Amend the init() function like this:

```
function init()
{
  Spry.$$('li:nth-child(odd)').addClassName('odd');
  Spry.$$('li:nth-child(even)').addClassName('even');
  Spry.$$('p.hideMe').removeClassName('hideMe');
}
```

This removes the hideMe class from any paragraph that has the hideMe class.

12. Save and test the page again. Check your code, if necessary, against spry_selector.html in examples/ch08.

This has been only a brief example of what you can do with SpryDOMUtils.js, but I hope it will encourage you to experiment more. Working your way through the samples included with the Spry framework download should give you further ideas.

8

Reducing download times with smaller files

One drawback with using a JavaScript library is the size of the files. Spry effects make your pages livelier, but they add 77KB to the download size. That's quite a lot of code just to add one or two pleasing effects, particularly if some of your users are still on dial-up connections. Even if your target audience uses broadband, file size remains a consideration because bigger files consume more bandwidth, and on a popular site, that can cost you or your clients a lot of money.

However, it's not quite as bad as it sounds. JavaScript files are stored in the user's browser cache, so they are normally downloaded only the first time they are required. Still, if you're concerned about the size of the Spry external files, you can replace them with smaller versions. If you download the full Spry framework from Adobe Labs, as described earlier, the ZIP file contains two folders, includes_minified and includes_packed. These contain versions of the library files that have been compressed to reduce their size. The files have exactly the same names as the versions installed by Dreamweaver, so all you need to do is swap your existing files for ones of the same name from either includes_minified or includes_packed. The two folders use different techniques to reduce file size, but those in includes_packed are considerably smaller. To give just one example, the version of SpryEffects.js installed by Dreamweaver is 77KB, the one in includes_minified is 62KB, whereas the one in includes_packed is just 29KB. On a popular site, the bandwidth savings could be considerable.

Creating unobtrusive JavaScript

If implemented skillfully, CSS separates a page's content from instructions about how it should be presented. This has inspired many developers to apply the same principle to JavaScript, separating behavior from structure. "Wouldn't it be better," the argument goes, "to add JavaScript to a page only if the browser is capable of handling it?"

Since JavaScript lets you manipulate the DOM, you can. This is a technique known as **unobtrusive JavaScript**. Instead of embedding onclick and other event handling attributes in the HTML code, unobtrusive JavaScript uses DOM manipulation to add them on the fly in just the same way as the previous exercise added the odd and even classes to the list items.

The difficulty with unobtrusive JavaScript is that it requires a lot of careful planning. Because you can't see the features being added to the HTML code, you need to work out exactly how everything can be added dynamically.

Using the JavaScript Extractor to externalize scripts

Dreamweaver CS4 has come up with a feature designed to take all the guesswork out of creating unobtrusive JavaScript: the JavaScript Extractor. This works on the simple principle that you embed the JavaScript elements in a page in the normal way. Once you're happy with the way the page works, you extract the JavaScript and externalize it. The drawback with this is that it's like squeezing toothpaste from a tube: it's easy to do, but don't try getting it back in afterward. . .

Moving JavaScript to an external file

This exercise demonstrates how to use the JavaScript Extractor using `spry_selector.html` from the preceding section.

1. Because the JavaScript Extractor cannot restore JavaScript once it has been removed from a page, it's always a good idea to create a new copy of the file that you want to work on. Save `spry_selector.html` from the previous exercise (or from examples/ch08) as `spry_unobtrusive.html` in workfiles/ch08.

2. Close the original file and work with `spry_unobtrusive.html`.

3. Select Commands ➤ Externalize JavaScript. Dreamweaver analyzes the page and opens the following dialog box:

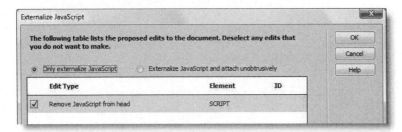

The radio buttons at the top of the dialog box offer the following two options:

- Only externalize JavaScript: This simply moves functions to an external file and attaches the file to the page.

- Externalize JavaScript and attach unobtrusively: This attempts to move everything and creates the necessary external script to add inline event handlers, such as `onclick`, through DOM manipulation.

With the first option selected, Dreamweaver finds only the function definitions in the `<head>` of `spry_unobtrusive.html`.

4. Select the second radio button. Dreamweaver displays a warning that behaviors will no longer be editable through the Behaviors panel (this includes Spry effects). When you click OK to dismiss the warning, the Externalize JavaScript dialog box changes to this:

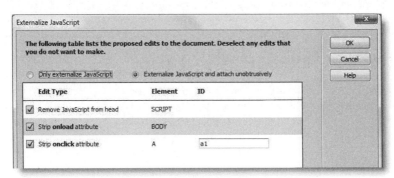

Dreamweaver lists all the JavaScript that it can find in the page. The checkbox alongside each proposed edit lets you decide whether to implement a particular suggestion. In this case, each edit is selected by default. However, Dreamweaver automatically deselects any scripts that use document.write, because these cannot be externalized.

To be able to manipulate the DOM, Dreamweaver automatically creates IDs for inline elements that don't already have them. As you can see in the preceding screenshot, it says it will add a1 as the ID for the onclick attribute. If you want to change the ID, the field is editable.

5. Click OK when you're happy with your selections. Dreamweaver then presents you with a report of what it has done, like this:

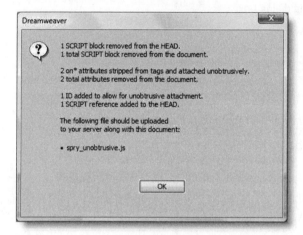

The important thing about this report is the last section, which tells you the name of the external JavaScript file that it has created. You must upload this to your website. Otherwise, none of the JavaScript will work.

The external file is given the same name as the file you have just extracted the JavaScript from, except with a .js filename extension. If a file with that name already exists, Dreamweaver adds a number just before the filename extension.

The external JavaScript file is created in the same folder, but you can move it to a dedicated scripts folder through the Files panel. If you move the file, don't forget to update the links when Dreamweaver prompts you.

Using other JavaScript libraries

Adobe realizes that not everyone will want to use Spry, so support for all flavors of JavaScript has been greatly improved in Dreamweaver CS4. As explained in Chapter 1, Dreamweaver now provides code hints for all the main data types and the DOM. More significantly, Dreamweaver constantly analyzes the JavaScript attached to a page, providing code hints for custom functions and classes. This includes popular JavaScript frameworks, such as Prototype and jQuery, as shown in Figure 8-7.

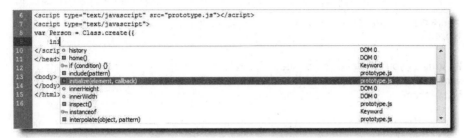

Figure 8-7. Dreamweaver's code introspection provides code hints for Prototype and other JavaScript libraries.

Code hints normally pop up when you type a period or opening parenthesis. You can also trigger them by pressing Ctrl+spacebar (the combination is the same on Windows and Mac).

Code hints generated by code introspection are available only in pages that are directly attached to the file that contains the function or class definition. For example, if you attach prototype.js to a page, you get Prototype hints in that page. However, if you attach an external file to the same page, you don't get any Prototype hints in the external file. Spry's code hints, on the other hand, are hardwired into Dreamweaver, so they're available in any page. Consequently, if you want to use JavaScript libraries other than Spry—and you want code hints—you need to attach the external library directly to the page where you create your JavaScript. The simple way to do this is to build your JavaScript in the <head> of the page and then use the JavaScript Extractor, as described in the previous section, to export it to an external file. That's how I created jquery_selector.html and jquery_selector.js in examples/ch08.

The other drawback with external libraries is that the level of hinting is determined by the structure of those libraries. Although you get hints for all the methods available to a Spry.$$ selector, similar hints are not generated for the Prototype $$ or jQuery $ selectors. Let's hope this situation will be improved either in a future version of Dreamweaver or by the release of a third-party extension to provide code hints for all the main frameworks.

Talking of third-party extensions, perhaps the best support of all for other JavaScript libraries comes through Adobe's decision to release the Web Widgets Software Development Kit (SDK). This enables JavaScript developers to package web widgets as Dreamweaver extensions. Prior to the release of Dreamweaver CS4, Adobe contacted the teams behind jQuery (http://jquery.com/) and the Yahoo! User Interface (YUI) Library (http://developer.yahoo.com/yui/) and asked them to adapt some of their widgets so they can be easily installed in Dreamweaver. Other leading developers are also being encouraged to package JavaScript widgets for Dreamweaver. To find out what widgets are available, open the Extend Dreamweaver control on the Application bar, as shown in Figure 8-8, and select Browse for Web Widgets.

8

Figure 8-8. The Extend Dreamweaver control on the Application bar is your gateway to JavaScript widgets.

As long as you're connected to the Internet, this takes you directly to a dedicated web widget section on the Adobe Exchange. Choose the widgets you want, download, and install them.

The next section walks you through the installation process for all Dreamweaver extensions. Then, to round out the chapter, I'll show you how to use two of the new web widgets, the jQuery Dialog and the YUI calendar.

Installing Dreamweaver extensions

One of the main reasons for Dreamweaver's enduring dominance as the leading website development program is its extensibility. Extensions created by third-party developers add new functionality to the program. Some extensions are quite simple. Others are much more powerful and are designed to take your productivity to a whole new level. For example, Cartweaver (http://www.cartweaver.com), the PHP version of which was created by my partner in crime on this book, Tom Muck, greatly simplifies the construction of a fully featured ecommerce site. The following is a short—and by no means exhaustive—list of some of the most respected third-party developers (the more sophisticated extensions, such as Cartweaver, are sold on a commercial basis, but many others are free):

- Community MX (http://communitymx.com/)
- DMXzone (http://dmxzone.com/)
- Kaosweaver (http://kaosweaver.com/)
- Project Seven (http://www.projectseven.com)
- Tom Muck (http://tom-muck.com/)

Adobe has also taken the decision to focus some aspects of Dreamweaver functionality in extensions, rather than make them part of the core product. This makes it easier to update that functionality between releases of the program itself. So, you're likely to see more extensions in the future.

Regardless of whether an extension is free or commercial, the method of installation is identical and is done through the Adobe Extension Manager.

Using the Adobe Extension Manager

In previous versions of Dreamweaver, the Extension Manager was installed automatically. However, the CS4 installer now gives you the option not to install many of the shared programs, such as Device Central, Bridge, and the Extension Manager. If you accepted the default selection of programs when installing Dreamweaver CS4, you should see Adobe Extension Manager CS4 listed among the programs in the Windows Start menu or in your Applications folder on a Mac. If it's not there, you need to install it from your Dreamweaver or Creative Suite DVD. You should also ensure that you have the Adobe Integrated Runtime (AIR) installed, because the Extension Manager is now an AIR application (AIR is included in the default Dreamweaver installation).

You can launch the Extension Manager in several ways, but perhaps the quickest way is by selecting Extension Manager in the Extend Dreamweaver control on the Application bar (see Figure 8-8). If you have hidden the Application bar on a Mac, alternative ways of opening the Extension Manager are by selecting Commands ➤ Manage Extensions or Help ➤ Manage Extensions. You can also open the program directly from the Windows Start menu or the Applications folder on a Mac. As if that weren't enough, you can usually also launch the Extension Manager by double-clicking the .mxp file of the extension you want to install.

Migrating extensions from a previous version

If you're upgrading from an earlier version of Dreamweaver, you'll immediately notice that the Extension Manager looks completely different. However, most of its functionality is unchanged. The first time you launch the Extension Manager, it detects any extensions installed in a previous version of Dreamweaver on the same computer account and presents you with the following options:

If you click Yes, the Extension Manager copies details of existing extensions to your CS4 configuration folder. It then tells you to relaunch the Extension Manager. Migrating extensions like this does not automatically enable them in CS4. You need to do that manually for each one, because some older extensions might not be compatible. However, it's a useful way to preserve functionality between versions.

To enable an extension, put a check mark in the Enabled checkbox to the left of the extension name, as shown in Figure 8-9. Some extensions require you to restart Dreamweaver, but you don't need to do so until you have selected all those you want to migrate. However, it's a wise policy to install extensions only one at a time, because this makes it

8

easier to detect which extension is responsible if Dreamweaver starts behaving erratically. Sometimes changes to Dreamweaver make older extensions incompatible with the latest version.

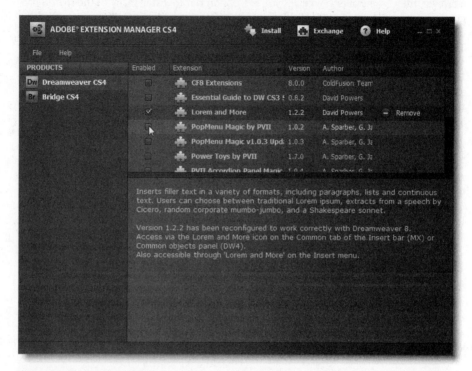

Figure 8-9. The Extension Manager provides a simple interface to add and remove Dreamweaver extensions.

Installing an extension

The Extension Manager is shared by several Creative Suite programs, so it's important to check that you have the correct program selected in the Products column on the left of the Extension Manager (see Figure 8-9). If you launched the Extension Manager from Dreamweaver CS4, it should automatically select the correct program.

> *Unlike previous versions, Extension Manager CS4 cannot be used to manage extensions in older programs. It recognizes only programs in Creative Suite 4.*

Installing an extension involves the following simple steps:

1. Click the Install button at the top of the Extension Manager.
2. In the Select Extension to Install dialog box, navigate to the folder where you downloaded the extension, select the extension's .mxp file, and click Open.

3. You're then presented with a disclaimer notice that tells you Adobe does not offer technical support for the extension and that any license is between you and its creator. In addition to a standard disclaimer that applies to all extensions, there might also be a license specific to the extension. You must click Accept to proceed with the installation.

4. The extension now installs. Small extensions install almost instantaneously. Larger ones may take several minutes. Extensions created by the same developer often share common files, so you might see warnings that an older or newer version of a particular file already exists. Click Yes to replace older versions and No if the existing version is newer.

When the process is complete, the Extension Manager will tell you whether you need to restart Dreamweaver. This usually happens with extensions that need to rebuild part of the menu system. The pane at the bottom of the Extension Manager provides a brief description of the extension and how to use it (see Figure 8-9).

Some commercial extensions require registration or activation. Follow the instructions onscreen the first time you launch Dreamweaver after installing such an extension.

Removing an extension

Removing an extension is easy. Just launch the Extension Manager, and click the Remove button alongside the name of the extension you want to remove (see Figure 8-9).

If you don't want to remove an extension completely from Dreamweaver, disable it temporarily by deselecting the Enabled checkbox alongside the extension name. Just select the checkbox again when you want to restore the extension.

Extensions install files in your personal configuration folder, so they are visible only to the current user account. If there is more than one user account on the computer, the extension needs to be installed separately in each one. Because extensions make changes to your configuration files, you should install extensions only from sources that you can trust.

Right, after that brief detour, let's get on with the jQuery and YUI web widgets.

Using jQuery and YUI web widgets

After downloading the extensions from the Adobe Exchange and installing them as described in the previous section, you need to restart Dreamweaver. The jQuery and YUI web widgets are then accessible through their own tabs on the Insert bar, as shown in the following screenshot, or submenus added at the bottom of the Insert menu. The icons and menu listings appear in the same order as you install each widget.

Both jQuery and YUI have packaged several of their best widgets for Dreamweaver, including calendars and sliders. The jQuery collection also includes an accordion and tabbed panels, which you might want to use in preference to the Spry versions described in Chapter 7, particularly if you're already at home with jQuery and want to incorporate other jQuery features into the widgets. A quick look at the jQuery accordion demonstrates the difference between the Spry widgets that are a core part of Dreamweaver CS4 and the third-party widgets.

To install a web widget, just position your cursor where you want to insert the widget, and click its icon on the Insert bar or select it from the Insert menu. Figure 8-10 shows a default jQuery UI Accordion widget inserted in `stroll.html`, the sample page that I showed you how to create in Chapter 5.

As you can see from the files listed in the Related Files toolbar in Figure 8-10, the jQuery accordion widget comes complete with three external JavaScript files, including the basic jQuery library, and a style sheet. However, no styles are applied in Design view, and the Property inspector simply has a link to online help. To see what the widget will look like when the page is deployed on the Web and to use the Code Navigator to inspect the widget's CSS, you need to turn on Live view (see Figure 8-11).

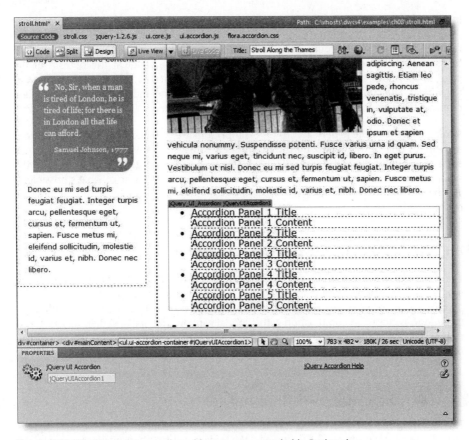

Figure 8-10. The jQuery UI accordion widget appears unstyled in Design view.

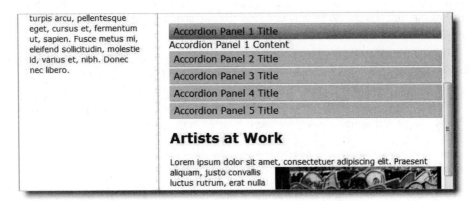

Figure 8-11. Turn on Live view to see what third-party widgets will look like in the finished page.

In spite of the lack of styling in Design view, using one of these web widgets is a huge time-saver. All the necessary files are attached and stored in a dedicated jQuery or YUI folder ready to be uploaded to your website. Inserting a widget also creates the necessary code to initialize it. However, instead of placing the initialization script at the bottom of the page, as Spry does, the third-party widgets insert it immediately after the HTML portion of the widget. Selecting the turquoise tab at the top-left of the widget and pressing Delete removes the widget, its contents, the initialization script, and all links to dependent files.

Adding content to the jQuery accordion is simply a matter of substituting the placeholder text, so it's one of the easiest third-party widgets to use. Other widgets require a knowledge of jQuery or the YUI Library API. Using jQuery and the YUI Library API is beyond the scope of this book, but the following sections give you a brief taster of what's possible. If you have a basic understanding of JavaScript, it doesn't take long to achieve impressive results.

Inserting a jQuery UI dialog widget

The jQuery UI dialog widget (http://docs.jquery.com/UI/Dialog) creates modeless and modal floating windows and dialog boxes. A **modeless** window is a pop-up window **that** permits access to the originating page, whereas a **modal** one blocks access until the pop-up window is closed. In combination with a modal window, the dialog widget makes it easy to dim the rest of the page so that the user's concentration is focused on the content of the pop-up—a technique that has become popular with image galleries (see Figure 8-13).

Displaying a larger image with a dialog widget

The following exercise uses the jQuery UI dialog widget to display a larger version of living_statues.jpg in stroll.html. Initially, the widget will be physically inserted into the page, but it will then be converted to use unobtrusive JavaScript so the page degrades gracefully in browsers that have JavaScript turned off. The exercise uses some basic jQuery techniques, but you should be able to follow the instructions even if you have never used jQuery before.

1. Copy stroll.html from examples/ch08, and save it as stroll_dialog.html in workfiles/ch08. Also copy stroll.css to the same folder.

2. Position your cursor at the end of the first paragraph, just before the Artists at Work heading. Insert a jQuery UI dialog widget from the Insert bar or Insert menu. A widget with some placeholder text is inserted in the page like this:

mi, eleifend sollicitudin, molestie id, varius et, nibh. Donec nec libero.

jQuery_UI_Dialog: jQueryUIDialog1

I'm in a dialog!

Artists at Work

3. Save `stroll_dialog.html`. Dreamweaver presents you with a dialog box informing you that it's copying dependent files to your site. These are all located in a dedicated folder called `jQuery.ui-1.5.2` in the site root (the name of the folder is likely to change when new versions are released).

4. Click the Live View button or load the page into a browser to view the default dialog widget (see Figure 8-12). The dialog box loads immediately. It's both resizable and draggable, and it closes when you click the close button at the top-right of the dialog box. It's not very practicable in its default state, but it doesn't take much effort to change.

Figure 8-12. The default widget displays a dialog box in the center of the page as soon as it loads.

5. Close the dialog box, and deactivate Live view. Switch to Code view to examine the code inserted by the widget. It's just above the second heading and looks like this:

```
50    <div id="jQueryUIDialog1" class="flora" title="This is my title">I'm in a dialog!</div>
51    <script type="text/javascript">
52 // BeginWebWidget jQuery_UI_Dialog: jQueryUIDialog1
53 jQuery("#jQueryUIDialog1").dialog({draggable: true, resizable: true});
54
55 // EndWebWidget jQuery_UI_Dialog: jQueryUIDialog1
56    </script>
57 <h2>Artists at Work </h2>
```

As you can see, the dialog box is simply a `<div>`. The text in the dialog box title bar is taken from the `title` attribute of the `<div>`, and the content of the `<div>` determines what is displayed inside the dialog box.

The code shown on line 53 of the preceding screenshot initializes the widget. To avoid conflicts with other JavaScript libraries, it uses the jQuery() function instead of the shorthand $() notation.

6. You're going to use the dialog box to display a larger version of living_statues.jpg, so replace the title attribute shown on line 50 with Living Statues on the South Bank.

7. Delete the placeholder text between the <div> tags, and with your cursor between the empty tags insert living_statues_680.jpg from the images folder. Add some alternative text when prompted to do so.

8. Enclose the entire <div> in *single* quotes, cut it to your clipboard, and paste it as the argument to the jQuery function in place of "jQueryUIDialog1". You might see the following warning when you try to select the code, but you can safely ignore it:

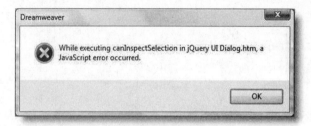

The code inside the <script> block should now look like this:

```
// BeginWebWidget jQuery_UI_Dialog: jQueryUIDialog1
jQuery('<div id="jQueryUIDialog1" class="flora" title="Living Statues ➥
on the South Bank"><img src="../../images/living_statues_680.jpg" ➥
width="680" height="449" alt="Living Statues" /></div>').dialog( ➥
{draggable: true, resizable: true});
// EndWebWidget jQuery_UI_Dialog: jQueryUIDialog1
```

9. If you save the page and test it now, the dialog box still appears immediately. It remains the same size, but you can resize it to see the larger image. By using the code for the <div> as the argument to jQuery(), the <div> and its contents are now being generated on the fly by JavaScript. This means the larger image won't be loaded in a browser that has JavaScript disabled.

10. The jQuery UI dialog() constructor method takes an object literal containing the options you want to set. At the moment, the options object has two properties: draggable and resizable, both of which are set to true. Let's set two more, height and width, so the image fits the dialog box. Amend the object literal like this:

```
{draggable: true,
 resizable: true,
 height: 515,
 width: 720}
```

Although adding newlines to JavaScript statements usually causes them to malfunction, you can use newlines in objects for ease of reading without causing problems.

11. To make the dialog box modal, all you need to do is add `modal: true` to the options object like this:

```
{draggable: true,
 resizable: true,
 height: 515,
 width: 720,
 modal:true}
```

12. To dim the background, you also need to use the overlay property, which expects its values as an object, so you nest it within the options object like this:

```
{draggable: true,
 resizable: true,
 height: 515,
 width: 720,
 modal:true,
 overlay: {
   opacity: 0.5,
   background: 'black'
 }
}
```

13. Test the page to make sure everything is working as expected. You should see the larger image displayed fully inside a modal dialog box, with the rest of the window dimmed (see Figure 8-13 on the next page).

14. To prevent the dialog box from opening automatically when the page loads, you need to set the autoOpen property of the options object to false. You also need a reference to the dialog box so that it can be opened when the user clicks the smaller image. Add the autoOpen property, and assign the whole declaration to a variable called bigImage. The complete code should look like this:

```
var bigImage = jQuery('<div id="jQueryUIDialog1" class="flora" ➥
title="Living Statues on the South Bank"><img ➥
src="../../images/living_statues_680.jpg" width="680" height="449" ➥
alt="Living Statues" /></div>').dialog({
  draggable: true,
  resizable: true,
  height: 515,
  width: 720,
  modal: true,
  overlay: {
    opacity: 0.5,
    background: 'black'
  },
  autoOpen:false
});
```

15. You can now attach an onclick event handler dynamically to the smaller image, which can be identified using the following attribute selector:

```
jQuery('img[src$=living_statues.jpg]')
```

8

This looks for an image with a src attribute that ends with living_statues.jpg. Add the following code immediately after the code in step 14:

```
jQuery('img[src$=living_statues.jpg]').css('cursor', 'pointer')
.attr('title', 'Click for a larger image')
.click(function(e){bigImage.dialog('open')});
```

In typical jQuery fashion, this chains several methods and applies them to living_statues.jpg. First, the css() method converts the cursor to a hand pointer whenever anyone mouses over the image. Then the attr() method adds a title attribute, which will be displayed as a tooltip, inviting users to click the image to see a larger version. Finally, the click() method is passed a function that references the dialog box using the variable bigImage and passes 'open' as an argument to its dialog() method.

16. Save stroll_dialog.html, and test it. When you mouse over living_statues.jpg, the cursor should turn to a hand and display a tooltip inviting you to view a larger image. Click, and you should see a much bigger version centered in a dialog box with the rest of the window dimmed, as shown in Figure 8-13.

Figure 8-13. The dialog widget displays the larger image and dims the rest of the page.

17. Finally, to tidy up the page and remove the JavaScript from the middle of the HTML, cut the script block and paste it into the <head> of the document after the links to the jQuery external files (or put it in an external file of its own, linked to the page after the other jQuery files). Once you move the script outside the body of the page, you need to wrap the script in a jQuery document ready handler like this:

```
jQuery(function() {
    var bigImage = jQuery('<div id="jQueryUIDialog1" class="flora" ➥
title="Living Statues on the South Bank"><img ➥
src="../../images/living_statues_680.jpg" width="680" height="449" ➥
alt="Living Statues" /></div>').dialog({
        draggable: true,
        resizable: true,
        height: 515,
        width: 720,
        modal: true,
        overlay: {
          opacity: 0.5,
          background: 'black'
        },
        autoOpen:false
    });
    jQuery('img[src$=living_statues.jpg]').css('cursor', 'pointer')
    .attr('title', 'Click for a larger image')
    .click(function(e){bigImage.dialog('open')}});
});
```

I have used jQuery() instead of the shorthand $(), but you can use $() if you're not mixing jQuery with other JavaScript libraries that use the same shorthand.

Check your code, if necessary, against stroll_dialog.html in examples/ch08.

Selecting dates with a YUI calendar

The YUI Library is a massive collection of utilities, controls, and components written in JavaScript. Just to give you a taste of the type of things available, I have chosen the YUI Calendar, which is one of the first web widgets to have been released for Dreamweaver. Inserting a calendar requires nothing more than clicking its icon in the YUI tab of the Insert bar or selecting it from the Insert menu and saving the external files to your site. However, you need to write your own JavaScript functions to do anything with selected dates.

Displaying the selected date

This exercise shows how to capture the date selected in a YUI calendar and display it as a JavaScript alert.

1. Create a new page called yui_calendar.html in workfiles/ch08, and insert a YUI Calendar widget from the Insert bar or Insert menu.

8

2. Save the page to copy the external JavaScript files and style sheet to your site. Dreamweaver stores them in a dedicated folder called YUI.

3. When you look at the page in Design view, you might be distinctly underwhelmed, because all you get is a turquoise border and tab with nothing inside.

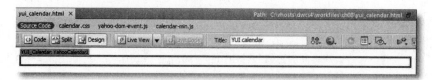

4. Click the Live View button, and everything comes to life, with the current month and date selected, as shown in Figure 8-14 (so now you know when I wrote this part of the book). The calendar is fully functional in the sense that you can move back and forth through the months and select dates, but nothing happens when you select a particular date. It's up to you to add that functionality yourself.

Figure 8-14.
The YUI calendar is generated entirely dynamically by JavaScript.

5. Deactivate Live view, and switch to Code view. As you can see in the following screenshot, the calendar is an empty <div>, and there are just a few lines of script. The code shown on lines 17–20 initializes the calendar, assigning it to a variable called oCalendar_YahooCalendar1. The code on line 21 loads the calendar into the page when the DOM is ready.

```
12  <div id="YahooCalendar1"></div>
13  <script type="text/javascript">
14  // BeginWebWidget YUI_Calendar: YahooCalendar1
15
16  document.body.className += " yui-skin-sam";
17  YAHOO.init_YahooCalendar1 = function() {
18      var oCalendar_YahooCalendar1 = new YAHOO.widget.Calendar("YahooCalendar1");
19      oCalendar_YahooCalendar1.render();
20  }
21  YAHOO.util.Event.onDOMReady(YAHOO.init_YahooCalendar1);
22
23
24  // EndWebWidget YUI_Calendar: YahooCalendar1
25  </script>
```

6. When you select one or more dates in the calendar, it dispatches an event called selectEvent, which contains the selected date(s) as a multidimensional array in the format [[YYYY, MM, DD], [YYYY, MM, DD] . . .]. So, you can define an event handler function to capture the selection. You need to add it inside the initialization function like this:

```
YAHOO.init_YahooCalendar1 = function() {
  function selectHandler(type, args, obj)
  {
    var dates = args[0];
    var date = dates[0];
    var months = ['Jan', 'Feb', 'Mar', 'Apr', 'May', 'June', 'July', ➡
'Aug', 'Sep', 'Oct', 'Nov', 'Dec'];
    var year = date[0], month = months[date[1]-1], day = date[2];
    alert('Selected date is : ' +  month + ' ' + day + ', ' + year);
  }
  var oCalendar_YahooCalendar1 = new YAHOO.widget.Calendar( ➡
"YahooCalendar1");
  oCalendar_YahooCalendar1.render();
}
```

The event handler needs to take three arguments: the type of event, the arguments dispatched by the event, and the object that was the event's target. The function needs the first and third arguments to know what to expect, but all you're interested in is extracting the value of the arguments passed by the event.

The selectEvent dispatches a single multidimensional array of dates, so there's only one argument, which can be extracted as args[0] and is assigned to a variable called dates.

For the purposes of this exercise, you want to extract just the first date in the dates array. This can be identified as dates[0] and is assigned to a variable called date.

Since each date is in itself an array in the format [YYYY, MM, DD], you can extract the day as date[2], the month as date[1], and the year as date[0].

To avoid confusion with different national conventions regarding date formats, I have created an array of month names. JavaScript counts arrays from zero, so you get the month name by subtracting one from the month number like this: months[date[1]-1].

Finally, the function passes the selected date to an alert.

7. The event handler function needs to be registered to listen for the selectEvent by using the subscribe() method after the calendar object has been instantiated like this:

```
var oCalendar_YahooCalendar1 = new YAHOO.widget.Calendar( ➡
"YahooCalendar1");
oCalendar_YahooCalendar1.selectEvent.subscribe(selectHandler, ➡
oCalendar_YahooCalendar1, true);
oCalendar_YahooCalendar1.render();
```

8

The subscribe() method takes three arguments: the event handler function, the object, and the Boolean variable true.

8. Save yui_calendar.html, and test it in Live view or a browser. Select a date in the calendar, and you should see its value displayed in a JavaScript alert, as shown in Figure 8-15.

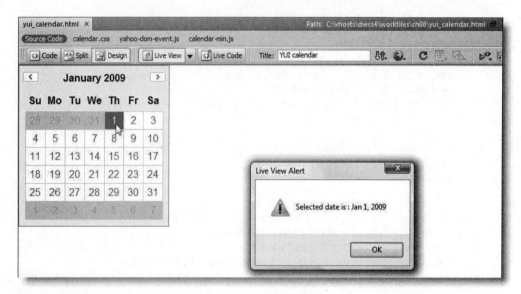

Figure 8-15. The event handler extracts and formats the selected date.

Check your code, if necessary, against yui_calendar.html in examples/ch08.

Of course, displaying the date as a JavaScript alert serves no practical value. The purpose of this exercise has been to demonstrate how to create an event handler to respond to the selection of dates. You can use the data gathered by the event handler for a variety of things, including populating date fields in online forms or triggering a request to display events related to that date. Your ability to do that depends on your JavaScript skills.

Chapter review

This has been very much a hands-on chapter, digging into the mysteries of JavaScript, Spry, and other web widgets. However, it has barely managed to scratch the surface of a vast subject. Spry, jQuery, and the YUI Library have many enthusiastic fans, but JavaScript remains an uphill struggle for many others. While the web widgets are an attractive addition, they are not integrated into Dreamweaver to the same extent as Spry. Their principal advantage is that they speed up the deployment of sophisticated UI components by bringing together all the necessary external files, installing them, and creating the initialization script with a single mouse click. After that, it's up to you. I hope this chapter has whetted your appetite to experiment further with the framework(s) of your choice.

In the next chapter, we take an in-depth look at creating online forms, which lay the foundation for much of the rest of this book. Forms are the principal way of communicating with a database. You'll also continue your exploration of Spry, because Dreamweaver incorporates an impressive set of validation widgets that check user input before submitting it to the server for processing.

8

9 BUILDING ONLINE FORMS AND VALIDATING INPUT

Online forms are the gateway to the server and lie at the very heart of working with PHP, the focus of most of the remaining chapters. You use forms for logging into restricted pages, registering new users, placing orders with online stores, entering and updating information in a database, and sending feedback by email. But gateways need protection.

You need to filter out incomplete or wrong information: a form isn't much use if users forget to fill in required fields or enter an impossible phone number. It's also important to make sure that user input doesn't corrupt your database or turn your website into a spam relay. That's what **input validation** is all about—checking that user input is safe and meets your requirements. This is different from validating your HTML or CSS against W3C standards, and it's much more important because it protects your data.

Validating user input is a theme that will run through much of the rest of this book. In this chapter, we'll look at client-side validation with the assistance of Spry. Then, in Chapter 11, I'll show you how to process the form and validate its content on the server with PHP. Server-side validation is more important, because it's possible for users to evade client-side filters. Even so, client-side validation is useful for catching errors before a form is submitted, improving user experience.

In this chapter, you'll learn about the following:

- Creating a PHP page
- Creating forms to gather user input
- Understanding the difference between GET and POST
- Passing information through a hidden form field
- Making online forms accessible
- Using Spry widgets to validate input
- Displaying and controlling the number of characters in a text area

Building a simple feedback form

All the components for building forms are on the Forms tab of the Insert bar. They're also on the Form submenu of the Insert menu, but for the sake of brevity, I'll refer only to the Insert bar in this chapter.

Most form elements use the `<input>` tag, with their function and look controlled by the type attribute. The exceptions are the multiline text area, which uses the `<textarea>` tag, and drop-down menu and scrollable lists, which use the `<select>` tag. Dreamweaver handles all the coding for you, but you need to dive into Code view frequently when working with forms and PHP, so if your knowledge of the tags and attributes is a bit rusty, brush it up with a good primer, such as *HTML and CSS Web Standards Solutions: A Web Standardista's Approach* by Christopher Murphy and Nicklas Persson (friends of ED, ISBN: 978-1-43021-606-3).

Choosing the right page type

HTML contains all the necessary tags to construct a form, but it doesn't provide any means to process the form when submitted. For that, you need a server-side solution, such as

PHP. In the past, you may have used FormMail or a similar script to send the contents of a form by email. Such scripts normally reside in a directory called `cgi-bin` and work with `.html` pages. The `action` attribute in the opening `<form>` tag tells the form where to send the contents for processing. It usually looks something like this:

```
<form id="sendcomments" method="post" action="/cgi-bin/formmail.cgi">
```

You can do the same with PHP: build the form in an `.html` page, and send the contents to an external PHP script for processing. However, it's far more efficient to put the form in a page with a `.php` file name extension and use the same page to process the form. This makes it a lot easier to redisplay the contents with error messages if any problems are found. So, from now on, we'll start using PHP pages. Before going any further, you should have specified a PHP testing server, as described in Chapter 2.

Creating a PHP page

You can create a PHP page in Dreamweaver in several ways, namely:

- Select Create New ➤ PHP in the Dreamweaver welcome screen.
- Select File ➤ New to open the New Document dialog box, and select Blank Page and PHP as the Page Type. As Figure 9-1 shows, this offers the same choice of CSS layouts as an HTML page. Click Create when you have made your selection.
- Right-click in the Files panel, and select New File. If you have defined a PHP testing server, Dreamweaver creates a default blank page with a `.php` file name extension.
- Change the file name extension of an existing page to `.php` in the Files panel or Save As dialog box.

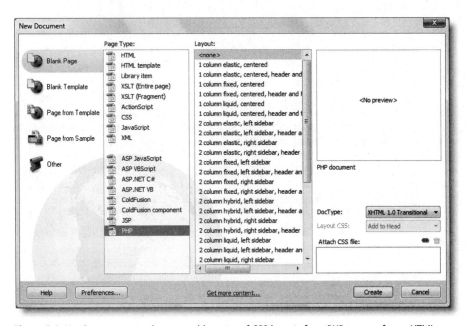

Figure 9-1. You have access to the same wide range of CSS layouts for a PHP page as for an HTML one.

9

The file name extension is the only difference between a blank PHP page and an HTML one. If you switch to Code view, you'll see the same DOCTYPE declaration and HTML tags. The .php extension tells the server to send the page to the PHP engine for processing before sending it to the browser.

Mixing .php and .html pages in a site

It's perfectly acceptable to mix .html and .php files in the same site. However, when building a new site, it's a good idea to create all pages with a .php extension, even if they don't contain dynamic code. That way, you can always add dynamic content to a page without needing to redirect visitors from an .html page. If you are converting an old site, you can leave the main home page as a static page and use it to link to your PHP pages.

A lot of people ask whether you can treat .html (or any other file name extension) as PHP. The answer is yes, but it's not recommended, because it places an unnecessary burden on the server and makes the site less portable. Also, reconfiguring Dreamweaver to treat .html files as PHP is messy and inconvenient.

Inserting a form in a page

It's time to get to work and build a feedback form. To concentrate on how the form is validated and processed, let's work in a blank page and keep the styling to a minimum.

> **Building the basic form**

The final code for this page is in feedback.php in examples/ch09.

1. Create a new PHP page as described in the previous section, and save it in workfiles/ch09 as feedback.php. If you use the New Document dialog box, set Layout to <none>, and make sure no style sheets are listed under Attach CSS file.

2. Add a heading, followed by a short paragraph. Make sure you're in Design view or, if Split view is open, that the focus is in Design view. Inserting a form is completely different when the focus is in Code view, as explained in "Inserting a form in Code view" later. With the insertion point at the end of the paragraph, click the Form button in the Forms tab of the Insert bar. It's the first item, as shown here:

3. This inserts the opening and closing <form> tags in the underlying code. In Design view, the form is surrounded by a red dashed line, as shown in the next screenshot:

All form elements must be inserted inside the red line, so don't click anywhere else in Design view. Otherwise, you might end up outside the form. Of course, once you start inserting form elements, the boundary expands to accommodate the content.

> *If you try to insert a form element outside the dashed red line, Dreamweaver asks you whether you want to insert a form tag. Unless you want to create two separate forms, this is normally an indication that your insertion point is in the wrong place. Although you can have as many forms as you like on a page, each one is treated separately. When a user clicks a form's submit button, only information in the same form is processed; all other forms are ignored.*

4. The Property inspector displays the form's settings, as shown here:

Dreamweaver gives forms a generic name followed by a number. This is applied to both the name and id attributes in the underlying code. If you change the value in the Form ID field of the Property inspector, Dreamweaver updates both attributes.

The Action field is where you enter the path of the script that processes the form. Since this will be a self-processing form, leave the field empty.

The Method menu has three options: Default, GET, and POST. This determines how the form sends data to the processing script. Leave the setting on POST. I'll explain the difference between GET and POST shortly. If you select the Default option, Dreamweaver omits the method attribute from the <form> tag. This results in the form behaving the same way as if you had selected GET. I recommend against using it, because you're less likely to make mistakes by selecting GET or POST explicitly.

You can ignore the Target and Enctype options. Target should normally be used only with frames, and Dreamweaver automatically selects the correct value for Enctype if required. The only time it needs a value is for uploading files. Dreamweaver server behaviors don't handle file uploads. See my book *PHP Solutions: Dynamic Web Design Made Easy* (friends of ED, ISBN: 978-1-59059-731-6) for details of how to do it by hand-coding.

9

375

Inserting a form in Code view

If you insert a form in Code view or in Split view with the focus in Code view, Dreamweaver displays the Tag Editor (see Figure 9-2). This offers the same options as the Property inspector, but you need to fill in all the details yourself. Inserting a form in Design view is much more user-friendly.

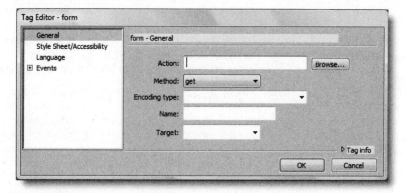

Figure 9-2. The Tag Editor is a less user-friendly way to insert a form.

The Tag Editor selects get as the default value for Method. (GET and POST are case-insensitive in the HTML method attribute.) If you enter a value in the Name field, Dreamweaver inserts the name attribute, even if you're using a strict DOCTYPE declaration, and doesn't assign the same value to the id attribute. To insert an ID, you need to select Style Sheet/Accessibility in the left column and enter the value manually.

Adding text input elements

Most online forms have fields for users to enter text, either in a single line, such as for a name, password, or telephone number, or a larger area, where the text spreads over many lines. Let's insert a couple of single-line text fields and a text area for comments.

Opinions vary on the best way to lay out a form. A simple way to get everything to line up is to use a table, but this creates problems for adding accessibility features, such as <label> tags. The method that I'm going to use is to put each element in a paragraph and use CSS to tidy up the layout.

Inserting text fields and a text area

Continue working with the form from the preceding exercise.

1. With your insertion point inside the red outline of the form, press Enter/Return. This inserts two empty paragraphs inside the form. Press your up arrow key once to return to the first paragraph, and click the Text Field button in the Forms tab of the Insert bar, as shown here:

2. By default, this launches the Input Tag Accessibility Attributes dialog box (see Figure 9-3).

Figure 9-3.
Dreamweaver makes it easy to build forms that follow accessibility guidelines.

The ID field uses the same value for the <input> tag's id and name attributes.

The Label field is for the label you want to appear next to the form element, including any punctuation, such as a colon, that you want to appear onscreen.

The Style option lets you choose how to associate the <label> tag with the form element. If you choose the first radio button, Wrap with label tag, it creates code like this:

```
<label>Name:
<input type="text" name="name" id="name" />
</label>
```

The second radio button, Attach label tag using 'for' attribute, creates code like this:

```
<label for="name">Name:</label>
<input type="text" name="name" id="name" />
```

From an accessibility point of view, either method is fine. However, using the for attribute often makes the page easier to style with CSS because the <label> and <input> tags are independent of each other.

The final radio button, No label tag, inserts no label at all. You normally use this with form buttons, which don't need a label because their purpose is displayed as text directly on the button.

This Style option is sticky, so Dreamweaver remembers whichever radio button you chose the last time.

The Position option, on the other hand, automatically chooses the recommended position for a form label. In the case of a text field, this is in front of the item, but with radio buttons and checkboxes, it's after the item. You can, however, override the default choice if you want to.

The final two options let you specify an access key and a tab index. Finally, if you don't want to use these accessibility features, there's a link that takes you to the relevant section of the Preferences panel to prevent this dialog box from appearing again. However, since accessibility is such an important issue in modern web design, I recommend you use these attributes as a matter of course.

Use the following settings, and click OK to insert a text field and label in the form:

- ID: name
- Label: Name:
- Style: Attach label tag using 'for' attribute
- Position: Before form item
- Access key/Tab index: **Leave blank**

3. Move your insertion point into the empty paragraph below, and insert another text field. Enter email in the ID field, and enter Email: in the Label field. Leave the other settings the same as in the previous step, and click OK.

4. Position your cursor after the new text field, and press Enter/Return twice to insert two more blank paragraphs in the form.

5. Put your cursor in the first blank paragraph, and click the Text Area button in the Forms tab of the Insert bar, as shown in the following screenshot:

In the Input Tag Accessibility Attributes dialog box, set ID to comments and Label to Comments:, leave the other settings as before, and click OK.

6. Move into the final blank paragraph, and select Button in the Forms tab of the Insert bar, as shown here:

In the Input Tag Accessibility Attributes dialog box, set ID to send, leave the Label field empty, select No label tag as Style, and click OK. This inserts a submit button.

7. In the Property inspector, change Value from Submit to Send comments. This changes the label on the button (press Enter/Return or move the focus out of the Value field for the change to take effect). Leave Action on the default Submit form. The form should now look like this in Design view:

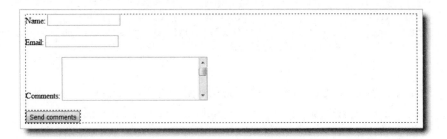

> If you select Reset form in the Property inspector, this creates a reset button that clears all user input from the form. However, in Chapter 11, you'll learn how to preserve user input when a form is submitted with errors. This technique relies on setting the value attribute of each form element, which prevents Reset form from working after the form has been submitted.

If you switch to Code view, the underlying HTML for the form should look like this:

```
<form action="" method="post" name="form1" id="form1">
  <p>
    <label for="name">Name:</label>
    <input type="text" name="name" id="name" />
  </p>
  <p>
    <label for="email">Email:</label>
    <input type="text" name="email" id="email" />
  </p>
  <p>
    <label for="comments">Comments:</label>
    <textarea name="comments" id="comments" cols="45" rows="5"> ➡
</textarea>
  </p>
  <p>
    <input type="submit" name="send" id="send" value="Send comments" />
  </p>
</form>
```

The XHTML 1.0 specification (http://www.w3.org/TR/xhtml1) lists a number of elements, including <form>, for which the name attribute has been deprecated. If you select a strict

9

DOCTYPE declaration, Dreamweaver omits the name attribute from the <form> tag. However, it's important to realize that this applies *only* to the opening <form> tag and not to elements within a form. The name attribute doesn't play a significant role in the <form> tag, which is why it has been deprecated, but its role on input elements in the form is crucial.

> The name *attribute not only remains valid for* <input>, <select>, *and* <textarea>; *PHP and other scripting languages cannot process data without it. Although the* id *attribute is optional, you must use the* name *attribute for each element you want to be processed. The* name *attribute should consist only of alphanumeric characters and the underscore and should contain no spaces.*

Setting properties for text fields and text areas

In the preceding exercise, you inserted two text fields and a text area. A text field permits user input only on a single line, whereas a text area allows multiple lines of input. The Property inspector offers almost identical options for both types of text input and even lets you convert from one to the other. Figure 9-4 shows the Property inspector for the Name text field. Notice that Type is set to Single line. This is Dreamweaver trying to be user-friendly by adopting descriptive terms, rather than using the official attribute names.

Figure 9-4. The Property inspector for a text field lets you convert it into a text area, and vice versa.

Unfortunately, if you're familiar with the correct HTML terminology, the labels in the Property inspector can be more confusing than enlightening. Let's run through the various options and their meanings:

- Type: The radio buttons determine the type of text input, as follows:
  - Single line: This creates an <input> tag and sets its type attribute to text. In other words, it creates a single-line text input field.
  - Multi line: This is what Dreamweaver uses to indicate a text area. If you select this radio button after inserting a single-line input field, Dreamweaver converts the <input> tag to a pair of <textarea> tags, as described in the next section.
  - Password: Select this option to change the type attribute of a single-line input field from text to password. This makes browsers obscure anything typed into the field by displaying a series of stars or bullets. It doesn't encrypt the input but prevents anyone from seeing it in plain text.

- Char width: This specifies the width of the input field, measured in characters. For a text field, this inserts the `size` attribute in the `<input>` tag. I normally use CSS to style the width of input fields, so you can leave this blank. This setting has no impact on the number of characters that can be typed into the field.

- Max chars: This sets the maximum number of characters that a field accepts by setting the `maxlength` attribute of a text field. If left blank, no limit is imposed.

- Init val: This lets you specify a default value for the field. It sets the `value` attribute, which is optional and normally left blank.

- Disabled: This is a new addition in Dreamweaver CS4. It adds the `disabled` attribute to the opening tag. This grays out the field when the form is displayed in a browser, preventing users from entering anything in the field.

- Read-only: This is also new to Dreamweaver CS4. Selecting this checkbox adds the `readonly` attribute to the opening tag. There's no change to the look of the field, but it prevents the user from deleting or changing the existing value.

> *The* Disabled *and* Read-only *checkboxes are visible only if you have the Property inspector expanded to its full height. Hiding the bottom half of the Property inspector saves a small amount of screen real estate but is normally a false economy.*

Figure 9-5 shows the Property inspector for the Comments text area. As you can see, it looks almost identical to Figure 9-4, although Type is set to Multi line. This time, Type has no direct equivalent in the underlying HTML. Selecting Multi line changes the tag from `<input>` to `<textarea>`.

The other important differences are that Max chars has changed to Num lines and default values have been set for Char width and Num lines. These determine the width and height of the text area by inserting the `rows` and `cols` attributes in the opening `<textarea>` tag. Both attributes are required for valid HTML and should be left in, even if you plan to use CSS to set the dimensions of the text area.

Figure 9-5. When you insert a text area, Dreamweaver gives it a default width and height.

An important change from previous versions of Dreamweaver is the removal of the Wrap option. This used to insert the invalid `wrap` attribute, which was ignored by most browsers. All modern browsers automatically wrap user input in a text area, so its removal is no loss. In its place are the Disabled and Read-only checkboxes, which work the same way as for a text input field.

9

Converting a text field to a text area, and vice versa

Although text fields and text areas use completely different tags, Dreamweaver lets you convert from one type to the other by changing the Type option in the Property inspector. If you change Type from Single line to Multi line, the <input> tag is replaced by a pair of <textarea> tags, and vice versa. Dreamweaver makes the process seamless by changing or removing attributes. For example, if you convert a text area to a text field, the cols attribute changes to size, and the rows attribute is deleted.

This is convenient if you change your mind about the design of a form, because it saves deleting one type of text input field and restarting from scratch. However, you need to remember to set both Char width and Num lines if converting a single-line field to a text area; Dreamweaver sets the defaults only when inserting a text area from the Insert bar or menu.

The Password option works only with single-line input. It cannot be used with a text area.

Styling the basic feedback form

The form looks a bit unruly, so let's give it some basic styling.

Styling the form

With the exception of a single class, all the style rules use type selectors (in other words, they redefine the style for individual HTML tags). Rather than using the New CSS Style dialog box to create them, it's quicker and easier to type them directly into a new style sheet in Code view.

1. Create a new style sheet by selecting File ➤ New. In the New Document dialog box, select Blank Page and CSS for Page Type. Insert the following rules, and save the page as contact.css in the workfiles/ch09 folder. (If you don't want to type everything yourself, there's a copy in the examples/ch09 folder. The version in the download files contains some extra rules that will be added later.)

```css
body {
    background-color:#FFF;
    color:#252525;
    font-family:Arial, Helvetica, sans-serif;
    font-size:100%;
}
h1 {
    font-family:Verdana, Arial, Helvetica, sans-serif;
    font-size:150%;
}
p {
    font-size:85%;
    margin:0 0 5px 25px;
    max-width:650px;
}
form {
```

```
  width:600px;
  margin:15px auto 10px 20px;
}
label {
  display:block;
  font-weight:bold;
}
textarea {
  width:400px;
  height:150px;
}
.textInput {
  width:250px;
}
```

The style rules are very straightforward, mainly setting fonts and controlling the size and margins of elements. By setting the display property for label to block, each <label> tag is forced onto a line of its own above the element it refers to.

2. Switch to feedback.php in the Document window, and attach contact.css as its style sheet. There are several ways of doing this. One is to open the Class drop-down menu in the HTML view of the Property inspector and select Attach Style Sheet. Alternatively, you can use the menu option, Format ➤ CSS Styles ➤ Attach Style Sheet, or click the Attach Style Sheet icon at the bottom right of the CSS Styles panel.

   Browse to contact.css, and attach it to feedback.php. The form should now look a lot neater.

3. Select the Name text field, and set its class to textInput to set its width to 250 pixels. Do the same with the Email text field.

4. Save feedback.php, and press F12/Opt+F12 to preview it in a browser. The form should look like Figure 9-6.

9

Figure 9-6.
The basic feedback form is ready for business.

Understanding the difference between GET and POST

Now that you have a form to work with, this is a good time to see how information is passed from the form and demonstrate the difference between choosing GET and POST as the method attribute. With feedback.php displayed in a browser, type anything into the form, and click the Send comments button. Whatever you typed into the text fields should disappear. It hasn't been processed because there's no script to handle it, but the content of the text fields hasn't entirely disappeared. Click the browser's reload button, and you should see a warning that the data will be resent if you reload the page.

If the action attribute is empty, the default behavior is to submit the data in the form to the same page. As the warning indicates, the data has been passed to the page, but since there's no script to process it, nothing happens. Processing the data is the subject of Chapter 11, but let's take a sneak preview to see the different ways POST and GET submit the data.

Examining the data submitted by a form

In this exercise, you'll add a simple PHP conditional statement to display the data transmitted by the POST method. You'll also see what happens when the form is submitted using the GET method. Use feedback.php from the preceding exercise. If you just want to test the code, use feedback_post.php in examples/ch09.

1. Save a copy of feedback.php as feedback_post.php in workfiles/ch09. Open it in Code view, and scroll to the bottom of the page.

2. Add the following code shown in bold between the closing </form> and </body> tags:

```
</form>
<pre>
<?php if ($_POST) {print_r($_POST);} ?>
</pre>
</body>
```

As soon as you type the underscore after the dollar sign, Dreamweaver pops up a PHP code hint, as shown in the screenshot alongside. Type p (uppercase or lowercase—it doesn't matter), and press Enter/Return. Dreamweaver completes $_POST and automatically places an opening square bracket after it. Delete the square bracket. $_POST is a PHP superglobal array, which is created automatically.

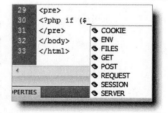

As the name suggests, it contains data sent by the POST method. (The role of superglobal arrays is explained in Chapter 11.)

Don't worry about the meaning of the PHP code. Just accept it for the moment, and concentrate on what it does.

3. Save the page, and load it into a browser. Enter some text in the form, and click Send comments. This time, you should see the value of each field identified by its name attribute displayed at the bottom of the page as in Figure 9-7.

Figure 9-7.
The PHP $_POST superglobal array contains the data submitted from the form.

The values gathered by the $_POST array contain not only the information entered into the text fields but also the value attribute of the submit button.

4. Change the value of method in the opening <form> tag from post to get like this:

```
<form action="" method="get" name="form1" id="form1">
```

5. Save the page, and display it again in the browser by clicking inside the address bar and pressing Enter/Return. Don't use the reload button, because you don't want to resend the POST data.

6. Type anything into the form, and click Send comments. This time, nothing will be displayed below the form, but the contents of the form fields will be appended to the URL, as shown in Figure 9-8. Again, each value is identified by its name attribute.

Figure 9-8. Data sent using the GET method is appended to the URL as a series of name/value pairs.

As you have just seen, the GET method sends your data in a very exposed way, making it vulnerable to alteration. Also, most browsers limit the amount of data that can be sent through a URL. The effective maximum is determined by Internet Explorer, which accepts no more than 2,083 characters, including both the URL and variables (http://support. microsoft.com/kb/208427). The POST method is more secure and can be used for much larger amounts of data. By default, PHP permits up to 8MB of POST data, although hosting companies may set a smaller limit.

Because of these advantages, you should normally use the POST method with forms. The GET method is used mainly in conjunction with database searches and has the advantage that you can bookmark a search result because all the data is in the URL.

> *Although the POST method is more secure than GET, you shouldn't assume that it's 100-percent safe. For secure transmission, you need to use encryption or the Secure Sockets Layer (SSL).*

9

Passing information through a hidden field

Frequently, you need to pass information to a script without displaying it in the browser. For example, a form used to update a database record needs to pass the record's ID to the update script. You can store the information in what's called a hidden field.

Adding a hidden field

Although you don't need a hidden field in this feedback form, let's put one in to see how it works. Hidden fields play an important role in later chapters. Continue working with feedback_post.php from the preceding exercise. The finished code is in feedback_hidden.php.

1. Set the value of method back to post. Do this in Code view or by selecting the form in Design view and setting Method to POST in the Property inspector.

2. A hidden field isn't displayed, so it doesn't matter where you locate it, as long as it's inside the form. However, it's normal practice to put hidden fields at the bottom of a form. Switch back to Design view, and click to the right of the Send comments button.

3. Click the Hidden Field button in the Forms tab of the Insert bar, as shown here:

4. Dreamweaver inserts a hidden field icon alongside the Send comments button. Type a name for the hidden field in the left text field in the Property inspector and the value you want it to contain in the Value field, as shown in Figure 9-9.

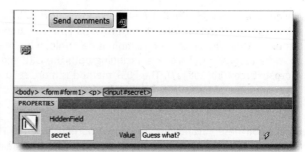

Figure 9-9.
Select a hidden field's icon in Design view to edit its name and value in the Property inspector.

Note that the PHP script at the bottom of the page is indicated by a gold PHP icon. If you can't see the hidden field or PHP icons in Design view, select View ➤ Visual Aids ➤ Invisible Elements.

> *The option on the* View *menu controls the display of invisible elements only on the current page. To change the default, open the* Preferences *panel from the* Edit *menu (*Dreamweaver *menu in a Mac), and select the* Invisible Elements *category. Make sure there's a check mark alongside* Hidden form fields *and* Visual Server Markup Tags, *and then click* OK. *The* Visual Aids *submenu is useful for turning off the display of various tools when they get in the way of the design of a page. You can toggle currently selected visual aids on and off with the keyboard shortcut Ctrl+Shift+I/Shift+Cmd+I.*

5. Switch to Code view. You'll see that Dreamweaver has inserted the following code at the end of the form:

```
<input name="secret" type="hidden" id="secret" value="Guess what?" />
```

6. Save feedback_post.php, and press F12/Opt+F12 to load the page in a browser (or use feedback_hidden.php in examples/ch09). The hidden field should be, well . . . hidden. Right-click to view the page's source code. The hidden field and its value are clearly visible. Test the form by entering some text and clicking Send comments. The value of secret should be displayed with the rest of the form input.

Just because a hidden field isn't displayed in a form doesn't mean that it really is hidden. Frequently, the value of a hidden field is set dynamically, and the field is simply a device for passing information from one page to another. Never use a hidden field for information that you genuinely want to keep secret.

Using multiple-choice form elements

9

Useful though text input is, you have no control over what's entered in the form. People spell things wrong or enter inappropriate answers. There's no point in a customer ordering a yellow T-shirt when the only colors available are white and black. Multiple-choice form elements leave the user in no doubt what the options are, and you get answers in the format you want.

Web forms have four multiple-choice elements, as follows:

- **Checkboxes**: These let the user select several options or none at all. They're useful for indicating the user's interests, ordering optional accessories, and so on.
- **Radio buttons**: These are often used in an either/or situation, such as male or female and yes or no, but there's no limit to the number of radio buttons that can be used in a group. However, only one option can be chosen.
- **Drop-down menus**: Like radio buttons, these allow only one choice but are more compact and user-friendly when more than three or four options are available.
- **Multiple-choice lists**: Like checkboxes, these permit several options to be chosen, but present them as a scrolling list. Often, the need to scroll back and forth to see all the options makes this the least user-friendly way of presenting a multiple choice.

Let's add them to the basic feedback form to see how they work.

Offering a range of choices with checkboxes

There are two ways to use checkboxes. One is to give each checkbox a different name; the other is to give the same name to all checkboxes in the same group. Which you choose depends on the circumstances. Use the first when the options represented by checkboxes aren't related to each other; create a checkbox group when there's a logical relationship between them. Normally, Dreamweaver uses the same values for the id and name attributes of form elements. Since an ID must always be unique, treating checkboxes as a group in previous versions of Dreamweaver involved adjusting the name attribute of each checkbox in Code view.

That's no longer a problem in Dreamweaver CS4, because you have the choice of creating individual checkboxes or a checkbox group. Individual checkboxes have the same value for both name and id attributes. Members of a checkbox group have separate id attributes but share a common name. You create a checkbox group through the simple dialog box shown in Figure 9-10. Access the dialog box through the Checkbox Group button in the Forms tab of the Insert bar or by selecting Insert ➤ Form ➤ Checkbox Group.

Figure 9-10. The new Checkbox Group dialog box speeds up the creation of related checkboxes.

The Checkbox Group dialog box has the following options:

- Name: This field is where you enter the name attribute that you want to assign to all checkboxes within the group. If you're feeling lazy, you can just accept the default. Dreamweaver automatically increments the number at the end of the default name if there is more than one checkbox group on a page.

- Checkboxes: This field is prefilled with two dummy checkboxes. To change the placeholder text, click inside the first Label field to open it for editing. You can move to the other prefilled fields with the Tab key or by clicking directly inside them. Add or remove checkboxes with the plus and minus buttons at the top left of the Checkboxes field. Change their order with the up and down arrows at the top right.

- Label: This is for the text you want to appear alongside the checkbox.
- Value: This is the value you want the checkbox to represent, if selected, when the form is submitted for processing.
- Lay out using: Choose whether to lay out the checkbox group using line breaks (`<br />` tags are used with an XHTML DOCTYPE declaration) or a single-column table.

However, you can't reopen the dialog box to add new checkboxes after the group has been created. Any extra checkboxes need to be added individually. The next exercise shows you how to do both.

Inserting a group of checkboxes

Continue working with feedback_post.php from the preceding exercise. Alternatively, copy feedback_multi_start.php from examples/ch09 to workfiles/ch09. The finished code for this exercise is in feedback_checkbox.php.

1. Save the page as feedback_checkbox.php in workfiles/ch09.

2. With the page open in Design view, click immediately to the right of the Comments text area. Press Enter/Return to insert a new paragraph.

3. Each checkbox has its own label, so you need a heading for the checkbox group that uses the same font size and weight as the `<label>` tags.

    Make sure that the HTML view of the Property inspector is selected, and click the Bold button (the large B just to the right of the CSS button). Although the tooltip says Bold, this inserts the `<strong>` tag in accordance with current standards, rather than the presentational `<b>` tag.

    > *When clicking the Bold button, it's vital that you're in the* HTML *view of the Property inspector. If you're in the* CSS *view, clicking the* Bold *button adds* font-weight: bold; *to the current selection in* Targeted Rule. *Since you're inside a paragraph, this makes the text in* all *paragraphs bold, not just the current one.*

4. Type a heading for the checkbox group. I used What aspects of London most interest you? Click the Bold tag again to move the cursor outside the closing `</strong>` tag in the underlying code.

5. Checkboxes usually have short labels, so it's often a good idea to display them in columns. The Checkbox Group dialog box has two layout options. You can display the checkboxes in a single-column table or use line breaks (`<br />` tags).

    If you choose line breaks, Dreamweaver automatically wraps the checkbox group in a pair of `<p>` tags unless the insertion point is already in a paragraph, in which case it uses the existing tags.

    Rather than use a table, I'm going to use a couple of floated paragraphs. You need to create a style rule for them later, but let's start by creating the checkbox group.

    With your insertion point at the end of the paragraph you entered in step 4, press Enter/Return to create a new paragraph.

9

6. Click the Checkbox Group button in the Forms tab of the Insert bar, as shown here:

> *Make sure you select the correct button. The* Checkbox Group *button uses the same icon as the* Radio Group *button (two buttons farther right). I find them easy to tell apart because each group button is immediately to the right of the button that inserts a single checkbox or radio button. However, if you find the plethora of icons in Dreamweaver confusing, either use the menu alternatives or display the* Insert *bar as a panel with labels (see Chapter 1).*

This opens the Checkbox Group dialog box shown in Figure 9-10.

7. In Chapter 11, you will build a PHP script to process this form. If more than one form item has the same name attribute, PHP expects the values to be submitted as an array (PHP arrays are described in the next chapter). To get PHP to treat all values in the checkbox group as an array, you need to add an empty pair of square brackets after the name attribute. I want to use interests as the name for this checkbox group, so enter interests[] in the Name field (there should be no space between interests and the square brackets).

8. Click the plus button alongside Checkboxes twice to add two checkboxes, and edit the Label and Value fields using the following values:

- Classical concerts   Classical concerts
- Rock & pop events   Rock/pop
- Drama   Drama
- Guided walks   Walks

9. Select Line breaks (
 tags) for the layout. The Checkbox Group dialog box should now look like this:

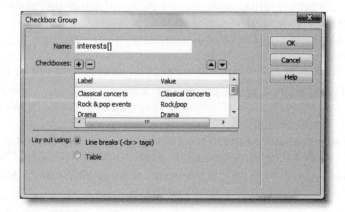

10. Click OK to insert the checkbox group. The new code should look like this in Split view:

As the preceding screenshot shows, Dreamweaver wraps the `<label>` tags around the checkbox `<input>` tags, rather than using the for attribute. This doesn't affect the way the checkboxes are displayed in this form, so I'm going to leave them as they are. You can also see that each checkbox has the same name attribute, but the id attributes are all unique. Dreamweaver has numbered them incrementally as interests_0, interests_1, and so on.

11. As explained earlier, you cannot reopen the Checkbox Group dialog box to add more checkboxes. The simple way to add another checkbox is to open Code view and copy and paste an existing checkbox. For example, to add a checkbox for Art, you could copy and paste the code shown on lines 39–41 in the preceding screenshot and edit them like this (new code is shown in bold):

```
<label>
  <input type="checkbox" name="interests[]" value="Art" ➥
id="interests_4" />
Art</label>
```

Alternatively, you need to add a single checkbox using the Checkbox button immediately to the left of the Checkbox Group button in the Forms tab of the Insert bar (or Insert ➤ Form ➤ Checkbox). The next few steps show you how to do that.

12. One of the trickiest aspects of adding a checkbox to an existing group is getting the insertion point in the right place. As with the `<form>` tag, you get a far less user-friendly dialog box if you position your cursor in Code view. To get to the right position in Design view, open Split view, and keep an eye on the position of the insertion point in Code view.

Click to the right of the label of the last checkbox (Guided walks) in Design view, and press the down arrow key twice. This should move the insertion point to just inside the closing `</p>` tag of the checkbox group, as shown.

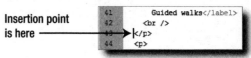

9

13. Click the Checkbox button in Forms tab of the Insert bar, as shown in the following screenshot:

14. In the Input Tag Accessibility Attributes dialog box, enter the following values, and click OK.

- ID: interests_4

- Label: Art

- Style: Wrap with label tag

- Position: After form item (Dreamweaver selects this automatically)

15. Dreamweaver inserts the following code in Code view:

```
<label>
  <input type="checkbox" name="interests_4" id="interests_4" />
Art</label>
```

You need to change the value of the name attribute to match the other checkboxes like this:

```
<label>
  <input type="checkbox" name="interests[]" id="interests_4" />
Art</label>
```

You must do this in Code view. If you use the Property inspector, Dreamweaver uses the same value for both name and id attributes. Square brackets are permitted in the name attribute, but not in an ID.

16. Save the page, and load it into a browser. Select some of the checkboxes, and click the Send comments button. The checked values should appear at the bottom of the page. Try it with no boxes checked. This time, interests isn't listed.

Check your code, if necessary, with feedback_checkbox.php in examples/ch09. Keep the file open, because you'll continue working with it in the next exercise.

As you can see, adding an extra checkbox to an existing checkbox group is rather fiddly, because you can't set the name and id attributes separately at the time of creation. However, if you are creating a stand-alone checkbox, for example one that asks users to confirm they agree to the terms and conditions of the site, it doesn't matter if the name and id are the same.

Displaying the checkboxes in columns

Currently, the checkboxes are stacked one on top of the other. Moving them into two columns is simply a matter of splitting them into two paragraphs and floating them left. Continue working with the same file as in the previous exercise.

1. To split the checkboxes into separate paragraphs, you need to go into Code view and replace the `<br />` tag between the third and fourth checkboxes with a closing `</p>` tag and an opening `<p>` one like this:

```
Drama</label>
</p>
<p>
  <label>
    <input type="checkbox" name="interests[]" value="Walks" ➥
id="interests_3" />
```

2. You now need to create a couple of style rules to float the paragraphs. Select contact.css in the Related Files toolbar, and add the following rules at the bottom of the page:

```
.chkRad {
  float: left;
  margin-bottom: 15px;
  margin-left: 50px;
}
.clearIt {
  clear: both;
}
```

The first rule creates the chkRad class, which will be applied to both checkboxes and radio buttons, floating them left and adding margins on the bottom and left.

The .clearIt selector uses the clear property, which prevents other elements from moving up into empty space alongside a floated element. This will be applied to the paragraph containing the submit button.

3. Click inside any of the first three checkboxes, and right-click the `<p>` tag in the Tag selector at the bottom of the Document window. Select Set Class ➤ chkRad from the context menu, as shown here:

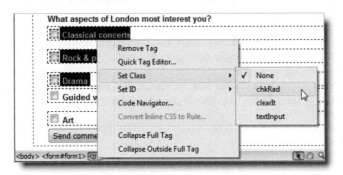

9

4. Do the same for the second paragraph containing checkboxes. This results in the Send comments button floating up alongside the second column of checkboxes, as shown here:

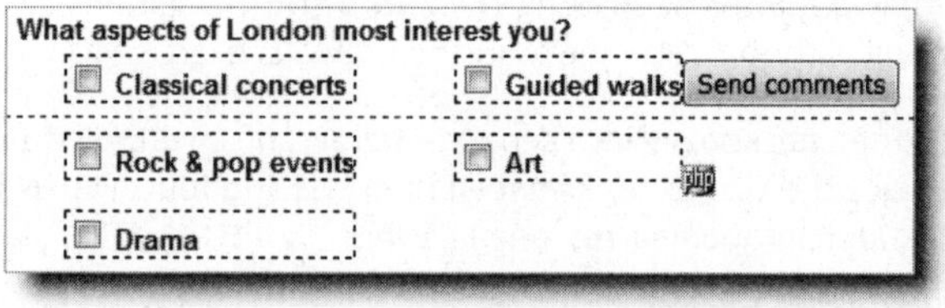

5. Fix this by selecting the Send comments button in Design view and then right-clicking the <p> tag in the Tag selector at the bottom of the Document window. Select Set Class ➤ clearIt from the context menu.

The Send comments button should move down to its original position, as shown in the following screenshot:

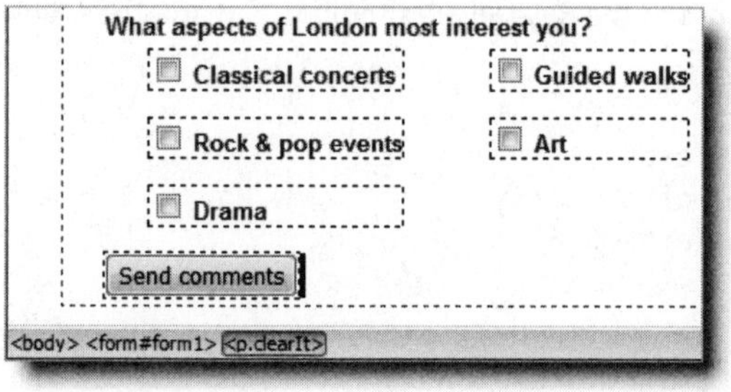

If the button remains floating, make sure you applied the class to the surrounding paragraph, not to the button itself.

Check your code, if necessary, with feedback_checkbox_cols.php in examples/ch09.

Using radio buttons to offer a single choice

The term **radio buttons** is borrowed from the preset buttons common on radios: you push a button to select a station and the currently selected one pops out; only one can be selected at any given time. Like a radio, there shouldn't be too many buttons to choose from. Otherwise, the user gets confused.

As with checkboxes, Dreamweaver offers you the choice of inserting radio buttons one at a time or as a group in a single operation. Similarly, there's no way of relaunching the Radio Group dialog box to edit the radio buttons or add a new one to the group. The options in the Radio Group dialog box are identical to the Checkbox Group dialog box (see Figure 9-10), so refer to the previous section for details.

The following exercise shows how to insert individual radio buttons.

Creating a radio button group with individual buttons

Continue working with the form from the preceding exercise, or copy feedback_checkbox_cols.php from examples/ch09 to workfiles/ch09. The finished code is in feedback_radio.php.

1. Save the file as feedback_radio.php.

2. Like checkboxes, each radio button has its own label, so you need to create a heading to indicate the question being asked. To add a new paragraph below the checkbox group, click in the last checkbox label in the right column (Art) in Design view, and press Enter/Return. Instead of the cursor moving below the checkbox group, it lines up alongside the Guided walks label. This is because Dreamweaver automatically applies the same style as the preceding paragraph when you press Enter/Return.

3. You need to remove the chkRad class from the new paragraph and replace it with the clearIt class. Right-click <p.chkRad> in the Tag selector at the bottom of the Document window, and select Set Class ➤ clearIt from the context menu. This is the same technique as in step 3 of the previous exercise, only this time you are changing the class rather than applying a new one.

> *You cannot use the Tag selector or Property inspector to apply multiple classes to the same element. The only ways to do so in Dreamweaver are through the* Tag Inspector *panel or in Code view.*

4. Click the Bold button in the HTML view of the Property inspector, and type a question. I used Would you like to receive regular details of events in London?

5. At the end of the line, click the Bold button again to move the insertion point outside the closing </strong> tag, and press Enter/Return to create a new paragraph.

6. Click Radio Button in the Forms tab of the Insert bar, as shown here:

7. Enter the following settings in the Input Tag Accessibility Attributes dialog box:

- ID: subscribeYes
- Label: Yes
- Style: Wrap with label tag
- Position: After form item (Dreamweaver selects this automatically)

9

8. When you click OK, Dreamweaver inserts the radio button and its associated label. Select the radio button element in Design view to display its details in the Property inspector, which should look like this:

The field on the left immediately below Radio Button sets the name attribute for the radio button. Change it to subscribe. Unlike other form elements, the name and id attributes of radio buttons aren't automatically linked in the Property inspector because Dreamweaver is smart enough to know that all buttons in a radio group share the same name, but they must have unique IDs. However, since only one value is submitted from a radio group, unlike a checkbox group, you don't need to add square brackets after the name.

Dreamweaver automatically enters the same value as the ID in Checked value. While this is OK, you can change the value here without affecting the ID. Just type the letter y in the Checked value field.

Leave the other values unchanged. Although the Class field displays clearIt, this is inherited from the surrounding paragraph. You need to change the paragraph's class, but it's better to do it after you have finished inserting the other radio button because it's easier to position the insertion point in Design view in nonfloated elements.

9. Click to the right of the Yes label in Design view, and press Enter/Return to insert a new paragraph. Repeat steps 6 and 7 to insert a second radio button, setting ID to subscribeNo and Label to No.

10. Select the second radio button element in Design view to display its details in the Property inspector. Change its name from radio to subscribe, and shorten Checked value to the letter n. It's always a good idea to set a default value for a radio button group, so set Initial state to Checked.

11. All that remains to do is change the class of the paragraphs surrounding the two radio buttons and float them alongside each other. However, to make it easy to insert the next form element in the following exercise, click to the right of the No label, and press Enter/Return to insert a new paragraph. This inherits the clearIt class, so it won't float alongside the radio buttons.

12. Click to the right of the Yes label in Design view, right-click <p.clearIt> in the Tag selector at the bottom of the Document window, and select Set Class ➤ chkRad

from the context menu. Do the same with the paragraph surrounding the No radio button. The radio buttons should float alongside each other like this:

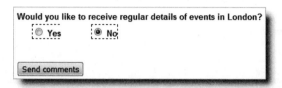

13. Save the page, and load it in a browser. Test it to make sure that the value of subscribe is y or n depending on the radio button selected.

Check your code, if necessary, against feedback_radio.php in examples/ch09.

Offering a single choice from a drop-down menu

Drop-down menus and multiple-choice lists both use the HMTL <select> tag, with each individual item in an <option> tag. Apart from two attributes in the opening <select> tag, their underlying structure is identical, so Dreamweaver uses the same tools to insert and configure them. First, let's take a look at a single-choice menu. The following instructions show you how to add one to the feedback form.

Inserting and configuring a drop-down menu

Continue working with the form from the preceding exercise, or copy feedback_radio.php from examples/ch09 to workfiles/ch09. The finished code is in feedback_select.php.

1. Save the file as feedback_select.php.

2. Insert your cursor in the empty paragraph between the radio buttons and the Send comments button, and click the List/Menu button on the Forms tab of the Insert bar, as shown here:

3. Enter the following settings in the Input Tag Accessibility Attributes dialog box:

- ID: visited
- Label: How often have you been to London?
- Style: Attach label tag using 'for' attribute
- Position: Before form item (Dreamweaver selects this automatically)

9

4. When you click OK, Dreamweaver inserts the label and a blank menu element in Design view. Click the menu element to select it and display its details in the Property inspector, as shown in the following screenshot:

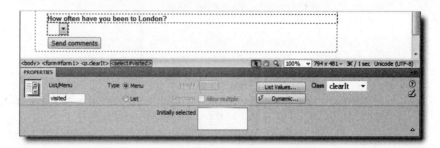

> *If you have difficulty selecting the menu element in Design view, open Split view, and click anywhere inside the `<select>` tag.*

5. Type is set by default to Menu, which builds a single-choice drop-down menu. The List option creates a scrolling list. You'll see how that works in the next section.

To populate the menu, click the List Values button in the Property inspector. This opens the List Values dialog box, as shown in the following screenshot:

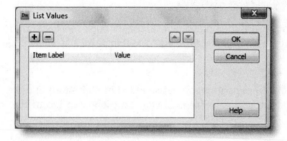

Item Label is what you want to be shown in the menu, and Value is the data you want to be sent if the item is selected when the form is submitted. The value attribute of the `<option>` tag is optional, so the Value field needs to be set only if you want the label and the data to be different.

> *This is another example of Dreamweaver using what it regards as user-friendly expressions.* Item Label *is the text element that goes between the `<option>` tags of a `<select>` menu. While this is, no doubt, helpful to some users, it can also be confusing because it bears no relation to the `<label>` tags that are used to improve the accessibility of online forms.*

The easiest way to fill in the dialog box is to tab between the fields. Tabbing from the Value field creates the next item. You can also click inside an existing field to edit it. Use the minus (–) button to delete a selected item and the up and down arrows to reorder the list.

I used the following values:

- -- Select one --   0
- Never been   Never
- Once or twice   1-2 times
- Less than once a year   Not yearly
- I go most years   Yearly
- I live there   Resident

The first item simply asks users to select one of the options. I have set the Value field to 0 to indicate that nothing has been selected. Without an explicit value, the text contents of the <option> tag is submitted by the form.

Click OK when you are finished.

6. Dreamweaver normally displays the longest option in Design view. To specify the one you want to be displayed when the form first loads, select it in the Initially selected field in the Property inspector. This adds selected="selected" to the <option> tag.

   By default, browsers show the first item in the menu if you don't set the Initially selected field. However, it's often useful to select an item that's lower down the list. For example, you may want to display a list of countries in alphabetical order, but if most of your visitors are from the United States, it's a courtesy to display that by default rather than forcing them to scroll all the way down the list to select it.

7. Save feedback_select.php, and load it in a browser. Select a menu item, and click Send comments. The value should be displayed as visited at the bottom of the page.

   Check your code, if necessary, against feedback_select.php in examples/ch09.

Creating a multiple-choice scrollable list

The way you build a multiple-choice list is almost identical to a drop-down menu. It involves only a couple more steps to set the size and multiple attributes in the opening <select> tag. Strictly speaking, the multiple attribute is optional. If it's omitted, the user can select only a single item.

You could convert the menu from the preceding section by changing Type from Menu to List in the Property inspector. However, the way you process data from a multiple-choice list is different, so let's add a separate list to the same form.

9

Inserting and configuring a scrollable list

Continue working with the form from the preceding exercise, or copy feedback_select.php from examples/ch09 to workfiles/ch09. The finished code is in feedback_multiselect.php.

1. Save the file as feedback_multiselect.php.

2. In Design view, click immediately to the right of the drop-down menu you inserted in the previous exercise, and press Enter/Return to insert a new paragraph. Because the clearIt class was applied to the preceding paragraph, Dreamweaver applies the same class to the new paragraph. Leaving it does no harm, but you don't really need it either, so reset Class to None in the HTML view of the Property inspector.

3. Click the List/Menu button on the Forms tab of the Insert bar.

4. Enter the following settings in the Input Tag Accessibility Attributes dialog box:

- ID: views
- Label: What image do you have of London?
- Style: Attach label tag using 'for' attribute
- Position: Before form item **(Dreamweaver selects this automatically)**

5. When you click OK, Dreamweaver inserts a blank drop-down menu into the page in the same way as in step 4 of the preceding exercise. Select the menu element in Design view to display its details in the Property inspector.

Change Type to List. This activates the Height and Selections options. These are more examples of Dreamweaver's attempt at user-friendly names instead of using the HTML attributes. Height sets the size attribute, which determines the number of items visible in the list; the browser automatically adds a vertical scrollbar. Change the value to 6, and put a check mark in the Selections checkbox to permit multiple choices. This adds multiple="multiple" in the <select> tag. The menu is converted into a tall, narrow rectangle, as shown here:

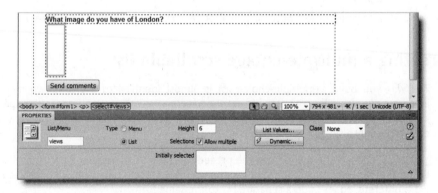

6. Click the List Values button to enter the labels and data values the same as for a drop-down menu. Leave Value blank if you want the data sent by the form to be the same as the label. The following screenshot shows the first five values I used:

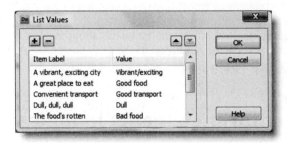

I set the sixth Item Label to A transport nightmare, and its Value to Transport nightmare.

7. Save the page, and load it into a browser. Select several items in the list (holding down the Shift or Ctrl/Cmd key while clicking), and click the Send comments button.

Uh, oh . . . something is wrong. Only the last selected item appears at the bottom of the page. To get all items, you need to use an array in the same way as with the checkbox group by appending a pair of square brackets to the end of the name attribute. Fortunately, there's only one name attribute to change.

The problem with the Property inspector is that it uses the same field for the name and id attributes. If you add the square brackets to views in the Property inspector, it affects both name and id. You could dive into Code view to fix the problem, but let me show you another way—using the Tag Inspector panel.

8. Make sure the list is selected in Design view, and open the Tag Inspector panel (F9/Shift+Opt+F9 or Window ➤ Tag Inspector). If the Behaviors button is selected, click the Attributes button at the top left of the Tag Inspector panel. This gives you direct access to the attributes of the element currently selected in the Document window. It has two views: listing attributes by category or in alphabetical order.

Expand the General and CSS/Accessibility categories in category view to reveal the name and id attributes. Click inside the name field to add a pair of square brackets after views, as shown in the screenshot alongside. (Depending on your monitor's resolution, they might appear to merge into an upright rectangle. This doesn't matter.)

9. Press Enter/Return to save the change. Save the page, and test it again in a browser. This time, all selected items from the multiple-choice list should be displayed as an array at the bottom of the page.

10. Click Send comments without selecting anything in the list. This time, views won't be among the items displayed at the bottom of the page. This is the same as with a checkbox group, and it has important implications for how you process the output of a form, as you'll see in Chapter 11.

Compare your code, if necessary, with feedback_multiselect.php in examples/ch09.

Organizing form elements in logical groups

An important element in designing a usable form is making sure that everything is laid out logically so that users can see at a glance what sort of information is required. It can also help to divide the form into a number of clearly labeled sections. HTML provides two tags for this purpose: `<fieldset>` and `<legend>`, which most browsers automatically style with a border (see Figure 9-11).

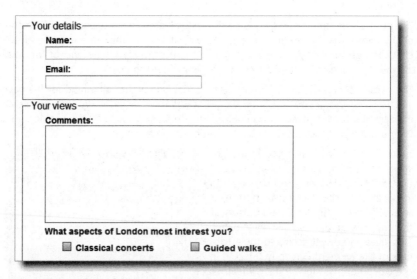

Figure 9-11. Fieldsets give forms a visual and logical structure that help make them more accessible to all users.

Inserting a fieldset

You can add fieldsets to your form before inserting the individual form elements or after you have finished. To insert a fieldset, click the Fieldset button on the Forms tab of the Insert bar, as shown here:

This opens the Fieldset dialog box. It has just one field: Legend, which is the title you want to give to the group of form elements within the fieldset.

When you click OK, Dreamweaver inserts the following code in your form:

```
<fieldset>
<legend>Your details</legend>
</fieldset>
```

If you create the fieldset before inserting the individual form elements, press your right keyboard arrow after clicking OK in the Fieldset dialog box. This positions the insertion point between the closing </legend> and </fieldset> tags ready for adding the form elements that belong to the fieldset.

To add a fieldset to existing form elements, select the elements you want to include by dragging your mouse across them in Design view. If you have Split view open, you will see that Dreamweaver doesn't select the opening and closing tags of your selection. However, when you insert the fieldset, it's smart enough to put the <fieldset> and <legend> tags in the correct place. If the fieldset border and legend appear in the wrong place, it probably means that you failed to select the form elements correctly. Press Ctrl+Z/Cmd+Z or Edit ➤ Undo, and try again. Alternatively, go into Code view, and make sure the target form elements are between the closing </legend> and </fieldset> tags.

To see the effect of adding fieldsets to the form you have been using throughout this chapter and to study the code, take a look at feedback_fieldsets.php in examples/ch09. You can alter the look of fieldsets with CSS by adding fieldset and legend type selectors to your style sheet.

Now that I've covered all the main form input and layout elements, let's turn our attention to checking user input before submitting the form to the server for processing.

Validating user input before submission

Validation of user input plays a very important role in the design and processing of online forms. Let's say you're building a form that offers to send customers more information. There's no point processing the form if it doesn't contain certain details, such as email or postal address. Similarly, a form that asks for the user's age needs to make sure the information supplied falls within an acceptable range. For example, it must be a number. Is there a minimum age, such as 16? Setting a maximum age is more difficult, but obviously a figure such as 402 should be rejected. Validation can't stop people from entering false information; its role is to ensure that you get the type of information you expect—an email address in an email field and something that looks like a phone number in a phone number field. Well-designed sites usually perform validation twice—on the client side before the data is submitted to the server and once again on the server side.

The problem with client-side validation is that it relies on JavaScript. A visitor simply needs to turn off JavaScript in the browser and press the submit button; all your client-side filters are rendered useless. Consequently, some developers argue that client-side validation is a waste of time. Nevertheless, most visitors to your sites aren't deliberately trying to abuse your forms and are likely to have JavaScript enabled. So, it's generally a good idea to detect errors before a form is submitted. JavaScript validation is conducted locally and is usually instantaneous. It's done as a courtesy to the user, who doesn't need to wait for a response from the server if there's a mistake in the information submitted. It also helps reduce the burden on the server, because forms aren't submitted with incomplete information.

Nevertheless, the fact that client-side validation can be so easily evaded raises the question of how thorough it should be. Since the real checks need to be done on the server, there's a strong argument for keeping client-side checks to the absolute minimum or eliminating them altogether. Client-side validation is optional; server-side validation should never be omitted. We'll look at server-side validation in Chapter 11. The rest of this chapter is devoted to client-side validation with Spry validation widgets.

> *In addition to Spry validation widgets, the* Validate Form *behavior can be accessed through the* Behaviors *panel. However, the checks it performs are so rudimentary as to be virtually worthless.*

Using Spry validation widgets

The Spry validation widgets, which were first introduced in Dreamweaver CS3, are anything but rudimentary. They're capable of performing a wide range of checks and use a combination of JavaScript and CSS to display customized alerts alongside the affected field. Three new validation widgets were added in Dreamweaver CS4, bringing the types of form input they can handle to seven, as follows:

- Text fields
- Text areas
- Checkboxes
- Radio button groups
- Menus and lists
- Password fields
- Password confirmation fields

The text field widget is particularly impressive, because it lets you test for a wide range of formats, including numbers, currency, IP addresses, Social Security numbers, and credit card numbers. You can even set up your own custom patterns without the need to master the complex subject of regular expressions. The text area validation widget also provides one of the most frequently requested features—the ability to display how many characters the user has entered or still has left before reaching a predetermined limit. The validation widgets also display warning messages that you can easily edit and style with CSS.

You can access the validation widgets on both the Forms and Spry tabs of the Insert bar. As Figure 9-12 shows, the icons are very similar to those of their related form elements. However, if you prefer menus to icons, the same options are also available on the Spry submenu of the Insert menu.

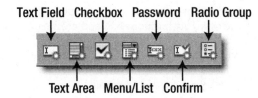

Figure 9-12.
Spry validation widgets have an orange sunburst on the same icons as their related form elements.

Spry validation widgets are certainly powerful, but they greatly increase page size. If you add all seven widgets to a form, the external JavaScript files and style sheets weigh in at more than 200KB. The text field widget is responsible for roughly one third that amount because of its extensive pattern-matching features. It's overkill for a very basic form, but could be extremely useful in validating user input on a form for a job application or an insurance policy quote.

> *The external files are cached by the user's browser, so are downloaded only once. However, if you're concerned about file size, you can use optimized versions of the Spry JavaScript files by downloading the Spry framework from* http://labs.adobe.com/technologies/spry/. *The versions of the files in the* includes_packed *folder weigh in at just 85KB. The files have the same names as those inserted by Dreamweaver, so just swap them over.*

If you insert a widget into a blank part of a form, Dreamweaver inserts both the validation code and the form element. Alternatively, you can apply a widget to an existing form element. Whichever approach you use, the method of configuration is exactly the same. In the remaining pages of this chapter, I'm going to show you how to apply validation widgets to an existing form.

I suggest you study carefully the first section of "Validating a text field with Spry," because it contains most of the knowledge you need to work with all validation widgets, particularly with regard to editing and controlling the display of alert messages.

Inserting a Spry validation widget

As with all Spry widgets, the page must have been saved at least once before you can apply a validation widget. Save the page again immediately afterward to attach the external JavaScript code and style sheet, and copy them to the Spry assets folder if necessary.

> Unless you're a JavaScript expert, don't try to use other JavaScript validation functions, such as the Validate Form behavior, on the same form with Spry validation widgets, because they're likely to conflict and cease functioning.

Removing a validation widget

Removing a widget immediately after you have applied it is easy. Unfortunately, the standard method of removing a Spry widget (selecting its turquoise tab and pressing Delete) removes the form element with it. The simple way to get around this problem is to select the form element (and label, if necessary) in Design view and cut it to your clipboard (Ctrl+X/Cmd+X). Then select the turquoise tab to delete the widget. If you see the following warning that the widget has been damaged, you can safely ignore it:

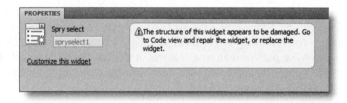

Once you have removed the widget, paste (Ctrl+V/Cmd+V) the form element back into the page.

> Dreamweaver is context-sensitive. If you cut from Design view, always paste back into Design view; the same with Code view. If you don't, Dreamweaver is likely to mess up your page.

Validating a text field with Spry

To validate a text field, either select an existing text field or position your cursor inside a form where you want to insert a new text field, and click the Spry Validation Text Field button on the Insert bar. If you are inserting a new text field, fill in the ID and Label fields in the Input Tag Accessibility Attributes dialog box as described earlier in the chapter.

Figure 9-13 shows what happens when you apply a validation widget to the first text field in the form that you have been working with throughout the chapter. The screenshot was taken with the Document window open in Split view, so you can see the underlying code (the section highlighted on lines 19–21).

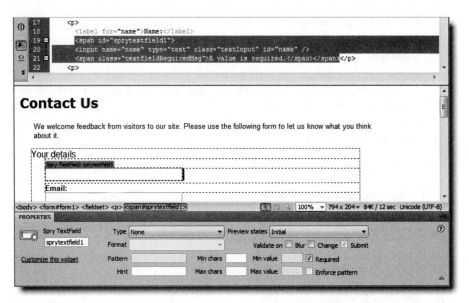

Figure 9-13. Validation widgets insert <span> tags and control their display with JavaScript.

The <input> tag has been surrounded by a <span> tag with the ID set to sprytextfield1. Immediately after the <input> tag is another <span>, which contains the text: A value is required. As you can see in Figure 9-13, that text isn't displayed in Design view. This is because the display of all validation messages in Spry widgets is controlled by JavaScript.

As you can see in Figure 9-13, the text field validation widget has a lot of options in the Property inspector. Let's run through them quickly before a practical exercise to show them in action:

- Type: This is where the real power of the text field validation widget lies. It lets you check user input against a wide range of formats, summarized in Table 9-1. All options, except None, insert an Invalid format <span> in the underlying code. Use the Preview states menu to display this in Design view for editing and/or styling.

- Format: This displays a drop-down menu of available formats, depending on the value of Type (see Table 9-1). It is disabled if the validation type is not associated with any formats.

- Pattern: Some validation types accept a custom pattern, which should be entered in this field. See "Building your own custom pattern" later in this chapter.

- Hint: This displays default text that disappears as soon as the text field has focus or anything is entered into it. It's useful for indicating the type of input or format expected. The value is displayed dynamically, so it won't be submitted as part of the form data if the user enters nothing in the field.

- Preview states: This controls the display of validation messages in Design view, allowing you to see what they look like and edit them and their associated styles.

9

- Validate on: This determines when the field is validated, namely:

  - Blur: This validates the input when focus moves from the field to another part of the page, for example when the user moves to the next input field.

  - Change: This validates the input each time the field changes. You should rarely use this on a text field, because it performs the validation each time the user types or deletes a character.

  - Submit: Validation is always performed when the form is submitted, so this checkbox is read-only.

- Min/Max chars: These fields let you specify the minimum or maximum number of characters required for validation. They add an alert message in a <span>, and the Preview states menu is updated to include an option to display and edit the alert.

- Min/Max value: These let you set a minimum or maximum value for validation.

- Required: This makes the field required. It is selected by default.

- Enforce pattern: This blocks invalid characters. For example, if Type is set to Integer, nothing is entered in the field if the user attempts to type a letter.

Table 9-1. Formats that the text field validation widget can recognize

Type	Available formats	Notes
None		Use this when no other suitable format is available.
Integer		This validates whole numbers only. Negative numbers are accepted but not decimal fractions or thousands separators. Use Real Number/Scientific Notation for decimals or Currency for whole numbers with thousands separators.
Email address		This performs only a rudimentary check for an email address, making sure that it contains a single @ mark followed by at least one period.
Date	mm/dd/yy mm/dd/yyyy dd/mm/yyyy dd/mm/yy yy/mm/dd yyyy/mm/dd mm-dd-yy dd-mm-yy yyyy-mm-dd mm.dd.yyyy dd.mm.yyyy	This checks not only the format but also the validity of the date, rejecting impossible dates, such as September 31. Leap years are recognized. A bug in Dreamweaver CS3 that incorrectly rejected February 29, 2000, has been fixed.
Time	HH:mm HH:mm:ss hh:mm tt hh:mm:ss tt hh:mm t hh:mm:ss t	HH represents the 24-hour clock, hh the 12-hour clock. Hours before 10 *must* have a leading zero. When using the 12-hour clock, tt stands for AM or PM; t stands for A or P. Lowercase is not accepted.

Type	Available formats	Notes
Credit Card	All Visa MasterCard American Express Discover Diner's Club	Matches basic patterns for major credit cards but should not be relied upon to check for a valid card number. Numbers must be entered without hyphens or spaces.
Zip Code	US-5 US-9 UK Canada Custom Pattern	This tests only that the right combination of numbers and/or letters is used. It doesn't check whether the code exists or matches other parts of an address. See "Building your own custom pattern" for details of how to use the Custom Pattern format.
Phone Number	US/Canada Custom Pattern	US/Canada must be in the same format as (212) 555-0197. For Custom Pattern, see "Building your own custom pattern."
Social Security Number	US/Canada Custom Pattern	This has been updated since Dreamweaver CS3 to accept a custom pattern.
Currency	1,000,000.00 1.000.000,00	In both formats, the thousands separator is optional, as is the decimal fraction. This makes it possible to validate currencies, such as yen, which aren't normally quoted with a smaller unit.
Real Number/ Scientific Notation		Used for numbers with a decimal fraction, which can optionally be expressed in scientific (exponential) notation, for example, 3.14159, 1.56234E+29, or 1.56234e29. The letter E can be uppercase or lowercase, but it must not be preceded by a space.
IP Address	IPv4 only IPv6 only IPv6 and IPv4	Covers all formats of IP address.
URL		This converts the URL to punycode (http://en.wikipedia.org/wiki/Punycode) before validation, so it should also accept international URLs that contain non-Latin characters.
Custom		This allows you to define your own format as described in "Building your own custom pattern."

9

Editing and controlling the display of validation alerts

The following exercise shows you how to control the display of validation alerts in a form. It uses the same form as has been used throughout this chapter. Continue using the form you built earlier. Alternatively, copy feedback_spry_start.php from examples/ch09, and save it in workfiles/ch09 as feedback_spry.php.

1. Select the Name text input field in Design view, and click the Spry Validation Text Field button in the Forms or Spry tab of the Insert bar (or use Insert ➤ Spry ➤ Spry Validation Text Field). Save the page to copy the external JavaScript file and style sheet to your site.

2. Make sure there's a check mark in the Required checkbox in the Property inspector (it should be selected by default), and choose Required from the Preview states drop-down menu. The text field should now look like this in Design view:

Not only is the text displayed, the background color of the text field has turned an alarming shade of pink.

3. Both the text field and the validation message are highlighted, so click inside the message so you can edit it. Shorten the text to Required.

4. With your cursor still inside the validation message, select the CSS view of the Property inspector, and click the Bold button, as shown here:

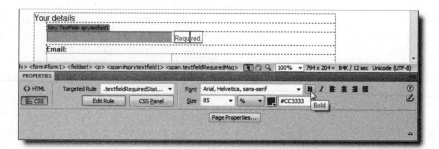

It's very important to use the CSS view of the Property inspector because this changes the targeted rule in the external style sheet, SpryValidationTextField.css, rather than in the underlying HTML. As a result, *all* validation messages will now be styled with bold text, not just the one you're currently editing.

5. Select the text field in Design view. The CSS view of the Property inspector is no longer visible, so you need to access the style sheet directly to change the background color of the text field. Hold down the Alt key (or Opt+Cmd keys on a Mac) to open the Code Navigator. As you can see in the following screenshot, the background color of the text field is controlled by a very complex selector:

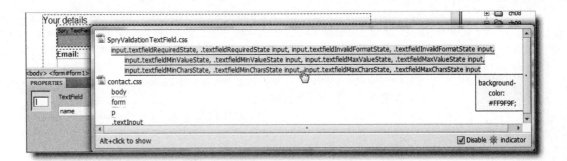

The selector is complex because it controls the look of the text field when validation fails in a wide range of circumstances. Don't worry about the selector. Just click its link in the Code Navigator to open the style sheet in Split view. Your cursor should automatically be located inside the right style rule.

6. Change the value of the background-color property from #FF9F9F to a less dramatic pink. I chose #FFDFDF. You can check the result by pressing F5 to refresh Design view.

7. Click the turquoise tab at the top left of the widget. In the Property inspector, change Preview states to Valid. The background color of the text field changes to green.

8. Select the text field, and then hold down the Alt/Opt+Cmd key(s) to open the Code Navigator. Select the style rule from SpryValidationTextField.css, as shown in the following screenshot:

> It's important to select the text field first. If you open the Code Navigator by holding down Alt/Opt+Cmd and clicking without first selecting the input field, Dreamweaver cannot detect the correct style rule. This is because the classes are dynamically generated by Spry, not hard-coded into the HTML tags.

9. Change the value of the background-color property from #B8F5B1 to a different shade of green. I chose #E3FBE1.

9

10. Select File ➤ Save All to save the page and style sheet, and load feedback_spry.php into a browser. Click inside the Name field. Assuming you're using a modern browser and JavaScript is enabled, the field should turn yellow, indicating that it has focus.

11. Don't enter anything in the field, but move the focus to another field. The Name field reverts to its previous state.

12. Click the Send comments button. The background of the text field turns pink, and the word Required is displayed alongside in bold crimson text. Also note that nothing is displayed below the Send comments button. The file feedback_spry.php contains the PHP script used earlier to display the data submitted by the form, so this is confirmation that the validation widget prevented the form from being submitted.

13. Type your name in the Name field, and move the focus to another field. Although the field turns yellow while you're typing, it turns pink again when the focus moves to another field, and the Required alert isn't cleared, as the following screenshot shows:

This is because the default behavior is to validate form elements only when the form is submitted, although you can easily change that.

14. Click the Send comments button. If your monitor is large enough for you to still see the text field, you'll see the background momentarily turn green indicating that it passed validation. You'll also see the form data displayed at the bottom of the page.

15. Back in Dreamweaver, select the turquoise tab at the top left of the validation widget to display its details in the Property inspector. Select the Blur checkbox, save the page, and repeat steps 10–14 to test it again. This time, the field turns green, and the Required message disappears in step 13.

Check your code, if necessary, against feedback_spry_text.php and SpryValidationTextField_edit.css in examples/ch09.

The styles changed in the preceding exercise affect all text field validation widgets in the same page, and they apply equally to all text field validation alerts. Although the Preview states menu gives you access to most style rules, you might want to edit the following two selectors directly in SpryValidationTextField.css:

- .textfieldFocusState input, input.textfieldFocusState: This gives the text field a yellow background when it has focus. The default color is #FFFFCC.

- .textfieldFlashText input, input.textfieldFlashText: This applies only when you select Enforce pattern in the Property inspector, and it makes the text briefly flash red if an invalid character is inserted.

Styling the alert messages for all remaining validation widgets follows the same principles as for a text field. Study the style sheets in the Spry assets folder, or click the Customize this widget *link in the Property inspector to display the help file, which explains which style rules to change.*

Building your own custom pattern

Spry makes it easy to build custom patterns using special pattern characters that act as a mask for the user's input. Spry custom patterns aren't as powerful as regular expressions, but they're a lot easier to use, so it's a reasonable trade-off for most people. Table 9-2 describes the special pattern characters.

Table 9-2. Special characters used for building custom patterns in Spry

Character	Matches	Case sensitivity
0	Any number 0–9	
A	Any letter A–Z	Converted to uppercase
a	Any letter a–z	Converted to lowercase
B	Any letter A–Z	Original case preserved
b	Any letter A–Z	Original case preserved
X	Any alphanumeric character (A–Z and 0–9)	Letters converted to uppercase
x	Any alphanumeric character (A–Z and 0–9)	Letters converted to lowercase
Y	Any alphanumeric character (A–Z and 0–9)	Letters preserve original case
y	Any alphanumeric character (A–Z and 0–9)	Letters preserve original case
?	Any character	

Although there are ten special pattern characters, you need concern yourself with only eight of them, because uppercase and lowercase B are identical. So are uppercase and lowercase Y.

When using a custom pattern, you must select the Enforce pattern *checkbox at the bottom right of the Property inspector (see Figure 9-13 earlier in the chapter).*

9

Any other character included in a custom pattern is treated as an auto-complete character. For example, let's say you have a stock code that looks like this: BC-901/c. If all stock codes follow the same pattern of two uppercase letters followed by a hyphen, three digits, a forward slash, and a lowercase letter, you could use the following custom pattern:

AA-000/a

Immediately after the first two letters are inserted, Spry automatically inserts the hyphen. Then after the next thee digits, it inserts the forward slash ready for the user to insert the final letter.

If you want to use any of the special characters listed in Table 9-2, you must precede them with a backslash (for example, \A). To insert a backslash as part of an auto-complete sequence, use a double backslash (\\).

Validating a text area with Spry

Unlike a text field, the `<textarea>` tag doesn't have any way in HTML to control the acceptable number of characters, so the text area validation widget optionally displays a counter that tells the user how many have been entered or can still be entered. This is important when inserting text in a database, because the text is truncated if the user inputs more than the maximum accepted by the database column. With Spry, this is no longer a problem, because you can block further input once the maximum has been reached.

To validate a text area, either select an existing text area or position your cursor in a form where you want to insert a new text area, and click the Spry Validation Text Area button in the Forms or Spry tab in the Insert bar or select Insert ➤ Spry ➤ Spry Validation Text Area. If you are inserting a new text area, fill in the ID and Label fields in the Input Tag Accessibility Attributes dialog box as described earlier in the chapter. Figure 9-14 shows the options available in the Property inspector for a text area validation widget.

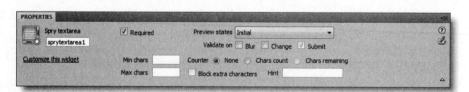

Figure 9-14. The text area validation widget has options to control and monitor the number of characters entered.

The layout of options in the Property inspector is slightly different, but Required, Preview states, Validate on, Min chars, Max chars, and Hint all work exactly the same as for a text field, so I won't explain them again (refer to "Validating a text field with Spry" if you need to refresh your memory).

Let's take a look at the two new options:

- Counter: There are three settings to choose from, as follows:

  - None: This is the default. It turns off automatic counting of characters entered.

  - Chars count: This displays the total number of characters entered. If you combine this with Validate on Change, it displays a constantly updated total (see Figure 9-15).

  - Chars remaining: This is grayed out until you enter a value in Max chars. It uses this value to calculate how many more characters can be accepted. If combined with Validate on Change, it displays a running total of characters left (see Figure 9-15).

- Block extra characters: This is self-explanatory. It prevents the user from entering more characters than the number specified in Max chars. The checkbox remains grayed out if Max chars is not specified.

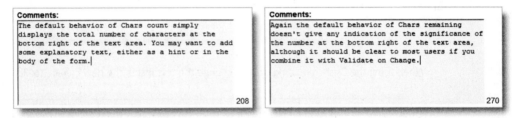

Figure 9-15. The character counter appears at the bottom right of the text area but gives no indication of its meaning.

Improving the character counter

As Figure 9-15 shows, the Spry character counter simply displays a number at the bottom right of the text area. Although most users will probably guess its meaning, it's more user-friendly to add a label to the counter. The following instructions show you how to do this. I have used feedback_spry.php from the previous exercise, but you can use any form with a text area.

1. In Design view, select the Comments text area, and apply a validation widget by clicking the Spry Validation Text Area button on the Insert bar (or use the Insert menu). Save the page to copy the external JavaScript file and style sheet to your site.

2. In the Property inspector, select Validate on Change, and set Counter to Chars count.

3. Open Split view to inspect the code inserted by Dreamweaver. It should look like this:

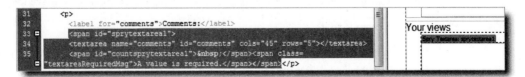

415

The first `<span>` shown on line 35 in the preceding screenshot contains a non-breaking space (` `). Spry uses this to display the character count. Because the content of the `<span>` is generated dynamically, the label needs to go outside.

4. Click in Code view, position your cursor immediately to the left of the first `<span>` shown on line 35, and insert the following code shown in bold:

`<span> Count: </span>``<span id="countsprytextarea1"> </span>`

5. Save the page and test it. You should now see a more user-friendly display like this:

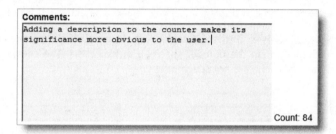

When using the Chars remaining option, change the text inside the new `<span>` to Remaining:.

> *By default, Dreamweaver puts all alerts in `<span>` tags and styles them to display inline alongside the form element. This can result in the alert splitting across two lines, which makes the default border look very messy. Either shorten the text or change the style rules so that they blend in with your design. In fact, there is nothing to stop you from moving the alerts to a different position. As long as you keep the classes and IDs assigned by Dreamweaver, you can change the `<span>` tags to other HTML elements, as demonstrated in the next exercise.*

Validating checkboxes with Spry

A common requirement on forms is a checkbox to confirm that the user agrees with certain terms and conditions. Creating this with Dreamweaver couldn't be simpler. If you already have the checkbox in your form, select it, and click the Spry Validate Checkbox button on the Insert bar. Save the page to copy the external JavaScript file and style sheet to your Spry assets folder.

If you don't have a checkbox, position your cursor where you want it to go inside the form, and click the Spry Validate Checkbox button in the Forms or Spry tab of the Insert bar. Fill in the ID and Label fields in the Input Tag Accessibility Attributes dialog box, and save the page.

That's all there is to it.

Validating a checkbox group is also easy, but the default use of `<span>` tags makes it difficult to create a layout that uses valid code and looks halfway decent. However, this is also a good opportunity to show you that you don't need to be constrained by Dreamweaver's way of doing things. The best way to explain is with a practical example based on the form you have been using throughout the chapter.

The form has a group of five checkboxes displayed in two columns, each of which is formed by a paragraph floated left. The Dreamweaver documentation tells you to add multiple checkboxes in the <span> created by the validation widget, but <span> tags cannot contain block-level elements like <div>, <table>, or <p>. So the best way to validate a checkbox group is to apply the widget first to a single checkbox. You can then convert the Dreamweaver code to wrap the entire group in <div> tags.

Applying a checkbox validation widget to a checkbox group

Continue using the page from the preceding exercises, or copy feedback_spry_start.php from examples/ch09 to workfiles/ch09 and save it as feedback_spry.php.

1. In Design view, select the checkbox labeled Classical concerts, and click the Spry Validation Checkbox button on the Insert bar (or use the Insert menu). Save the page to copy the external style sheet and JavaScript file to your site.

2. In the Property inspector, select the Enforce range (multiple) radio button, and type 2 in the Min # of selections field. Press Enter/Return or Tab to make sure Dreamweaver updates the validation code.

3. Open Split view to inspect the code inserted by Dreamweaver. It should look like Figure 9-16.

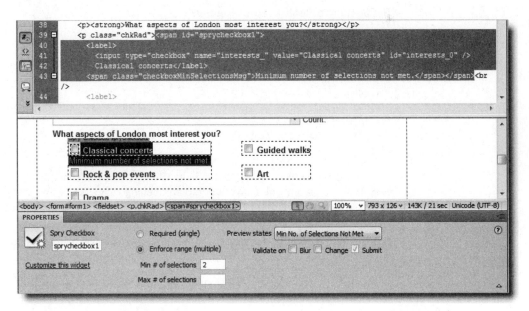

Figure 9-16. Apply a validation widget to a single checkbox, and edit the code to validate a group.

As you can see on line 39 in Figure 9-16, Dreamweaver creates an opening `<span>` tag with the ID sprycheckbox1 to wrap the checkbox (the closing `</span>` tag is at the end of line 43). Another `<span>` at the beginning of line 43 is assigned the class checkboxMinSelectionsMsg and contains the alert message.

With Preview states set to Min No. of Selections Not Met, you can see that the alert is displayed between the checkbox and its label. It looks a mess, but not for long . . .

4. What you need to do is to convert the sprycheckbox1 `<span>` into a `<div>` and wrap it around the entire checkbox group.

   Switch to Code view, select the following tag shown on line 39 of Figure 9-16, and cut it to your clipboard:

   ```
   <span id="sprycheckbox1">
   ```

5. Create a new line immediately above, paste the code back into the new line, and change span to div. The resulting code should look like this (the lines above and below are included for context):

   ```
   <p><strong>What aspects of London most interest you?</strong></p>
   <div id="sprycheckbox1">
   <p class="chkRad">
   ```

6. Cut the following `<span>` (it's shown on line 43 of Figure 9-16), and paste immediately below the line you moved in the previous step:

   ```
   <span class="checkboxMinSelectionsMsg">Minimum number of selections ➥
   not met.</span>
   ```

   The resulting code should look like this:

   ```
   <div id="sprycheckbox1">
   <p class="chkRad">
   <span class="checkboxMinSelectionsMsg">Minimum number of selections ➥
   not met.</span>
     <label>
     <input type="checkbox" name="interests_" value="Classical concerts" ➥
   id="interests_0" />
     Classical concerts</label>
   </span><br />
   ```

7. The closing `</span>` tag highlighted in bold after the Classical concerts label is left over from the `<span>` you converted into an opening `<div>` tag in step 5. It needs to be converted to a closing `</div>` tag and moved right to the end of the checkbox group.

   This is where a good understanding of HTML and your page structure comes in. Although it's just a case of moving a closing tag, you must get it in the correct position after the closing tag of the second chkRad class paragraph (it should now be on line 62). The following code shows the new tag in bold in its surrounding context:

```
    <label>
      <input type="checkbox" name="interests_4" id="interests_4" />
    Art</label>
  </p>
  </div>
  <p class="clearIt"><strong>Would you like to receive regular details ➥
  of events in London?</strong></p>
```

8. Switch back to Design view, and click the turquoise tab at the top left of the checkbox validation widget. The checkbox group should now look like this:

You can tell whether you have inserted the closing `</div>` tag in the right place by looking at the Spry widget's thin turquoise border. It should wrap all the checkboxes but not extend into the following line of text.

You can still display and hide the alert message using the Preview states menu in the Property inspector. The heavy blue outline around the validation widget doesn't enclose the checkboxes because they're floated. If you put the checkbox group in a nonfloated element, such as a table, the outline would enclose the whole group.

9. Select Validate on Change in the Property inspector, save the page, and test it in a browser. Select one checkbox, and the alert message should appear above the checkbox group. Select a second checkbox, and the alert disappears.

You might want to make some changes to the CSS, but this shows you how you can adapt the basic code created by Dreamweaver. This is something you will appreciate even more during the second half of this book when working with PHP. Dreamweaver provides a solid basis, but the rest is up to you.

This exercise just lifts the lid on the possibilities. I'll leave you to experiment with other variations.

Validating a radio button group with Spry

The Spry radio button group validation widget is unusual in that you cannot apply it to an existing radio button group. If anything is selected on the page, even a radio button, Dreamweaver opens the Spry Validation Radio Group dialog box and inserts a new radio button group after the selected element. If nothing is selected on the page, the new radio button group is inserted at the current insertion point.

To insert a radio button group validation widget, click the Spry Validation Radio Group button on the Forms or Spry tab of the Insert bar (or use the Insert menu). The options in the

Spry Validation Radio Group dialog box are identical to the Checkbox Group dialog box (see Figure 9-10), so refer to the description earlier in the chapter if you need help.

Figure 9-17 shows the Property inspector for a Spry radio button group validation widget. It has very few options. Most are the same as for other validation widgets, but the following two require explanation:

- Empty Value: This is used when you want to force the user to select a radio button other than the default. For example, rather than two buttons with the values yes and no, you might have a default button with the value unspecified. If you enter unspecified in this field, validation will fail until one of the other values is chosen.

- Invalid Value: This is for a button that contains an unacceptable answer. For example, if users must agree to terms and conditions before submitting a form, you could have two radio buttons with the values accept and decline. If you enter decline in this field, validation will fail, and a message will be displayed when the user selects the decline button.

Figure 9-17. The Spry radio button group validation widget has only a small number of options.

You edit and style the validation messages in the same way as other validation widgets. To edit individual radio buttons after creating the validation widget, select the radio button element in Design view to display the normal radio button Property inspector.

Validating a drop-down menu with Spry

The Spry validation widget for <select> elements does not have an option to enforce multiple choices. It has options only to reject a blank or invalid value. Consequently, it's more suited to single-choice drop-down menus than multiple-choice lists.

To apply the validation widget to an existing <select> element, highlight the menu object in Design view, and click the Spry Validation Select button in the Forms or Spry tab of the Insert bar (or use the Insert menu). Figure 9-18 shows the available options in the Property inspector.

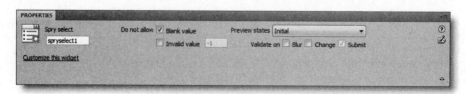

Figure 9-18. The select validation widget checks only whether a single value is blank or invalid.

Apart from those common to all validation widgets, there are just two options, namely:

- Blank value: This option is selected by default. Validation fails if the user selects a menu item that doesn't have a value. Spry considers a blank value to be an <option> tag either without a value attribute or with value="".

  The value attribute is not required in the <option> tag. When it's omitted, forms use the contents of the <option> tag as the submitted value. If you build a menu that doesn't set the value attribute for each item, you *must* deselect the Blank value checkbox. Otherwise, the menu will fail validation, even when an option is selected.

- Invalid value: If you select this option, enter the value you want to be treated as invalid in the field alongside. For example, in the form built in the exercises earlier in the chapter, the value for -- Select one -- was set to 0. To prevent this from being accepted, select Invalid value, and enter 0 in the field alongside.

Validating passwords with Spry

There are two validation widgets for passwords, both of which are new to Dreamweaver CS4. Since they work in combination with each other, I'll deal with them together. The first widget lets you specify criteria against which the password should be validated, while the second simply checks whether the password entered in a confirmation field matches the original password.

You can apply the password validation widget to an existing password field or use it to insert a new field. To apply it to an existing password field, select the field in Design view, and click the Spry Validation Password button on the Forms or Spry tab of the Insert bar (or use the Insert menu).

If the selected element is not a password field, Dreamweaver opens the Input Tag Accessibility Attributes dialog box for you to enter the ID and label for the password field. Even if you click OK or Cancel without filling in any of the fields, Dreamweaver inserts a new password field immediately after the currently selected element and assigns it default values.

Figure 9-19 shows the options in the Property inspector for a password validation widget. There are a lot of them, but their meaning is self-explanatory. They let you specify the strength of the password by setting a minimum and maximum number of characters, as well as upper and lower limits for letters, numbers, uppercase, and special characters. Letters are defined as unaccented letters of the Roman alphabet (A–Z, both uppercase and lowercase). Special characters are anything other than a number or unaccented letter.

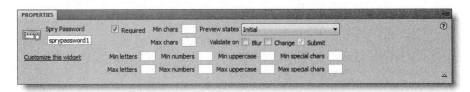

Figure 9-19. The password validation widget lets you specify the strength of the password.

You can apply the password confirmation validation widget to an existing text input or password field, or you can use it to insert a new field. However, there must already be at least one other text input or password field in the form. Otherwise, the widget will generate errors.

The password confirmation field should normally be positioned below the original password field. Dreamweaver scans the page upward to locate the first password field and uses its ID to associate the two fields with each other. As you can see in Figure 9-20, there's an option to change the field against which the password is validated.

Figure 9-20. The password confirmation widget has very few options.

Chapter review

This has been a long chapter, crammed with detail, but it's an important one. You'll use forms time and again when building dynamic sites, and making sure that user input is in the right format saves endless headaches later. Spry does a lot to help with validation and is fairly easy to use, but the Dreamweaver interface could still do with some improvement. However, it's important to remember that client-side validation is only half the story. Because JavaScript can be turned off in the browser, you also need to check user input on the server side with PHP.

Moreover, forms are useless without a script capable of processing the data. The next chapter serves as a crash course in PHP basics for readers new to PHP. Then in Chapter 11, we get down to the nitty-gritty of server-side programming, using PHP to validate user input and then send it to your mail inbox.

This chapter is a cross between a crash course in PHP and a handy reference. It's aimed at readers who are completely new to PHP or who may have dabbled without really getting to grips with the language. The intention is not to teach you all there is to know but to arm you with sufficient knowledge to dig into Code view to customize Dreamweaver code with confidence. Dreamweaver's automatic code generation does a lot of the hard work for you, but you need to tweak the code to get the best out of it, and when it comes to sending an email from an online form, you have to do everything yourself.

In this chapter, you'll learn about the following:

- Writing and understanding PHP scripts
- Using variables to represent changing values
- Understanding the difference between single and double quotes
- Organizing related information with arrays
- Creating pages that make decisions for themselves
- Using loops and functions for repetitive work

If you're already comfortable with PHP, just glance at the section headings to see what's covered, because you might find it useful to refer to this chapter if you need to refresh your memory about a particular subject. Then move straight to the next chapter and start coding.

If you're new to PHP, don't try to learn everything at one sitting, or your brain is likely to explode from information overload. On the first reading, look at the headings and maybe the first paragraph or two under each one to get a general overview. Also read the section "Understanding PHP error messages."

Understanding what PHP is for

Back in the early 1990s, web pages consisted of nothing but text. Things didn't stand still for long, and it soon became possible to add images and scrolling text. But even if some things moved around the page in an irritating way, everything on the Web was **static** in the sense that the content was fixed at the time the developer created the page. Genuinely dynamic features began to be added around 1995 with the help of two distinct types of technology: client-side and server-side. The primary distinction between the two is concerned not with *how* dynamic features are generated but with *where*.

At its most basic level, the Internet involves a simple request and response between the user's computer (the **client**) and the remote website (the **server**), as illustrated in Figure 10-1. JavaScript is the most common example of a **client-side** technology. The scripts that control the Spry widgets you used in previous chapters are downloaded with the web page and loaded into the client's memory. When a user clicks a collapsible panel or tabbed interface, all the action takes place in the browser on the client computer.

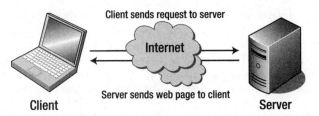

Figure 10-1. The basic relationship on the Internet is between client and server.

With **server-side** technology, on the other hand, all the action takes place on the web server before it's sent to the client. PHP is the most widely used server-side language for web development. In spite of its power, it's relatively easy to learn, and it has the advantage of being cross-platform. In other words, with only a handful of minor differences, it works the same on Windows, Mac OS X, and Linux.

> *Server-side technology encompasses a much broader range, but I'm concerned here with the way it integrates with the Web.*

Increasing user interactivity with server-side technology

With a static web page, everything is fixed at the time of design. All text, links, images, and client-side scripts are hard-coded into the underlying markup. Dynamic web pages built with a server-side language like PHP work in a very different way. Instead of all content being embedded in the underlying code, much of it is automatically generated by the server-side language or drawn from a database. Figure 10-2 illustrates this extra stage in the process.

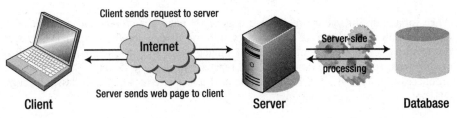

Figure 10-2. Server-side technology involves processing on the server before the web page is sent back to the client.

Generating content dynamically on the server makes it possible to offer the user a much richer variety of content. Perhaps the best known example is http://www.amazon.com. The Amazon catalog contains many thousands of items, something that would be impossible if it were necessary to create and store a separate web page for every item. International news providers, such as the BBC (http://www.bbc.com/news) or CNN (http://www.cnn.com), are able to update their pages constantly in response to breaking news because most of the content is stored in a database. The web server uses server-side technology to extract the relevant information and build web pages on the fly. Although this involves extra processing, it's normally very quick, and the whole sequence appears seamless to the user.

By the end of this book, you will be able to create web pages that do the same: querying or searching a database, extracting the information, and displaying it as part of your website. You'll also be able to insert new material in the database and update or delete existing material. Admittedly, the projects in the remaining chapters won't be as grandiose as Amazon or a major news site, but they work on the same principles. It will involve getting your hands dirty from time to time with code, but Dreamweaver will do most of the hard work for you.

Writing PHP scripts

The web server processes your PHP code and sends only the results—usually as HTML—to the browser. Because all the action is on the server, you need to tell it that your pages contain PHP code. This involves two simple steps, namely:

- Give every page a PHP filename extension. Do not use anything other than .php unless you are told to specifically by your hosting company.
- Enclose all PHP code within PHP tags.

The opening tag is <?php, and the closing tag is ?>. You may come across <? as a short version of the opening tag. However, <? doesn't work on all servers. Stick with <?php, which is guaranteed to work.

Embedding PHP in a web page

When somebody visits your site and requests a PHP page, the server sends it to the PHP engine, which reads the page from top to bottom looking for PHP tags. HTML passes through untouched, but whenever the PHP engine encounters a <?php tag, it starts processing your code and continues until it reaches the closing ?> tag. If the PHP code produces any output, it's inserted at that point. Then, any remaining HTML passes through until another <?php tag is encountered.

> *You can have as many PHP code blocks as you like on a page, but they cannot be nested inside each other.*

PHP doesn't always produce direct output for the browser. It may, for instance, check the contents of form input before sending an email message or inserting information into a database. So, some code blocks are placed above or below the main HTML code. You can also store code in external files. Code that produces direct output, however, always goes where you want the output to be displayed.

A typical PHP page uses some or all of the following elements:

- **Variables** to act as placeholders for unknown or changing values
- **Arrays** to hold multiple values
- **Conditional statements** to make decisions
- **Loops** to perform repetitive tasks
- **Functions** to perform preset tasks

Ending commands with a semicolon

PHP is written as a series of commands or statements. Each **statement** normally tells the PHP engine to perform a particular action, and it must always be followed by a semicolon, like this:

```
<?php
do this;
now do something else;
finally, do that;
?>
```

PHP is not like JavaScript or ActionScript. It won't automatically assume there should be a semicolon at the end of a line if you leave it out. This has a nice side effect: you can spread long statements over several lines and lay out your code for ease of reading. PHP, like HTML, ignores whitespace in code. Instead, it relies on semicolons to indicate where one command ends and the next one begins.

> *To save space, I won't always surround code samples with PHP tags.*

10

Using variables to represent changing values

A **variable** is simply a name you give to something that may change or that you don't know in advance. The *name* that you give to a variable remains constant, but the *value* stored in the variable can be changed at any time.

Although this concept sounds abstract, you use variables all the time in everyday life. When you meet somebody for the first time, one of the first things you ask is, "What's your name?" It doesn't matter whether the person you've just met is Tom, Dick, or Harry, *name* remains constant, but the value you store in it varies for different people. Similarly, with your bank account, money goes in and out all of the time (mostly out, it seems), but it doesn't matter whether you're scraping the bottom of the barrel or as rich as Croesus, the amount of money in your account is always referred to as the *balance*. In computer terms, *name* and *balance* are variables.

Naming variables

You can choose just about anything you like as the name for a variable, as long as you keep the following rules in mind:

- Variables always begin with $ (a dollar sign).
- The first character after the dollar sign cannot be a number.
- No spaces or punctuation are allowed, except for the underscore (_).
- Variable names are case-sensitive: $name and $Name are not the same.

A variable's name should give some indication of what it represents: $name, $email, and $totalPrice are good examples. Because you can't use spaces in variable names, it's a good idea to capitalize the first letter of the second or subsequent words when combining them (sometimes called **camel case**). Alternatively, you can use an underscore (for example, $total_price).

Don't try to save time by using really short variables. Using $n, $e, and $tp instead of descriptive ones makes code harder to understand. More important, it makes errors more difficult to spot.

> Although you have considerable freedom in the choice of variable names, you can't use $this, because it has a special meaning in PHP object-oriented programming. It's also advisable to avoid using any of the keywords listed at http://docs.php.net/manual/en/reserved.php.

Assigning values to variables

Variables get their values from a variety of sources, including the following:

- User input through online forms
- A database
- An external source, such as a news feed or XML file
- The result of a calculation
- Direct inclusion in the PHP code

Wherever the value comes from, it's always assigned in the same way with an equal sign (=), like this:

```
$variable = value;
```

Because it assigns a value, the equal sign is called the **assignment operator**. Although it's an equal sign, get into the habit of thinking of it as meaning "is set to" rather than "equals." This is because, in common with many other programming languages, PHP uses two equal signs (==) to mean "equals" when comparing items—something that catches out a lot of beginners (experienced PHP programmers are not immune to the occasional lapse, either).

Use the following rules when assigning a value to a variable:

- Text must be enclosed in single or double quotes (the distinction between the different types of quotes is explained later in the chapter).
- Numbers should not be in quotes—enclosing a number in quotes turns it into a string.

You can also use a variable to assign a value to another variable, for example:

```
$name = 'David Powers';
$author = $name;  // both $author and $name are now 'David Powers'
```

If the value of $name changes subsequently, it doesn't affect the value of $author. As this example shows, you don't use quotes around a variable when assigning its value to another. However, as long as you use double quotes, you can embed a variable in text like this:

```
$blurb = "$author has written several best-selling books on PHP.";
```

The value of $blurb is now "David Powers has written several best-selling books on PHP." There's a more detailed description on the use of variables with double quotes in "Choosing single or double quotation marks" later in the chapter.

> In common with other computer languages, PHP refers to a block of text as a **string**. This comes from the fact that text is a string of characters. From now on, I'll use the correct terminology.

Displaying PHP output

The most common ways of displaying dynamic output in the browser are to use echo or print. The differences between the two are so subtle you can regard them as identical. I prefer echo, because it's one fewer letter to type. It's also the style used by Dreamweaver.

Put echo (or print) in front of a variable, number, or string like this to output it to the browser:

```
$name = 'David';
echo $name;       // displays David
echo 5;           // displays 5
echo 'David';     // displays David
```

You may see scripts that use parentheses with echo and print, like this:

```
echo('David'); // displays David
print('David'); // displays David
```

The parentheses make no difference. Unless you enjoy typing purely for the sake of it, leave them out.

10

> *The important thing to remember about* echo *and* print *is that they work only with variables that contain a single value. You cannot use them to display more complex structures that are capable of storing multiple values.*

Commenting scripts for clarity and debugging

Even if you're an expert programmer, code is not always as immediately understandable as something written in your own human language. That's where comments can be a life-saver. You may understand what the code does five minutes after creating it, but when you come back to maintain it in six months' time—or if you have to maintain someone else's code—you'll be grateful for well-commented code.

In PHP, there are three ways to add comments. The first will be familiar to you if you write JavaScript. Anything on a line following a double slash is regarded as a comment and will not be processed:

```
// Display the name
echo $name;
```

You can also use the hash sign (#) in place of the double slash:

```
# Display the name
echo $name;
```

Either type of comment can go to the side of the code, as long as it doesn't go onto the next line:

```
echo $name;    // This is a comment
echo $name;    #  This is another comment
```

The third style allows you to stretch comments over several lines by sandwiching them between /* and */ (just like CSS comments):

```
/* You might want to use this sort of comment to explain
the whole purpose of a script. Alternatively, it's a
convenient way to disable part of a script temporarily.
*/
```

As the previous example explains, comments serve a dual purpose: they not only allow you to sprinkle your scripts with helpful reminders of what each section of code is for; they can also be used to disable a part of a script temporarily. This is extremely useful when you are trying to trace the cause of an error.

Choosing single or double quotation marks

As I mentioned earlier, strings must always be enclosed in single or double quotes. If all you're concerned about is what ends up on the screen, most of the time it doesn't matter which quotes you use, but behind the scenes, PHP uses single and double quotes in very different ways:

- Anything between single quotation marks is treated as plain text.
- Anything between double quotation marks is processed.

Quotation marks need to be in matching pairs. If a string begins with a single quote, PHP looks for the next single quote and regards that as the end of the string. Since an apostrophe uses the same character as a single quote, this presents a problem. A similar problem arises when a string in double quotes contains double quotes. The best way to explain this is with a practical example.

Experimenting with quotes

This simple exercise demonstrates the difference between single and double quotes and what happens when a conflict arises with an apostrophe or double quotes inside a string.

1. Create a new PHP page called quotes.php in workfiles/ch10. If you just want to look at the finished code, use quotes.php in examples/ch10.

2. Switch to Code view, and type the following code between the `<body>` tags:

```php
<?php
$name = 'David Powers';
echo 'Single quotes: The author is $name<br />';
echo "Double quotes: The author is $name";
?>
```

3. Save the page, and load it into a browser. As you can see from the following screenshot, $name is treated as plain text in the first line but is processed and replaced with its value in the second line, which uses double quotes.

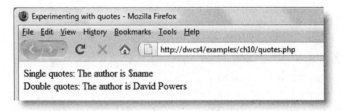

> To display the output on separate lines, you have to include HTML tags, such as `<br />`, because echo outputs only the values passed to it—nothing more.

4. Slightly change the text in lines 3 and 4 of the code, as follows:

```php
echo 'Single quotes: The author's name is $name<br />';
echo "Double quotes: The author's name is $name";
```

10

As you type, the change in Dreamweaver syntax coloring should alert you to a problem, but save the page nevertheless, and view it in a browser (it's quotes2.php in examples/ch10). You should see something like this:

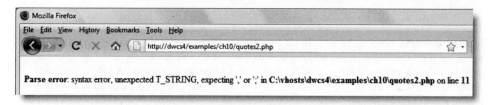

As far as PHP is concerned, an apostrophe and a single quote are the same thing, and quotes must always be in matching pairs. What's happened is that the apostrophe in author's has been regarded as the closing quote for the first line, what was intended as the closing quote of the first line becomes a second opening quote, and the apostrophe in the second line becomes the second closing quote. This is all quite different from what was intended—and if you're confused, is it any wonder that PHP is unable to work out what's meant to happen?

> The meaning of parse error and other error messages is explained in "Understanding PHP error messages" later in this chapter.

5. To solve the problem, insert a backslash in front of the apostrophe in the first sentence, like this (see quotes3.php in examples/ch10):

```php
echo 'Single quotes: The author\'s name is $name<br />';
```

You should now see the syntax coloring revert to normal. If you view the result in a browser, it should display correctly like this:

Using escape sequences in strings

Using a backslash like this is called an **escape sequence**. It tells PHP to treat a character in a special way. Double quotes within a double-quoted string? You guessed it—escape them with a backslash:

```php
echo "Swift's \"Gulliver's Travels\""; // displays the double quotes
```

The next line of code achieves exactly the same thing, but by using a different combination of quotes:

```
echo 'Swift\'s "Gulliver\'s Travels"';
```

> When creating strings, the outside pair of quotes must match—any quotes of the same style in the string must be escaped with a backslash. However, putting a backslash in front of the opposite style of quote will result in the backslash being displayed. To see the effect, put a backslash in front of the apostrophe in the doubled-quoted string in the previous exercise.

So, what happens when you want to include a literal backslash? You escape it with a backslash (\\).

The backslash (\\) and the single quote (\') are the only escape sequences that work in a single-quoted string. Because double quotes are a signal to PHP to process any variables contained within a string, there are many more escape sequences for double-quoted strings. Most of them are to avoid conflicts with characters that are used with variables, but three of them have special meanings: \n inserts a newline character, \r inserts a carriage return (needed mainly for Windows), and \t inserts a tab. Table 10-1 lists the main escape sequences supported by PHP.

Table 10-1. The main PHP escape sequences

Escape sequence	Character represented in double-quoted string
\"	Double quote
\n	Newline
\r	Carriage return
\t	Tab
\\	Backslash
\$	Dollar sign
\{	Opening curly brace
\}	Closing curly brace
\[	Opening square bracket
\]	Closing square bracket

10

> *The escape sequences listed in Table 10-1, with the exception of \\, work only in double-quoted strings. If you use them in a single-quoted string, they are treated as a literal backslash followed by the second character.*

Joining strings together

PHP has a rather unusual way of joining strings. Although many other computer languages use the plus sign (+), PHP uses a period, dot, or full stop (.), like this:

```
$firstName = 'David';
$lastName = 'Powers';
echo $firstName.$lastName; // displays DavidPowers
```

As the comment in the final line of code indicates, when two strings are joined like this, PHP leaves no gap between them. Don't be fooled into thinking that adding a space after the period will do the trick. It won't. You can put as much space on either side of the period as you like; the result will always be the same, because PHP ignores whitespace in code. You must either include a space in one of the strings or insert the space as a string in its own right, like this:

```
echo $firstName.' '.$lastName; // displays David Powers
```

> *The period—or **concatenation operator**, to give it its correct name—can be difficult to spot among a lot of other code. Make sure the font size in Code view is large enough to read without straining to see the difference between periods and commas. You can adjust the size in the* Fonts *category of the* Preferences *panel (*Edit *menu on Windows or* Dreamweaver *menu on a Mac).*

Adding to an existing string

Often you need to add more text at the end of an existing string. One way to do it is like this:

```
$author = 'David';
$author = $author.' Powers'; // $author is now 'David Powers'
```

Basically, this concatenates Powers (with a leading space) on the end of $author and then assigns everything back to the original variable.

Adding something to an existing variable is such a common operation that PHP offers a shorthand way of doing it—with the **combined concatenation operator**. Don't worry about the highfalutin name; it's just a period followed by an equal sign. It works like this:

```
$author = 'David';
$author .= ' Powers'; // $author is now 'David Powers'
```

There should be no space between the period and equal sign. You'll find this shorthand very useful when building the string to form the body of an email message in the next chapter.

How long can a string be? As far as PHP is concerned, there's no limit. In practice, you are likely to be constrained by other factors, such as server memory; but in theory, you could store the whole of War and Peace *in a string variable.*

Using quotes efficiently

Award yourself a bonus point if you spotted a better way of adding the space between $firstName and $lastName in the preceding example. Yes, that's right . . . Use double quotes, like this:

```
echo "$firstName $lastName"; // displays David Powers
```

Choosing the most efficient combination of quotation marks isn't easy when you first start working with PHP, but it can make your code a lot easier to use. The coding standard for the Zend Framework (http://framework.zend.com/manual/en/coding-standard.html) lays down the following rules:

- Use single quotes for literal strings (ones that contain no variables to be processed).

- When a literal string contains apostrophes, use double quotes around the whole string.

- Use double quotes when the string contains variables that need to be processed.

The Zend Framework is a set of advanced PHP scripts written by leading programmers, including members of the core PHP development team. By following its rules, you start out writing scripts the way an expert would. One of the main objectives is to make code efficient and readable, avoiding unnecessary escaping. I frequently see scripts written by inexperienced developers that contain lines like this:

```
echo "<img src=\"me.jpg\" width=\"300\" height=\"216\" alt=\"Me\" />";
```

Compare it with the following line, which wraps the whole literal string in single quotes:

```
echo '<img src="me.jpg" width="300" height="216" alt="Me" />';
```

It doesn't take a genius to work out which version is easier to read, not to mention type.

Special cases: true, false, and null

Although text should be enclosed in quotes, three special cases—true, false, and null—should never be enclosed in quotes unless you want to treat them as strings. The first two mean what you would expect; the last one, null, means "nothing" or "no value."

PHP makes decisions on the basis of whether something evaluates to true or false. Putting quotes around false has surprising consequences. The following code:

```
$OK = 'false';
```

does exactly the opposite of what you might expect: it makes $OK true! Why? Because the quotes around false turn it into a string, and PHP treats strings as true (see "The truth

10

according to PHP" later in this chapter). The other thing to note about true, false, and null is that they are *case-insensitive*. The following examples are all valid:

```
$OK = TRUE;
$OK = tRuE;
$OK = true;
```

Working with numbers

PHP can do a lot with numbers—from simple addition to complex math. Numbers can contain a decimal point or use scientific notation, but they must contain no other punctuation. Never use a comma as a thousands separator. The following examples show the right and wrong ways to assign a large number to a variable:

```
$million = 1000000;     // this is correct
$million = 1,000,000;   // this generates an error
$million = 1e6;         // this is correct
$million = 1e 6;        // this generates an error
```

When using scientific notation, the letter *e* can be uppercase or lowercase and optionally followed by a plus or minus sign. No spaces are permitted.

Negative numbers are preceded by a minus sign (use the hyphen on your keyboard or the minus key on a numeric keypad) with no space before the first digit, for example:

```
$loss = -50000;
```

Performing calculations

The standard arithmetic operators all work the way you would expect, although some of them look slightly different from those you learned at school. For instance, an asterisk (*) is used as the multiplication sign, and a forward slash (/) is used to indicate division.

Table 10-2 shows examples of how the standard arithmetic operators work. To demonstrate their effect, the following variables have been set:

```
$x = 20;
$y = 10;
$z = 3;
```

Table 10-2. Arithmetic operators in PHP

Operation	Operator	Example	Result
Addition	+	$x + $y	30
Subtraction	-	$x - $y	10

Operation	Operator	Example	Result
Multiplication	*	$x * $y	200
Division	/	$x / $y	2
Modulo division	%	$x % $z	2
Increment (add 1)	++	$x++	21
Decrement (subtract 1)	--	$y--	9

You may not be familiar with the modulo operator. This returns the remainder of a division, as follows:

```
26 % 5    // result is 1
26 % 27   // result is 26
10 % 2    // result is 0
```

A quirk with the modulo operator in PHP is that it converts both numbers to integers before performing the calculation. Consequently, if $z is 4.5 in Table 10-2, it gets rounded up to 5, making the result 0, not 2, as you might expect.

A practical use of the modulo operator is to work out whether a number is odd or even. $number % 2 will always produce 0 or 1.

The increment (++) and decrement (--) operators can come either before or after the variable. When they come before the variable, 1 is added to or subtracted from the value before any further calculation is carried out. When they come after the variable, the main calculation is carried out first, and then 1 is either added or subtracted. Since the dollar sign is an integral part of the variable name, the increment and decrement operators go before the dollar sign when used in front:

```
++$x
--$y
```

You can set your own values for $x, $y, and $z in calculation.php in examples/ch10 to test the arithmetic operators in action. The page also demonstrates the difference between putting the increment and decrement operators before and after the variable.

As noted earlier, numbers should not normally be enclosed in quotes, although PHP will usually convert to its numeric equivalent a string that contains only a number or that begins with a number.

Calculations in PHP follow the same rules as standard arithmetic. Table 10-3 summarizes the precedence of arithmetic operators.

10

Table 10-3. Precedence of arithmetic operators

Precedence	Group	Operators	Rule
Highest	Parentheses	()	Operations contained within parentheses are evaluated first. If these expressions are nested, the innermost is evaluated foremost.
Next	Multiplication and division	* / %	These operators are evaluated next. If an expression contains two or more operators, they are evaluated from left to right.
Lowest	Addition and subtraction	+ -	These are the final operators to be evaluated in an expression. If an expression contains two or more operators, they are evaluated from left to right.

If in doubt, use parentheses all the time to group the parts of a calculation that you want to make sure are performed as a single unit. For example:

```
4 * 5 - 2    // result is 18
4 * (5 - 2)  // result is 12
```

Combining calculations and assignment

You will often want to perform a calculation on a variable and assign the result back to the same variable. PHP offers the same convenient shorthand for arithmetic calculations as for strings. Table 10-4 shows the main combined assignment operators and their use.

Table 10-4. Combined arithmetic assignment operators used in PHP

Operator	Example	Equivalent to
+=	$a += $b	$a = $a + $b
-=	$a -= $b	$a = $a - $b
*=	$a *= $b	$a = $a * $b
/=	$a /= $b	$a = $a / $b
%=	$a %= $b	$a = $a % $b

Don't forget that the plus sign is used in PHP *only as an arithmetic operator*.

- **Addition**: Use += as the combined assignment operator.
- **Strings**: Use .= as the combined assignment operator.

Using arrays to store multiple values

Arrays are an important—and useful—part of PHP. You met one of PHP's built-in arrays, $_POST, in the previous chapter, and you'll work with it a lot more through the rest of this book. Arrays are also used extensively with a database, because you fetch the results of a search in a series of arrays.

An **array** is a special type of variable that stores multiple values rather like a shopping list. Although each item might be different, you can refer to them collectively by a single name. Figure 10-3 demonstrates this concept: the variable $shoppingList refers collectively to all five items—wine, fish, bread, grapes, and cheese.

Figure 10-3. Arrays are variables that store multiple items, just like a shopping list.

Individual items—or **array elements**—are identified by means of a number in square brackets immediately following the variable name. PHP assigns the number automatically, but it's important to note that the numbering always begins at 0. So, the first item in the array, wine, is referred to as $shoppingList[0], not $shoppingList[1]. And although there are five items, the last one (cheese) is $shoppingList[4]. The number is referred to as the array **key** or **index**, and this type of array is called an **indexed array**.

10

Instead of declaring each array element individually, you can declare the variable name once and assign all the elements by passing them as a comma-separated list to array(), like this:

```
$shoppingList = array('wine', 'fish', 'bread', 'grapes', 'cheese');
```

> The comma must go outside the quotes, unlike American typographic practice. For ease of reading, it's recommended to insert a space following each comma, but omitting the space is perfectly valid.

PHP numbers each array element automatically, so this creates the same array as in Figure 10-3. To add a new element to the end of the array, use a pair of empty square brackets like this:

```
$shoppingList[] = 'coffee';
```

PHP uses the next number available, so this becomes $shoppingList[5].

Using names to identify array elements

Numbers are fine, but it's often more convenient to give array elements meaningful names. For instance, an array containing details of this book might look like this:

```
$book['title'] = 'Essential Guide to Dreamweaver CS4';
$book['author'] = 'David Powers';
$book['publisher'] = 'friends of ED';
```

This type of array is called an **associative array**. Note that the array key is enclosed in quotes (single or double; it doesn't matter). It mustn't contain any spaces or punctuation, except for the underscore.

The shorthand way of creating an associative array uses the => operator (an equal sign followed by a greater-than sign) to assign a value to each array key. The basic structure looks like this:

```
$arrayName = array('key1' => 'element1', 'key2' => 'element2');
```

So, this is the shorthand way to build the $book array:

```
$book = array('title'     => 'Essential Guide to Dreamweaver CS4',
              'author'    => 'David Powers',
              'publisher' => 'friends of ED');
```

It's not essential to align the => operators like this, but it makes code easier to read and maintain.

> *Technically speaking, all arrays in PHP are associative. This means you can use both numbers and strings as array keys in the same array. Don't do it, though, because it can produce unexpected results. It's safer to treat indexed and associative arrays as different types.*

Inspecting the contents of an array with print_r()

As you saw in the previous chapter, you can inspect the contents of an array using print_r(). This is the code you inserted at the bottom of feedback.php:

```
<pre>
<?php if ($_POST) {print_r($_POST);} ?>
</pre>
```

It displays the contents of the array like this:

```
Array
(
    [name] => David
    [email] => david@example.com
    [comments] => Hi there!
    [send] => Send comments
)
```

The <pre> tags are simply to make the output more readable. What really matters here is that print_r() displays the contents of an array. As explained earlier, echo and print work only with variables that contain a single value. However, print_r() is no good in a live web page; it's used only to inspect the contents of an array for testing purposes. To display the contents of an array in normal circumstances, you need to use a loop. This gives you access to each array element one at a time. Once you get to an element that contains a single value, you can use echo or print to display its contents. Loops are covered a little later.

Making decisions

Decisions, decisions, decisions . . . Life is full of decisions. So is PHP. They give it the ability to display different output according to circumstances. Decision making in PHP uses **conditional statements**. The most common of these uses if and closely follows the structure of normal language. In real life, you may be faced with the following decision (admittedly not very often if you live in Britain):

    If the weather's hot, I'll go to the beach.

In PHP pseudo-code, the same decision looks like this:

```
if (the weather's hot) {
  I'll go to the beach;
}
```

10

The condition being tested goes inside parentheses, and the resulting action goes between curly braces. This is the basic decision-making pattern:

```
if (condition is true) {
    // code to be executed if condition is true
}
```

> Confusion alert: I mentioned earlier that statements must always be followed by a semi-colon. This applies only to the statements (or commands) inside the curly braces. Although called a conditional statement, this decision-making pattern is one of PHP's control structures, and it shouldn't be followed by a semicolon. Think of the semicolon as a command that means "do it." The curly braces surround the command statements and keep them together as a group.

The code inside the curly braces is executed *only* if the condition is true. If it's false, PHP ignores everything between the braces and moves on to the next section of code. How PHP determines whether a condition is true or false is described in the following section.

Sometimes, the if statement is all you need, but you often want a default action to be invoked. To do this, use else, like this:

```
if (condition is true) {
    // code to be executed if condition is true
} else {
    // default code to run if condition is false
}
```

What if you want more alternatives? One way is to add more if statements. PHP will test them, and as long as you finish with else, at least one block of code will run. However, it's important to realize that *all* if statements will be tested, and the code will be run in every single one where the condition equates to true. If you want only one code block to be executed, use elseif like this:

```
if (condition is true) {
    // code to be executed if first condition is true
} elseif (second condition is true) {
    // code to be executed if first condition fails
    // but second condition is true
} else {
    // default code to run if both conditions are false
}
```

You can use as many elseif clauses in a conditional statement as you like. It's important to note that *only the first one* that equates to true will be executed; all others will be ignored, even if they're also true. This means you need to build conditional statements in the order of priority that you want them to be evaluated. It's strictly a first-come, first-served hierarchy.

> *Although* elseif *is normally written as one word, you can use* else if *as separate words.*

The truth according to PHP

Decision making in PHP conditional statements is based on the mutually exclusive **Boolean values**, true and false (the name comes from a 19th-century mathematician, George Boole, who devised a system of logical operations that subsequently became the basis of much modern-day computing). If the condition equates to true, the code within the conditional block is executed. If false, it's ignored. Whether a condition is true or false is determined in one of the following ways:

- A variable set explicitly to true or false
- A value PHP interprets implicitly as true or false
- The comparison of two values

Explicit true or false values

This is straightforward. If a variable is assigned the value true or false and then used in a conditional statement, the decision is based on that value. As explained earlier, true and false are case-insensitive and must *not* be enclosed in quotes.

Implicit true or false values

PHP regards the following as false:

- The case-insensitive keywords false and null
- Zero as an integer (0), a floating-point number (0.0), or a string ('0' or "0")
- An empty string (single or double quotes with no space between them)
- An empty array
- A SimpleXML object created from empty tags

All other values equate to true.

> *This definition explains why* "false" *(in quotes) is interpreted by PHP as* true. *The value* –1 *is also treated as* true *in PHP.*

How comparisons equate to true or false is described in the next section.

Using comparisons to make decisions

Conditional statements often depend on the comparison of two values. Is this bigger than that? Are they both the same? If the comparison is true, the conditional statement is executed. If not, it's ignored.

10

To test for equality, PHP uses two equal signs (==) like this:

```
if ($status == 'administrator') {
  // send to admin page
} else {
  // refuse entry to admin area
}
```

Don't use a single equal sign in the first line like this:

```
if ($status = 'administrator') {
```

Doing so will open the admin area of your website to everyone. Why? This automatically sets the value of $status *to administrator; it doesn't compare the two values. To compare values, you must use two equal signs. It's an easy mistake to make, but one with potentially disastrous consequences.*

Size comparisons are performed using the mathematical symbols for less than (<) and greater than (>). Let's say you're checking the size of a file before allowing it to be uploaded to your server. You could set a maximum size of 50KB like this:

```
if ($bytes > 51200) {
  // display error message and abandon upload
} else {
  // continue upload
}
```

If you're wondering why I used 51200 instead of 50000, it's because when measuring computer storage capacity, a kilobyte is traditionally calculated as 1,024 (2^{10}) bytes. International standards organizations insist this should be called a kibibyte (KiB) instead of a kilobyte, but this doesn't seem to have caught on in general usage (http:// en.wikipedia.org/wiki/Kilobyte).

Comparison operators

These compare two values (known as **operands** because they appear on either side of an operator). If both values pass the test, the result is true (or to use the technical expression, it **returns** true). Otherwise, it returns false. Table 10-5 lists the comparison operators used in PHP.

Table 10-5. PHP comparison operators used for decision-making

Symbol	Name	Use
==	Equality	Returns true if both operands have the same value; otherwise, returns false.
!=	Inequality	Returns true if both operands have different values; otherwise, returns false.

Symbol	Name	Use
<>	Inequality	This has the same meaning as !=. It's rarely used in PHP but has been included here for the sake of completeness.
===	Identical	Determines whether both operands are identical. To be considered identical, they must not only have the same value but also be of the same datatype (for example, both floating-point numbers).
!==	Not identical	Determines whether both operands are not identical (according to the same criteria as the previous operator).
>	Greater than	Determines whether the operand on the left is greater in value than the one on the right.
>=	Greater than or equal to	Determines whether the operand on the left is greater in value than or equal to the one on the right.
<	Less than	Determines whether the operand on the left is less in value than the one on the right.
<=	Less than or equal to	Determines whether the operand on the left is less in value than or equal to the one on the right.

Testing more than one condition

Frequently, comparing two values is not enough. PHP allows you to set a series of conditions using **logical operators** to specify whether all, or just some, need to be fulfilled.

All the logical operators in PHP are listed in Table 10-6. **Negation**—testing that the opposite of something is true—is also considered a logical operator, although it applies to individual conditions rather than a series.

Table 10-6. Logical operators used for decision-making in PHP

Symbol	Name	Use
&&	Logical AND	Evaluates to true if both operands are true. If the left-hand operand evaluates to false, the right-hand operand is never tested.
and	Logical AND	Exactly the same as &&, but it takes lower precedence.

Continued

10

Table 10-6. *Continued*

Symbol	Name	Use
||	Logical OR	Evaluates to true if either operand is true; otherwise, returns false. If the left-hand operand returns true, the right-hand operand is never tested.
or	Logical OR	Exactly the same as ||, but it takes lower precedence.
xor	Exclusive OR	Evaluates to true if only one of the two operands returns true. If both are true or both are false, it evaluates to false.
!	Negation	Tests whether something is not true.

Technically speaking, there is no limit to the number of conditions that can be tested. Each condition is considered in turn from left to right, and as soon as a defining point is reached, no further testing is carried out. When using && or and, every condition must be fulfilled, so testing stops as soon as one turns out to be false. Similarly, when using \|\| or or, only one condition needs to be fulfilled, so testing stops as soon as one turns out to be true.

```
$a = 10;
$b = 25;
if ($a > 5 && $b > 20) // returns true
if ($a > 5 || $b > 30) // returns true, $b never tested
```

The implication of this is that when you need all conditions to be met, you should design your tests with the condition most likely to return false as the first to be evaluated. When you need just one condition to be fulfilled, place the one most likely to return true first. If you want a particular set of conditions considered as a group, enclose them in parentheses.

```
if (($a > 5 && $a < 8) || ($b > 20 && $b < 40))
```

Operator precedence is a tricky subject. Stick with && and \|\|, rather than and and or, and use parentheses to group expressions to which you want to give priority. The xor operator is rarely used.

Using the switch statement for decision chains

The switch statement offers an alternative to if . . . else for decision making. The basic structure looks like this:

```
switch(variable being tested) {
  case value1:
    statements to be executed
    break;
  case value2:
```

```
    statements to be executed
    break;
  default:
    statements to be executed
}
```

The case keyword indicates possible matching values for the variable passed to switch().
When a match is made, every subsequent line of code is executed until the break keyword
is encountered, at which point the switch statement comes to an end.

You can group several instances of the case keyword together to apply the same block of
code to them. For example:

```
switch($httpStatus) {
  case 200:
    $message = 'File OK';
    break;
  case 301:
  case 302:
  case 303:
  case 307:
  case 410:
    $message = 'File moved or does not exist';
    break;
  case 404:
    $message = 'File not found';
    break;
  default:
    $message = 'Other error';
}
```

Dreamweaver uses a switch statement in the GetSQLValueString() function (see Figure 15-1
in Chapter 15), which it inserts into pages that insert or update records in a database.

The main points to note about switch are as follows:

- The expression following the case keyword must be a number or a string.
- You can't use comparison operators with case. So, case > 100: isn't allowed.
- Each block of statements should normally end with break, unless you specifically
  want to continue executing code within the switch statement.
- If no match is made, any statements following the default keyword will be
  executed. If no default has been set, the switch statement will exit silently and
  continue with the next block of code.

Using the conditional (ternary) operator

The **conditional operator** (?:) is a shorthand method of representing a simple conditional statement. Because it uses three operands, it's also called the **ternary operator**.
The basic syntax looks like this:

```
condition ? value if true : value if false;
```

10

What this means is that, if the condition to the left of the question mark is true, the value immediately to the right of the question mark is used. However, if the condition evaluates to false, the value to the right of the colon is used instead. Here is an example of it in use:

```
$age = 17;
$fareType = $age > 16 ? 'adult' : 'child';
```

The conditional operator can be quite confusing when you first encounter it, so let's break down this example section by section.

The first line sets the value of $age to 17.

The second line sets the value of $fareType using the conditional operator. The condition is between the equal sign and the question mark—in other words, $age > 16.

If $age is greater than 16, the condition evaluates to true, so $fareType is set to the value between the question mark and the colon—in other words, 'adult'. Otherwise, $fareType is set to the value to the right of the colon—or 'child'. The equivalent code using if . . . else looks like this:

```
if ($age > 16) {
    $fareType = 'adult';
} else {
    $fareType = 'child';
}
```

The if . . . else version is much easier to read, but the conditional operator is more compact, and it's used frequently by Dreamweaver. Most beginners hate this shorthand, but you need to understand how it works if you want to customize Dreamweaver code.

Using loops for repetitive tasks

Loops are huge time-savers, because they perform the same task over and over again yet involve very little code. They're frequently used with arrays and database results. You can step through each item one at a time looking for matches or performing a specific task. Loops frequently contain conditional statements, so although they're very simple in structure, they can be used to create code that processes data in often sophisticated ways.

Loops using while and do . . . while

The simplest type of loop is called a while loop. Its basic structure looks like this:

```
while (condition is true) {
    do something
}
```

The following code displays every number from 1 through 100 in a browser (you can see it in action in while.php in examples/ch10). It begins by setting a variable ($i) to 1 and then using the variable as a counter to control the loop, as well as display the current number onscreen.

```
$i = 1;  // set counter
while ($i <= 100) {
  echo "$i<br />";
  $i++; // increase counter by 1
}
```

A variation of the while loop uses the keyword do and follows this basic pattern:

```
do {
  code to be executed
} while (condition to be tested);
```

The only difference between a do . . . while loop and a while loop is that the code within the do block is executed at least once, even if the condition is never true. The following code (in dowhile.php in examples/ch10) displays the value of $i once, even though it's greater than the maximum expected.

```
$i = 1000;
do {
  echo "$i<br />";
  $i++; // increase counter by 1
} while ($i <= 100);
```

Dreamweaver uses a do . . . while loop in its Repeat Region server behavior to loop through the results of a database query (what Dreamweaver calls a **recordset**) and display them on your page.

The danger with creating while and do . . . while loops yourself is forgetting to set a condition that brings the loop to an end or setting an impossible condition. When this happens, you create an infinite loop that either freezes your computer or causes the browser to crash.

The versatile for loop

The for loop is less prone to generating an infinite loop, because you specify in the first line how you want the loop to work. The for loop uses the following basic pattern:

```
for (initialize counter; test; increase or decrease the counter) {
  code to be executed
}
```

The three expressions inside the parentheses control the action of the loop (note that they are separated by semicolons, not commas):

- The first expression initializes the counter variable at the start of the loop. You can use any variable you like, but the convention is to use $i. When more than one counter is needed, $j and $k are frequently used. This is the exception to the rule about using descriptive names for variables. The convention of using $i (or another single letter) as a counter is so deeply entrenched in programming and mathematic culture, it's unnecessary to use anything else.

- The second expression is a test that determines whether the loop should continue to run. This can be a fixed number, a variable, or an expression that calculates a value.

- The third expression shows the method of stepping through the loop. Most of the time, you will want to go through a loop one step at a time, so using the increment (++) or decrement (--) operator is convenient.

The following code does the same as the previous while loop, displaying every number from 1 to 100 (see forloop.php in examples/ch10):

```php
for ($i = 1; $i <= 100; $i++) {
  echo "$i<br />";
}
```

There is nothing stopping you from using bigger steps. For instance, replacing $i++ with $i+=10 in this example would display 1, 11, 21, 31, and so on.

Looping through arrays with foreach

The final type of loop in PHP is used exclusively with arrays. It takes two forms, both of which use temporary variables to handle each array element. If you need to do something only with the value of each array element, the foreach loop takes the following form:

```php
foreach (array_name as temporary_variable) {
  do something with temporary_variable
}
```

> The foreach *keyword is one word. Inserting a space between* for *and* each *doesn't work.*

The following example loops through the $shoppingList array and displays the name of each item (see shopping_list.php in examples/ch10):

```php
$shoppingList = array('wine', 'fish', 'bread', 'grapes', 'cheese');
foreach ($shoppingList as $item) {
  echo $item.'<br />';
}
```

The preceding example accesses only the value of each array element. An alternative form of the foreach loop gives access to both the key and the value of each element. It takes this slightly different form:

```php
foreach (array_name as key_variable => value_variable) {
  do something with key_variable and value_variable
}
```

This next example uses the $book array from "Using names to identify array elements" earlier in the chapter and incorporates the key and value of each element into a simple string, as shown in the screenshot (see book.php in examples/ch10):

```php
foreach ($book as $key => $value) {
  echo "The value of '$key' is '$value'<br />";
}
```

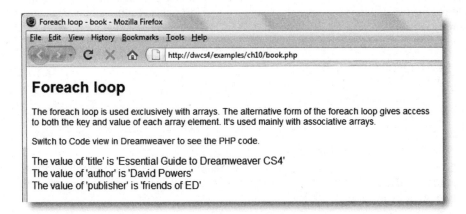

The use of $key and $value as the variables in a foreach loop has also become something of a convention. In this example, it makes sense because the loop is exposing the keys and values of array elements. However, it's a good idea to use descriptive variables where appropriate. For example, when looping through an array of book titles, it's much more meaningful to use something like this:

```php
foreach ($titles as $title) {
  echo $title . '<br />';
}
```

Descriptive variables make code much easier to read and understand.

Breaking out of a loop

To bring a loop prematurely to an end when a certain condition is met, insert the break keyword inside a conditional statement. As soon as the script encounters break, it exits the loop. For example, the following loop comes to an end as soon as a banned word is found in $input:

```php
foreach ($bannedWords as $word) {
  if (strpos($input, $word) !== false) {
    $reject = true;
    break;
  }
}
```

The strpos() function reports the position of a substring inside a longer string, counting from zero. If the presence of a single banned word is sufficient to reject $input, there's no point in looping through the whole array, so break terminates the loop as soon as the condition is met. (The reason for using !== false is to avoid a false negative; a matching word at the beginning of $input would return 0, which PHP treats as false.)

To skip an iteration of the loop when a certain condition is met, use the continue keyword. Instead of exiting, it returns to the top of the loop and executes the next iteration. In the next example, the loop goes through an array of prices, counting how many items are less than $20.

```
$total = 0;
foreach ($prices as $price) {
  if ($price > 20) {
    continue;
  }
  $total++;
}
```

The continue keyword forces the script to abandon the rest of the current iteration if $price is higher than 20, so $total isn't incremented. Of course, you could achieve the same result by using the following code:

```
$total = 0;
foreach ($prices as $price) {
  if ($price < 20) {
    $total++;
  }
}
```

But then it wouldn't demonstrate how continue works . . .

Using functions for preset tasks

Functions do things . . . lots of things, mind-bogglingly so in PHP. The last time I counted, PHP had nearly 3,000 built-in functions, and more have been added since. Don't worry: you'll only ever need to use a handful, but it's reassuring to know that PHP is a full-featured language capable of industrial-strength applications.

The functions you'll be using in this book do really useful things, such as send email, query a database, format dates, and much, much more. You can identify functions in PHP code, because they're always followed by a pair of parentheses. Sometimes the parentheses are empty. Often, though, the parentheses contain variables, numbers, or strings, like this:

```
$thisYear = date('Y');
```

This calculates the current year and stores it in the variable $thisYear. It works by feeding the string 'Y' to the built-in PHP function date(). Placing a value between the parentheses like this is known as **passing an argument** to a function. The function takes the value in the argument and processes it to produce (or **return**) the result. For instance, if you pass the string 'M' as an argument to date() instead of 'Y', it will return the current month as a three-letter abbreviation (for example, Mar, Apr, May). The date() function is covered in detail in Chapter 17.

Some functions take more than one argument. When this happens, separate the arguments with commas inside the parentheses, like this:

```
$mailSent = mail($to, $subject, $message);
```

It doesn't take a genius to work out that this sends an email to the address stored in the first argument, with the subject line stored in the second argument and the message stored in the third one. You'll see how this function works in the next chapter.

> You'll often come across the term *parameter* in place of argument. There is a technical difference between the two words, but for all practical purposes, they are interchangeable.

As if the 3,000-odd built-in functions weren't enough, PHP lets you build your own custom functions. Even if you don't relish the idea of creating your own, throughout this book you'll use some that I have made. You use them in exactly the same way.

Understanding PHP error messages

There's one final thing you need to know about before savoring the delights of PHP: error messages. They're an unfortunate fact of life, but it helps a great deal if you understand what they're trying to tell you. The following illustration shows the structure of a typical error message:

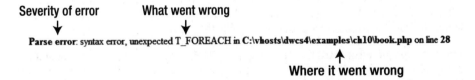

The first thing to realize about PHP error messages is that they report the line where PHP discovered a problem. Most newcomers—quite naturally—assume that's where they have to look for their mistake. Wrong . . .

What PHP is telling you most of the time is that something unexpected has happened. In other words, the mistake frequently lies *before* that point. The preceding error message means that PHP discovered a foreach command where there shouldn't have been one. (Error messages always prefix PHP elements with T_, which stands for token. Just ignore it.)

Instead of worrying what might be wrong with the foreach command (probably nothing), start working backward, looking for anything that might be missing. Usually, it's a semicolon or closing quote. In this example, the error was caused by omitting the semicolon at the end of line 27 in book.php. In other words, the error was on the previous line, not the line in the error message.

Sometimes you'll see an error message that tells you it found a problem on or after the last line on the page. That normally means you left out a closing curly brace earlier in the script. Use the Balance Braces tool, as described in the next chapter, to find the cause of the problem.

There are five main categories of error, presented here in descending order of importance:

- **Fatal error**: Any HTML output preceding the error will be displayed, but once the error is encountered—as the name suggests—everything else is killed stone dead. A fatal error is normally caused by referring to a nonexistent file or function.

- **Parse error**: This means there's a mistake in your code, such as mismatched quotes, or a missing semicolon or closing brace. Like a fatal error, it stops the script in its tracks and doesn't even allow any HTML output to be displayed.

- **Warning**: This alerts you to a serious problem, such as a missing include file. (Include files are covered in Chapter 12.) However, the error is not serious enough to prevent the rest of the script from being executed.

- **Deprecated**: This is a new type of error introduced in PHP 5.3 that warns you about code that won't work in future versions. Don't say you haven't been warned.

- **Notice**: This advises you about relatively minor issues, such as the use of a nondeclared variable. Although you can turn off the display of notices, you should always try to eliminate the cause, rather than sweep the issue under the carpet. Any error is a threat to your output.

Hosting companies have different policies about the level of error checking. If error checking is set to a high level and the display of errors is turned off, any mistakes in your code will result in a blank screen. Even if your hosting company has a more relaxed policy, you still don't want mistakes to be displayed for all to see. Test your code thoroughly, and eliminate all errors before deploying it on a live website.

Another type of error, **strict**, was introduced in PHP 5.0, mainly for the benefit of advanced developers. Strict error messages are not displayed by default, but this will change in PHP 6. The official definition of a strict message is that it suggests changes to "ensure the best interoperability and forward compatibility of your code." Quite how this differs from deprecated is unclear, although the implication appears to be that deprecated means a feature will definitely be removed, whereas strict means a change is under consideration.

Chapter review

After that crash course, I hope you're feeling not like a crash victim but invigorated and raring to go. Although you have been bombarded with a mass of information, you'll discover that it's easy to make rapid progress with PHP. In the next chapter, you'll use most of the techniques from this chapter to send user input from an online form to your email inbox. To begin with, you'll probably feel that you're copying code without much comprehension, but I'll explain all the important things along the way, and you should soon find things falling into place.

10

In Chapter 9, I showed you how to build a feedback form and validate the input on the client side with Spry validation widgets. In this chapter, we'll take the process to its next stage by validating the data on the server side with PHP. If the data is OK, we'll send the contents by email and display an acknowledgment message. If there's a problem with any of the data, we'll redisplay it in the form with messages prompting the user to correct any errors or omissions. Figure 11-1 shows the flow of events.

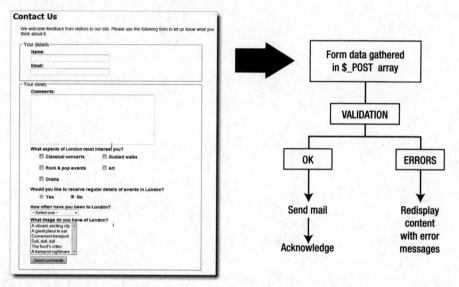

Figure 11-1. The flow of events in processing the feedback form

Sending an email from an online form is just the sort of task that Dreamweaver should automate, but unfortunately it doesn't. Commercial extensions are available to automate the process for you, but not everyone will have—or want to buy—a commercial extension in addition to Dreamweaver CS4, so I think it's important to show you how to hand-code this vital feature. At the same time, it gives you practical experience working with PHP code, which is essential unless you are willing to be limited to very basic tasks. The Dreamweaver server behaviors and data objects that you will use in later chapters take a lot of the hard work out of creating dynamic applications, but like the CSS layout that you used in Chapter 5, they lay a solid foundation for you to build on, rather than do absolutely everything for you.

In this chapter, you'll learn about the following:

- Gathering user input and sending it by email
- Using PHP conditional logic to check required fields
- Displaying errors without losing user input
- Saving frequently used code as a snippet

- Filtering out suspect material
- Avoiding email header injection attacks
- Processing multiple-choice form elements
- Blocking submission by spam bots

The flow of events shown in Figure 11-1 is controlled by a series of conditional statements (see "Making decisions" in the previous chapter). The PHP script will be in the same page as the form, so the first thing it needs to know is if the form has been submitted. If it has, the contents of the $_POST array will be checked. If it's OK, the email will be sent and an acknowledgment displayed, else a series of error messages will be displayed. In other words, everything is controlled by if . . . else statements.

Activating the form

As you saw in Chapter 9, data entered into the form can be retrieved by using print_r($_POST); to inspect the contents of the $_POST array. This is one of PHP's so-called superglobal arrays. They're such an important part of PHP that it's worth pausing for a moment to take a look at what they do.

Getting information from the server with PHP superglobals

Superglobal arrays are built-in associative arrays that are automatically populated with really useful information. They all begin with a dollar sign followed by an underscore. The most important superglobal arrays are as follows:

- **$_POST**: This contains values sent through the post method.
- **$_GET**: This contains values sent through the get method or a URL query string.
- **$_SERVER**: This contains information stored by the web server, such as file name, pathname, hostname, and so on.
- **$_SESSION**: This stores information that you want to preserve so that it's available to other pages. Sessions are covered in Chapter 15.
- **$_FILES**: This contains details of file uploads. File uploads are not covered in this book. See http://docs.php.net/manual/en/features.file-upload.php or my book *PHP Solutions: Dynamic Web Design Made Easy* (friends of ED, ISBN: 978-1-59059-731-6) for details.

The keys of $_POST and $_GET are automatically derived from the names of form elements. Let's say you have a text input field called address in a form; PHP automatically creates an array element called $_POST['address'] when the form is submitted by the post method or $_GET['address'] if you use the get method. As Figure 11-2 shows, $_POST['address'] contains whatever value a visitor enters in the text field, enabling you

11

to display it onscreen, insert it in a database, send it to your email inbox, or do whatever you want with it.

Figure 11-2. The $_POST array automatically creates variables with the same name and value as each form field.

It's important to realize that variables like $_POST['address'] or $_GET['address'] don't exist until the form has been submitted. So, before using $_POST or $_GET variables in a script, you should always test for their existence with isset() or wrap the entire section of script in a conditional statement that checks whether the form has been submitted. You'll see both of these techniques in action in this chapter and the rest of this book.

You may come across old scripts or tutorials that tell you PHP automatically creates variables with the same name as form fields. In this example, it would be $address. This relies on a setting called register_globals being on. The default for this setting has been off since 2002, because it leaves your site wide open to malicious attacks. Most hosting companies now seem to have turned it off, but don't be tempted to try to find a way to turn it back on. It has been removed from PHP 6, so scripts that rely on register_globals will break in future.

Some scripts also recommend the use of $_REQUEST, which is another PHP superglobal. It's much less secure. Always use $_POST for data submitted using the post method and $_GET for the get method or when values are passed through a query string at the end of a URL.

> *Don't forget that PHP is case-sensitive. All superglobal array names are written in uppercase. $_Post or $_Get, for example, won't work.*

Dreamweaver code hints make it easy to type the names of superglobals. As soon as you type the underscore after the dollar sign, it displays a list of the array names; and for arrays such as $_SERVER with predefined elements, a second menu with the predefined elements is also displayed, as you'll see when you start scripting the form.

Sending email

To send an email with PHP, you use the mail() function, which takes up to five arguments, as follows (the first three are required):

- **Recipient(s)**: The email address(es) to which the message is being sent. Addresses can be in either of the following formats:

  ```
  'user@example.com'
  'Some Guy <user2@example.com>'
  ```

To send to more than one address, use a comma-separated string like this:

`'user@example.com, another@example.com, Some Guy <user2@example.com>'`

- **Subject**: A string containing the subject line of the message.
- **Body**: This is the message being sent. It should be a single string, regardless of how long it is. However, the email standard imposes a maximum line length. I'll describe how to handle this later.
- **Additional headers**: This is an optional set of email headers, such as From, Cc, Reply-to, and so on. They must be in a specific format, which is described later in this chapter.
- **Additional parameters**: As an antispam measure, some hosting companies require verification that the email originates from the registered domain. I'll explain how to use this argument later in the chapter.

It's important to understand that mail() isn't an email program. It passes data to the web server's mail transport agent (MTA). PHP's responsibility ends there. It has no way of knowing whether the email is delivered to its destination. It doesn't handle attachments or HTML email. Still, it's efficient and easy to use.

These days, most Internet service providers (ISPs) enforce Simple Mail Transfer Protocol (SMTP) authentication before accepting email for relay from another machine. However, mail() was designed to communicate directly with the MTA on the same machine, without the need for authentication. This presents a problem for testing mail() in a local testing environment. Since mail() doesn't normally need to authenticate itself, it's not capable of doing so. More often than not, when you attempt to use mail() on your local computer, it can't find an MTA or the ISP rejects the mail without authentication.

Although I normally recommend testing everything locally before uploading PHP scripts to a remote server, it's usually not possible with mail(), especially if you need to log into your normal email account. Some parts of the following script can be tested locally, but when it comes to the sections that actually send the mail, the overwhelming majority of readers will need to upload the script to their website and test it from there.

11

Scripting the feedback form

To make things simple, I'm going to break up the PHP script into several sections. To start off, I'll concentrate on the text input fields and sending their content by email. Then I'll move onto validation and the display of error messages before showing you how to handle checkboxes, radio buttons, menus, and multiple-choice lists.

Most readers should be able to send a simple email after the following exercise, but even if you are successful, you should implement the server-side validation described later in the chapter. This is because, without some simple security precautions, you risk turning your online forms into a spam relay. Your hosting company might suspend your site or close down your account altogether.

This involves a lot of hand-coding—much more than you'll encounter in later chapters. To reduce the amount of typing you need to do, I have created an extension that contains several PHP functions stored as Dreamweaver snippets (small pieces of code that can be easily inserted into any page). I suggest you install them now so they're ready for use in this and subsequent chapters.

Installing the PHP snippets

To install the snippets, you need to have installed the Extension Manager when you originally installed Dreamweaver CS4. If you accepted the default options when installing Dreamweaver, you should have access to the Extension Manager. However, if you deselected all the optional programs and components, you will need to install the Extension Manager from your Dreamweaver or Creative Suite 4 DVD. The extension file is called dwcs4_snippets.mxp and is in the extras folder of the download files for this book.

1. Launch the Extension Manager as described in Chapter 8.
2. Click the Install button, navigate to dwcs4_snippets.mxp, and install it.
3. Close and relaunch Dreamweaver.
4. The snippets should have been installed in a folder called PHP-DWCS4 in the Dreamweaver Snippets panel (see Figure 11-3). They are now accessible for use in any site.

I'll show you how to insert a snippet in a page later in this chapter.

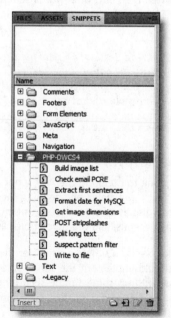

Figure 11-3.
The extension installs a set of useful PHP scripts.

This is a long script. Give yourself plenty of time to absorb the details. You can check your progress at each stage with the files in examples/ch11. The final code is in feedback_12.php. Even if you don't want to do a lot of PHP programming, it's important to get a feel for the flow of a script, because this will help you customize the Dreamweaver code once you start working with a database. The script uses a lot of PHP's built-in functions. I explain the important ones but don't always go into the finer points of how they work. The idea is to give you a working solution, rather than overwhelm you with detail. In the next chapter, I'll show you how to put the main part of the script in an external file so that you can reuse it with other forms without the need to hand-code everything from scratch every time.

Processing and acknowledging the message

The starting point is in feedback_01.php in examples/ch11. It's the same as feedback_fieldsets.php from Chapter 9 but with the small block of PHP code removed from the bottom of the page. If you want to use your own form, I suggest you remove any client-side validation from it, because the client-side validation makes it difficult to check whether the more important server-side validation with PHP is working correctly. You can add the client-side validation back at the final stage.

1. Copy feedback_01.php and contact.css from examples/ch11 to workfiles/ch11. Rename feedback_01.php to feedback.php. If Dreamweaver asks you whether to update links, click No.

2. Select contact.css in the Related Files toolbar to open it in Split view, and add the following style rule:

```css
.warning {
  font-weight:bold;
  color:#F00;
}
```

This adds a class called warning, which displays text in bold red. Save contact.css.

3. Select Source Code in the Related Files toolbar to display the underlying code of feedback.php in Split view, click anywhere in the form, and use the Tag selector at the bottom of the Document window to select the entire form. This should bring the opening tag of the form into view in Code view. Click in Code view so that your cursor is between the quotes of the action attribute. Although you can set the action for the form through the Property inspector, doing so in Code view greatly reduces the possibility of making a mistake.

4. Select the PHP tab on the Insert bar, and click the Echo button (the menu option is Insert ➤ PHP Objects ➤ Echo). This will insert a pair of PHP tags followed by echo

11

between the quotes of the action attribute, and Dreamweaver positions your cursor in the correct place to start typing, as shown in the following screenshot:

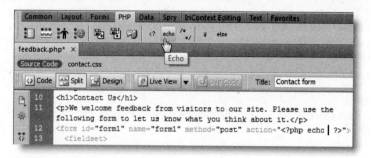

5. To set the action attribute of the form to process itself, you need to use a variable from the $_SERVER superglobal array. As noted before, superglobals always begin with $_, so type just that at the current position. Dreamweaver automatically presents you with a pop-up menu containing all the superglobals, as shown here:

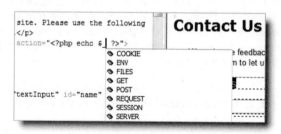

You can navigate this pop-up menu in several ways: continue typing server in either uppercase or lowercase until SERVER is highlighted or use your mouse or the arrow keys to highlight it. Then double-click or press Enter/Return. Dreamweaver will present you with another pop-up menu. Locate PHP_SELF as shown here, and either double-click or press Enter/Return:

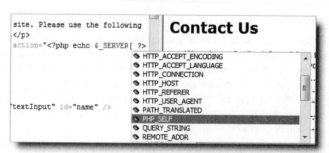

6. Although it's not strictly necessary for a single command, get into the habit of ending all statements with a semicolon, and type one after the closing square bracket

(]) of the superglobal variable that's just been entered. The code in the opening <form> tag should look like this (new code is highlighted in bold type):

```
<form id="form1" name="form1" method="post" action="<?php echo ➥
$_SERVER['PHP_SELF']; ?>">
```

The predefined variable $_SERVER['PHP_SELF'] always contains the name of the current page, so using echo between the quotes of the action attribute automatically sets it to the current page, making this a self-processing form. As you saw in Chapter 9, leaving out the value of action also results in the form attempting to process itself. So, technically speaking, this isn't 100-percent necessary, but it's common practice in PHP scripts, and it's useful to know what $_SERVER['PHP_SELF'] does.

7. You now need to add the mail-processing script at the top of the page. As you saw in Chapter 9, the $_POST array contains not only the data entered into the form but also the name and value of the submit button. You can use this information to determine whether the submit button has been clicked. From this point onward, it will be easier to work in Code view. Switch to Code view, and insert the following block of PHP code immediately above the DOCTYPE declaration:

```php
<?php
if (array_key_exists('send', $_POST)) {
  // mail processing script
  echo 'You clicked the submit button';
}
?>
<!DOCTYPE html PUBLIC "-//W3C//DTD XHTML 1.0 Transitional//EN" ➥
"http://www.w3.org/TR/xhtml1/DTD/xhtml1-transitional.dtd">
```

This uses the PHP function array_key_exists() to check whether the $_POST array contains a key called send, the name attribute of the form submit button. If you don't want to type the function name yourself, you can press Ctrl+Space to bring up an alphabetical list of all PHP functions. Type just the first few letters, and then use your arrow keys to select the right one. When you press Tab or Enter/Return, Dreamweaver finishes the rest of the typing and pops up a code hint. Alternatively, just type the function name directly, and the code hint appears as soon as you enter the opening parenthesis after array_key_exists, as shown here:

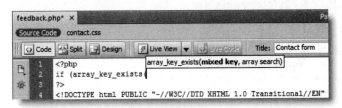

The mixed data type refers to the fact that array keys can be either numbers or strings. In this case, you are using a string, so enclose send in quotes, and then after a comma, type $_POST. Because it's a superglobal, you are presented with the same pop-up menu as in step 5. If you select POST, Dreamweaver assumes you want to add the name of an array key and will automatically add an opening square bracket after the T. On this occasion, you want to check the whole $_POST array, not just a single element, so remove the bracket by pressing Backspace. Make sure you use two closing parentheses—the first belongs to the function array_key_exists(), and the second encloses the condition being tested for by the if statement.

If the send array key exists, the submit button must have been clicked, so any script between the curly braces is executed. Otherwise, it's ignored. Don't worry that echo will display text above the DOCTYPE declaration. It's being used for test purposes only and will be removed eventually.

> Remember, an if statement doesn't always need to be followed by else or elseif. When the condition of a solitary if statement isn't met, PHP simply skips to the next block of code.

8. Save feedback.php, and test it in a browser. It should look no different from before.

9. Click the Send comments button. A message should appear at the top of the page saying "You clicked the submit button."

10. Reload the page without using the browser's reload button. Click inside the address bar, and press Enter/Return. The message should disappear. This confirms that any code inside the curly braces runs only if the submit button has been clicked.

11. Change the block of code you entered in step 7 so it looks like this:

```php
<?php
if (array_key_exists('send', $_POST)) {
  //mail processing script
  $to = 'me@example.com'; // use your own email address
  $subject = 'Feedback from Essential Guide';

  // process the $_POST variables
  $name = $_POST['name'];
  $email = $_POST['email'];
  $comments = $_POST['comments'];

  // build the message
  $message = "Name: $name\r\n\r\n";
  $message .= "Email: $email\r\n\r\n";
  $message .= "Comments: $comments";

  // limit line length to 70 characters
  $message = wordwrap($message, 70);

  // send it
  $mailSent = mail($to, $subject, $message);
}
?>
```

The code that does the processing consists of five stages. The first two lines assign your email address to $to and the subject line of the email to $subject.

Next, $_POST['name'], $_POST['email'], and $_POST['comments'] are reassigned to ordinary variables to make them easier to handle.

The shorter variables are then used to build the body of the email message, which must consist of a single string. As you can see, I have used the combined concatenation operator (.=) to build the message and escape sequences to add carriage returns and newline characters between each section (see "Adding to an existing string" and "Using escape sequences in strings" in Chapter 10).

Once the message body is complete, it's passed to the wordwrap() function, which takes two arguments: a string and an integer that sets the maximum length of each line. Although most mail systems will accept longer lines, it's recommended to limit each line to 70 characters.

After the message has been built and formatted, the recipient's address, subject line, and body of the message are passed to the mail() function. There is nothing magical about the variable names $to, $subject, and $message. I chose them to describe what each one contains, making much of the script self-commenting.

The mail() function returns a Boolean value (true or false) indicating whether it succeeded. By capturing this value as $mailSent, you can use it to redirect the user to another page or change the contents of the current one.

> *The official format for email is described in a document known as Request For Comments (RFC) 2822 (http://tools.ietf.org/html/rfc2822). Among other things, it says that carriage returns and newline characters must not appear independently in the body of a message; they must always be together as a pair. It also sets the maximum length of a line in the body at 998 characters but recommends restricting lines to no more than 78. The reason I have set wordwrap() to a more conservative 70 characters is to avoid problems with some mail clients that automatically wrap messages. If you set the value too high, you end up with alternating long and short lines.*

11

12. For the time being, let's keep everything in the same page, because the rest of the chapter will add further refinements to the basic script. Scroll down, and insert the following code just after the page's main heading (new code is highlighted in bold):

```
<h1>Contact us</h1>
<?php
if ($_POST && !$mailSent) {
?>
  <p class="warning">Sorry, there was a problem sending your message.
Please try later.</p>
<?php
} elseif ($_POST && $mailSent) {
?>
  <p><strong>Your message has been sent. Thank you for your feedback.
</strong></p>
<?php } ?>
<p>We welcome feedback from visitors . . .</p>
```

Many beginners mistakenly think you need to use echo or print to display HTML in a PHP block. However, except for very short pieces of code, it's more efficient to switch back to HTML, as I've done here. Doing so avoids the need to worry about escaping quotes. Also, Dreamweaver code hints and automatic tag completion speed things up for you. As soon as you type a space after <p in the first paragraph, Dreamweaver pops up a code hint menu like this:

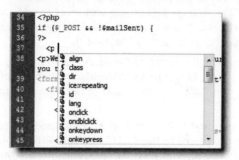

Select class. As soon as you do so, Dreamweaver checks the available classes in the attached style sheet and pops up another code hint menu, as shown in the next screenshot, so you can choose warning:

This makes coding much quicker and more accurate. Dreamweaver's context sensitivity means you get the full range of HTML code hints only when you're in a section of HTML code. When you're in a block of PHP code, you get a list of HTML tags when you type an opening angle bracket, but there are no attribute hints or autocompletion. So, it makes more sense to use PHP for the conditional logic but keep the HTML separate. The only thing you need to watch carefully is that you balance the opening and closing curly braces correctly. I'll show you how to do that in "Using Balance Braces" a little later in the chapter.

So, what does this code do? It may look odd if you're not used to seeing scripts that mix HTML with PHP logic, but it can be summarized like this:

```
<h1>Contact us</h1>
<?php
if ($_POST && !$mailSent) {
  // display a failure message
} elseif ($_POST && $mailSent) {
  // display an acknowledgment
 }
?>
<p>We welcome feedback from visitors . . .</p>
```

Both parts of the conditional statement check the Boolean values of $_POST and $mailSent. Although the $_POST array is always set, it doesn't contain any values unless the form has been submitted. Since PHP treats an empty array as false (see "The truth according to PHP" in Chapter 10), you can use $_POST on its own to test whether a form has been submitted. So, the code in both parts of this conditional statement is ignored when the page first loads.

However, if the form has been submitted, $_POST equates to true, so the next condition is tested. The exclamation mark in front of $mailSent is the negative operator, making it the equivalent of *not* $mailSent. So, if the email hasn't been sent, both parts of the test are true, and the HTML containing the error message is displayed. However, if $mailSent is true, the HTML containing the acknowledgment is displayed instead.

13. Save feedback.php, and switch to Design view. The top of the page should now look like this:

There are three gold shields indicating the presence of PHP code, and both the error and acknowledgment messages are displayed. You need to get used to this sort of thing when designing dynamic pages.

If you don't see the gold shields, refer to "Passing information through a hidden field" in Chapter 9 for details of how to control invisible elements in Design view.

14. To see what the page looks like when the PHP is processed, click the Live View button in the Document toolbar. Dreamweaver will ask whether you want to update the copy on the testing server. Click Yes.

If you have coded everything correctly, the error message and acknowledgment should disappear. Click the Live View button to toggle it off again.

If you got a PHP error message, read "Using Balance Braces," and then check your code against feedback_02.php.

> *The script in step 11 is theoretically all you need to send email from an online form. Don't be tempted to leave it at that. Without the security checks described in the rest of the chapter, you run the risk of turning your website into a spam relay.*

11

Using Balance Braces

Even if you didn't encounter a problem in the preceding exercise, Balance Braces is a tool that you definitely need to know about. Like quotes, curly braces must always be in matching pairs, but sometimes the opening and closing braces can be dozens, even hundreds, of lines apart. If one of a pair is missing, your script will collapse like a house of cards. Balance Braces matches pairs in a highly visual way, making troubleshooting a breeze.

Let's take a look at the code in step 12 that I suspect will trip many people up. I deliberately removed an opening curly brace at the end of line 39 in the following screenshot. That triggered a parse error, which reported an unexpected closing curly brace on line 42. Now, that could mean either of the following:

- There's a missing opening brace to match the closing one.
- There's an extra closing brace that shouldn't be there.

The way to resolve the problem is to place your cursor anywhere between a pair of curly braces, and click the Balance Braces button in the Coding toolbar. This highlights the code between the matching braces. I started by placing my cursor on line 37. As you can see, it highlighted all the code between the braces on lines 35 and 38.

Next, I positioned my cursor on line 41. When I clicked the Balance Braces button again, nothing was highlighted, and my computer just beeped. So there was the culprit. All I needed to work out was where the opening brace should go. My first test showed that I had a logical block on lines 35–38 (the closing brace is at the beginning of line 39), so it was just a process of elimination tracking down the missing brace. If the problem had been an extra curly brace that shouldn't have been there, the code would have been highlighted, giving me a clear indication of where the block ended.

Although it can't tell you whether your code logic is right or where a missing brace should go, you'll find this tool a great time-saver. It works not only with braces but also with square brackets and parentheses. Just position your cursor inside any curly brace, square bracket, or parenthesis, and click the Balance Braces button to find the other one of the pair. You may need to test several blocks to find the cause of a problem, but it's an excellent way of visualizing code blocks and the branching logic of your scripts.

You can also access Balance Braces through the Edit menu, and if you're a keyboard shortcut fan, the combination is Ctrl+'/Cmd+' (single quote).

Testing the feedback form

Assuming that you now have a page that displays correctly in Live view, it's time to test it. As mentioned earlier, testing mail() in a local PHP testing environment is unreliable, so I suggest you upload feedback.php to a remote server for the next stage of testing. Once you have established that the mail() function is working, you can continue testing locally.

Upload feedback.php and contact.css to your remote server. Enter some text in the Name, Email, and Comments fields. Make sure your input includes at least an apostrophe or quotation mark, and click Send comments. The form should clear, and you should see a confirmation message, as in Figure 11-4.

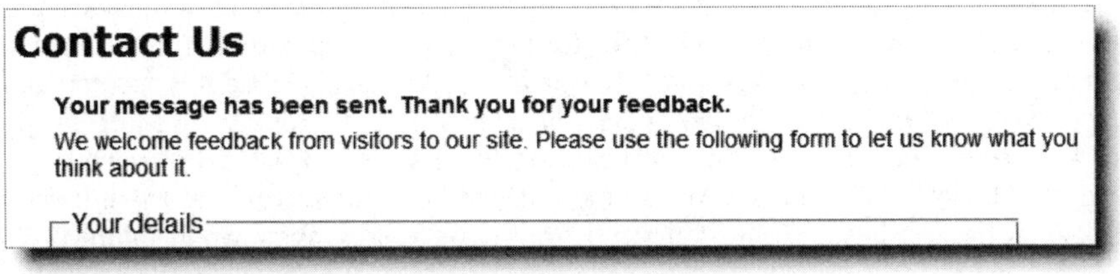

Contact Us

Your message has been sent. Thank you for your feedback.
We welcome feedback from visitors to our site. Please use the following form to let us know what you think about it.

Your details

Figure 11-4. Confirmation that the mail() function has passed the message to the server's mail transport agent

Shortly afterward, you should receive the message in your inbox. Most of the time, it should work, but there are several things that might go wrong. The next section should help you resolve the problem.

If you see an error message saying that the From header wasn't set or that sendmail_from isn't defined in php.ini, keep building the script as described in each section, and I'll tell you when you can test your page on the remote server again. If you get a blank page, it means you have a syntax error in your PHP script, use the File Compare feature (see Chapter 2) to compare your code with feedback_02.php in examples/ch11.

Troubleshooting mail()

If you don't receive anything, the first thing to check is your spam trap, because the email may appear to come from an unknown or a suspicious source. For example, it may appear to come from Apache or a mysterious nobody (the name often used for web servers). Don't worry about the odd name; that will be fixed soon. The main thing is to check that the mail is being sent correctly.

Improving the security of the mail-processing script

As the preceding exercise showed, the basic principles of processing the contents of a form and sending it by email to your inbox are relatively simple. However, you can improve the script in many ways; indeed, some things must be done to improve its security. One of the biggest problems on the Internet is caused by insecure scripts. As the mail processing script currently stands, it's wide open to abuse. If you received an error

11

message about the From header not being set, it indicates that your hosting company has taken measures to increase security and prevent poorly written mail scripts from being used as spam relays. Your script won't work until you implement the security measures in the following sections.

Most of the rest of this chapter is devoted to improving the security and user experience of the existing script. First I'll deal with unwanted backslashes that might appear in your email.

Getting rid of unwanted backslashes

Some day back in the mists of time, the PHP development team had the "brilliant" idea of creating a feature known as magic quotes . . . only it wasn't so brilliant after all. When inserting data into a database, it's essential to escape single and double quotes. So, the idea of magic quotes was to make life simpler for beginners by doing this automatically for all data passed through the $_POST and $_GET arrays, and cookies. While this seemed like a good idea at the time, it has caused endless problems. To cut a long story short, magic quotes are being officially phased out of PHP (they'll be gone in PHP 6), but they're still enabled on a lot of shared servers. You will know whether your server uses them if your test email has backslashes in front of any apostrophes or quotes, as shown in Figure 11-5.

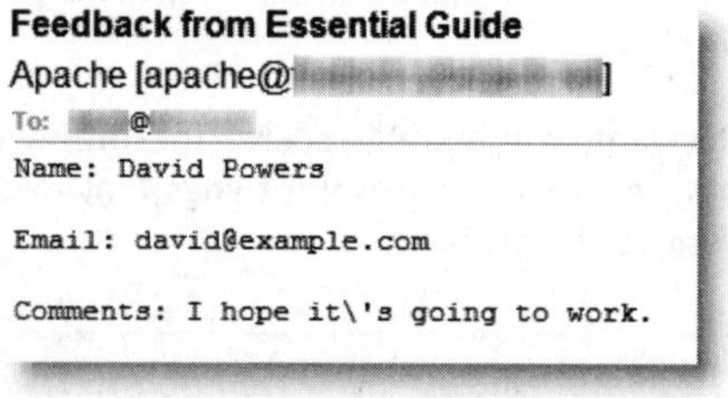

Figure 11-5.
PHP magic quotes insert unwanted backslashes in the email.

Feedback from Essential Guide
Apache [apache@██████ ████████]
To: ████@████████

Name: David Powers

Email: david@example.com

Comments: I hope it\'s going to work.

Dreamweaver's server behaviors automatically handle magic quotes by stripping the backslashes, if necessary, and preparing data for database input. However, when you're handcoding like this, you need to deal with the backslashes yourself.

I have created a Dreamweaver snippet so that you can drop a ready-made script into any page that needs to get rid of unwanted backslashes. It automatically detects whether magic quotes are enabled, so you can use it safely on any server. If magic quotes are on, it removes the backslashes. If magic quotes are off, it leaves your data untouched. It's part of the collection of snippets that you should have installed as a Dreamweaver extension at the beginning of this chapter.

Using the POST stripslashes snippet

These instructions continue the creation of the form processing script. So, continue working with feedback.php from the previous section. They also show you how to insert code from the Snippets panel.

1. Open feedback.php in Code view. Position your cursor at the beginning of line 4, just under the mail processing script comment, and insert a couple of blank lines.

   Move your cursor onto one of the blank lines, and open the Snippets panel by clicking the Snippets tab in the Files panel group or selecting Window ➤ Snippets.

On Windows, you can also use the keyboard shortcut Shift+F9, but this doesn't work on the Mac version.

Highlight the POST stripslashes snippet in the PHP-DWCS4 folder, and double-click it, or click the Insert button at the bottom of the panel.

2. This inserts the following block of code into your page:

```
// remove escape characters from $_POST array
if (PHP_VERSION < 6 && get_magic_quotes_gpc()) {
  function stripslashes_deep($value) {
    $value = is_array($value) ? array_map('stripslashes_deep', ➥
$value) : stripslashes($value);
    return $value;
  }
  $_POST = array_map('stripslashes_deep', $_POST);
}
```

Lying at the heart of this code is the PHP function stripslashes(), which removes the escape backslashes from quotes and apostrophes. Normally, you just pass the string that you want to clean up as the argument to stripslashes(). Unfortunately, that won't work with an array. This block of code checks whether the version of PHP is prior to PHP 6 and, if so, whether magic quotes have been turned on (magic quotes have been removed from PHP 6); and if they have, it goes through the $_POST array and any nested arrays, cleaning up your text for display either in an email or in a web page.

3. Save feedback.php, and send another test email that includes apostrophes and quotes in the message. The email you receive should be nicely cleaned up. This won't work yet if you weren't able to send the first test email.

If you have any problems, check your page against feedback_03.php.

Making sure required fields aren't blank

When required fields are left blank, you don't get the information you need, and the user may never get a reply, particularly if contact details have been omitted. The following instructions make use of arrays and the foreach loop, both of which are described in Chapter 10. So if you're new to PHP, you might find it useful to refer to the relevant sections in the previous chapter before continuing.

11

Checking required fields

In this part of the script, you create three arrays to hold details of variables you expect to receive from the form, those that are required, and those that are missing. This not only helps identify any required items that haven't been filled in; it also adds an important security check before passing the user input to a loop that converts the names of $_POST variables to shorter ones that are easier to handle.

1. Start by creating two arrays: one listing the name attribute of each field in the form and the other listing all *required* fields. Also, initialize an empty array to store the names of required fields that have not been completed. For the sake of this

demonstration, make the email field optional so that only the name and comments fields are required. Add the following code just before the section that processes the $_POST variables:

```
$subject = 'Feedback from Essential Guide';

// list expected fields
$expected = array('name', 'email', 'comments');
// set required fields
$required = array('name', 'comments');
// create empty array for any missing fields
$missing = array();

// process the $_POST variables
```

2. At the moment, the $_POST variables are assigned manually to variables that use the same name as the $_POST array key. With three fields, manual assignment is fine, but it becomes a major chore with more fields. Let's kill two birds with one stone by checking required fields and automating the naming of the variables at the same time. Replace the three lines of code beneath the $_POST variables comment as follows:

```
// process the $_POST variables
foreach ($_POST as $key => $value) {
  // assign to temporary variable and strip whitespace if not an array
  $temp = is_array($value) ? $value : trim($value);
  // if empty and required, add to $missing array
  if (empty($temp) && in_array($key, $required)) {
    array_push($missing, $key);
  } elseif (in_array($key, $expected)) {
    // otherwise, assign to a variable of the same name as $key
    ${$key} = $temp;
  }
}

// build the message
```

If studying PHP code makes your brain hurt, you don't need to worry about how this works. As long as you create the $expected, $required, and $missing arrays in the previous step, you can just copy and paste the code for use in any form.

So, what does it do? In simple terms, this foreach loop goes through the $_POST array, strips out any whitespace from user input, and assigns its contents to a variable with the same name (so $_POST['email'] becomes $email, and so on). If a required field is left blank, its name attribute is added to the $missing array.

The code uses several built-in PHP functions, all of which have intuitive names:

- is_array() tests whether a variable is an array.
- trim() trims whitespace from both ends of a string.
- empty() tests whether a variable contains nothing or equates to false.

- in_array() checks whether the first argument is part of the array specified in the second argument.
- array_push() adds a new element to the end of an array.

At this stage, you don't need to understand how each function works, but you can find details in the PHP online documentation at http://docs.php.net/manual/en/index.php. Type the name of the function in the search for field at the top right of the page (see Figure 11-6), and click the right-facing arrow alongside function list. The PHP documentation has many practical examples showing how functions and other features are used.

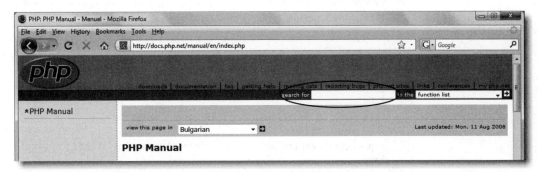

Figure 11-6. Refer often to the excellent PHP online documentation, and your skills will increase rapidly.

> *Why is the $expected array necessary? It's to prevent an attacker from injecting other variables in the $_POST array in an attempt to overwrite your default values. By processing only those variables that you expect, your form is much more secure. Any spurious values are ignored.*

3. You want to build the body of the email message and send it only if all required fields have been filled in. Since $missing starts off as an empty array, nothing is added to it if all required fields are completed, so empty($missing) is true. Wrap the rest of the script in the opening PHP code block like this:

```
// go ahead only if all required fields OK
if (empty($missing)) {

  // build the message
  $message = "Name: $name\r\n\r\n";
  $message .= "Email: $email\r\n\r\n";
  $message .= "Comments: $comments";

  // limit line length to 70 characters
  $message = wordwrap($message, 70);
```

11

```
    // send it
    $mailSent = mail($to, $subject, $message);
    if ($mailSent) {
      // $missing is no longer needed if the email is sent, so unset it
      unset($missing);
    }
  }
}
```

This ensures that the mail is sent only if nothing has been added to $missing. However, $missing will be used to control the display of error messages in the main body of the page, so you need to get rid of it if the mail is successfully sent. This is done by using unset(), which destroys a variable and any value it contains.

4. Let's turn now to the main body of the page. You need to display a warning if anything is missing. Amend the conditional statement at the top of the page content like this:

```
<h1>Contact us</h1>
<?php
if ($_POST && isset($missing) && !empty($missing)) {
?>
  <p class="warning">Please complete the missing item(s) indicated.</p>
<?php
} elseif ($_POST && !$mailSent) {
?>
  <p class="warning">Sorry, there was a problem sending your message.
Please try later.</p>
```

This adds a new condition. The isset() function checks whether a variable exists. If $missing doesn't exist, that means that all required fields were filled in and the email was sent successfully, so the condition fails, and the script moves on to consider the elseif condition. However, if all required fields were filled in but there was a problem sending the email, $missing still exists, so you need to make sure it's empty. An exclamation mark is the negative operator, so !empty means "not empty."

On the other hand, if $missing exists and *isn't* empty, you know that at least one required field was omitted, so the warning message is displayed.

I've placed this new condition first. The $mailSent variable won't even be set if any required fields have been omitted, so you must test for $missing first.

5. To make sure it works so far, save feedback.php, and load it in a browser. You don't need to upload it to your remote server, because you want to test the message about missing items. Don't fill in any fields. Just click Send comments. The top of the page should look like this (check your code against feedback_04.php if necessary):

Contact Us

Please complete the missing item(s) indicated.

We welcome feedback from visitors to our site. Please use the following form to let us know what you think about it.

6. To display a suitable message alongside each missing required field, add a PHP code block to display a warning as a `<span>` inside the `<label>` tag like this:

```
<label for="name">Name: <?php
if (isset($missing) && in_array('name', $missing)) { ?>
<span class="warning">Please enter your name</span><?php } ?>
</label>
```

Since the $missing array is created only after the form has been submitted, you need to check first with isset() that it exists. If it doesn't exist—such as when the page first loads or if the email has been sent successfully—the `<span>` is never displayed. If $missing does exist, the second condition checks whether the $missing array contains the value name. If it does, the `<span>` is displayed as shown in Figure 11-7.

7. Insert a similar warning for the comments field like this:

```
<label for="comments">Comments: <?php
if (isset($missing) && in_array('comments', $missing)) { ?>
<span class="warning">Please enter your comments</span><?php } ?>
</label>
```

The PHP code is the same except for the value you are looking for in the $missing array. It's the same as the name attribute for the form element.

8. Save feedback.php, and test the page again locally by entering nothing into any of the fields. The page should look like Figure 11-7. Check your code against feedback_05.php if you encounter any problems.

Contact Us

Please complete the missing item(s) indicated.

We welcome feedback from visitors to our site. Please use the following form to let us know what you think about it.

Your details

Name: Please enter your name

Email:

Your views

Comments: Please enter your comments

Figure 11-7. The PHP script displays alerts if required information is missing, even when JavaScript is disabled.

9. Try one more test. Open Code view, and amend the line that sends the email like this:

```
$mailSent = false; // mail($to, $subject, $message);
```

This temporarily sets the value of $mailSent to false and comments out the code that actually sends the email.

10. Reload `feedback.php` into your browser, and type something in the Name and Comments fields before clicking Send comments. This time you should see the message telling you there was a problem and asking you to try later.

11. Reverse the change you made in step 9 so that the code is ready to send the email.

Preserving user input when a form is incomplete

Imagine you have just spent ten minutes filling in a form. You click the submit button, and back comes the response that a required field is missing. It's infuriating if you have to fill in every field all over again. Since the content of each field is in the $_POST array, it's easy to redisplay it when an error occurs.

When the page first loads or the email is successfully sent, you don't want anything to appear in the input fields. But you do want to redisplay the content if a required field is missing. So, that's the key: if the `$missing` variable exists, you want the content of each field to be redisplayed. You can set default text for a text input field by setting the value attribute of the `<input>` tag.

At the moment, the `<input>` tag for name looks like this:

```
<input name="name" type="text" class="textInput" id="name" />
```

To add the value attribute, all you need is a conditional statement that checks whether `$missing` exists. If it does, you can use echo to display value="" and put the value held in `$_POST['name']` between the quotes. It sounds simple enough, but this is one of those situations where getting the right combination of quotes can drive you mad. It's made even worse by the fact that the user input in the text field might also contain quotes. Figure 11-8 shows what happens if you don't give quotes in user input special treatment. The browser finds the first matching quote and throws the rest of the input away.

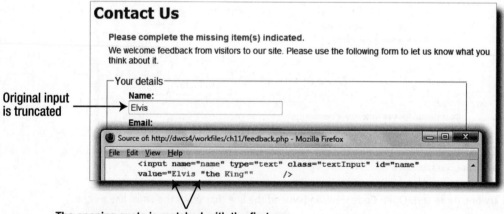

Figure 11-8. Quotes within user input need special treatment before form fields can be redisplayed.

You might be thinking that this is a case where magic quotes would be useful. Unfortunately, they won't work either. If you don't use the POST stripslashes snippet, this is what you get instead:

Magic quotes work only with input into a database (and not very well, either, which is why they are being phased out). The browser still sees the first matching quote as the end of the value attribute. The solution is simple: convert the quotes to the HTML entity equivalent ("), and PHP has a function called—appropriately— htmlentities(). Passing the $_POST array element to this function converts all characters (except space and single quote) that have an HTML entity equivalent to that entity. As a result, the content is no longer truncated. What's cool is that the HTML entity " is converted back to double quotes when the form is resubmitted, so there's no need for any further conversion.

The htmlentities() function was created in the days before widespread support for Unicode (UTF-8), so it uses Latin-1 or Western European encoding (ISO-8859-1) as its default. Since Dreamweaver uses UTF-8 as the default encoding for web pages, you need to pass an argument to htmlentities() to tell it to use the correct encoding. Unfortunately, to set the encoding argument, you need to pass a total of three arguments to htmlentities(): the string you want converted, a PHP constant describing how to handle quotes, and a string containing the encoding. Tables 11-1 and 11-2 list the available values for the second and third arguments.

Table 11-1. PHP constants for handling quotes in htmlentities()

Constant	Meaning
ENT_COMPAT	Converts double quotes to " but leaves single quotes alone. This is the default. You don't need to use this unless you also pass a third argument to htmlentities().
ENT_QUOTES	Converts double quotes to " and single quotes to '.
ENT_NOQUOTES	Leaves both double and single quotes alone.

Table 11-2. Character encodings supported by htmlentities()

Encoding	Aliases	Description
ISO-8859-1	ISO8859-1	Western European (Latin-1). This is the default and not normally required as an argument to htmlentities().
ISO-8859-15	ISO8859-15	Western European (Latin-9). Includes the euro symbol and characters used in French and Finnish.
UTF-8		Unicode, the default encoding in Dreamweaver CS4.

Continued

11

Table 11-2. *Continued*

Encoding	Aliases	Description
cp866	ibm866, 866	DOS-specific Cyrillic character set.
cp1251	Windows-1251, win-1251, 1251	Windows-specific Cyrillic character set.
cp1252	Windows-1252, 1252	Windows-specific character set for Western European.
KOI8-R	koi8-ru, koi8r	Russian.
GB2312	936	Simplified Chinese; national standard character set used in People's Republic of China.
BIG5	950	Traditional Chinese; mainly used in Taiwan.
BIG5-HKSCS		Big5 with Hong Kong extensions.
Shift_JIS	SJIS, 932	Japanese.
EUC-JP	EUCJP	Japanese.

If you are using the Dreamweaver default encoding, passing a value to htmlentities() involves using all three arguments like this:

```
htmlentities(value, ENT_COMPAT, 'UTF-8');
```

This converts double quotes but leaves single quotes alone. More importantly, it preserves accented characters and any other characters outside the Latin-1 character set.

If you are using a different encoding for your web pages or want quotes to be handled differently, substitute the appropriate values for the second and third arguments using Tables 11-1 and 11-2. The third argument must be a string, so it should be enclosed in quotes. The aliases in Table 11-2 are alternative spellings or names for the character encoding supported by PHP.

So, to summarize, the way you redisplay the user's input in the Name field if one or more required fields are missing is like this:

```
<input name="name" type="text" class="textInput" id="name"
<?php if (isset($missing)) {
  echo 'value="'.htmlentities($_POST['name'], ENT_COMPAT, 'UTF-8').'"';
} ?>
/>
```

This code is quite short, but the line inside the curly braces contains a tricky combination of quotes and periods. The first thing to realize is that there's only one semicolon—right at the end—so the echo command applies to the whole line. You can break down the rest of the line into three sections, as follows:

- 'value="'.
- htmlentities($_POST['name'], ENT_COMPAT, 'UTF-8')
- .'"'

The first section outputs value=" as text and uses the concatenation operator (a period—see "Joining strings together" in Chapter 10) to join it to the next section, which passes $_POST['name'] and the two arguments from Tables 11-1 and 11-2 to the htmlentities() function. The final section uses the concatenation operator again to join the next string, which consists solely of a double quote. So if $missing has been set and $_POST['name'] contains Joe, you'll end up with this inside the <input> tag:

```
<input name="name" type="text" class="textInput" id="name" ➡
value="Joe" />
```

Whenever you need this code, the only thing that changes is the name of the $_POST array element. So, rather than laboriously type it out every time, it's a good idea to convert it into a snippet.

Saving frequently used code as a snippet

Although I have provided some snippets for you in the extension that you installed at the beginning of this chapter, it's easy enough to create snippets of your own. The following instructions show you how to turn the code described in the previous section into a snippet that leaves your cursor in the correct position to insert the name of the $_POST array element. You can use the same technique to create a snippet from any frequently used code.

1. Open the Snippets panel, right-click, and select New Folder from the context menu. Name the new folder PHP.

2. With the PHP folder selected in the Snippets panel, right-click, and select New Snippet from the context menu. This opens the Snippet dialog box shown in Figure 11-9.

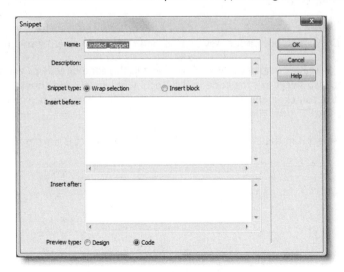

11

Figure 11-9.
Snippets are a useful way of storing short pieces of frequently used code.

The Snippets panel has the following options:

- Name: This is the name that appears in the Snippets panel. Choose a short but descriptive name. Spaces are permitted.

- Description: This is for a more detailed description. It appears alongside the name in the Snippets panel (you might need to expand the panel horizontally to see it). When you mouse over it, the full description appears as a tooltip.

- Snippet type: Wrap selection creates a wraparound snippet that leaves the cursor in the correct place to type in a value. Insert block inserts a single block of code.

- Insert before: This is the first section of code in a wraparound snippet. The cursor will be positioned immediately after the code you enter here. If you select the Insert block radio button, the Insert before and Insert after fields are merged into a single one labeled Insert code.

- Insert after: This applies only to a wraparound snippet. Enter the code you want to appear after the cursor.

- Preview type: This determines how the snippet is displayed in the preview pane at the top of the Snippets panel. Snippets can consist of HTML code. So, selecting Design shows the output rather than the underlying code in the preview pane.

3. Enter Sticky input value in the Name field.

4. Type a brief description in the Description field. I used this: Redisplays user input by inserting value attribute when $missing is set.

5. Select the Wrap selection radio button, and enter the following code in the Insert before field:

```php
<?php if (isset($missing)) {
  echo 'value="' . htmlentities($_POST['
```

6. Enter the following code in the Insert after field:

```php
'], ENT_COMPAT, 'UTF-8') . '"';
} ?>
```

7. Select the Code radio button for Preview type, and click OK to save the snippet.

That's all there is to creating a snippet. As well as typing in the code directly as you have done here, you can also select existing code in the Document window and choose Create New Snippet from the context menu. Dreamweaver automatically inserts the selected code in the Insert before field.

To edit a snippet, select it in the Snippets panel, right-click, and select Edit from the context menu.

Creating sticky form fields

Now that you have a new snippet to cut down on the coding, let's put it to work.

1. Insert a blank line just before the closing /> of the <input> tag for the Name text field like this:

```
<input name="name" type="text" class="textInput" id="name"

/>
```

2. With your cursor on the blank line, double-click Sticky input value in the Snippets panel. Alternatively, select the snippet, and click the Insert button at the bottom of the Snippets panel, or right-click and select Insert from the context menu.

   Dreamweaver should insert the code in the snippet and leave your cursor in the right position to type the name of the $_POST array element, as shown here:

```
89          <input name="name" type="text" class="textInput" id="name"
90          <?php if (isset($missing)) {
91      echo 'value="' . htmlentities($_POST['|'], ENT_COMPAT, 'UTF-8') . '"';
92      } ?>
93              />
```

> *In my testing, I found that Dreamweaver inserted the cursor after the pair of single quotes instead of between them. The only way I could correct this problem was by adding a space before the closing quote in the Insert after field of the Snippets dialog box (see Figure 11-9). I decided that moving the cursor one character to the left with my arrow keys was still a lot easier than typing the full code every time.*

3. Make sure your cursor is between the single quotes of $_POST[''], and enter name so that it reads $_POST['name'].

4. Repeat steps 1–3 to amend the email input field in the same way, entering email instead of name between the quotes of $_POST['']

5. The comments text area needs to be handled slightly differently, because <textarea> tags don't have a value attribute. You place the PHP block between the opening and closing tags of the text area like this (new code is shown in bold):

```
<textarea name="comments" id="comments" cols="45" rows="5"><?php
  if (isset($missing)) {
    echo htmlentities($_POST['comments'], ENT_COMPAT, 'UTF-8');
  } ?></textarea>
```

It's important to position the opening and closing PHP tags right up against the <textarea> tags. If you don't, you'll get unwanted whitespace in the text area.

11

6. Save feedback.php, and test the page. If the first test message earlier in the chapter was successful, you can upload it to your remote server. If any required fields are omitted, the form displays the original content along with any error messages. However, if the form is correctly filled in, the email is sent, an acknowledgment is displayed, and the input fields are cleared.

If your remote server test didn't succeed earlier in the chapter, just test locally. You'll probably get a PHP error message if all required fields are filled in, but that's nothing to worry about. We're almost at the stage to get your remote server working.

You can check your code with feedback_06.php.

You might want to save the PHP code inserted in step 5 as another snippet. The easiest way is to highlight the whole section of PHP code, right-click, and select New Snippet from the context menu. You can then cut and paste the code inside the Snippets panel to split it between the Insert before and Insert after fields.

Filtering out potential attacks

A particularly nasty exploit known as **email header injection** emerged in mid-2005. It seeks to turn online forms into spam relays. A simple way of preventing this is to look for the strings "Content-Type:", "Cc:", and "Bcc:", because these are email headers that the attacker injects into your script in an attempt to trick it into sending HTML email with copies to many people. If you detect any of these strings in user input, it's a pretty safe bet that you're the target of an attack, so you should block the message. An innocent message may also be blocked, but the advantages of stopping an attack outweigh that small risk.

Blocking emails that contain specific phrases

In this section, we'll create a pattern to check for suspect phrases and pass the form input to a custom-built function that checks for any matches. The function is one of the snippets that you installed earlier in the chapter, so the most complex part of the coding is already done for you. If a match is found, a conditional statement prevents the email from being sent.

1. PHP conditional statements rely on a true/false test to determine whether to execute a section of code. So, the way to filter out suspect phrases is to create a Boolean variable that is switched to true as soon as one of those phrases is detected. The detection is done using a search pattern or regular expression. Insert the code for both of these just above the section that processes the $_POST variables:

```
// create empty array for any missing fields
$missing = array();

// assume that there is nothing suspect
$suspect = false;
```

```
// create a pattern to locate suspect phrases
$pattern = '/Content-Type:|Bcc:|Cc:/i';

// process the $_POST variables
```

The string assigned to $pattern will be used to perform a case-insensitive search for any of the following: "Content-Type:", "Bcc:", or "Cc:". It's written in a format called Perl-compatible regular expression (PCRE). The search pattern is enclosed in a pair of forward slashes, and the i after the final slash makes the pattern case-insensitive.

2. You can now use $pattern to filter out any suspect user input from the $_POST array. At the moment, each element of the $_POST array contains only a string. However, multiple-choice form elements, such as checkboxes, return an array of results. So, you need to tunnel down any subarrays and check the content of each element separately. In the snippets collection you installed earlier in the chapter, you'll find a custom-built function to do precisely that.

Insert two blank lines immediately after the $pattern variable from step 1. Then open the Snippets panel, and double-click Suspect pattern filter in the PHP-DWCS4 folder to insert the code shown here in bold:

```
// create a pattern to locate suspect phrases
$pattern = '/Content-Type:|Bcc:|Cc:/i';

// function to check for suspect phrases
function isSuspect($val, $pattern, &$suspect) {
  // if the variable is an array, loop through each element
  // and pass it recursively back to the same function
  if (is_array($val)) {
    foreach ($val as $item) {
      isSuspect($item, $pattern, $suspect);
    }
  } else {
    // if one of the suspect phrases is found, set Boolean to true
    if (preg_match($pattern, $val)) {
      $suspect = true;
    }
  }
}
```

3. I won't go into detail about how this code works. All you need to know is that calling the isSuspect() function is very easy. You just pass it three values: the $_POST array, the pattern, and the $suspect Boolean variable. Insert the following code immediately after the code in the previous step:

```
// check the $_POST array and any subarrays for suspect content
isSuspect($_POST, $pattern, $suspect);
```

4. If any suspect phrases are detected, the value of $suspect changes to true, so you need to set $mailSent to false and delete the $missing array to prevent the email from being sent and to display an appropriate message in the form. There's also no

11

point in processing the $_POST array any further. Wrap the code that processes the $_POST variables in the second half of an `if . . . else` statement like this:

```
if ($suspect) {
  $mailSent = false;
  unset($missing);
} else {
  // process the $_POST variables
  foreach ($_POST as $key => $value) {
    // assign to temporary variable and strip whitespace if not an array
    $temp = is_array($value) ? $value : trim($value);
    // if empty and required, add to $missing array
    if (empty($temp) && in_array($key, $required)) {
      array_push($missing, $key);
      }
    // otherwise, assign to a variable of the same name as $key
    elseif (in_array($key, $expected)) {
      ${$key} = $temp;
      }
    }
  }
```

Don't forget the extra curly brace to close the `else` statement.

5. If suspect content is detected, you don't want the code that builds and sends the email to run, so amend the condition in the opening `if` statement like this:

```
// go ahead only if not suspect and all required fields OK
if (!$suspect && empty($missing)) {
  // build the message
```

6. Save feedback.php, and check your code against feedback_07.php.

Because the `if` statement in step 4 sets $mailSent to false and unsets $missing if it detects any suspect pattern, the code in the main body of the page displays the same message that's displayed if there's a genuine problem with the server. A neutral message reveals nothing that might assist an attacker. It also avoids offending anyone who may have innocently used a suspect phrase.

You can use isSuspect() with any array or pattern, but it always requires the following three arguments:

- An array that you want to filter. If the array contains other arrays, the function burrows down until it finds a simple value against which it can match the pattern.

- A regular expression containing the pattern(s) you want to search for. There are two types of regular expression, Perl-compatible regular expression (PCRE) and Portable Operating System Interface (POSIX). You must use a PCRE. This function won't work with a POSIX regular expression. A good online source is http://regexlib.com.

- A Boolean variable set to false. If the pattern is found, the value is switched to true.

Safely including the user's address in email headers

Up to now, I've avoided using one of the most useful features of the PHP mail() function: the ability to add extra email headers with the optional fourth argument. A popular use of extra headers is to incorporate the user's email address into a Reply-To header, which enables you to reply directly to incoming messages by clicking the Reply button in your email program. It's convenient, but it provides a wide open door for an attacker to supply a spurious set of headers. With the isSuspect() function in place, you can block attacks and safely use the fourth argument with the mail() function.

The most important header you should add is From. Email sent by mail() is often identified as coming from nobody@*servername*. Adding the From header not only identifies your mail in a more user-friendly way, but it also solves the problem you might have encountered on the first test of there being no setting for sendmail_from in php.ini.

You can find a full list of email headers at http://www.faqs.org/rfcs/rfc2076, but some of the most well-known and useful ones enable you to send copies of an email to other addresses (Cc and Bcc) or to change the encoding (often essential for languages other than Western European ones).

Like the body of the email message, headers must be passed to the mail() function as a single string. Each new header, except the final one, must be on a separate line terminated by a carriage return and newline character. This means using the \r and \n escape sequences in double-quoted strings.

Let's say you want to send copies of messages to other departments, plus a copy to another address that you don't want the others to see. This is how you pass those additional email headers to mail():

```
$headers = "From: Essential Guide<feedback@example.com>\r\n";
$headers .= "Cc: sales@example.com, finance@example.com\r\n";
$headers .= 'Bcc: secretplanning@example.com';

$mailSent = mail($to, $subject, $message, $headers);
```

The default encoding for email is iso-8859-1 (English and Western European). If you want to use a different encoding, set the Content-Type header. Dreamweaver uses Unicode (UTF-8) as its default, so you need to add a header like this:

```
$headers .= "Content-Type: text/plain; charset=utf-8\r\n";
```

The web page that the form is embedded in must use the same encoding (usually set in a <meta> tag). The preceding code assumes other headers will follow. If it's the final header, omit the \r\n sequence at the end of the line.

Hard-coded additional headers present no security risk, but anything that comes from user input must be filtered before it's used.

11

Adding email headers and automating the reply address

This section incorporates the user's email address into a Reply-To header. Although isSuspect() should sanitize user input, it's worth subjecting the email field to a more rigorous check to make sure that it doesn't contain illegal characters or more than one address.

1. At the moment, the $required array doesn't include email, and you may be happy to leave it that way. So, to keep the validation routine flexible, it makes more sense to handle the email address outside the main loop that processes the $_POST array.

   - If email is required but has been left blank, the loop will have already added email to the $missing array, so the message won't get sent anyway.

   - If it's not a required field, you need to check $email only if it contains something. So, you need to wrap the validation code in an if statement that uses !empty().

   Insert the code shown in bold after the loop that processes the $_POST array.

   ```
       // otherwise, assign to a variable of the same name as $key
       elseif (in_array($key, $expected)) {
         ${$key} = $temp;
       }
     }
   }

   // validate the email address
   if (!empty($email)) {

   }

   // go ahead only if not suspect and all required fields OK
   if (!$suspect && empty($missing)) {
   ```

2. Position your cursor on the blank line between the curly braces of the conditional statement you have just inserted. Open the Snippets panel, and double-click Check email PCRE in the PHP-DWCS4 folder. This inserts the following regular expression:

   ```
   $checkEmail = '/^[^@]+@[^\s\r\n\'";,@%]+$/';
   ```

   Designing a regular expression to recognize a valid-looking email address is notoriously difficult. So, instead of striving for perfection, $checkEmail, takes a negative approach by rejecting characters that are illegal in an email address. However, to make sure that the input resembles an email address in some way, it checks for an @ mark surrounded by at least one character on either side.

3. Now add the code shown in bold to check $email against the regular expression:

   ```
   // validate the email address
   if (!empty($email)) {
     // regex to ensure no illegal characters in email address
     $checkEmail = '/^[^@]+@[^\s\r\n\'";,@%]+$/';
   ```

```
    // reject the email address if it doesn't match
    if (!preg_match($checkEmail, $email)) {
      $suspect = true;
      $mailSent = false;
      unset($missing);
    }
  }
```

The conditional statement uses the preg_match() function, which takes two arguments: a PCRE and the string you want to check. If a match is found, the function returns true. Since it's preceded by the negative operator, the condition is true if the contents of $email *don't* match the PCRE.

If there's no match, $suspect is set to true, $mailSent is set to false, and $missing is unset. This results in the neutral alert saying that the message can't be sent and clears the form. This runs the risk that someone who has accidentally mistyped the email address will be forced to enter everything again. If you don't want that to happen, you can omit unset($missing);. However, the PCRE detects illegal characters that are unlikely to be used by accident, so I have left it in.

> *Many popular PHP scripts use pattern-matching functions that begin with* ereg. *These work only with POSIX regular expressions. I recommend you always use the PCRE functions that begin with* preg_. *Not only is PCRE more efficient, support for the* ereg *family of functions has been removed from PHP 6.*

4. Now add the additional headers to the email. Place them immediately above the call to the mail() function, and add $headers as the fourth argument like this:

```
// limit line length to 70 characters
$message = wordwrap($message, 70);

// create additional headers
$headers = "From: Essential Guide<feedback@example.com>\r\n";
$headers .= 'Content-Type: text/plain; charset=utf-8';
if (!empty($email)) {
  $headers .= "\r\nReply-To: $email";
}

// send it
$mailSent = mail($to, $subject, $message, $headers);
```

Use your own email address in the first header, rather than the dummy one shown here.

The second header assumes you are using the Dreamweaver default encoding. If you are using a different character encoding on your page, you need to change charset=utf-8 to the appropriate value for your character set. You can find the correct value by inspecting the Content-Type <meta> tag in the <head> of your web page.

11

If you don't want email to be a required field, there's no point in using a nonexistent value in the Reply-To header, so I have wrapped it in a conditional statement. Since you have no way of telling whether the Reply-To header will be created, it makes sense to put the carriage return and newline characters at the beginning of the second header. It doesn't matter whether you put them at the end of one header or the start of the next one, as long as a carriage return and newline character separate each header. For instance, if you wanted to add a Cc header, you could do it like this:

```
$headers = "From: Essential Guide<feedback@example.com>\r\n";
$headers .= "Content-Type: text/plain; charset=utf-8\r\n";
$headers .= 'Cc: admin@example.com';
if (!empty($email)) {
  $headers .= "\r\nReply-To: $email";
}
```

Or like this:

```
$headers = "From: Essential Guide<feedback@example.com>\r\n";
$headers .= 'Content-Type: text/plain; charset=utf-8';
$headers .= "\r\nCc: admin@example.com";
if (!empty($email)) {
  $headers .= "\r\nReply-To: $email";
}
```

5. Save feedback.php, upload it to your remote server, and test the form. When you receive the email, click the Reply button in your email program, and you should see the address that you entered in the form automatically entered in the recipient's address field. You can check your code against feedback_08.php.

> *When building your own forms, don't forget to add the name of each text field to the $expected array. Also add the name of required fields to the $required array, and add a suitable alert as described in "Checking required fields."*

What if you still don't get an email?

For security reasons, some hosting companies require a fifth argument to mail(). Normally, it takes the form of a string comprised of -f followed by your email address like this:

```
'-fdavid@example.com'
```

Add it to the line of code that sends the mail like this:

```
$mailSent = mail($to,$subject,$message,$headers,'-fdavid@example.com');
```

If using this fifth argument does not work, ask your hosting company for a sample script for sending email. Some companies tell you to use ini_set() to adjust a setting called sendmail_from. The $headers in the previous section should avoid the need to do this.

However, if you still get an error message about sendmail_from, amend the preceding code like this (use your own email address instead of david@example.com):

```
ini_set('sendmail_from', 'david@example.com');
$mailSent = mail($to,$subject,$message,$headers,'-fdavid@example.com');
```

Handling multiple-choice form elements

You now have the basic knowledge to process text input from an online form and email it to your inbox. The principle behind handling multiple-choice elements is exactly the same: the name attribute is used as the key in the $_POST array. However, as you saw in Chapter 9, checkboxes and multiple-choice lists don't appear in the $_POST array if nothing has been selected, so they require different treatment.

The following exercises show you how to handle each type of multiple-choice element. If you're feeling punch drunk at this stage, come back later to study how to handle multiple-choice elements when you need to incorporate them into a script of your own.

Getting data from checkboxes

In Chapter 9, I showed you how to create a checkbox group, which stores all checked values in a subarray of the $_POST array. However, the subarray isn't even created if all boxes are left unchecked. So, you need to use isset() to check the existence of the subarray before attempting to process it.

1. Add the name of the checkbox group to the $expected array like this:

   ```
   $expected = array('name', 'email', 'comments', 'interests');
   ```

   In the form, interests is followed by square brackets like this:

   ```
   <input type="checkbox" name="interests[]" . . .
   ```

   The square brackets in the form tell the $_POST array to store all checked values in a subarray called $_POST['interests']. However, *don't* add square brackets to interests in the $expected array. Doing so would bury the checked values in a subarray one level deeper than you want. See "Using arrays to store multiple values" in Chapter 10 for a reminder of how arrays are created.

2. If you want the checkboxes to be required, add the name of the checkbox group to the $required array in the same way.

3. Because the checkbox array might never be created, you need to set a default value before processing the $_POST variables. You need to do this even if you're not making the checkbox group required, because it affects the way the message is built. The following code in bold goes after the $missing array is initialized:

   ```
   // create empty array for any missing fields
   $missing = array();
   // set default values for variables that might not exist
   if (!isset($_POST['interests'])) {
     $_POST['interests'] = array();
   }
   ```

11

This uses a conditional statement to check whether $_POST['interests'] has been set. If it hasn't, it's initialized as an empty array. This will trigger the code that processes the $_POST variables to add interests to the $missing array if no checkbox has been selected.

4. If you want more than one checkbox to be required, you need to add another test immediately after the code in the previous step like this:

```
// minimum number of required checkboxes
$minCheckboxes = 2;
// if fewer than required add to $missing array
if (count($_POST['interests']) < $minCheckboxes) {
  $missing[] = 'interests';
}
```

This sets a variable containing the minimum number of required checkboxes (I'm using a variable so the number can be reused in the error message) and then compares it with the number of elements in $_POST['interests']. The count() function, as you might expect, counts the number of elements in an array.

5. To extract the values of the checkbox array, you can use the oddly named implode() function, which joins array elements. It takes two arguments: a string to be used as a separator and the array. So, implode(', ', $interests) joins the elements of $interests as a comma-separated string. Add the following code shown in bold to the script that builds the body of the email:

```
$message .= "Comments: $comments\r\n\r\n";
$message .= 'Interests: '.implode(', ', $interests);
```

Note that I added two newline characters at the end of the line that adds the user's comments to the email. On the following line, I put Interests: in single quotes because there are no variables to be processed, and I used the concatenation operator to join the result of implode(', ', $interests) to the end of the email message. You cannot include a function inside a string.

6. If you have made the checkbox group required, add an alert like this:

```
<p><strong>What aspects of London most interest you?</strong>
<?php if (isset($missing) && in_array('interests', $missing)) { ?>
<span class="warning">Please choose at least
<?php echo $minCheckboxes; ?></span><?php } ?>
</p>
```

This assumes you have set a value for $minCheckboxes in step 4. If you want only one checkbox selected, you can replace <?php echo $minCheckboxes; ?> with the word "one" inside the <span>.

7. The next listing shows the code for the first two checkboxes in the body of the page. The code in bold preserves the user's checkbox selections if any required field is missing.

```
<label>
<input type="checkbox" name="interests[]" value="Classical concerts" ➥
id="interests_0"
```

```php
<?php
if (isset($missing) && in_array('Classical concerts', ➡
$_POST['interests'])) {
    echo 'checked="checked"';
} ?>
/>Classical concerts</label>
<br />
<label>
<input type="checkbox" name="interests[]" value="Rock/pop" ➡
id="interests_1"
<?php
if (isset($missing) && in_array('Rock/pop', $_POST['interests'])) {
    echo 'checked="checked"';
} ?>
/>Rock & pop events</label>
```

The PHP code for each checkbox tests whether the $missing variable exists and whether the value of the checkbox is in the $_POST['interests'] subarray. If both are true, echo inserts checked="checked" into the <input> tag. (If you're using HTML instead of XHTML, use just checked.) Although it looks like a lot of hand-coding, you can copy and paste the code after creating the first one. Just change the first argument of in_array() to the value of the checkbox. The complete code is in feedback_09.php.

Getting data from radio button groups

Radio button groups allow you to pick only one value. This makes it easy to retrieve the selected one. All buttons in the same group must share the same name attribute, so the $_POST array contains the value attribute of whichever radio button is selected. However, if you don't set a default button in your form, the radio button group's $_POST array element remains unset.

1. Add the name of the radio button group to the $expected array.

2. If you haven't set a default button and you want a choice to be compulsory, also add it to the $required array. This isn't necessary if a default choice is set in the form.

3. If you haven't set a default button, you need to set a default value before building the body of the email message. You do this in a similar way to a checkbox group, but since a radio button group can have only one value, you set the default as an empty string, not an array, as shown in this example:

```php
if (!isset($_POST['radioGroup'])) {
    $_POST['radioGroup'] = '';
}
```

4. Add the value of the radio button group to the body of the message like this:

```php
$message .= 'Interests: '.implode(', ', $interests)."\r\n\r\n";
$message .= "Subscribe: $subscribe";
```

5. Assuming a default button has been defined, amend the radio button group like this:

```
<label>
  <input type="radio" name="subscribe" id="subscribeYes" value="y"
  <?php
  if (isset($missing) && $_POST['subscribe'] == 'y') {
    echo 'checked="checked"';
  } ?>
  />
Yes</label>
<label>
  <input name="subscribe" type="radio" id="subscribe-no" value="n"
  <?php
  if (!$_POST || isset($missing) && $_POST['subscribe'] == 'n') {
    echo 'checked="checked"';
  } ?>
  />
No</label>
```

The conditional statement for the default radio button begins with !$_POST ||, which means "if the $_POST array is empty *or* . . ." So, if the form hasn't been submitted or if the user has selected No and the form is incomplete, this button will be checked.

The completed script is in feedback_10.php.

You need to add a required alert only if no default has been defined in the original form.

Getting data from a drop-down menu

Drop-down menus created with the <select> tag normally allow the user to pick only one option from several. One item is always selected, even if it's only the first one inviting the user to select one of the others. Setting the value of this first <option> to 0 has the advantage that the empty() function, which is used to check required fields, returns true when 0 is passed to it either as a number or string.

1. Add the name of the drop-down menu to the $expected array. Also add it to the $required array if you want a choice to be compulsory.

2. Add the value of the drop-down menu to the email message like this:

```
$message .= "Subscribe: $subscribe\r\n\r\n";
$message .= "Visited: $visited";
```

One option will always be selected, so this doesn't need special treatment. However, change the value of the first <option> tag in the menu to No response if it isn't a required field. Leave it as 0 if you want the user to make a selection.

3. The following code shows the first two items of the drop-down menu in feedback.php. The PHP code highlighted in bold assumes that the menu has been made a required field and resets the selected option if an incomplete form is submitted. When the page first loads, the $_POST array contains no elements, so you can select the first <option> by testing for !$_POST. Once the form is submitted, the $_POST array always contains an element from a drop-down menu, so you don't need to test for it.

```
<label for="visited">How often have you been to London? <?php
if (isset($missing) && in_array('visited', $missing)) { ?>
  <span class="warning">Please select a value</span><?php } ?></label>
  <select name="visited" id="visited">
    <option value="0"
    <?php
    if (!$_POST || $_POST['visited'] == '0') {
      echo 'selected="selected"';
    } ?>
    >-- Select one --</option>
    <option value="Never"
    <?php
    if (isset($missing) && $_POST['visited'] == 'Never') {
      echo 'selected="selected"';
    } ?>
    >Never been</option>
    . . .
  </select>
```

When setting the second condition for each <option>, it's vital that you use the same spelling and mixture of uppercase and lowercase as contained in the value attribute. PHP is case-sensitive and won't match the two values if there are any differences.

The finished code is in feedback_11.php.

Getting data from a multiple-choice list

Multiple-choice lists are similar to checkboxes: they allow the user to choose zero or more items, so the result is stored in an array. If no items are selected, the $_POST array contains no reference to the list, so you need to take that into consideration both in the form and when processing the message.

1. Add the name of the multiple-choice list to the $expected array. Also add it to the $required array if you want a choice to be compulsory.

2. Set a default value for a multiple-choice list in the same way as for an array of checkboxes.

```
// set default values for variables that might not exist
if (!isset($_POST['interests'])) {
  $_POST['interests'] = array();
}
if (!isset($_POST['views'])) {
  $_POST['views'] = array();
}
```

3. When building the body of the message, use implode() to create a comma-separated string, and add it to the message like this:

```
$message .= "Visited: $visited\r\n\r\n";
$message .= 'Impressions of London: '.implode(', ', $views);
```

4. The following code shows the first two items from the multiple-choice list in feedback.php. The code works in an identical way to the checkboxes, except that you echo 'selected="selected"' instead of 'checked="checked"'. It also assumes you have made at least one selection required.

```
<label for="views">What image do you have of London? <?php
if (isset($missing) && in_array('views', $missing)) { ?>
  <span class="warning">Please select a value</span><?php } ?>
</label>
<select name="views[]" size="6" multiple="multiple" id="views">
  <option value="Vibrant/exciting"
  <?php
  if (isset($missing) && in_array('Vibrant/exciting', ➥
$_POST['views'])) {
     echo 'selected="selected"';
  } ?>
  >A vibrant, exciting city</option>
  <option value="Good food"
  <?php
  if (isset($missing) && in_array('Good food', $_POST['views'])) {
     echo 'selected="selected"';
  } ?>
  >A great place to eat</option>
  . . .
</select>
```

The completed code is in feedback_12.php.

If you want to make more than one item in the multiple-choice list required, create a variable for the minimum number of items, and use count() to add the name of the multiple-choice list to the $missing array in the same way as in step 4 of "Getting data from checkboxes."

Redirecting to another page

Everything has been kept within the same page, even if the message is sent successfully. To redirect the visitor to a different page, change the code at the end of the message-processing section like this:

```
// send it
$mailSent = mail($to, $subject, $message, $headers);
if ($mailSent) {
```

```
            // redirect the page with a fully qualified URL
            header('Location: http://www.example.com/thanks.php');
            exit;
        }
    }
}
```

The HTTP/1.1 protocol stipulates a fully qualified URL for a redirect command, although most browsers will perform the redirect correctly with a relative pathname.

When using the header() function, you must be careful that no output is sent to the browser before PHP attempts to call it. If, when testing your page, you see an error message warning you that headers have already been sent, check that there are no characters, including newline characters, spaces, or tabs, ahead of the opening PHP tag.

Blocking submission by spam bots

The battle against spam is never ending. The filters used in this chapter should prevent turning your form into a spam relay, but they won't stop spammers from using the form to send unwanted mail to your inbox. Most spam is sent by automated bots, so several techniques have been developed to try to prevent forms from being submitted automatically.

Using a CAPTCHA

One of the most common methods of combating spam is to use a CAPTCHA (Completely Automated Public Turing Test to Tell Computers and Humans Apart). This requires the user to decipher distorted text and type it into a field before submitting the form. Figure 11-10 shows a typical example. The idea is that such text is easy for humans to read but that it's beyond the capability of current computer programs.

Figure 11-10.
If a CAPTCHA is hard to read, it deters humans just as much as spam bots.

11

The problem with using a CAPTCHA is that, for the text to defeat optical character recognition, it needs to be difficult to read. I have pretty good eyes, but I found the first word in Figure 11-10 difficult to make out. If it weren't a real word, I would have difficulty guessing some of the letters. For anyone who is not a native speaker of English or with poor eyesight, it would be a major challenge. This particular example also has an audio button, but—for me at least—the audio test was even more difficult. It also assumes that the user has an audio player and speakers installed.

In theory, CAPTCHA is a good idea, but its major drawback lies in the need to make the test too difficult for computer programs to solve. As a result, it becomes more difficult for humans. So, there's a danger that using a CAPTCHA will prevent not only the spammers but also the people you want to use the form.

You can learn more about CAPTCHA at http://www.captcha.net.

Using a question in plain text

A simpler form of CAPTCHA asks a question in plain text, for example "What is the sum of three plus four?" If the answer is entered in a text input field called test, you could add the following code to the script in feedback.php after the $missing array is initialized:

```
if (empty($_POST['test']) || $_POST['test'] != 7 || ➡
strtolower($_POST['test']) != 'seven') {
  $missing[] = 'test';
}
```

This checks whether any value has been entered in the test field and whether its value gives the right answer either as a number or in words (strtolower() converts the answer to lowercase, so any combination of uppercase and lowercase is acceptable). If the field hasn't been filled in or the answer is wrong, test is added to the $missing array, preventing the mail from being processed.

The problem with this sort of solution is that its simplicity makes it relatively easy to break. It could be strengthened by rotating the questions on a random basis, but that makes the code much more complex.

Using a honeypot

Another technique is based on the principle that just like bears can't resist honey, spam bots can't resist filling in every field they find. A honeypot is a form field that's hidden from view in normal browsers, so it shouldn't contain any input. Give the field a name attribute that a spammer is likely to want to fill in, and give its surrounding paragraph an ID that gives no indication that you're using it as a honeypot, for example:

```
<p id="website">
  <label for="url">Website: </label>
  <input type="text" name="url" id="url" />
</p>
```

In your style sheet, create a style rule for the surrounding paragraph's ID like this:

```
#website {
  display: none;
}
```

In the form processing script, check whether $_POST['url'] contains a value. If it does, the form has almost certainly been filled in by a spam bot, so can be rejected. If you want to check that genuine form submissions aren't rejected by mistake, change the address and subject line of the email like this:

```
if (!empty($_POST['url'])) {
  $to = 'spamtrap@example.com';
  $subject = 'Suspected bot submission from feedback form';
} else {
  $to = 'me@example.com'; // use your own email address
  $subject = 'Feedback from Essential Guide';
}
```

On the other hand, if you want to dump all suspect submissions, set $suspect to true when $_POST['url'] contains a value like this:

```
// check the $_POST array and any subarrays for suspect content
isSuspect($_POST, $pattern, $suspect);
if (!empty($_POST['url'])) {
  $suspect = true;
}
```

No doubt, spammers will get wise to the existence of honeypots, but this technique appears to be reasonably successful at the time of this writing.

Chapter review

If that was your first encounter with PHP, your head will probably be reeling. This has been a tough chapter. In the next chapter, you'll adapt this script so that it can be reused as an external file with most forms. The external file never changes, and the hand-coding is cut down to about a dozen lines. I could, of course, have given you the external file without explanation, but if you don't understand the code, you can't adapt it to your own requirements. Even if you never write an original PHP script of your own, you should know what the code in your page is doing. If you don't, you're storing up trouble for the future.

What makes PHP pages dynamic—and so powerful—is the fact that your code makes decisions, even though you have no way of knowing in advance what is going to be input into the form. The Dreamweaver code that you'll encounter in subsequent chapters tries to anticipate a lot of these unknown factors, but its beauty lies in the fact that it's configurable. If you know how to hand-code, you can get Dreamweaver to do a lot of the hard work for you and then take it beyond the basics.

However, it's no fun spending all your time churning out code. Life becomes simpler if you can reuse code. So, that's what the next chapter is about—saving time with PHP includes.

11

Wouldn't it be wonderful if you could make changes to just a single page and have them reflected through the site in the same way as CSS? Well, with PHP includes, you can. As the name suggests, the contents of an include file are included and treated as an integral part of the page. They can contain anything you would normally find in a PHP page: plain text, HTML, and PHP code. The file name extension doesn't even need to be .php, although for security it's common practice to use it.

Dreamweaver makes working with includes easy thanks to its ability to display the contents of an include in Design view (or Live view for dynamic content).

In this chapter, you'll learn about the following:

- Using PHP includes for common page elements
- Applying CSS to page fragments with design-time style sheets
- Exporting a navigation menu to an external file
- Adapting the mail processing script to work with other forms
- Avoiding the "headers already sent" error with includes

To start with, let's take a quick look at how you create a PHP include.

Including text and code from other files

The ability to include code from other files is a core part of PHP. All that's necessary is to use one of PHP's include commands and tell the server where to find the file.

Introducing the PHP include commands

PHP has four separate commands for creating an include: include(), include_once(), require(), and require_once(). Why so many? And what's the difference?

They all do the same thing, but "require" is used in the sense of "mandatory"; everything comes to a grinding halt if the external file is missing or can't be opened. The "include" pair of commands, on the other hand, soldier bravely on. The purpose of _once is to prevent variables being accidentally overwritten and functions from being redefined (defining the same function more than once triggers a fatal error). The PHP engine uses the first instance it encounters and ignores any duplicates. If in doubt about which to use, choose include_once() or require_once(). Using them does no harm and could avoid problems.

Telling PHP where to find the external file

The include commands take a single argument: a string containing the path of the external file. While this sounds simple enough, it confuses many Dreamweaver users. PHP looks for the external file in what's known as the include_path. By default, this includes the current directory (folder), although some hosting companies configure PHP to restrict you to including files only from specified locations. In any case, PHP expects either a relative or an absolute path to an include file. *It won't work with a path relative to the site root.*

If Links relative to is set to Document in the Local Info category of your site definition (see Figure 12-1), Dreamweaver automatically uses the correct path for include files. However, if you have selected Site root as your default style for links, includes won't work unless you override the default setting to change the path to a document-relative one or take alternative measures to set the include_path.

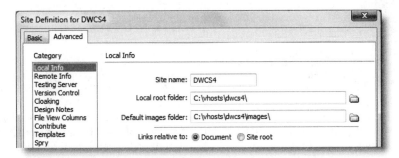

Figure 12-1. Dreamweaver's site definition dialog box lets you specify the default format of internal links.

A practical exercise should clarify the situation.

Including a text file

In this exercise, you'll see what happens if you use the wrong type of path for an include file. You'll also learn how to override the default setting so that you can use includes successfully even if your site definition specifies using links relative to the site root.

1. Create a new subfolder called includes in your workfiles folder, and copy include.txt from examples/includes to the new folder.

2. Go to File ➤ New. Select Blank Page and PHP for Page Type. Choose any of the predefined layouts. The one I chose was 2 column fixed, left sidebar. This is only going to be a test page, so you can leave Layout CSS on Add to Head. Click Create, and save the file as include_test.php in workfiles/ch12.

3. Position your cursor at the beginning of the first paragraph under the Main Content headline. Press Enter/Return to insert a new paragraph, and then press your up keyboard arrow to move the insertion point into the empty paragraph.

4. Select the PHP tab on the Insert bar, and click the Include button as shown in the following screenshot (alternatively use the menu option Insert ➤ PHP Objects ➤ Include). Dreamweaver opens Split view, inserts a PHP code block complete with an include() command, and positions the insertion point between the parentheses, ready for you to enter the path of the external file (it's on line 72 in the following screenshot).

12

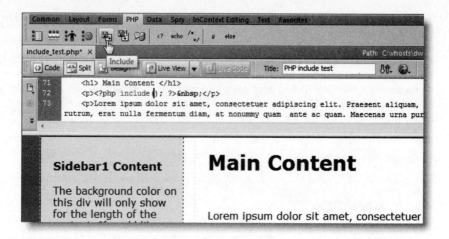

5. The path needs to be a string, so enter a quotation mark (I prefer a single quote, but it doesn't matter, as long as the closing quote matches). Dreamweaver's syntax coloring turns all the subsequent code red, but this reverts to normal once you have finished. Inserting the quotation mark places a tiny Browse icon at the insertion point like this:

> *Bringing up the* Browse *icon automatically is a small but welcome productivity improvement in Dreamweaver CS4. In previous versions, you needed to select* URL Browser *from* Code Hint Tools *on the context menu.*

6. Click the Browse icon to open the Select File dialog box. Navigate to the workfiles/includes folder, and select include.txt. Before clicking OK, check the setting of Relative to at the bottom of the dialog box. It displays Document or Site Root, depending on the default in your site definition (see Chapter 2 and Figure 12-1). If necessary, change it to Site Root, as shown here, and click OK:

7. Type a closing quote after the path that has just been entered into the include() command. Syntax coloring turns the rest of the code back to its normal color—a useful reminder of the importance of matching quotes. Move your cursor further along the line to remove the   just before the closing </p> tag.

The code in that line should now look like this:

```
<p><?php include('/workfiles/includes/include.txt'); ?></p>
```

8. Click inside Design view. The content of the external text file should be displayed just below the main heading. Magic . . . well, not quite.

9. Click the Live View button. Dreamweaver will ask whether you want to save the page and update it on the testing server. Click Yes in both cases. You should see something like Figure 12-2.

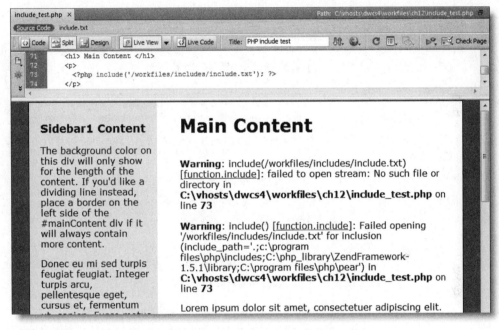

Figure 12-2. If PHP can't find the include file, it displays ugly warning messages.

The first warning says there was no such file or directory, but of course, there is. The second warning gives a cryptic clue as to why PHP can't open the file. The include_path is where PHP looks for include files. The value shown on your computer for include_path won't necessarily be the same as in Figure 12-2; the default on most web servers is . (a period), which is shorthand for the current working directory, and either the main PHP folder or pear (PEAR—the PHP Extension and Application Repository—is a library of extensions to PHP).

What these warnings are telling you is that PHP doesn't understand a leading forward slash as meaning the site root, so it starts from the current folder and ends up in a nonexistent part of the site.

10. Switch off Live view, and delete the value between the parentheses of include().

12

11. Repeat steps 5 and 6 to include `.txt` again, but this time make sure that Relative to is set to Document. Switch on Live view again, saving and updating the files when prompted. The content of the include file should now be correctly displayed, as shown in Figure 12-3.

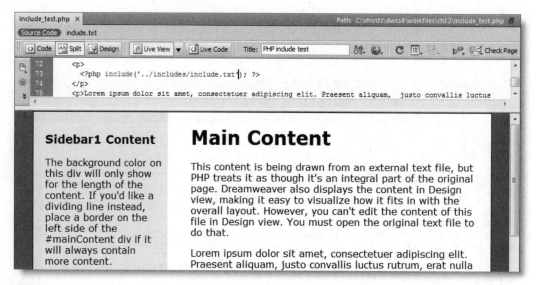

Figure 12-3. The include file is displayed correctly when a relative path is used.

12. Switch off Live view, and change the command from `include` to `require` like this:

```php
<?php require('../includes/include/txt'); ?>
```

13. Test the page again in Live view. It should look identical to Figure 12-3.

14. Change the path to point to a nonexistent file, such as `includ.txt`. When you test the page in Live view, it should look similar to Figure 12-2, but instead of the second warning, you should see Fatal error. The other difference is that there's no text after the error message. As explained in "Understanding PHP error messages" in Chapter 10, any output preceding a fatal error is displayed, but once the error is encountered, everything else is killed stone dead.

Using site-root-relative links with includes

As you have just seen, PHP cannot find include files referenced by a link relative to the site root. My recommendation is that, if you have selected links relative to the site root as your default, you simply select Relative to Document in the Select File dialog box (as described in step 11 of the preceding exercise) when creating an include.

Nevertheless, there are a couple of alternatives if you have a pressing reason for wanting to use links relative to the site root. The problem is that they don't work on all servers.

The virtual() function accepts both document-relative and site-root-relative paths and can be used as a direct replacement for include() and require(). It works only when PHP is run as an Apache module.

$_SERVER['DOCUMENT_ROOT'] is a predefined PHP variable that contains the path of the server's root folder, so adding it to the beginning of a site-root-relative link has the effect of turning it into an absolute path. The following works on most servers:

```
<?php include($_SERVER['DOCUMENT_ROOT'].'/workfiles/includes/ ➡
include/txt'); ?>
```

Unfortunately, $_SERVER['DOCUMENT_ROOT'] isn't supported by IIS running PHP in CGI mode.

To check whether your server supports either method, run server_check.php in examples/ch12. If both are supported, you should see output similar to this:

The preceding screenshot shows the output from my local testing server, but it's important to test your remote server as well. If neither virtual() nor $_SERVER['DOCUMENT_ROOT'] is supported and you still want to use site-root-relative links, you need to define a **constant** containing the path to the site root. A constant is like a variable, except that once defined in a script, its value cannot be changed. Constants don't begin with a dollar sign, and by convention, they are always in uppercase. You define a constant like this:

```
define('SITE_ROOT', 'C:\inetpub\wwwroot\dwcs4');
```

You could then use SITE_ROOT with a site-root-relative link like this:

```
<?php include(SITE_ROOT.'/workfiles/includes/include/txt'); ?>
```

The disadvantage with this approach is that you need to include the definition of the constant in every page that uses includes.

> *The restriction on site-root-relative links applies only to the include command. Inside include files, all links should be site-root-relative. Document-relative links inside an include file will be broken if the file is included at a different level of the site hierarchy.*

12

Lightening your workload with includes

So far, you have seen only a fairly trivial use of an include to insert a block of text inside a paragraph. This might be useful in a situation where you want to change the content of part of a page on a frequent basis without going to the bother of building a database-driven content management system. A much more practical use of includes is for content that appears on many pages, for example a navigation menu or footer. Any changes made to the include file are immediately reflected throughout the site.

Choosing the right file name extension for include files

As I explained at the beginning of the chapter, the external file doesn't need to have a .php file name extension. Many developers use .inc as the default file name extension to make it clear that the file is an include. Although this a common convention, Dreamweaver doesn't automatically recognize an .inc file as containing PHP code, so you don't get code hints or syntax coloring. More importantly, browsers don't understand .inc files. So, if anybody accesses an .inc file directly through a browser (as opposed to it being included as part of a PHP page), everything is displayed as plain text.

This is a potential security risk if you put passwords or other sensitive information in external files. One way around this problem is to store include files outside the server root folder. Many hosting companies provide you with a private folder, which cannot be reached by a browser. As long as the PHP script knows where to find the external file *and* has permission to access it, include files can be outside the server root. However, this creates problems for Dreamweaver site management.

A simpler, widely adopted solution is to use .inc.php as the file name extension. Browsers and servers treat only the final .php as the file name extension and automatically pass the file to the PHP engine if requested directly. The .inc is simply a reminder to you as the developer that this is an include file.

As long as you store passwords and other sensitive information as PHP variables within PHP code blocks and you use .php as the final file name extension, your data cannot be seen by anyone accessing the page directly in a browser (of course, it will be revealed if your code uses echo or print to display that information, but I assume you have the sense not to do that).

Displaying HTML output

When PHP includes an external file, it automatically treats the contents of the external file as plain text or HTML. This means that you can cut a section out of an existing page built in HTML and convert it into an include file. In order to preserve your sanity, it's important to put only complete, logical elements in external files. Putting the opening part of a <div> in one external file and the closing part in another file is a disaster waiting to happen. It becomes impossible to keep track of opening and closing tags, and Dreamweaver is likely to start trying to replace what it regards as missing tags.

Usually, I find the best approach is to build the complete page first and then convert common elements into include files.

Converting a navigation menu into an include

This exercise shows you how to extract the menu from the "Stroll along the Thames" site in Chapter 6 and convert it into an include file. The menu bar currently contains only dummy links. I'll show you later in this chapter how to edit the menu to update the links.

1. Copy `stroll_horiz.php` and `stroll.css` from examples/ch12 to workfiles/ch12. This is an identical copy of the completed page from Chapter 6. The only difference is that the file name extension has been changed to `.php` so that the PHP engine knows to process it and include the external files you are about to create. Test the page in a browser to make sure it displays correctly. It should look like Figure 12-4.

Figure 12-4. The menu is the same on every page of the site, so it is a prime candidate for an include file.

2. Create a new PHP file, and save it in the workfiles/includes folder as `menu.inc.php`. You don't need one of the CSS layouts, because you need a completely blank page. Switch to Code view in `menu.inc.php`, and delete everything, including the DOCTYPE declaration. There should be nothing left in the page.

3. Switch to `stroll_horiz.php` in the Document window. Click anywhere inside the navigation menu, and click <div#nav> in the Tag selector to select the entire menu. Switch to Code view, and then cut the menu to your computer clipboard (Ctrl+X/Cmd+X or Edit ➤ Cut).

You must be in Code view when cutting the menu to the clipboard. If you remain in Design view, Dreamweaver cuts all the Spry-related code and pastes it into the include file. You want to move only the HTML code and the Spry object initialization, but they're in different parts of the page, so it has to be done in two steps. Click No if Dreamweaver displays the warning shown in the preceding screenshot at any time during the next few steps. Once you move the initialization script, the warning message no longer appears.

4. Without moving the insertion point, click the Include button on the PHP tab of the Insert bar (or use the menu alternative). This inserts a PHP code block and positions your cursor between the parentheses of an `include()` command.

5. Type a single quote, and click the Browse icon to navigate to `menu.inc.php` in the `workfiles/includes` folder in the same way as in "Including a text file" earlier in the chapter. In the Select File dialog box, make sure Relative to is set to Document. Click OK, and type a closing quote after the path. Save `stroll_horiz.php`.

6. Switch to `menu.inc.php` in the Document window. Make sure you are in Code view, and paste the menu that you cut from `stroll_horiz.php`. (If you are in Design view, you won't get all the HTML code. Always cut and paste in the same view in Dreamweaver—Design view to Design view or Code view to Code view.)

7. Go back to `stroll_horiz.php`, scroll down to the bottom of the page, and cut to your clipboard the section of code highlighted on lines 53–57 in the following screenshot:

```
52    <!-- end #container --></div>
53 ▤  <script type="text/javascript">
54    <!--
55    var MenuBar1 = new Spry.Widget.MenuBar("MenuBar1", {imgDown:"../../SpryAssets/SpryMenuBarDownHover.gif",
      imgRight:"../../SpryAssets/SpryMenuBarRightHover.gif"});
56    //-->
57 ▤  </script>
58    </body>
59    </html>
```

This is the initialization script for the Spry menu bar. Make sure you have the opening and closing <script> tags.

8. Paste the Spry object initialization script into menu.inc.php after the closing </div> tag. Save menu.inc.php, and close the file.

9. Switch to Design view in stroll_horiz.php. The menu should be visible as it was before. If you can't see the menu, open Preferences from the Edit menu (Dreamweaver menu on a Mac), select the Invisible Elements category, and make sure there's a check mark in Server-Side includes: Show contents of included file.

10. Hover your mouse pointer over the navigation menu, and click the turquoise Spry Menu Bar tab at the top-left corner. The Property inspector recognizes it as a server-side include (SSI) and displays the name of the file, together with an Edit button, as shown in Figure 12-5. If the Spry Menu Bar tab doesn't appear, make sure there's a check mark alongside Invisible Elements in the View ➤ Visual Aids submenu.

Figure 12-5. The Property inspector provides a direct link to edit the include file.

If the Related Files feature is enabled, clicking the Edit button in the Property inspector opens the include file in Split view ready for editing. Frequently, though, it's better to open the include file as a separate file so that you can edit it in Design view as well as in Code view. To do so, right-click the include file's name in the Related Files toolbar, and select Open as Separate File.

If you have disabled Related Files, clicking Edit opens the file in a separate tab.

11. Test stroll_horiz.php in a browser. It should look like Figure 12-4, and the menu should work as before. You can check your code against stroll_horiz_menu.php in examples/ch12 and menu.inc.php in examples/includes.

> An annoying quirk in the way Dreamweaver handles PHP includes in Design view is that the include command must be in its own PHP code block. If you put any other PHP code in the same block—even a comment—Dreamweaver just displays the gold PHP shield.

12

Putting the Spry object initialization script at the end of menu.inc.php results in it being called earlier than it was in the original page, but it's still in the right order and doesn't result in invalid code. It also prevents the warning in step 3 from being displayed every time you open the parent page.

An added advantage is that you can edit the Spry menu through the Property inspector in the same way as in Chapter 6. Even though the include file has no direct link to the Spry menu bar external JavaScript file, Dreamweaver automatically finds it because the Spry assets folder is specified in the site definition.

However, what you put in an external file doesn't always have such benign consequences.

Avoiding problems with include files

The server incorporates the content of an include file into the page at the point of the include command. If you pasted all the Spry-related code into menu.inc.php, rather than just the constructor, you would end up with the link to the external style sheet within the <body> of stroll_horiz.php. Although some browsers might render the page correctly, <style> blocks are invalid outside the <head> of a web page. If it doesn't break now, it probably will sooner or later as browsers get increasingly standards-compliant.

The most common mistake with include files is adding duplicate <head> and <body> tags. Keep your include files free of extraneous code, and make sure when everything fits back together that you have a DOCTYPE declaration, a single <head> and <body>, and that everything is in the right order.

Dreamweaver depends on the DOCTYPE declaration at the top of a page to determine whether to use XHTML rules. Code added to an include will normally use HTML style, so when editing an include, you need to keep a close eye on what is happening in Code view. This is why I recommend extracting code into include files only toward the end of a project or if the external file uses mainly dynamic code.

Another common problem is a broken link in an include file. Always use links relative to the site root inside include files. As explained in Chapter 2, root-relative links provide a constant reference to a page or an asset, such as an image. If you use document-relative links inside an include file, the relationship—and therefore the link—is broken if the file is included at a different level of the site hierarchy than where it was originally designed.

Let's test that with the menu bar that was extracted to an external file in the preceding exercise.

Updating links in the menu bar

This exercise demonstrates the importance of using root-relative links in an include file. It updates two of the links in menu.inc.php, the include file created in the preceding exercise. Continue working with the same files.

1. With stroll_horiz.php open in the Document window, right-click menu.inc.php in the Related Files toolbar, and select Open as Separate File, as shown here:

2. This opens menu.inc.php in a separate tab. The menu bar displays as an unstyled unordered list (see Figure 12-6). In the next section, I'll show you how you can display the styles while working on an include file like this. However, that's not important at the moment. What you're interested in is updating the links.

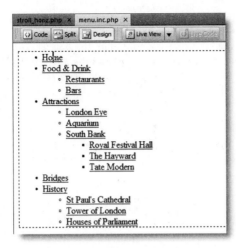

Figure 12-6.
The menu bar is unstyled
in the include file.

If you prefer working with the Spry menu bar Property inspector, select the Spry
Menu Bar turquoise tab at the top left of the unordered list. However, I think it's
quicker to just click inside the individual links and use the HTML view of the
Property inspector.

Whichever method you use, select the Home link, click the Browse for File icon to the
right of the Link field in the Property inspector, and navigate to stroll_horiz.php
in the workfiles/ch12 folder. Make sure Relative to in the Select File dialog box is set
to Document, as shown in the following screenshot (I'm deliberately doing this to
demonstrate what happens when you use document-relative links in an include file):

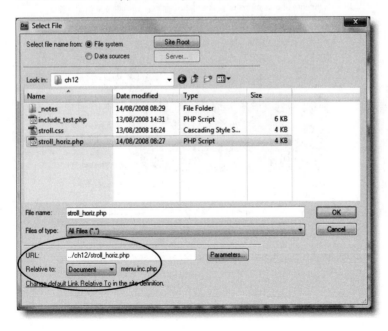

3. Click OK to update the link. Then select the London Eye link, and create a link to eye.php, which is in the examples/ch12/attractions folder. Also make sure Relative to is set to Document, and click OK to update the link. There is no need to move eye.php to the workfiles folder. I have created the page so that it automatically includes your version of menu.inc.php from workfiles/includes.

4. Save menu.inc.php, switch back to horiz_stroll.php, and press F12/Opt+F12 to load the page into a browser. Click Yes when asked whether you want to update the page on the testing server.

5. Mouse over Attractions in the menu bar to reveal the drop-down menu, and click London Eye. You should see the page shown in Figure 12-7.

Figure 12-7. The menu navigates successfully to a page at a different level in the site hierarchy.

6. Now click the Home link in the new page. This time, you should see something similar to Figure 12-8.

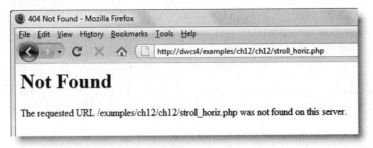

Figure 12-8. Document-relative links prevent the menu from navigating back to the correct location.

If you're using the same site structure as I am, you'll see that the menu has tried to find stroll_horiz.php in the examples folder, rather than return to your workfiles folder. Not only that, but it's trying to find two levels of ch12. Although the browser was able to find the correct file the first time, document-relative links make it impossible for an include file to navigate through a complex site structure. Using document-relative links works only if you keep everything in the same folder.

7. Return to menu.inc.php, and update the Home and London Eye links. They should still point to the same pages, but this time select Site Root as the value for Relative to. The values in the URL field should look like this:

```
/workfiles/ch12/stroll_horiz.php
/examples/ch12/attractions/eye.php
```

This works only if you have set up your testing server as a virtual host in Apache or as a web site in IIS7.

If you defined your site in a subfolder of the server root, you need to prefix these values with the name of the subfolder preceded by a forward slash. For example, if you created the site in a subfolder of the server root called dwcs4 and you use http://localhost/dwcs4/workfiles/ch12/stroll_horiz.php to display the first page, you need to manually adjust the preceding values like this:

```
/dwcs4/workfiles/ch12/stroll_horiz.php
/dwcs4/examples/ch12/attractions/eye.php
```

If you have built the site in your Sites folder on a Mac, you need to add your username as well, like this:

```
/~username/dwcs4/workfiles/ch12/stroll_horiz.php
/~username/dwcs4/examples/ch12/attractions/eye.php
```

8. The script that initializes the menu bar also uses document-relative links like this:

```
var MenuBar1 = new Spry.Widget.MenuBar("MenuBar1", ➡
{imgDown:"../../SpryAssets/SpryMenuBarDownHover.gif", ➡
imgRight:"../../SpryAssets/SpryMenuBarRightHover.gif"});
```

12

Because the include file always remains in the same location relative to the SpryAssets folder, you don't need to edit these links. However, for the sake of consistency, it's a good idea to do so. Remove the `../..` from the beginning of both links like this:

```
var MenuBar1 = new Spry.Widget.MenuBar("MenuBar1", ➥
{imgDown:"/SpryAssets/SpryMenuBarDownHover.gif", ➥
imgRight:"/SpryAssets/SpryMenuBarRightHover.gif"});
```

9. Save `menu.inc.php` and reload `stroll_horiz.php` in a browser. You should now be able to navigate successfully between the Home and London Eye pages.

> *The instructions in step 7 for prefixing the links with the server root subfolder are purely for the benefit of this exercise. When deploying the file on a live site, you would need to remove the /dwcs4 or /~username/dwcs4 from each link, making the process cumbersome and prone to error. If you plan to use links in include files, it's essential to set up your testing server in a virtual host or a standalone web site in IIS7 (see Chapter 2 for details).*

Applying styles with design-time style sheets

Although Dreamweaver displays the menu normally in `stroll_horiz.php`, it looks completely different in `menu.inc.php`. As Figure 12-6 shows, the menu is completely unstyled; all you can see is the underlying series of nested unordered lists. Design-time style sheets let you apply the styles in an external style sheet to a page or code fragment without the need to attach the style sheet directly to the page. As the name suggests, the style sheet is applied only at design time; in other words, it's applied in Design view.

To apply design-time style sheets to a page or an include file, select CSS Styles ➤ Design-time from either the Format menu or from the context menu when right-clicking in Design view. This opens the Design-Time Style Sheets dialog box, as shown in the following screenshot:

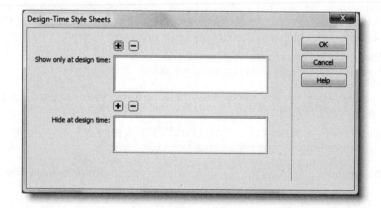

The dialog box has two sections. The first one, Show only at design time, lets you apply a style sheet without attaching it to the file. The second one, Hide at design time, works with style sheets that are attached to a file, letting you hide the effect of selected style sheets while working in Design view. It's particularly useful when working with style sheets for different media, such as print and screen.

Both sections work the same way: add a style sheet to the list by clicking the plus (+) button and navigating to the style sheet in the site file system. The rules of the CSS cascade apply, so add multiple style sheets in the same order as to the original page. To remove a style sheet, highlight it, and click the minus (–) button. Figure 12-9 shows menu.inc.php after applying workfiles/ch12/stroll.css and SpryAssets/SpryMenuBarHorizontal_stroll.css as design-time style sheets. It now looks the same as in the page it was extracted from.

Figure 12-9. After applying design-time style sheets, the include file looks the same as in the original page.

With the design-time style sheets applied, you can manipulate the styles of the include file by changing the class or ID of individual elements. You can also change the style rules in the external style sheets through the CSS Styles panel or the CSS view of the Property inspector. But—and it's a rather large one—you should remember that the code fragment you're working with is no longer in the context of its parent page. As a result, you cannot access the Code Navigator by holding down Alt/Opt+Cmd and clicking in the page, nor are the styles preserved in Live view. More importantly, the full effect of the CSS cascade may not be accurately reflected if particular styles are dependent on being inside a parent element that's not part of the code fragment. Also, changes made to the external style sheet may have unexpected consequences on other parts of your design. Although useful, design-time style sheets have their limitations.

Another drawback is that design-time style sheets can be applied to only one page at a time. There is a commercial extension available that lets you apply design-time style sheets to an entire site. See http://www.communitymx.com/abstract.cfm?cid=61265 for details. Dreamweaver stores details of style sheets applied to a page in this way in a subfolder called _notes. The subfolder is hidden in the Files panel but can be inspected in Windows Explorer or Finder.

Adding dynamic code to an include

The footer of a page frequently contains details that might change, such as company address or telephone number, making it an ideal candidate for an include file.

12

Automatically updating a copyright notice

The footer in stroll_horiz.php contains only a copyright notice, which normally changes only once a year, but with a little PHP magic, you can get it to update automatically at the stroke of midnight on New Year's Eve every year. Continue working with the files from the previous exercise.

1. Create a PHP page, and save it in workfiles/includes as footer.inc.php. Switch to Code view, and remove all code so the file is completely blank. Switch to Design view.

2. Open stroll_horiz.php in Design view, and click anywhere inside the copyright notice at the bottom of the page. Select the entire footer by clicking <div#footer> in the Tag selector, and cut it to your clipboard.

3. Without moving the insertion point, click the Include button on the PHP tab of the Insert bar. Dreamweaver opens Split view with the cursor placed between the parentheses of an include() block. Type a single quote, click the Browse icon as before to insert the path to footer.inc.php, and type a closing quote.

4. Switch to footer.inc.php, and paste the contents of your clipboard into Design view (do *not* paste into Code view—remember always to paste back to the same view as you cut from). The footer is unstyled, but if you save footer.inc.php, switch to stroll_horiz.php, and click in Design view, then you'll see the footer properly styled as though you had never moved it.

5. Close the separate tab containing footer.inc.php. The rest of the work on the include file needs to be done in Code view, so you can now access it through the Related Files toolbar. Select footer.inc.php in the Related Files toolbar to open it in Split view, as shown in the following screenshot:

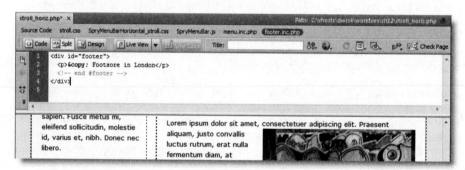

6. A copyright notice should have a year. You could just type it in, but the PHP date() function generates the current year automatically. Add the following code like this:

```
<p>&copy;
<?php
ini_set('date.timezone', 'Europe/London');
echo date('Y');
?>
Footsore in London</p>
```

Chapter 17 explains dates in PHP and MySQL in detail, but let's take a quick look at what's happening here. The core part of the code is this line:

```
echo date('Y');
```

This displays the year using four digits. Make sure you use an uppercase Y. If you use a lowercase y instead, only the final two digits of the year will be displayed.

The reason for the preceding line is because PHP 5.1.0 or higher requires a valid time-zone setting. This should be set in php.ini, but if your hosting company forgets to do this, you may end up with ugly error messages in your page.

What if your hosting company is using an earlier version of PHP? No problem. Earlier versions simply ignore this line.

Setting the time zone like this is not only good insurance against error messages, but it also allows you to override the hosting company setting, if your host is in a different time zone from your own. The second argument for ini_set() must be one of the time zones listed at http://docs.php.net/manual/en/timezones.php.

7. Save both stroll_horiz.php and footer.inc.php, and click the Live View button. You should see the current year displayed alongside the copyright symbol, as shown in Figure 12-10.

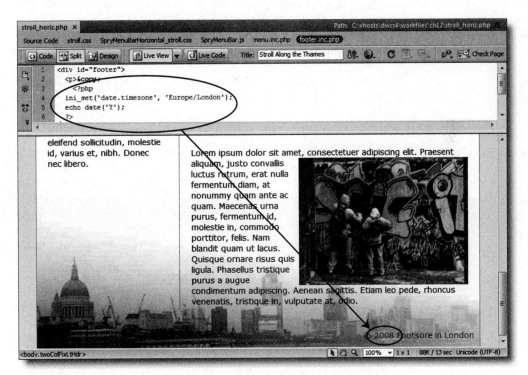

Figure 12-10. The PHP code generates the current year and displays it in the page.

12

8. Click the Live Code button, and scroll down to the bottom of the Code view section of the Document window. This shows you the actual code being sent to the browser. As you can see in the following screenshot, the PHP code remains on the server, and only the generated output is visible. The line numbers are different because Live Code merges the include files into the main page.

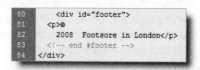

9. Copyright notices normally cover a range of years, indicating when a site was first launched. To improve the copyright notice, you need to know two things: the start year and the current year. Turn off both Live view and Live Code. Select footer.inc.php in the Related Files toolbar, if necessary, and change the PHP code like this:

```php
<p>&copy;
<?php
ini_set('date.timezone', 'Europe/London');
$startYear = 2008;
$thisYear = date('Y');
if ($startYear == $thisYear) {
  echo $startYear;
} else {
  echo "{$startYear}-{$thisYear}";
}
?>
Footsore in London</p>
```

This uses simple conditional logic (if you're new to PHP, see "Using comparisons to make decisions" in Chapter 10, and take particular note of the use of two equal signs in the conditional statement). The static value of $startYear is compared to the dynamically generated value of $thisYear. If both are the same, only the start year is displayed; if they're different, you need to display both with a hyphen between them.

I've used curly braces around the variables in the following line:

```php
echo "{$startYear}-{$thisYear}";
```

This is because they're in a double-quoted string that contains no whitespace. The curly braces enable the PHP engine to identify the beginning and end of the variables. Since hyphens aren't permitted in variable names, you could omit the curly braces on this occasion. However, their presence makes the code easier to read.

10. Save footer.inc.php, and toggle Live view on again. Assuming you used the current year for $startYear, you'll see no difference, so experiment by changing the value of $startYear and alternating between uppercase and lowercase y in the date() function.

Depending on the value of $startYear and the current date, you should see something like © 2007–2008 if you used an uppercase Y, and © 2007–08 with a lowercase y.

The values of $startYear, $thisYear, and the name of the copyright owner are the only things you need to change, and you have a fully automated copyright notice. You can check your code against footer.inc.php in examples/includes and stroll_horiz_footer.php in examples/ch12.

Using includes to recycle frequently used PHP code

Includes become really useful when you create PHP code that can be used in any site. A simple example is the POST stripslashes snippet you used in the previous chapter. Instead of putting the code directly inside your script, you could put it in an external file and use include() to incorporate it.

Let's take a look at the code again:

```
// remove escape characters from POST array
if (PHP_VERSION < 6 && get_magic_quotes_gpc()) {
  function stripslashes_deep($value) {
    $value = is_array($value) ? array_map('stripslashes_deep', ➡
$value) : stripslashes($value);
    return $value;
  }
  $_POST = array_map('stripslashes_deep', $_POST);
}
```

It contains nothing but PHP code, and the code itself consists of a conditional statement that removes backslashes from the $_POST array if magic quotes are enabled on the server. To use it successfully as an include, you must do the following two things:

- The code in the external file must be surrounded by PHP tags. Although include() and its related commands are part of PHP, the PHP engine treats everything in an include file as plain text or HTML until it encounters an opening PHP tag. The opening tag must be matched by a closing one at or before the end of the include file.

- The code must be included at the point in the script where you want to run it. In this respect, it's the same as the text and HTML includes earlier in the chapter.

PHP can be used in two main ways: as a **procedural** language and as an **object-oriented** one. In a procedural language, everything is usually in the same page, and the code is executed from top to bottom. However, to avoid the need to retype frequently used sections of script, you can package them up as custom-built functions. An object-oriented language takes the concept of functions much further and packages most of the code in libraries called **classes**.

12

For an in-depth look at object-oriented PHP, see my PHP Object-Oriented Solutions *(friends of ED, ISBN: 978-1-4302-1011-5).*

That's a vast oversimplification, but in both approaches, unless the contents of an external file define functions or classes, the include command must come at the point in the code where you want to run it. The POST stripslashes snippet does include the definition of the stripslashes_deep() function, but it's buried inside a conditional statement. So, the snippet itself is a chunk of procedural code that must be included at the point of the script where it's needed.

However, you can convert the snippet into a new function called nukeMagicQuotes() like this:

```php
<?php
function nukeMagicQuotes() {
  // remove escape characters from POST array
  if (get_magic_quotes_gpc()) {
    function stripslashes_deep($value) {
      $value = is_array($value) ? array_map('stripslashes_deep', ➥
$value): stripslashes($value);
      return $value;
    }
    $_POST = array_map('stripslashes_deep', $_POST);
  }
}
?>
```

If you save this as nukequotes.inc.php, you can include the external file at the beginning of your script and run this function at any stage in your script like this (you can see the code in feedback_nuke.php in examples/ch12 and nukequotes.inc.php in examples/includes):

```php
nukeMagicQuotes();
```

The difference of this approach is that the include file initializes the function, but the function doesn't actually run until it's called in the main body of the script. Since this particular piece of code runs only once, there's no immediate advantage of doing it this way. However, let's say you find a way of improving this script; the changes need to be made only in the external file, saving you the effort of hunting through every page where it might have been used. External files can define more than one function, so you can store frequently used functions together. In this respect, includes are the PHP equivalent of linking external JavaScript files or style sheets.

> *When functions or classes are stored in an external file, the include command must come before you use the functions or classes in your main script.*

Although building your own function library is an important use of includes, you shouldn't ignore the opportunity to recycle procedural code.

Adapting the mail processing script as an include

The mail processing script in the previous chapter performs a series of tasks, some of them specific to the feedback form, others more generic in nature. The next section shows you how to adapt the script and make it generic so that it can handle the output of any feedback form. If you glance ahead at the next few pages, you'll see there's a lot of PHP code. Don't despair. Most of the work involves cutting and pasting from one page to another. At the end, you will have an include file that can be used with just about any online form to process the input and send it by email. This considerably reduces the amount of coding that needs to be done in the page that contains the form itself.

Analyzing the script

To make the script reusable, you need to identify what's specific, what's generic, and whether any of the specific tasks can be made generic. Once you have identified the nature of each task, you need to concentrate the generic ones into a single unit that can be exported to an external file.

Table 12-1 lists the tasks in the order they are currently performed and identifies their roles. You can study the code in feedback_orig.php in examples/ch12.

Table 12-1. Analysis of the mail processing script

Step	Description	Type
1	Check whether form has been submitted.	Specific
2	Remove magic quotes.	Generic
3	Set to address and subject.	Specific
4	List expected and required fields.	Specific
5	Initialize $missing array.	Generic
6	Set default values for checkbox group and multiple-choice list.	Specific
7	Filter suspect content.	Generic
8	Process $_POST variables and check for missing fields.	Generic
9	Validate email address.	Generic
10	Build the message body.	Specific
11	Create additional headers.	Specific
12	Send email.	Generic

12

As you can see from Table 12-1, most tasks are generic, but they don't form a single block. However, step 2 can easily be moved after step 6. That leaves just steps 6, 10, and 11 that get in the way. The easy way to deal with step 6 is to initialize the $missing array as part of the specific script. After all, it's only one line.

So, what about step 10? This builds the body of the message, which would appear to be something that's always specific to each form. Let's take another look at that part of the script:

```
// build the message
$message = "Name: $name\r\n\r\n";
$message .= "Email: $email\r\n\r\n";
$message .= "Comments: $comments\r\n\r\n";
$message .= 'Interests: '.implode(', ', $interests)."\r\n\r\n";
$message .= "Subscribe: $subscribe\r\n\r\n";
$message .= "Visited: $visited\r\n\r\n";
$message .= 'Impressions of London: '.implode(', ', $views);
```

It doesn't take a genius to work out that the message is built using text labels followed by variables with the same name as the label. Since the variable names come from the name attributes in the form, all you need is a way of displaying the name attributes as well as the values of each input field. That's easily done with PHP. It's also easy to set default values for variables that contain nothing.

That leaves just step 11, the creation of additional headers. With the exception of the return email address, it doesn't matter when you specify the additional headers. They simply need to be passed to the mail() function in step 12. So, you can move the creation of most headers to the form-specific section at the beginning of the script. Table 12-2 shows the revised order of tasks.

Table 12-2. The revised mail processing script

Where defined	Step	Description
Main script		
	1	Check whether form has been submitted.
	2	Set to address and subject.
	3	Set form-specific email headers.
	4	List expected and required fields.
	5	Initialize missing array.
	6	Set default values for checkbox group and multiple-choice list.

Where defined	Step	Description
Include file		
	1	Remove magic quotes.
	2	Filter suspect content.
	3	Process $_POST variables, and check for missing fields.
	4	Validate email address.
	5	Build the message body.
	6	Add return email address to headers.
	7	Send email.

Building the message body with a generic script

Loops and arrays take a lot of the hard work out of PHP scripts, although they can be difficult to understand when you're new to PHP. You may prefer just to use the completed script, but if you're interested in the details, take a look at the following code, and I'll explain how it works:

```
// initialize the $message variable
$message = '';
// loop through the $expected array
foreach($expected as $item) {
  // assign the value of the current item to $val
  if (isset(${$item}) && !empty(${$item})) {
    $val = ${$item};
  } else {
    // if it has no value, assign 'Not selected'
    $val = 'Not selected';
  }
  // if an array, expand as comma-separated string
  if (is_array($val)) {
    $val = implode(', ', $val);
  }
  // add label and value to the message body
  $message .= ucfirst($item).": $val\r\n\r\n";
}
```

12

This replaces the code for step 10 that was listed in the preceding section. It begins by initializing $message as an empty string. Everything else is inside a foreach loop (see "Looping through arrays with foreach" in Chapter 10), which iterates through the $expected array. This array consists of the name attributes of each form field (name, email, and so on).

A foreach loop assigns each element of an array to a temporary variable. In this case, I have used $item. So, the first time the loop runs, $item is name; the next time it's email, and so on. This means you can use $item as the text label for each form field, but before you can do that, you need to know whether the field contains any value. The code that processes the $_POST variables assigns the value of each field to a variable based on its name attribute ($name, $email, and so on). The rather odd-looking ${$item} is what's known as a **variable variable** (the repetition is deliberate, not a misprint). Since the value of $item is name the first time the loop runs, ${$item} refers to $name. On the next pass through the loop, it refers to $email, and so on.

In effect, what happens is that on the first iteration the following conditional statement

```
if (isset(${$item}) && !empty(${$item})) {
  $val = ${$item};
}
```

becomes this:

```
if (isset($name) && !empty($name)) {
  $val = $name;
}
```

If the variable doesn't exist (which would happen if nothing was selected in a checkbox group) or if it doesn't contain a value, the else clause assigns $val the string Not selected.

So, you now have $item, which contains the label for the field, and $val, which contains the field's value.

The next conditional statement uses is_array() to check whether the field value is an array (as in the case of checkboxes or a multiple-choice list). If it is, the values are converted into a comma-separated string by implode().

Finally, the label and field value are added to $message using the combined concatenation operator (.=). The label ($item) is passed to the ucfirst() function, which converts the first character to uppercase. The concatenation operator (.) joins the label to a double-quoted string, which contains a colon followed by the field value ($val) and two pairs of carriage returns and newline characters.

This code handles all types and any number of form fields. All it needs is for the name attributes to make suitable labels and to be added to the $expected array.

Converting feedback.php to use the generic script

The following instructions show you how to adapt feedback.php from the previous chapter so that it can be recycled for use with most forms. If you don't have a copy of the file from the previous chapter, copy feedback_orig.php from examples/ch12 to workfiles/ch12, and save it as feedback.php.

1. Create a new PHP file, and save it as process_mail.inc.php in workfiles/includes. Switch to Code view, and strip out all existing code.

2. Insert the following code:

```php
<?php
if (isset($_SERVER['SCRIPT_NAME']) && strpos($_SERVER['SCRIPT_NAME'],➡
'.inc.php')) exit;

?>
```

   This uses the predefined variable $_SERVER['SCRIPT_NAME'] and the strpos() function to check the name of the current script. If it contains .inc.php, that means somebody is trying to access the include file directly through a browser, so the exit command brings the script to a halt. When accessed correctly as an include file, $_SERVER['SCRIPT_NAME'] contains the name of the parent file, so unless you also give that the .inc.php file name extension, the conditional statement returns false and runs the rest of the script as normal.

   Calling process_mail.inc.php directly shouldn't have any negative effect, but if display_errors is enabled on your server, it generates error messages that might be useful to a malicious attacker. This simple security measure prevents the script running unless it's accessed correctly.

3. Cut the POST stripslashes code from the top of feedback.php, and paste it on the blank line before the closing PHP tag in process_mail.inc.php.

4. Leave $to, $subject, $expected, and $required in feedback.php. Cut the remaining PHP code above the DOCTYPE declaration (DTD), except for the closing curly brace and PHP tag. The following code should be left above the DTD in feedback.php:

```php
<?php
if (array_key_exists('send', $_POST)) {
  //mail processing script
  $to = 'me@example.com'; // use your own email address
  $subject = 'Feedback from Essential Guide';

  // list expected fields
  $expected = array('name', 'email', 'comments', 'interests', ➡
'subscribe', 'visited', 'views');
  // set required fields
  $required = array('name', 'comments', 'interests', 'visited', ➡
'views');
```

12

```
// create empty array for any missing fields
$missing = array();
// set default values for variables that might not exist
if (!isset($_POST['interests'])) {
  $_POST['interests'] = array();
}
if (!isset($_POST['views'])) {
  $_POST['views'] = array();
}
// minimum number of required checkboxes
$minCheckboxes = 2;
// if fewer than required, add to $missing array
if (count($_POST['interests']) < $minCheckboxes) {
  $missing[] = 'interests';
}
}
?>
```

5. Paste into process_mail.inc.php just before the closing PHP tag the code you cut from feedback.php.

6. Cut the following two lines from process_mail.inc.php:

```
// create additional headers
$headers = "From: Essential Guide<feedback@example.com>\r\n";
$headers .= 'Content-Type: text/plain; charset=utf-8';
```

7. Paste them into feedback.php just before the closing curly brace of the code shown in step 4 like this:

```
if (count($_POST['interests']) < $minCheckboxes) {
  $missing[] = 'interests';
}
// create additional headers
$headers = "From: Essential Guide<feedback@example.com>\r\n";
$headers .= 'Content-Type: text/plain; charset=utf-8';
}
?>
```

8. Replace the code that builds the message with the generic version shown at the beginning of this section. The full listing for process_mail.inc.php follows, with the new code highlighted in bold:

```
<?php
if (isset($_SERVER['SCRIPT_NAME']) && strpos($_SERVER['SCRIPT_NAME'],➥
'.inc.php')) exit;
// remove escape characters from POST array
if (get_magic_quotes_gpc()) {
  function stripslashes_deep($value) {
    $value = is_array($value) ? array_map('stripslashes_deep', ➥
$value) : stripslashes($value);
```

```php
    return $value;
  }
  $_POST = array_map('stripslashes_deep', $_POST);
}

// assume that there is nothing suspect
$suspect = false;
// create a pattern to locate suspect phrases
$pattern = '/Content-Type:|Bcc:|Cc:/i';

// function to check for suspect phrases
function isSuspect($val, $pattern, &$suspect) {
  // if the variable is an array, loop through each element
  // and pass it recursively back to the same function
  if (is_array($val)) {
    foreach ($val as $item) {
      isSuspect($item, $pattern, $suspect);
    }
  } else {
    // if one of the suspect phrases is found, set Boolean to true
    if (preg_match($pattern, $val)) {
      $suspect = true;
    }
  }
}

// check the $_POST array and any subarrays for suspect content
isSuspect($_POST, $pattern, $suspect);

if ($suspect) {
  $mailSent = false;
  unset($missing);
} else {
  // process the $_POST variables
  foreach ($_POST as $key => $value) {
    //assign to temporary variable and strip whitespace if not an array
    $temp = is_array($value) ? $value : trim($value);
    // if empty and required, add to $missing array
    if (empty($temp) && in_array($key, $required)) {
      array_push($missing, $key);
    } elseif (in_array($key, $expected)) {
      // otherwise, assign to a variable of the same name as $key
      ${$key} = $temp;
    }
  }
}
```

12

```php
    // validate the email address
    if (!empty($email)) {
      // regex to identify illegal characters in email address
      $checkEmail = '/^[^@]+@[^\s\r\n\'";,@%]+$/';
      // reject the email address if it deosn't match
      if (!preg_match($checkEmail, $email)) {
        $suspect = true;
        $mailSent = false;
        unset($missing);
      }
    }

    // go ahead only if not suspsect and all required fields OK
    if (!$suspect && empty($missing)) {
      // initialize the $message variable
      $message = '';
      // loop through the $expected array
      foreach($expected as $item) {
        // assign the value of the current item to $val
        if (isset(${$item}) && !empty(${$item})) {
          $val = ${$item};
        } else {
          // if it has no value, assign 'Not selected'
          $val = 'Not selected';
        }
        // if an array, expand as comma-separated string
        if (is_array($val)) {
          $val = implode(', ', $val);
        }
        // add label and value to the message body
        $message .= ucfirst($item).": $val\r\n\r\n";
      }

      // limit line length to 70 characters
      $message = wordwrap($message, 70);

      // create Reply-To header
      if (!empty($email)) {
        $headers .= "\r\nReply-To: $email";
      }

      // send it
      $mailSent = mail($to, $subject, $message, $headers);
      if ($mailSent) {
        // $missing is no longer needed if the email is sent, so unset it
        unset($missing);
      }
    }
?>
```

9. All that remains is to include the mail processing script. Since the form won't work without it, it's a wise precaution to check that the file exists and is readable before attempting to include it. The following is a complete listing of the amended code above the DOCTYPE declaration in feedback.php. The new code, including the $header pasted in the previous step, is highlighted in bold.

```php
<?php
if (array_key_exists('send', $_POST)) {
  //mail processing script
  $to = 'me@example.com'; // use your own email address
  $subject = 'Feedback from Essential Guide';

  // list expected fields
  $expected = array('name', 'email', 'comments', 'interests', ➥
'subscribe', 'visited', 'views');
  // set required fields
  $required = array('name', 'comments', 'interests', 'visited', ➥
'views');
  // create empty array for any missing fields
  $missing = array();
  // set default values for variables that might not exist
  if (!isset($_POST['interests'])) {
    $_POST['interests'] = array();
  }
  if (!isset($_POST['views'])) {
    $_POST['views'] = array();
  }
  // minimum number of required checkboxes
  $minCheckboxes = 2;
  // if fewer than required, add to $missing array
  if (count($_POST['interests']) < $minCheckboxes) {
    $missing[] = 'interests';
  }
  $headers = "From: Essential Guide<feedback@example.com>\r\n";
  $headers .= 'Content-Type: text/plain; charset=utf-8';
  $process = '../includes/process_mail.inc.php';
  if (file_exists($process) && is_readable($process)) {
    include($process);
  } else {
    $mailSent = false;
  }
}
?>
```

The path to process_mail.inc.php is stored in $process. This avoids the need to type it three times. The conditional statement uses two functions with self-explanatory names: file_exists() and is_readable(). If the file is OK, it's included. If not, $mailSent is set to false. This displays the warning that there was a problem sending the message.

12

10. To be super-efficient, send yourself an email alerting you to the problem with the include file by amending the conditional statement like this:

```
if (file_exists($process) && is_readable($process)) {
  include($process);
} else {
  $mailSent = false;
  mail($to, 'Server problem', "$process cannot be read", $headers);
}
```

You can check the final code in feedback_process.php in examples/ch12 and process_mail.inc.php in examples/includes.

Because process_mail.inc.php uses generic variables, you can slot this include file into any page that processes a form and sends the results by email. The only proviso is that you must use the same variables as in step 9, namely, $to, $subject, $expected, $required, $missing, $minCheckboxes, $headers, and $mailSent. If you don't want to set a minimum number of checkboxes, set $minCheckboxes to 0.

Programming purists would criticize this use of procedural code, arguing that a more robust solution should be built with object-oriented code. An object-oriented solution would be better. In fact, I have created one in my book, *PHP Object-Oriented Solutions*, but it would be more difficult for a PHP beginner to adapt. It also requires a minimum of PHP 5.2. The purpose of this exercise has been to demonstrate how even procedural code can be recycled with relatively little effort. It also prepares the ground for customizing the PHP code automatically generated by Dreamweaver. With the exception of the XSL Transformations server behavior (covered in Chapter 18), Dreamweaver uses procedural code.

Avoiding the "headers already sent" error

A problem that you're bound to encounter sooner or later is this mysterious error message:

Warning: Cannot add header information - headers already sent

It happens when you use header() to redirect a page, as described in the previous chapter, or with PHP sessions (covered in Chapter 15). Frequently, the cause of the problem lies in an include file. The other main culprit lurks inside the main file just before you include the external file.

Using header() or starting a PHP session must be done before any output is sent to the browser. This includes not only HTML but also any whitespace. As far as PHP is concerned, *whitespace means any space, tab, carriage return, or newline character* outside a PHP block. Why the error message is so mysterious—and causes so much head banging—is because the whitespace is often at the end of an include file. Use the line numbers in Code view, as shown in Figure 12-11, to make sure there are no blank lines at the end of an include file. Also make sure that there is no whitespace after the closing PHP tag on the final line.

Whitespace *inside* the PHP tags is unimportant, but the PHP code must not generate any HTML output before using header() or starting a session. The same applies to the parent page: there must be no whitespace before the opening PHP tag.

On rare occasions, the error is triggered by an invisible control character at the beginning of the file. Use View ➤ Code View Options ➤ Hidden Characters to check, and delete the character.

> *Since Dreamweaver CS3 adopted UTF-8 as its default encoding, an increasing number of people have reported problems with headers being already sent, even if they've removed all of the whitespace as specified earlier. The reason is because they have selected* Include Unicode Signature (BOM) *in the* New Document *category of* Preferences (Edit ➤ Preferences, *or* Dreamweaver ➤ Preferences *on a Mac) or in the* Title/Encoding *category of* Page Properties *(see Chapter 4). BOM stands for byte-order mark, which is used by some versions of Unicode to indicate how the data is stored. PHP interprets a BOM as output, preventing the use of* header() *or sessions. UTF-8 does not require a BOM. Make sure the option to include it is deselected in all PHP pages (this is the Dreamweaver default setting).*

Make sure the opening PHP tag is flush with the beginning of line 1

This empty line will prevent the use of header() and PHP sessions

Figure 12-11. Eliminate whitespace outside the PHP tags to avoid the "headers already sent" error.

Chapter review

This chapter has given you a thorough overview of PHP includes, their advantages, and their pitfalls. Once you understand the potential pitfalls, includes are very easy to use. The PHP code generated by Dreamweaver uses them all the time, so at a minimum you need to know how to deal with the "headers already sent" error even if you don't yet have the confidence to start creating your own include files.

When you first start working with PHP, the idea of splitting a page into its various component parts can be a difficult concept to come to terms with, particularly if you come from a nonprogramming background. So, in the next chapter, we're going to take a brief respite from PHP coding to look at Dreamweaver templates and a new feature called Adobe InContext Editing. Templates are a way of building a master page that contains all the common elements for a site, spawning child pages from the master, and updating all the child pages automatically whenever changes are made to the master. InContext Editing bears many similarities to templates but is an online hosted service that lets authorized users update the content in certain parts of a page.

13 PRESERVING DESIGN INTEGRITY WITH TEMPLATES AND INCONTEXT EDITING

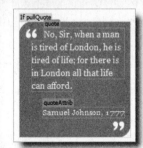

To give a unified look to a website, most pages have common elements, such as a header, navigation menu, and footer. Nobody likes repeating work just for the sake of it, so the ability to build page templates has long been one of Dreamweaver's most popular features. All common features can be defined and locked, but Dreamweaver propagates to all child pages any changes that you make to the master template. This sounds like a wonderful idea until you realize that every time you make a change all the affected pages must be uploaded again to your remote server. On a large site, this can be a major undertaking. Nevertheless, templates can be useful on small sites or in a team environment. Because you can lock the main design elements of the page, you can generate a child page and hand it to a less experienced developer in the knowledge that only the editable regions can be changed.

Adobe InContext Editing is a new online service that shares many similarities with templates in that it permits the developer to designate certain areas of a web page as editable. The main difference is that the editing is done through a browser. It's designed mainly for simple updates to the content of a page. A typical scenario where it might be used is where a web developer creates individual or small business websites on behalf of clients who want to be able to update content themselves. The developer designates which parts of a page can be edited and sets rules for how the content can be changed, for example, whether fonts and colors can be edited. All the tools for creating pages ready for InContext Editing are included in Dreamweaver CS4, but the service itself is hosted on Adobe servers and must be purchased through a monthly or annual subscription (http://www.adobe.com/products/incontextediting/).

You don't need PHP to use either templates or InContext Editing. In fact, they are arguably more suited to sites created in static HTML. I'm covering them in the PHP section of the book because there are certain things you need to be aware of when using templates or InContext Editing with PHP pages.

In this chapter, you'll learn about the following:

- Converting an existing page into a template
- Defining editable, optional, and repeating regions in a template
- Generating and editing child pages
- Resolving inconsistencies when editing a template
- Locking PHP code outside the <html> tags
- Preparing a page for InContext Editing
- Editing a page using the Adobe InContext Editing service

The information in this chapter is not a prerequisite to working with later chapters. So if you're keen to start using Dreamweaver's PHP server behaviors to build a database-driven content management system, skip ahead to the next chapter. You can come back to this chapter at any time.

Using Dreamweaver templates

In the previous chapter, I showed you how to extract two sections from the "Stroll along the Thames" site and turn them into includes. You could go further and convert the header and fixed parts of the document <head> into includes so that each page consists of several includes, with just the sidebar and main content forming the actual content of the page. As long as you keep each include as a coherent block, it's relatively easy to manage, and Design view preserves the unified look of the page.

However, it's not an approach that everybody feels comfortable with. That's where Dreamweaver templates can be a useful alternative. A template locks the fixed elements of the design but lets you designate editable regions for the content you want to change on each page. Dreamweaver templates allow you to control what can and can't be edited with a great degree of precision, right down to the individual attributes of a tag. If you change anything in a locked region of a master template, Dreamweaver automatically updates all child pages (as long as you accept the option to do so). Although this is convenient, you still need to upload the changed pages manually to the live website.

Templates are a vast subject. The following pages give a broad overview of creating a template, designating editable regions, and creating child pages. I'll also touch on issues that apply specifically to working with PHP in a Dreamweaver template.

Creating a template

In theory, you can create a template from scratch by selecting Blank Template from the New Document dialog box. However, this is not the most efficient way of working. It's much easier to design a page in the Document window in the normal way. It's then a simple matter of saving the page as a template and designating the editable regions. The following exercise shows how it's done.

Converting an existing page into a template

This exercise uses one of the exercise files from the previous chapter and converts it into a Dreamweaver template, combining the benefits of both templates and PHP includes. The menu and footer are PHP includes, so can be edited separately, while the rest of the page as a template locks down the main design elements.

1. Open stroll_horiz_footer.php from examples/ch12 in the Document window. There is no need to copy or move it, because converting it into a template takes care of that.

2. Choose Make Template from the Common tab of the Insert bar, as shown in the following screenshot. Alternatively, use the menu option File ➤ Save as Template.

3. This opens the following dialog box:

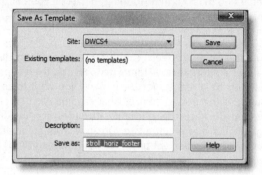

In theory, you can choose to save the template in a different site, but this is likely to cause problems with images, so leave Site unchanged. Existing templates displays a list of templates that you have already defined, if any. Optionally enter a description of the template in the Description field. The Save as field suggests using the current file name. You can change this, if you like, but don't add a file name extension, because Dreamweaver uses a special extension for templates. Click Save.

4. Dreamweaver asks whether you want to update links. You *must* click Yes, or your template will have broken links and cause endless trouble.

5. Although it may appear as though nothing happens, this saves the file as a template in a new folder called Templates in the site root. You can tell that it's a template because it has a `.dwt.php` file name extension, as shown here (templates created from static HTML pages simply have a `.dwt` extension):

The file with the `.dwt.php` file name extension is now the master template from which you create child pages. Any changes to the design of this page will affect all child pages created from it—as long as you accept the option to update them.

> *You must never move templates from the* Templates *folder. This is perhaps the single most common mistake with templates—moving the master template to another folder will cause you endless grief. Don't do it.*

Adding editable regions to the master template

Everything in a template is locked, except for the `<title>` tag and an editable region in the `<head>` of the document. This is needed so that external JavaScript files and style sheets can be added to a child page. It's also where Dreamweaver behaviors insert the JavaScript functions that they require. However, the area above the DOCTYPE declaration and below the closing </html> tag is not locked in templates for server-side languages, such as PHP. I'll come back to this issue a little later, because it causes a lot of confusion.

> *It's important to note that template code is locked only in Dreamweaver. You can edit locked regions in any other text or HTML editor. The whole concept of templates breaks down unless everyone responsible for handling the pages uses only Dreamweaver to edit them.*

It goes without saying that you must unlock at least one part of the page for the template to be of any real value. Otherwise, every child page would be identical. Deciding what to lock and unlock depends entirely on the level of control that you want over a page. For instance, you could create separate editable regions for each of the headings on the page. If you select the entire heading, including its surrounding tags, the heading can be replaced by anything: a table, a <div>, an <iframe>, or whatever you like. If you select just the content of an <h2> tag and convert it into an editable region, only the content can be changed in a child page. You can't even change it to an <h1> tag.

Since the remaining chapters of this book are about building dynamic content with PHP, you don't want such rigid control. So, you could make everything inside the container <div> one big editable region. However, we'll take a slightly different approach.

Making the sidebar and main content areas editable

This exercise shows you how to create separate editable regions for the sidebar heading and paragraphs, as well as for the whole main content area.

1. Open stroll_horiz_footer.dwt.php in the Templates folder if it's not already open.

2. Open Split view. Click immediately to the left of the heading that reads The pleasures of London. Hold down your mouse button, and drag to the end of the heading. Alternatively, hold down the Shift key while pressing the keyboard right arrow to select the content of the heading. Make sure you have just the text and not the surrounding <h3> tags, as shown in the following screenshot:

3. There are several ways to make this an editable region. If you're a fan of the Insert bar, click the down arrow next to the Make Template button on the Common tab, and select Editable Region. The Insert bar remembers your last selection, so the Editable Region button remains displayed, ready for the creation of more editable regions.

   Alternatively, right-click and select Templates ➤ New Editable Region from the context menu, or select Insert ➤ Template Objects ➤ Editable Region.

4. This opens the New Editable Region dialog box. It has just one field for a name for the editable region. It can be anything you like, but each region must have a different name. Enter sidebarHead, and click OK.

5. This wraps the contents of the <h3> tag in two special HTML comment tags, as shown in Figure 13-1. These tell Dreamweaver to treat this as an editable region in child pages. Dreamweaver also displays a turquoise border around the region in Design view, with a tab at the top left indicating the name of the editable region.

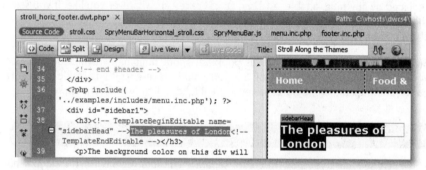

Figure 13-1. Editable regions are easily identified in both Code view and Design view.

> *Always check the position of the* TemplateBeginEditable *and* TemplateEndEditable *comments in Code view, because you can easily move them or any of the surrounding code while still in the template. Checking now saves a lot of frustration later, when you discover that you didn't select the region accurately in Design view and your child pages don't work the way you expect. These comments are an integral part of the template control mechanism and are propagated to the child pages, where they remain part of the HTML.*

6. Select the first paragraph in the sidebar by clicking inside it and selecting <p> in the Tag selector at the bottom of the Document window. Repeat steps 3 and 4 to turn it into an editable region called sidebarTop.

7. Do the same with the bottom paragraph in the sidebar, and call it sidebarFollow.

8. This leaves the <blockquote> outside the editable regions in the sidebar. Because the pull quote is styled in a particular way, you probably don't want an inexperienced person to do anything other than change the text. So, select the text in the

first paragraph of the <blockquote> element, and apply an editable region called quote. Even if you don't select the surrounding <p> tags, Dreamweaver usually assumes you want them included in the editable region, so you need to move them manually in Code view.

9. Do the same with the quote_attrib paragraph, and call the editable region quoteAttrib. After you have moved the <p> tags, the TemplateBeginEditable and TemplateEndEditable comments should be inside the paragraphs like this:

```
<blockquote>
    <p><!-- TemplateBeginEditable name="quote" -->No, Sir, when a man is ➥
tired of London, he is tired of life; for there is in London all that ➥
life can afford.<!-- TemplateEndEditable --></p>
    <p id="quote_attrib"><!-- TemplateBeginEditable name="quoteAttrib" -->
Samuel Johnson, 1777<!-- TemplateEndEditable --></p>
</blockquote>
```

You can tell if you have positioned the tags correctly because the turquoise outlines of the editable regions should now hug the text in Design view, rather than surround the quotation marks of the pull quote's background images, as shown here:

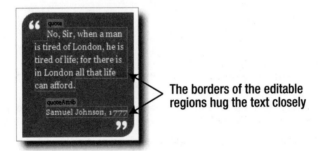

The borders of the editable regions hug the text closely

10. Select all the content in the mainContent <div>, but not the surrounding <div> tags, and create an editable region called mainContent. Check that the template comments are in the right place in Code view, and save stroll_horiz_footer.dwt.php.

11. Dreamweaver should display a warning that sidebarHead is inside a block tag and that users of the template won't be able to create new blocks in this region. This is because the <h3> tags are outside the sidebarHead editable region, which prevents anything other than a level-three heading being created. That's fine. So, click OK.

Creating child pages from a template

Now that you have a template, you can build pages based on it. The editable regions can be freely changed, but the other areas remain locked and can be changed only by editing the master template.

13

Creating and editing a template-based page

This exercise uses the template from the previous exercise to create a child page and explores the way editable regions control the extent of editing you can do.

1. Go to File ➤ New. When the New Document dialog box opens, select Page from Template from the options on the left side. Assuming you created the template in the preceding exercises, the dialog box should look similar to Figure 13-2.

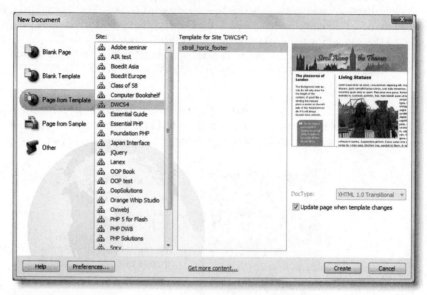

Figure 13-2. The New Document dialog box gives you access to all the templates you have created.

Dreamweaver lists all your sites. Select the current site and the template you want to use as the basis for a new page (you can have as many templates as you like in a site, using different designs for pages that serve different functions).

The New Document dialog box shows a preview of the selected template, together with the description you entered when it was first created.

The idea of a template is that all changes to common elements are propagated automatically to child pages when the master template is updated. Unless you want to create a page that doesn't automatically update, make sure that there's a check mark in Update page when template changes, and click Create.

2. A new page is created in the Document window. At first glance, it looks identical to the template, but several features tell you that it's a child page (see Figure 13-3) and that you can make changes only to the editable regions indicated by the turquoise borders and tabs. Whenever your mouse is over a locked part of the page, the pointer turns into a circle with a diagonal bar to warn you that no changes can be made.

Cursor changes shape over locked areas
to indicate they cannot be edited

Yellow tab displays
name of master template

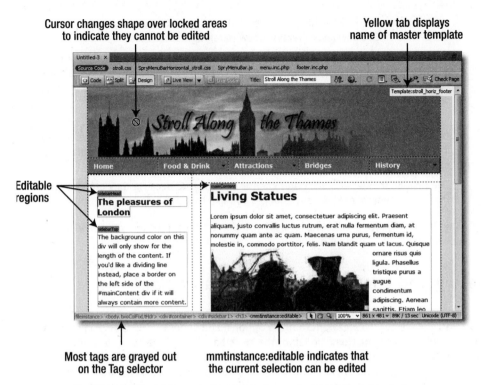

Editable
regions

Most tags are grayed out
on the Tag selector

mmtinstance:editable indicates that
the current selection can be edited

Figure 13-3. The child page is identical to the master template, but locked areas can no longer be edited.

3. Save the page as `stroll_index.php` in `workfiles/ch13`.

4. Insert your cursor in the sidebar heading (The pleasures of London). Select the HTML view of the Property inspector, and change Format from Heading 3 to Heading 2. You should see the warning shown in Figure 13-4.

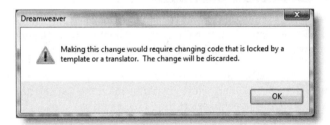

Figure 13-4.
Dreamweaver refuses to make any changes that violate the rules laid down in the master template.

13

It doesn't matter how hard you try; you cannot change the level of the heading because the <h3> tags are outside the editable region. Even if you attempt to change the tags in Code view, Dreamweaver rejects the changes.

5. Insert your cursor anywhere in the sidebarTop editable region, and press Enter/Return. Dreamweaver creates a new paragraph as normal.

6. Now try the same in the quote editable region. The text moves down a line but doesn't form a new paragraph. If you check the code in Split view, you'll see that a `<br />` tag has been inserted. The difference in behavior is determined by the rules you set when creating the editable regions.

   In sidebarTop, the paragraph tags are inside the editable region, so you can edit the content freely. You can even replace the paragraphs with any HTML elements. The same is true of the mainContent editable region: everything is replaceable, except for the `<div>` tags that define the region.

   The header, menu bar, and footer cannot be changed, because they are locked by the master template. Make any changes you like to stroll_index.php, and save it.

Although the pull quote is editable, let's say you don't want it on every page. The answer is to convert it into an optional region.

Creating and controlling an optional region

Creating an optional region in a template is very similar to creating an editable region. You just select the element(s) you want to make optional and choose Optional Region from the Template submenu on the Common tab of the Insert bar or from the Template Objects submenu of the Insert menu. You can also right-click and choose Templates ➤ New Optional Region from the context menu. Like editable regions, you can have more than one optional region in a template, but you must give each one a unique name. Optional regions can contain editable regions, but not the other way round.

You can control the display of an optional region in a child page in several ways, but the simplest is to open the Template Properties dialog box from the Modify menu and select whether to display the optional region.

Converting the pull quote into an optional region

This exercise shows you how to convert the `<blockquote>` element in stroll_horiz_footer.dwt.php into an optional region and control its display in a child page. Continue working with the same template as in the previous exercises.

1. Open stroll_horizon_footer.dwt.php, and insert your cursor anywhere inside the pull quote in the sidebar. Then select `<blockquote>` in the Tag selector at the bottom of the Document window to select the whole element.

2. Select Optional Region from the Templates submenu on the Common tab of the Insert bar as shown in Figure 13-5 (or use one of the menu options). Do *not* choose Editable Optional Region, because this works a different way and will be explained later.

Figure 13-5. The Template submenu on the Insert bar

3. This opens the New Optional Region dialog box shown in Figure 13-6.

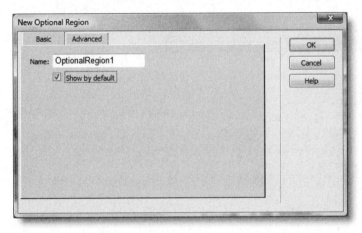

Figure 13-6. The Basic tab just sets a name for the optional region and whether to show it by default.

Just enter pullQuote in the Name field of the Basic tab, and check that Show by default is selected. If you want to use an optional region only occasionally, simply deselect the Show by default checkbox.

You don't need to touch the Advanced tab now, because I'll explain it later.

4. Click OK to create the optional region. The entire pull quote should now be surrounded by a pale blue border with an If tab at the top left, as shown here:

5. Save stroll_horiz_footer.dwt.php. Dreamweaver displays a dialog box asking whether you want to update all files based on this template (there's only one: stroll_index.php). Click Update. Dreamweaver displays another dialog box reporting that the updates have been completed. Click Close to dismiss it.

13

6. Check `stroll_index.php`. It should look exactly the same as before. If the pull quote in the sidebar has disappeared, you must have deselected Show by default in the New Optional Region dialog box (see Figure 13-6). It doesn't matter, because you'll soon see how to enable or disable an optional region in a child page.

7. Open the New Document dialog box, and create another child page from the `stroll_horiz_footer` template. Save the new page as `parliament.php` in a new subfolder called `history` in `workfiles/ch13`.

8. Just so you can distinguish the pages from each other, change the main heading in parliament.php to Mother of Parliaments, and replace `living_statues.jpg` with `bigben.jpg`.

9. To remove the pull quote in the sidebar, select Modify ➤ Template Properties to open the dialog box shown in Figure 13-7.

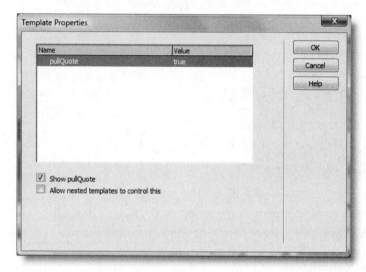

Figure 13-7. The Template Properties dialog box controls the display of optional regions.

Deselect the Show pullQuote checkbox (if you have more than one optional region in the template, you need to select it in the upper pane first). The Value field should turn from true to false. Click OK.

10. The pull quote has gone away, as shown in Figure 13-8.

11. Check in the sidebar in Code view. The `<blockquote>` and its content are not there. Dreamweaver doesn't use CSS or HTML comments to hide an optional region. The code is physically removed from the child page.

Figure 13-8. The optional region has been removed from the sidebar.

12. To see how Dreamweaver knows whether to include the code from an optional region, scroll up in Code view until you reach the `<head>` section. Just before the closing `</head>` tag, you'll see the code shown on line 27 of Figure 13-9.

```
25   <!-- InstanceBeginEditable name="head" -->
26   <!-- InstanceEndEditable -->
27   <!-- InstanceParam name="pullQuote" type="boolean" value="false" -->
28   </head>
```

Figure 13-9.
Dreamweaver controls the optional region with a template parameter in the `<head>` of the page.

This code creates a **template parameter**, which is basically an instruction to the template engine telling it whether to display the optional region. Although you can edit this code, changing `false` to `true` in Code view won't restore the pull quote. You need to do that through the Template Properties dialog box (see Figure 13-7).

13. Save parliament.php. You can close it, because it won't be needed in the next exercise.

Using advanced options with an optional region

Unless you plan to make heavy use of Dreamweaver templates, you don't need to concern yourself with the Advanced tab of the New Optional Region dialog box (see Figure 13-10).

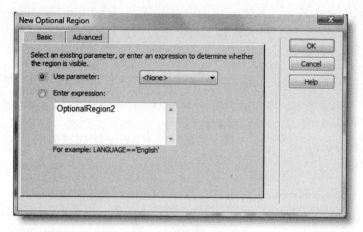

Figure 13-10. The Advanced tab automates the visibility of an optional region.

The Advanced tab has the following two options:

- Use parameter: This determines whether to display the optional region depending on another template parameter. The drop-down menu alongside this option lists the parameters defined in the current template. So, for example, you could create a new optional region and select pullQuote from the drop-down menu. This ties the two optional regions together. If pullQuote is displayed, so is the other optional region. If pullQuote is not displayed, both are removed from the page.

- Enter expression: This option lets you craft sophisticated rules to govern the display of an optional region. To learn about this feature, enter template expressions in the Search for Help field on the Application bar. Many of the results refer to earlier versions of Dreamweaver, but they are still applicable to Dreamweaver CS4. Template expressions have not changed since they were introduced in Dreamweaver MX. They are a complex subject beyond the scope of this book.

Using editable optional regions

You may have noticed in Figure 13-5 that there are menu options for Optional Region and Editable Optional Region. By default an optional region is not editable, but as you saw in the previous exercise, it can contain editable regions. This gives you great control over the content of the optional region.

On the other hand, the entire content of an editable optional region can be edited, so you have no control over what goes into it. More important, you cannot select existing content and turn it into an editable optional region. An editable optional region is created at the current insertion point and contains nothing. If you want to add any default content to an editable optional region, you must do so after creating it. Normally, it's more efficient to use an ordinary optional region.

Creating a repeating region

Templates give you a further level of control over content with repeating regions and repeating tables. I don't intend to cover repeating tables because they are of little use in a PHP site. In template terms, a repeating table creates the basic table structure and lets you determine the number of rows and content in individual child pages. As you'll see in the following chapters, Dreamweaver's PHP server behaviors populate tables automatically and far more efficiently.

However, using repeating regions in a template can be useful for things like bulleted or numbered lists. You can also use them to ensure that everything is in identically styled paragraphs. To add a repeating region, select the element you want to repeat (it's a good idea to use the Tag selector to make sure you get the opening and closing tags) and choose Repeating Region from the Template submenu on the Common tab of the Insert bar (see Figure 13-5), or use the menu option, Insert ➤ Template Objects ➤ Repeating Region.

By default, a repeating region is not editable, so it should contain at least one editable region unless you want the same content (such as an icon) repeated several times. The next exercise shows how to use a repeating region.

Removing or changing template regions

Inevitably the time comes when you change your mind about the design or your requirements change. If no child pages have been created from a template, the solution is simple: right-click the tab at the top left of the template region you want to remove, and select Templates ➤ Remove Template Markup from the context menu. Alternatively, you can select the tab and choose Modify ➤ Templates ➤ Remove Template Markup. Dreamweaver removes the template comments cleanly from the underlying code.

Things become more complicated if you have already created child pages. When you remove a template region, Dreamweaver needs to be told what to do with the existing content. After saving the changes to the template, you are presented with the Inconsistent Region Names dialog box (see Figure 13-11) indicating any unresolved regions. You can either move the content to another template region or tell Dreamweaver to delete it. If you have a large number of child pages generated from the template, this can be a major headache causing the loss of vital content.

> **Converting editable regions in the sidebar**
>
> This exercise takes you through the process of changing template regions and resolving what to do with the affected content. It also shows you how to create a repeating region with an unordered list. Continue working with the same template as in the previous exercises.
>
> 1. In `stroll_horiz_footer.dwt.php`, right-click the tab at the top left of the sidebarHead editable region, and select Templates ➤ Remove Template Markup.
> 2. Change the text in the `<h3>` tags from The pleasures of London to In this section:. This is now a locked region, so this heading will appear on all child pages.

13

3. Remove the template markup from the sidebarTop editable region, and replace the text in the existing paragraph with Feature.

4. Convert the paragraph you have just edited into an unordered list by clicking the Unordered List button in the HTML view of the Property inspector or by selecting Format ➤ Lists ➤ Unordered List.

5. You're going to convert this to a repeating region, so the text inside the <li> tags needs to be converted to an editable region. Select the word Feature in Design view, and open Split view to make sure you have selected only the text and not the surrounding <li> tags.

6. Apply an editable region, and call it feature.

7. To apply the repeating region, you need to select the surrounding <li> tags. You can do that either in Code view or by clicking <li> in the Tag selector.

8. Select Repeating Region from the Templates submenu on the Common tab of the Insert bar (see Figure 13-5), or use the Insert menu. The New Repeating Region dialog box has just one field for the name of the new region. Call it featureList.

The section you have just edited should look like this in Split view:

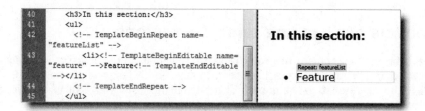

The <h3> header shown on line 40 of the preceding screenshot has no template markup, so it's now locked. The same text will appear in all child pages.

The template markup for the beginning of the repeating region is on line 42 between the opening <ul> and <li> tags. The editable region markup is on line 43 inside the <li> tags, and the end of the repeating region is on line 44 between the closing </li> and </ul> tags.

9. Save stroll_horiz_footer.dwt.php. Ignore the message about placing an editable region inside a block tag. That's exactly what you want to do. When Dreamweaver asks whether you want to update all files based on the template, click Update.

10. Because you have removed two editable regions from the original template, Dreamweaver needs to know what to do with the content in those regions in the child pages and presents you with the Inconsistent Region Names dialog box, as shown in Figure 13-11.

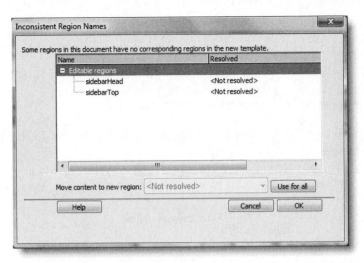

Figure 13-11. Before updating child pages, you need to decide what to do with content from regions that no longer exist.

11. You want the new content in the <h3> heading to replace the original text. So, highlight sidebarHead in the Inconsistent Region Names dialog box, and open the Move content to new region drop-down menu. This contains a list of all editable regions in the page, plus three other entries:

   - Nowhere: This discards the content.

   - doctitle: This is the page's <title> tag. Although it's an editable region, you should not move the content here.

   - head: This is an editable area just before the closing </head> tag, which is intended to let you add links to style sheets and external JavaScript files in child pages. Dreamweaver also uses it to insert JavaScript functions for behaviors. Again, you should not move content here.

   Select Nowhere to discard the old <h3> heading that was in sidebarHead.

12. The child pages that you have created contain only dummy text in what used to be the sidebarTop editable region, so you could tell Dreamweaver to discard it, too. However, let's imagine that it contains vital content. To avoid losing it, you must move it elsewhere. Since it's already in the sidebar, I suggest moving it to the sidebarFollow editable region.

   Highlight sidebarTop in the Inconsistent Region Names dialog box, and select sidebarFollow in the Move content to new region drop-down menu.

   > The Use for all *button moves all unresolved content to the same location as selected for the currently highlighted region.*

13

13. The settings in the Inconsistent Region Names dialog box should now look like this:

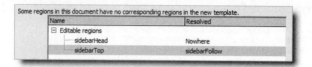

Click OK to save the changes and update the child pages. Click Close to dismiss the update report.

14. The top of both child pages now contains a fixed `<h3>` heading and a repeating region containing a dummy item for an unordered list, as shown in Figure 13-12.

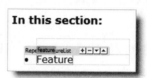

Figure 13-12.
The repeating region uses familiar icons to show how to edit it.

Editing the repeating region follows a familiar pattern common to many Dreamweaver dialog boxes. Click the plus and minus buttons at the top right of the repeating region, and use the up and down arrows to change their order (see Figure 13-12).

15. Replace the dummy text in the list item, click the plus button, and add another. The result should look like this:

You can add as many list items as you like, but you cannot add any other element.

Comparing templates with PHP includes

The main drawback with using templates is that any change to the master template involves updating all child pages. Although Dreamweaver handles the updating automatically on your local computer, you still need to upload all the revised pages to the live server on the Internet. As the site grows in size, this becomes a heavier burden. This means that if your navigation menu is part of the template, every page on the site needs to be updated whenever you add a new item to the menu. Any advantages offered by templates rapidly fade in comparison with includes.

However, the template you have been working on throughout this chapter doesn't actually contain the code for the navigation menu. The code for the menu is in a PHP include file, menu.inc.php. All that's in the template is an include command. Consequently, any changes to the menu can be made in menu.inc.php, and that's the only file you need to upload to the server.

Updating the menu

This exercise demonstrates how changes to an include file are propagated automatically to template child pages without the need to update each page individually. It assumes you have created stroll_index.php and parliament.php in the exercises earlier in this chapter.

1. When you created the template at the beginning of the chapter, it was based on a file in the examples folder, so the include command points to the version of menu.inc.php in examples/includes. For testing purposes, you need to point to the version in workfiles/includes (if you didn't create menu.inc.php in the previous chapter, copy it from examples/includes to workfiles/includes).

   Open stroll_horiz_footer.dwt.php if it's not already open, and click the turquoise Spry Menu Bar tab at the top left of the navigation menu. This displays the details of the include file in the Property inspector, as shown here (**SSI** stands for server-side include):

2. Click the icon that looks like a folder to the right of the Filename field, and navigate to menu.inc.php in the workfiles/includes folder. Click OK (Choose on a Mac) to close the Select File dialog box. The value in the Filename field should now be ../workfiles/includes/menu.inc.php.

   When linking a template to other files within the site, always use the Dreamweaver interface to navigate to the correct location. Dreamweaver adjusts document-relative links automatically when creating child pages, so it needs to know where the file is in relation to the master template. Unless you are using links relative to the site root, typing the link directly into the Property inspector is likely to result in broken links.

3. Save stroll_horiz_footer.dwt.php, and click Update when Dreamweaver asks whether you want to update all files based on the template.

4. Before clicking Close to dismiss the next dialog box, select the Show log checkbox. As you can see in the screenshot alongside, Dreamweaver presents a report of the number of files examined and updated. On this occasion, it has updated two files.

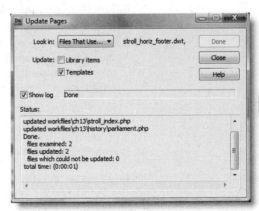

5. Launch stroll_index.php in a browser. Use the navigation menu to try to go to History ➤ Houses of Parliament. It should come as no surprise that nothing happens, because you haven't created that link yet.

   If you did the exercises with menu.inc.php in the previous chapter, click the Home link. You'll be taken to the old version of the Stroll Along the Thames page because the menu links to stroll_horiz.php in workfiles/ch12.

13

6. In Dreamweaver, open `menu.inc.php` in `workfiles/includes`. Update the Home link to point to `stroll_index.php` in `workfiles/ch13`. Because this is in an include file, the link *must* be relative to the site root. If necessary, adjust the Relative to menu in the Select File dialog box to Site Root, as shown in Figure 13-13.

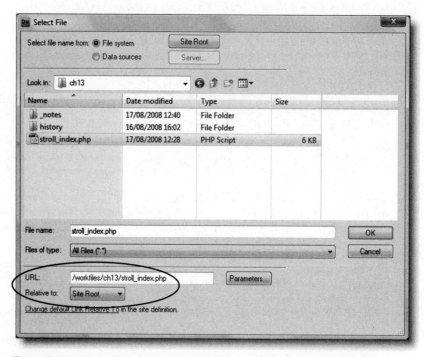

Figure 13-13. Links inside an include file should always be relative to the site root.

7. Update the Houses of Parliament link to point to `parliament.php` in the `workfiles/ch13/history` folder. Also make sure the link is relative to the site root.

8. Save `menu.inc.php`. Note that the file saves just like an ordinary file. You are not prompted to update child files.

9. Reload `stroll_index.php` in a browser. The History ➤ Houses of Parliament link should now take you to `parliament.php`, and the Home link should take you back to `stroll_index.php`. If you did the exercises in the previous chapter, the Attractions ➤ London Eye link should also load `eye.php`.

   As noted in the previous chapter, the menu works only if you are using a virtual host in Apache or a stand-alone web site in IIS7. If you are using a subfolder of the server root to test your site, you need to prefix the links in the menu with the name(s) of the subfolder(s), as described in Chapter 12.

This final exercise with Dreamweaver templates should help convince you of the value of includes. In this exercise, only two child pages were involved, but imagine if you had a site of 50 pages or more. Instead of updating every page, you need to update only the include file for the changes to be available in each page that uses the include.

Locking code outside the <html> tags

To round out this discussion of Dreamweaver templates, I'd like to deal with a question that often appears in online forums from people puzzled by the fact that the code isn't propagated to child pages when a server behavior is applied to a template. Although coverage of server behaviors begins in the next chapter, it makes sense to discuss this issue here, while still on the subject of templates.

Dreamweaver uses the space above the DOCTYPE declaration and below the closing </html> tag to create the PHP scripts used for server behaviors, such as inserting or updating records in a database. This is the same technique as you used in Chapter 11 to build the mail processing script. The reason for doing this is quite simple: the PHP engine reads the page from top to bottom and processes the dynamic code in the order that it encounters it. So if you have a page that displays the results of a database search, it stands to reason that you need to conduct the search before displaying the results as HTML. Dreamweaver uses the area after the closing </html> tag to clean up any resources used by the script.

Templates are intended to lock common elements, but dynamic code is almost always unique to a page. As a result, Dreamweaver doesn't lock the code outside the <html> tags. So even if you apply a server behavior to a master template (or write your own custom script above the DOCTYPE declaration), the code outside the <html> tags will not be propagated to any child pages.

If, for any reason, you want to create a template that propagates code outside the <html> tags, add the following code anywhere inside the <head> of the master template:

```
<!-- TemplateInfo codeOutsideHTMLIsLocked="true" -->
```

This is an all or nothing option. The PHP code will be propagated to child pages, but you cannot apply any other server behaviors to such child pages. The circumstances in which this option is useful are extremely rare, so use with care—if at all.

Breaking the link between a page and a template

Sometimes, it's useful to create a page from a template, but then break the link between the two. This lets you edit locked regions and no longer updates the page when the template is changed. Breaking the link is simple. Just select Modify ➤ Templates ➤ Detach from Template. All template markup is removed, and the page acts just like an ordinary one.

13

Updating Content with Adobe InContext Editing

A common dilemma for web developers is a request from a client or department manager who wants to be able to update content directly. The thought of letting unskilled people loose on a painstakingly crafted website gives many a developer nightmares. "Don't worry;

I only want to change a little bit of text." Rather than soothing nerves, these words set them jangling. That little bit of text almost certainly contains HTML tags marked up with classes or IDs. Once they're deleted, the site begins to fall apart. Even worse, the semi-skilled dabbler might decide to add extra flourishes such as <font> tags or features that destroy the unity of the design.

One solution is to create a content management system (CMS) allowing users to enter only plain text or use a limited set of HTML tags. But creating a CMS is time-consuming and expensive because each one normally needs to be tailored to the needs of the particular website. Another solution is to use a program like Adobe Contribute (http://www.adobe.com/products/contribute/), which uses Dreamweaver templates but gives the developer a much finer level of control over how pages can be updated. The drawback of Contribute is that it requires each person responsible for updating pages to have a copy of the program. It's cheaper than Dreamweaver but still represents a barrier to some users.

Adobe's latest attempt to solve this problem is InContext Editing, a hosted service that requires no software other than a modern browser. It doesn't give the same level of control as Contribute, and Adobe says it's not intended as a replacement for Contribute. Because the service is hosted on Adobe servers, it's not free, but Adobe says it's aware that pricing will be a sensitive factor in the adoption and success of the service. From the developer's point of view, everything needed to make a website ready for use with InContext Editing is included in Dreamweaver CS4. There's nothing to pay unless you want to use the online service.

InContext Editing is designed to make it easy for developers to give clients the opportunity to update their own web pages either because the developer doesn't have time to devote to minor updates or the client doesn't want the expense of a maintenance contract. The editing interface is easy to use, so this is likely to suit a lot of clients. However, problems are likely to arise with clients who make changes but forget to publish them or who realize they have made a mess and need the developer to put things right. Because InContext Editing uses inline styles in <span> tags and some presentational markup, cleaning up a page that has been heavily edited through this service will involve a lot of work. On the other hand, a well-designed page with InContext Editing markup that carefully controls the available options should work well. It's ideal for a restaurant page with a special dish that changes every day or an organization site listing this week's guest speaker. In most cases, it's probably better suited to one or two pages in a site, rather than applied to every page.

InContext Editing is a new service, so it's impossible to give a considered opinion based on experience. My initial assessment is that the underlying technology is impressive, but the level of control that it offers the designer still has some way to go. For example, authorized users can upload files to the web server, but there is no limit on the size or type of file that is accepted. Also, the range of tags that can be used for editable and repeating regions is severely limited, making InContext Editing much less flexible than either templates or Contribute. Because the service is likely to evolve in response to user feedback, the following sections give just a brief overview of how to prepare a page for InContext Editing and updating it online.

How InContext Editing works

To use InContext Editing, the developer adds special markup to pages that authorized users will be permitted to edit through the service. The pages are then uploaded to the site's normal web server. The Adobe server comes into the picture only when the user browses to a page that contains the special markup and presses a preset key combination (the default is Ctrl+E/Cmd+E). This prompts the user to log into the Adobe server. Once logged in, InContext Editing uses JavaScript and the Adobe Flash Player to display editing tools in the user's browser. All changes are made to a local copy of the page directly within the user's browser. The user can save the changes to the Adobe server, where they remain until a decision is taken whether to discard or publish them. Up to this point, the live website remains unaffected.

When the authorized user is ready to publish the revised page, the Adobe server transfers it via FTP (File Transfer Protocol) or SFTP (Secure File Transfer Protocol) to the live website on the server where the page is normally hosted, overwriting the original file. On logging out, the user is returned to the updated page on the live website. Once changes have been published, they cannot be rolled back, except by connecting to the Adobe server and editing the page again. From the user's point of view, the whole operation is seamless. Although all the updating process is done through the Adobe server, the web page remains in the browser the whole time, but with an editing toolbar at the top of the viewport, as shown in Figure 13-14.

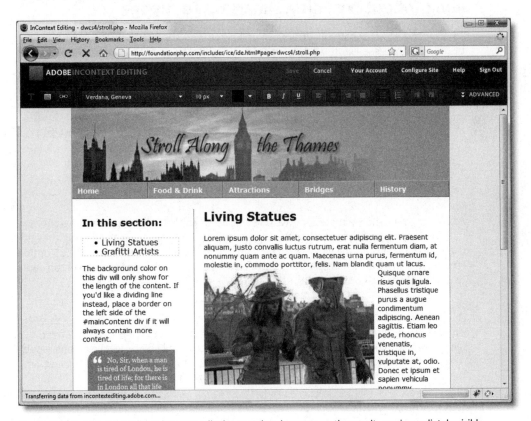

Figure 13-14. InContext Editing lets you edit the page in a browser, so the results are immediately visible.

Minimum requirements for InContext Editing

The requirements for using InContext Editing are relatively simple.

- The web server must be publicly accessible. InContext Editing cannot be used with an intranet.
- It must be possible to connect to the server via FTP or SFTP.
- To edit files, the user must access the site using one of the following browsers:
  - Internet Explorer 6
  - Internet Explorer 7
  - Safari 3
  - Firefox 3
- JavaScript must be enabled in the browser
- The browser must have Flash Player (minimum version 9.0.124) installed.

It's important to note that Safari 2 and Firefox 2 are *not* supported. Support will probably be added for Internet Explorer 8 when the final version is released.

Adding InContext Editing markup to a page

To add the necessary markup for InContext Editing, you can use the InContext Editing tab of the Insert bar (see Figure 13-15) or the menu option Insert ➤ InContext Editing. You can also add the markup directly in Code view with the help of code hints.

Figure 13-15.
InContext Editing has a more limited range of options than templates.

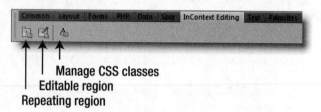

Manage CSS classes
Editable region
Repeating region

As Figure 13-15 shows, there are just three options: editable and repeating regions, and CSS. The concepts of editable and repeating regions are very similar to the way they are used in templates, but they can be applied only to a limited range of tags. The CSS option lets you designate external style sheets that contain classes that authorized users can apply to elements in an editable region.

Creating an editable region

An editable region can be applied to only three tags: <div>, <th>, and <td>. In effect, this means that, with the exception of table headers and cells, only block-level elements—such as headings, paragraphs, and lists—can be designated as editable regions, because anything else you want to make editable must be wrapped in a <div>.

To create an editable region, select the element(s) you want to make editable, and click the Create Editable Region button on the InContext Editing tab of the Insert bar or use the menu option Insert ➤ InContext Editing ➤ Create Editable Region. If you choose a single <div>, <th>, or <td> element, Dreamweaver automatically converts it into an editable region. If you choose anything else, Dreamweaver presents you with the following dialog box:

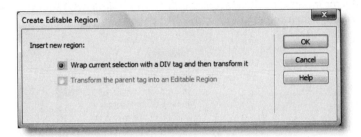

Normally, it offers to wrap the selection in a <div> tag. However, if the immediate parent tag of the current selection is a <div>, <th>, or <td>, you can choose to apply the editable region to the parent tag instead.

If, for example, you select a single paragraph, Dreamweaver adds the following code:

```
<div ice:editable="*">
    <p>This content is editable in InContext Editing.</p>
</div>
```

However, if you select all the content inside a <div> and choose to convert the parent tag into and editable region, Dreamweaver simply adds the ice:editable attribute to the parent <div> like this:

```
<div id="mainContent" ice:editable="*">
    <h2>Living Statues</h2>
    <p>Lorem ipsum . . .</p>
    <h2>Artists at work</h2>
    <p> Lorem ipsum . . .</p>
</div>
```

You need to be very careful when selecting content in Design view. If you just drag your mouse across a paragraph or several elements, Dreamweaver doesn't normally select the opening and closing tags. Attempting to apply an editable region to an incomplete selection like this brings up this warning:

13

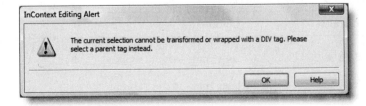

When selecting a single element to convert into an editable region, always use the Tag selector at the bottom of the Document window to ensure that you select the whole element. When selecting several elements, it's best to do so in Code view.

An editable region is identified in Design view by a turquoise tab at the top-left corner, as shown in Figure 13-16. Unlike an editable region in a template, the tab is not always visible. The tabs for InContext Editing act in the same way as JavaScript widgets in that they are displayed only when you mouse over the element or select it.

Editable Region
Donec eu mi sed turpis
feugiat feugiat. Integer turpis
arcu, pellentesque eget,
cursus et, fermentum ut,
sapien. Fusce metus mi,
eleifend sollicitudin, molestie
id, varius et, nibh. Donec nec
libero.

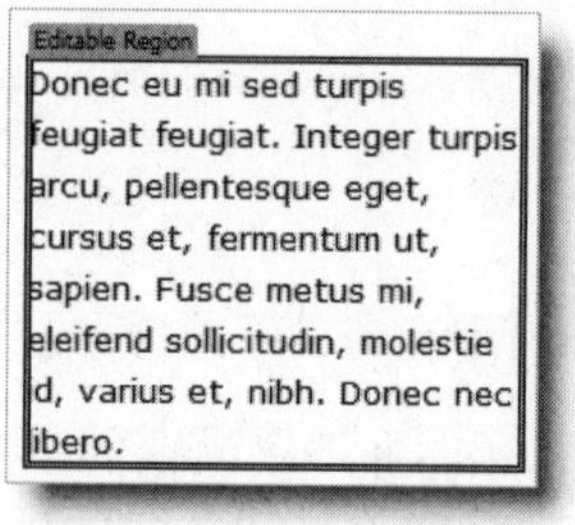

Figure 13-16. Editable regions are identified by a turquoise tab.

Controlling what can be edited in an editable region

In its initial state, an editable region gives the user complete freedom to change just about everything. However, you can control the range of tools available to users through the Property inspector. To display the editable region options in the Property inspector (see Figure 13-17), select the turquoise tab at the top left of the region.

PROPERTIES
Editable Region
Remove Region
Options:
Class
twoColFi...
Get started with InContext Editing
Check all
Uncheck all

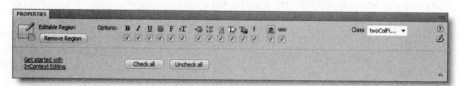

Figure 13-17. The options for an editable region give the developer considerable control over what can be changed.

As you can see in Figure 13-17, there are a lot of options, all of which are enabled by default. To enable just a few, click the Uncheck all button, and select the checkboxes you want.

Some of the icons are intuitive, but others are less so. Table 13-1 describes the editing options made available to the user by selecting each icon.

Table 13-1. Options for InContext Editing editable regions

Icon	Permits	Comments
B	Bold text	Uses `font-weight: bold`.
I	Italic text	Uses `font-style: italic`.

Icon	Permits	Comments
U	Underline text	Uses text-decoration: underline.
≡	Align text	Text can be aligned left, right, centered, and justified. Uses the deprecated align attribute.
F	Change font	User can choose from a selection of fonts. Uses font-family style property.
T	Change font size	User can select one of the following sizes: 10px, 13px, 16px, 18px, 24px, 32px, and 48px. Uses font-size style property.
⇥	Indent text	Wraps the text in a <div> and applies the margin-left property as an inline style. If the selection is already inside a block-level tag, the style is applied to the existing tag.
≔	Insert and edit lists	Numbered and bulleted lists only. Uses standard HTML <ol>, <ul>, and <li> tags.
A	Create headings	The tooltip for this icon misleadingly describes it as Paragraph Styles. Paragraphs are simulated by inserting tags. This option controls only heading styles (<h1> to <h6>). There is no way to restrict the range of available heading levels.
T	Change background color	Colors must be chosen from the 216 in the same basic color picker as used in Dreamweaver. Uses background-color style property.
T	Change text color	Allows the user to pick one of 216 colors for selected text. Uses color style property.
s	Use CSS classes	Gives the user access to all classes defined in selected external style sheets. The class is applied via a <span> wrapped around the selection.
▦	Insert media or image files	Files can be sourced from the Internet, the user's local hard disk, or a designated media folder in the site.
⊂⊃	Create links	Links can be to other pages, external websites, and files in the site's designated media folder. InContext Editing automatically inserts a title attribute. If the user doesn't enter anything in the tooltip field, title="" is added to the <a> tag. Optionally inserts target="_blank" to open the target page in a new browser window or tab.

13

Depending on the options you choose, the `ice:editable` attribute in the editable region's parent tag changes. If all options are selected, the opening `<div>` tag looks like this:

```
<div ice:editable="*">
```

If you select only bold, italic, CSS classes, media and images, and links, it looks like this:

```
<div ice:editable="bold,italic,css_styles,media,hyperlink" >
```

Understanding the code created through selecting the options in the Property inspector gives you a finer level of control. For example, the icon to align text inserts the following values into the parent tag:

```
<div ice:editable="align_justify,align_right,align_center,align_left">
```

You can restrict this to centering text by amending the attribute like this:

```
<div ice:editable="align_center">
```

Most options result in wrapping content in `<span>` tags. Wherever possible, InContext Editing uses CSS properties as inline styles. However, you can disable these features and create your own classes as described later in the chapter.

Copying the InContext Editing files to your site

The first time you save a page containing InContext Editing markup, Dreamweaver displays the dialog box shown in Figure 13-18 advising you that three files are being copied to a folder called `includes/ice` in your site root. You must upload these files to your remote server in order to use the InContext Editing service.

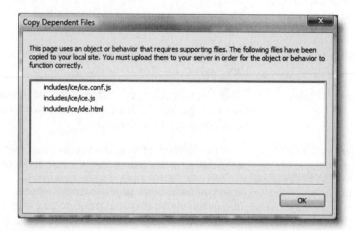

Figure 13-18. InContext Editing relies on external files that must be saved and uploaded to your server.

Changing the InContext Editing login shortcut

One of the files, `ice.conf.js`, determines the keyboard shortcut used to log into the InContext Editing server. The default shortcut is Ctrl+E/Cmd+E. However, you can change this by editing this file.

All you need to do is edit these two lines of code:

```
ICE.USER_LOGIN_PC = "CTRL+E";
ICE.USER_LOGIN_MAC = "CMD+E";
```

To change the login shortcut to Ctrl+Alt+Shift+W/Cmd+Opt+Shift+W, amend the two lines like this:

```
ICE.USER_LOGIN_PC = "CTRL+ALT+SHIFT+W";
ICE.USER_LOGIN_MAC = "CMD+ALT+SHIFT+W";
```

When setting a new shortcut, you need to be careful not to override any of the keyboard shortcuts used by the browsers listed earlier in "Minimum requirements for InContext Editing." Otherwise, anyone who uses that shortcut will be prompted to log into InContext Editing, rather than getting the browser to respond as expected.

Creating a repeating region

As with templates, repeating regions are not automatically editable, so you will normally apply an editable region first and then convert it to a repeating region. To convert the whole of an editable region into a repeating region, select the turquoise tab at the top left of the region and click the Create Repeating Region button on the InContext Editing tab (see Figure 13-15) of the Insert bar, or use the menu option Insert ➤ InContext Editing ➤ Create Repeating Region.

This adds the `ice:repeating` attribute to the opening tag like this:

```
<div ice:repeating="true" ice:editable="*">
```

The turquoise tab at the top left of the region changes from Editable Region to Repeating Region, but the options in the Property inspector remain the same as in Figure 13-17 and Table 13-1.

If you apply a repeating region to content that cannot be edited or to content that contains a mixture of material that can and cannot be edited, the Property inspector looks like Figure 13-19.

13

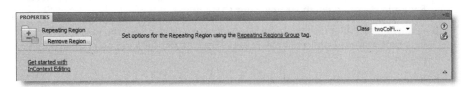

Figure 13-19. Unless the entire repeating region is editable, it has no options.

This is because options common to repeating regions need to be set through the repeating regions group they belong to. When you insert a repeating region, Dreamweaver automatically converts its parent element into a repeating regions group by adding the ice:repeatinggroup attribute to the parent element's opening tag. Clicking the Repeating Regions Group link in the Property inspector selects the parent element and reveals options that affect all repeating regions within the same group (see Figure 13-20).

Controlling actions within a repeating regions group

The purpose of a repeating regions group is to control the scope of repeating regions, as well as what the user can do with all repeating regions within the same group. Select the Repeating Regions Group turquoise tab at the top left of the parent element to display the group options, as shown in Figure 13-20.

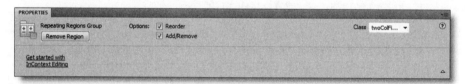

Figure 13-20. The Repeating Regions Group controls all repeating regions within the same parent element.

As Figure 13-20 shows, there are just two options for a repeating regions group:

- Reorder: Selecting this allows the user to change the order of repeating regions within the group.

- Add/Remove: This option allows the user to add or remove repeating regions. The type of new content that can be added is controlled by the options set in each editable region within the repeating regions group.

Removing editable and repeating regions

The Remove Region button on the Property inspector removes the ice:editable, ice:repeating, or ice:repeatinggroup attribute from the opening tag of the selected region. This is a nondestructive operation, because it leaves intact all the content within the region. However, you should note the following points:

- The Remove Region button does not remove any <div> tags inserted when an editable region was created. To remove redundant tags, right-click the tag in the Tag selector, and select Remove Tag from the context menu. If you're not careful, failure to do so could affect how your CSS works.

- Removing an editable repeating region involves clicking Remove Region twice. The first time removes the editable region. The second time removes the repeating region.

- When you remove the last repeating region from a repeating region group, Dreamweaver selects the parent tag ready for you to remove the group markup.

Enabling the use of CSS classes

Although the editable region options cover most aspects of presentation, the range of colors is very limited. There's also a danger that the integrity of your design could be quickly ruined by inexperienced users selecting inappropriate fonts, font sizes, and colors. A much greater level of control can be achieved by deselecting most of the options in Table 13-1 and creating dedicated styles for the user.

InContext Editing lets you designate one or more external style sheets for use with the hosted service. The only restrictions are as follows:

- Only class selectors can be used. They must be simple class selectors. For example, .warning is supported; p.warning is not.

- Only style sheets attached to the page using the <link> tag are supported. Styles attached using @import are ignored.

- Styles embedded in the <head> of the document are ignored.

It's important to emphasize that these restrictions affect *only* what is accessible to the user when amending a page through the InContext Editing server. This means you can utilize all your CSS skills to design the overall look of the site and restrict the user to a small subset.

To enable CSS classes in an InContext Editing page, click the Manage Available CSS Classes button (see Figure 3-15) in the InContext Editing tab of the Insert bar, or use the menu option Insert ➤ InContext Editing ➤ Manage Available CSS Classes. This opens the dialog box shown in Figure 13-21.

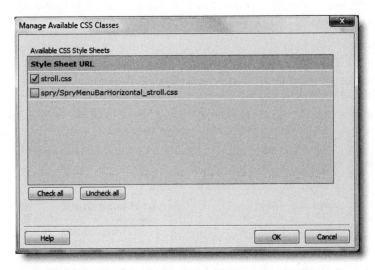

Figure 13-21. You can choose which style sheets to make available to users.

13

The dialog box lists all style sheets attached to the page through the `<link>` tag. Select those you want to make available through InContext Editing, and click OK. This inserts the `ice:classes` attribute into the `<link>` tags of selected style sheets like this:

```
<link href="stroll.css" rel="stylesheet" type="text/css" ➥
ice:classes="*" />
```

Listing the class names in place of the asterisk has no effect. The only way to limit the classes available to users appears to be by creating a separate style sheet.

To disable the use of a style sheet with InContext Editing, open the Manage Available CSS Classes dialog box (see Figure 13-21), and deselect the style sheet. To remove all style sheets, click Uncheck all.

Preparing a page for InContext Editing

This section guides you through the process I used to adapt the Stroll Along the Thames page for use with InContext Editing. If you worked through the template exercises in the first half of this chapter, you'll see that I needed to take a different approach. Instead of making the entire mainContent `<div>` an editable region, I turned it into two repeating editable regions. By contrast, it proved impossible to turn the bulleted list at the top of the sidebar into a repeating region, so I wrapped it in an editable region restricted to using only lists.

If you want to follow along as a hands-on exercise, use stroll_ice_start.php in examples/ch13. The finished code is in stroll_ice.php. However, to edit the page with InContext Editing, you need to sign up for an account (see http://www.adobe.com/products/incontextediting/ for details).

1. To convert the bulleted list at the top of the sidebar into an editable region, click inside the list, and select `<ul>` in the Tag selector.

2. Click the Create Editable Region button in the InContext Editing tab of the Insert bar, and accept the option to wrap the selection in a `<div>`.

3. With the editable region still selected, click Uncheck all in the Property inspector, and select the Numbered List and Bulleted List checkbox.

4. Open Split view, and edit the ice:editable attribute in the opening `<div>` tag to remove ordered_list. The bulleted list should now look like this:

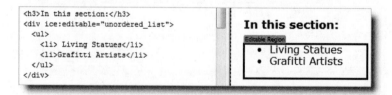

In theory, this should restrict the editable region to creating or editing bulleted lists. However, in my tests, it still permitted numbered lists as well.

Although this would seem ideal to turn into a repeating region, you can't do so because the <li> elements need to be wrapped in <div> tags. When you publish the page through InContext Editing, the <div> tags remain, but the <li> tags are deleted, leaving you with no bullets alongside each item.

5. In the mainContent <div>, select the Living Statues heading and the following paragraph. Turn it into an editable region in the same way as in step 2.

6. With the editable region still selected, deselect all options except for bold, italic, numbered and bulleted lists, paragraph styles, CSS classes, images, and links. The selections in the Property inspector look like this:

7. With the editable region still selected, click the Create Repeating Region button in the InContext Editing tab of the Insert bar to convert it into an editable repeating region.

Since this is the first repeating region that has been created, Dreamweaver converts the mainContent <div> into a repeating regions group and selects the entire <div>. Because there is no margin above the Living Statues heading, the turquoise tabs of the repeating region and its parent group overlap, making them difficult to distinguish or select. Clicking the right end of the turquoise tab selects the group, whereas clicking the left of the tab selects the first repeating region.

8. Select the Artists at Work heading and the following paragraph. Convert it into an editable region with the same options as in step 6. Then convert it into a repeating region.

9. Click the Manage Available CSS Classes button in the InContext Editing tab of the Insert bar, and select stroll.css, as shown in Figure 13-21 in the preceding section.

10. Save stroll_ice.php. If this is the first InContext Editing page in the site, click OK to save the external files to the inserts/ice folder (see Figure 13-18).

These changes give anyone authorized to edit the page through InContext Editing relatively limited scope to damage the overall integrity of the design yet sufficient freedom to add new material to the page.

Editing a page with InContext Editing

Before you can use InContext Editing, the web designer or whoever administers the account needs to set up details of the website. This is a relatively simple process to register the FTP details of the site you want to edit through InContext Editing. Follow the instructions given by Adobe when you sign up for the service.

Upload your website to your remote server in the same way as usual. The only extra step involves uploading the contents of the includes/ice folder. The site operates in the same way as an ordinary site.

13

The following pages describe the editing process immediately prior to the official launch. Because InContext Editing is an online service, it can be updated more easily than a desktop program. So, some aspects of the service are likely to change in response to user feedback. Consult the online help for the most up-to-date information.

Logging into InContext Editing

The difference starts when you press the InContext Editing keyboard shortcut (Ctrl+E/Cmd+E unless you change it as described in "Changing the InContext Editing login shortcut") in one of the supported browsers listed earlier.

Within a few seconds, you should see a login screen, as shown in Figure 13-22.

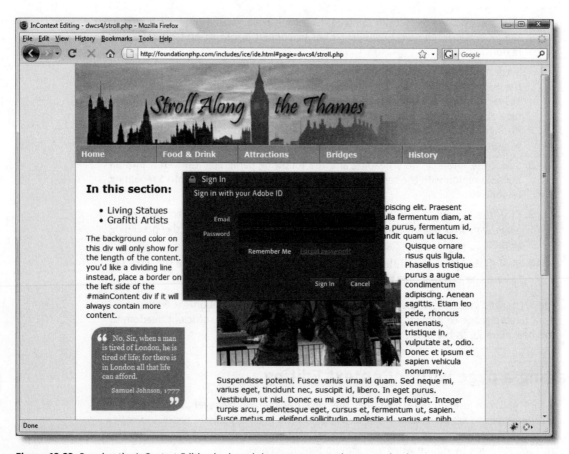

Figure 13-22. Pressing the InContext Editing keyboard shortcut prompts the user to log in.

> With some keyboards, the login screen inserts a double quote when you type the @ sign in your email address. If this happens, press the double quote key instead of the @ one.

Once you have logged in, the InContext Editing toolbar (Figure 13-23) is displayed at the top of your page.

Figure 13-23. The InContext Editing toolbar sits at the top of the page inside the browser.

Updating an editable region

To start editing, click Edit. This adds a second toolbar at the top of the page, and as you move the mouse over the different elements, a tooltip indicates which elements are editable. A heavy border and mini-toolbar are also displayed on repeating regions, as shown in Figure 13-24.

Figure 13-24. The editing interface is intuitive to use.

13

When you click inside an editable region, the rest of the page is dimmed (see Figure 13-25), as are the editing tools that the developer deselected when adding the InContext Editing markup.

Figure 13-25. The rest of the page is dimmed when editing, giving a clear indication of the section being worked on.

The editing toolbar is controlled by three buttons on the left. As shown in the screenshot alongside, they give access to tools for editing text, inserting images and media files, and creating links.

Editing text

The editing toolbar always displays the full range of options, but items that have been disabled by the developer are dimmed and have no effect. All of the options should be familiar to users from word processing programs and use the same icons. With the text button selected on the editing toolbar, the following options are available (see Figure 13-24):

- Font: The drop-down menu offers a choice of web-safe fonts.
- Font size: The user can choose one of the following sizes: 10px, 13px, 16px, 18px, 24px, 32px, and 48px.
- Font color: The color of the font is displayed in an unlabeled square alongside the font size. Clicking the down arrow to the right of the square reveals a color picker with 216 web-safe colors.
- Bold, Italic, Underline: Formatting can either be applied to a selection or toggled on and off as text is being typed.

- Align: Content can be aligned left, centered, right, or justified. All text up to the following line break is affected.

- Bulleted/numbered lists: These buttons work in the same way as a word processor.

- Indent/outdent: These have the effect of indenting text by adding or removing a `margin-left` style to the parent block-level tag.

- Advanced: Clicking the Advanced button reveals the options shown in Figure 13-26, namely:

  - Styles: This can be used to apply a class from an external style sheet enabled as described in "Enabling the use of CSS classes" earlier in this chapter.

  - Headings: This applies <h1> though <h6> to all text up to the next line break.

  - Highlight: This applies a background color to the current selection.

Figure 13-26.
Advanced text editing options

Inserting images and media files

Selecting the second button on the left of the editing toolbar reveals the initial set of options for inserting an image or other media file, as shown in Figure 13-27.

Figure 13-27. Before inserting an image or media file, you need to tell InContext Editing where to find it.

The Media Location drop-down menu offers three options:

- The Internet: Enter the URL of the asset in the field alongside, and click Insert media.

- My Computer: This displays a dialog box for the user to locate a file on your local computer and upload it to the website's designated media folder.

- My Site: This displays the contents of the designated media folder to select a file.

After the file has been inserted, the editing toolbar displays the options shown in Figure 13-28.

13

Figure 13-28. The editing toolbar lets the user change an image, delete it, or alter its size.

The meaning of most options is self-explanatory. The padlock icon on the right is selected by default; it constrains the proportions of the image. For example, if the width of the image in Figure 13-28 is reset to 150 (pixels), the height is automatically adjusted to 200. Although both dimensions are displayed in the toolbar, InContext Editing inserts neither in the <img> tag when the image is left at its default size. When an image is proportionally resized, it inserts only the width or height attribute, but not both.

Figure 13-29 shows the Advanced options for images. The Tooltip option inserts the same value for the alt and title attributes of the <img> tag. If this field is left blank, InContext Editing inserts alt="" title="" into the <img> tag.

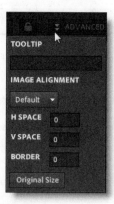

Figure 13-29.
Advanced image editing options

The Image Alignment options insert align, hspace, vspace, and border attributes. Standards warriors will be horrified at the description of deprecated presentational attributes as "advanced," but it seems that label was chosen for options for which there was no room on the main toolbar.

The Original Size button restores the image to its original size by removing its dimensions from the underlying code.

Creating links

Selecting the third button on the left of the toolbar reveals the options for creating links, as shown in Figure 13-30.

Figure 13-30. Links can be created to other web pages, files on the same site, and email addresses.

The Link To drop-down menu has the following four options:

- Web Page: Enter the URL in the field alongside. Use this for external links.
- Document from My Website: This creates a text link to a file in the designated media folder. Selecting this option displays a dialog box for the user to choose a file.
- Page in My Website: Use this for internal links. Selecting this option displays a dialog box for the user to choose a file. It gives access to *all* files in the site.
- Email Address: This inserts a `mailto` link. Enter the email address in the field alongside.

Select the text or image that is to be used for the link, choose the appropriate option, and click the Insert Link button to create the link. Once the link has been created, this button serves to remove the link.

The Open in new window checkbox adds `target="_blank"` to the `<a>` tag.

The Advanced option is visible only when a link exists. It has a single field, Tooltip, which adds a `title` attribute to the `<a>` tag. If nothing is entered in this field, a link to a web page contains `title=""`. Links to an email address or file are automatically populated with the email address or file name. However, this can be replaced with any text.

Editing a repeatable region

Clicking inside an editable repeatable region displays the mini-toolbar in the following screenshot:

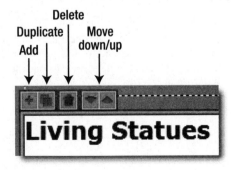

13

Clicking each icon performs the following operation:

- Add a region: This adds a blank editable region immediately above the current selection. What can be added to the new region depends on the settings selected by the developer when adding the InContext Editing markup.

- Duplicate region: This creates a duplicate of the currently selected region immediately below it. Both content and editing capabilities are duplicated.

- Delete region: This deletes the selected repeating region.

- Move region down/up: This lets you change the order of repeating regions within the parent group.

Saving drafts and publishing

After making an edit, you can save it as a draft by clicking Save in the main InContext Editing toolbar. To undo all changes, click Cancel.

Clicking Save does not publish the changes to the live website. They're saved only to the Adobe server. User accounts for InContext Editing can be set up with different access levels, so a junior person can be given permission to make changes but not publish them. This provides an opportunity to show the proposed changes to another person for approval, to make further changes, or to discard them altogether. When you have finished editing, click Done on the main InContext Editing toolbar. The options on the toolbar change to let you edit the current draft, discard it, or publish it, as shown in Figure 13-31.

Return to live website

Figure 13-31. After saving, you can make further edits, discard the changes, or publish the revised page.

The draft remains on the Adobe server until you or another authorized user decide what to do with it. However, if you click the Publish button and confirm that you want to update the live site, that's it. There is no way of rolling back. The page is immediately updated on the live website. The only ways of restoring it to its former state are to edit the page through InContext Editing again, or upload the original version of the page from the developer's computer.

After working on a page, you can return to the live website by clicking the icon at the bottom right of the toolbar. This keeps you signed into the InContext Editing server, so you can choose another page to edit without the need to sign back in again. Once you have finished, click the Sign Out button at the top right.

Assessing the pros and cons of InContext Editing

It's too early at the time of this writing to offer a considered judgment of InContext Editing. In my testing, adding the markup to a web page was very easy once I understood the limitations of using only <div>, <th>, and <td> as editable elements. Editing through the InContext Editing service was also very easy. However, I also found it very easy to turn a unified design into a hideous mess by changing fonts, colors, and backgrounds. To avoid this, you need to disable many of the editing options.

Used carefully on a handful of pages to make limited edits, this could be a very useful service. However, I don't believe it is suitable for editing whole pages or websites.

The following points also need to be taken into consideration:

- Once a page has been edited through InContext Editing, the version on the development computer is out of date. Uploading a page from the development computer restores the page to its original state but deletes any new content.

- Although InContext Editing uses CSS wherever possible and you can enable your own classes, most presentational markup is applied through <span> tags and inline styles. This produces a modern version of tag soup little different from old-style markup with <font> tags. Editing pages that have been updated through InContext Editing could be time-consuming for the developer.

- Dynamic code, such as PHP or JavaScript, *must not be included* in an editable area. Otherwise, it is likely to be overwritten when changes are made to the page through InContext Editing.

- Repeating regions should not contain elements with IDs because this will result in multiple instances of the same IDs if a repeating region is duplicated. This will prevent any JavaScript that interacts with those IDs from working.

- The InContext Editing markup inserts nonstandard attributes inside HTML tags, preventing pages from validating. To get around this problem, Adobe has developed an unobtrusive version of the markup using CSS classes. This requires the installation of a Dreamweaver extension that was released just as this book went to the printers. For details and a tutorial, see http://www.adobe.com/devnet/dreamweaver/articles/incontext_applying_unob_code.html.

- Even if unobtrusive markup is used, InContext Editing relies on easily identifiable markup within the HTML. This could be used by a hacker to identify sites to try to break into. All communication with the Adobe server is done through the secure sockets layer, and Adobe encrypts the site's FTP login details; but if individual users choose passwords that are simple to guess or share their login details with others, pages that are enabled for InContext Editing could easily be compromised.

13

Chapter review

Templates and InContext Editing both offer solutions to the problem of allowing less skilled people to update a website's content without destroying the overall integrity of the design. However, templates currently offer the developer a much finer level of control. They can also be useful even when no one else is involved in the creation or updating of a site, because they allow the developer to lock fixed elements of the design and generate identical child pages in seconds. When used in combination with PHP includes, they become even more versatile because the contents of the include file are propagated to all files without the need to update every page in the site. Adobe has developed InContext Editing in response to what it perceives as a market demand for simple updates to web pages. It will be interesting to see how the market responds.

This chapter has covered most aspects of working with templates apart from repeating tables and advanced features, such as nested templates and editable attributes. I have omitted them because I believe that PHP offers a more flexible solution to similar issues. The next chapter begins an in-depth exploration of Dreamweaver's PHP server behaviors, which make light work of storing information in a MySQL database, retrieving the information for display in a web page, as well as updating and deleting it. Even if you have never used a database before, you will have a basic content management system up and running in surprisingly little time.

Dynamic websites take on a whole new meaning in combination with a database. Drawing content from a database allows you to present material in ways that would be impractical—if not impossible—with a static website. Examples that spring to mind are online stores, such as Amazon.com; news sites, such as the International Herald Tribune (http://www.iht.com); and the big search engines, including Google and Yahoo!. Database technology allows these websites to present thousands, sometimes millions, of unique pages with remarkably little underlying code. Even if your ambitions are nowhere near as grandiose, a database can increase your website's richness of content with relatively little effort.

Although PHP is capable of interacting with most popular databases (and some less well-known ones, too), Dreamweaver has made the choice for you. All the server behaviors are designed to work with MySQL. In one respect, this is a good choice, because it's widely available, free, and very fast and it offers an excellent range of features. The downside is that the server behaviors work *only* with MySQL. If you want to use a different database, such as PostgreSQL (http://www.postgresql.org/), SQLite (http://www.sqlite.org/), or Microsoft Access (http://office.microsoft.com/access), you have to do all the coding by hand.

Although Dreamweaver does a lot of the hard work for you when building a database-driven website, it's important to remember that you're combining several technologies. So, there's a lot to learn. A big mistake that most beginners make is to rush headlong into creating a database and cram it full of data without understanding how databases work (I know, I did it myself many years ago). I'll try not to overburden you with too much heavy theory, but this chapter starts with some of the basic knowledge that you'll need to start working with a MySQL database.

In this chapter, you'll learn about the following:

- Creating MySQL user accounts
- Defining a database table through the phpMyAdmin graphical interface
- Choosing the appropriate data types for database columns
- Using Dreamweaver server behaviors to insert, update, and delete records
- Creating a simple user registration system

I assume you already have access to a MySQL database, preferably in a local testing environment. The current stable version of MySQL is 5.0, but MySQL 5.1 should be released around the time this book is published. Dreamweaver is compatible with MySQL as far back as MySQL 3.23, but you should ideally be using a minimum of MySQL 4.1, because older versions do not support UTF-8 encoding.

Introducing MySQL

If you have ever worked with Microsoft Access, your first encounter with MySQL might come as something of a shock. For one thing, it doesn't have a glossy interface. As

Figure 14-1 shows, it looks like a throwback to the old days of DOS before the friendly interfaces of Mac and Windows. Its beauty lies, however, in its simplicity. What's more, most of the time you'll never see MySQL in its raw state like this. You'll use either Dreamweaver or a graphic front end. Several graphic front ends for MySQL are available—some free, others commercial products. The one I'll be using in this book is a free application called phpMyAdmin (http://www.phpmyadmin.net/). Best of all, you'll be designing your own personalized interface by creating PHP pages.

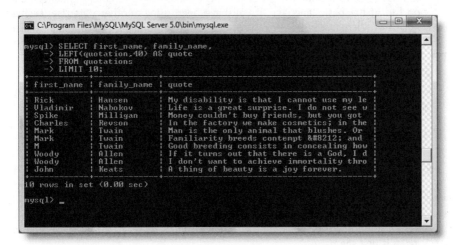

Figure 14-1. The unadorned interface of MySQL in a Windows Command Prompt window

The other thing that comes as a surprise to Access users is that your database is not kept in a single file that you can upload to your remote server. MySQL keeps all databases in a central data folder, and each database table normally consists of three separate files. The way you transfer data from one server to another is by creating a text file that contains all the necessary commands to build the database and its contents—in other words, a backup file. All you need to know now is that there isn't "a database file"—there are lots of them, and normally, you should never handle them directly.

Understanding basic MySQL terminology

If you haven't worked with a relational database before, you may find your head spinning with some of the names that crop up throughout the rest of this book. So, here's a quick guide:

- **SQL**: Structured Query Language is the international standard behind all major relational databases. It's used to insert and otherwise manipulate data and is based on natural English. For instance, let's say you have a database table called members that stores each person's details as first_name, family_name, and username. You

14

would use the following command (or SQL query) to find the first_name and family_name for the person whose username is dpowers:

```
SELECT first_name, family_name
FROM members
WHERE username = 'dpowers'
```

As you can see, it's very human-readable, unlike many other computer languages. Although SQL is a standard, all of the main databases have added enhancements on top of the basic language. If you have been using another database, such as Access or Microsoft SQL Server, be prepared for some slight differences in the use of functions. Some people pronounce SQL "sequel," while others say "Ess-queue-ell." Both are right.

- **MySQL**: This refers to the entire database system created by MySQL AB, originally a Swedish company but now part of Sun Microsystems (http://www.sun.com). It's always spelled in uppercase, except for the "y," and the official pronunciation is "My-ess-queue-ell." It's not just a single program, but a client/server system with a number of related programs that perform various administrative tasks. The two main components are mysql and mysqld, with both terms entirely in lowercase.

- mysql: This has three distinct meanings. The first is the client program used to feed requests to the database. mysql is also the name of the main administrative database that controls user accounts, and on Windows, it is the name of the Windows service that starts and stops the database server. Once you start working with MySQL, differentiating between the different meanings of "mysql" is not as confusing as it first seems.

Using MySQL with a graphic interface

Although you can use MySQL in a Windows Command Prompt window or Mac Terminal, it's a lot easier to use a graphic interface. There are several to choose from, both commercial and free. Among the free offerings are two from MySQL: MySQL Administrator and MySQL Query Browser (http://www.mysql.com/products/tools). Three other popular graphical front ends for MySQL are Navicat (http://www.navicat.com), a commercial product, and DBTools Manager (http://www.dbtools.com.br/EN/dbmanagerpro/) and SQLyog (http://www.webyog.com), which are available in both commercial and free versions.

However, the most popular graphical interface for MySQL is phpMyAdmin (http://www.phpmyadmin.net). It's a PHP-based administrative system for MySQL that has been around since 1998, and it constantly evolves to keep pace with MySQL developments. It works on Windows, Mac OS X, and Linux. What's more, many hosting companies provide it as the standard interface to MySQL. For that reason, I plan to use phpMyAdmin throughout the rest of this book.

If you installed XAMPP or MAMP, phpMyAdmin is already installed on your local computer. However, for the benefit of readers who need to install phpMyAdmin, the next section describes the process.

Setting up phpMyAdmin on Windows and Mac

Like a lot of open source applications, phpMyAdmin is constantly evolving. At the time of this writing, a major rewrite of the application, phpMyAdmin 3, had reached release candidate status. The upgrade to version 3 has been necessitated by the imminent release of MySQL 5.1, which is not supported by phpMyAdmin 2. Fortunately, the installation process for the new version remains unchanged—at least it was at the time I wrote the following instructions. Any changes of a substantial nature will be listed on my website at http://foundationphp.com/dwcs4/updates.php.

Downloading and installing phpMyAdmin

Since phpMyAdmin is PHP-based, all that's needed to install it is to download the files, unzip them to a website in your local testing environment, and create a simple configuration file. phpMyAdmin 3 requires a minimum of PHP 5.2 and MySQL 5.0. If you are running earlier versions, you must install phpMyAdmin 2.

1. Go to http://www.phpmyadmin.net, and download the version you require. The files can be downloaded in three types of compressed file: BZIP2, GZIP, and ZIP. Choose whichever format you have the decompression software for.

2. Unzip the downloaded file. It will extract the contents to a folder called phpMyAdmin-x.x.x, where x represents the version number.

3. Highlight the folder icon, and cut it to your clipboard. On Windows, paste it inside the folder designated as your web server root (with an Apache server, this is usually a folder called htdocs). If you're on a Mac and want phpMyAdmin to be available to all users, put the folder in Macintosh HD:Library:WebServer:Documents rather than in your own Sites folder.

4. Rename the folder you have just moved to this: phpMyAdmin.

5. Create a new subfolder called config within the phpMyAdmin folder. Windows users skip to step 7. Mac users continue with step 6.

6. On Mac OS X, use Finder to locate the config folder you have just created. Ctrl-click and select Get Info. In Ownership & Permissions, expand Details, and click the lock icon so that you can make changes to the settings. Change the setting for Others to Read & Write. Close the config Info panel.

7. Open a browser, and type the following into the address bar:

   http://localhost/phpmyadmin/scripts/setup.php

   If you created the phpMyAdmin folder inside your Sites folder on a Mac, use the following address, substituting *username* with your Mac username:

   http://localhost/~*username*/phpmyadmin/scripts/setup.php

8. You should see the page shown in Figure 14-2.

14

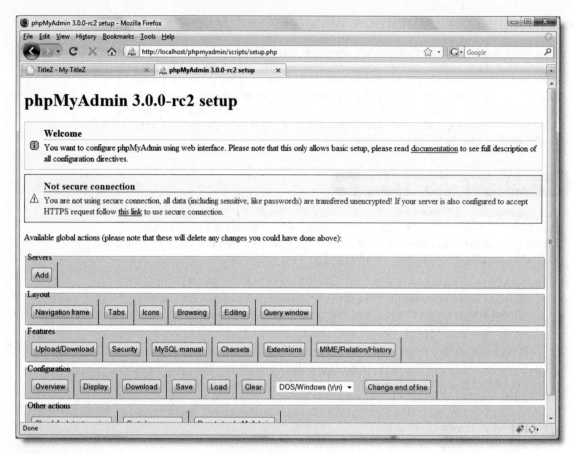

Figure 14-2. A built-in script automates the configuration of phpMyAdmin.

Ignore any warning about the connection not being secure. This is intended for server administrators installing phpMyAdmin on a live Internet server. If, on the other hand, you see the following warning, it means you have not set up the config folder correctly and should go back to step 5.

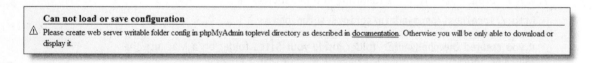

9. Click the Add button in the Servers section. This loads a form with most of the necessary information already filled in. Check the following settings:

   - Server hostname: localhost

   - Server port: Leave blank unless your web server is running on a nonstandard port, such as 8080

- Server socket: Leave blank
- Connection type: tcp
- PHP extension to use: mysqli

10. The default setting for Authentication type is config. If you don't need to password protect access to phpMyAdmin, check that User for config auth is set to root, and enter your MySQL root password in the next field, Password for config auth.

If you want to restrict access to phpMyAdmin by prompting users for a password, change Authentication type to http, and delete root from the User for config auth field.

11. Scroll down to the Actions field, and click Add. As shown here, there are two Add buttons close to each other; click the one circled in the screenshot:

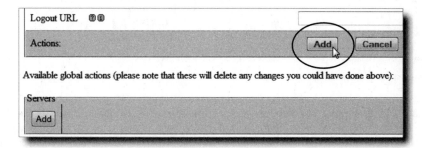

12. The next screen will probably warn you that you didn't set up a phpMyAdmin database, so you won't be able to use all the phpMyAdmin features. This is not important. You can set up one later if you decide to use the advanced features of phpMyAdmin.

13. Scroll down to the Configuration section near the bottom of the page, and click Save.

14. Open the config folder in Explorer or Finder. You should see a new file called config.inc.php. Move it to the main phpMyAdmin folder. The official instructions tell you to delete the config folder, but this isn't necessary in a local testing environment.

Launching phpMyAdmin

To use phpMyAdmin, launch a browser, and enter http://localhost/phpMyAdmin/index.php in the address bar (on a Mac, use http://localhost/~*username*/phpMyAdmin/index.php if you put phpMyAdmin in your Sites folder). If you stored your root password in config.inc.php, phpMyAdmin should load right away, as shown in Figure 14-3. If you chose to password protect phpMyAdmin, enter root as the username and whatever you specified as the MySQL root password when prompted.

14

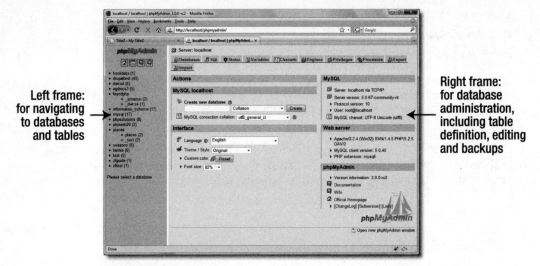

Left frame:
for navigating
to databases
and tables

Right frame:
for database
administration,
including table
definition, editing
and backups

Figure 14-3. phpMyAdmin is a very user-friendly and stable graphical interface to MySQL.

I have a large number of databases on my computer, so you'll have a much shorter list in the left frame than shown in Figure 14-3. If you're used to glossy software design, your initial impression of phpMyAdmin may not be all that favorable, particularly if you don't have a large monitor. The interface is sorely in need of a face-lift, but don't let that fool you; phpMyAdmin is both powerful and easy to use. The layout is slightly different in phpMyAdmin 2, so don't be surprised if your version doesn't look exactly like the screenshots in this book.

Troubleshooting

The following common errors occur when launching phpMyAdmin:

- If you get a message saying that the server is not responding or that the socket is not correctly configured, make sure that the MySQL server is running.

- If you get a message that the `mysqli` module cannot be loaded, there's a mistake in your installation of PHP. This normally happens only on Windows. Display your server's PHP configuration details by creating a script with `<?php phpinfo(); ?>` in it (and nothing else), and load it in a browser. Scroll roughly halfway down the page to locate sections for mysql and mysqli. If they're not there, you need to reinstall PHP and select both MySQL and MySQLi in the list of extensions to be enabled.

- If you get messages about failing to write session data or not being able to start a session without errors, it means that the folder PHP uses to save session information doesn't exist or is read-only. Use `phpinfo()` to display your PHP configuration details, and find the value of `session.save_path` (it's close to the bottom of the page in the session section). Make sure that the folder exists and is writable.

  If the folder doesn't exist, create it. On Windows, you don't normally need to set any permissions to make the folder writable. On a Mac, select the folder in Finder, and press Cmd+I to display a Get Info panel. In the Ownership & Permissions section, expand Details, and set Others to Read & Write.

Logging out of phpMyAdmin

If you opted to password protect phpMyAdmin, a Log out link is added to the front page. When you click the link, you are immediately prompted for your username and password. Click Cancel, and you are presented with a screen informing you that you supplied the wrong username/password—in other words, you have been logged out. Odd, but that's the way it works. You cannot log back in to phpMyAdmin from the wrong username/password screen. You must enter the original URL into the browser address bar.

Setting up a database in MySQL

MySQL isn't a single database, but a relational database management system (RDBMS). The screenshot in Figure 14-3 was taken on my development computer, which contains more than a dozen databases listed in the left frame of phpMyAdmin. However, if you examine a new installation of MySQL in phpMyAdmin, you'll see it contains the following three databases:

- `information_schema`: This is a virtual database that contains details of other databases within the RDBMS.
- `mysql`: This contains all the user account and security information and should never be edited directly unless you're really sure what you're doing.
- `test`: This contains nothing. You can either use it for testing or delete it.

The numbers phpMyAdmin displays in parentheses alongside each database name indicate how many tables that database contains.

If you're using a remote server and your hosting company provides phpMyAdmin, the list of databases will be limited to those on your account, or you may be limited to only one database.

Creating a local database for testing

Assuming you have set up a local testing environment, you need to create a test database to work with the remaining chapters. I'm going to call the database dwcs4, and that's how I'll refer to it from now on. However, if you already have a hosting package, I suggest you use the name of a database on your remote server, because this will make things a lot easier when it comes to testing your pages on the Internet.

Type the name of the database in the field labeled Create new database in the phpMyAdmin welcome screen, and click Create, as shown in Figure 14-4. Most readers can leave Collation in its default position. However, if you're working in a language other than English, Swedish, or Finnish, *and* your remote server runs MySQL 4.1 or later, read "Understanding collation" before clicking Create.

14

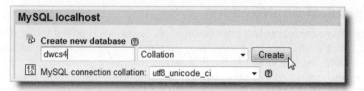

Figure 14-4. To create a new database, just type its name into the phpMyAdmin welcome screen, and click Create.

Because phpMyAdmin is a browser-based application, the precise layout of what you see onscreen depends on the size of your monitor and browser viewport. The layout of phpMyAdmin 3 also differs slightly from phpMyAdmin 2. However, the basic functionality remains the same.

The database should be created instantly, and phpMyAdmin will invite you to create a new table. Before doing that, you need to create at least one user account for the database. Leave phpMyAdmin open.

Understanding collation

Collation determines the sort order of records. Different languages have their own sorting rules, so MySQL 4.1 and above let you set the default sort order at different levels: for the entire database, for individual tables, and for individual columns. MySQL was originally developed in Sweden, so the default sort order is `latin1_swedish_ci`. English and Finnish share the same sort order.

If you work in a different language and your remote server is MySQL 4.1 or above, click the Charsets tab (or the Character Sets and Collations link in phpMyAdmin 2) on the phpMyAdmin welcome screen to see the full range of supported sort orders. When defining a new database or table, select the appropriate sort order from the Collation drop-down menu.

You can change the collation of an existing database or table in phpMyAdmin by selecting it in the left frame and then clicking the Operations tab. Since collation can be set at different levels, this sets the default only for new tables or columns. Existing tables and columns preserve their original collation unless you edit them individually.

If you are working in a language, such as Spanish or French, that uses accented characters, MySQL 3.23 and 4.0 do not support UTF-8 (Unicode). This affects the way accented characters are stored. If accented characters are garbled when retrieving records from MySQL, change the default encoding of your web pages from UTF-8 to the encoding appropriate for your language. Alternatively, store accented characters as HTML entities (for example, é for é). Better still, upgrade to MySQL 5.

Creating user accounts for MySQL

A new installation of MySQL has only one registered user—the superuser account called **root**, which has complete control over everything. A lot of beginners use root for everything and don't even bother setting up a password for root. This is a big mistake. The root user should *never* be used for anything other than administration, and you should get into the good habit of using a password for root. XAMPP and MAMP both have instructions for setting the root password. If you need to change the root password in phpMyAdmin, follow the instructions in the next section. Otherwise, skip ahead to "Granting user privileges."

Changing the MySQL root password in phpMyAdmin

Changing the MySQL root password in phpMyAdmin is quick and easy. Just follow these steps:

1. Launch phpMyAdmin, and click the Privileges tab in the welcome screen (it's a link on the left side of the main frame in phpMyAdmin 2).

2. This displays a list of MySQL user accounts, as shown in Figure 14-5 (if it's a new installation, the only one listed is root). Click the Edit privileges icon alongside root.

Edit privileges

	User	Host	Password	Global privileges [1]	Grant	
☐	dw8admin	localhost	Yes	USAGE	No	⚡
☐	dw8query	localhost	Yes	USAGE	No	⚡
☐	egadmin	localhost	Yes	USAGE	No	⚡
☐	eguser	localhost	Yes	USAGE	No	⚡
☐	flexbuilder	localhost	Yes	USAGE	No	⚡
☐	psadmin	localhost	Yes	USAGE	No	⚡
☐	psquery	localhost	Yes	USAGE	No	⚡
☐	root	localhost	Yes	ALL PRIVILEGES	Yes	⚡
☐	zfguide	%	Yes	USAGE	No	⚡

Figure 14-5. Click the icon in the right column to edit a user's privileges.

3. This opens the Edit Privileges screen. Scroll down until you find the following section:

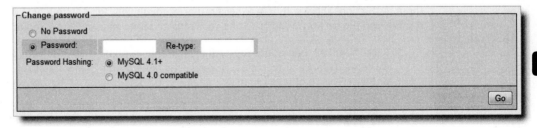

14

4. Select the Password radio button, and enter the new password in both fields. Unless you are using an old version of MySQL, leave Password Hashing on the default, MySQL 4.1+.

5. Click Go in the Change password section. There are several Go buttons on the page. Make sure you select the one in the right section.

6. If you selected config as the authentication type when setting up phpMyAdmin, don't forget to update config.inc.php. You can do this manually by opening the file and changing the following line:

```
$cfg['Servers'][$i]['password'] = 'newRootPassword';
```

Granting user privileges

MySQL stores all databases in a common directory. So, on shared hosting, your database—with all its precious information—rubs shoulders with everyone else's. Clearly, you need a way to prevent unauthorized people from seeing or altering your data. The answer is to create user accounts that have the fewest number of privileges necessary to perform essential tasks, preferably on a single database.

You normally want visitors to your site to be able to see the information it contains but not to change it. However, as administrator, you need to be able to insert new records and update or delete existing ones. This involves four types of privileges, all named after the equivalent SQL commands:

- SELECT: Retrieves records from database tables
- INSERT: Inserts records into a database
- UPDATE: Changes existing records
- DELETE: Deletes records but not tables or databases (the command for that is DROP)

In an ideal setup, you create two separate user accounts: one for administrators, who require all four privileges, and another one for visitors, limited to SELECT. If your hosting company lets you set up user accounts with different privileges, I suggest you create two accounts like this. However, if you have no choice, set up one account and use the same username and password as on your remote server.

Setting up MySQL user accounts

These instructions show you how to set up user accounts in a local testing environment. You can skip this section if you are using your remote server as your testing server.

1. Click the home icon at the top of the left frame in phpMyAdmin to return to the welcome screen, and then click Privileges. In phpMyAdmin 3, this is a tab at the top of the screen. In phpMyAdmin 2, it's a link in the left column of the main frame.

> *To create a new user account, you must use the link in the welcome screen. The* Privileges *tab in other screens displays details of existing accounts only.*

2. The User overview screen opens. Click Add a new User halfway down the page.

3. In the page that opens, enter the name of the user account that you want to create in the User name field. Select Local from the Host drop-down menu. This automatically enters localhost in the field alongside. This option restricts the user to connecting to MySQL only from the same computer. Enter a password in the Password field, and confirm it in the Re-type field. The Login Information table should look like this:

Dreamweaver needs these details later to make a connection to the database. The password I used for the cs4admin user when creating the download files is humpty. If you want to use the download files exactly as they are, you need to use the same password and username as I did. However, I suggest you use your own username and password both here and when creating the MySQL connection in Dreamweaver later in the chapter.

4. Beneath the Login Information table is one labeled Global privileges. Granting such extensive privileges is insecure, so scroll past the Global privileges table, and click the Go button at the bottom of the page.

5. The next page confirms that the user has been created and displays many options, beginning with the Global privileges again. Scroll down to the section labeled Database-specific privileges. Activate the drop-down menu, as shown here, to display a list of all databases. Select the name for the database you plan to use for testing.

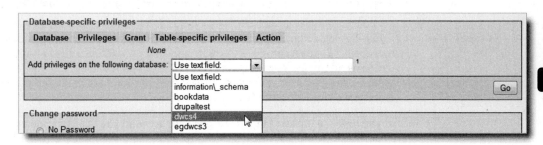

14

6. The next screen allows you to set the user's privileges for just this database. You want the admin user to have all four privileges listed earlier, so click the SELECT, INSERT, UPDATE, and DELETE checkboxes (if you hover your mouse pointer over each option, phpMyAdmin displays a tooltip describing what it's for). After selecting the four privileges, as shown here, click the top Go button.

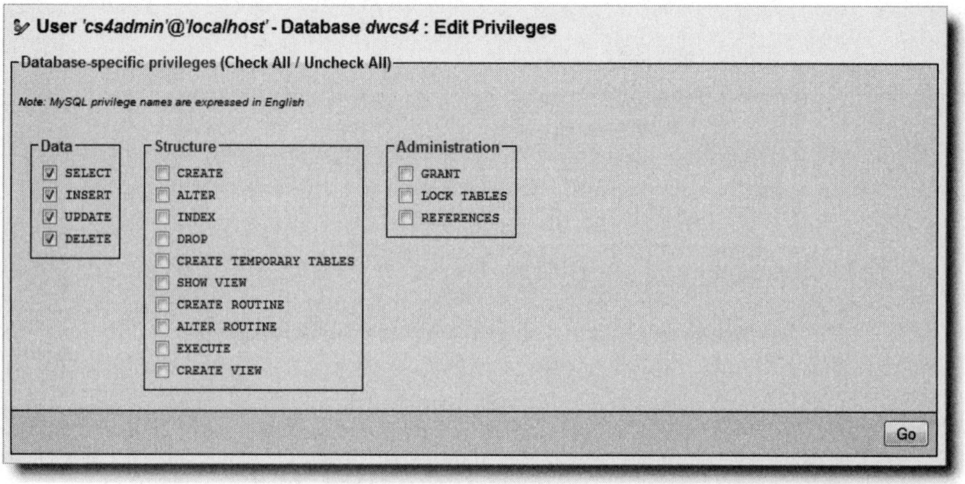

phpMyAdmin frequently offers you a variety of options on the same page, each of which normally has its own Go button. Always click the one at the foot of or alongside the section that relates to the options you want to set.

7. phpMyAdmin presents you with confirmation that the privileges have been updated for the user account. The page displays the Database-specific privileges table again, in case you need to change anything. Assuming you got it right, click the Privileges tab at the top right of the page. You should now see the new user listed in the User overview.

If you ever need to make any changes to a user's privileges, click the Edit Privileges icon to the right of the listing (see Figure 14-5 in the previous section). You can also delete users by selecting the checkbox to the left of the User column and then clicking Go.

8. If your hosting company permits you to create multiple user accounts, click Add a new User, and repeat steps 3–7 to create a second user account. If you want to use the same username and password as in the download files, call the account cs4user, and give it the password dumpty. This user will have restricted privileges, so in step 6, check only the SELECT option.

Now that you have a database and at least one user account, you can start adding tables to store information. However, first, you need to understand the principles behind table construction.

How a database stores information

All data in MySQL is stored in tables, with information organized into rows and columns very much like a spreadsheet. Figure 14-6 shows a simple database table as seen in phpMyAdmin.

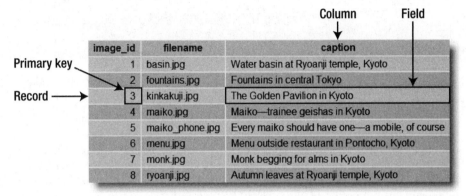

Figure 14-6. Information in a database table is stored in rows and columns, just like in a spreadsheet.

Each **column** has a name (image_id, filename, and caption) indicating what it stores.

The rows aren't labeled, but the first column (image_id) contains a unique identifier known as a **primary key**, which can be used to identify the data associated with a particular row. Each row contains an individual **record** of related data. The significance of primary keys is explained in the next section.

The intersection of a row and a column, where the data is stored, is called a **field**. So, for instance, the caption field for the third record in Figure 14-6 contains the value The Golden Pavilion in Kyoto, and the primary key for that record is 3.

> *The terms "field" and "column" are often used interchangeably. A field holds one piece of information for a single record, whereas a column contains the same field for all records.*

How primary keys work

Although Figure 14-6 shows image_id as a consecutive sequence from 1 to 8, they're not row numbers. Figure 14-7 shows the same table with the captions sorted in alphabetical order. The field highlighted in Figure 14-6 has moved to the seventh row, but it still has the same image_id and filename.

14

image_id	filename	caption ▴
8	ryoanji.jpg	Autumn leaves at Ryoanji temple, Kyoto
5	maiko_phone.jpg	Every maiko should have one—a mobile, of course
2	fountains.jpg	Fountains in central Tokyo
4	maiko.jpg	Maiko—trainee geishas in Kyoto
6	menu.jpg	Menu outside restaurant in Pontocho, Kyoto
7	monk.jpg	Monk begging for alms in Kyoto
3	kinkakuji.jpg	The Golden Pavilion in Kyoto
1	basin.jpg	Water basin at Ryoanji temple, Kyoto

Now in the seventh row, but image_id remains unchanged →

Figure 14-7. Even when the table is sorted in a different order, each record can be identified by its primary key.

Although the primary key is rarely displayed, it identifies the record and all the data stored in it. If you know the primary key, you can update a record, delete it, or use it to display data. Don't worry about how you find the primary key; it's easy using Structured Query Language (SQL), the standard means of communicating with all major databases. The important thing is to assign a primary key to every record.

- A primary key doesn't need to be a number, but *it must be unique*.
- Social Security, staff ID, or product numbers make good primary keys. They may consist of a mixture of numbers, letters, and other characters but are always different.
- MySQL will generate a primary key for you automatically.
- Once a primary key has been assigned, it should never—repeat, never—be changed.

Because a primary key must be unique, MySQL doesn't normally reuse the number when a record is deleted, leaving holes in the sequence. *Don't even think about renumbering.* By changing the numbers to close the gaps, you put the integrity of your database at serious risk. Some people want to remove gaps to keep track of the number of records, but you can easily get the same information with SQL.

Although Figures 14-6 and 14-7 show the similarity between a database table and a spreadsheet, there's an important difference. With a spreadsheet, you can enter data without the need to specify beforehand what type of data it is or how it's to be structured. You can't do that with a database.

Designing a database table

Before entering data, you need to define the table structure. This involves the following decisions:

- The name of the table
- How many columns it will have

- The name of each column
- What type of data will be stored in each column
- Whether the column must always have data in each field
- Which column contains the table's primary key

Don't be tempted to choose the first thing that comes into your head. Experienced database developers often say at least half the total development time is spent deciding the structure of a database. Although the structure of a database can be altered, some decisions tie your hands so badly you need to redesign everything from scratch. That's not much fun when the database contains several thousand records. The time spent on these early decisions can save a lot of agony and frustration later.

Because each database is different, it's impossible to prescribe one simple formula, but the next few pages should help guide you in the right direction. Don't attempt to commit everything to memory at the first read-through. Come back later when you need to refresh your memory or check a particular point.

Choosing the table name

The basic MySQL naming rules for databases, tables, and columns are as follows:

- Names can be up to 64 characters long.
- Legal characters are numbers, letters, the underscore, and $.
- Names can begin with a number but cannot consist exclusively of numbers.

Some hosting companies seem blissfully ignorant of these rules and assign clients databases that contain one or more hyphens (an illegal character) in their names. If a name contains spaces or illegal characters, you must surround it by backticks (`) in SQL queries. Note that this is not a single quote (') but a different character. Dreamweaver and phpMyAdmin normally do this for you automatically.

Choose names that are meaningful. Tables hold groups of records, so it's a good strategy to use plural nouns. For example, use products rather than product. Don't try to save on typing by using abbreviations, particularly when naming columns. Explicit names make it much easier to build SQL queries to extract the information you want from a database. SQL is designed to be as human-readable as possible, so don't make life difficult for yourself by using cryptic naming conventions.

When choosing column names, there is a danger that you might accidentally choose one of MySQL's many reserved words (http://dev.mysql.com/doc/refman/5.0/en/reserved-words.html), such as date or time. A good technique is to use compound words, such as arrival_date, arrival_time, and so on. These names also tell you much more about the data held in the column.

Case sensitivity of names

Windows and Mac OS X treat MySQL names as case-insensitive. However, Linux and Unix servers respect case sensitivity. To avoid problems when transferring databases and PHP code from your local computer to a remote server, I recommend you use only lowercase

14

in database, table, and column names. Using camel case (for example, arrivalDate) is likely to cause your code to fail when transferring a database from your local computer to a Linux server.

Deciding how many columns to create

How should you store each person's name? One column? Or one each for the family and personal names? A commercial contacts management program like Microsoft Outlook goes even further, splitting the name into five parts. In addition to first and last name, it stores a title (Mr., Mrs., and so on), a middle name, and a suffix (I, II, III, Jr., and Sr.). Addresses are best broken down into street, town, county, state, ZIP code, and so on. Think of all the possible alternatives, and add a column for each one. Things like company name, apartment number, and extra lines in an address can be made optional, but you need to make provision for them. This is an important principle of a relational database: *break down complex information into its component parts, and store each part separately.*

This makes searching, sorting, and filtering much easier. Breaking information into small chunks may seem a nuisance, but you can always join them together again. It's much easier than trying to separate complex information stored in a single field.

Choosing the right column type in MySQL

MySQL 5.0 has 28 different column types. Rather than confuse you by listing all of them, I'll explain just the most commonly used. You can find full details of all column types in the MySQL documentation at http://dev.mysql.com/doc/refman/5.0/en/data-types.html.

Storing text

The difference between the main text column types boils down to the maximum number of characters that can be stored in an individual field and whether you can set a default value.

- CHAR: A fixed-length width text column up to a maximum of 255 characters. You must specify the size when building the table, although this can be altered later. Shorter strings are OK. MySQL adds trailing space to store them and automatically removes it on retrieval. If you attempt to store a string that exceeds the specified size, excess characters are truncated. You can define a default value.

- VARCHAR: A variable-length character string. The maximum number must be specified when designing the table, but this can be altered later. Prior to MySQL 5.0, the limit is 255; this has been increased to 65,535 in MySQL 5.0. Another change in MySQL 5.0 affects the way trailing space is treated. Prior to MySQL 5.0, trailing space is stripped at the time of storing a record. Since MySQL 5.0, trailing space is retained for both storage and retrieval. You can define a default value.

- TEXT: Stores a maximum of 65,535 characters (approximately two thirds of this chapter). You cannot define a default value.

TEXT is convenient, because you don't need to specify a maximum size (in fact, you can't). Although the maximum length of VARCHAR is the same as TEXT in MySQL 5.0, other factors such as the number of columns in a table reduce this.

Prior to MySQL 5.0, you cannot use CHAR in a table that also contains VARCHAR, TEXT, or BLOB. When creating the table, MySQL silently converts any CHAR columns to VARCHAR.

> Keep it simple: use VARCHAR *for short text items and* TEXT *for longer ones.*

Storing numbers

The most frequently used numeric column types are as follows:

- TINYINT: Any whole number (integer) between –128 and 127. If the column is declared as UNSIGNED, the range is from 0 to 255. This is particularly suitable for storing people's ages, number of children, and so on.

- INT: Any integer between –2,147,483,648 and 2,147,483,647. If the column is declared as UNSIGNED, the range is from 0 to 4,294,967,295.

- FLOAT: A floating-point number.

- DECIMAL: A floating-point number *stored as a string. This column type is best avoided.*

DECIMAL is intended for currencies, but you can't perform calculations with strings inside a database, so it's more practical to use INT. For dollars or euros, store currencies as cents; for pounds, use pence. Then use PHP to divide the result by 100, and format the currency as desired.

> *Don't use commas or spaces as the thousands-separator. Apart from numerals, the only characters permitted in numbers are the negative operator (-) and the decimal point (.). Although some countries use a comma as the decimal point, MySQL accepts only a period.*

Storing dates and times

MySQL stores dates in the format YYYY-MM-DD. This may come as a shock, but it's the ISO (International Organization for Standardization) standard, and it avoids the ambiguity inherent in national conventions. The most important column types for dates and times are as follows:

- DATE: A date stored as YYYY-MM-DD. The supported range is 1000-01-01 to 9999-12-31.

- DATETIME: A combined date and time displayed in the format YYYY-MM-DD HH:MM:SS.

- TIMESTAMP: A timestamp (normally generated automatically by the computer). Legal values range from the beginning of 1970 to partway through 2037.

MySQL timestamps are based on a human-readable date and, since MySQL 4.1, use the same format as DATETIME. As a result, they are incompatible with Unix and PHP

14

timestamps, which are based on the number of seconds elapsed since January 1, 1970. Don't mix them.

> Attempting to insert a date in any format other than YYYY-MM-DD results in the date being stored as 0000-00-00. Handling dates in different formats is covered in Chapter 17.

Storing predefined lists

MySQL lets you store two types of predefined lists that could be regarded as the database equivalents of radio button and checkbox states:

- ENUM: This column type stores a single choice from a predefined list, such as "yes, no, don't know" or "male, female." The maximum number of items that can be stored in the predefined list is a mind-boggling 65,535—some radio-button group!
- SET: This stores zero or more choices from a predefined list, up to a maximum of 64. Although this violates the principle of storing only one piece of information in a field, it's useful when the items form a coherent unit (for example, optional extras on a car).

The values stored in the ENUM and SET columns are stored as a comma-separated string. Individual values can include spaces and other characters but not commas.

Storing binary data

Binary data, such as images, bloat your tables and cannot be displayed directly from a database. However, the following column types are designed for binary data:

- TINYBLOB: Up to 255 bytes
- BLOB: Up to 64KB
- MEDIUMBLOB: Up to 16MB
- LONGBLOB: Up to 4GB

With such whimsical names, it's a bit of a letdown to discover that BLOB stands for **binary large object**.

Deciding whether a field can be empty

When defining a database table, specifying a column as NOT NULL is the equivalent of designating a required field. Since the phpMyAdmin default is NOT NULL, you need to manually override this to make a field optional. You can change a column definition from NOT NULL to NULL, and vice versa, at any time.

> If you set a default value for a NOT NULL column, MySQL automatically uses that value if nothing is entered in the field. Unfortunately, Dreamweaver doesn't support this useful feature.

Creating a user registration system

After that essential introduction, it's now time to get down to business and create a simple application that registers a person's name, username, and password. This will become the basis of a user registration system that controls access to selected pages in your website. Once you have created the database table, Dreamweaver's Insert Record, Update Record, and Delete Record server behaviors make light work of creating the forms that add the user's details to the database. They are easy to use, and they protect you against a type of malicious attack known as **SQL injection**. An injection attack can be used to reveal sensitive information or even delete all your data by passing spurious values through form fields or URL query strings. That's the good news . . . .

The not-so-good news is that the server behaviors do nothing to ensure that user input meets your criteria for suitable data. So, you could end up with someone just pressing the spacebar a couple of times, rather than typing a username or a password. However, that's an issue that can wait until the next chapter. To begin with, I'll concentrate on getting your first database application up and running.

To register users for your site, you need the following elements:

- A database table to store user details, such as username and password
- A registration form
- A page to display a list of registered users
- A form to update user details
- A form to delete users

Defining the database table

Let's start with creating the necessary table to store user details in the database. I plan to use the same table for both site administrators and ordinary visitors. So, it will also store the level of user privileges. This means the table needs a total of six columns to store the user's first name, family name, username, password, and privilege level. That's only five . . . . The missing column is needed for the primary key.

Creating the users table

These instructions show you how to define the users table in phpMyAdmin. If you're new to working with MySQL, I suggest you work through this section step-by-step to familiarize yourself with table definition. More experienced users might prefer to use the phpMyAdmin Import tab to build the table structure with ch14_users.sql in the extras folder of the download files (for MySQL 4.0 use ch14_users40.sql).

1. Launch phpMyAdmin, and select the dwcs4 database from the list of databases in the left frame. Since the database doesn't yet have any tables, you should see a message that no tables were found and a form to create a new one. You want to

14

create new table called users. It needs to have six columns, so fill in the form as shown here, and click Go.

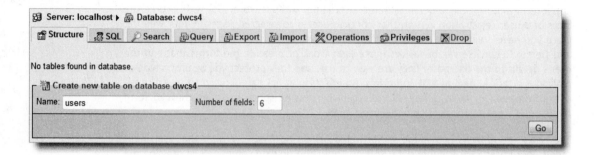

2. This opens a huge matrix where you define the table. Although it looks intimidating at first glance, it's quite straightforward to fill in. The layout in phpMyAdmin 3 has changed since the previous version, so both versions are shown in Figures 14-8 and 14-9.

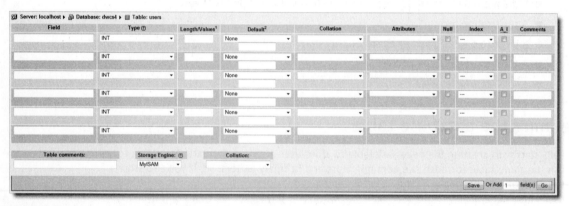

Figure 14-8. The new table definition layout in phpMyAdmin 3

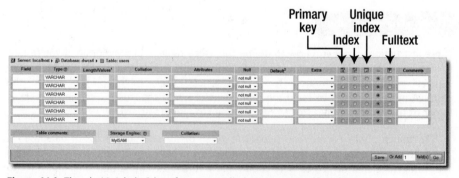

Figure 14-9. The phpMyAdmin 2 interface uses radio buttons to specify indexes.

For the sake of consistency, I will use screenshots of phpMyAdmin 3. If you are using phpMyAdmin 2 or need to switch between versions because your hosting company still uses phpMyAdmin 2, you should be aware of the following differences:

- When setting a default value in phpMyAdmin 3, you need to select a value from the drop-down menu. The options are None, As defined, NULL, and CURRENT_TIMESTAMP. If you select As defined, type the value in the field below. In phpMyAdmin 2, you simply enter a default value or leave the field blank.

- Both versions of phpMyAdmin set all columns to NOT NULL—in other words, required. To make a column optional in phpMyAdmin 3, select the Null check-box; in phpMyAdmin 2, select null from the drop-down menu.

- phpMyAdmin 3 uses a drop-down menu to specify whether the column should have an index (this includes setting the table's primary key). In phpMyAdmin 2, use the radio buttons labeled in Figure 14-9.

- To create an auto incrementing column (normally used in conjunction with the primary key), select the A_I checkbox in phpMyAdmin 3. In phpMyAdmin 2, select auto_increment from the Extra drop-down menu.

The settings for each column are summarized in Table 14-1.

Table 14-1. Settings for the users table

Field	Type	Length/Values	Default	Attributes	Null	Index	A_I
user_id	INT		None	UNSIGNED	No	PRIMARY	Yes
username	VARCHAR	15	None		No	UNIQUE	No
pwd	VARCHAR	40	None		No		No
first_name	VARCHAR	30	None		No		No
family_name	VARCHAR	30	None		No		No
admin_priv	ENUM	'n', 'y'	n		No		No

The table's primary key is user_id. Setting the Attributes field to UNSIGNED restricts the column to use only positive numbers. By selecting A_I (auto_increment), the value will automatically increase by one each time a record is added to the table.

The next column, username, has Type set to VARCHAR with a length of 15, which should be long enough for a username. You don't want anyone to have the same username as anyone else, so a unique index is applied to the column ensuring that the same value can never be entered more than once.

14

The next three columns—pwd, first_name, and family_name—all have Type set to VARCHAR. I have set the length of pwd to 40, because the function used to encrypt the passwords always produces a hexadecimal string exactly 40 characters long.

Thirty characters each for first_name and family_name might seem a lot, but it's better to be overgenerous than to end up with truncated data.

The final column, admin_priv, uses the ENUM column type. As explained earlier, this is typically used for "choose one of the following" situations. In this case, it's whether a user has administrative privileges. Type the permitted values in the Length/Values field as comma-separated strings like this:

'n', 'y'

In the Default column for admin_priv, enter n without any quotes (in phpMyAdmin 3, you also need to set the Default drop-down menu to As defined).

All columns have been set to not null. This is because I want all of them to be required fields. Click Save.

3. Check that the table structure displayed in phpMyAdmin looks like this:

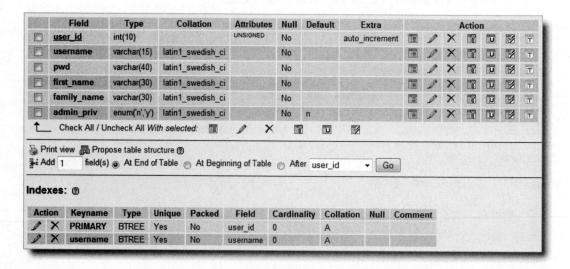

Note that the Indexes table at the bottom left of the screenshot lists user_id as the primary key and both user_id and username are listed as unique indexes. The primary key is always unique.

If you need to make any changes, click the pencil icon in the row that needs amending. To change several rows, select the checkbox alongside the column names, and click the pencil icon at the bottom of the table structure. If you make a complete mess and need to start again, click the Drop tab at the top right of the screen and confirm that you want to delete the table.

Telling Dreamweaver how to connect to the database

Before you can communicate with your database inside Dreamweaver, you need to create a MySQL connection. If you defined your site correctly in Chapter 2, it should take no more than a minute or two.

Creating a MySQL connection

A MySQL connection is simply a convenient way of storing the details needed to connect to MySQL: the server address, username, password, and database name. Dreamweaver stores them in an include file, which it automatically attaches to a web page whenever you select the connection in a server behavior.

1. Before you can create a MySQL connection, you need to have a PHP page open in the Document window. Create a blank PHP page, and save it as register_user.php in workfiles/ch14.

2. With register_user.php open in the Document window, open the Databases panel. If you can't see the panel, you can open it from the menu system (Window ➤ Databases) or use the keyboard shortcut Ctrl+Shift+F10/Shift+Cmd+F10.

3. Click the plus (+) button, and select MySQL Connection, as shown here:

4. The dialog box that opens asks you for the following details:

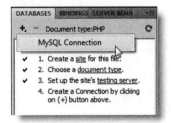

- Connection name: You can choose any name you like, but it must not contain any spaces or special characters. This connection will be used by the administrator user account, so I have entered connAdmin.

- MySQL server: This is the address of the database server. If MySQL is on the same computer as Dreamweaver, you should enter localhost.

- If you are running MySQL on a port other than the default 3306 (this happens with some of the all-in-one PHP packages, such as MAMP), add the port number after a colon (for example, localhost:8889).

- If you are using your remote server as a testing server, use the address your hosting company gave you. In most cases, this is also localhost. Dreamweaver uploads hidden files to your remote server and creates a local connection there.

- Some hosting companies locate the MySQL server on a different computer from your web files. If you are doing remote testing and have been given a server name other than localhost, enter that name now. If you are testing locally but know that your host doesn't use localhost, you will have to change this field when you finally upload your site to the remote server.

- User name: Enter the name of the MySQL user account that you want to use. This connection will be used for administrative pages, so I have entered cs4admin.

14

- Password: Enter the password for the user account. This should be the password you registered when creating the MySQL account.

- Database: Enter the name of the database that you want to use. You can also use the Select button to get Dreamweaver to show you a list of databases that the named user has access to.

Fill in the necessary details. The completed dialog box should look something like the following screenshot. When you have finished, click the Test button. If all goes well, Dreamweaver will tell you that the connection was made successfully.

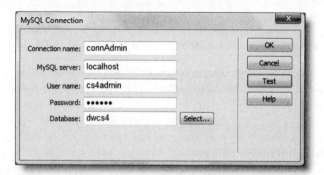

5. If you got the thumbs-up from Dreamweaver, click OK to close both dialog boxes. If you failed to make the connection, cancel the connection setup, and check the points listed in step 4 before trying again. If that fails, see "Troubleshooting the connection."

6. In the Databases panel, you should see a database icon that has been created for connAdmin. Expand the tree menu by clicking the tiny plus button (it's a triangle on the Mac) to the left of connAdmin. It displays the database features available to the connection, including a brief description of every column in the users table. The columns are listed in alphabetical order, not the order they appear in the database. The little key icon alongside user_id indicates that it's the table's primary key. Both Stored procedures and Views are empty. Although MySQL 5.0 supports these features, support for them has not been implemented in Dreamweaver CS4.

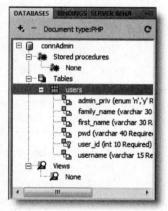

If you ever need to change the connection details, double-click the database icon in the Databases panel to reopen the MySQL Connection dialog box, make your changes, and click OK. Alternatively, right-click the connection name, and choose Edit Connection from the context menu.

7. If you have created two user accounts for MySQL, create another MySQL connection called connUser for the second account that has only SELECT privileges.

Dreamweaver stores the MySQL connection details in a file with the same name as the connection. So, connAdmin becomes connAdmin.php, which is stored in a folder called Connections that Dreamweaver creates in the site root. Don't forget to upload the contents of this folder to your remote server when deploying a PHP site on the Internet.

Troubleshooting the connection

Hopefully, everything went OK, but this section should help identify what might have gone wrong if you get an error message. Normally, you get a message about there being no testing server or saying that the testing server doesn't map to a particular URL.

All communication between Dreamweaver and MySQL is conducted through two files, MMHTTPDB.php and mysql.php, located in a hidden folder called _mmServerScripts. Dreamweaver automatically creates the hidden folder and files in the site root of your testing server. If you have defined the URL prefix incorrectly in your site definition, the folder will be in the wrong place. The solution is to use an Explorer window or Finder to see where the folder has been created. Then adjust the testing server site definition (see Chapter 2) so that both the testing server folder and URL prefix point to the site root.

If you're using your remote server as the testing server, Dreamweaver uploads the hidden folder and files to your remote server. Even if you have defined the URL prefix correctly, Dreamweaver might not be able to create the _mmServerScripts folder because of permission problems. Create the folder yourself, and make sure it has read and write permissions.

You may see a rather unhelpful message about an unidentified error. Things to check when this happens are that MySQL and your web server are running. Also check your username and password—both are case-sensitive and will fail if you use the wrong case (make sure Caps Lock isn't on by accident). A software firewall may also be blocking communication between Dreamweaver and MySQL. Try turning it off temporarily. If that solves the problem, adjust the firewall settings.

Inserting user details into the database

Although you can use phpMyAdmin or another graphical interface to insert records in a database table, it's more common to build a dedicated form to do so. Building dedicated forms gives you control over which parts of your database can be accessed by different people. The form you'll build over the next few pages is intended to be used by an administrator to control who has access to different parts of a website, but you could use a similar form in a public part of your site for users to register their details, such as email address.

There are two ways to create a form to insert records into a database table: either you can design your own form and use the Insert Record server behavior or you can use the Record Insertion Form Wizard to build the form and apply the server behavior in a single

14

operation. Personally, I think the insert wizard creates ugly forms, but it offers a quick way to build a form to interact with a database. I'll use the wizard in this chapter, but in subsequent chapters, I'll show you how to adapt your own forms.

Using a wizard to build the registration form

These instructions step through the process of building a form to insert records in the users table. Continue working with register_user.php from the previous section.

1. Create another blank PHP page, and save it as list_users.php in workfiles/ch14. This will be used later to display a list of registered users. You don't need the page for the time being, so you can close it if you want.

2. Return to register_user.php. Give the page a title, such as Register User. Select Heading 1 from the Format menu in the HTML view of the Property inspector, and type the same heading at the top of the page. Then select the <h1> tag in the Tag selector at the bottom of the Document window, and press your right keyboard arrow to move the insertion point out of the heading. If you forget to do this, Dreamweaver embeds the entire form inside the <h1> tags.

3. Open the Data tab of the Insert bar, and locate the fifth icon from the right. It should display Insert Record as a tooltip. If this is the first time you have accessed this icon, clicking it opens a submenu, as shown in the following screenshot. Select Record Insertion Form Wizard from the submenu. On subsequent occasions, Dreamweaver remembers the option you used most recently, so you can just click the button.

   If you're not sure whether you have used this option before, click the small down arrow alongside the icon to access the submenu directly.

   If you prefer working with the main menu system, use Insert ➤ Data Objects ➤ Insert Record ➤ Record Insertion Form Wizard.

4. This opens the Record Insertion Form dialog box (see Figure 14-10). When it first loads, you need to select a MySQL connection with INSERT privileges. If you created two user accounts for MySQL, use the administrator connection (connAdmin).

   This populates the Table drop-down menu with a list of tables in the database. They are listed in alphabetical order, so you need to select users. The dialog box then presents you with its suggested values for the record insertion form, as shown in Figure 14-10.

Edit the form labels here →

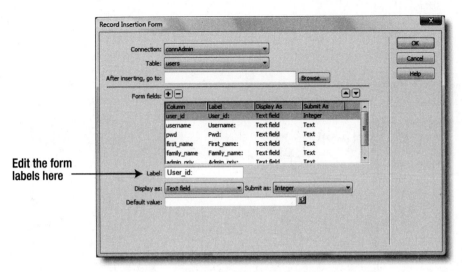

Figure 14-10. The Record Insertion Form Wizard helps build the insertion form automatically.

5. Dreamweaver uses the table column names to suggest labels and appropriate types of input fields for the form. The columns are listed in the same order as they appear in the database, but you can use the up and down arrow buttons at the top right of the Form fields area to rearrange the order they will be displayed in the record insertion form. If you don't want to display a particular field, remove it by clicking the minus button. To restore a deleted item, click the plus button, and select it from the list.

You can also specify where you want to go to after the record has been inserted. If you leave the option blank, the same page will be redisplayed ready for another record.

6. The primary key is generated automatically, so you don't want a field for it in the form. Select user_id in the Form fields area, and click the minus button to delete it.

7. The suggested labels for the pwd, first_name, family_name, and admin_priv columns all need amending. Select each one in turn, and edit the value in the Label field (see Figure 14-10). Expand Pwd: to Password: and change the value of Display as to Password field; remove the underscore from First_name: and Family_name:, and change admin_priv to Administrator:.

8. The admin_priv column uses the ENUM column type, so you want to use a radio button group. With admin_priv selected in Form fields, change Display as to Radio group, and then click the Radio Group Properties button that appears. This opens the Radio Group Properties dialog box. Use the plus button to create two Radio items: Yes with a value of y, and No with a value of n, as shown in the following screenshot. These match the values defined in the ENUM column in the database

14

611

table. To make No the default value, enter n in the field labeled Select value equal to, and click OK.

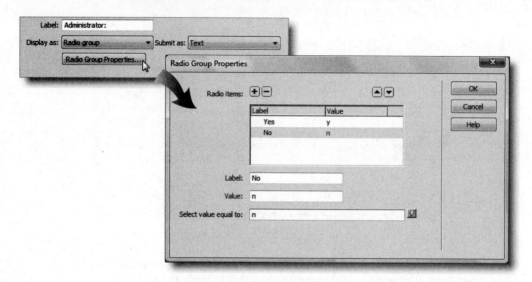

9. Reorder the items with the up and down arrows at the top right of the Form fields area so that they look like this:

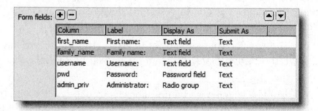

10. Click the Browse button alongside the field labeled After inserting, go to. Navigate to list_users.php, and select it. This will redirect the user to list_users.php after a record has been inserted in the database table.

11. Click OK to create the form. In Design view, the page should now look like Figure 14-11. The form's light blue coloring indicates that it contains dynamic code.

> *Once you click* OK *in the* Record Insertion Form *dialog box, you cannot reopen it to make any changes. All further changes to the form need to be made in the Document window. If you want to start afresh, use the minus button in the* Server Behaviors *panel to remove the Insert Record code before deleting the form. Otherwise, you'll end up with a tangle of impossible code.*

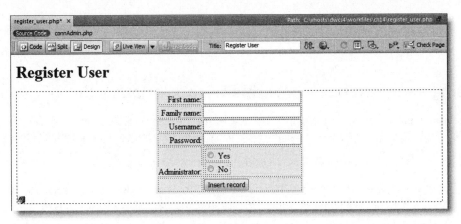

Figure 14-11. The Record Insertion Form Wizard creates the form and the necessary PHP code in a single operation.

12. Save `register_user.php`, and load it into a browser (don't use Preview in Browser with a temporary file). Enter some details in each field, and click Insert Record. Don't worry if you see a blank page; you should have been taken to `list_users.php`, which doesn't yet contain anything.

13. Launch phpMyAdmin, select the `dwcs4` database, and then select the `users` table. When you click the Browse tab, you should see the details of the record you just inserted listed like this:

user_id	username	pwd	first_name	family_name	admin_priv
1	dpowers	codeslave	David	Powers	y

Compare your code, if necessary, with `register_user.php` in examples/ch14.

It's as easy as that!

Before you start celebrating too soon, I should warn you that there are lots of things wrong with this registration form. The password is stored in the database in plain text, which is insecure. Also, the form is incapable of handling the database error if someone chooses the same username as another person. In fact, there's nothing to prevent someone from entering a single space in each field and registering that. This form is functional, but a lot of work still needs to be done on it.

We'll come back to server-side validation in the next chapter. The next stage is to create a page that displays a list of entries in the database table, but first a quick word about things that might have gone wrong:

- If you get a string of errors about `mysql_real_escape_string()` and the ODBC connection, it means you have used Preview in Browser with a temporary file. Load the actual page into a browser, and try again.

- If you get a fatal error about a call to undefined function virtual(), it means your site defaults to links relative to the site root and you're not using Apache as the web server. See the next section.

Using server behaviors with site-root-relative links

If you open register_user.php in Code view to see the PHP code that Dreamweaver has added to the page and you use document-relative links, the top section will look like this:

```php
<?php require_once('../../Connections/connAdmin.php'); ?>
```

This code uses require_once() to include the MySQL connection details. However, if your site definition uses links relative to the site root, this will be replaced by the following:

```php
<?php virtual('/Connections/connAdmin.php'); ?>
```

The virtual() function *works only on Apache*. If your code uses virtual(), make sure it is supported on both your testing and remote servers before going any further (see "Using site-root-relative links with includes" in Chapter 12 for details of how to do this).

All Dreamweaver server behaviors need to include the MySQL connection. If your server doesn't support virtual(), you have two options, namely:

- Change your site definition to use document-relative links, and manually override the default when creating links that you want to be relative to the site root. You do this in the Select File dialog box by changing the Relative to drop-down menu to Site Root, as described in "Including a text file" in Chapter 12.
- Manually replace virtual() with require_once() and a document-relative link in pages that use server behaviors. The require_once() command works on all servers.

Neither solution is ideal. I believe that Dreamweaver needs a platform-neutral way of connecting to MySQL when site-root-relative links are used, or it should use require_once() regardless of the default link type.

Retrieving information from the database

Inserting information into a database is fine, but there's not much point unless you can retrieve it and do something useful with it. Retrieving information from a database involves creating a SQL SELECT query. As the name suggests, it selects information from the database according to your criteria and returns the results. Dreamweaver calls this a **recordset**. Once you have created a recordset, you can use it to display the results of the query in a web page. Although there's currently only one record in the users table, let's build a page to display a list of all registered users, because this is an essential prerequisite to being able to update and delete information stored in the database.

Creating a recordset

These instructions show you how to use the Recordset dialog box in Simple mode to query the users table in preparation for displaying the results in a web page.

1. Open list_users.php, and give it a title and heading, such as Registered Users. Insert a link to register_user.php and a table with two rows and three columns. I made the table 500 pixels wide, with no border, cellpadding, or cellspacing. I also set Header to Top.

   Type Name, Username, and Administrator in the first row. The page should look like this:

2. Open the Recordset dialog box by clicking the plus button in the Server Behaviors panel and selecting Recordset. The Server Behaviors panel is normally grouped with the Database and Bindings panels. If you can't see it, select Window ➤ Server Behaviors to open it, or press Ctrl+F9/Cmd+F9.

   You can also click the Recordset button on the Data tab of the Insert bar or select Insert ➤ Data Objects ➤ Recordset.

   The Recordset dialog box has two modes: Simple and Advanced. If this is the first time you have opened the dialog box, it will be in Simple mode, as shown in Figure 14-12.

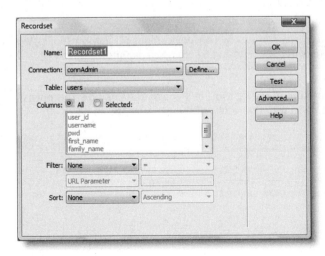

Figure 14-12.
The Recordset dialog box in Simple mode is used for basic SELECT queries.

14

You can tell which mode you're in by looking at the buttons on the right side of the dialog box. If you're in Simple mode, the fourth button is labeled Advanced; and if you're in Advanced mode, it's labeled Simple (because it switches to the opposite mode).

3. By default, Dreamweaver enters a generic value such as Recordset1, Recordset2, and so on, in the Name field. However, the name is used to create several PHP variables, so it's better to choose something that tells you what the recordset is for. Use only letters, numbers, and the underscore. Don't use any spaces. Some people use the convention of beginning recordset names with rs, but this isn't necessary. The name I have chosen is listUsers.

4. Dreamweaver CS4 now remembers the most recent connection you used, so the connAdmin connection is automatically selected. Although this recordset performs only a SELECT operation, you'll be editing the records later, so it's more consistent to use the administrator connection for all the pages.

5. There's only one table in the database at the moment, so the users table is also selected automatically.

6. The Columns field has two radio buttons: All and Selected. By default, the All radio button is selected, and the columns are grayed out. A lot of beginners select All every time, even if they need only one or two columns. It's easy, and it makes the SQL query a lot easier to read (we'll study SQL syntax in Chapter 16). However, it's a bad habit. Even if you need all columns, it's considered best practice to select them individually because it makes the meaning of your code much clearer.

   Choose the Selected radio button, and Ctrl-click/Cmd-click username, first_name, family_name, and admin_priv.

7. You can ignore the Filter settings this time. I'll explain their use later.

8. Although there's only one record at the moment, it's a good idea to decide how the results should be sorted when there are more records in the table. Open the drop-down menu labeled Sort. It lists all the columns in the table. Choose family_name. This enables the drop-down menu to the right. It has two options: Ascending and Descending. Select Ascending. This will sort all results by the family name in alphabetical order.

> In Simple mode, you can sort by only one column. In Chapter 16, I'll show you how to use Advanced mode to sort by multiple columns.

9. Click the Test button on the right of the Recordset dialog box. This opens the Test SQL Statement panel with the results of the query, as shown here:

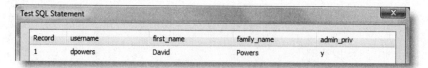

Record	username	first_name	family_name	admin_priv
1	dpowers	David	Powers	y

10. Click OK to close the test panel, and then click OK again to close the Recordset dialog box and create the recordset.

11. The listUsers recordset should now be listed at the top of the Server Behaviors panel, as shown in the following screenshot:

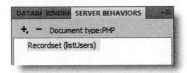

12. Save list_users.php. Leave the page open ready to insert the code that will display the results of the recordset. If you want to check your page so far, compare it with list_users_01.php in examples/ch14.

Editing and removing server behaviors

Whenever you create a recordset or apply a server behavior, Dreamweaver adds it to the list in the Server Behaviors panel (some server behaviors add several items to the list). If you need to edit a server behavior, double-click its listing in the Server Behaviors panel to reopen its dialog box. To delete a server behavior, *always* select it from this list and click the minus button at the top of the panel. Failure to do so will result in code that is likely to behave erratically.

> *Dreamweaver creates a lot of PHP code behind the scenes when working with server behaviors. You'll examine a lot of it in coming chapters to get to know what it's for. Until you understand the code, it's dangerous to highlight PHP elements in Design view and press Delete. Using the minus button in the* Server Behaviors *panel removes the code cleanly.*

Displaying the results of a recordset

Once you have created a recordset, Dreamweaver makes its results available through the Bindings panel, which displays a list of the database columns retrieved by each recordset you create. You use the panel to insert PHP code into your web page and display the results of the database query.

Creating the list of registered users

The following instructions show how to insert dynamic text from the Bindings panel and display the results of the listUsers recordset. Continue working with list_users.php from the previous section.

1. Open the Bindings panel by selecting its tab, selecting Window ➤ Bindings, or pressing the keyboard shortcut Ctrl+F10/Cmd+F10.

14

2. Expand the `listUsers` recordset as shown in Figure 14-13 by clicking to the left of the icon alongside Recordset (listUsers).

Figure 14-13.
The Bindings panel gives
access to the query result.

3. To insert the database results into a page, you can drag the column names from the Bindings panel into the Document window. Alternatively, position your cursor in the Document window where you want to display the result, select the column name in the Bindings panel, and click the Insert button at the bottom of the panel.

Use either method to insert first_name from the Bindings panel into the first cell of the second row of the table. This inserts a dynamic text placeholder in the page like this:

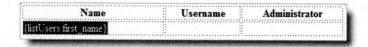

4. Click to the right of the dynamic text placeholder, and insert a space. Then insert family_name from the Bindings panel alongside. Insert username into the second cell of the second row, and insert admin_priv into the third cell. The table should now look like this:

It doesn't matter if the dynamic text placeholders in the first cell stack on top of each other like this, because the placeholders are longer than the actual text that will be displayed.

5. Save list_users.php, and press F12/Opt+F12 to load it into a browser. You should see the details of the record you inserted into the users table displayed in the page like this:

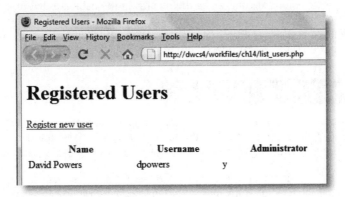

Don't worry about the way the page looks. That's cosmetic and can be easily fixed with CSS. At the moment, I just want to concentrate on working with the server behaviors. If anything went wrong, compare your code with list_users_02.php in examples/ch14.

6. Assuming everything went OK, click the Register new user link to go to register_user.php, and enter a new record in the database. Choose a family name that comes before the existing record in alphabetical order. When you click the Insert record button in register_user.php, list_users.php should automatically load and display the new name, as shown here:

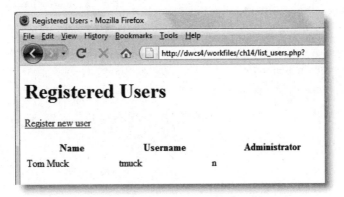

This is progress. The results have been sorted in alphabetical order, but only the first result is displayed. Keep list_users.php open in Dreamweaver, and we'll fix that next.

14

Displaying multiple results with a repeat region

Unless you explicitly limit the results of a database query (you'll learn how to do that later in the book), a recordset contains all the records in the database that match your search criteria. However, the dynamic text placeholders inserted from the Bindings panel display only the first result. To display the remaining ones, you need to apply the Repeat Region server behavior. Let's do that now so you can see both results.

Adding a Repeat Region server behavior

These instructions show you how to display multiple results from a recordset by applying a Repeat Region server behavior to the table row that contains the dynamic text place-holders. Continue working with list_users.php from the preceding section.

1. Position your cursor inside the second table row in list_users.php, and click <tr> in the Tag selector at the bottom of the Document window to select the entire row.

It's important to select the entire row, including the opening and closing <tr> tags. If you simply drag across the table cells to select them in Design view, there's a danger that Dreamweaver will select only the <td> tags. Using the Tag selector ensures you get the correct selection every time.

2. Open the Server Behaviors panel. Note that the four instances of dynamic text have been added to the list, as shown here:

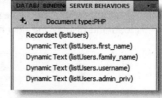

3. Click the plus button in the Server Behaviors panel, and select Repeat Region from the menu that appears. Alternatively, click the Repeat Region button on the Data tab of the Insert panel, or use the menu option, Insert ➤ Data Objects ➤ Repeat Region.

This opens the Repeat Region dialog box shown in Figure 14-14.

Figure 14-14.
A repeat region can display a selected number of records or all of them.

4. There's only one recordset on the page, so the Repeat Region dialog box auto-matically selects listUsers. The Show option lets you choose whether to show a limited number of records or all of them. The default is to show a maximum of ten records, but you can change this by entering your own value in the text field.

You'll learn in Chapter 16 how to page through a long recordset several records at a time. On this occasion, though, select All records, and click OK to apply the repeat region.

5. Save list_users.php, and reload it in a browser. You should now see both records listed, as shown in Figure 14-15.

Figure 14-15.
The repeat region now displays all records in the table.

If the results end up being displayed across the page as shown in the following screenshot, it means that you failed to select the entire table row in step 1:

If this happened to you, select Repeat Region (listUsers) in the Server Behaviors panel, click the minus button to remove it cleanly, and start again from step 1.

Check your code, if necessary, against list_users_03.php in examples/ch14. You'll improve the page further in the next section, so keep it open in the Document window.

Updating and deleting records

To update a record in a database, you need to populate a form with the existing details so they can be edited and reinserted into the database. This is where a table's primary key plays a vital role. If you know the primary key of a record, you can easily retrieve it and populate the update form. Equally important, you can use the primary key to delete a record when it's no longer wanted. So, how do you find the primary key? Simple . . . Look it up in the database, and store it in a link that loads the update form or triggers the delete mechanism.

The listUsers recordset that you created earlier retrieves the first_name, family_name, username, and admin_priv columns. All you need to do is to edit the recordset to get it to retrieve the primary key, user_id, as well. You can then use that information to create edit and delete links in list_users.php.

Time to get back to work . . . .

14

Adding a record's primary key to a query string

These instructions show you how to edit the listUsers recordset to retrieve the primary key of each record and then incorporate the primary key into links that will be used to update and delete individual records.

1. Create two new blank PHP pages called update_user.php and delete_user.php. You don't need them for the time being, so you can close them if you want.

2. You need to add two columns on the right of the table in list_users.php. The easiest way to do this is to right-click in the last column and select Table ➤ Insert Row or Columns from the context menu. In the dialog box that opens, select the Columns radio button, set Number of columns to 2, and select After current Column, as shown here:

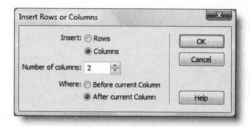

3. When you click OK to insert the extra columns, you might find it difficult to insert your cursor in the new cells. To make it easier to work in the table, turn on Expanded Tables mode by pressing Alt+F6/Opt+F6 (you can also click the Expanded button on the Layout tab of the Insert bar or select View ➤ Table Mode ➤ Expanded Tables Mode.

   Type EDIT in the fourth cell of the second row, and type DELETE in the final cell. Once you have entered the text in the new cells, you can exit Expanded Tables mode by clicking Exit at the top of the Document window.

4. Open the Server Behaviors panel, and double-click Recordset (listUsers) to open the Recordset dialog box. Edit the settings by holding down the Ctrl/Cmd key and selecting user_id in the Columns field.

5. Click the Test button to make sure the query now includes the user_id primary key, as shown in the following screenshot:

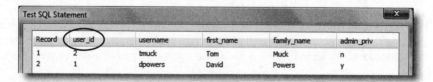

6. Close the test panel, and save the amended recordset.

7. Select the text in the fourth cell (EDIT). You need to turn it into a link to the update page and add the record's primary key to a query string at the end of the URL.

Begin by clicking the Browse for File button to the right of the Link field in the HTML view of the Property inspector. In the Select File dialog box that opens, select update_user.php. Then click the Parameters button alongside the URL field.

8. In the Parameters dialog box, type user_id in the Name field. Click the lightning bolt icon on the right of the Value field. In the Dynamic Data dialog box, highlight user_id, as shown in Figure 14-16.

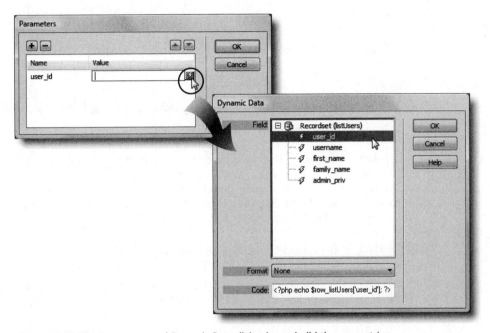

Figure 14-16. The Parameters and Dynamic Data dialog boxes build the query string.

This is where many people go wrong. The Name *field in the* Parameters *dialog box takes a* static *value, which you type in yourself. The* Value *field takes a* dynamic *value, which you insert by clicking the lightning bolt icon and selecting the primary key from the* Dynamic Data *dialog box.*

9. Click OK to close both the Dynamic Data and Parameters dialog boxes. Then click OK (Choose on the Mac) to close the Select File dialog box.

10. Repeat steps 7 through 9 with the text in the fifth cell (DELETE). In step 7, select delete_user.php.

11. Save list_users.php, and preview it in a browser. Mouse over the EDIT and DELETE links. The status bar of your browser should display links to update_user.php and delete_user.php and have a query string containing user_id and the user's primary key, as shown in Figure 14-17.

14

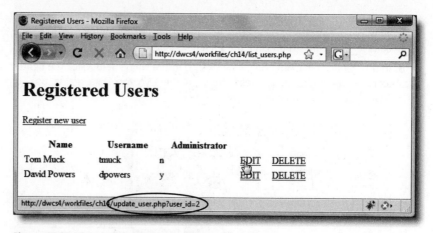

Figure 14-17. The query string has been added to the URL.

Make sure the query string is correctly formed at the end of the URL when you mouse over the links. This is very important; the update and delete pages won't work unless the query string displays user_id= followed by a number. Review steps 7–10 again if the URL doesn't look right. If necessary, check your code against list_users_04.php in examples/ch14.

Retrieving a database record using its primary key

The wizard that builds update forms is almost identical to the one that inserts new records into a database. The main difference is that you can't use it until you have already created a recordset to retrieve the existing details of the record you want to update. So, the process involves three basic steps, namely:

1. Create a recordset to retrieve a single record.

2. Display the results of the recordset in a form ready for editing.

3. Submit the edited information to update the existing record.

Since each record has a unique primary key, you can retrieve the details of a specific record by using its primary key as a filter. You don't need to know the actual primary key to create the recordset. All you need to know is the name of the variable containing the primary key and where it's coming from. The query string you added at the end of the URL in the EDIT link of list_users.php in the previous section contains the individual record's primary key as a variable called user_id. So, this is the value you use to filter the recordset.

Using the primary key to filter a recordset

The following instructions show you how to retrieve a record identified by its primary key:

1. Open update_user.php. Give the page a suitable title and a heading, such as Update User Record.

2. Click the plus button in the Server Behaviors panel, and select Recordset from the menu that appears. The Recordset dialog box should still be in Simple mode from the last time you used it.

3. Name the recordset getUser.

4. Check that the Connection field has been set to connAdmin (Dreamweaver should remember from the most recent time you used it).

5. Since you have only one table, users should be automatically selected. Click the Selected radio button, and Shift-click all the columns.

6. The Filter section consists of three drop-down menus and a text field. The first drop-down menu lists all the columns in the users table. You want to use the primary key to select the record, so choose user_id from the list.

   The drop-down menu on the right contains a range of comparison operators that determine how the filter is used. You want the variable passed through the query string to be equal to the user_id column, so the default, =, is fine.

   The drop-down menu in the second row determines where the value comes from. On this occasion, it's being passed in through a query string, so select URL Parameter.

   The text field on the right of the second row is where you enter the name of the variable whose value you want to match in the selected column. Dreamweaver assumes you want to use the same name as the column, which is why I used user_id in the query string. If you use a different variable name, you can type it in here, but it's not necessary on this occasion.

   The settings in the Recordset dialog box should now look like this:

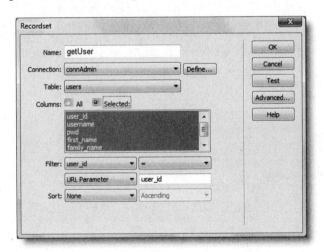

7. Click the Test button. Because you're filtering the recordset, Dreamweaver asks you to provide a test value for user_id. Assuming you haven't deleted any records in the table, enter 1 or 2, and click OK. You should see details of the record that has that primary key.

8. Click OK to dismiss the test panel, and then click OK again to save the recordset. You're now ready to create the update form. Leave update_user.php open to continue with the next section.

14

Using the Record Update Form Wizard

Now that you have a recordset that retrieves the details of the record you want to update, you can use the Record Update Form Wizard (if you attempt to use the wizard without first creating the recordset, Dreamweaver displays a message telling you to do so).

Building the update form

You use the wizard in almost the same way as the one that created the form to insert new records. Here's how . . . .

1. You need to make sure the wizard builds the update form outside the <h1> tags of the page heading in update_user.php. So, insert your cursor in the page heading, select <h1> in the Tag selector, and press your right arrow key once.

2. Select Record Update Form Wizard in the Data tab of the Insert bar (it's the fourth icon from the right), as shown in the following screenshot. Alternatively, use the menu option, Insert ➤ Data Objects ➤ Update Record ➤ Record Update Form Wizard.

3. This opens the Record Update Form dialog box shown in Figure 14-18. It's very similar to the dialog box used to create the form for new records, but there are some important differences. The wizard recognizes the getUser recordset you created in the previous section and automatically fills most fields to use it.

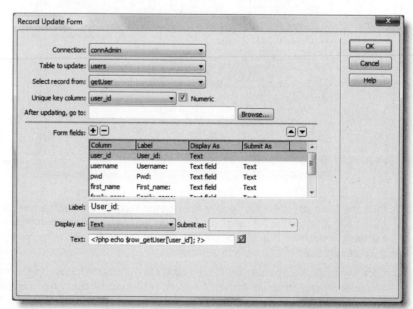

Figure 14-18.
The update wizard automatically populates the dialog box with most options.

The first four options (Connection, Table to update, Select record from, and Unique key column) already have the correct details and don't need to be changed. The Unique key column refers to the primary key you're using to identify the correct record to update. The Numeric checkbox alongside is selected because the user_id column was defined as an INT type when you built the users table earlier in the chapter. This is an important security check that Dreamweaver makes to help protect your database from malicious attack.

4. The field labeled After updating, go to is where you want to redirect the user after the record has been updated. Click the Browse button, navigate to list_users.php, and select it.

5. Form fields lists all the columns retrieved in the getUser recordset. You use it in the same way as when you built the form to insert new records. You should never change the primary key of a record, so select user_id in Form fields, and click the minus button to remove it from the list.

6. Amend the labels for the pwd, first_name, family_name, and admin_priv columns in the same way as before by selecting each one and editing it in the Label field. Expand Pwd to Password, remove the underscores from First_name and Family_name, and change Admin_priv to Administrator. Use the up key at the top right of Form fields to move the first and family name items to the top of the list.

Notice that the Text field at the bottom of the dialog box is automatically populated with PHP code. This uses the getUser recordset results to display the record's existing value in the update form.

7. Leave the Display as drop-down menu set to Text for all columns except admin_priv.

8. Select admin_priv in Form fields, and select Radio group from the Display as drop-down menu. Click the Radio Group Properties button to open the following dialog box:

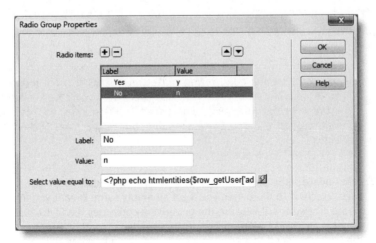

Set the values for the two radio buttons as shown in the screenshot. Notice that, this time, you don't need to fill in the field labeled Select value equal to. Dreamweaver automatically populates this field with PHP code to select the correct

14

radio button according to the value stored in the getUser recordset. Click OK to close the Radio Group Properties dialog box.

9. The update wizard is like the one you used earlier—once you click OK to close the Record Update Form dialog box, there's no way to reopen it to edit it. Check that you have made all the necessary changes, and click OK to create the update form, which should look like Figure 14-19. The form is basically the same as the one used to insert a new record, but each field contains a dynamic text placeholder that uses the getUser recordset to insert the existing value stored in the database. At the bottom left of the update form, you should see two gold shields. These are hidden form fields that Dreamweaver has created to send the record's primary key and details of the form to the update script.

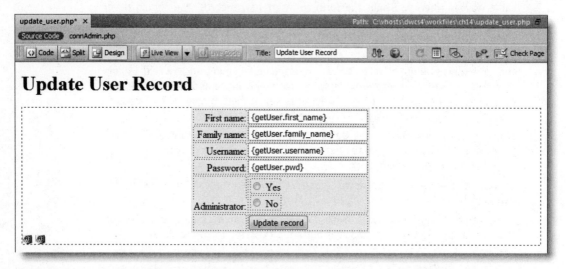

Figure 14-19. The update form contains dynamic text placeholders to display the record's details.

If you can't see the gold shields, make sure there's a check mark alongside Invisible Fields *in* View ➤ Visual Aids. *Also check the* Invisible Elements *category in the Dreamweaver* Preferences *panel (*Edit ➤ Preferences *or* Dreamweaver ➤ Preferences *on a Mac). Make sure that the* Hidden *form fields checkbox is selected.*

10. Save update_user.php. You now need to test the update form, but if you load the page directly into a browser, you'll get an empty form. Even if you fill it in, it won't create a new record because the underlying code uses the SQL UPDATE command, rather than INSERT. Without a primary key, there's nothing to update. So, to test the page, you need to load list_users.php into a browser.

11. Click the EDIT link alongside one of the records. The update form should load into the browser with the record's details ready for updating, as shown in Figure 14-20.

The primary key is passed through the query string, telling the update form which record to display

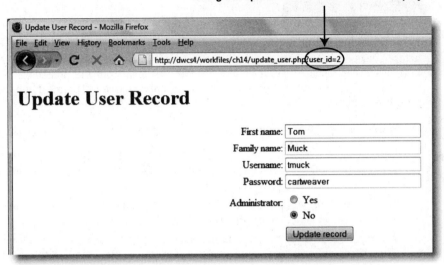

Figure 14-20. The update form displays the existing details ready for editing.

If the form is empty, check that the query string has been added correctly to the end of the URL. Also check the spelling of the variable in the query string. It must match exactly the way you spelled the primary key in the users table.

12. Make some changes to the record, such as changing the first name and administrator status, and click Update record. The amended details (apart from the password) are displayed immediately in list_users.php, as shown here:

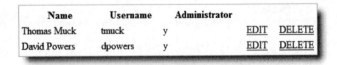

Check your code, if necessary, against update_users.php in examples/ch14.

Deleting a record

Deleting a record is an irreversible action, so it's essential to get confirmation not only that the deletion should go ahead but also that the correct record is being deleted. There isn't a wizard for creating a delete page, but it's not difficult to build the page yourself. As when updating a record, you need a recordset to identify whether Dreamweaver can apply the necessary server behavior. The good news is that you can save time by copying the recordset from the update page.

Building the delete page

These instructions show you how to create a page that asks the user for confirmation before deleting a record from the database. They assume you have created list_users.php, update_user.php, and delete_user.php from the preceding sections. You should also be familiar with form building techniques (see Chapter 9 if you need to refresh your memory).

1. Open delete_user.php in the Document window.

2. Open update_user.php, or switch to it if it's still open.

3. In the Server Behaviors panel, highlight Recordset (getUser), right-click, and select Copy from the context menu.

4. Switch back to delete_user.php, right-click inside the Server Behaviors panel, and select Paste. Bingo, one quick, easy recordset.

5. Give the page a heading and title, and insert a form. Use the Bindings panel to insert some details that will identify the user (this is the same as displaying details in list_users.php earlier in the chapter), and add a submit button named delete with a suitable label. The screenshot shows a suggested layout:

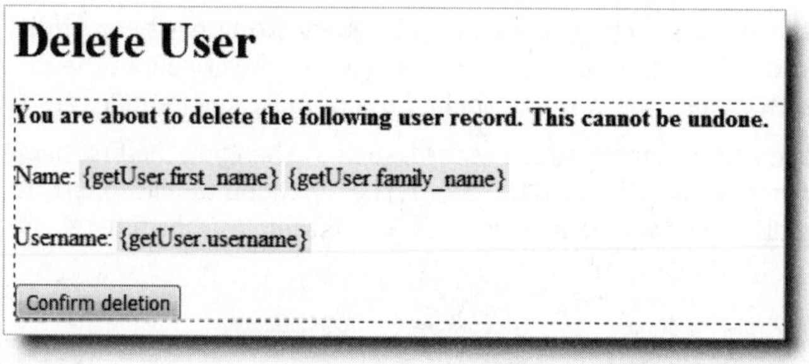

6. Insert a hidden field into the form. This will be used to pass the primary key to the DELETE command, so name the field user_id. You need to get its value from the getUser recordset, so click the lightning bolt icon to the right of the Value field to open the Dynamic Data dialog box, and select user_id from the getUser recordset, as shown in Figure 14-21.

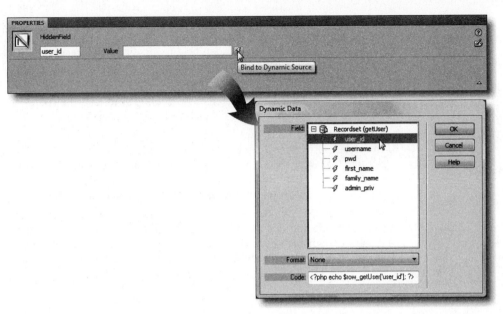

Figure 14-21. Bind the value of a form field to a recordset result by clicking the lightning bolt icon alongside the field.

7. You're now ready to apply the Delete Record server behavior. Use the plus button in the Server Behaviors panel, and select Delete Record from the menu that opens. Alternatively, use the Delete Record button on the Data tab of the Insert bar, or the menu option, Insert ➤ Data Objects ➤ Delete Record.

This opens the Delete Record dialog box, as shown in Figure 14-22. Most of the values are selected automatically by Dreamweaver, but you should always check them.

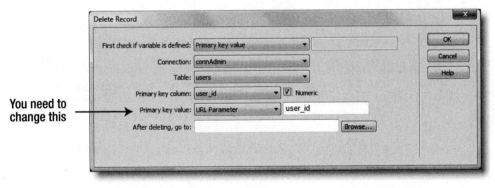

You need to change this

Figure 14-22. The Delete Record server behavior needs to use the primary key submitted by the form.

14

Make sure the connection that has administrative privileges and the correct table are selected.

When you select the table from which the record is to be deleted, Dreamweaver should automatically select the correct value for the Primary key column. However, the server behavior uses the hidden field to identify the correct record to delete, so make sure you select Form Variable as the Primary key value and that the primary key's name (user_id) is entered in the text field alongside.

After the record has been deleted, it's a good idea to load the complete list, so enter list_users.php in the final field labeled After deleting, go to. Click OK to insert the server behavior.

8. The delete user page is now fully operational, but what happens if you have selected the wrong record or change your mind about deletion? The easy way is to use the browser back button or a text link to return to the list of registered users. However, it looks more professional to add a cancel button.

   You'll notice that the Delete Record server behavior has inserted a hidden field icon alongside the Confirm deletion button in Design view. Position your cursor alongside the hidden field icon, and insert another submit button. In the Property inspector, enter cancel in the Button name field, and set the Value field to Cancel.

9. You need to be very careful where you put the code to cancel the delete operation.

   Switch to Code view, and locate the code shown in the following screenshot:

Cancel code MUST go here →

```
30    return $theValue;
31  }
32  }
33
34  if ((isset($_POST['user_id'])) && ($_POST['user_id'] != "")) {
35    $deleteSQL = sprintf("DELETE FROM users WHERE user_id=%s",
36                          GetSQLValueString($_POST['user_id'], "int"));
37
38    mysql_select_db($database_connAdmin, $connAdmin);
39    $Result1 = mysql_query($deleteSQL, $connAdmin) or die(mysql_error());
40
41    $deleteGoTo = "list_users.php";
42    if (isset($_SERVER['QUERY_STRING'])) {
43      $deleteGoTo .= (strpos($deleteGoTo, '?')) ? "&" : "?";
44      $deleteGoTo .= $_SERVER['QUERY_STRING'];
45    }
46    header(sprintf("Location: %s", $deleteGoTo));
47  }
```

The code shown on lines 34–47 is the Delete Record server behavior. The important thing to notice is the conditional statement on line 34. It simply checks whether $_POST['user_id'] is set and that it's not an empty string. Because the hidden field inserted by the server behavior sets $_POST['user_id'], you *must* cancel the delete operation before the script gets to this line.

10. Insert the following code at the point indicated in the preceding screenshot:

```
if (array_key_exists('cancel', $_POST)) {
  header('Location: http://dwcs4/workfiles/ch14/list_users.php');
  exit;
}
```

The first argument to array_key_exists() must be the name you give to the cancel button. It's case-sensitive, so make sure you spell it correctly. The code inside the braces uses header() to redirect the user back to list_users.php. Change the URL to the page you want users to be sent to when cancelling a delete operation. Calling exit after header() terminates the PHP script, ensuring that the form is not displayed again. Technically speaking, exit is not a function, so it doesn't need to be followed by a pair of parentheses. However, exit; and exit(); are both equally correct.

11. Load list_users.php into a browser, and click the DELETE link alongside one of the names. Make sure that delete_user.php displays the details of the record you selected for deletion. If the details aren't there, check the query string at the end of the URL. Make sure it's correctly formed with the variable and primary key number. Also check the spelling, paying careful attention to uppercase and lowercase.

If the details display correctly, test the Cancel button first. When you're taken back to the list of users, the record should still be listed. If it isn't, check the location of the code inserted in step 10.

Finally, test the Confirm deletion button. This time, the record should be deleted. Don't worry that you're losing data that has already been saved. Testing is essential. You should always be prepared to sacrifice data while making sure everything works as expected.

That's all there is to it. You can check your code against delete_user.php in examples/ch14.

You now have a basic but nevertheless fully functional user registration system. In the next chapter, you'll improve it considerably, but to round out this chapter, I want to show you how to control what is displayed onscreen when a recordset produces no results.

Displaying different content when a recordset is empty

Use list_users.php to delete all records in the users table. When the final record has been deleted, the page looks rather odd, as shown in Figure 14-23.

Figure 14-23. The list of users looks untidy when no records are left in the table.

14

Dreamweaver has a convenient set of server behaviors that can display different content depending on whether a recordset is empty. Let's put them into action in list_users.php.

Applying the Show Region server behavior

These instructions show you how to hide the table and display a different message onscreen when the listUsers recordset is empty.

1. Open list_users.php in the Document window.

2. Insert a new paragraph between the Register new user link and the table that displays the listUsers recordset. Type No records found.

3. Select the paragraph you have just created by clicking <p> in the Tag selector at the bottom of the Document window.

4. Click the plus button in the Server Behaviors panel, and select Show Region ➤ Show If Recordset Is Empty from the menu that appears. The same options are available on the Data tab of the Insert bar and the Insert ➤ Show Region menu.

5. This opens a dialog box that asks you to select the recordset. Since there's only one on the page, listUsers is chosen automatically, so just click OK to apply the server behavior.

6. Select the table that displays the results of the listUsers recordset, and repeat steps 4 and 5. However, this time select Show If Recordset Is Not Empty. The paragraph and table should now be surrounded by Show If tabs, as shown in Figure 14-24.

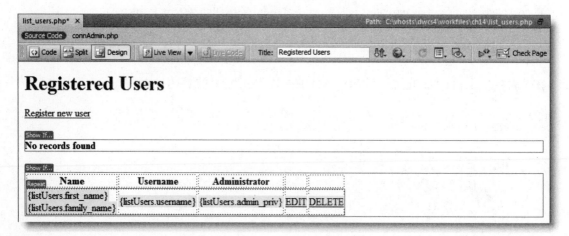

Figure 14-24. Dreamweaver surrounds optional regions with Show If tabs.

7. Save list_users.php, and load it into a browser. This time, you should see No records found. The empty table is hidden.

8. Click the Register new user link, and add a new record to the users table. When list_users.php reloads, you should see the details in the table, and the No records found message has disappeared. A simple but effective solution.

You can check your code, if necessary, against list_users_05.php in examples/ch14.

When you mouse over the EDIT and DELETE links in list_users.php, you'll see that the number used for the primary key has *not* been reset to 1. MySQL continues assigning new numbers as the primary key. As I wrote earlier in this chapter, *don't even think about renumbering*. The primary key is intended as a unique identifier and should not be reused even when a record is deleted. If you need to find out how many records there are in a database table, it's easy to do with the following SQL:

```
SELECT COUNT(*) AS total FROM tableName
```

I'll show you in Chapter 17 how to build your own SQL queries like this.

Chapter review

This chapter has taken you through all the basic commands in SQL: INSERT, SELECT, UPDATE, and DELETE. With the exception of activating the Cancel button on the delete page, I have deliberately avoided diving into the code that Dreamweaver has created on your behalf. What you have built is only a simple table, but the principle behind creating a more complex table to store much more information is identical. Most of your work with a database involves these four commands.

Dreamweaver has taken virtually all the hard work out of creating this user registration system, but if you're hoping to leave all the coding to Dreamweaver, you'll rapidly discover that you're very limited in what you can do with a database. The Adobe development team says it regards the server behaviors as serving two main purposes: rapid prototype development and as a learning tool. Rapid prototype development lets you build a database-driven site as a proof of concept to demonstrate how the site will work. Once the plan has been approved, it's necessary to add server-side validation to the basic code generated by Dreamweaver. As a learning tool, Dreamweaver takes a lot of the tedium and uncertainty out of connecting with a database and building the basic SQL queries to manage and display database content.

The next chapter begins the learning process by examining the code created by Dreamweaver for the user registration system and then makes it more secure by adding server-side validation. You'll also use the details stored in the users table to control access to different parts of your website.

14

First name:

Welcome!

Hello, {getName.first_name} {getName.family_name} . You logged in successfully.

Dreamweaver provides you with the basic functionality of inserting and updating records in a database, but it's up to you to make sure that the data entered by a user meets the criteria you envisaged when designing the database structure. When designing database forms, you must remember the GIGO principle—garbage in, garbage out. Unless you control carefully what you allow to go into a database, a lot of your results will be useless garbage. Many developers rely on JavaScript validation to filter user input before it's submitted to the database, but JavaScript is easily turned off in the browser leaving your site vulnerable. JavaScript validation, such as that provided by Spry validation widgets (see Chapter 9), should be regarded as a convenience offered to the user. The only way to make sure data is safe to insert into a database is to validate it with PHP.

In this chapter, we're going to get down and dirty with PHP code. If you don't come from a programming background, that thought might fill you with horror, but you should never deploy dynamic code on a website without understanding what it's for. In any case, PHP is not difficult. A major reason for its popularity is that it's relatively easy to learn. If the code looks strange to you, it's because it's unfamiliar. The more you work with it, the more familiar—and easier—it becomes. If you feel inspired to study PHP more, for a hands-on approach take a look at my *PHP Solutions: Dynamic Web Design Made Easy* (friends of ED, ISBN: 978-1-59059-731-6). Or if you prefer a reference book, grab hold of *Beginning PHP and MySQL: From Novice to Professional, Third Edition* by W. Jason Gilmore (Apress, ISBN: 978-1-59059-862-7).

We'll start by examining the code that Dreamweaver created when you built the insert and update forms in the previous chapter. There's no need to study every line of code. The key thing is to recognize the code Dreamweaver generates, where it puts it, and what it's for. This makes it easy to adapt the code to do much more than the basic functionality provided by the server behaviors. I'll also show you how to create simple server behaviors of your own to speed up the process of creating interactive web pages.

By the end of this chapter you will have enhanced the insert and update forms and made them much more user-friendly by preventing invalid input, displaying error messages, and preserving user input when it fails validation. Once the forms have been updated, you'll be able to use the user registration system to control access to sensitive or protected areas of your site.

In this chapter, you'll learn about the following:

- Recognizing the code generated by Dreamweaver server behaviors
- Preventing the creation of duplicate usernames
- Building your own custom server behaviors
- Preserving information related to an individual visitor with PHP sessions
- Restricting access to your pages

This chapter builds on the user registration system created in the previous chapter, so it assumes you have built register_user.php, list_users.php, update_user.php, and delete_user.php. However, to make sure everyone begins from the same starting point, I have included versions of each file in the download files for this chapter. Let's begin by examining the code that Dreamweaver generated for you.

Analyzing the code generated by Dreamweaver

My first attempt at developing a database-driven website was with Dreamweaver UltraDev 4 using ASP. It was a disaster. There were two major problems. First, I didn't realize the importance of removing server behaviors cleanly through the Server Behaviors panel if I changed my mind about how I wanted the page to work. Second, the code didn't look anything like the ASP in any of the books I consulted. I was so frustrated; I went away and learned to hand-code everything in PHP.

Even if you have studied some PHP, you might find the code generated by Dreamweaver overwhelming at first sight. However, it's actually quite straightforward, and it's organized in blocks that are relatively easy to recognize. It needs to be, because Dreamweaver needs to recognize them in order to let you edit or remove them through the Server Behaviors panel. Once you learn to recognize the blocks, you can begin to modify them yourself to add much greater functionality and flexibility to your websites. Wherever possible, I try to leave Dreamweaver's code blocks intact, because that preserves the ability to edit them through the Server Behaviors panel. However, that's not always possible, but if you keep a cool head, you'll quickly find that Dreamweaver speeds up development by creating the basic code for you to improve upon. I have no difficulty hand-coding a database query, but Dreamweaver accomplishes in seconds what it would take me many minutes to type.

As I said before, I don't intend to go through the code line by line, nor will I cover all the code generated by Dreamweaver when building the user registration system in the previous chapter. This is intended as a quick overview so you can recognize the code associated with the main server behaviors. It should also help you troubleshoot some common problems.

Inspecting the server behavior code

I suggest you open the pages in Code view as you read through this section to help familiarize yourself with the code. Copies of the finished pages from the previous chapter are in examples/ch15. The insert and update pages are called register_user_start.php and update_user_start.php, because they will be used as the starting point for building the server-side validation later in this chapter. The other two pages, list_users.php and delete_user.php, don't need further improvement, so their names are unchanged.

Connecting to the database

If you open each of the pages, you'll see that they all begin with the following line of code:

```php
<?php require_once('../../Connections/connAdmin.php'); ?>
```

If your site definition uses links relative to the site root, require_once() is replaced by virtual() like this:

```php
<?php virtual('/Connections/connAdmin.php'); ?>
```

15

This includes the login details for the MySQL user account. If this code or the include file is missing, the rest of the script cannot connect to the database, so nothing will work. As explained in the previous chapter, virtual() is supported only by the Apache web server. So, a page that works perfectly on Apache will suddenly stop working if you move the site to any other web server.

Preventing SQL injection

Immediately following the line of code that includes the database connection details is the lengthy block of code shown in Figure 15-1. This defines a custom function called GetSQLValueString(), which prepares values submitted through a form or query string for insertion into a database query. Its main task is to prevent a malicious attack known as **SQL injection**, which attempts to pass spoof values to a database in the hope of extracting confidential information or corrupting the data.

```
 2  <?php
 3  if (!function_exists("GetSQLValueString")) {
 4  function GetSQLValueString($theValue, $theType, $theDefinedValue = "", $theNotDefinedValue = "")
 5  {
 6    if (PHP_VERSION < 6) {
 7      $theValue = get_magic_quotes_gpc() ? stripslashes($theValue) : $theValue;
 8    }
 9
10    $theValue = function_exists("mysql_real_escape_string") ? mysql_real_escape_string($theValue) :
    mysql_escape_string($theValue);
11
12    switch ($theType) {
13      case "text":
14        $theValue = ($theValue != "") ? "'" . $theValue . "'" : "NULL";
15        break;
16      case "long":
17      case "int":
18        $theValue = ($theValue != "") ? intval($theValue) : "NULL";
19        break;
20      case "double":
21        $theValue = ($theValue != "") ? doubleval($theValue) : "NULL";
22        break;
23      case "date":
24        $theValue = ($theValue != "") ? "'" . $theValue . "'" : "NULL";
25        break;
26      case "defined":
27        $theValue = ($theValue != "") ? $theDefinedValue : $theNotDefinedValue;
28        break;
29    }
30    return $theValue;
31  }
32  }
```

Figure 15-1. The GetSQLValueString() function helps protect your database from malicious attack.

The function also ensures that strings are correctly enclosed in quotes when incorporated in a SQL query.

Inserting a record into a database

Figure 15-2 shows the rest of the code Dreamweaver inserted above the DOCTYPE declaration in register_user_start.php.

```
34  $editFormAction = $_SERVER['PHP_SELF'];
35  if (isset($_SERVER['QUERY_STRING'])) {
36    $editFormAction .= "?" . htmlentities($_SERVER['QUERY_STRING']);
37  }
38
39  if ((isset($_POST["MM_insert"])) && ($_POST["MM_insert"] == "form1")) {
40    $insertSQL = sprintf("INSERT INTO users (first_name, family_name, username, pwd, admin_priv) VALUES (%s, %s,
      %s, %s, %s)",
41                         GetSQLValueString($_POST['first_name'], "text"),
42                         GetSQLValueString($_POST['family_name'], "text"),
43                         GetSQLValueString($_POST['username'], "text"),
44                         GetSQLValueString($_POST['pwd'], "text"),
45                         GetSQLValueString($_POST['admin_priv'], "text"));
46
47    mysql_select_db($database_connAdmin, $connAdmin);
48    $Result1 = mysql_query($insertSQL, $connAdmin) or die(mysql_error());
49
50    $insertGoTo = "list_users.php";
51    if (isset($_SERVER['QUERY_STRING'])) {
52      $insertGoTo .= (strpos($insertGoTo, '?')) ? "&" : "?";
53      $insertGoTo .= $_SERVER['QUERY_STRING'];
54    }
55    header(sprintf("Location: %s", $insertGoTo));
56  }
```

Figure 15-2. The Insert Record server behavior inserts a record and redirects the user to the next page.

The first four lines (34–37) set a variable called $editFormAction to the name of the current page and preserve any query string in the URL. The variable is used later in the page to set the value of the action attribute in the insert form. You can normally leave this block of code alone unless you want to add anything to the query string.

Immediately following these four lines of code is the core of the Insert Record server behavior.

The server behavior is wrapped in a conditional statement that makes sure the code is run only when the insert form has been submitted. It's easy to tell that this is an Insert Record server behavior because all the variables begin with $insert (Dreamweaver's variables and functions use names that make it easy to guess their purpose). As you can see on lines 41–45 of Figure 15-2, the value of each form field is passed to the GetSQLValueString() function to prepare it for insertion in the SQL query.

Lines 40–45 build the SQL query; line 47 selects the correct database; and line 48 executes the query, inserting the new record into the database table.

The remaining lines redirect the user to the next page (in this case, list_users.php), preserving any values in the query string. The actual redirect is performed by the header() function on line 55.

> If you don't specify a page to redirect to after the record is inserted, the code shown on lines 50–55 is omitted.

15

Understanding why a redirect doesn't work

A question that turns up regularly in online forums is why an insert or update form doesn't redirect the user to the next page after inserting or updating the record. The key to understanding the problem lies in knowing how the header() function works. I have mentioned this several times already, but it confuses so many people, it's worth repeating here. The header() function cannot do its job if any output is sent to the browser before you call the function.

This means you can't use echo, print, or any other function that outputs content anywhere before a call to header(). Nor can any HTML appear before header(). Other things that prevent header() from working are using the byte-order mark or whitespace outside PHP tags. A common cause of failure is extra whitespace at the end of an include file (see "Avoiding the 'headers already sent' error" in Chapter 12).

Updating a database record

Now take a look at update_user_start.php. Figure 15-3 shows the code immediately following the GetSQLValueString() function. Compare it with the code in Figure 15-2. It's almost identical. The differences are that all the variables begin with $update and the SQL query built on lines 40–46 uses the UPDATE command rather than INSERT.

```
34  $editFormAction = $_SERVER['PHP_SELF'];
35  if (isset($_SERVER['QUERY_STRING'])) {
36    $editFormAction .= "?" . htmlentities($_SERVER['QUERY_STRING']);
37  }
38
39  if ((isset($_POST["MM_update"])) && ($_POST["MM_update"] == "form1")) {
40    $updateSQL = sprintf("UPDATE users SET first_name=%s, family_name=%s, username=%s, pwd=%s, admin_priv=%s
    WHERE user_id=%s",
41                         GetSQLValueString($_POST['first_name'], "text"),
42                         GetSQLValueString($_POST['family_name'], "text"),
43                         GetSQLValueString($_POST['username'], "text"),
44                         GetSQLValueString($_POST['pwd'], "text"),
45                         GetSQLValueString($_POST['admin_priv'], "text"),
46                         GetSQLValueString($_POST['user_id'], "int"));
47
48    mysql_select_db($database_connAdmin, $connAdmin);
49    $Result1 = mysql_query($updateSQL, $connAdmin) or die(mysql_error());
50
51    $updateGoTo = "list_users.php";
52    if (isset($_SERVER['QUERY_STRING'])) {
53      $updateGoTo .= (strpos($updateGoTo, '?')) ? "&" : "?";
54      $updateGoTo .= $_SERVER['QUERY_STRING'];
55    }
56    header(sprintf("Location: %s", $updateGoTo));
57  }
```

Figure 15-3. The Update Record server behavior code is almost identical to the Insert Record server behavior.

Everything else works exactly the same way as an Insert Record server behavior.

Deleting a record

Figure 15-4 shows the Delete Record server behavior in delete_user.php. It's easy to recognize because all the variables begin with $delete. It simply deletes a record and redirects to another page.

```
38   if ((isset($_POST['user_id'])) && ($_POST['user_id'] != "")) {
39       $deleteSQL = sprintf("DELETE FROM users WHERE user_id=%s",
40                            GetSQLValueString($_POST['user_id'], "int"));
41
42       mysql_select_db($database_connAdmin, $connAdmin);
43       $Result1 = mysql_query($deleteSQL, $connAdmin) or die(mysql_error());
44
45       $deleteGoTo = "list_users.php";
46       if (isset($_SERVER['QUERY_STRING'])) {
47           $deleteGoTo .= (strpos($deleteGoTo, '?')) ? "&" : "?";
48           $deleteGoTo .= $_SERVER['QUERY_STRING'];
49       }
50       header(sprintf("Location: %s", $deleteGoTo));
51   }
```

Figure 15-4.
The Delete Record server behavior deletes a record without confirmation.

The key point to note about this server behavior, as I explained in the previous chapter, is that the conditional statement surrounding the server behavior checks only that the variable being used to identify the record exists. If it does, it goes ahead and deletes the record.

In the previous chapter, I told you to set the Primary key value in the Delete Record dialog box to Form Variable. This makes the server behavior use the $_POST array and gives you the opportunity to confirm that the correct record is being deleted. If, on the other hand, you use the default setting, URL Parameter, the server behavior uses the $_GET array. This results in the record being deleted immediately without confirmation.

Distinguishing between Form Variable and URL Parameter

A lot of server behavior dialog boxes ask you to specify the origin of a variable. The two most frequently used values are Form Variable and URL Parameter, so it's important to understand the difference.

- Form Variable: This uses the $_POST array and takes the value from a form submitted using the post method.

- URL Parameter: This uses the $_GET array and takes the value from a query string at the end of a URL or from a form submitted using the get method.

If a server behavior doesn't pick up a variable, check that you haven't selected the wrong one.

Many beginners get mixed up between get and post, but it makes a crucial difference to how your page works. If you're still unclear about the difference, skip back to Chapter 9 and refresh your memory.

Retrieving database records with a recordset

Figure 15-5 shows the remaining code inserted above the DOCTYPE declaration in update_user_start.php. This is the code for the getUser recordset.

```
59   $colname_getUser = "-1";
60   if (isset($_GET['user_id'])) {
61       $colname_getUser = $_GET['user_id'];
62   }
63   mysql_select_db($database_connAdmin, $connAdmin);
64   $query_getUser = sprintf("SELECT user_id, username, pwd, first_name, family_name, admin_priv FROM users WHERE
         user_id = %s", GetSQLValueString($colname_getUser, "int"));
65   $getUser = mysql_query($query_getUser, $connAdmin) or die(mysql_error());
66   $row_getUser = mysql_fetch_assoc($getUser);
67   $totalRows_getUser = mysql_num_rows($getUser);
```

Figure 15-5.
Dreamweaver uses the recordset name to create the variables.

15

If you cast your mind back to the previous chapter, I told you that you needed to create the recordset *before* using the Record Update Form Wizard, yet the recordset code has been inserted *after* the Update Record server behavior. This is the way that Dreamweaver works—the code for a recordset is always inserted immediately above the DOCTYPE declaration. Normally, this is fine, but a recordset often produces information that can be useful for validation and needs to be moved. The good news is that Dreamweaver doesn't mind you moving the code, just as long as you keep it all together.

The first thing to notice about a recordset is that the names of all the variables are based on the name you give the recordset. So, giving a recordset a name that describes its purpose makes it a lot easier to recognize the right code. This is what the variables mean (*recordsetName* changes depending on the name you give the recordset):

- $colname_*recordsetName*: This is the variable being used as a filter for the recordset. In the getUser recordset, you set the primary key, user_id, as the filter, so this holds the value of user_id passed in through the query string of the URL. As you'll see in later chapters, you can use more than one variable to filter results. When you use more than one variable, colname is replaced by the variable name you choose yourself.

- $query_*recordsetName*: This contains the SQL query used to create the recordset.

- $*recordsetName*: This contains the results of the database query.

- $row_*recordsetName*: This is an array that contains the results from the current record. Dreamweaver automatically gets the first record so that it's ready for display inside the page.

- $totalRows_*recordsetName*: This contains the number of records retrieved from the database. This is extremely useful in determining whether the query produced any results.

The basic recordset code is on lines 63–67 of Figure 15-5. All recordsets contain these five lines of code. The code shown on lines 59–62 defines the variable for the filter. If more than one variable is used as a filter, each one is defined in the same way.

> All the server behavior code you have looked at so far is placed above the DOCTYPE declaration. This is perfectly OK because it doesn't send any output to the browser, except when redirecting the user to another page. When adapting server behaviors or writing PHP code of your own, don't put anything above the DOCTYPE that will send output to the browser, because it will render your CSS in quirks mode, possibly breaking your design. The only exception is when debugging code. Sometimes, it's useful to display the value of variables to see why your code isn't working as expected, but you should remove the debugging code when you have finished testing.

Creating a repeat region

The code used to create a repeat region is very simple. It consists of just two lines wrapped around the code that you want to repeat. Figure 15-6 shows the repeat region that you applied to the second table row in list_users.php. The two lines that repeat the table row are highlighted on lines 62 and 70. They create a simple do . . . while loop (see Chapter 10). Dreamweaver uses a do . . . while loop because the first record is already stored in $row_*recordsetName*, as explained in the preceding section. The code inside the parentheses at the end of the loop on line 70 gets the next row of results from the recordset.

```
62    <?php do { ?>
63      <tr>
64        <td><?php echo $row_listUsers['first_name']; ?> <?php echo $row_listUsers['family_name']; ?></td>
65        <td><?php echo $row_listUsers['username']; ?></td>
66        <td><?php echo $row_listUsers['admin_priv']; ?></td>
67        <td><a href="update_user.php?user_id=<?php echo $row_listUsers['user_id']; ?>">EDIT</a></td>
68        <td><a href="delete_user.php?user_id=<?php echo $row_listUsers['user_id']; ?>">DELETE</a></td>
69      </tr>
70    <?php } while ($row_listUsers = mysql_fetch_assoc($listUsers)); ?>
```

Figure 15-6. The code for a repeat region is simple, but its location is vital.

Usually when a repeat region goes haywire, it's the result of selecting the wrong elements in Design view before applying the server behavior. A quick look at the code should confirm what the problem is.

Adding server-side validation

The user registration form created by the Record Insertion Form Wizard has several problems. Figure 15-7 shows what happens if you submit the form without filling in any fields (top screenshot) or if a username is used more than once (bottom screenshot).

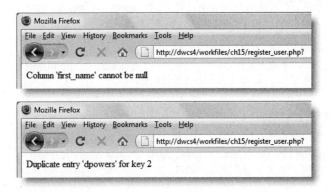

Figure 15-7. The default error messages are not user-friendly.

Setting all columns to NOT NULL in the table definition prevents anyone from submitting the form without filling in each field, but there's no guarantee that the right type of information will be input. As things currently stand, a single space would satisfy the form's definition of a required field. Applying a unique index to the username column certainly prevents duplicate entries, but the error message isn't very informative. More important, the form has disappeared, and the only way to get back to it is to click the back button in the browser.

Of course, you could prevent this sort of problem by applying the Spry validation widgets that you studied in Chapter 9. This would probably be sufficient for most bona fide users, but the Web is a dangerous place filled with people with less honorable intentions. Anyone intent on a malicious attack normally disables JavaScript, and even if the information in

15

your database remains intact, it could easily be filled with unwanted garbage. So, it's important to validate input on the server before inserting it into your database.

The registration form created by the Dreamweaver wizard needs the following improvements:

- All required fields must contain specified minimum content.
- When a field fails to validate, a suitable error message must be displayed.
- Existing input must be preserved when an error occurs.

Let's begin by making sure that each field is filled in with a minimum amount of content.

Verifying that required fields have been filled in

All fields are required, so you need to check that they contain at least something. If a problem is detected, the validation code needs to prevent the INSERT command from being executed. The series of tests that you'll add to the code in register_user.php perform only simple checks on the user input. You can make them much more rigorous. The purpose of the following exercises is to demonstrate the principles behind server-side validation, rather than incorporate exhaustive tests. The level of testing you choose depends entirely on what the form is for. An insurance proposal form is likely to warrant far more rigorous validation than one for a community forum.

Adding server-side validation to the Insert Record server behavior is easy to implement, but it involves editing the server behavior, so it's no longer accessible through the Server Behaviors panel. The idea of losing access to server behaviors through the panel instills terror into the mind of most newcomers to dynamic design, but it's important to remember that Dreamweaver server behaviors cannot do everything. To get the best out of them, you frequently need to amend the code. If you cling tenaciously to the dialog box interface, you'll be severely limited in what you can achieve.

Checking required fields

This section uses the PHP functions, trim(), empty(), and strlen(), to trim whitespace from user input and check whether it's empty or how many characters it contains. If any problems are encountered, error messages are created for display later in the registration form. You can continue using register_user.php from the previous chapter. Alternatively, copy register_user_start.php from examples/ch15 to workfiles/ch15, and rename it register_user.php.

1. With register_user.php open in the Document window, switch to Code view. The validation code should run only if the form has been submitted. Locate the following code (it should be on or around line 39):

   ```
   if ((isset($_POST["MM_insert"])) && ($_POST["MM_insert"] == "form1")) {
   ```

   This conditional statement checks the value of a hidden field to see whether the insert form has been submitted. So, if you place the validation code inside the braces of this conditional statement, your new code runs only at the same time as the Insert Record server behavior. Doing so means that the server behavior ceases to be editable through a dialog box, but this is a sacrifice you must make in the interests of data integrity.

Place your cursor at the end of this line, and press Enter/Return a couple of times to make room for the validation code, as shown in the following screenshot:

Insert validation code here

```
39   if ((isset($_POST["MM_insert"])) && ($_POST["MM_insert"] == "form1")) {
40
41
42       $insertSQL = sprintf("INSERT INTO users (first_name, family_name, username, pwd, admin_priv) VALUES (%s, %s,
         %s, %s, %s)",
43                            GetSQLValueString($_POST['first_name'], "text"),
```

Insert the following code:

```
// Initialize array for error messages
$error = array();
// Remove whitespace and check first and family names
$_POST['first_name'] = trim($_POST['first_name']);
$_POST['family_name'] = trim($_POST['family_name']);
if (empty($_POST['first_name']) || empty($_POST['family_name'])) {
  $error['name'] = 'Please enter both first name and family name';
}
```

This initializes $error as an empty array. PHP treats an array with zero elements as false (see "The truth according to PHP" in Chapter 10), so this can be used later to test whether any errors have been found and, if so, to prevent the Insert Record server behavior from attempting to execute the INSERT query.

The remaining lines use trim() to remove leading and trailing whitespace from the first_name and family_name fields and then pass them to empty(). If either field has no value, an appropriate message is added to the $error array.

> *You might wonder why I haven't reassigned the values of the $_POST array variables to shorter ones, as with the mail processing script in Chapter 11. It's because they're required by the Insert Record server behavior. Changing them here would involve further changes to the code generated by Dreamweaver, increasing not only your workload but also the likelihood of errors creeping in.*

2. The next check makes sure that the username contains at least six characters. It uses the PHP function strlen(), which determines the number of characters in any string passed to it. Add the following code immediately after the code in the preceding step:

```
// Check the username for length
$_POST['username'] = trim($_POST['username']);
if (strlen($_POST['username']) < 6) {
  $error['length'] = 'Please select a username that contains at least ➥
    6 characters';
}
```

15

3. A similar check is done next on the password. The following code goes immediately after the code in the previous step:

```
// set a flag that assumes the password is OK
$pwdOK = true;
// trim leading and trailing white space
$_POST['pwd'] = trim($_POST['pwd']);
// if less than 6 characters, create alert and set flag to false
if (strlen($_POST['pwd']) < 6) {
    $error['pwd_length'] = 'Your password must be at least 6 characters';
    $pwdOK = false;
}
```

This code starts by setting a variable that assumes the password is OK. After trimming any whitespace, strlen() is used to check that the trimmed password contains at least six characters. If it doesn't, an error message is added to the $error array, and $pwdOK is set to false. You'll see the purpose of the $pwdOK variable in the next section.

If you would like to check your code so far, compare it against register_user_01.php in examples/ch15.

Verifying and encrypting the password

Since the password won't appear onscreen, you should get the user to type it in twice to confirm the spelling. Also, to keep the password secure, it should be encrypted before it's stored in the database. Encryption is important because it keeps the passwords secret, even if someone manages to compromise the security of the database and expose the stored passwords.

Improving password validation

In this section, you'll add an extra field for the user to retype the password to ensure that both versions match. You'll also encrypt the password before it's passed to the SQL query. Continue working with the same file as in the preceding section.

1. Adding a new field for the user to confirm the password means adding a new row to the table that contains the registration form. You can do this in several ways. Start by switching back to Design view and clicking inside the table cell that contains the Administrator label. If you have a good memory for keyboard shortcuts, the quickest and easiest way to add a new table row is to press Ctrl+M/Cmd+M. This always inserts a new row *above* the current one.

Alternative ways of adding a new row are to use the menu system. Modify ➤ Table ➤ Insert Row does the same as the keyboard shortcut: the new row goes above the current one. Modify ➤ Table ➤ Insert Rows or Columns opens a dialog box that lets you specify the number of rows or columns to be inserted and on which side of the current selection to put them. Finally, the Layout tab of the Insert bar offers a visual way of doing it.

Use whichever method you prefer to create a new row between Password and Administrator. Then type Confirm password as the label in the left cell, and insert a text field in the right cell. Name the text field conf_pwd, and set Type to Password in the Property inspector (form creation was covered in Chapter 9).

> *The table layout for the insert form created by the wizard doesn't use <label> tags, so choose the No label tag option in the Input Tag Accessibility Attributes dialog box. Using the wizard is best avoided except when you're developing a prototype as a proof of concept, which will be rebuilt using your own forms and designs later. I'll show you how to apply Insert Record and Update Record server behaviors to custom-built forms in the next chapter.*

2. You can now compare the content of the pwd and conf_pwd fields. Switch to Code view, and add the following code immediately after the code you inserted in step 3 of the previous section:

```
    $error['pwd_length'] = 'Your password must be at least 6 characters';
    $pwdOK = false;
}
// if no match, create alert and set flag to false
if ($_POST['pwd'] != trim($_POST['conf_pwd'])) {
    $error['pwd'] = "Your passwords don't match";
    $pwdOK = false;
}
```

This trims whitespace off both ends of $_POST['conf_pwd'] and compares the result with $_POST['pwd']. There's no need to pass the original password to trim() because that was already done in the previous section and the value reassigned to $_POST['pwd']. Also, there's no need to store the result of trim($_POST['conf_pwd']), because you're using it only to make sure the two entries match. If they do, this conditional statement will be ignored. However, if there's a mismatch, an error message is created, and $pwdOK is set to false.

3. Finally, if $pwdOK is still true, you can encrypt the password by passing it to the sha1() function like this (the code goes immediately after the code in the previous step):

```
// if password OK, encrypt it
if ($pwdOK) {
    $_POST['pwd'] = sha1($_POST['pwd']);
}
```

The sha1() function converts any string passed to it into a 40-character hexadecimal number—in effect, encrypting the string ready for insertion into the database.

You can check your code, if necessary, against register_user_02.php in examples/ch15.

15

Dealing with duplicate usernames

Dreamweaver has a server behavior called Check New User that queries your database to find out whether a username is already in use. Unfortunately, it's badly designed and guaranteed to enrage visitors to your site. If it finds a duplicate username, it takes the visitor to another page and wipes out all the information that had been entered into the form. Applying a unique index to the username column, as you did in the previous chapter, is a much more elegant way of handling the situation, but you need a way to prevent the form from disappearing when a duplicate entry is detected. This is done by checking the error code returned by MySQL.

Creating an error message for duplicate usernames

The following instructions show you how to amend the Insert Record server behavior to generate a user-friendly error message when the INSERT query fails as the result of a duplicate username being submitted. Continue working with the same file.

1. Approximately ten lines below the last section of code you have just inserted, locate the line that looks like this (it should be on or around line 80):

   ```
   $Result1 = mysql_query($insertSQL, $connAdmin) or die(mysql_error());
   ```

   What this line does is execute the INSERT query; but if there's a problem, the section highlighted in bold displays an error message and brings all further processing to a halt.

   The draconian-sounding function die() tells a PHP script to terminate immediately if it encounters an error. It takes a single argument: the error message you want to display onscreen. In this case, the message is generated by another function, mysql_error(), which gives you access to the most recent error message from MySQL.

   Instead of bringing the script to a halt, it's far more user-friendly to redisplay the form ready for the user to submit an alternative username.

2. Remove the section highlighted in bold so the line of code looks like this:

   ```
   $Result1 = mysql_query($insertSQL, $connAdmin);
   ```

   Make sure you don't lose the semicolon at the end of the line.

3. In addition to mysql_error(), PHP has a function called mysql_errno(), which returns an error code from MySQL. Although error messages are easier for human beings to understand, it's easier for PHP to work with numbers. Add the conditional statement highlighted in bold, as shown here:

   ```
   $Result1 = mysql_query($insertSQL, $connAdmin);
   if (!$Result1 && mysql_errno() == 1062) {
     $error['username'] = $_POST['username'] . ' is already in use. ➥
       Please choose a different username.';
   } elseif (mysql_error()) {
   ```

```
   $error['dbError'] = 'Sorry, there was a problem with the database. ➦
      Please try later.';
}
$insertGoTo = "list_users.php";
```

If the Insert Record server behavior succeeds, $Result1 is true. So, placing the negative operator (!) in front of $Result1 tests whether it is *not* true—in other words, whether it fails. A duplicate value entered into a unique index column produces the MySQL error code 1062. So if the Insert Record server behavior fails and the error code is 1062, you know it's because of a duplicate value.

The code inside the first conditional statement uses $_POST['username'], the value submitted from the registration form, to create an error message and stores the message in $error['username'].

You should never display the contents of MySQL error messages in a live web page, because it can reveal information that might be helpful to an attacker. So, the second conditional statement checks for any other MySQL error and creates a generic error message.

If you encounter problems when testing the page, substitute the line of code in the second conditional statement with the following:

```
$error['dbError'] = mysql_error();
```

This gives you access to the MySQL error message. Once you have identified the problem, replace mysql_error() with the neutral message.

4. If the database returns an error, you need to prevent the script from redirecting the user to the next page, so wrap the code that redirects the page in a final else statement like this:

```
   $error['dbError'] = 'Sorry, there was a problem with the database.
Please try later.';
   } else {
      $insertGoTo = "list_users.php";
      if (isset($_SERVER['QUERY_STRING'])) {
      $insertGoTo .= (strpos($insertGoTo, '?')) ? "&" : "?";
        $insertGoTo .= $_SERVER['QUERY_STRING'];
      }
      header(sprintf("Location: %s", $insertGoTo));
   }
}
```

By placing the redirection code in the final else block of the conditional statement, the redirect goes ahead only if the database doesn't return an error (you can see the full chain of conditions in Figure 15-8).

You can check your code so far against register_user_03.php in examples/ch15.

> *MySQL error messages can appear rather cryptic. Chapter 17 contains advice on understanding them and troubleshooting problems with SQL queries.*

15

Displaying the error messages

Now that the checks are complete, you need to build the logic that determines whether the record is inserted in the database. If there are no errors, the new record is inserted into the database, and the user is redirected to the next page. However, if errors are detected, the INSERT command is ignored, and the form needs to be redisplayed with the appropriate error messages.

Building the error detection logic

This section completes the validation process by wrapping the code that inserts the record in a conditional statement to prevent it from being executed if any errors are discovered. You will also add code to the insert form to display any error messages. Continue working with the same file.

1. If no errors have been found, the $error array will contain zero elements, which, as you know, PHP treats as false. Wrap the remaining section of the Insert Record server behavior code with this conditional statement (the exact location is shown in Figure 15-8):

```
// if no errors, insert the details into the database
if (!$error) {
    // Insert Record server behavior code
}
```

Insert conditional statement here

```
67  // if password OK, encrypt it
68  if ($pwdOK) {
69      $_POST['pwd'] = sha1($_POST['pwd']);
70  }
71
72  // if no errors, insert the details into the database
73  if (!$error) {
74      $insertSQL = sprintf("INSERT INTO users (first_name, family_name, username, pwd, admin_priv) VALUES (%s,
    %s, %s, %s, %s)",
75                      GetSQLValueString($_POST['first_name'], "text"),
76                      GetSQLValueString($_POST['family_name'], "text"),
77                      GetSQLValueString($_POST['username'], "text"),
78                      GetSQLValueString($_POST['pwd'], "text"),
79                      GetSQLValueString($_POST['admin_priv'], "text"));
80
81      mysql_select_db($database_connAdmin, $connAdmin);
82      $Result1 = mysql_query($insertSQL, $connAdmin);
83      if (!$Result1 && mysql_errno() == 1062) {
84          $error['username'] = $_POST['username'] . ' is already in use. Please choose a different username.';
85      } elseif (mysql_error()) {
86          $error['dbError'] = 'Sorry, there was a problem with the database. Please try later.';
87      } else {
88          $insertGoTo = "list_users.php";
89          if (isset($_SERVER['QUERY_STRING'])) {
90              $insertGoTo .= (strpos($insertGoTo, '?')) ? "&" : "?";
91              $insertGoTo .= $_SERVER['QUERY_STRING'];
92          }
93          header(sprintf("Location: %s", $insertGoTo));
94      }
95
96  }
97  ?>
98  <!DOCTYPE html PUBLIC "-//W3C//DTD XHTML 1.0 Transitional//EN"
```

Figure 15-8. The conditional statement prevents the record from being inserted if any errors are found.

The negation operator (an exclamation mark) gives you the reverse meaning of a value. So if $error is an empty array, this test equates to true, and the Insert Record server behavior is executed. If errors are found, the test equates to false, and the server behavior is ignored.

2. Scroll down to the page heading (around line 106) just below the <body> tag, and insert the following code block between the heading and the opening <form> tag:

```
<h1>Register user </h1>
<?php
if (isset($error)) {
  echo '<ul>';
  foreach ($error as $alert) {
    echo "<li class='warning'>$alert</li>\n";
  }
  echo '</ul>';
}
?>
<form action="<?php echo $editFormAction; ?>" method="post" ➥
name="form1" id="newUser">
```

This begins by checking whether the $error array exists, because it's created only when the form is submitted. If it doesn't exist, the whole block is ignored. If it does exist, a foreach loop iterates through the array and assigns each element to the temporary variable $alert, which is used to display the error messages as a bulleted list. (See Chapter 10 if you need to refresh your memory about foreach loops.)

3. Save register_user.php, and load it into a browser. Click the Insert record button without filling in any fields. The page should reload and display the following warnings:

> **Register User**
>
> - Please enter both first name and family name
> - Please select a username that contains at least 6 characters
> - Your password must be at least 6 characters

4. Now try filling in all fields, but with a username that is already registered. This time, you should see something similar to this:

> **Register User**
>
> - dpowers is already in use. Please choose a different username.

If you have any problems, check your code against register_user_04.php in examples/ch15. The page contains no style rules, but if you add a warning class, you could make the error messages stand out in bold, red text.

15

This has improved the insert form considerably, but imagine the frustration of being forced to fill in all the details again because of a mistake in just one field. What you really need is a server behavior to provide the same solution you used in the contact form in Chapter 11. There isn't one, but you can make it yourself.

Building custom server behaviors

One reason for the great success of Dreamweaver is that, in addition to its massive range of features, it's also extensible. You can build your own server behaviors to take the tedium out of repetitive tasks.

To redisplay the contents of a text field after a form has been submitted, all you need to do is insert a PHP conditional statement between the quotes of the <input> element's value attribute like this:

```
value="<?php if (isset($_POST['field'])) {echo htmlentities( ➡
$_POST['field'], ENT_COMPAT, UTF-8);} ?>"
```

This checks whether the $_POST array element exists. If it does, it's passed to htmlentities() to avoid any problems with quotes, and the resulting output is inserted into the value attribute using echo. It's very similar to the snippet you created in Chapter 11. Apart from *field*, the code never changes. This consistency makes it ideal for creating a new server behavior, which involves the following steps:

1. Create a unique name for each block of code that the server behavior will insert into your page. The Server Behavior Builder generates this automatically for you.

2. Type the code into the Server Behavior Builder, replacing any changeable values with Dreamweaver parameters. The parameters act as placeholders until you insert the actual value through a dialog box when the server behavior is applied.

3. Tell Dreamweaver where to insert the code.

4. Design the server behavior dialog box.

Creating a Sticky Text Field server behavior

These instructions show you how to create your own server behavior to insert a conditional statement in the value attribute of a text field to preserve user input in any page. You must have a PHP page open in the Document window before you start.

1. In the Server Behaviors panel, click the plus button, and select New Server Behavior. In the dialog box that opens, make sure that Document type is set to PHP MySQL. Type Sticky Text Field in the Name field, and click OK.

2. This opens the Server Behavior Builder dialog box. Click the plus button next to Code blocks to insert. Dreamweaver suggests a name for the new code block based

on the name of the new server behavior. Click OK to accept it. Dreamweaver fills in the remaining fields of the Server Behavior Builder, as shown in Figure 15-9.

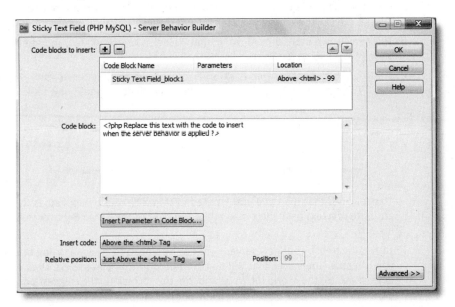

Figure 15-9. The Server Behavior Builder makes it easy to create your own server behaviors.

3. The Code block area in the center is where you insert the PHP code that you want to appear on the page. The value of *field* will change every time, so you need to replace it with a parameter. Parameter names must not contain any spaces, but they are used to label the server behavior dialog box, so it's a good idea to choose a descriptive name, such as FieldName. To insert a parameter, click the Insert Parameter in Code Block button at the appropriate point in the code, type the name in the dialog box, and click OK. Dreamweaver places it in the code with two @ characters on either side. You can also type the parameters in the code block directly yourself. Whichever method you use, replace the dummy text in the Code block area with this:

```php
<?php if (isset($_POST['@@FieldName@@'])) {
echo htmlentities($_POST['@@FieldName@@'], ENT_COMPAT, 'UTF-8');} ?>
```

> *I am using the optional second and third arguments to* htmlentities(), *as described in Chapter 11. If you want to encode single quotes or are using a different encoding from Dreamweaver's default UTF-8, change the second and third arguments to suit your own requirements (see Tables 11-1 and 11-2 for the available options).*

15

4. As soon as you add any parameters in the Code block area, the label on the OK button changes to Next, but first you need to tell Dreamweaver where you want the code to appear in the page. It needs to be applied to the value attribute of <input> tags, so select Relative to a Specific Tag from the Insert code drop-down menu.

5. This reveals two more drop-down menus. Select input/text for Tag, and select As the Value of an Attribute for Relative position.

6. This triggers the appearance of another drop-down menu labeled Attribute. Select value. The bottom section of the Server Behavior Builder should now look like this:

This specifies that the code you entered in step 3 should be applied as the value attribute of a text field. Click Next at the top right of the Server Behavior Builder dialog box.

7. To be able to use your new server behavior, you need to create a dialog box where you can enter the values that will be substituted for the parameters. Dreamweaver does most of the work for you, and on this occasion, the suggestions in the Generate Behavior Dialog Box dialog box are fine, so just click OK.

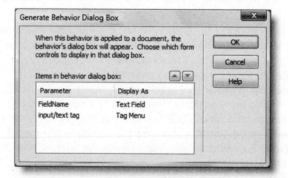

Creating a server behavior for Sticky Text Areas

The server behavior you have just built works only with text fields, so it's worth building another to handle text areas. Unlike text fields, text areas don't have a value attribute.

1. Repeat steps 1 and 2 of the previous section, only this time call the new server behavior Sticky Text Area.

2. In step 3 of the previous section, enter the following code in the Code block area:

```php
<?php if (isset($_POST['@@TextArea@@'])) {echo ➡
htmlentities($_POST['@@TextArea@@'], ENT_COMPAT, 'UTF-8');} ?>
```

I have split the code over two lines because of printing constraints, but you should enter the code all on a single line to avoid adding any whitespace between the <textarea> tags when this code is executed. Although the value is inserted directly between the tags as plain text, it's still a good idea to use htmlentities() to prevent malicious users from attempting to embed executable script, such as JavaScript, in your page.

3. Fill in the bottom section of the Server Behavior Builder, as shown in the following screenshot. This places the content of the $_POST variable between the opening and closing <textarea> tags.

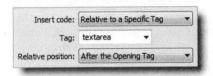

4. Click Next, and accept the defaults suggested for the server behavior dialog box.

Both server behaviors will be available in all PHP sites from the menu in the Server Behaviors panel.

Completing the user registration form

Now that you have built your own server behaviors, you can complete register_user.php. What remains to be done is to redisplay the user's input if any errors are detected by the server-side validation. In the case of the text fields, this is done by the Sticky Text Field server behavior that you have just built. However, the radio buttons need to be handled differently. First, let's deal with the text fields.

Preserving user input in text fields

Applying the Sticky Text Field server behavior to each text field ensures that data already inserted won't be lost through the failure of any validation test.

Applying the Sticky Text Field server behavior

This section shows you how to use the Sticky Text Field server behavior. Continue working with register_user.php from earlier in the chapter.

1. In Design view, select the first_name text field. Click the plus button in the Server Behaviors panel. The new server behaviors are now listed. Select Sticky Text Field.

2. The Sticky Text Field dialog box appears. If you have selected the first_name text field correctly, the input/text tag field should automatically select first_name. If it's

15

not selected, activate the drop-down menu to select it. Type the field's name in FieldName, as shown here, and click OK:

3. Dreamweaver inserts a dynamic content placeholder inside the text field in Design view. Open Split view, and as the next screenshot shows, the conditional statement you created in the Code block area of the Server Behavior Builder has been inserted, but @@FieldName@@ has been replaced by the actual name of the field:

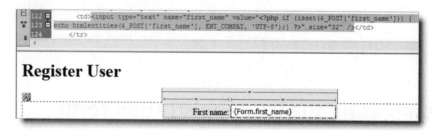

4. Apply the Sticky Text Field server behavior to the family_name and username fields. Dreamweaver doesn't include password fields in the drop-down menu, so you can't apply the server behavior to them. In any case, the password is encrypted by sha1(), so you shouldn't attempt to redisplay it.

5. All instances of Sticky Text Field are now listed in the Server Behaviors panel. If you ever need to edit one, highlight it and double-click, or use the minus (–) button to remove it cleanly from your code.

6. Save register_user.php, and load it into a browser. Test it by entering an incomplete set of details. This time, the content of text fields is preserved. Check your code, if necessary, against register_user_05.php in examples/ch15.

Applying a dynamic value to a radio group

The Administrator radio buttons still don't respond to the changes. We'll fix that next. Dreamweaver lets you bind the value of radio buttons to a dynamic value, such as from a recordset or a variable. You can type the variable directly into the dialog box, but Dreamweaver also lets you define superglobal variables, such as from the $_POST and $_GET arrays, for use throughout the site.

Making the radio buttons sticky

In this section, you'll define the $_POST variable that contains the value of the selected radio button and apply it to the radio button group so that it displays the value selected by the user when an error is detected. Continue working with register_user.php from the previous section.

1. When any errors are detected, you need checked="checked" to be inserted in the tag of the radio button that the user selected. Since the radio group is called admin_priv, the value you want is contained in $_POST['admin_priv']. Although you can type this directly into the Dynamic Radio Group dialog box, Dreamweaver lets you define $_POST, $_GET, and other super-global variables in the Bindings panel.

   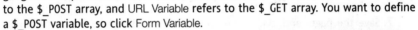

   In the Bindings panel, click the plus button to display the menu shown alongside.

   Dreamweaver uses generic names because the same menu applies to other server-side languages. As explained earlier, Form Variable refers to the $_POST array, and URL Variable refers to the $_GET array. You want to define a $_POST variable, so click Form Variable.

2. Type admin_priv in the Name field of the Form Variable dialog box, and click OK. The new dynamic variable is now listed in the Bindings panel like this:

   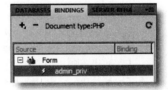

3. Select one of the radio buttons in Design view, and click the Dynamic button in the Property inspector.

4. The admin_priv radio group will be automatically selected in the Dynamic Radio Group dialog box and grayed out, because the Record Insertion Form Wizard bound the value of the radio group to n. Change the binding by clicking the lightning bolt icon to the right of the Select value equal to field. Then choose admin_priv from the Dynamic Data panel (click the tiny plus sign or triangle alongside Form if you can't see admin_priv). Click OK twice to close both panels.

5. The problem with binding the value of the radio button group to $_POST['admin_priv'] is that this variable doesn't exist when the registration form first loads. As a result, neither radio button is selected. If PHP error reporting is set to its highest level, this displays unsightly error messages. And even if the display of errors is turned off, you're still left without a default radio button checked, which could lead to the user forgetting to select one and generating another error. So, this needs to be fixed—and it involves another journey into Code view.

659

In Design view, highlight one of the radio buttons so that you can easily locate the relevant code, and switch to Code view. The radio button code looks like this:

```
147        <td><input type="radio" name="admin_priv" value="y"   <?php if (!(strcmp($_POST['admin_priv'],"y")))
    {echo "checked=\"checked\"";} ?> />
148            Yes</td>
149        </tr>
150        <tr>
151        <td><input type="radio" name="admin_priv" value="n"   <?php if (!(strcmp($_POST['admin_priv'],"n")))
    {echo "checked=\"checked\"";} ?> />
152            No</td>
```

Dreamweaver uses a rather unusual PHP function called strcmp() to check whether $_POST['admin_priv'] is y or n. The function takes two arguments and returns 0 if they're exactly the same. Since 0 equates to false, the negation operator (!) converts it to true. If you find the logic difficult to follow, just take my word for it—it works.

6. You need to check whether the form has been submitted. Although the POST array is always set, it will be empty if the form hasn't been submitted. And as you should know by now, an empty array equates to false. Amend the beginning of both sections of radio button code (shown on lines 147 and 151 in the preceding screenshot) like this:

```
<input <?php if ($_POST && !(strcmp($_POST['admin_priv'],
```

7. Save the page, and load it into your browser. The radio buttons should now be back to normal. The only problem is that you don't have a default checked value when the page first loads. In one respect, it shouldn't be a problem, because you set a default value when defining the users table earlier. Unfortunately, Dreamweaver server behaviors treat unset values as NULL, causing your form to fail because admin_priv was defined as "not null."

8. Change the code for the No radio button shown on line 151 in the preceding screenshot like this (the change made in step 6 is also shown in bold):

```
<input <?php if (($_POST && !(strcmp($_POST['admin_priv'],"n"))) ➥
|| !$_POST) {echo "checked=\"checked\"";} ?> name="admin_priv" ➥
type="radio" value="n" />
```

I have enclosed the original test (as adapted in step 6) in an extra pair of parentheses to ensure that it's treated as a single unit. Then I added a second test:

```
|| !$_POST
```

This tests whether the $_POST array is empty. The result is this (in pseudocode):

```
if ((the form has been sent AND admin_priv is "n")
OR the form has not been sent) {mark the button "checked"}
```

9. Just one thing remains to be tidied up. If your PHP configuration has magic quotes turned on (and many hosting companies seem to use this setting), your sticky text fields will end up with backslashes escaping apostrophes in users' names. So, scroll

down to the section of code that displays the error messages, and insert a new line just before the closing curly brace. Open the Snippets panel, and insert the POST stripslashes snippet that you installed in the PHP-DWCS4 folder in Chapter 11. The amended code at the top of the body of the page should now look like this:

```php
<?php
if (isset($error) && $error) {
  echo '<ul>';
  foreach ($error as $alert) {
    echo "<li class='warning'>$alert</li>\n";
  }
  echo '</ul>';
  // remove escape characters from POST array
  if (PHP_VERSION < 6 && get_magic_quotes_gpc()) {
    function stripslashes_deep($value) {
      $value = is_array($value) ? array_map('stripslashes_deep', ➡
        $value) : stripslashes($value);
      return $value;
    }
    $_POST = array_map('stripslashes_deep', $_POST);
  }
}
?>
```

10. Save `register_user.php`. You now have a user registration form that performs all the necessary checks before entering a new record into your database, but all the input fields will still be populated if an error is detected.

Check your code, if necessary, against `register_user_06.php` in examples/ch15.

Building server-side validation into a simple user registration form has taken a lot of effort. You could have used the version from the previous chapter right away, but before long, you would have ended up with a lot of unusable data in your database, not to mention the frustration of users when an input error results in all their data being wiped from the screen. The more time you spend refining the forms that interact with your database, the more time you will save in the long run.

Applying server-side validation to the update form

The validation tests required by the update form are the same as those for the insert form, so there's considerably less new script involved. However, you need to take the following points into consideration:

- The password has been encrypted, so it can no longer be displayed in the update form. The code needs to be amended so that the password is updated only if a value is inserted into the form. If the password fields are left empty, the original password is retained.

- When the update form first loads, it populates the form fields with values from the database, but you need to preserve any changes if the server-side validation detects errors when the form is submitted. This means adapting the Sticky Text Field server behavior to work with an update form.

Right, let's get to work.

Merging the validation and update code

Much of the work involved in adapting the code created by the Record Update Form Wizard can be done by copying and pasting the server-side validation code from the insert form.

Adapting update_user.php

These instructions show how to apply the same validation tests to update_user.php. You can use your own version from the previous chapter. Alternatively, copy update_user_start.php from examples/ch15 to workfiles/ch15, and rename it update_user.php. Continue working with the amended version of register_user.php from the preceding section. However, if you want to start with a clean copy, use register_user_06.php in examples/ch15.

1. Open both register_user.php and update_user.php in Code view.

2. In update_user.php, locate the conditional statement that controls the update server behavior, and insert a couple of blank lines, as shown in the following screenshot. This is where you will paste the validation script from register_user.php.

Paste validation script here

```
39  if ((isset($_POST["MM_update"])) && ($_POST["MM_update"] == "form1")) {
40
41
42    $updateSQL = sprintf("UPDATE users SET first_name=%s, family_name=%s, username=%s, pwd=%s, admin_priv=%s
      WHERE user_id=%s",
43                    GetSQLValueString($_POST['first_name'], "text"),
```

3. Switch to register_user.php, and copy the validation script shown highlighted in Figure 15-10.

4. Paste the code into update_user.php in the location indicated in the screenshot in step 2.

```
39   if ((isset($_POST["MM_insert"])) && ($_POST["MM_insert"] == "form1")) {
40     // Initialize array for error messages
41     $error = array();
42     // Remove whitespace and check first and family names
43     $_POST['first_name'] = trim($_POST['first_name']);
44     $_POST['family_name'] = trim($_POST['family_name']);
45     if (empty($_POST['first_name']) || empty($_POST['family_name'])) {
46       $error['name'] = 'Please enter both first name and family name';
47     }
48     // Check the username for length
49     $_POST['username'] = trim($_POST['username']);
50     if (strlen($_POST['username']) < 6) {
51       $error['length'] = 'Please select a username that contains at least 6 characters';
52     }
53     // set a flag that assumes the password is OK
54     $pwdOK = true;
55     // trim leading and trailing white space
56     $_POST['pwd'] = trim($_POST['pwd']);
57     // if less than 6 characters, create alert and set flag to false
58     if (strlen($_POST['pwd']) < 6) {
59       $error['pwd_length'] = 'Your password must be at least 6 characters';
60       $pwdOK = false;
61     }
62     // if no match, create alert and set flag to false
63     if ($_POST['pwd'] != trim($_POST['conf_pwd'])) {
64       $error['pwd'] = "Your passwords don't match";
65       $pwdOK = false;
66     }
67     // if password OK, encrypt it
68     if ($pwdOK) {
69       $_POST['pwd'] = sha1($_POST['pwd']);
70     }
71
72     // if no errors, insert the details into the database
73     if (!$error) {
```

Figure 15-10. Most of the validation script can be copied and pasted into the update page.

5. There's just one change you need to make to the validation script you have pasted into update_user.php. When a user's record is being updated, you want either to preserve the same password or to set a new one. The simplest way to handle this is to decide that if pwd is left blank, the existing password will be maintained. Otherwise, the password needs to be checked and encrypted as before.

Amend the password validation code as follows (new code shown in bold):

```
$_POST['pwd'] = trim($_POST['pwd']);
// if password field is empty, use existing password
if (empty($_POST['pwd'])) {
  $_POST['pwd'] = $row_getUser['pwd'];
} else {
  // otherwise, conduct normal checks
  // if less than 6 characters, create alert and set flag to false
  if (strlen($_POST['pwd']) < 6) {
    $error['pwd_length'] = 'Your password must be at least 6➥
characters';
    $pwdOK = false;
  }
```

15

663

```
// if no match, create alert and set flag to false
if ($_POST['pwd'] != trim($_POST['conf_pwd'])) {
    $error['pwd'] = 'Your passwords don\'t match';
    $pwdOK = false;
}
// if new password OK, encrypt it
if ($pwdOK) {
    $_POST['pwd'] = sha1($_POST['pwd']);
}
}
```

This checks whether $_POST['pwd'] is empty. If it is, the value of the existing password is taken from the getUser recordset and assigned to $_POST['pwd']. Because the existing password is already encrypted, there is no need to pass it to sha1(). If $_POST['pwd'] isn't empty, the else clause executes the checks inherited from register_user.php.

6. You now need to prevent the update query from being executed if there are any errors. This involves wrapping the section of code immediately below the validation script in a conditional statement in the same way as in register_user.php. Figure 15-11 shows where to insert the code.

Insert conditional statement here

```
72    // if password OK, encrypt it
73    if ($pwdOK) {
74        $_POST['pwd'] = sha1($_POST['pwd']);
75    }
76    }
77
78    // update the record if there are no errors
79    if (!$error) {
80        $updateSQL = sprintf("UPDATE users SET first_name=%s, family_name=%s, username=%s, pwd=%s, admin_priv=%s
      WHERE user_id=%s",
81                            GetSQLValueString($_POST['first_name'], "text"),
82                            GetSQLValueString($_POST['family_name'], "text"),
83                            GetSQLValueString($_POST['username'], "text"),
84                            GetSQLValueString($_POST['pwd'], "text"),
85                            GetSQLValueString($_POST['admin_priv'], "text"),
86                            GetSQLValueString($_POST['user_id'], "int"));
87
88        mysql_select_db($database_connAdmin, $connAdmin);
89        $Result1 = mysql_query($updateSQL, $connAdmin) or die(mysql_error());
90
91        $updateGoTo = "list_users.php";
92        if (isset($_SERVER['QUERY_STRING'])) {
93            $updateGoTo .= (strpos($updateGoTo, '?')) ? "&" : "?";
94            $updateGoTo .= $_SERVER['QUERY_STRING'];
95        }
96        header(sprintf("Location: %s", $updateGoTo));
97    }
98    }
99
100   $colname_getUser = "-1";
```

Figure 15-11. The conditional statement prevents the update code from being run if there are validation errors.

7. You also need to make the same changes as before to the code that runs the update query to catch any database errors and prevent the page from being redirected if any are found. Remove or die(mysql_error()) shown on line 89 of Figure 15-11, and amend the code on lines 89–96 like this:

```
$Result1 = mysql_query($updateSQL, $connAdmin);
if (!$Result1 && mysql_errno() == 1062) {
  $error['username'] = $_POST['username'] . ' is already in use. ➥
    Please choose a different username.';
} elseif (mysql_error()) {
  $error['dbError'] = 'Sorry, there was a problem with the ➥
    database. Please try later.';
} else {
  $updateGoTo = "list_users.php";
  if (isset($_SERVER['QUERY_STRING'])) {
    $updateGoTo .= (strpos($updateGoTo, '?')) ? "&" : "?";
    $updateGoTo .= $_SERVER['QUERY_STRING'];
  }
  header(sprintf("Location: %s", $updateGoTo));
}
}
```

You can copy and paste the first two conditions from register_user.php, because they are identical. Don't forget to add the closing curly brace after the code that redirects to the next page.

8. That deals with the changes to the validation script in Code view, but the update form doesn't have the password confirmation field. You also need to add some text to inform the user to leave the password fields blank if the same password is to be kept.

   So, switch to Design view, and add (leave blank if unchanged) to the Password label.

9. The original update form showed the password in plain text, so select the pwd field, and change the Type radio button from Single line to Password in the Property inspector.

10. Create a new table row between Password and Administrator. Type Confirm password as the label in the left cell, and insert a text field in the right cell. Name the text field conf_pwd, and set Type to Password in the Property inspector.

11. The change you made to the password validation in step 6 compares $_POST['pwd'] with $row_getUser['pwd']. However, as I explained at the beginning of the chapter, Dreamweaver always inserts the code for recordsets immediately above the DOCTYPE declaration. Consequently, $row_getUser['pwd'] won't have been created unless you move the recordset script to an earlier position.

15

Cut the recordset code shown on lines 105–113 of the following screenshot, and paste it in the position indicated (I used Code Collapse to hide most of the validation script).

```
34  $editFormAction = $_SERVER['PHP_SELF'];
35  if (isset($_SERVER['QUERY_STRING'])) {
36    $editFormAction .= "?" . htmlentities($_SERVER['QUERY_STRING']);
37  }
38
39  if ((isset($_POST["MM_update"])) && ($_POST["MM_update"] == "form1")) {
40    // Initialize array for error messages
41    $error = array();
42    // Remo...
100       header(sprintf("Location: %s", $updateGoTo));
101     }
102   }
103  }
104
105  $colname_getUser = "-1";
106  if (isset($_GET['user_id'])) {
107    $colname_getUser = $_GET['user_id'];
108  }
109  mysql_select_db($database_connAdmin, $connAdmin);
110  $query_getUser = sprintf("SELECT user_id, username, pwd, first_name, family_name, admin_priv FROM users WHERE
     user_id = %s", GetSQLValueString($colname_getUser, "int"));
111  $getUser = mysql_query($query_getUser, $connAdmin) or die(mysql_error());
112  $row_getUser = mysql_fetch_assoc($getUser);
113  $totalRows_getUser = mysql_num_rows($getUser);
114  ?>
115  <!DOCTYPE html PUBLIC "-//W3C//DTD XHTML 1.0 Transitional//EN"
```

12. Save the page, and leave it open for the next section. There have been a lot of important changes, so check your code against update_user_01.php in examples/ch15.

The final set of changes you need to make to the update page involves removing the existing code that binds the values from the database to the input fields and replacing it with code that not only displays the values retrieved from the database but also preserves the user's input if there are any errors when the update form is submitted. The Sticky Text Field server behavior won't work in these circumstances, but it's easy to adapt.

Adapting the Sticky Text Field server behavior

As you have already seen, it's only when the form has been submitted—and errors detected—that the Sticky Text Field code executes. So if the $_POST variables haven't been set, you know the form hasn't been submitted and that you need to display the values stored in the database instead.

Dreamweaver always uses the following naming convention to refer to the results of a recordset: $row_*RecordsetName*['*FieldName*']. So, all that's needed is to add an else clause to the existing code:

```php
<?php if (isset($_POST['field'])) {
  echo htmlentities($_POST['field'], ENT_COMPAT, 'UTF-8');
} else {
  echo htmlentities($row_RecordsetName['FieldName'], ENT_COMPAT, ➥
    'UTF-8');
} ?>
```

Most of the settings are identical to the Sticky Text Field server behavior that you built earlier, so you can use the existing server behavior to create the new one.

1. Make sure you have a PHP page open, and click the plus button in the Server Behaviors panel. Select New Server Behavior.

2. Name the new server behavior Sticky Edit Field, and place a check mark in the box labeled Copy existing server behavior. This will populate a drop-down menu with the names of server behaviors you have already built (unfortunately, the dialog box won't let you base a new server behavior on one of Dreamweaver's). Select Sticky Text Field, and click OK.

3. Edit the contents of the Code block area like this:

```php
<?php if (isset($_POST['@@FieldName@@'])) {
  echo htmlentities($_POST['@@FieldName@@'], ENT_COMPAT, 'UTF-8');
} else {
  echo htmlentities($row_@@RecordsetName@@['@@FieldName@@'], ➡
    ENT_COMPAT, 'UTF-8');
} ?>
```

Dreamweaver will use the new parameter—@@RecordsetName@@—in combination with @@FieldName@@ to build a variable like $row_getUser['family_name'].

> Sometimes Dreamweaver prevents you from using the same parameter name in more than one server behavior. If that happens, change both instances of @@FieldName@@ to @@Field@@.

4. Click Next. Dreamweaver warns you that the server behavior's HTML file already exists and asks whether you want to overwrite it. The HTML file is actually a copy, so there's no problem overwriting it. It controls the server behavior's dialog box, which needs to be redesigned, so the answer is Yes.

5. In the Generate Behavior Dialog Box dialog box, reset Display as for RecordsetName by clicking to the right of the existing value and selecting Recordset Menu. Set FieldName to Recordset Field Menu, and reorder the items as shown here. Click OK.

To create a similar server behavior for text areas, name it Sticky Edit Area, and select Sticky Text Area in step 2. The code block in step 3 is identical for both Sticky Edit Area and Sticky Text Area.

15

Binding the field values to the update form

Now that you have the Sticky Edit Field server behavior, you can bind the results of the getUser recordset to the form fields so that the existing values are ready for editing but will be replaced by the user's input if the update process fails for any reason. The text fields are quite easy, but the radio button group needs special handling.

Completing the update form

These instructions show how to apply the Sticky Edit Field server behavior and adapt the code in the radio button group. Continue working with update_user.php from before.

1. Before you can apply the Sticky Edit Field server behavior, you need to remove the existing code from the form fields. In the Server Behaviors panel, Shift-click to select the Dynamic Text Field entries for first_name, family_name, username, and pwd. Then click the minus button, as shown in the screenshot alongside, to remove them cleanly from the update form.

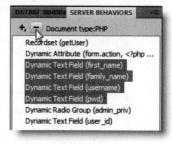

2. In Design view, select the first_name field, click the plus button in the Server Behaviors panel, and select Sticky Edit Field.

Since getUser is the only recordset on this page, it's selected automatically in the Sticky Edit Field dialog box, but make sure you choose the right one if you use this server behavior on a page that has two or more recordsets. Select the field's name from the FieldName drop-down menu, as shown here:

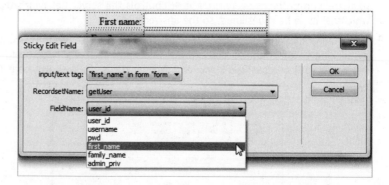

3. Apply the Sticky Edit Field server behavior in the same way to the family_name and username fields. In Design view, the form should end up looking like the following screenshot, with dynamic text placeholders in the first three fields.

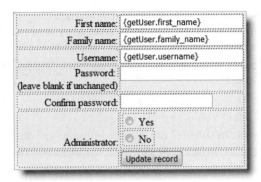

The dynamic text placeholders in the three fields look the same as before in Design view, but if you inspect the underlying code in Split view, you'll see that Dreamweaver has inserted the code you used to build the Sticky Edit Field server behavior.

4. The radio buttons present an interesting challenge. When the page first loads, you want the value stored in the database for admin_priv to be selected; but if the form is submitted with errors and the value of admin_priv has been changed, you want the new value to be shown.

Select one of the radio buttons in Design view to help locate the code for the radio group; then switch to Code view to actually see it. The code looks like this:

```
160        <td><input type="radio" name="admin_priv" value="y" <?php if (!(strcmp(htmlentities($row_getUser[
'admin_priv'], ENT_COMPAT, 'utf-8'),"y"))) {echo "checked=\"checked\"";} ?> />
161          Yes</td>
162        </tr>
163        <tr>
164        <td><input type="radio" name="admin_priv" value="n" <?php if (!(strcmp(htmlentities($row_getUser[
'admin_priv'], ENT_COMPAT, 'utf-8'),"n"))) {echo "checked=\"checked\"";} ?> />
165          No</td>
```

Let's first map out in terms of pseudocode what needs to happen inside the Yes radio button's <input> tag. The logic goes like this:

```
if (the form has NOT been submitted
    AND the value of admin_priv in the database is "y") {
        mark the button "checked"
} elseif (the form has been submitted
            AND the form value of admin_priv is "y") {
        mark the button "checked"
}
```

You can create this code by copying and pasting the existing conditional statements and making a few changes. It's not difficult, but you need to follow the next steps carefully.

5. When the page first loads, the form hasn't been submitted, so the $_POST array will have zero elements (and therefore equate to false). This means the first check can be performed by inserting !$_POST into the conditional statement like this:

```
if (!$_POST && !(strcmp(htmlentities($row_getUser['admin_priv'], ➥
ENT_COMPAT, 'utf-8'),"y"))) {echo "checked=\"checked\"";}
```

15

6. You now need to deal with the alternative scenario. Begin by copying the amended conditional statement and pasting it immediately after the closing curly brace. So, now you have two identical conditional statements.

7. You want the second statement to run only if the first one fails, so change the second if to elseif.

8. In the alternative scenario, you want $_POST to be true, so remove the negative operator from in front of $_POST.

9. You also want the value of admin_priv to come from the form input, rather than the database, so change $row_getUser['admin_priv'] to $_POST['admin_priv'].

10. Repeat steps 5–9 for the No button. The completed radio button code looks like this:

```
    <td><input type="radio" name="admin_priv" value="y"
    <?php if (!$_POST && !(strcmp(htmlentities($row_getUser['admin_priv'], ➥
    ENT_COMPAT, 'utf-8'),"y"))) {echo "checked=\"checked\"";}
    elseif ($_POST && !(strcmp(htmlentities($_POST['admin_priv'], ➥
    ENT_COMPAT, 'utf-8'),"y"))) {echo "checked=\"checked\"";} ?> />
    Yes</td>
    </tr>
    <tr>
      <td><input type="radio" name="admin_priv" value="n"
    <?php if (!$_POST && !(strcmp(htmlentities($row_getUser['admin_priv'], ➥
    ENT_COMPAT, 'utf-8'),"n"))) {echo "checked=\"checked\"";}
    elseif ($_POST && !(strcmp(htmlentities($_POST['admin_priv'], ➥
    ENT_COMPAT, 'utf-8'),"n"))) {echo "checked=\"checked\"";} ?> />
    No</td>
```

11. One more thing, and you're done. Copy the code that displays the error messages from register_user.php (shown on lines 107–123 of the following screenshot), and paste it just above the update form in update_user.php.

```
106  <h1>Register User</h1>
107  <?php
108  if (isset($error)) {
109    echo '<ul>';
110    foreach ($error as $alert) {
111      echo "<li class='warning'>$alert</li>\n";
112    }
113    echo '</ul>';
114    // remove escape characters from POST array
115    if (PHP_VERSION < 6 && get_magic_quotes_gpc()) {
116      function stripslashes_deep($value) {
117        $value = is_array($value) ? array_map('stripslashes_deep', $value) : stripslashes($value);
118        return $value;
119      }
120      $_POST = array_map('stripslashes_deep', $_POST);
121    }
122  }
123  ?>
124  <form action="<?php echo $editFormAction; ?>" method="post" name="form1" id="form1">
```

12. Save update_user.php. Compare your code with update_user_02.php in examples/ch15 if you have any problems.

You can now update existing records by loading `list_users.php` into a browser and clicking the EDIT link alongside the username of the account you want to change. Adapting the update form has also required considerable effort. It's a pity that Dreamweaver doesn't offer more help in the way of server-side validation, but if you value your data, you need to customize the code that Dreamweaver creates for you.

You might want to take a break at this stage, but now that you have a simple user registration system, you can use it to password protect various parts of your website. You'll be relieved to know that Dreamweaver's user authentication server behaviors don't need anywhere near the same level of customization. They rely on the use of PHP sessions, so before showing you how to build a login system, let's take a quick look at sessions and what they're for.

What sessions are and how they work

The Web is a brilliant illusion. When you visit a well-designed website, you get a great feeling of continuity, as though flipping through the pages of a book or a magazine. Everything fits together as a coherent entity. The reality is quite different. Each part of an individual page is stored and handled separately by the web server. Apart from needing to know where to send the relevant files, the server has no interest in who you are, nor is it interested in the PHP script it has just executed. PHP **garbage collection** (yes, that's what it's actually called) destroys variables and other resources used by a script as soon as they're no longer required. But it's not like garbage collection at your home, where it's taken away, say, once a week. With PHP, it's instant: the server memory is freed up for the next task. Even variables in the $_POST and $_GET arrays persist only while being passed from one page to the next. Unless the information is stored in some other way, such as a hidden form field, it's lost.

To get around these problems, PHP (in common with other server-side languages) uses **sessions**. A session ensures continuity by storing a random identifier on the web server and on the visitor's computer (as a cookie). Because the identifier is unique to each visitor, all the information stored in session variables is directly related to that visitor and cannot be seen by anyone else.

> *The security offered by sessions is adequate for most user authentication, but it is not 100-percent foolproof. For credit card and other financial transactions, you should use an SSL connection verified by a digital certificate. To learn more about this and other aspects of building security into your PHP sites,* Pro PHP Security *by Chris Snyder and Michael Southwell (Apress, ISBN: 978-1-59059-508-4) is essential reading. Although aimed at readers with an intermediate to advanced knowledge of PHP, it contains a lot of practical advice of value to all skill levels.*

15

Creating PHP sessions

Creating a session is easy. Just put this command in every PHP page that you want to use in a session:

```
session_start();
```

Once you call that command, the page has access to the visitor's session variables. This command should be called only once in each page, and it must be called before the PHP script generates any output, so the ideal position is immediately after the opening PHP tag. If any output is generated before the call to session_start(), the command fails, and the session won't be activated for that page. Even a single blank space, newline character, or byte-order mark is considered output. This is the same issue that affects the header() function, if any output is generated before you call the function. The solution is the same and was described in "Avoiding the 'Headers already sent' error" in Chapter 12.

Creating and destroying session variables

You create a session variable by adding it to the $_SESSION superglobal array in the same way you would assign an ordinary variable. Say you want to store a visitor's name and display a greeting. If the name is submitted in a login form as $_POST['name'], you assign it like this:

```
$_SESSION['name'] = $_POST['name'];
```

$_SESSION['name'] can now be used in any page that begins with session_start(). Because session variables are stored on the server, you should get rid of them as soon as they are no longer required by your script or application. Unset a session variable like this:

```
unset($_SESSION['name']);
```

To unset *all* session variables—for instance, when you're logging someone out—set the $_SESSION superglobal array to an empty array, like this:

```
$_SESSION = array();
```

> *Do not be tempted to try* unset($_SESSION). *It not only clears the current session but also prevents any further sessions from being stored.*

Destroying a session

By itself, unsetting all the session variables effectively prevents any of the information from being reused, but you should also destroy the session with the following command:

```
session_destroy();
```

By destroying a session like this, there is no risk of an unauthorized person gaining access either to a restricted part of the site or to any information exchanged during the session. However, a visitor may forget to log out, so it's not always possible to guarantee that the session_destroy() command will be triggered, which is why it's so important not to store sensitive information in a session variable.

> *You may find the deprecated functions* session_register() *and* session_unregister() *in old scripts. Use* $_SESSION['*variable_name*'] *and* unset($_SESSION['*variable_name*']) *instead.*

Checking that sessions are enabled

Sessions should be enabled by default in PHP. A quick way to check is to load session1.php in examples/ch15 into a browser. Type your name in the text field, and click the Submit button. When session2.php loads, you should see your name and a link to the next page. Click the link. If session3.php displays your name and a confirmation that sessions are working, your setup is fine. Click the link to page 2 to destroy the session.

If you don't see the confirmation on the third page, create a PHP page containing the single line of code <?php phpinfo(); ?> to display details of your PHP configuration. Make sure that session.save_path points to a valid folder that the web server can write to. Also make sure that a software firewall or other security system is not blocking access to the folder specified in session.save_path.

Registering and authenticating users

As you have just seen, session variables enable you to keep track of a visitor. If you can identify visitors, you can also determine whether they have the right to view certain pages. Dreamweaver has four user authentication server behaviors, as follows:

- **Log In User:** This queries a database to check whether a user is registered and has provided the correct password. You can also check whether a user belongs to a particular group to distinguish between, say, administrators and ordinary users.
- **Restrict Access to Page:** This prevents visitors from viewing a page unless they have logged in and (optionally) have the correct group privileges. Anyone not logged in is sent to the login page but can be automatically redirected to the originally selected page after login.
- **Log Out User:** This brings the current session to an end and prevents the user from returning to any restricted page without first logging back in again.
- **Check New Username:** This checks whether a particular username is already in use. I don't recommend using it, because it's rather badly designed. Using a unique index and testing for MySQL error 1062, as described earlier in this chapter, is more user-friendly.

15

Creating a login system

Now that you have a way of registering users, you need to create a way for them to log in to restricted areas of your site. Building the login system is a lot simpler than building the registration system.

> *The login system uses encrypted passwords. You must encrypt the passwords of records that were created with the forms from the previous chapter before server-side validation was added. Do this by clicking the EDIT link in* list_users.php *and reentering the password in the update form.*

Creating the login page

The first element of a login system is the form where registered users enter their username and password. To keep things simple, the following instructions use a dedicated login page, but you can embed the login form on any public page of a site.

1. Create a PHP page called login.php in workfiles/ch15. Lay out the page with a form, two text fields, and a submit button, as shown here. Since you'll be applying a server behavior, there is no need to set the action or method attributes of the form.

Text field: username →
Password-type text field: pwd →
Submit button: doLogin →

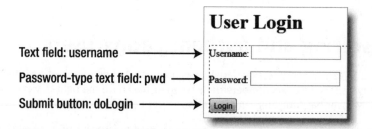

2. The Log In User server behavior expects you to designate two pages: one that the user will be taken to if the login is successful and another if it fails. Create one page called success.php, and enter some content to indicate that the login was successful. Call the other page loginfail.php, and insert a message telling the user that the login failed, together with a link back to login.php.

3. Make sure login.php is the active page in the Dreamweaver workspace. Click the plus button in the Server Behaviors panel, and select User Authentication ➤ Log In User. (You can also apply the server behavior from the Data tab of the Insert bar or from the Data Objects submenu of the Insert menu.)

4. The Log In User dialog box has a lot of options, but their meaning should be obvious, at least for the first two sections. Select the connAdmin connection, the users table, and the username and password columns, using the settings shown alongside.

The third section asks you to specify which pages to send the user to, depending on whether the login succeeds or fails. Between the text fields for the filenames is a check box labeled Go to previous URL (if it exists). This works in conjunction with the Restrict Access to Page server behavior that you will use shortly. If someone tries to access a restricted page without first logging in, the user is redirected to the login page. If you select this option, after a successful login, the user will be taken directly to the page that originally refused access. Unless you always want users to view a specific page when first logging in, this is quite a user-friendly option.

The final section of the dialog box allows you to specify whether access should be restricted on the basis of username and password (the default) or whether you also want to specify an access level. The access level must be stored in one of your database columns. For this login page, set Get level from to admin_priv. Click OK to apply the server behavior.

5. A drawback with the Dreamweaver Log In User server behavior is that it has no option for handling encrypted passwords, so you need to make a minor adjustment by hand. Open Code view, and place your cursor immediately to the right of the opening PHP tag on line 2. Press Enter/Return to insert a new line, and type the following code:

```
if (isset($_POST['pwd'])) { $_POST['pwd'] = sha1($_POST['pwd']); }
```

This checks whether the form has been submitted, and it uses sha1() to encrypt the password. I have reassigned the value back to $_POST['pwd'] so that Dreamweaver continues to recognize the server behavior; this way, you can still edit it through the Server Behaviors panel. Although Dreamweaver doesn't object to you placing the line of code here, it will automatically remove it if you ever decide to remove the server behavior.

> It's important to realize that you're not decrypting the version of the password stored in the database. You can't—the sha1() function performs one-way encryption. You verify the user's password by encrypting it again and comparing the two encrypted versions.

6. Save login.php. You can check your code against login.php in examples/ch15.

15

Restricting access to individual pages

Now that you have a means of logging in registered users, you can protect sensitive pages in your site. When working with PHP sessions, there is no way of protecting an entire folder. Sessions work on a page-by-page basis, so you need to protect each page individually.

1. Open success.php. Click the plus button in the Server Behaviors panel, and select User Authentication ➤ Restrict Access to Page.

2. In the Restrict Access to Page dialog box, select the radio button to restrict access based on Username, password, and access level. Then click the Define button.

3. The Define Access Levels dialog box lets you specify acceptable values. What may come as a bit of a surprise is that it's not the column name that Dreamweaver is interested in but the value retrieved from the column. Consequently, it's not admin_priv that you enter here but y or n.

   As you might have noticed, although Dreamweaver gives you the option to specify different access levels, the Log In User server behavior sends all successful logins to the same page. If you have different login pages for each type of user, this is fine; you select the appropriate value. So, for an administrator's login page, just enter y in the Name field, and click the plus button to register it in the Access levels area.

   However, if you want to use the same login form for everyone, you need to register all access levels for the first page and then use PHP conditional logic to distinguish between different types of users. So, for success.php, also enter n in the Name field, and click the plus button to register it. Then click OK.

4. After defining the access levels, hold down the Shift key, and select them all in the Select level(s) field. Then, either browse to login.php, or type the filename directly in the field labeled If access denied, go to. The dialog box should look like this:

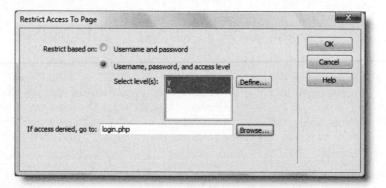

5. Click OK to apply the server behavior, and save success.php.

6. Try to view the page in a browser. Instead of success.php, you should see login.php. You have been denied access and taken to the login page instead.

7. Enter a username and password that you registered earlier, and click Log in. You should be taken to success.php. You can check your code against success_01.php in examples/ch15.

When developing pages that will be part of a restricted area, I find it best to leave the application of this server behavior to the very last. Testing pages becomes an exercise in frustration if you need to be constantly logging in and out.

I'll come back to the question of how to deal with different access levels, but first, let's look at logging out.

Logging out users

The Dreamweaver Log Out User server behavior is quick and easy to apply. It automatically inserts a logout link in your page, so you need to position your cursor at the point you want the link to be created.

1. Press Enter/Return to create a new paragraph in success.php.
2. Click the plus button in the Server Behaviors panel, and select User Authentication ➤ Log Out User.
3. The Log Out User dialog box gives you the option to log out when a link is clicked or when the page loads. In this case, you want the default option, which is to log out when a link is clicked and to create a new logout link. Browse to login.php, or type the filename directly into the field labeled When done, go to. Click OK.
4. Save success.php, and load the page into a browser. Click the Log out link, and you will be taken back to the login page. Type the URL of success.php in the browser address bar, and you will be taken back to the login page until you log in again. You can check your code against success_02.php in examples/ch15.

Displaying different content depending on access levels

As I mentioned earlier, PHP sessions are the technology that lies behind the user authentication server behaviors. The Log In User server behavior creates the following two session variables that control access to restricted pages:

- $_SESSION['MM_Username']: This stores the user's username.
- $_SESSION['MM_UserGroup']: This stores the user's access level.

You can use these in a variety of ways. The simplest, and perhaps most important, use is to present different content on the first page after logging in. The following exercises are based on success.php but can be used with any page that begins with session_start() after a user has logged in.

> The following instructions assume you have created at least one administrator and an ordinary user in the users table.

1. In success.php, insert two paragraphs: one indicating that it's for administrators, the other indicating that it's for non-administrators. The actual content is unimportant.

15

2. Switch to Code view, and add the PHP code highlighted in bold around the two paragraphs like this:

```php
<?php if ($_SESSION['MM_UserGroup'] == 'y') { ?>
<p>Content and links for administators</p>
<?php } else { ?>
<p>Content and links for non-administrators</p>
<?php } ?>
```

This is simple PHP conditional logic. If the value of $_SESSION['MM_UserGroup'] is y, display the HTML inside the first set of curly braces. If it's not, show the other material. There's only one paragraph in each conditional block, but you can put as much as you want.

3. Save the page, and log in as an administrator. You'll see only the first paragraph. Log out and log back in as an ordinary user. This time you'll see the second paragraph. You can compare your code with success_03.php in examples/ch15.

Any content that you want to be seen by both groups should go outside this PHP conditional statement. (In success_03.php, you'll see that the page heading and the log out link are common to both groups.) By using this sort of branching logic in the first page, you can restrict access to subsequent pages according to the specific access level. So, the links in the first section would point to pages that only administrators are permitted to see.

Greeting users by name

Since the user's username is stored in $_SESSION['MM_Username'], you could use that to display a greeting, but it's much friendlier to use the person's real name. All that's needed is a simple recordset.

1. In success.php, create a recordset using the following settings in Simple mode:

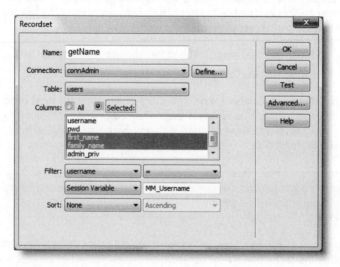

By setting Filter to username = Session Variable MM_Username, the recordset retrieves the values of the first_name and family_name columns for the currently logged in user.

2. Open the Bindings panel, and drag the first_name and family_name dynamic text placeholders into the page like this:

Welcome!

Hello, {getName.first_name} {getName.family_name} . You logged in successfully.

When the page loads, the dynamic text placeholders will be replaced by the values drawn from the recordset. You can check your code against success_04.php.

Of course, if you want other details about the user, such as user_id, amend the settings in the Recordset dialog box to retrieve all the columns you need.

Creating your own $_SESSION variables from user details

To avoid the need to create a recordset on every page, store these details as $_SESSION variables. The code needs to be inserted *after* the recordset code, which Dreamweaver places immediately above the DOCTYPE declaration. The pattern Dreamweaver uses for recordset results looks like this:

```
$row_recordsetName['fieldName']
```

So, to create $_SESSION variables from first_name and family_name in session.php, you would add the following code immediately before the closing PHP tag above the DOCTYPE declaration:

```
$_SESSION['first_name'] = $row_getName['first_name'];
$_SESSION['family_name'] = $row_getName['family_name'];
```

You're not restricted to using the same element names for the variables. You could do this instead:

```
$_SESSION['full_name'] = $row_getName['first_name'].' '. ➡
$row_getName['family_name'];
```

You can see this code in action in success_05.php in examples/ch15.

Redirecting to a personal page after login

You might want to provide users with their own personal page or folder after logging in. This is very easy to do, particularly if you base the name of the personal name or folder on the username. Before the Log In User server behavior creates the session variables, it stores the submitted username as $loginUsername, so you can use this variable to redirect users to pages or folders based on their username.

15

If the name of the personal page is in the form *username*.php, enter the following in the Log In User dialog box in the field labeled If login succeeds, go to (see step 4 of "Creating the login page"):

```
$loginUsername.php
```

If the personal page is in a folder named after the username, use the following:

```
$loginUsername/index.php
```

This assumes that the folder is a subfolder of the folder where the login page is located. If the username is dpowers, these values would redirect the user to dpowers.php and dpowers/index.php, respectively.

Encrypting and decrypting passwords

These are common questions: What happens when a user forgets his or her password? How can I send a reminder? If you encrypt passwords using sha1(), as described in this chapter, you can't. The sha1() algorithm is one-way; you can't decrypt it. Although this sounds like a disadvantage, it actually ensures a considerable level of security. Since the password cannot be decrypted, even a corrupt system administrator has no way of discovering another person's password. The downside is that you can't send out password reminders.

If a password is forgotten, you need to verify the user's identity and issue a new password. You can also create a form for users to change their own passwords after logging in. It's simply a question of using $_SESSION['MM_Username'] as the filter for the Update Record server behavior. Don't worry if you feel that's currently beyond your capability. In the next chapter, you'll learn about the four basic SQL commands that are the key to database management.

However, it is possible to store passwords using two-way encryption. For more information, see my book *PHP Solutions: Dynamic Web Design Made Easy* (friends of ED, ISBN: 978-1-59059-731-6) and the MySQL documentation at http://dev.mysql.com/doc/refman/5.0/en/encryption-functions.html.

Chapter review

If you're beginning to wobble because of the constant need to dive into Code view, take heart. This has been a tough chapter. The danger with Dreamweaver server behaviors is they make it very easy to create record insertion and update forms, giving you a false sense of achievement. If you're just creating a dynamic website as a hobby, you might be happy with minimum checks on what's inserted into your database. But even if it's a hobby, do you really want to waste your time on a database that gets filled with unusable data? And if you're doing it professionally, you simply can't afford to.

PHP is like the electricity or kitchen knives in your home: handled properly, it's very safe; handled irresponsibly, it can do a lot of damage. Get to know what the code you're putting into your pages is doing. The more hands-on experience you get, the easier it becomes. A lot of PHP coding is simple logic: if this, do one thing; else do something different.

Take a well-earned rest. In the next chapter, we'll delve into the mysteries of SQL, the language used to communicate with most databases, and joining records from two or more tables.

15

Table options

Rename table to	authors
Table comments	
Storage Engine ⑦	InnoDB
Collation	latin1_swedish_ci
AUTO_INCREMENT	1
ROW_FORMAT	COMPACT

Go

❝ Democracy is the worst form of government except all those other forms that have been tried from time to time.

Winston Churchill ❞

❝ My age is as a lusty winter, frosty, but kindly.

William Shakespeare ❞

❝ The way to ensure summer in England is to have it framed and glazed in a comfortable room.

Horace Walpole ❞

❝ Money couldn't buy friends, but you got a better class of enemy.

Spike Milligan ❞

Quotations Listed by Author

Name	Quotation		
	It is only with the heart that one can see rightly; what is essential is invisible to the eye.	EDIT	DELETE
Woody Allen	I don't want to achieve immortality through my work... I want to achieve it by not dying.	EDIT	DELETE
Woody Allen	If it turns out that there is a God, I don't think that he's evil. But the worst that you can say about him is that basically, he's an underachiever.	EDIT	DELETE

The wizards you used in Chapter 14 offer a quick way to create, insert, and update forms, but they suffer from inflexibility. You need to make all your decisions about what to include in the form at the time of launching the wizard; and if you change your mind, it's often quicker to delete everything and start again. There's also the problem of fitting the forms into the overall design of your site. For these reasons, I prefer to design my own forms and apply the Insert Record and Update Record server behaviors separately. The dialog boxes used by the independent server behaviors are very similar to the wizards, so they're easy to use. You'll see how to use them in this chapter, at the same time as learning how to work with multiple tables.

As I explained in Chapter 14, an important principle of working with a relational database is the need to break larger units, such as addresses or names, into their component elements and store them in separate columns. Another equally important principle is to get rid of columns that contain repetitive data and move them to a separate table. The advantages of doing this are that it eliminates inconsistency and improves efficiency. Let's say you're creating a product catalog and store everything in a single table; you might spell a company name in different ways. For instance, friends of ED might sometimes be entered as foED, freinds of ED, or—heaven forbid—fiends of ED. Run a search for friends of ED, and anything spelled a different way will not turn up in the results. Consequently, vital data could be lost forever. Even if you never make a spelling mistake, storing frequently repeated information in a separate table means you change it only once instead of updating every instance in the database.

In this chapter, you'll learn about the following:

- Applying the rules of normalization to decide what to store in a table
- Linking related information in different tables
- Applying insert and update server behaviors to custom forms
- Building SQL queries with SELECT, INSERT, UPDATE, and DELETE
- Using MySQL functions and aliases
- Creating a navigation bar to page through database results

As long as each record has a primary key to identify it, records in separate tables can be linked by storing the primary key from one table as a reference in the other. This is known as creating a **foreign key**. The disadvantage of using multiple tables is that it's conceptually more difficult than a single table. Also, you need to make sure that deleting a record doesn't leave references to its primary key in dependent tables. This chapter shows you how to overcome these difficulties.

Storing related information in separate tables

The example in this chapter uses two tables to store a selection of famous—and not so famous—quotations. The same principles apply to most multiple-table databases, so once you have mastered this chapter, you'll be equipped to create a wide variety of practical applications, such as a product catalog, contacts list, or content management system.

Deciding on the best structure

Each database is different, so there is no single "right" way to design one. However, a process known as **normalization** lays down the principles of good design. The main rules can be summarized as follows:

- Give each data record a primary key as a unique means of identification (I covered this in Chapter 14).
- Put each group of associated data in a table of its own.
- Cross-reference related information by using the primary key from one table as a foreign key in other tables.
- Store only one item of information in each field.

These principles are sometimes summed up as "Stay DRY"—don't repeat yourself.

You can find more detailed advice in *Beginning MySQL Database Design and Optimization: From Novice to Professional* by Jon Stephens and Chad Russell (Apress, ISBN: 978-1-59059-332-5).

Using foreign keys to link records

Figure 16-1 shows how most beginners would construct a database table to store their favorite quotations. Everything is held in one table, resulting in the need to enter the author's first name and family name for each individual record. It's not only tedious to retype the names every time; it has resulted in inconsistency. The five quotations from Shakespeare list him in three different ways. In records 25 and 34, he's William Shakespeare; in record 33, he's W Shakespeare; and in records 31 and 32, he's just plain Shakespeare.

quote_id	quotation	first_name	family_name
25	Sweet lovers love the spring.	William	Shakespeare
26	O, Wind, If Winter comes, can Spring be far behin...	Percy Bysshe	Shelley
27	In the spring a young man's fancy lightly turns to...	Alfred, Lord	Tennyson
28	It is not spring until you can plant your foot on ...		Proverb
29	The way to ensure summer in England is to have it ...	Horace	Walpole
30	’Tis the last rose of summer Left blooming ...	Thomas	Moore
31	Shall I compare thee to a summer's day? Thou art ...		Shakespeare
32	Now is the winter of our discontent Made glorious...		Shakespeare
33	Blow, blow, thou winter wind, Thou art not so unk...	W	Shakespeare
34	My age is as a lusty winter, frosty, but kindly.	William	Shakespeare

Figure 16-1. Storing repetitive information in a single table leads to redundancy and inconsistency.

It's more logical to create a separate table for names—I've called it authors—and store each name just once. So instead of storing the name with each quotation, you can store the appropriate primary key from the authors table (on the right of Figure 16-2) as a foreign key in the quotations table (on the left).

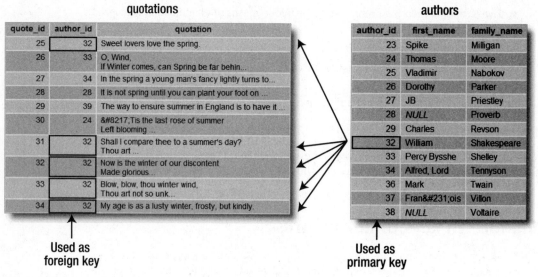

Figure 16-2. Shakespeare's primary key in the authors table (right) identifies him in the quotations table (left).

- The primary key of the authors table is author_id. Because primary keys must be unique, each number is used only once.

- The author_id for William Shakespeare is 32.

- All quotations attributed to William Shakespeare are identified in the quotations table by the same author_id (32). Because author_id is being used as a foreign key in this table, there can be multiple references to the same number.

> *As long as* author_id *remains unique in the* authors *table—where it's the primary key—you know that it always refers to the same person.*

I've drawn arrows in Figure 16-2 linking only Shakespeare with his quotations, but you can see that quote_id 26 comes from the poet Shelley (author_id 33) and that quote_id 27 comes from Tennyson (author_id 34). Before any sense of panic sets in about how you are going to remember all these numbers, relax. When you communicate with the database, you tell it to find the appropriate number for you. In other words, if you want to conduct a search for all quotations by Shakespeare, you issue a command that tells the database to do something like this (in pseudo-code):

SELECT all records in the quotation column
FROM the quotations table
WHERE the author_id in the quotations table is the same as
the author_id for "William Shakespeare" in the authors table

This type of structure creates what's known as a **one-to-many relationship**: one record in one table refers to one or more records in another. In this example, it allows you to associate one author with many quotations. However, it's not suitable for a database of books, where an author is likely to be associated with multiple books and each book might have several authors. This is known as a **many-to-many relationship** and needs to be resolved through the creation of a **lookup table** (sometimes called a **linking table**). In the case of a book database, each record in the lookup table stores a single pair of foreign keys linking an individual author with a particular book. To learn more about lookup tables, see my book *PHP Solutions: Dynamic Web Design Made Easy* (friends of ED, ISBN: 978-1-59059-731-6).

Avoiding orphaned records

The relationship between the two tables in Figure 16-2 isn't an equal one. If William Shakespeare is deleted from the authors table, author_id 32 will no longer have a value attached to it, orphaning the five Shakespeare quotations in the quotations table. However, even if you delete all five quotations from the quotations table, the authors table is unaffected. Sure, there won't be any quotations by Shakespeare (at least not in the section shown in Figure 16-2), but nothing in the authors table actually depends on the quotations table. The primary key author_id 32 continues to identify Shakespeare and can be reused if you decide to add new quotations attributed to him.

Because the foreign keys in the quotations table depend on the authors table, authors is considered to be the **parent table**, and quotations is the **child table**. Although deleting records from a child table doesn't affect the parent, the opposite is not true. Before deleting records from a parent table, you need to check whether there are any dependent records in the child table. If there are, you need to do one of the following:

- Prevent the deletion of the record(s) in the parent table.
- Delete all dependent records in the child table as well.
- Set the foreign key value of dependent records in the child table to NULL.

Making sure that the foreign key relationship between parent and child tables remains intact is known as maintaining **referential integrity**. In simple terms, it maintains the integrity of records that reference each other and means that you don't end up with incomplete records.

There are two ways to maintain referential integrity. The best way is to use **foreign key constraints**. These establish a foreign key relationship in the table definition and specify what should happen when a record in a parent table is deleted. If your hosting company supports the InnoDB storage engine in MySQL, you can use foreign key constraints to automate referential integrity.

Unfortunately, most hosting companies offer only the default MyISAM storage engine, which doesn't support foreign key constraints (support on all storage engines is now planned for MySQL 6.1, so is still some way off). However, you can reproduce the same effect with PHP. All that's required is a little conditional logic like this (in pseudo-code):

```
if (no dependent records) {
  delete;
} else {
  don't delete;
}
```

I'll show you both approaches in this chapter. First of all, let's define the authors and quotations tables.

Defining the database tables

The basic table definition is the same for MyISAM and InnoDB tables. Since I gave step-by-step instructions for defining tables in phpMyAdmin in Chapter 14, I won't go through the process in great detail again. Create two new tables in the dwcs4 database, call them authors and quotations, and give them each three columns (fields) using the settings in Table 16-1. You don't need to set any values for the Default or Collation fields.

When you create a table with only a few columns, phpMyAdmin displays the table definition matrix vertically, rather than horizontally, as shown in Figure 16-3. Both Table 16-1 and Figure 16-3 show the settings in phpMyAdmin 3. If you are using phpMyAdmin 2, refer to Figure 14-9 in Chapter 14 for the radio buttons that set a column's index and auto_increment (called A_I in phpMyAdmin 3).

Table 16-1. Settings for the authors and quotations tables

Table	Field	Type	Length/Values	Attributes	Null	Index	A_I
authors							
	author_id	INT		UNSIGNED	No	PRIMARY	Yes
	first_name	VARCHAR	30		Yes		No
	family_name	VARCHAR	30		No		No
quotations							
	quote_id	INT		UNSIGNED	No	PRIMARY	Yes
	author_id	INT		UNSIGNED	Yes	INDEX	No
	quotation	VARCHAR	255		No		No

If your remote server supports InnoDB, set Storage Engine *to* InnoDB *when defining the tables in phpMyAdmin. On older versions of phpMyAdmin,* Storage Engine *is called* Table type.

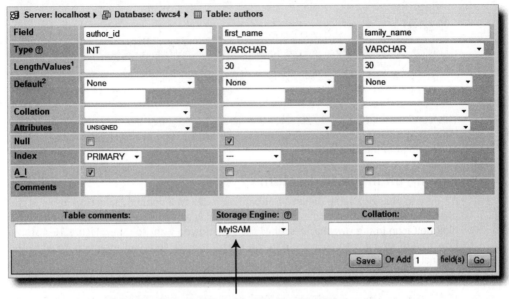

Set this to InnoDB if your remote server supports it

Figure 16-3. When a table has only a few columns, the definition matrix in phpMyAdmin is displayed vertically.

Some records in the authors table don't have a value for first_name, so I have specified null in the table definition (select the Null checkbox in phpMyAdmin 3 or null from the drop-down menu in phpMyAdmin 2). I have done this because Dreamweaver treats not null as meaning "required," so the Insert Record and Update Record server behaviors reject a blank field.

The other thing to note is the different settings for author_id in two tables. In the authors table, it is the primary key and uses auto_increment. However, in the quotations table, it's a foreign key, so it has an ordinary index and does not use auto_increment. A foreign key must *not* be automatically incremented. I have also set author_id to null in the quotations table because you might not always be able to assign author_id as a foreign key—for instance, when inserting a new quotation for someone not yet registered in the authors table.

You can use a foreign key as a primary key in some circumstances (for example, in a lookup table where two foreign keys form a joint primary key), but on this occasion it's not appropriate.

After defining the quotations table, check the Indexes section at the bottom of the screen that displays the table structure (in phpMyAdmin 3, you might need to click the Details link at the bottom left of the screen). It should look similar to this (the output looks slightly different in phpMyAdmin 2):

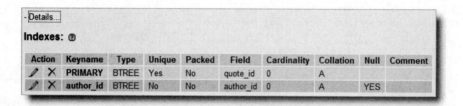

This confirms that quote_id remains the table's primary key but that author_id is also indexed. If author_id isn't listed in the Indexes section, you can alter the table structure, as described in the next section.

Adding an index to a column

It's easy to change a table definition to add an index to a column. Select the table in the phpMyAdmin navigation frame on the left to display its structure grid, and click the lightning bolt icon in the row that describes the column you want to index. Figure 16-4 shows how to add an index to author_id in the quotations table if you forgot to do so in the original table definition.

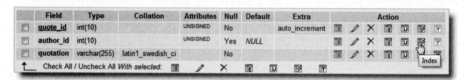

Figure 16-4. You can add an index to a column by clicking the Index icon in the table's structure grid in phpMyAdmin.

Although adding an index to a column can speed up searches, don't apply them indiscriminately. Indexing has drawbacks, the main one being that it increases the size of a table. The most important index is always the primary key. At this stage, index only foreign key columns, or use a unique index on columns that shouldn't have duplicate entries.

Defining the foreign key relationship in InnoDB

The default MyISAM storage engine in MySQL doesn't support foreign key constraints. If your remote server doesn't support InnoDB, skip ahead to "Populating the tables."

> *This section applies only if you are using InnoDB tables. If you have converted your tables to InnoDB by mistake, refer to "Converting a table's storage engine."*

The normal way to define a foreign key relationship in MySQL is in the initial table definition. However, you can alter the structure of a table at any time, and this is the approach that phpMyAdmin takes. Defining a foreign key relationship in phpMyAdmin involves the following steps:

1. Define both parent and child tables, and set Storage Engine (Table type in older versions of phpMyAdmin) to InnoDB.

2. Confirm that the foreign key column in the child table is indexed.

3. Use Relation view to add the foreign key constraint to the child table.

Steps 1 and 2 have already been covered in the preceding sections, but you might want to convert MyISAM tables to InnoDB at a later stage, so I'll briefly describe the process.

Checking the storage engine of a table

To find out whether a table uses the MyISAM or InnoDB storage engine, click the database name at the top of the main frame in phpMyAdmin or in the navigation frame on the left to display the database structure. The value for Type shows the current storage engine for each table. Figure 16-5 shows that the authors and quotations tables use InnoDB, while the users table uses MyISAM.

Table	Action	Records¹	Type	Collation	Size	Overhead
authors		0	InnoDB	latin1_swedish_ci	16.0 KiB	–
quotations		0	InnoDB	latin1_swedish_ci	32.0 KiB	–
users		1	MyISAM	latin1_swedish_ci	3.1 KiB	20 B
3 table(s)	**Sum**	**1**	**MyISAM**	**latin1_swedish_ci**	**51.1 KiB**	**20 B**

Server: localhost ▸ Database: dwcs4

Structure · SQL · Search · Query · Export · Import · Operations · Privileges · Drop

Figure 16-5. Check the storage engine used by each table by viewing the database structure in phpMyAdmin.

It's perfectly acceptable to mix different types of storage engines in MySQL. In fact, it's recommended that you use the most appropriate type for each table. MyISAM has the advantage of speed, but it currently lacks support for foreign key constraints and transactions.

> In database terminology, a **transaction** is a linked series of SQL queries, in which every query must succeed. If any part of the series fails, the whole series is abandoned, and the database remains unchanged. Transactions are an advanced subject beyond the scope of this book. For details, see http://dev.mysql.com/doc/refman/5.0/en/transactional-commands.html.

Converting a table's storage engine

You can change a table's storage engine at any time, even if it already contains data. The following instructions explain how:

1. Select the table name in the list of links in the phpMyAdmin navigation frame (or click the Structure icon alongside the table name under Action in the main frame).

2. With the table structure displayed in the main frame, click the Operations tab.

3. Select InnoDB or MyISAM from the Storage Engine drop-down menu in the Table options section, as shown in the following screenshot (you might see different options, but Storage Engine is the only one you're interested in here), and click Go:

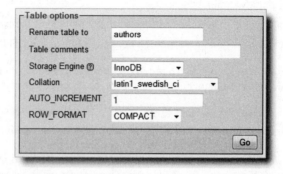

Converting a table from MyISAM to InnoDB shouldn't cause any problems. However, if foreign key constraints have been defined in an InnoDB table relationship, you must first remove them before converting from InnoDB to MyISAM. Removing a foreign key relationship simply involves reversing the process described in the next section.

Setting foreign key constraints in phpMyAdmin

When a table uses the InnoDB storage engine, phpMyAdmin adds a new option called Relation view beneath the table structure (see Figure 16-6). This is where you define foreign key constraints.

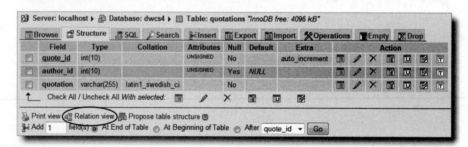

Figure 16-6. The Relation view option lets you define foreign key constraints with InnoDB tables.

The foreign key constraint must always be defined in the child table. In the case of authors and quotations, this is quotations, because it uses the authors primary key (author_id) as a foreign key. The following instructions show you how to establish the relationship:

1. Select the child table (quotations) in phpMyAdmin, and click the Structure tab to display the table grid, as shown in Figure 16-6.

2. Click the Relation view link beneath the structure grid (it's circled in Figure 16-6). This displays the screen shown in Figure 16-7.

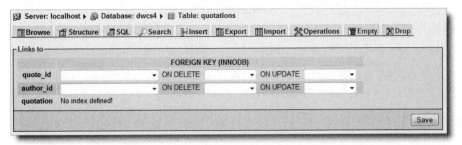

Figure 16-7. Relation view lets you specify what happens when a record in a parent table is deleted or updated.

Foreign key relationships can be established only on indexed columns. The quotations table has two indexed columns: quote_id is the table's primary key, and author_id is the foreign key. As you can see in Figure 16-7, phpMyAdmin displays three drop-down menus alongside both indexed columns. These are for you to set the foreign key constraint options, so the ones you are interested in are alongside author_id. The first drop-down is where you specify which indexed column you want to *reference*. (The underlying SQL command uses the keyword REFERENCES to establish the foreign key relationship.)

3. Click the down arrow on the right of the first drop-down menu. This lists all indexed columns in InnoDB tables in the database. As you can see from the screenshot alongside, they are listed in the format databaseName.tableName.columnName (phpMyAdmin 2 omits the name of the database, and uses -> as a separator). Since there are only two InnoDB tables in the database, the list is very short, but in a larger database, it would be considerably longer, so you need to make sure you select the right one.

4. You need to establish a reference between the author_id columns in the child (quotations) and parent (authors) tables. Select dwcs4.authors.author_id in the first drop-down menu alongside author_id.

5. Activate the ON DELETE drop-down menu alongside author_id. It displays the options shown here:

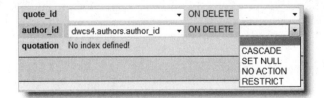

This is what each option means:

■ CASCADE: If you delete a record in the parent table, MySQL cascades the delete operation to the child table. So if you delete the record for Shakespeare in the authors table, all records in the quotations table with an author_id of 32 are automatically deleted (see Figure 16-2 earlier in the chapter). This is a silent operation, and you have no way of restoring the records once they have been deleted.

- SET NULL: If you delete a record in the parent table, the foreign key of related records in the child table is set to NULL. For this to work, the foreign key column in the child table must accept NULL values. Taking the Shakespeare example again from Figure 16-2, if Shakespeare is deleted from the authors table, the value of author_id is set to NULL in all records that currently have a value of 32. This leaves the quotations intact, but they are no longer related to Shakespeare. If you subscribe to literary conspiracy theories, you could now reassign those quotations to Christopher Marlowe.

- NO ACTION: This doesn't mean what you might expect. Some database systems allow you to delay foreign constraint checks. NO ACTION means a delayed check, but this is not supported in MySQL. If you select this option, MySQL treats it the same as RESTRICT.

- RESTRICT: This rejects any attempt to delete records in the parent table if related records still exist in the child table. So, attempting to delete Shakespeare from the authors table would fail unless all records with an author_id of 32 in the quotations table have already been deleted.

The fifth option is to select nothing. This applies the default action, which is the same as RESTRICT. The same options are available for ON UPDATE, although they are less useful, especially if the foreign key is the primary key in the parent table. In normal circumstances, you should never change the primary key of a record. However, in the rare cases where this might be appropriate, the most useful options are RESTRICT and CASCADE. The former prevents changes if there are dependent records in the child table; the latter propagates the changes automatically to all dependent records.

6. Set both ON DELETE and ON UPDATE to RESTRICT, and click Save.

7. When it confirms the creation of the foreign key constraint, phpMyAdmin displays the SQL query that it used to change the table definition. It looks like this:

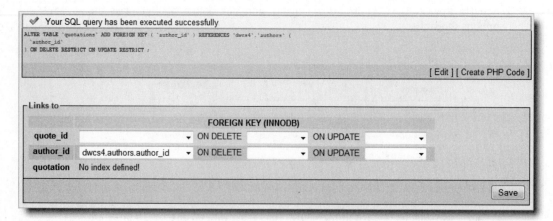

Although the field at the top of the page shows that phpMyAdmin used ON DELETE RESTRICT ON UPDATE RESTRICT, the Links to section gives the impression that your instructions were ignored. This isn't the case, because RESTRICT is the same as the default action. In other words, the only time you need to set values for ON DELETE or ON UPDATE is if you want to set them to either CASCADE or SET NULL.

If you need to remove a foreign key constraint (for example, when converting an InnoDB table to MyISAM), set all drop-down menus to the default value, and click Save.

Populating the tables

Later in the chapter, I'll show you how to build a content management system to insert, update, and delete records from the authors and quotations tables. First, though, I'd like to show you how to display the contents of tables linked through a foreign key. So, to save you the trouble of typing out lots of quotations and authors' names, I have created SQL scripts to populate the tables automatically.

The extras folder of the download files contains four different scripts. They all contain the same data but are designed to work with different versions of MySQL and storage engines. If your server is running MySQL 4.1 or 5.0, use ch16_MyISAM.sql or ch16_InnoDB.sql, depending on the storage engine that is supported. The versions of files that end in 40.sql are for MySQL 4.0. The following instructions show you how to load them into your database:

1. Launch phpMyAdmin, if it's not open, and select the dwcs4 database.
2. If you are using InnoDB, to prevent errors when loading from the SQL file, select the quotations table, and click the Drop tab. Confirm that you want to delete the table. Do the same with the authors table. The SQL file will rebuild them for you.

   You don't need to delete the tables if you're using MyISAM.
3. Click the Import tab at the top of the main frame (on versions of phpMyAdmin prior to 2.7.0, click the SQL tab instead).
4. Click the Browse button alongside the File to import field, navigate to the appropriate SQL file for your version of MySQL and the storage engine, and select it.
5. Click Go. That's it!

Restoring the content of the tables

When learning, it's a good strategy to experiment. From time to time, you may need to restore the authors and quotations tables to their original states. To do so, select each table in turn in phpMyAdmin, and click the Empty tab. Click OK when phpMyAdmin asks you to confirm that you want to TRUNCATE the table. This removes all existing records in the table. After removing all records from the authors and quotations tables, you can use the SQL script to populate them again with the original records. With InnoDB tables,

16

use the Drop tab to delete the tables if you encounter errors when trying to reload the contents from the SQL file.

Selecting records from more than one table

To select records from multiple tables, you need to join them—not in the literal sense but by using SQL commands that tell the database you want to retrieve results from more than one table. We'll look in more detail at the basic SQL commands shortly, but first let's try it out for real by displaying quotations and their associated authors from the authors and quotations tables.

Displaying a random quotation

The "Stroll Along the Thames" page you've used in several chapters has a pull quote with a quotation from Samuel Johnson. In this exercise, you'll replace that static quotation with one drawn at random from the authors and quotations tables. This demonstrates three useful techniques: how to join multiple tables, randomize the order of recordset results, and limit the number of results. You can use an existing version of the page, as long as it has a .php extension. However, you will probably find it easier to use the version in examples/ch16, because it contains no other PHP script, so you can see the new code in isolation.

1. Copy stroll_quote_start.php from examples/ch16, and save it as stroll_quote.php in workfiles/ch16. Click Update if Dreamweaver prompts you to update links in the page.

2. Click the plus button in the Server Behaviors panel, and select Recordset from the menu. Because you'll be selecting columns from more than one table, you need to use the Recordset dialog box in Advanced mode (see Figure 16-7). If necessary, click the Advanced button on the right of the dialog box to switch from Simple mode.

3. Your recordset should have a meaningful name, so type getQuote in the Name field.

4. The recordset will be used in a public page, so choose the nonadministrative user account for Connection. If you're using the same connections as me, select connQuery. If you have only one user account, use connAdmin as before.

   If Dreamweaver inserted a SELECT query in the SQL field when you switched from Simple mode, clear the field by selecting any code and pressing Delete. The Recordset dialog box should now look like Figure 16-8.

   The SQL field in the top half of the dialog box is where you build the query that will be sent to the database. If you're familiar with SQL, you can type your query here manually, but the Database items field takes a lot of the hard work out of typing. It also reduces the likelihood of spelling mistakes.

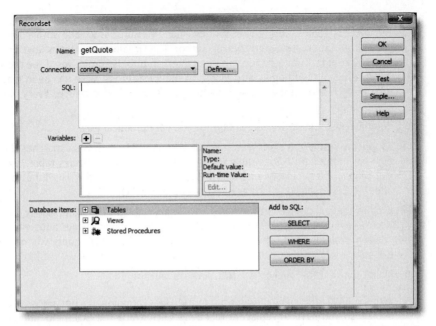

Figure 16-8. The Advanced mode of the Recordset dialog box lets you create more complex SQL queries.

5. In the Database items field, expand Tables. You should now see the authors, quotations, and users tables listed. Expand quotations, highlight quotation, and click the SELECT button, as shown here:

This starts building the SQL query. You should now see this code in the SQL field:

```
SELECT quotations.quotation
FROM quotations
```

6. Expand authors in the Database items area, and highlight first_name. Click SELECT.

7. Highlight family_name, and click SELECT. The SQL query should now look like this:

```
SELECT quotations.quotation, authors.first_name, authors.family_name
FROM quotations, authors
```

8. If you click Test now, you will see the first quotation attributed everyone listed in the authors table, starting with Woody Allen, Matsuo Basho, and so on. Then the second quotation attributed to each author. The Dreamweaver test shows only the first 100 results, but if you run the same query in phpMyAdmin, you'll see there are 2,000 results altogether—every record in the quotations table has been matched with every record in the authors table. In other words, it produces every possible combination.

You have just joined two tables but not in a very practical way.

9. To get the result you want, you need to add a WHERE clause that matches the foreign key in the quotations table to the primary key in the authors table. Highlight author_id in the quotations tree in Database items, and click the WHERE button. This adds WHERE quotations.author_id to the end of the SQL.

10. Expand the authors tree in Database items, and highlight the other author_id. Click WHERE again. Each time you click WHERE, Dreamweaver always adds whichever column is highlighted using AND, so the final line of the SQL query will now look like this:

```
WHERE quotations.author_id AND authors.author_id
```

Although AND is often what you want in a WHERE expression, it's not always the right choice, so you have to replace it manually. Click inside the SQL field, and replace AND with =. The SQL should now look like this:

```
SQL:  SELECT quotations.quotation, authors.first_name, authors.family_name
      FROM quotations, authors
      WHERE quotations.author_id = authors.author_id
```

11. Click the Test button now, and you'll see that each quotation has now been correctly matched with the right name. Adding the WHERE clause uses the foreign key to select only those records where author_id matches in both tables. Click OK to close the Test SQL Statement panel.

12. If you click Test again, the recordset appears in exactly the same order, which is the order the quotations were entered into the table. To change the order, select family_name in the authors tree in Database items, and click the ORDER BY button.

The SQL query should now look like this:

```
SELECT quotations.quotation, authors.first_name, authors.family_name
FROM quotations, authors
WHERE quotations.author_id = authors.author_id
ORDER BY authors.family_name
```

13. Click the Test button again. The quotations should be ordered according to family name.

14. Close the test panel, and add DESC at the end of the final line of the SQL query like this:

```
ORDER BY authors.family_name DESC
```

When you test the query this time, a quotation from Wordsworth will be at the top of the list, with the authors listed in reverse alphabetical order (DESC stands for "descending").

15. You want to display a random quotation in the page, so edit the last line of the SQL query like this:

```
ORDER BY RAND()
```

This uses the MySQL function RAND() to generate a random order. *Make sure there is no space between* RAND *and the parentheses.*

16. Since you need only one quotation to display in the page, it's inefficient to create a full recordset, so let's limit the result to just one record. How do you do that? Easy—change the final line of the SQL query like this:

```
ORDER BY RAND() LIMIT 1
```

17. Use the test panel several times to make sure you're getting just one random quotation and the associated names. Once you're happy that everything is as expected, click OK to close the Recordset dialog box.

18. In Design view, highlight the quotation from Samuel Johnson, open the Bindings panel, select quotation from Recordset (getQuote), and click Insert. Then replace Samuel Johnson's name and the date with dynamic text for first_name, family_name, and a space in between.

19. Save stroll_quote.php, and load it into a browser. Each time you click the browser's reload button, you should see a quotation picked at random from the 50 in the quotations table (see Figure 16-9). Occasionally, you'll see the same quotation twice in succession, but that's no different from rolling two 6s twice in succession from a pair of dice.

You can check your code against stroll_quote.php in examples/ch16.

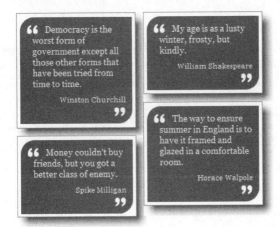

Figure 16-9. The quotations and authors' names are drawn seamlessly from separate tables.

The four essential SQL commands

As you have just seen, Advanced mode of the Recordset dialog box helps build SQL queries that work with multiple tables. Using the SELECT, WHERE, and ORDER BY buttons in conjunction with the table trees in the Database items field helps avoid spelling mistakes and always creates unambiguous references to columns. However, it cannot do everything. Not only do you need to hand-code some parts of SQL queries, you also need to have a reasonable understanding of the basic syntax. Fortunately, you don't need to be a SQL genius.

The Recordset dialog box handles only SELECT queries, but it's important to know about the four essential commands: SELECT, INSERT, UPDATE, and DELETE. The following sections provide a brief overview of how each command is structured. Read through them to get a basic understanding of how SQL works, and use them later as a reference. This is not an exhaustive listing of every available option, but it concentrates on the most important ones. I have used the same typographic conventions as the MySQL online manual at http://dev.mysql.com/doc/refman/5.0/en (which you may also want to consult):

- Anything in uppercase is a SQL command.
- Expressions in square brackets are optional.
- Lowercase italics represent variable input.
- A vertical pipe (|) separates alternatives.

When working with SQL, you should follow these simple rules:

- Keywords in SQL commands are case-insensitive. Although the convention is to use uppercase, SELECT, select, and SeLeCt are all acceptable.
- Whitespace is ignored. This means you can split queries over several lines for increased readability.
- The one exception where whitespace is not ignored concerns MySQL functions, such as RAND(). There must be *no* whitespace between the function name and the opening parenthesis.
- Each section of a query *must* be in the same order as presented here. For instance, in a SELECT query, LIMIT cannot come before ORDER BY.
- Pay particular attention to punctuation. A missing or superfluous comma will cause a query to fail; so will missing quotes around a string used in a WHERE expression. However, you should read carefully "Using variables in a SQL query" later in this chapter. Since version 8.0.2, Dreamweaver automatically adds quotes where necessary around runtime variables. This subject is also discussed in depth in Chapter 17.

SELECT

SELECT is used for retrieving records from one or more tables. Its basic syntax is as follows:

```
SELECT [DISTINCT] select_list
FROM table_list
[WHERE where_expression]
```

```
[ORDER BY col_name | formula] [ASC | DESC]
[LIMIT [skip_count,] show_count]
```

The DISTINCT option tells the database you want to eliminate duplicate rows from the results.

select_list is a comma-separated list of columns that you want included in the result. *table_list* is a comma-separated list of tables from which the results are to be drawn. For example, the following selects the first_name and family_name columns from the users table:

```
SELECT first_name, family_name
FROM users
```

The shorthand to retrieve all columns is an asterisk (*) like this:

```
SELECT * FROM users
```

The preceding example selects all columns from the users table. Although this can be useful, particularly when dealing with small tables, it's inefficient. Inexperienced developers frequently create tables with a large number of columns and records and use * to select everything even when they need only one or two items. If you have ten fields but need the data from only five of them, your query takes twice as long to execute. It's better to be explicit when formulating SELECT queries: get only the data you actually need.

When working with multiple tables, you must use unambiguous references if the same column name is used in more than one table. The syntax for unambiguous references is to use the table name followed by a period separating it from the column name like this:

```
quotations.family_name
```

In Advanced mode, the Dreamweaver Recordset dialog box always uses this syntax. Unambiguous references are not required unless there's a conflict, but it's considered good practice to use them.

When the query draws data from more than one table, all tables you want to be included in the results *must* be listed.

The WHERE clause specifies search criteria, for example:

```
SELECT first_name, family_name
FROM users
WHERE user_id = 2

SELECT quotations.quotation, authors.first_name, authors.family_name
FROM quotations, authors
WHERE quotations.author_id = authors.author_id
```

WHERE expressions can use comparison, arithmetic, logical, and pattern-matching operators. The most important ones are listed in Table 16-2.

Table 16-2. The main operators used in MySQL WHERE expressions

Comparison		Arithmetic	
<	Less than	+	Addition
<=	Less than or equal to	-	Subtraction
=	Equal to	*	Multiplication
<>	Not equal to	/	Division
!=	Not equal to	DIV	Integer division
>	Greater than	%	Modulo
>=	Greater than or equal to		
IN()	Included in list		
BETWEEN *min* AND *max*	Between (and including) two values		
Logical		**Pattern matching**	
AND	Logical and	LIKE	Case-insensitive match
&&	Logical and	NOT LIKE	Case-insensitive nonmatch
OR	Logical or	LIKE BINARY	Case-sensitive match
||	Logical or (best avoided)	NOT LIKE BINARY	Case-sensitive nonmatch

Table 16-2 contains two operators that are not part of standard SQL: != (not equal to) and || (logical or). The first of these is widely used in other major database systems, but I suggest you avoid using || instead of OR because it has a completely different meaning in standard SQL.

DIV is the counterpart of the modulo operator. It produces the result of division as an integer with no fractional part, whereas modulo produces only the remainder.

```
5 / 2      /* result 2.5 */
5 DIV 2    /* result 2   */
5 % 2      /* result 1   */
```

IN() evaluates a comma-separated list of values inside the parentheses and returns true if one or more of the values is found. Although BETWEEN is normally used with numbers, it also applies to strings. For instance, BETWEEN 'a' AND 'd' returns true for *a*, *b*, *c*, and *d* (but not their uppercase equivalents). Both IN() and BETWEEN can be preceded by NOT to perform the opposite comparison.

LIKE, NOT LIKE, and the related BINARY operators are used for text searches in combination with the following two wildcard characters:

- % matches any sequence of characters or none.
- _ (an underscore) matches exactly one character.

So, the following WHERE clause matches Dennis, Denise, and so on, but not Aiden:

```
WHERE first_name LIKE 'den%'
```

To match Aiden, put % at the front of the search pattern. Because % matches any sequence of characters or none, '%den%' still matches Dennis and Denise. To search for a literal percentage sign or underscore, precede it with a backslash (\% or _). The next chapter covers the use of wildcard characters in more detail.

Conditions are evaluated from left to right but can be grouped in parentheses if you want a particular set of conditions to be considered together. For example, let's say you want to find all the Smiths whose first name begins with "Den" or "Dan." The following WHERE clause would produce the wrong results:

```
WHERE first_name LIKE 'den%' OR first_name LIKE 'dan%'
AND family_name = 'Smith'
```

The OR takes precedence, so the WHERE clause succeeds as soon as first_name matches "Den" or "Dan." As a result, you not only get Dennis Smith but Daniel Short as well. Dan may be a nice guy, but . . . .

To ensure that the AND part of the WHERE clause is also evaluated, you need to group the first two conditions in parentheses like this:

```
WHERE (first_name LIKE 'den%' OR first_name LIKE 'dan%')
AND family_name = 'Smith'
```

ORDER BY specifies the sort order of the results. This can be specified as a single column, a comma-separated list of columns, or an expression such as RAND(), which randomizes the order. The default sort order is ascending (a–z, 0–9), but you can specify DESC (descending) to reverse the order.

LIMIT followed by one number stipulates the maximum number of records to return. If two numbers are given separated by a comma, the first tells the database how many rows to skip. For instance, LIMIT 10, 10 produces results 11–20. If fewer results exist than the limit specified, you get however many fall within the specified range. You don't get a series of empty or undefined results to make up the number.

For more details on SELECT, see http://dev.mysql.com/doc/refman/5.0/en/select.html.

INSERT

The INSERT command is used to add new records to a database. The general syntax is as follows:

```
INSERT [INTO] table_name (column_names)
VALUES (values)
```

In MySQL, the word INTO is optional; it simply makes the command read a little more like human language. The column names and values are comma-delimited lists, and both must be in the same order. So, to insert the forecast for New York (blizzard), Detroit (smog), and Honolulu (sunny) into a weather database, this is how you would do it:

```
INSERT INTO forecast (new_york, detroit, honolulu)
VALUES ('blizzard', 'smog', 'sunny')
```

The reason for this rather strange syntax is to allow you to insert more than one record at a time. Each subsequent record is in a separate set of parentheses, with each set separated by a comma:

```
INSERT INTO numbers (x,y)
VALUES (10,20),(20,30),(30,40),(40,50)
```

You'll use this multiple insert syntax in the next chapter. Any columns omitted from an INSERT query are set to their default values. *Never set an explicit value for the primary key where the column is set to* auto_increment; leave the column name out of the INSERT statement. For more details, see http://dev.mysql.com/doc/refman/5.0/en/insert.html.

UPDATE

This command is used to change existing records. The basic syntax looks like this:

```
UPDATE table_name
SET col_name = value [, col_name = value]
[WHERE where_expression]
```

The WHERE expression tells MySQL which record or records you want to update (or perhaps in the case of the following example, dream about):

```
UPDATE sales SET q1_2009 = 25000
WHERE title = 'Essential Guide to Dreamweaver CS4'
```

For more details on UPDATE, see http://dev.mysql.com/doc/refman/5.0/en/update.html.

DELETE

DELETE can be used to delete single records, multiple records, or the entire contents of a table. The general syntax for deleting from a single table is as follows:

```
DELETE FROM table_name [WHERE where_expression]
```

Although phpMyAdmin prompts you for confirmation before deleting a record, MySQL itself takes you at your word and performs the deletion immediately. DELETE is totally unforgiving—once the data is deleted, it is gone *forever*. The following query will delete all records from a table called subscribers where the date in expiry_date has already passed (as you can probably guess, NOW() is a MySQL function that returns the current date and time):

```
DELETE FROM subscribers WHERE expiry_date < NOW()
```

For more details, see http://dev.mysql.com/doc/refman/5.0/en/delete.html.

> *Although the* WHERE *clause is optional in both* UPDATE *and* DELETE, *you should be aware that if you leave* WHERE *out, the entire table is affected. This means that a careless slip with either of these commands could result in every single record being identical—or wiped out.*

Managing content with multiple tables

Now that you've seen how to use a foreign key to join tables and retrieve related records, the great mystery in life remains: "How do I insert the right foreign key in the first place?" The answer is disarmingly simple: you look it up in the database. Before I describe how to do it, let me anticipate another question: "What happens if the record I want to use as a foreign key doesn't yet exist?"

Rather than talk in abstract terms, let's use the authors and quotations tables as concrete examples. The authors table is the parent, and quotations is the child.

You can add a new record to authors or update an existing one at any time, because it isn't dependent on any other table. Deleting, however, is a different matter, because you shouldn't delete a record from authors if it has any dependent records in the child table (quotations). If you're using InnoDB tables, you can't anyway, but we'll come back to that issue later.

Adding a new record to the quotations table presents us with a chicken-and-egg situation. If the author has already been registered in the authors table, it's easy to look up the author's primary key and insert it in the foreign key column. What happens, though, when you want to insert a new quotation and a new author at the same time? The SQL INSERT command works with only one table, so the record in the parent table *must* exist before you can use its primary key as a foreign key in a child table. However, there's a simple way around this. The author_id column in the quotations table (where author_id is the foreign key) accepts NULL values. This means you can insert a new quotation without assigning the foreign key. After registering the new author, you simply update the record in the quotations table to add the foreign key.

With PHP conditional logic, it is possible to build an insert form with the option to add a new author at the same time as a quotation. I have chosen this simpler approach so that you can concentrate on the basic technique of inserting the foreign key in a child table. You need four management pages for each table—insert, list, update, and delete—so you have plenty on your hands without adding further complications.

Inserting new quotations

So, what's the magic secret of looking up the primary key from the authors table so you can use it as a foreign key? In the insert form for a new quotation, you have a drop-down menu that's dynamically populated by a recordset containing the names of all the authors. The drop-down menu displays the name of each author, and the value attribute contains the author's primary key. Simple, really. If you're still confused, I promise that all will come clear once you see the insert form in action.

> *From now on, I will assume you are familiar with all the basics of building web pages and forms in Dreamweaver and will concentrate my instructions mainly on the server behaviors that interact with the database. I'll also assume you know how to access the* Recordset *dialog box from the* Server Behaviors *panel, the* Data *tab of the Insert bar, or the* Data Objects *submenu of the* Insert *menu. I'll just tell you to open it in Advanced or Simple mode.*

Creating the quotation insert form

First, you need to design the insert form for a new quotation. It contains a text area for the quotation, a select menu for the authors' names, and a submit button.

1. Create a new PHP page, and save it in workfiles/ch16 as quote_insert.php.
2. Attach the form.css style sheet from examples/ch16 to give the page some minimal styling. Give the page a suitable title and heading, insert a form, and lay it out using the following illustration as a guide:

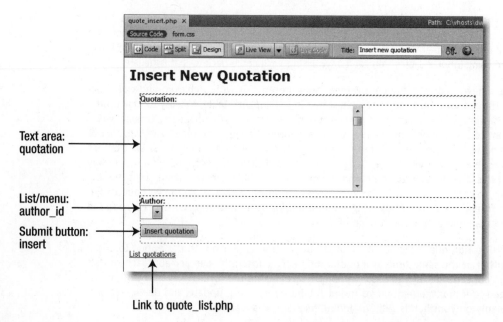

Text area: quotation

List/menu: author_id

Submit button: insert

Link to quote_list.php

When inserting the form, set Method to POST, and leave Action empty.

Note that the names I've chosen for the text area and the list/menu are the same as the column names in the database. This makes working with the Insert Record server behavior much simpler.

The link to quote_list.php will display a list of all quotations (you'll create this page later). You can check your code against quote_insert_01.php in examples/ch16.

Before you can add the Insert Record server behavior, you need to populate the author_id select menu with each author's name and primary key.

Populating a drop-down menu from a database

When building drop-down menus in a static web page, you have to go through the tedious process of typing in all the values and labels manually. With a dynamic site, all this is done automatically. First, you create a recordset containing the details you want displayed in the menu. Dreamweaver then does the rest by creating a PHP loop that runs through the recordset filling in the details for you.

1. Continue working in the same page. Open the Recordset dialog box in Advanced mode. In the Name field, type listAuthors, and select connAdmin from the Connection drop-down menu. The recordset doesn't require administrative privileges, but the rest of the form does, so it makes more sense to use the same MySQL connection throughout.

2. Build the SQL query by expanding Tables and then authors in the Database items area at the bottom of the dialog box. Highlight author_id in the authors table tree, and click the SELECT button. Do the same with first_name and family_name.

3. With family_name still highlighted, click ORDER BY. Do the same with first_name. The top half of the Recordset dialog box should now look like this:

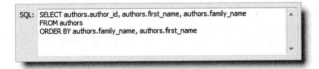

This selects all columns from the authors table and orders them first by family_name and then by first_name. Click Test to make sure you get the right results. Close the test panel, and click OK to save the recordset.

4. To populate the author_id drop-down menu with the recordset results, you need to open the Dynamic List/Menu dialog box. There are at least four ways to do this: from Insert ➤ Data Objects ➤ Dynamic Data ➤ Dynamic Select List, from the Dynamic Data submenu on the Data tab of the Insert bar, from the Server Behaviors panel (choose Dynamic Form Elements ➤ Dynamic List/Menu), and the quickest way of

all—through the Property inspector. Highlight the author_id menu in Design view, and click the Dynamic button, as shown here:

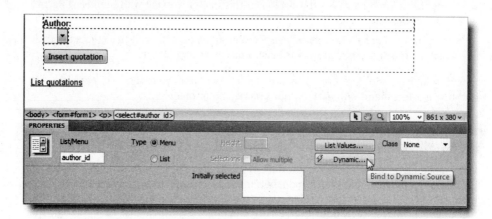

Whichever method you use, the Dynamic List/Menu dialog box automatically selects the author_id menu because it's the only one on the page.

5. In addition to the results from the database, you need a default option for the drop-down menu. Click the plus button alongside Static options. Make sure the Value field is blank, and insert Not registered in the Label field. This ensures that the foreign key will be set to NULL if Not registered is selected when inserting a new record.

> Give yourself a bonus point if you spotted an apparent inconsistency with what I said in Chapter 9. The value attribute of the <option> tag is optional in a drop-down menu. If it's omitted, the label is submitted instead. So, how does "Not registered" become NULL? The Insert Record server behavior knows that the author_id column uses the INT datatype, and it converts any value that's not a whole number to NULL to protect the integrity of your data.

6. Activate the Options from recordset drop-down menu, and select listAuthors. This will automatically populate the Values and Labels drop-down menus with the names of the available columns in your recordset. Set Values to author_id and Labels to family_name. Leave the final field (Select value equal to) blank. This is used when you want a dynamic value to be displayed automatically. You'll use it later when building the update form. The settings in the Dynamic List/Menu dialog box should be the same as in Figure 16-10. Click OK.

7. Save quote_insert.php, and test it in a browser. Activate the drop-down menu, and you will see that it has been populated with all family names from the authors table. If you view the underlying code in your browser, you will also see that the author_id has been used as the value of each <option> tag. If necessary, check your code against quote_insert_02.php.

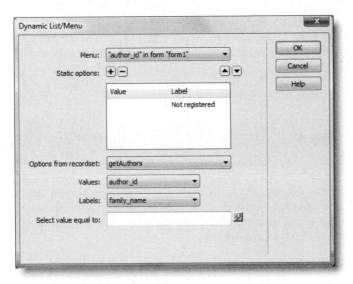

Figure 16-10. The Dynamic List/Menu dialog box allows you to use only one field as the label for each item.

This is impressive, but it's far from ideal. The Dynamic List/Menu dialog box won't let you choose more than a single field to populate the labels of the drop-down menu. A simple way to get around this is to dive into Code view, find the dynamic text object for family_name, and use the Bindings panel to insert first_name and a space alongside it. However, there's a much cooler way to do it—and that's to get MySQL to manipulate the data for you. All it requires is a function and an alias.

Using a MySQL function and alias to manipulate data

Many beginners use SQL to extract raw data and then rely on PHP or another server-side language to reformat it, whereas SQL is actually capable of doing most of the transformation itself. MySQL has an extensive range of functions (http://dev.mysql.com/doc/refman/5.0/en/functions.html) that allow you to manipulate the data in your tables in many ways. The data stored in the table remains unchanged, but you can use functions to perform calculations, format text and dates, and much, much more.

MySQL has two functions that concatenate (join together) strings, namely:

- CONCAT(): The arguments passed to CONCAT() can be literal strings (in quotes) or column names (without quotes). When a column name is used, the value of the current record is inserted into the string. CONCAT() returns NULL if any argument is NULL.

- CONCAT_WS(): This stands for "concatenate with separator." The first argument is a separator that you want inserted between the remaining arguments, which can be literal strings or column names. If the separator argument is NULL, CONCAT_WS() returns NULL, but it skips any NULL values in the remaining arguments.

Since some of the first_name fields contain NULL, you can't use CONCAT() to join the first_name and family_name columns, but CONCAT_WS() is ideal. To add a space between the two columns, you pass a pair of quotes with a space between them as the first argument like this:

```
CONCAT_WS(' ', first_name, family_name)
```

> Don't attempt to use + to concatenate strings. In MySQL, + is exclusively an arithmetic operator.

When manipulating data as part of a SQL query, you need a convenient way of referring to the result of the calculation or function. You do this by creating an **alias**. An alias is simply a temporary name that becomes part of the recordset. You assign an alias using the AS keyword. The basic syntax looks like this:

```
FUNCTION_NAME(column_name, other_arguments) AS alias_name
```

Combining the contents of two columns as a single field

In this section, you'll use CONCAT_WS() to join the first_name and family_name columns and assign the result to an alias called author.

1. Highlight Recordset (listAuthors) in the Server Behaviors panel, and double-click to edit the recordset.

2. Click inside the SQL field, and amend the SQL query like this (new code in bold):

```
SELECT authors.author_id,
CONCAT_WS(' ', authors.first_name, authors.family_name) AS author
FROM authors
ORDER BY authors.family_name, authors.first_name
```

Make sure there is no space before the opening parenthesis of CONCAT_WS()—leaving a space before the opening parenthesis of a MySQL function generates a SQL error.

3. Click the Test button. You should now see the authors' names correctly formatted as a single field called author, as shown in Figure 16-11. You can now use this to populate the Labels field in the Dynamic List/Menu dialog box.

Record	author_id	author
1	1	Woody Allen
2	2	Matsuo Basho
3	3	Jeremy Bentham

Figure 16-11. The results are displayed using the alias instead of the original column names.

4. Close the test panel, and click OK to save the revised recordset. If you look at the Server Behaviors panel, you'll notice there's a red exclamation mark next to Dynamic List/Menu (author_id). This is because the recordset no longer produces a result called family_name.

5. Highlight Dynamic List/Menu (author_id) in the Server Behaviors panel, and double-click to edit it. You will be presented with a warning that the column family_name was not found. Click OK, and select author as the value for the Labels field. Click OK to close the Dynamic List/Menu dialog box.

6. Save the page, and preview it in a browser again. This time, the authors' names should be correctly displayed. You can check your code against quote_insert_03.php.

All that remains to complete the quotation insert form is to apply the Insert Record server behavior.

Applying the Insert Record server behavior to a custom form

The Insert Record dialog box analyzes both your form and your database table, matching form fields with table columns of the same name. So if you adopt the practice of giving each form field the same name as its respective column, Dreamweaver does almost everything automatically for you. Even if there is a discrepancy between form and table names, it's easy to fix inside the dialog box.

Applying the Insert Record server behavior to the quotations table

These instructions take you through the process of applying an Insert Record server behavior to quote_insert.php. Continue working with the same file as in the preceding section.

1. With quote_insert.php open in the Document window, click the plus button in the Server Behaviors panel, and select Insert Record from the menu that appears. Alternatively, use the menu option, Insert ➤ Data Objects ➤ Insert Record ➤ Insert Record, or click the Insert Record button on the Data tab of the Insert bar.

2. This opens the Insert Record dialog box (see Figure 16-12). Since there's only one form on the page, the dialog box automatically selects form1 as the value for Submit values from.

3. The next field asks you to select the database connection. Since inserting records requires administrative privileges, choose connAdmin from the Connection drop-down menu.

4. As soon as you select the database connection, the Insert table drop-down menu is populated with a list of all tables for which the connection has INSERT privileges. Dreamweaver lists them in alphabetical order, so you need to select quotations from the drop-down menu.

5. Dreamweaver automatically populates the Columns field, matching the form fields with their respective columns, as shown in Figure 16-12.

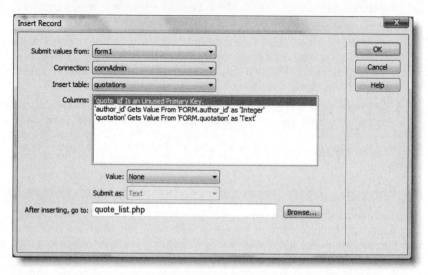

Figure 16-12. The Insert Record dialog box matches form fields with table columns.

The first entry might come as a bit of a surprise, because it describes quote_id as an Unused Primary Key. This is nothing to worry about. When you defined the table, you set the primary key column to increment automatically, so MySQL simply assigns the next available number.

As long as the remaining form fields have the same name as their respective columns, you don't need to make any changes to the Columns field. However, if any columns are listed as Does Not Get a Value (as shown in Figure 16-13), read the next section before proceeding to step 6.

6. After the record has been inserted into the database, you'll display a list of all records in quote_list.php, so enter the file name into the field labeled After inserting, go to, and click OK to apply the Insert Record server behavior.

You can check your code against quote_insert_04.php in examples/ch16.

Applying the Insert Record server behavior is so simple, I think it offers a much better solution than the Record Insertion Form Wizard, because it gives you greater control over the look of your site. A potential hazard with creating your own forms is that Dreamweaver might fail to match fields automatically with their respective table columns. However, it's easy to fix, as described in the next section.

Setting values manually in the Columns field

As you have just seen, Dreamweaver normally matches the names of form fields automatically with their respective columns in the Insert Record dialog box. However, you might need to set the value manually for one or more columns in two scenarios, namely:

- The names of the form fields and columns don't match—either through misspelling or the need to use an existing form that wasn't designed with the database table in mind.

- You want Dreamweaver to insert Y, N, -1, 0, or 1 into the database instead of the text of the value attribute of a checkbox.

Figure 16-13 shows what happened when I misnamed the Author drop-down menu in quote_insert.php. Dreamweaver was looking for a field named author_id to match the column name, but the name I had used was authorID—close enough for a human to recognize but sufficiently different to confuse a computer.

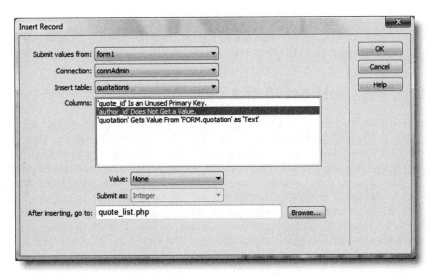

Figure 16-13. If the field name doesn't match a table column, you need to set the value manually.

Changing the value manually is very easy. Just select the column you want to change in the Columns field, and open the Value drop-down menu immediately below to display a list of available form fields. Select the appropriate one, as shown in the following screenshot:

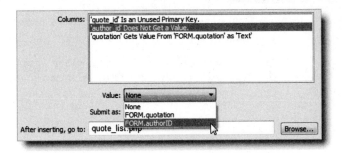

When you select the field that contains the value you want to insert into the column, Dreamweaver automatically uses the column's data type to set the value of the Submit as drop-down menu.

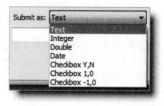

The only time you should ever need to change the value of the Submit as drop-down menu is if you want Dreamweaver to insert abbreviated values for a checkbox. As you can see from the screenshot alongside, the Submit as drop-down menu has three options for Checkbox. Select one of them if you want the first value to be inserted when the checkbox is selected and the second value to be inserted for an unselected checkbox.

This option works only for single checkboxes, not for checkbox groups. I'll show you how to handle checkbox groups in the next chapter.

Inserting new authors in the parent table

Since the authors' names are in a separate table, it's vital to ensure you don't insert the same name twice. Nothing is stopping you from inserting duplicate quotations either, but it won't really matter unless you decide to use quote_id as a foreign key in another table. Adding a unique index to the quotation column, as you did with the username column in the previous chapter, is not a good idea, because the spelling and punctuation would need to be identical to prevent duplicates. More importantly, attempting to index a column that contains a lot of text is wasteful of resources. If you end up with the same quotation more than once, you can delete duplicate entries in a child table without destroying the referential integrity of your database. The same cannot be said for the parent table.

So, what about using a unique index for authors? That won't work, because you need to check the values of two fields. Instead, I'll show you how to build the PHP logic yourself. In the process, you'll learn how to pass PHP variables to a SQL query, which forms the basis of all search operations.

Building the basic insert form

First you need to create the form to insert new authors. It requires two text fields and a submit button.

1. Create a new PHP page, save it in workfiles/ch16 as author_insert.php, attach the form.css style sheet, and lay out the form as shown in the following screenshot:

16

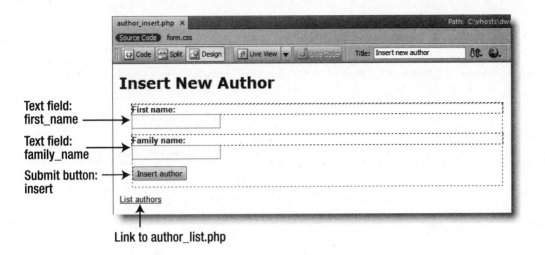

Text field:
first_name

Text field:
family_name

Submit button:
insert

Link to author_list.php

2. Apply an Insert Record server behavior in the same way as you did for quote_insert.php, this time using the following values in the Insert Record dialog box:

- Submit values from: form1
- Connection: connAdmin
- Insert table: authors
- After inserting, go to: author_list.php

Compare your code, if necessary, with author_insert_01.php in examples/ch16.

As it stands, author_insert.php is now ready to insert new records into the authors table. However, it doesn't validate the input in any way. You can use the Spry validation widgets described in Chapter 9 to make sure that required fields are filled in, but this won't prevent the insertion of duplicate records. For that, you need to roll up your sleeves and dive into Code view.

Using variables in a SQL query

To find out whether an author has already been registered, you need to check the authors table to see whether any record matches the values submitted in the first_name and family_name fields. In other words, you need to search the database (or in this case, a single table). If there's a match, you need to stop the Insert Record server behavior from executing. Otherwise, the insert operation can go ahead. Since you don't know what will be entered in the form fields, you need to pass their values as variables to the query that creates the recordset.

Passing form values to a SQL query

If you are upgrading from a version of Dreamweaver earlier than Dreamweaver 8.0.2, pay careful attention to the instructions in this section, because the way you do this changed in a subtle but important way. Continue working with author_insert.php.

1. Open the Recordset dialog box in Advanced mode. Name the recordset checkAuthor, and select connAdmin in the Connection field.

2. Expand Tables in the Database items area, expand the authors table, select each of the columns in turn, and click SELECT. Highlight first_name, and click WHERE. Then do the same with family_name. You should now have a SQL query that looks like this:

```
SELECT authors.author_id, authors.first_name, authors.family_name
FROM authors
WHERE authors.first_name AND authors.family_name
```

The WHERE expression needs to search for the names entered in the first_name and family_name fields. Although you don't know what the names will be, they will be stored in the $_POST array when the Insert author button is clicked. Instead of entering the PHP variables directly in the SQL query, you need to define runtime variables in the Variables area in the center of the Recordset dialog box. Dreamweaver replaces these variables with PHP format specifiers (normally %s or %d) and uses the GetSQLValueString() function (see "Inspecting the server behavior code" in Chapter 15) to handle quotes and other characters that might cause problems with the SQL query. It also automatically adds quotes around text values. *This is an important difference from standard SQL.*

The runtime variables are not PHP variables, so they shouldn't begin with a dollar sign. You can use any alphanumeric characters to create the variables, as long as they don't clash with the names of columns or any other part of the SQL query. I normally call the runtime variables var1, var2, and so on, but another common convention is to use col1, col2, and so on.

> *Dreamweaver uses these variables to prevent SQL injection, which exploits poorly written scripts to inject spurious code into SQL queries. SQL injection can be used to gain unauthorized access to a database and even wipe out all the stored data. In 2007, Adobe made significant changes to the way runtime variables are handled. If you have pages created in Dreamweaver 8.0.1 or earlier that have SQL queries with runtime variables, you need to remove the PHP code completely and apply the server behavior again. The code is incompatible with Dreamweaver CS4.*

3. I'm going to use var1 and var2 as my runtime variables, so change the last line of the SQL query like this:

```
WHERE authors.first_name = var1 AND authors.family_name = var2
```

16

4. You now need to define the runtime variables. Click the plus button alongside the Variables label in the Recordset dialog box. This opens the Add Variable dialog box, which has the following four fields:

- Name: This is the name of the runtime variable you want to define.

- Type: This is a drop-down menu with four options: Integer, Text, Date, and Floating point number. Integer and Text are self-explanatory. The Date option doesn't have any practical use in PHP, so you can ignore it. Floating point number accepts numbers with or without a decimal fraction. (In Dreamweaver 8.0.2 and CS3, Integer and Floating point number were called Numeric and Double, respectively. The change in names is for clarity only; it doesn't affect the code generated by Dreamweaver.)

- Default value: As you'll see in the next chapter, Dreamweaver handles this value in an unexpected way. The only time it's used is when you click the Test button in the Recordset dialog box or when the page first loads. You must enter a value in this field, because Dreamweaver uses it to prevent a MySQL error if the variable defined as Runtime value doesn't exist. Unless you want to display a default recordset result when a page first loads, set this to -1 or anything that produces no results.

- Runtime value: This is the value you want the runtime variable to represent when the SQL query is submitted.

5. When the form is submitted, you want var1 to use the value in the first_name field, so set Runtime value to $_POST['first_name']. Unless you want to check the SQL with the Test button, enter anything in the Default value field. Here are the settings that I used:

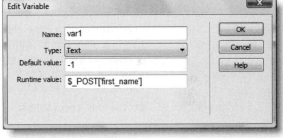

PHP is case-sensitive, so make sure $_POST is all uppercase. Click OK.

6. Define var2 in the same way, using $_POST['family_name'] as Runtime value. The central section of the Recordset dialog box should look like this:

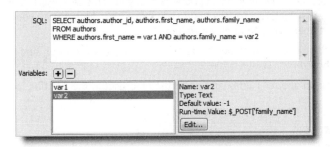

7. Click OK to close the Recordset dialog box, and save author_insert.php. You can check your code against author_insert_02.php.

Preventing duplicate entries

The recordset you created in the preceding section checks whether there's already an author of the same name registered in the table. Unfortunately, Dreamweaver puts the code for a recordset immediately above the DOCTYPE declaration, so it's *after* the Insert Record server behavior. I know what you're thinking, but it doesn't matter which order you enter them. Dreamweaver always puts recordsets beneath Insert Record and Update Record server behaviors, so you need to move it manually.

1. Open Code view. Locate the section of code in the following screenshot:

```
55  $var1_checkAuthor = "-1";
56  if (isset($_POST['first_name'])) {
57    $var1_checkAuthor = $_POST['first_name'];
58  }
59  $var2_checkAuthor = "-1";
60  if (isset($_POST['family_name'])) {
61    $var2_checkAuthor = $_POST['family_name'];
62  }
63  mysql_select_db($database_connAdmin, $connAdmin);
64  $query_checkAuthor = sprintf("SELECT authors.author_id, authors.first_name, authors.family_name FROM authors
    WHERE authors.first_name = %s AND authors.family_name = %s", GetSQLValueString($var1_checkAuthor, "text"),
    GetSQLValueString($var2_checkAuthor, "text"));
65  $checkAuthor = mysql_query($query_checkAuthor, $connAdmin) or die(mysql_error());
66  $row_checkAuthor = mysql_fetch_assoc($checkAuthor);
67  $totalRows_checkAuthor = mysql_num_rows($checkAuthor);
```

This is the code for the checkAuthor recordset. You can easily identify it, because the first line begins with $var1_checkAuthor, which is the way Dreamweaver defines var1, which you created in step 5 of the previous section. The part of the code that interacts with the database begins with mysql_select_db on line 63 and continues to the end of the line that reads as follows:

$totalRows_checkAuthor = mysql_num_rows($checkAuthor);

As I explained in the previous chapter, $totalRows_*recordsetName* tells you how many records were retrieved by the recordset. So, you can use $totalRows_checkAuthor to determine whether a record already exists for the same author. If the number of rows is zero, there are no matching records, and you can safely insert the new author. But if any matching records are found, you know it's a duplicate, so you need to skip the insert operation and display a warning.

2. Highlight the code shown on lines 55–67 in the screenshot, and cut them to the clipboard.

3. Scroll up about 17 lines, and paste the recordset in the position indicated here:

```
34  $editFormAction = $_SERVER['PHP_SELF'];
35  if (isset($_SERVER['QUERY_STRING'])) {
36    $editFormAction .= "?" . htmlentities($_SERVER['QUERY_STRING']);
37  }
38
39  if ((isset($_POST["MM_insert"])) && ($_POST["MM_insert"] == "form1")) {
40    $insertSQL = sprintf("INSERT INTO authors (first_name, family_name) VALUES (%s, %s)",
41                  GetSQLValueString($_POST['first_name'], "text"),
42                  GetSQLValueString($_POST['family_name'], "text"));
```

Paste code here →

4. Make sure your cursor is at the end of the code you have just pasted, and press Enter/Return to make room to insert the following code highlighted in bold:

```
$totalRows_checkAuthor = mysql_num_rows($checkAuthor);
// assume that no match has been found
$alreadyRegistered = false;

// check whether recordset found any matches
if ($totalRows_checkAuthor > 0) {
  // if found, reset $alreadyRegistered
  $alreadyRegistered = true;
} else {
  // go ahead with server behavior
if ((isset($_POST["MM_insert"])) && ($_POST["MM_insert"] == "form1")) {
```

> Note that false *and* true *in this code block are keywords. They must not be enclosed in quotes.*

5. Position your cursor right at the end of the code shown on line 39 in the previous screenshot (it should now be around line 61). This is the beginning of the Insert Record server behavior. Click the Balance Braces button on the Coding toolbar (or press Ctrl+'/Cmd+') to find the end of the server behavior, and insert a closing brace (}) to match the opening one of the else block at the end of the code in step 4.

   This prevents the Insert Record server behavior from running if a matching record is found in the authors table.

6. All that remains now is to display a warning message if the insert is abandoned. Scroll down until you find the following code (around line 87):

```
<h1>Insert new author</h1>
```

7. Add the following code immediately after it:

```
<?php
if ($_POST && $alreadyRegistered) {
  echo '<p class="warning">'.$_POST['first_name'].' '. ➡
$_POST['family_name'].' is already registered</p>';
}
?>
```

   This section of code will run only if the $_POST array contains any values (in other words, the insert form has been submitted) and if $alreadyRegistered has been set to true.

8. Save the page, and preview it in a browser. Try inserting a name that you know already exists in the table, such as William Shakespeare. You should see a warning that William Shakespeare is already registered.

Then try a name you know hasn't been registered. You'll see a warning that author_list.php wasn't found (you haven't created it yet), but when you reload quote_insert.php, the new name should be listed in the drop-down menu of authors' names. Check your code against author_insert_03.php if you have any problems.

> *Although this is an adequate safeguard for a basic content management system, it won't prevent you from entering similar names or misspelled ones.*

Paging through a long list of database results

As you have already seen, the way to update and delete records is to create a list of all records with EDIT and DELETE links that pass the record's primary key to the update or delete form through a query string appended to the URL. The authors table has a lot of records in it, so we'll improve the basic technique by adding a recordset navigation bar, which lets you page through a long set of search results a specified number of records at a time.

Inserting a recordset navigation bar

To save space and time, I have created the basic code for the page to display a list of authors. Refer to Chapter 14 if you need to refresh your memory on how to build this sort of page.

1. Copy author_list_01.php from examples/ch16, and save it as author_list.php in workfiles/ch16. The page has a recordset called listAuthors, which retrieves everything from the authors table, and the EDIT and DELETE links point to author_update.php and author_delete.php with the author_id primary key appended as a query string.

2. The page doesn't yet have a repeat region, so insert your cursor anywhere in the second row of the table, and click the <tr> tag in the Tag selector at the bottom of the Document window to select the entire row. Choose Repeat Region from the Server Behaviors panel. Alternatively, use the Data tab of the Insert bar or the Data Objects submenu of the Insert menu. Set the repeat region to show 15 records at a time.

3. Before inserting the recordset navigation bar, you need to make sure your insertion point is in the right place. Select <table> in the Tag selector, and press your right arrow key once to move the insertion point outside the table. Then select Recordset Navigation Bar from the Data tab of the Insert bar, as shown in the following screenshot (or select Insert ➤ Data Objects ➤ Recordset Paging ➤ Recordset Navigation Bar):

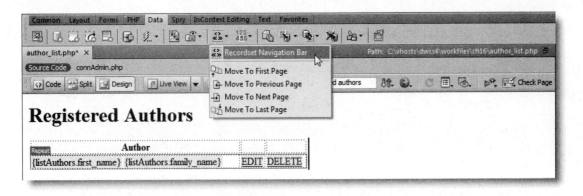

4. The Recordset Navigation Bar dialog box has two settings. The first lets you choose which recordset you want to use. There's only one on the current page, so listAuthors is selected automatically. The other setting lets you choose whether to use text or images. Select Images, and click OK.

5. The recordset navigation bar is inserted beneath the table that displays the recordset. As you can see from the following screenshot, it's a rather enigmatic jumble of images with gray tabs on top:

The HTML markup of the recordset navigation bar is a simple table. It's up to you to style it with CSS.

6. Click anywhere in the recordset navigation bar, and click the <table> tag in the Tag selector to select the whole table. Give the navigation bar an ID by typing recNav in the Table Id field in the Property inspector. Now, click the New CSS Rule icon at the bottom right of the CSS Styles panel, and create a rule for #recNav (the New CSS Rule dialog box automatically suggests the selector name if the navigation bar table is still selected).

For the purposes of this exercise, select This document only to embed the rule in the <head> of the page. In the Box category, set Width to 400 px, and click OK. This is 50 pixels narrower than the table that contains the recordset results, but it seems to fit better.

7. A simple way of formatting the recordset navigation bar is to click inside the first cell to the right of the double arrow image and insert a space. Next, hold down the

mouse button and drag-select the first two table cells. Merge the two cells by clicking the Merge selected cells icon in the Property inspector:

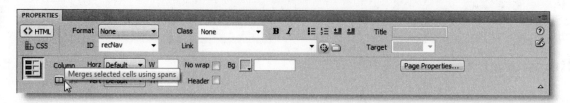

8. Do the same with the third and fourth cells by inserting a space to the right of the arrow in the third cell and merging the two cells. Finally, create a style rule (I used a class called `textRight` with the rule `text-align: right`) to move the right arrows to the right edge of the table.

A quick way to create and apply the `textRight` class to the merged cells is to select the CSS button in the Property inspector with the cells still selected. In the Targeted Rule drop-down menu, select <New CSS Rule>, and click the Align Right button, as shown in the following screenshot:

In the New CSS Rule dialog box, choose Class (can apply to any HTML element) as the Type Selector, and type textRight in the Selector Name field. When you click OK, the class is created and automatically applied to the current selection.

9. Save author_list.php, and test it in a browser. You should see two arrows at the bottom right of the list of authors, as shown here:

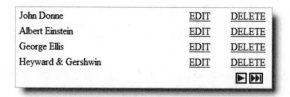

Click the single arrow, and you'll see the continuation of the list of authors, together with arrows at the bottom left of the table for you to navigate back. The double arrows take you to the beginning and end of the list—pagination for a long list of records made easy!

10. There's just one thing—the images are surrounded by ugly blue lines because they're links. To get rid of the lines, create a new CSS style rule. The quickest way do this is to go into Code view and add the following rule to the `<style>` block in the `<head>` of the page:

```
a img {
   border: none;
}
```

When you view the page again, the ugly blue border around the images is gone.

You can check your code against author_list_02.php in examples/ch16.

Now that you have a list of all authors registered in the database, you can adapt the insert form to handle updates. It's quicker to base the update page on author_insert.php, instead of building the whole page from scratch.

Adapting the author insert form for updates

Adapting the insert form involves removing the Insert Record server behavior—a simple, clean operation that involves just two clicks. You then create a recordset to retrieve the details of the record you want to update and bind the results to the fields in the form. This displays the existing contents of the record ready for editing. Finally, you apply the Update Record server behavior and move the code into the space originally occupied by the Insert Record server behavior.

1. Open author_insert.php, and save it (File ➤ Save As or Ctrl+Shift+S/Shift+Cmd+S) as author_update.php.

2. You now have an exact copy of author_insert.php. Change the title and heading to Update Author. Use the Property inspector to change the Button name and Value of the submit button to update and Update author, respectively.

3. In the Server Behaviors panel, highlight Insert Record, and click the minus button to delete it. Make sure you delete only the Insert Record server behavior, because you still need the checkAuthor recordset.

> *If you alter the code of a Dreamweaver server behavior, its name disappears from the* Server Behaviors *panel, or a red exclamation mark appears alongside, indicating the code is no longer editable through the server behavior's dialog box. However, when building the insert form, you simply moved the recordset code and wrapped the Insert Record server behavior in an* else *clause, without altering the actual code. Consequently, they still remain fully accessible through the* Server Behaviors *panel. When you remove the Insert Record server behavior in this way, the conditional statement you added to the insert form remains intact, ready for reuse in this page.*

4. An update form always needs a recordset for the Update Record server behavior to work with. Open the Recordset dialog box in Simple mode, and use the settings shown in the following screenshot. Click OK to create the getAuthor recordset. This selects just one author identified by author_id passed in the URL query string.

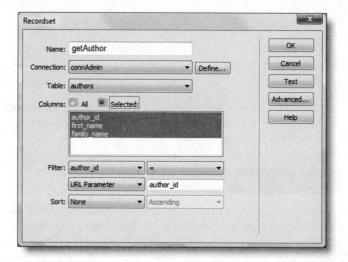

5. Open the Bindings panel. You should now have two recordsets listed there: checkAuthor and getAuthor. The second one will be used to set the initial values for the text fields in the updateAuthor form. Expand the getAuthor recordset in the Bindings panel, and highlight the first_name text field in the form, followed by first_name in the recordset, as shown alongside. The label on the Insert button at the bottom of the Bindings panel changes to Bind, and the drop-down menu alongside should display input.value. Click Bind, and a dynamic placeholder will appear inside the first_name text field. The Bind button changes to Unbind. Click this if you ever want to remove dynamic text bound in this way.

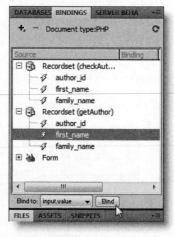

6. Repeat step 5 with the family_name text field and family_name in the recordset.

7. The Update Record server behavior also needs to know the author_id. Click any blank space inside the form, and insert a hidden field (see Chapter 9). In the Property inspector, change the name of the hidden field to author_id, and click the lightning bolt icon alongside the Value field.

8. In the Dynamic Data dialog box that opens, select author_id from Recordset (getAuthor), and click OK. Make sure you use the correct recordset.

9. Apply the Update Record server behavior by clicking the plus button in the Server Behaviors panel, and select Update Record. Alternatively, use the Update Record

button on the Data tab of the Insert bar, or select the menu option, Insert ➤ Data Objects ➤ Update Record ➤ Update Record.

If you have followed all the steps correctly, the Update Record dialog box will automatically apply the correct values as soon as you select connAdmin in the Connection field. As you can see in Figure 16-14, the Update Record dialog box is almost identical to the Insert Record one. The difference is that the first item in the Columns field identifies the record to be updated by its primary key. Dreamweaver automatically selects the Primary key checkbox for the first item, taking its value from the hidden form field you created in step 7. If this value isn't set, click Cancel, and retrace your steps.

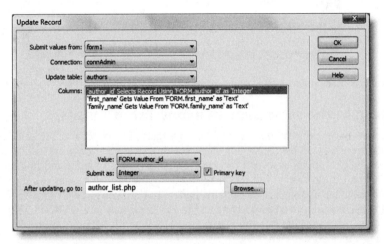

Figure 16-14. The Update Record dialog box uses the primary key to identify the record being updated.

Assuming everything is OK, set the final field to go to author_list.php after updating. Check your settings against those in Figure 16-14, and click OK.

10. As I explained in the previous chapter, Dreamweaver inserts server behavior code in a predetermined order. It works fine for basic pages, but it doesn't take into account any server-side validation that you might want to do. So, you need to move the Update Record server behavior code that has just been created.

Switch to Code view, and locate the following code:

```
39   if ((isset($_POST["MM_update"])) && ($_POST["MM_update"] == "form1")) {
40     $updateSQL = sprintf("UPDATE authors SET first_name=%s, family_name=%s WHERE author_id=%s",
41                          GetSQLValueString($_POST['first_name'], "text"),
42                          GetSQLValueString($_POST['family_name'], "text"),
43                          GetSQLValueString($_POST['author_id'], "int"));
44
45     mysql_select_db($database_connAdmin, $connAdmin);
46     $Result1 = mysql_query($updateSQL, $connAdmin) or die(mysql_error());
47
48     $updateGoTo = "author_list.php";
49     if (isset($_SERVER['QUERY_STRING'])) {
50       $updateGoTo .= (strpos($updateGoTo, '?')) ? "&" : "?";
51       $updateGoTo .= $_SERVER['QUERY_STRING'];
52     }
53     header(sprintf("Location: %s", $updateGoTo));
54   }
```

This is the Update Record server behavior code. Highlight it, making sure you don't miss the closing curly brace shown on line 54 in the screenshot, and cut it to your clipboard.

11. Scroll down until you find the empty else clause just above the DOCTYPE declaration, and paste the Update Record server behavior between the braces.

```
66   // check whether recordset found any matches
67   if ($totalRows_checkAuthor > 0) {
68     // if found, reset $alreadyRegistered
69     $alreadyRegistered = true;
70   } else {
71     // go ahead with server behavior
72
73   }
74   ?>
75   <!DOCTYPE html PUBLIC "-//W3C//DTD XHTML 1.0 Transitional//EN"
```

Paste code here ──→

You can check your code against author_update.php in examples/ch16 if necessary.

Returning to the same page in a long list of results

The recordset navigation bar does a nice job of paging through a long list of database results, but there's an annoying problem when you link to another page and return to the list. Let's say you're updating several records. You page through the list and find the first record you want to update on the third page. Clicking the EDIT link takes you directly to the update form, but as soon as you click the update button, you're taken back to the first page of the list, and you need to navigate all the way back to where you were. When this happens once, it's annoying, but you can live with it. When it happens all the time, you begin to get rather exasperated.

This is an issue that doesn't affect only update forms. It happens whenever you link to another page and then link back to the list. If you haven't already realized, linking from a list of records to an update form is the way you link from any list to a page that contains the details of a record stored in a database. So, you use this technique for product catalogs, search results, and so on.

The way that the recordset navigation bar works is by sending the page number through the query string at the end of the URL. So, all you need to do is add the page number to the query string that links to the update form. Because the Update Record server behavior preserves the query string and appends it to the return URL, you get back to where you started. Here's how it's done:

1. Load author_list.php into a browser, and click the navigation arrow at the bottom of the list of authors to display the next 15 names. Now, look at the URL in the browser address bar. As you can see in Figure 16-15, a long query string has been added.

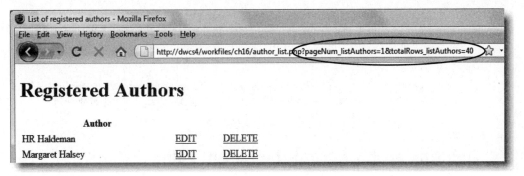

Figure 16-15. The Record Navigation Bar uses the recordset name in the query string to identify its current position.

What should strike you is that the name of the listAuthors recordset is incorporated into the query string. The code generated by Dreamweaver uses a combination of pageNum_*recordsetName* and totalRows_*recordsetName* to identify its current position within a recordset and determine which navigation links to display.

It's the value of pageNum_*recordsetName* that's of interest. Incorporate it into the EDIT link, and you'll be returned to the correct page after finishing the update.

2. Open author_list.php in Dreamweaver, insert your cursor in the EDIT link, and select <a> in the Tag selector at the bottom of the Document window. This selects the underlying code, which looks like this in Code view:

```
<a href="author_update.php?author_id=<?php echo ➥
$row_listAuthors['author_id']; ?>">EDIT</a>
```

3. Amend the code like this:

```
<a href="author_update.php?author_id=<?php echo ➥
$row_listAuthors['author_id'];
if ($pageNum_listAuthors) {
  echo '&amp;pageNum_listAuthors='.$pageNum_listAuthors;
} ?>">EDIT</a>
```

Dreamweaver uses the PHP convention of beginning a series of numbers at zero and initializes the value of $pageNum_listAuthors as 0. If the first set of results is being displayed, the value of $pageNum_listAuthors is 0, which equates to false, so the code inside the conditional statement is ignored. However, on subsequent pages, the value is greater than 0, which equates to true, so the conditional statement adds the variable and its value to the query string.

4. Save author_list.php, and load it into a browser. Click one of the navigation bar links, and select one of the authors to update. You don't need to make any changes in the update form. Just click Update record, and you'll be taken back to the previous page, rather than back to the beginning of the list.

Check your code, if necessary, against author_list_03.php in examples/ch16. I have made this enhancement only to the EDIT link, but you can also add it to the DELETE link if you want it to work the same way.

This works with the update form because the Update Record server behavior automatically preserves the query string. In detail pages that you create yourself, you need to capture pageNum_*recordsetName* from the $_GET array and insert it in the link back to the recordset list page like this:

```
<a href="list.php<?php if (isset($_GET['pageNum_recordsetName'])) {
    echo '?pageNum_recordsetName='.$_GET['pageNum_recordsetName'];
} ?>">Back to the list</a>
```

Deleting authors from the parent table

In "Avoiding orphaned records" earlier in the chapter, I told you that using foreign key constraints in InnoDB tables automates the preservation of referential integrity. It does—in the sense that it prevents you from deleting records in a parent table if there are still dependent records in a child table. Figure 16-16 shows what happened when I tried to delete William Shakespeare from the authors table using InnoDB with a foreign key constraint defined.

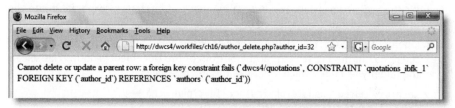

Figure 16-16. A foreign key constraint prevents the deletion of a record while it still has dependent records in a child table.

When I did the same thing with MyISAM tables, William Shakespeare vanished into cyber-oblivion without so much as a by-your-leave to his children. So, foreign key constraints are a good security measure, but you don't want an ugly MySQL error message like that in Figure 16-16 on your website. Consequently, even if you're using InnoDB tables, you need to incorporate the same sort of checks into a delete page as with MyISAM tables. In other words, when deleting a record from a parent table, you need to do the following:

1. Search the child table to see whether the record's primary key has any matches in the foreign key column. In the example in Figure 16-2 earlier in the chapter, Shakespeare's primary key is 32. So before you can delete his record, you need to check whether any records in the quotations table have the same value as the foreign key (author_id).

2. If there are any matches, display a message saying that the deletion cannot go ahead, and hide the delete button.

   If there are no matching records, display the delete button, asking for confirmation.

Adapting the author update page to handle deletes

The conditional logic that you used in the insert and update forms checked whether an author was already registered in the authors table. For the delete form, you need to perform a similar check, only this time in the quotations table. Although you're checking a different table, the script flow is exactly the same. If there are any matching records, you stop the server behavior from being executed. Otherwise, you let it go ahead. Consequently, you can adapt the existing script quite easily.

1. Open author_update.php, and save it as author_delete.php.

2. Change the title and heading to Delete Author. Use the Property inspector to change the Button name and Value of the submit button to delete and Delete author, respectively.

3. In the Server Behaviors panel, highlight Recordset (checkAuthor), and delete it by clicking the minus button.

4. Do the same with Update Record.

5. Click the plus button in the Server Behaviors panel, and select Delete Record. As in the previous chapter, you get the value of the record to be deleted from a hidden field, so make sure you choose Form Variable for Primary key value. Check that your settings are the same as shown in the screenshot, and click OK.

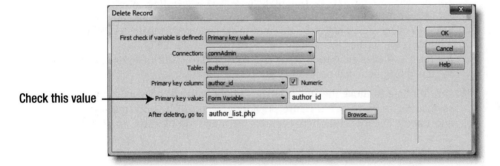

Check this value

6. Before deleting a record from the authors table, you must check whether its primary key is still in use in the quotations table. Create a new recordset called checkForeign. Use the Recordset dialog box in Advanced mode with the settings shown in the following screenshot:

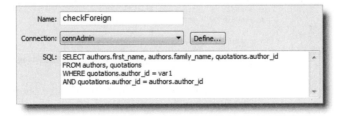

The WHERE clause selects records where quotations.author_id is equal to a variable (we'll define that in a moment) and where quotations.author_id is the same as authors.author_id. As explained in the "The four essential SQL commands" earlier in the chapter, the dot notation *tableName.columnName* eliminates ambiguity in a SQL query when columns in different tables have the same name. What this SQL query is looking for is any record where author_id matches the runtime variable var1.

7. The value of author_id is passed through the query string from author_list.php, so var1 needs to be defined in the Variables field. Click the plus button alongside Variables, and use the following settings:

The primary key, author_id, is a number, so Type needs to be set to Integer. I have set Default Value to -1 because I don't want the variable to default to a genuine value. Runtime value is set to $_GET['author_id'] because the value is passed through a query string in the URL. Remember, $_GET is used for URL variables and $_POST for form variables submitted using the POST method. Click OK to close the Add Variable dialog box, and click OK again to save the recordset.

8. Now it's time to move the Delete Record server behavior from its current position so that it's inside the else clause previously occupied by both the Insert Record and Update Record server behaviors. Locate the following code, and cut it to your clipboard:

```
34  if ((isset($_POST['author_id'])) && ($_POST['author_id'] != "")) {
35      $deleteSQL = sprintf("DELETE FROM authors WHERE author_id=%s",
36                          GetSQLValueString($_POST['author_id'], "int"));
37
38      mysql_select_db($database_connAdmin, $connAdmin);
39      $Result1 = mysql_query($deleteSQL, $connAdmin) or die(mysql_error());
40
41      $deleteGoTo = "author_list.php";
42      if (isset($_SERVER['QUERY_STRING'])) {
43          $deleteGoTo .= (strpos($deleteGoTo, '?')) ? "&" : "?";
44          $deleteGoTo .= $_SERVER['QUERY_STRING'];
45      }
46      header(sprintf("Location: %s", $deleteGoTo));
47  }
```

9. Paste the code from your clipboard to the position indicated here:

```
53   // assume that no match has been found
54   $alreadyRegistered = false;
55
56   // check whether recordset found any matches
57   if ($totalRows_checkAuthor > 0) {
58     // if found, reset $alreadyRegistered
59     $alreadyRegistered = true;
60   } else {
61     // go ahead with server behavior
62
63   }
64   ?>
65   <!DOCTYPE html PUBLIC "-//W3C//DTD XHTML 1.0 Transitional//EN"
```

Paste code here ──────▶

10. Next, amend the code shown on lines 54–59 of the preceding screenshot to match the name of the checkForeign recordset like this:

```
// assume that no match has been found
$recordsExist = false;

//check whether recordset found any matches
if ($totalRows_checkForeign > 0) {
  // if found, reset $recordsExist
  $recordsExist = true;
  }
else {
```

11. Scroll down until you find this line (it should be around line 90):

```
if ($_POST && $alreadyRegistered) {
```

The check for $_POST is not needed this time, because the checkForeign recordset will be created as soon as the page loads. You also need to change the variable to $recordsExist. Change the line to look like this:

```
if ($recordsExist) {
```

12. In the next line, $_POST['first_name'] and $_POST['family_name'] need to be replaced with dynamic data from the checkForeign recordset. Highlight $_POST['first_name'], and open the Bindings panel. Expand Recordset (checkForeign), select first_name, and click the Insert button. This will replace $_POST['first_name'] with $row_checkForeign['first_name']. Do the same with $_POST['family_name'], selecting family_name from the Bindings panel.

13. Change the remaining text in the warning paragraph, and add the opening part of an else clause so that the entire PHP code block now looks like this:

```
<?php
if ($recordsExist) {
echo '<p class="warning">'.$row_checkForeign['first_name'].' '. ➥
$row_checkForeign['family_name'].' has dependent records. Cannot ➥
be deleted.</p>';
} else {
?>
```

14. Scroll all the way down to just after the closing `</form>` tag (around line 107), and insert a closing curly brace inside a pair of PHP tags like this:

```
<?php } ?>
```

What you have done is enclose the entire form in an `else` clause, so it will be displayed only if there are no dependent records in the quotations table.

15. Switch back to Design view, click immediately to the right of the first PHP shield at the top of the page, and press Enter/Return to create a new paragraph. Type a warning that the delete operation cannot be undone, and apply the warning class to the paragraph.

16. Save author_delete.php, and load author_list.php into your browser. Select an author that you know has dependent records in the quotations table, and click DELETE. You should see a message like this:

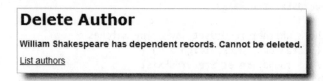

17. Now insert a new author. When the name appears in the list, click DELETE. This time you should see a screen like the following one. Click Delete author. You will be taken back to the list of authors, and the new entry will have disappeared without a trace. You can check your code against author_delete.php in examples/ch16.

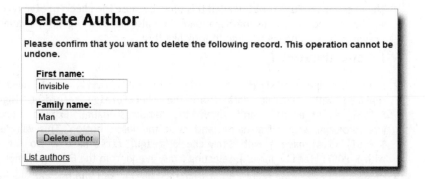

Improving the delete form

As the screenshot in step 16 shows, the warning message simply tells you that the author has dependent records. A simple improvement would be to display a list of the dependent records so that you can delete them, if required. All that's needed is to add quotation to the checkForeign recordset. You can then use a repeat region to display the dependent records if any are found. Sample code showing how this is done can be found in author_delete_display.php in examples/ch16. The code is fully commented, explaining how to incorporate the display of dependent records.

Another improvement would be to remove the text fields that display the name of the author to be deleted and just display the first_name and family_name values in the same way as with delete_user.php in Chapter 14. However, it doesn't matter that the names are displayed in editable text fields. Even if you edit the names, it has no effect on the database.

Performing a cascading delete with InnoDB tables

Although you still need to use PHP logic in the delete form for a parent table, one advantage that InnoDB tables have over MyISAM is the ability to perform a cascading delete. This means that when you delete a record in the parent table, all dependent records are automatically deleted from the child table. To enable this behavior, you need to change the foreign key constraint to ON DELETE CASCADE.

Deleting dependent records simultaneously

The following instructions show you how to adapt author_delete.php to perform a cascading delete with InnoDB tables. You can use author_delete.php in examples/ch16 as the starting point. The completed code is in author_delete_cascade.php.

These instructions apply only to InnoDB tables. They do not work with the default MyISAM tables.

1. In phpMyAdmin, select the quotations table in the dwcs4 database. Click the Structure tab to display the table structure, and select Relation view.

2. In the Links to area, change the value of ON DELETE for author_id to CASCADE, as shown in the following screenshot, and click Save:

3. Open author_delete.php, and double-click Recordset (checkForeign) in the Server Behaviors panel to edit it.

4. Expand the Tables tree in the Database items area at the bottom of the Recordset dialog box, highlight quotation in the quotations table, and click the SELECT button to add it to the SQL query. This will enable you to display the dependent records about to be deleted.

5. Save the edited recordset, and locate the following section in Code view:

```
87  <h1>Delete Author</h1>
88    <?php
89  if ($recordsExist) {
90    echo '<p class="warning">'.$row_checkForeign['first_name'].' '.$row_checkForeign['family_name'].' has
    dependent records. Cannot be deleted.</p>';
91  } else {
92  ?>
93  <p class="warning">Please confirm that you want to delete the following record. This operation cannot be
    undone.</p>
```

6. Delete the PHP code block shown on lines 88–92 of the preceding screenshot.

7. Delete the PHP code block immediately after the closing </form> tag. It contains only a closing curly brace to match the opening one on line 91 of the preceding screenshot.

8. Inside the form, delete the first_name and family_name text fields, leaving only the submit button and hidden field. The <body> section of the page should now look like this:

```
86  <body>
87  <h1>Delete Author</h1>
88  <p class="warning">Please confirm that you want to delete the following record. This operation cannot be
    undone.</p>
89  <form id="form1" name="form1" method="POST">
90    <p>
91      <input type="submit" name="delete" id="delete" value="Delete author" />
92      <input name="author_id" type="hidden" id="author_id" value="<?php echo $row_getAuthor['author_id']; ?>" />
93    </p>
94  </form>
95  <p><a href="author_list.php">List authors</a></p>
96  </body>
```

9. Select the words the following record (shown on line 88 of the preceding screenshot), and replace them with dynamic text from the getAuthor recordset to display the author's first name and family name. Add another sentence warning that all dependent records will also be deleted at the same time.

10. You could use the page like this, but it's much better to display the dependent records that are about to be deleted. Switch to Design view, position your cursor at the end of the warning paragraph, and press Enter/Return to insert a new paragraph. Type The following dependent records will also be deleted:.

11. Press Enter/Return, and click the Unordered List button in the HTML view of the Property inspector (or use Format ➤ List ➤ Unordered List).

12. Open the Bindings panel, select quotation in Recordset (checkForeign), and click Insert. Then click <li> in the Tag selector at the bottom of the Document window to select the whole <li> element, and apply a repeat region to show all records. This will display all dependent records from the quotations table.

13. Not every record in the parent table will have dependent records, so you need to say if no records were found. Click <ul> in the Tag selector to select the whole unordered list, and press the right arrow key once to move the insertion point after the closing </ul> tag. Press Enter/Return to insert a new paragraph, and type No dependent records.

14. You now have contradictory displays in the page. You want to show the unordered list only if there are dependent records, and the paragraph you have just typed if there are none. This is a case for using the Show Region server behavior, as described in Chapter 14.

Click the <p> tag in the Tag selector to select the paragraph you have just typed. Then, click the plus button in the Server Behaviors panel, and select Show Region ➤ Show If Recordset Is Empty. Unlike Chapter 14, this time the page has two record-sets, so you must choose the right one in the dialog box that opens. Select checkForeign, and click OK.

15. Position your cursor anywhere in the unordered list, and click the <ul> tag in the Tag selector to select the whole list. Select the Show Region submenu again, and choose Show If Recordset Is Not Empty. Again, select checkForeign for Recordset.

You now have a user-friendly cascading delete form for use with InnoDB tables. Check your code, if necessary, against author_delete_cascade.php in examples/ch16.

Updating quotations in the child table

Now that you've dealt with all the issues involved with the parent table, authors, you can return to the child table and finish the content management system for quotations. You'll be relieved to know that building the update and delete forms doesn't involve a great deal of work. However, the presence of the foreign key in a child table does add a slight compli-cation to creating the page that displays a list of all records. Let's start by building quote_list.php to display a list of all quotations with links to the update and delete forms.

Displaying a list of quotations

The layout of the page follows the same pattern as all other lists of records. The main dif-ference lies in the SQL query that you build in the Recordset dialog box, because you need to draw records from the child and parent tables, using the foreign key to match records in both tables.

1. Create a PHP page called quote_list.php in workfiles/ch16, and lay it out like this:

2. Open the Recordset dialog box in Advanced mode, and build the query shown alongside:

This selects the quotation and its primary key, as well as the author's first name and family name by matching the author_id in

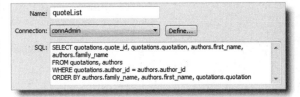

both tables. The results are ordered by family name, first name, and quotation, in that order.

3. Use the Bindings panel to add the dynamic text objects to the page, building the EDIT and DELETE links in the same way as before (linking to quote_update.php and quote_delete.php and passing quote_id as a parameter through the query string).

> *Passing the primary key through a query string is something a lot of people seem to get wrong. Refer to "Updating and deleting records" in Chapter 14 if you need a reminder of how to do it.*

4. Apply a repeat region and a recordset navigation bar. I won't give step-by-step instructions, because you've done this before. Check your code, if necessary, against quote_list_01.php in examples/ch16.

That was easy, wasn't it? Unfortunately, it was too easy, because there's a hidden flaw in the SQL.

Load quote_insert.php into a browser, and insert a new quotation. It doesn't matter what it is, as long as you don't select an author. Leave the author drop-down menu on Not registered. Now load quote_list.php into a browser, and look for the quotation you have just inserted. It's not listed. Double-check in phpMyAdmin— the new quotation should be at the end of the quotations table. What's going on?

Solving the mystery of missing records with a left join

The reason for the failure of quote_list.php to display quotations without an associated author lies in the WHERE expression:

```
WHERE quotations.author_id = authors.author_id
```

This works fine when there are matching records in both tables, but if the author_id foreign key hasn't been set in the quotations table, there's nothing to match it in the authors table. You need a way to find all records, even if there isn't a corresponding match for the foreign key. This is achieved in SQL by what is known as a **left join**.

The SQL queries generated by Dreamweaver are known as **inner joins**—there must be a complete match in both tables of all conditions in a WHERE expression. The difference with a left join is that when there's no match for a record in the table(s) to the "left" of the join, the result is still included in the recordset, but all the columns in the table to the "right" of the join are set to NULL. "Left" and "right" are used in the sense of which side of the keywords LEFT JOIN they appear in the SQL query. The syntax looks like this:

```
SELECT column_name(s) FROM first_table
LEFT JOIN second_table ON condition
```

If the condition is matching two columns of the same name (such as author_id), an alternative syntax can be used:

```
SELECT column_name(s) FROM first_table
LEFT JOIN second_table USING (column_name)
```

Using a left join to find incomplete records

You can now amend the SQL query in `quote_list.php` to use a left join. Dreamweaver doesn't have an automatic way of generating a left join, so you need to adjust the query manually. Continue working with `quote_list.php` from the preceding section.

1. Highlight Recordset (quoteList) in the Server Behaviors panel, and double-click it to open the Recordset dialog box.

2. Edit the SQL query by hand like this:

   ```
   SELECT quotations.quote_id, quotations.quotation, authors.first_name,
   authors.family_name
   FROM quotations LEFT JOIN authors USING (author_id)
   ORDER BY authors.family_name, authors.first_name, quotations.quotation
   ```

3. Click the Test button to make sure you haven't made any mistakes in the query. I find that I frequently forget to remove the comma after the first table name when replacing an inner join with a left join.

4. Click OK to save the recordset. Save the page, and refresh your browser. Any quotations without an `author_id` will now appear at the top of the list with the Name column blank, as shown in Figure 16-17.

Quotations Listed by Author

Name	Quotation		
	It is only with the heart that one can see rightly; what is essential is invisible to the eye.	EDIT	DELETE
Woody Allen	I don't want to achieve immortality through my work... I want to achieve it by not dying.	EDIT	DELETE
Woody Allen	If it turns out that there is a God, I don't think that he's evil. But the worst that you can say about him is that basically, he's an underachiever.	EDIT	DELETE

Figure 16-17. Using a left join finds records that don't have a match in both tables.

Compare your code, if necessary, with `quote_list_02.php` in examples/ch16.

Adapting the insert page for updates

Rather than build the update form from scratch, you can easily adapt the insert page again. Because you don't need to check for duplicate entries, this is simpler than the update page for authors. After removing the Insert Record server behavior, you create a recordset for the record being updated, bind the existing values to the quotation text area and author drop-down menu, and apply an Update Record server behavior.

1. Save `quote_insert.php` as `quote_update.php`. Change the title and heading to Update quotation. Also change the Button name and Value of the submit button to update and Update quotation, respectively.

2. Select the Insert Record server behavior in the Server Behaviors panel, and click the minus button to remove it.

3. When the EDIT link in quote_list.php is clicked, you need to display the details of the record. Open the Recordset dialog box in Simple mode, and create a recordset called getQuote using the following settings:

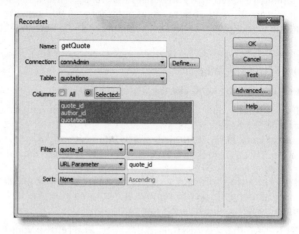

4. Expand Recordset (getQuote) in the Bindings panel. Select the quotation text area in the form, and then select quotation in the recordset. Click Bind.

5. You also need the author_id drop-down menu to display the correct value. Select the menu object in the form, and click the Dynamic button in the Property inspector. All the existing values are fine, but to display the selected value dynamically, click the lightning bolt icon to the right of the Select value equal to field at the bottom of the dialog box.

In the Dynamic Data dialog box, select author_id from Recordset (getQuote), as shown in the following screenshot. Make sure you choose the correct recordset—both of them include author_id. The other recordset contains *all* author_id numbers; you want only the specific one associated with the quotation identified by the URL query string.

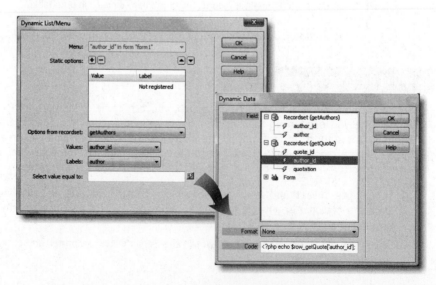

Click OK twice to close both dialog boxes. What you have just done creates the code to dynamically insert selected="selected" in the appropriate <option> tag to display the correct name from the authors table.

6. Before adding the Update Record server behavior, you need to create a hidden form field to store the correct quote_id. Click in a blank area of the form, and insert a hidden field. In the Property inspector, name the hidden field quote_id, and click the lightning bolt icon to insert dynamic data in the Value field. Choose quote_id from Recordset (getQuote), and click OK.

7. Click the plus button on the Server Behaviors panel, and choose Update Record. Use the following settings:

- Submit values from: updateQuote
- Connection: connAdmin
- Update table: quotations
- After updating, go to: quote_list.php

8. Save the page, and test it. Compare your code, if necessary, with quote_update.php in examples/ch16.

Deleting quotations

Nearly there! Just one more page to go—the page for deleting quotations is relatively simple to make, because there's no need to check for dependent records. It's only when a foreign key refers to a deleted record that you have a problem. Delete Shakespeare's records in the quotations table, and the integrity of your database remains intact. The only loss is some of the greatest sayings in the English language.

Adapting the update page for deletes

This is much simpler than the delete form for authors, because no dependent records are involved. It's a quick and easy adaptation of the update page.

1. Save quote_update.php as quote_delete.php. Change the title and heading to Delete quotation. Change the Button name and Value of the submit button to delete and Confirm deletion, respectively.

2. Insert a new paragraph between the heading and form asking for confirmation of the deletion and warning that it's not undoable. Apply the warning class to the paragraph.

3. Highlight Update Record in the Server Behaviors panel, and click the minus button to delete it.

4. Click the plus button in the Server Behaviors panel, and select Delete Record. Use the settings shown in the following screenshot. Make sure you choose the correct table and set Primary key value to Form Variable. The default value is URL Parameter,

which deletes the record without confirmation. Click OK to apply the server behavior.

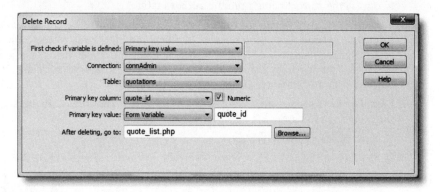

5. Save the page, and compare your code, if necessary, against quote_delete.php in examples/ch16.

You now have a complete management system for a parent and child set of tables.

Chapter review

Creating the content management system for two tables in a parent-child relationship requires a much more complex back-end than for a single table. You may be wondering whether it's really worth the effort. The answer is *yes*. Creating a database and its related content management system is a time-consuming process, but the time spent on building a solid foundation for your database will be well rewarded.

Although this chapter has involved a lot of steps and you've needed to dive into Code view from time to time, it's important to realize that the Dreamweaver server behaviors have taken an enormous coding burden off your shoulders. Remembering how to fill in the different dialog boxes takes time and practice, but this chapter has taken you much further by showing you how to join tables and maintain referential integrity when deleting records. This has been a relatively simple example, using just two tables. Databases frequently contain many tables with complex relationships, but the underlying principles remain the same.

In the next chapter, we'll take a more in-depth look at searching for records, as well as formatting dates.

The previous three chapters have covered the basic knowledge you need to work with a database: inserting records, updating them, and deleting them. Where you go now depends on your needs and your willingness to learn more about SQL and PHP. The reason both are so powerful lies in their flexibility. I'm constantly finding new ways of handling situations that previously puzzled me. The key to doing this lies not only in learning the features available in both languages but also in thinking about issues using the same conditional logic as PHP. As human beings we make decisions instinctively. Computers need to go through a lengthier process of making comparisons—at least, it seems lengthier to us as developers. It takes us far longer to type the code than it takes the computer to execute it. I find that, rather than beginning by writing code, it's often more productive to sketch how I think something will work by writing a series of comments. Once the logic is there, the code comes much more easily.

This chapter addresses several common issues you are likely to encounter when developing a website with PHP and MySQL. To start, I'll address the problem of storing input from multiple-choice form elements, such as checkbox groups and multiple-choice lists. Then, I'll turn to showing you some basic search techniques. Finally, I'll demonstrate how to handle dates in PHP and MySQL.

As you saw in Chapter 14, MySQL stores dates in the ISO format of YYYY-MM-DD. PHP takes a completely different approach, calculating dates by counting the number of seconds elapsed since January 1, 1970 (I explain why later in the chapter). It's not as complicated as it sounds, but you need to ensure that dates submitted to MySQL are in the correct format and—equally important—that you can display dates in a human-friendly way.

In this chapter, you'll learn about the following:

- Using SET columns to store multiple choices
- Displaying the number of results from a search
- Creating striped table rows
- Troubleshooting MySQL errors
- Searching for records based on full and partial matches
- Using FULLTEXT indexing
- Reusing a recordset after a repeat region
- Formatting dates with MySQL and PHP

This is a long chapter, but it ties up a lot of loose ends. Don't feel obliged to read through everything at one sitting. Everything follows a logical sequence, but the chapter is also designed for you to be able to dip in to find answers to issues you might encounter. To work with most of the examples in this chapter, you need to have created the authors and quotations tables and populated them with data, as described in Chapter 16.

Storing multiple values in a SET column

In the previous chapter, I told you that a process called **normalization** lays down the principles of good database design, and one of its main rules is to store only one item of information in the same field. The feedback form that you worked with in Chapters 9, 11, and 12 has a checkbox group, from which the user can choose up to five options, and a multiple-choice list with a choice of up to six options. If you follow the rule of only one item of information in the same field, you need to decide how to store each option. The beginner's answer is either to ignore the single-item rule and put everything in the same field or to create a separate column for each option.

Neither choice works well. Putting everything in the same column makes it difficult to search and retrieve information. Creating separate columns for each option might seem like a good idea to start with, but it rapidly becomes unwieldy. In the feedback form, there are 11 options, but many users will choose fewer than half of them, so you end up with a lot of wasted space in the database. Even worse, when you add new options, you need to add new columns. After a year or so, you could end up with dozens, or even hundreds, of columns.

The alternative solutions are to put the options in a separate table and use the record's primary key to identify which options are selected by each user or to use a SET column. As I explained in Chapter 14, SET is a MySQL column type that stores zero or more choices from a predefined list. The maximum number of items you can define is 64. This can be useful for storing multiple choices, where the range of options is fixed or unlikely to change frequently.

Although a SET column appears to break the rule of storing only one item of information in a field, it's actually a shorthand form of normalization. Instead of storing the actual text each time a record is created, MySQL stores a reference to each selection as a number. In other words, it creates an internal foreign key to look up the stored values. This not only saves space, but it speeds up searches. Databases search through numbers much faster than through text.

The values in the predefined list can contain any characters except a comma, because commas are used to separate values.

The following sections show you how to store data in a SET column and retrieve it.

Defining a SET column

Rather than build a complex table to demonstrate working with SET columns, I'm going to keep the structure as simple as possible by creating an online poll that asks visitors which operating systems they use. An online poll simply records results, so the database table doesn't really need a primary key. However, I'm going to use one because it makes it possible to get the most recent record.

Creating the table for the poll

To store the results of the poll, you need to create a table with a column that stores the visitors' choices in a SET column with four options: Windows, Mac, Linux, and none. The insert form will contain only the first three options. Adding none to the predefined list in the SET column avoids the problem of dealing with invalid submissions. If the form is submitted without any of the checkboxes selected, a conditional statement will set the value to none.

1. Launch phpMyAdmin, select the dwcs4 database, and create a new table called os_poll with just two fields like this:

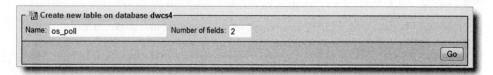

2. In the matrix where you define the table columns, use the following values for the primary key:

- Field: vote_id
- Type: INT
- Attributes: UNSIGNED
- Index: PRIMARY
- A_I: Yes

Use the following values for the second column:

- Field: operating_system
- Type: SET
- Length/Values: 'Windows', 'Mac', 'Linux', 'none'

The Length/Values field takes a comma-separated list of strings containing the options you want to store in the SET column. Searches of SET columns are case-insensitive, but when values retrieved from a SET column are displayed, the original combination of uppercase and lowercase is preserved. Because the field where you enter the options is rather narrow, I find it can be helpful to type the values in a text editor or Dreamweaver Code view first. This ensures that the spelling is correct and that the commas and quotes are in the right places. Then cut and paste the entire string into the Length/Values field.

Leave the other fields at their default values, and click Save when you have finished.

3. The structure of the os_poll table should look like Figure 17-1 in phpMyAdmin.

Field	Type	Collation	Attributes	Null	Default	Extra
vote_id	int(10)		UNSIGNED	No		auto_increment
operating_system	set('Windows','Mac','Linux','none')	latin1_swedish_ci		No		

Figure 17-1. The os_poll table consists of a primary key and a SET column listing four options.

Inserting data into a SET column

To save time and space, I have created a simple form with a checkbox group called operating_system[ ]. As you should recall from Chapter 9, the square brackets at the end of the name tell PHP to treat the values of selected checkboxes as an array. The checkboxes have their value attributes set to Windows, Mac, and Linux to match those specified in the table definition.

You can store any combination of these in the operating_system column for each record in the database. However, if you decide to change the form to add SunOS to the checkbox group, you cannot store SunOS in the operating_system column without first updating the table definition. Illegal values—and that includes misspellings—are ignored.

Inserting poll responses into the table

The values from a checkbox group or multiple-choice list need to be inserted into a SET column as a comma-separated string. However, the Dreamweaver Insert Record server behavior doesn't recognize SET columns, so you need to tweak the code manually. You do this by passing the array that contains the form values to implode() and then inserting the values into the database as text. The following exercise uses only a checkbox group, but the same technique applies to multiple-choice lists.

1. Copy set_insert_start.php from examples/ch17 to workfiles/ch17, and save it as set_insert.php. The page contains a simple form with three checkboxes and a submit button, as shown in Figure 17-2.

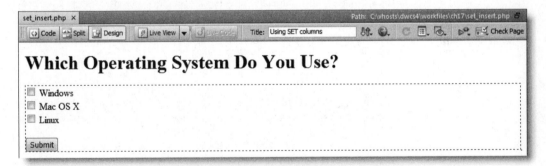

Figure 17-2. The values of a checkbox group can be stored efficiently in a SET column.

2. Open the Server Behaviors panel, click the plus button, and select Insert Record from the menu that appears (or use the Insert menu or Data tab of the Insert bar).

3. In the Insert Record dialog box, select connAdmin as the connection and os_poll as the table. Because the checkbox names end in square brackets, the server behavior cannot match them to the operating_system column in the table. So, it displays 'operating_system' Does Not Get a Value in the Columns field.

4. Select operating_system in the Columns field, and activate the Value drop-down menu. As Figure 17-3 shows, Dreamweaver lists the three checkboxes as FORM.operating_system[].

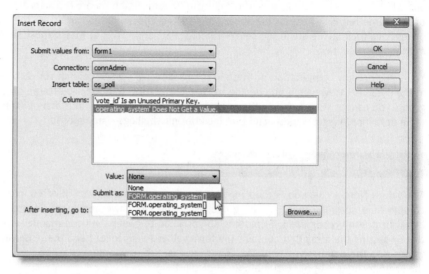

Figure 17-3. The square brackets prevent Dreamweaver from matching the checkbox group with the SET column.

5. Select one of the instances of FORM.operating_system[].

6. Dreamweaver automatically selects Checkbox 1,0 in the Submit as drop-down menu. You need to change this to Text.

7. You don't need to enter anything in the field labeled After inserting, go to, so just click OK to close the Insert Record dialog box.

> If you open the dialog box again for any reason, Dreamweaver sets operating_system *back to* Does Not Get a Value. *However, you're about to edit the server behavior in Code view, after which it ceases to be editable through the dialog box. Once you feel at home with editing server behaviors, you can leave Dreamweaver to do all the tedious coding, while you tidy up details, such as adjusting the code for* SET *columns.*

8. Switch to Code view; the section that builds the SQL query looks like this:

```
39  if ((isset($_POST["MM_insert"])) && ($_POST["MM_insert"] == "form1")) {
40    $insertSQL = sprintf("INSERT INTO os_poll (operating_system) VALUES (%s)",
41                   GetSQLValueString($_POST['operating_system[]'], "text"));
42
43    mysql_select_db($database_connAdmin, $connAdmin);
44    $Result1 = mysql_query($insertSQL, $connAdmin) or die(mysql_error());
45  }
```

9. Remove the square brackets after operating_system in $_POST['operating_ system[]'] (line 41 in the preceding screenshot) so that it looks like this:

```
GetSQLValueString($_POST['operating_system'], "text"),
```

This inserts the value of $_POST['operating_system'] into the table as a string, but the values being sent from the checkbox group are an array. So, they need to be reformatted before they can be inserted into the database.

10. To convert the array in $_POST['operating system'] into a comma-separated string, add the following code block highlighted in bold immediately after the code shown on line 39 in the preceding screenshot:

```
if ((isset($_POST["MM_insert"])) && ($_POST["MM_insert"] == "form1")) {
// convert the checkbox group subarray to a string
if (isset($_POST['operating_system'])) {
  $_POST['operating_system'] = implode(',', $_POST['operating_system']);
} else {
  $_POST['operating_system'] = 'none';
}
$insertSQL = sprintf("INSERT INTO os_poll (operating_system) ➥
VALUES (%s)",
```

The block is enclosed in the server behavior's conditional statement that executes the code only if the form has been submitted. Because checkboxes and multiple-choice lists don't appear in the $_POST array if nothing has been selected, the new code first checks whether any values have been selected for operating_system. If they have, they are converted to a comma-separated string with implode(). Otherwise, none is assigned as the value. This is needed to prevent the SQL query from throwing an error.

The first argument to the implode() function is the string you want to act as a separator between array elements. It's vital to use a comma with no space on either side like this:

```
$_POST['operating_system'] = implode(',', $_POST['operating_system']);
```

If you add a space after the comma inside the first argument, only the first value is inserted in the SET column. This is because the space is treated as part of the string. The extra space after the first comma in the following line of code will result in incomplete data being inserted into the SET column:

```
$_POST['operating_system'] = implode(', ', $_POST['operating_system']);
```

11. Save set_insert.php, and load it in a browser. Test the form by selecting at least two checkboxes and clicking Submit.

12. Check the results by clicking the Browse tab in phpMyAdmin. Confirm that you can see the selected values inserted in the table, as shown here:

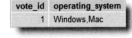

Check your code, if necessary, against set_insert_01.php in examples/ch17.

Retrieving data stored in a SET column

The MySQL documentation (http://dev.mysql.com/doc/refman/5.0/en/set.html) classifies the SET data type as a string, so that's what it expects you to insert, and that's what it returns when you retrieve data with a SELECT query. However, as I explained earlier, the values are stored numerically, rather than as text. This has the following important effects on the data that you get back from a SET column:

- Values are returned as a comma-separated list.
- Trailing spaces are automatically deleted.
- Even if the INSERT query contains duplicate values, each value is stored only once. This means you can't adapt the form in set_insert.php to record how many computers of a different type a person owns.
- Values are returned in the same order as the original table specification. The results from a search of the os_poll table will always be in the order Windows, Mac, Linux. You can't use a SET column to store items in order of preference. It's purely a yes or no choice.

The values stored for each record in a SET column can be accessed in the normal way through a recordset, as the following exercise shows.

Displaying the user's vote

This exercise shows different ways of displaying values retrieved from a SET column. Continue working with set_insert.php and the os_poll table from the previous exercise.

1. With set_insert.php open in the Document window, open the Recordset dialog box in Simple mode, and use the following settings to create a recordset called getVote:

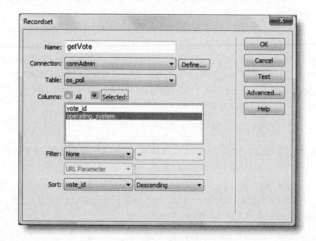

Even though this uses only a SELECT query, I'm using the administrative user account because it makes more sense to use the same connection as the INSERT query on the same page.

Setting Sort to vote_id Descending uses the primary key to sort the recordset in reverse order, so the most recent record will always be the first.

2. Underneath the insert form, add a paragraph with the text You selected:, and use the Bindings panel to insert a dynamic text placeholder for operating_system from the getVote recordset. The bottom of the page should look like this:

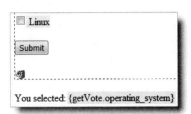

3. Save set_insert.php, and click the Live View button. Click Yes when asked about updating the copy on the testing server. The bottom of the page should look similar to this:

Hang on a moment . . . You can't submit the form in Live view, yet the dynamic text is displaying a result. It is, of course, the result from the previous vote. You want to display it only after the visitor has voted. So, the recordset code needs to go inside the conditional statement that controls the INSERT query, but it must come after the vote has been registered.

4. Open Code view, and locate the code shown in Figure 17-4. Study the code carefully. In Chapter 15, I told you that Dreamweaver always puts the code for recordsets immediately above the DOCTYPE declaration. On this occasion, though, the getVote recordset code is on lines 34–38, more than 20 lines above the DOCTYPE declaration, with the Insert Record server behavior in between.

```
34  mysql_select_db($database_connAdmin, $connAdmin);
35  $query_getVote = "SELECT operating_system FROM os_poll ORDER BY vote_id DESC";
36  $getVote = mysql_query($query_getVote, $connAdmin) or die(mysql_error());
37  $row_getVote = mysql_fetch_assoc($getVote);
38  $totalRows_getVote = mysql_num_rows($getVote);
39
40  $editFormAction = $_SERVER['PHP_SELF'];
41  if (isset($_SERVER['QUERY_STRING'])) {
42    $editFormAction .= "?" . htmlentities($_SERVER['QUERY_STRING']);
43  }
44
45  if ((isset($_POST["MM_insert"])) && ($_POST["MM_insert"] == "form1")) {
46    // convert the checkbox group subarray to a string
47    if (isset($_POST['operating_system'])) {
48      $_POST['operating_system'] = implode(',', $_POST['operating_system']);
49    } else {
50      $_POST['operating_system'] = 'none';
51    }
52    $insertSQL = sprintf("INSERT INTO os_poll (operating_system) VALUES (%s)",
53                         GetSQLValueString($_POST['operating_system'], "text"));
54
55    mysql_select_db($database_connAdmin, $connAdmin);
56    $Result1 = mysql_query($insertSQL, $connAdmin) or die(mysql_error());
57  }
58  ?>
59  <!DOCTYPE html PUBLIC "-//W3C//DTD XHTML 1.0 Transitional//EN"
```

Figure 17-4.
Because the Insert Record server behavior has been edited, the recordset has been inserted above it.

This has happened because you edited the Insert Record behavior in the previous exercise, so Dreamweaver no longer recognizes it. However, it recognizes the GetSQLValueString() function declaration as part of its own code, so it puts the recordset with it. Because you're moving the recordset code anyway, it doesn't really matter where Dreamweaver put it. However, this illustrates the importance of understanding what each block of code does and where it's located. PHP code is processed in the same order as it appears in the script. If you left the code in its current location and surrounded it with a conditional statement to run only after the form has been submitted, it would work, but it would always show the previous result rather than the current one because it's executed before the INSERT query.

5. Cut the getVote recordset code (lines 34–38 in Figure 17-4) to your clipboard, and paste it in front of the closing curly brace shown on line 57 of Figure 17-4. This ensures that the recordset is created only when the form is submitted and that it gets the most recent result.

6. Also, you want to show the result only when the recordset has been created. You can do this by surrounding the paragraph that displays it with a conditional statement that checks whether the recordset has been created like this:

```php
<?php if (isset($getVote)) { ?>
<p>You selected: <?php echo $row_getVote['operating_system']; ?></p>
<?php } ?>
```

The $getVote variable contains the recordset result, so it must exist if the recordset does. (See why it's a good idea to give recordsets meaningful names?)

7. Since the recordset is created only when the form is submitted, you also need a conditional statement around the code that clears the recordset result at the end of the script like this:

```php
</html>
<?php
if (isset($getVote)) {
  mysql_free_result($getVote);
}
?>
```

8. Save set_insert.php, and load it into a browser. When the page first loads, the form looks the same as before, but when you submit the form, it displays your choice immediately below as a comma-separated string, as shown in Figure 17-5.

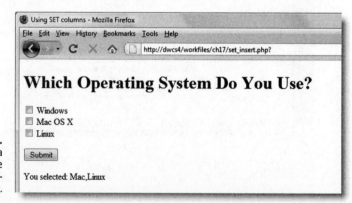

Figure 17-5.
The values stored in a SET column are returned as a comma-separated string.

If you select just one value, there is no comma, but when more than one value is returned, they are separated by commas with no space in between.

9. How you handle the comma-separated string depends on what you want to do with the results of a recordset that contains a SET column. If you simply want to add a space after each comma, you can use the str_replace() function like this:

```php
<?php echo str_replace(',', ', ', $row_getVote['operating_system']); ?>
```

The str_replace() function takes three arguments: the string you want to replace, what you want to replace it with, and the string you want to perform the replacement on. So, the first argument here is a comma on its own, the second argument is a comma followed by a space, and the final argument is the value from the recordset.

10. To format the comma-separated string in more complex ways, pass the value from the recordset to the explode() function, and store it in a variable like this:

```php
$selected = explode(',', $row_getVote['operating_system']);
```

The explode() function converts a string into an array. It normally takes two arguments: a string containing the character(s) that mark(s) the boundary between each array element, and the string you want to split. The boundary characters are discarded, so this converts a comma-separated string into an array, which you can then manipulate however you like. For example, you could display the results as a bulleted list like this:

```php
<p>You selected: <?php $selected = explode(',', ➥
$row_getVote['operating_system']); ?></p>
<ul>
<?php foreach ($selected as $item) {
  echo "<li>$item</li>";
}
?>
</ul>
```

You can check your code against set_insert_02.php in examples/ch17.

The purpose of this exercise is to demonstrate the use of SET columns, not to build a realistic online poll. To prevent multiple submissions by the same person, an online poll also needs a column that records a value that can be used to identify someone who has already voted. One way of doing this is to create a session variable that contains a randomly generated value like this:

```php
session_start();
if (!isset($_SESSION['random_id'])) {
  $_SESSION['random_id'] = md5(uniqid(rand(), true));
}
```

This uses the PHP function uniqid() (http://docs.php.net/manual/en/function.uniqid.php) in combination with md5(), an encryption function, and rand(), which generates a random value, to create a 32-character string. Store the session variable in a hidden form field, and check that it doesn't already exist in the database before inserting it with the poll data.

I'll come back later to showing you how to find records that contain specific values in a SET column.

Getting the information you want from a database

As you have probably realized by now, a recordset is the result of a database search. Controlling the search is a SQL query using the SELECT command. Dreamweaver builds the PHP code that passes the SQL query to the database and processes the result. It can also build the SQL query for very simple searches. For anything more sophisticated, it's up to you to build the query yourself. Over the next few pages, I'll show you how to tackle some common search problems. However, writing SELECT queries is a massive subject, about which whole books have been written (one of my favorite writers on MySQL is Paul DuBois). So, treat the following pages as an introduction to a fascinating and rewarding subject, rather than a definitive guide to search queries.

Books and online forums can provide a lot of help in formulating the appropriate SELECT query to extract the information that you want from a database. But to use that information successfully with Dreamweaver, you need to understand how the Recordset dialog box builds a SELECT statement.

Understanding how Dreamweaver builds a SQL query

The file find_author_01.php in examples/ch17 contains a form with a single text field called first_name and a submit button. Beneath the form is a table with a single row in a repeat region, which displays the results of the search. Load the page into a browser, type William in the text field, and click Search. You should see a list of authors whose first name is William, as shown here:

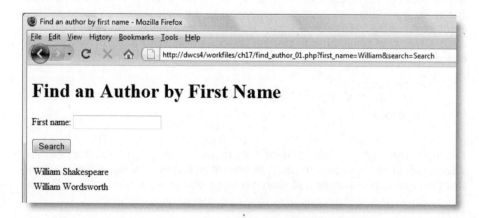

Try some other names, such as John, Dorothy, and Mae, and a list of matching records is displayed. By default, text searches in MySQL are case-insensitive, so it doesn't matter what combination of uppercase and lowercase you use. We'll get to case-sensitive and partial-word searches later, but let's look at the code that Dreamweaver uses to submit the query to the database.

I created the getAuthors recordset in find_author_01.php using the following settings in the Recordset dialog box in Simple mode:

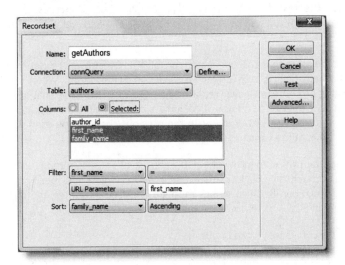

The same query looks like this in Advanced mode:

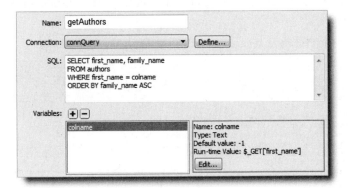

The first thing to note is that Dreamweaver doesn't add the table name in front of each column name when you use the Recordset dialog box in Simple mode. As explained in the previous chapter, adding the table name is necessary only when the same column name is used in more than one table (like author_id in the authors and quotations tables). Simple mode is capable of handling only single tables, so there's never any danger of ambiguity. However, Dreamweaver automatically adds the table names to all columns when you build a query in Advanced mode. It does so as a precautionary measure, even if there's no likelihood of ambiguity.

The other thing to note is that the Filter settings from Simple mode have been converted to this:

```
WHERE first_name = colname
```

Dreamweaver uses colname to represent the unknown value that will be passed to the SQL query through the text field in find_author_01.php. The properties of colname are defined in the Variables area below, with Type set to Text, Default value to -1, and Run-time Value to $_GET['first_name'].

It's important to realize that colname is not part of SQL. Dreamweaver uses the concept of replacement when dealing with unknown values in SQL queries. When you close the Recordset dialog box, Dreamweaver replaces colname with PHP code that inserts the run-time value into the query. The choice of colname is purely arbitrary. It can be anything that doesn't clash with the rest of the query. In the previous chapter, you used var1 and var2 as the names for runtime variables.

The other important thing to know about Dreamweaver's use of runtime variables is that the PHP code automatically encloses the value in quotes unless you specify Type as Integer or Floating point number. Because strings must be enclosed in quotes, the correct way to write this query in SQL is as follows (assuming that you're searching for "William"):

```
SELECT first_name, family_name
FROM authors
WHERE first_name = 'William'
ORDER BY family_name ASC
```

Because Dreamweaver handles the quotes automatically, you need to adapt SQL from other sources accordingly.

Now, look at the PHP code generated by these settings (see Figure 17-6).

```
34  $colname_getAuthors = "-1";
35  if (isset($_GET['first_name'])) {
36    $colname_getAuthors = $_GET['first_name'];
37  }
38  mysql_select_db($database_connQuery, $connQuery);
39  $query_getAuthors = sprintf("SELECT first_name, family_name FROM authors WHERE first_name = %s ORDER BY
    family_name ASC", GetSQLValueString($colname_getAuthors, "text"));
40  $getAuthors = mysql_query($query_getAuthors, $connQuery) or die(mysql_error());
41  $row_getAuthors = mysql_fetch_assoc($getAuthors);
42  $totalRows_getAuthors = mysql_num_rows($getAuthors);
```

Figure 17-6. The code Dreamweaver generates for a recordset that uses a variable passed through a query string

You have seen the recordset code on many occasions, and I described the meaning of the variables in Chapter 15. What I would like you to focus on here is the way Dreamweaver handles colname and uses it to insert the runtime variable into the SQL query. The following sequence of events takes place:

1. The name of the variable defined in the Recordset dialog box (in this case, colname) is combined with the recordset name on line 34 to create a PHP variable ($colname_getAuthors), which is assigned a default value of -1.

2. The conditional statement on lines 35–37 replaces the default value with the submitted value from the form. In this case, it uses $_GET['first_name']. So if a variable called first_name is passed through a query string at the end of the URL, $colname_getAuthors takes its value. Otherwise, $colname_getAuthors remains -1.

3. The code shown on line 39 of Figure 17-6 builds the SQL query using a PHP function called sprintf().

The sprintf() function can be difficult to get your head around, but it takes a minimum of two arguments. The first of these is a string that contains one or more predefined placeholders; the number of remaining arguments matches the number of placeholders in the first argument. When the script runs, sprintf() replaces each placeholder with its corresponding argument.

Why use such a convoluted way of inserting something into the SQL query? It's a shorthand way of passing the runtime variables to another function without the need to assign the result to a variable. Dreamweaver passes all runtime variables to a custom-built function called GetSQLValueString(), which is shown in Figure 15-1. As explained in Chapter 15, this function protects your database from malicious attacks known as **SQL injection**. If Dreamweaver didn't use sprintf(), it would need to store the result of passing each runtime variable to GetSQLValueString() before building the query. It also avoids complex problems with escaping quotes with a lot of variables.

The most commonly used predefined placeholder used with sprintf() is %s, which stands for "string." So, the colname that you saw in the Recordset dialog box becomes %s, and when the script runs, it is replaced by the result of GetSQLValueString($colname_getAuthors, "text").

When there's more than one runtime variable in a SQL query, Dreamweaver replaces each one with %s and passes it to GetSQLValueString() when listing the variable as an argument to sprintf().

Dreamweaver uses sprintf() to build all SQL queries, not just for recordsets. The important things to remember about editing SQL queries in Dreamweaver or adapting queries that you read about elsewhere are as follows:

- The number of arguments following the first one passed to sprintf() must be the same as the number of %s placeholders in the query.
- GetSQLValueString() automatically handles quotes around text values, so you should never add quotes around the %s placeholder in sprintf().

Troubleshooting SQL queries

At the end of line 40 in Figure 17-6 is this rather doom-laden command:

```
or die(mysql_error());
```

This tells the script to stop running if there's a problem with the SQL query and to display the error message returned by MySQL. Figure 17-7 shows what happens if you add single quotes around the %s placeholder in the SQL query in find_author_01.php.

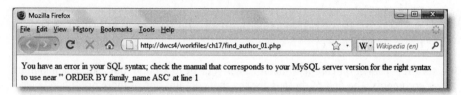

Figure 17-7. MySQL error messages look cryptic but are very useful.

The error is reported as being on line 1, because the message comes from MySQL, not PHP. MySQL sees only the query, so the error is always on line 1. The important information is the reference to the error being "near" a particular part of the query. The error is always immediately preceding the segment quoted in the message, but the only way to diagnose the problem is to study the contents of the query.

Don't waste time trying to analyze the code. As I explained in Chapter 15, the SQL query is stored in a variable called $query_*recordsetName*. Dive into Code view, and use echo to display the query onscreen, as shown in the following illustration (use line breaks to separate the query from the error message):

Add code to display the SQL query

```
39  $query_getAuthors = sprintf("SELECT first_name, family_name FROM authors WHERE first_name = '%s' ORDER BY
    family_name ASC", GetSQLValueString($colname_getAuthors, "text"));
40  echo $query_getAuthors . '<br /><br />';
41  $getAuthors = mysql_query($query_getAuthors, $connQuery) or die(mysql_error());
```

You can then load the page into a browser and see exactly what is being sent to the database. In the case of find_author_01.php, the query is displayed as soon as you load the page (see Figure 17-8). In some cases, you need to pass the necessary values to the query through the form or as part of a query string in the browser address bar. You might see a lot of error messages onscreen, but that's not important. As long as you can see what the SQL query contains, you can get to the root of the problem.

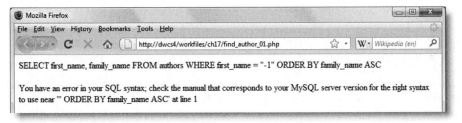

Figure 17-8. Displaying the contents of a SQL query onscreen is the best way to analyze MySQL errors.

At first glance, the output in Figure 17-8 seems OK, but on closer inspection, what looks like a pair of double quotes around -1 is, in fact, four single quotes (if you try this yourself, use the browser's View Source option to see the output in monospaced type). This is what MySQL actually sees:

```
SELECT first_name, family_name
FROM authors
WHERE first_name =''
-1'' ORDER BY family_name ASC
```

The extra pair of quotes around -1 results in the value of first_name being an empty string. This is followed by -1 and another pair of quotes, none of which makes any sense, so MySQL gives up.

Even if you can't spot the problem yourself, you can copy the output and paste it into a question in an online forum. You're much more likely to get a helpful response by showing what's being passed to the database and giving details of the MySQL error message.

You can use this technique with all SQL queries, not just SELECT ones.

Let's take a look at various search operations, beginning with the choice of method for search forms.

Choosing GET or POST for search forms

All the forms you have built so far in this book have used the POST method. This has been the appropriate choice for several reasons. First, the POST method is more secure than GET, because the values are not sent through a query string at the end of the URL. Moreover, the maximum length of 2,083 characters in a URL imposed by Internet Explorer makes the GET method impractical for many database insert forms.

So, if the POST method is more secure, why not use it for everything? The answer is convenience. Passing the search criteria as variables through a query string at the end of the URL makes it easy to save search results as bookmarks in a browser. So, it's usual to use the GET method when creating search forms.

When choosing between POST and GET, use the following as a general guide:

- If sending an email or modifying a database, use POST.
- If searching a database, use GET.

You might think there's a contradiction inherent in this advice. After all, when updating or deleting a record from a database, its primary key is sent through a query string and retrieved from the $_GET array. However, the primary key sent through the query string is used only to search for details of the record. The actual updating or deletion is done by a form that uses the POST method. That's why it's important to build a confirmation page for deleting records. Using GET for any operation that directly modifies database records is an invitation to disaster. That's why I also recommend setting up a user account that has only SELECT privileges to prevent an attacker from modifying your data.

Using numerical comparisons

As you've already seen, a single equal sign in a SQL query looks for an exact match. You can also use comparison operators, such as > (greater than) and < (less than). This would be of more practical value in a price list, where you're looking for something cheaper or more expensive than a particular amount, but you can see it in action using the primary key column of the authors table, which uses numbers.

In find_author_02.php, I changed the text input field in the form to author_id. Then I changed the Filter setting in the Recordset dialog box in Simple mode like this:

This changes the WHERE clause to this:

```
WHERE author_id < colname
```

The Type of colname is changed to Integer, and its Runtime Value is changed to $_GET['author_id']. Because the default is left at -1, nothing is displayed when the page first loads, but if you enter a number and click the Search button, you see a list of all authors with a primary key less than the figure entered.

> For a greater-than comparison, the default needs to be higher than any existing value in the column. If you leave it at -1, all records are displayed when the page first loads.

This is a rather trivial example, but if you go through the various Filter options in Simple mode and examine the SQL in Advanced mode, you'll quickly learn how the operators are used in a SQL query. Dreamweaver uses <> as the "not equal to" operator instead of !=. Either is perfectly acceptable.

At the bottom of the Filter drop-down menu are three options: begins with, ends with, and contains. These perform wildcard searches, where the user enters only part of the search term. In previous versions of Dreamweaver, this type of filter failed when you used any of these options with a numeric column. However, this problem has been fixed in Dreamweaver CS4. If you switch to Advanced mode, you'll see that the Type of colname is changed to Text. Although this might appear to be a bug, it is, in fact, the correct way to perform a wildcard search. The SQL generated by Dreamweaver uses LIKE, which *must* be followed by a string, not a number. I'll come back to wildcards when discussing text searches later in the chapter.

Although the Filter options in Simple mode have their uses, they're not very practical in a real-world situation. Normally, you want a search form to offer the user a variety of options. That's where an understanding of the code generated by Dreamweaver becomes invaluable.

Roll up your sleeves to create something a little more practical.

Performing user-controlled comparisons

This exercise enhances find_author_02.php by adding a drop-down menu that gives the user the option to choose how the comparison should be performed—greater than, less than, equal to, or not equal to. The selection is passed to the SQL query as a form variable. Since Dreamweaver has options only for numbers and text, you need to do some elementary hand-coding.

1. Copy find_author_02.php from examples/ch17, and save it as find_author_03.php in workfiles/ch17.

2. Click inside the Author_id label to the left of the text field, select the <label> tag in the Tag selector at the bottom of the Document window, and press the right arrow key once to position the insertion point correctly between the label and text field.

3. Select List/Menu from the Forms tab of the Insert bar (or use the Form submenu of the Insert menu). In the Input Tag Accessibility Attributes dialog box, enter operator in the ID field, leave Label blank, select No label tag, and click OK.

4. Click the List Values button in the Property inspector, and enter the following operators in both the Item Label and Value fields: =, !=, <, <=, >, and >=. Although you don't normally need to set the Value field if it's the same as Item Label, you need to do it on this occasion, because Dreamweaver replaces the less-than and greater-than operators with HTML entities.

5. Select the equal sign as Initially Selected.

6. Open Split view, and edit the value properties of the <option> tags to change the HTML entities to the less-than and greater-than operators. Leave the HTML entities intact between the opening and closing <option> tags. The page should look like this:

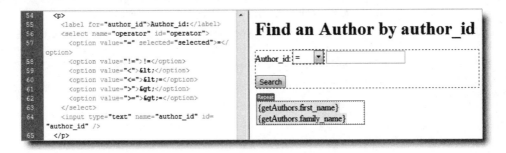

7. In Code view, scroll up to locate the following section of code:

```
33
34   $colname_getAuthors = "-1";
35   if (isset($_GET['author_id'])) {
36       $colname_getAuthors = $_GET['author_id'];
37   }
38   mysql_select_db($database_connQuery, $connQuery);
39   $query_getAuthors = sprintf("SELECT first_name, family_name FROM authors WHERE author_id < %s ORDER BY
     family_name ASC", GetSQLValueString($colname_getAuthors, "int"));
```

8. You need to replace the < in the WHERE clause (shown on line 39 of the preceding screenshot) with a variable and define it in the same way as Dreamweaver has done with colname. Begin by positioning your cursor on the blank line shown on line 33 and inserting the following code:

```
// define the operator variable and give it a default value
$operator = '=';
// define an array of acceptable operators
$permittedOperators = array('=', '!=', '<', '<=', '>', '>=');
// get operator value from form, if submitted
if (isset($_GET['operator']) && in_array($_GET['operator'], ➥
$permittedOperators)) {
  $operator = $_GET['operator'];
}
```

This sets $operator to a default value of an equal sign, defines an array of acceptable operators, and reassigns the value submitted from the form, if it exists and is one of the permitted operators. Using the $permittedOperators array and in_array() like this performs a similar security check to the $expected array that you used with the feedback form in Chapter 11. Any variable that's passed to a SQL query should be scrutinized to prevent SQL injection.

9. Now edit the SQL query (shown on line 39 of the preceding screenshot) like this (new code is highlighted in bold):

```
$query_getAuthors = sprintf("SELECT first_name, family_name ➥
FROM authors WHERE author_id %s %s ORDER BY family_name ASC", ➥
$operator, GetSQLValueString($colname_getAuthors, "int"));
```

As explained earlier in "Understanding how Dreamweaver builds a SQL query," sprintf() uses %s as a placeholder and replaces each one in order by the subsequent arguments passed to the function. So, the form values are both passed to the SQL query in a secure manner; the first %s is replaced by the operator, and the second one is replaced by the value entered in the text field.

10. Save the page, and test it in a browser. Enter 32 in the text field, and click Search. William Shakespeare should be displayed. Change the operator to !=, and perform the same search. All authors except Shakespeare are displayed, and so on.

You can check your code against find_author_03.php in examples/ch17.

The value of the drop-down menu in the preceding exercise always resets to the equal sign. If you want the previous selection to be redisplayed, you need to add conditional statements to each <option> tag. The following code shows the first two tags:

```
<option value="=" <?php if (isset($_GET['operator']) && ➡
$_GET['operator'] == '=' || !isset($_GET['operator'])) {
  echo 'selected="selected"';
} ?>>=</option>
<option value="!=" <?php if (isset($_GET['operator']) && ➡
$_GET['operator'] == '!=') {
  echo 'selected="selected"';
} ?>>!=</option>
```

Searching within a numerical range

There are two ways to specify a range in SQL. One is to use >= (greater than or equal to) for the bottom end of the range and <= (less than or equal to) for the top end. The alternative is BETWEEN . . . AND. Both require two input fields. This means setting two variables, so you're obliged to use the Recordset dialog box in Advanced mode. The files find_author_04.php and find_author_05.php in examples/ch17 have been modified by adding a second text input field and naming the two fields min and max. The recordset settings in find_author_04.php look like this:

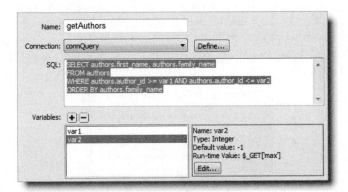

I have used var1 and var2 as the runtime variables and given them both the same settings, as shown in the preceding screenshot (Run-time Value for var1 is $_GET['min']).

The only difference in find_author_05.php is the WHERE clause in the SQL query, which looks like this:

```
WHERE authors.author_id BETWEEN var1 AND var2
```

If you test both pages in a browser, they produce identical results. As long as you enter a number in both fields, you should see a list of authors' names (unless, of course, the minimum is greater than the highest number in the table).

Now try entering a value in just the minimum field. As you might expect, there are no results. This is hardly surprising, because the default value of var2 (which controls the maximum) is set to -1. So, try just the maximum field. Again, no results. This is more puzzling, because the default for the minimum field is also -1, so you would expect to get a list of authors whose primary keys belong in the range from 1 (since primary keys can't be negative) to whatever you entered in the maximum field.

You need to look at the code to understand what's happening.

Experimenting with the default value

This exercise helps explain how the default value of a runtime variable is used in a SQL query. It also shows how to tweak the Dreamweaver code to influence the way default values are used. You can use either find_author_04.php or find_author_05.php, because the PHP code is identical.

1. In the Server Behaviors panel, double-click Recordset (getAuthors) to open the Recordset dialog box. Select var2 in the Variables field, click the Edit button, and change Default value to 10. Since var2 is the runtime variable for max, this resets the default maximum.

2. Save the changes, and load the page into a browser. The names of the first ten authors are displayed after the form.

3. Enter a number between 1 and 9 in the Minimum field, but leave the Maximum field empty. Click Search. It doesn't matter what number you choose; nothing is displayed. So, what's happened to the default you set in step 1?

4. To find out, open Code view, and locate the code that sets the default values. It looks like this:

```
34  $var1_getAuthors = "-1";
35  if (isset($_GET['min'])) {
36    $var1_getAuthors = $_GET['min'];
37  }
38  $var2_getAuthors = "10";
39  if (isset($_GET['max'])) {
40    $var2_getAuthors = $_GET['max'];
41  }
```

The code shown on line 38 sets the default value of $var2_getAuthors to 10. However, the conditional statement on lines 39–41 resets it if the value of $_GET['max'] has been defined. I imagine that many of you will be scratching your head at this point. Surely, if the field is left blank, the value isn't defined? Wrong. It is defined—as an empty string. As a result, if you enter 5 in the Minimum field, the WHERE clause in find_author_04.php is converted to this:

WHERE authors.author_id >= 5 AND authors.author_id <=

Similarly, the WHERE clause in find_author_05.php has no maximum. Without it, the SQL query returns no results. It doesn't trigger any error messages either, because a valid value is passed to the query. The problem is that it's a number you want, not an empty string.

5. To preserve the default number when a blank field is submitted, change the code shown on line 39 like this:

```
if (isset($_GET['max']) && !empty($_GET['max'])) {
```

6. Test the page again. This time, if you leave the Maximum field blank, the script uses 10 as its default value. Of course, you can override this by entering a different number in the field. But if you leave the Minimum field blank, you still get no results. It needs to be changed in the same way if you always want a default value to be used when the form is submitted.

Is this a bug in Dreamweaver? It depends on your point of view. When creating runtime variables in Simple mode, Dreamweaver always uses -1 as its default value. This ensures that a search form displays no results when the page first loads. This is usually what you want, but you should ask, "Why bother to run the SQL query when the page first loads?" It's inefficient to submit a query to the database when no search criteria have been defined.

The more efficient way to prevent the display of recordset results when a search form first loads is to wrap the recordset code in a conditional statement and execute the SQL query only when the search form has been submitted. If you name the submit button search, you can use the following code:

```
if (array_key_exists('search', $_GET)) {
   // recordset code goes here
}
```

This is the same technique as used in Chapter 11 to make sure that the client-side validation of the feedback form is run only after the form has been submitted. Since the recordset isn't created when the page first loads, you need to wrap the table that displays the recordset results in a similar conditional statement. You also need to amend this block of code below the closing </html> tag:

```
<?php
mysql_free_result($recordsetName);
?>
```

Change it like this:

```
<?php
if (isset($recordsetName)) mysql_free_result($recordsetName);
?>
```

A fully commented version of this code is in find_author_06.php in examples/ch17. Only the form is displayed when the page first loads. If nothing is entered in either or both of the text fields when the form is submitted, the default values are used. Otherwise, the search is based on the values entered into each field. This results in a much more efficient way of searching through a numerical range.

Searching for text

Searching for text follows the same basic principles, but there are more options, because you frequently need to base text searches on partial information. For example, you might want to find all authors whose family name begins with "S," or you might want to search for quotations that contain the word "winter." In some cases, you might also want the search to be case-sensitive.

Making a search case-sensitive

As explained earlier, text searches in MySQL are, by default, case-insensitive. To enforce case sensitivity, you simply add the keyword BINARY in front of the runtime variable.

In find_author_01.php (see "Understanding how Dreamweaver builds a SQL query" earlier in the chapter), the SQL query looks like this:

```
SELECT first_name, family_name
FROM authors
WHERE first_name = colname
ORDER BY family_name ASC
```

When the form is submitted, colname is replaced by the value in the first_name field. To make the search case-sensitive, change the WHERE clause like this:

```
WHERE first_name = BINARY colname
```

The SQL query in find_author_07.php performs a case-sensitive search. Enter John in the search field, and you get three results. Enter john, JOHN, or any other combination of uppercase and lowercase letters, and you'll see no results.

Displaying a message when no results are found

It's not very user-friendly to leave users wondering whether a search is still being performed or whether it simply produced no results. The Show Region server behavior, which was introduced in Chapter 14, makes it easy to display a special message if nothing is found, but it's inappropriate to show the message until a search has been executed.

Using the Show Region server behavior

This brief exercise shows you how to add a message to find_author_07.php to tell a user that no results were found. The default code generated by Dreamweaver needs to be edited slightly if you don't want the message to appear when the page first loads.

1. Copy find_author_07.php from examples/ch17, and save it in workfiles/ch17 as find_author_08.php.

2. Click inside the search form, select <form#form1> in the Tag selector at the bottom of the Document window, and press your right arrow key once to place the insertion point outside the closing </form> tag.

3. Press Enter/Return to insert a new paragraph, click the Bold button in the HTML view of the Property inspector, and type No results found.

4. Click the <p> tag in the Tag selector to highlight the paragraph that you have just inserted, and select Show Region ➤ Show If Recordset Is Empty from the Server Behaviors panel menu (the same options are also available on the Data tab of the Insert bar and the Data Objects submenu of the Insert menu).

5. The dialog box that opens has only one option: for you to select the recordset. Since there's only one on this page, it automatically selects the correct one, so just click OK. This surrounds the selected paragraph with a gray border and a Show If tab at the top-left corner, indicating that it's controlled by a conditional statement.

6. Save the page, and load it into a browser. As the following screenshot shows, the No results found message is automatically displayed:

This is because of the way Dreamweaver handles runtime variables (see "Searching within a numerical range" earlier in the chapter). Unless you wrap the recordset code in a conditional statement, as described earlier, the SQL query is submitted to the database when the page first loads. The default value of -1 deliberately prevents any results from being found, so the message is displayed.

There are two ways to get around this. One is to wrap the code in conditional statements as described earlier (the Show Region server behavior code needs to go inside the conditional statement that controls the display of results). The other, simpler solution is to edit the Show Region server behavior code. This time, we'll take the second option.

7. Select Show If Recordset is Empty (getAuthors) in the Server Behaviors panel to select the server behavior code, and switch to Code view. The code should be highlighted like this:

```
61    </form>
62    <?php if ($totalRows_getAuthors == 0) { // Show if recordset empty ?>
63      <p><strong>No results found</strong></p>
64      <?php } // Show if recordset empty ?>
65    <table width="200">
```

17

767

8. You want the code in this conditional statement to be executed only if the form has been submitted, so amend the code shown on line 62 like this:

```
<?php if (array_key_exists('search', $_GET) && $totalRows_getAuthors➥
== 0) { // Show if form submitted and recordset empty ?>
```

Changing the code like this prevents you from editing the Show Record server behavior in the Server Behaviors panel, but it tidies up the display of your search form. When you reload the page into a browser, the message is hidden until you conduct a search that genuinely produces no results.

Check your code, if necessary, against find_author_08.php in examples/ch17.

Searching multiple columns

Frequently, text searches are based on matching multiple criteria or alternatives. SQL uses AND and OR to build such queries. The meaning is self-explanatory. To search for an author by both first name and family name, create a second runtime variable, such as colname2, and change the WHERE clause to this:

```
WHERE first_name = colname AND family_name = colname2
```

To search on the basis of either first name or family name, change the WHERE clause to this:

```
WHERE first_name = colname OR family_name = colname2
```

Examples of this are in find_author_09.php and find_author_10.php, respectively, in examples/ch17. The file find_author_11.php shows an example of passing AND or OR as a runtime variable to the SQL query using the same technique as described earlier in "Performing user-controlled comparisons."

Using wildcard characters in a search

In SQL, the equal sign looks only for an exact match. All the examples so far have used the authors table, where each column normally contains only a single word. A search for "William" produces two results: William Shakespeare and William Wordsworth. However, a search for "Will" produces no results. You might also want to search for all family names beginning with "S" or search the quotations table for all entries that include "winter."

When searching through columns that contain short text entries or numbers, you can use wildcard characters in your search. For longer sections of text, you should consider creating a FULLTEXT index, which I'll describe later in this chapter.

MySQL has two wildcard characters: the underscore (_) matches a single character, and the percentage sign (%) matches any number of characters. A particularly useful feature about % is that it also matches nothing. This means that a search for "Will%" matches both William and Will on its own. Consequently, most wildcard searches use %.

To use a wildcard character in a SQL query in Dreamweaver, add it to the beginning, end, or both ends of the runtime variable. Also, replace the equal sign with the keyword LIKE.

So, to search for authors based on the first part of their name, change the WHERE clause in find_author_09.php like this:

```
WHERE first_name LIKE colname% AND family_name LIKE colname2%
```

You can test this in find_author_12.php. Start by entering the first part of a name in both fields. For example, if you type W in the First name field and S in the Family name field, the result is William Shakespeare. Try it again, just typing W in the First name field. You should see four results.

Pause a moment to think about this. The SQL query uses AND, so shouldn't there be something in both fields? To understand what's happened, repeat the test with find_author_13.php. The SQL query is identical, but the page displays the query along with the results, as shown in Figure 17-9.

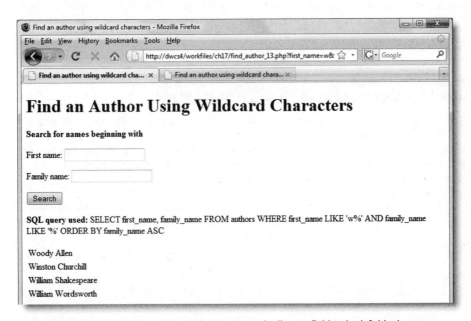

Figure 17-9. Using AND with a wildcard character search allows a field to be left blank.

Although nothing is entered in the second field, the wildcard character % is added to the end of the runtime variable. This results in the second condition matching the family_name column with %—in other words, anything.

Now try it with find_author_14.php, where the only difference is that AND has been changed to OR.

If you enter values in both fields, you'll get the results that you expect. However, if you leave one of the fields blank, you'll always get a full list of all records. This is because the query tells the database to match anything in one of the fields.

This illustrates an important difference between SQL and PHP. When it encounters OR, the PHP engine doesn't bother to evaluate the second half of the condition if the first half is true. In a SQL query, however, both sides are evaluated. So, in the first case, the SQL query finds authors whose first name begins with "W" AND whose family name is anything. In the second case, it finds authors whose first name begins with "W" OR whose family name is anything. Creating searches with wildcards can be confusing, so it's a good idea to display the SQL query onscreen while testing to understand why you get the results you do.

Adding % at the front of a runtime variable lets you search for words that end with a particular letter or series of characters. Putting % at both ends of a runtime variable finds the search expression in the middle of a string; and since % can also match nothing, it means the search term can be anywhere—at the beginning, in the middle, at the end—or it can even be the full string itself.

So, let's bring the quotations table into our search.

Searching for quotations that contain a word or phrase

This exercise adapts the SQL query used in quote_list.php in the previous chapter. Instead of displaying a list of all quotations and their authors, it uses a runtime variable with % at both ends to search for quotations that contain a specific word or phrase. To save you time, I have created find_quote_01.php in examples/ch17 for you to use as a starting point. The finished code is in find_quote_02.php.

1. Copy find_quote_01.php to workfiles/ch17, and open it in the Document window. The page contains a form with a single text input field called searchTerm, a submit button, and code to display the results of the search.

2. Double-click Recordset (getQuote) in the Server Behaviors panel to open the Recordset dialog box. The SQL query looks like this:

```
SELECT authors.first_name, authors.family_name, quotations.quotation
FROM quotations LEFT JOIN authors USING (author_id)
ORDER BY authors.family_name
```

It's based on the query in quote_list.php in Chapter 16 (it doesn't get quote_id and uses a simpler ORDER BY clause). Click the Test button, and you'll see every quotation listed with its author's name.

3. To search for quotations containing a particular word or phrase, you need to add the quotation column to the WHERE clause. In the Database items section at the bottom of the Recordset dialog box, expand Tables, and highlight quotation in the quotations tree menu. Click the WHERE button to add it to the SQL query. The query should now look like this:

```
SELECT authors.first_name, authors.family_name, quotations.quotation
FROM quotations LEFT JOIN authors USING (author_id)
WHERE quotations.quotation
ORDER BY authors.family_name
```

4. Add LIKE %var1% to the end of the WHERE clause, click the plus button alongside Variables, and define the runtime variable var1 using the following settings:

- Name: var1
- Type: Text
- Default value: -1
- Runtime value: $_GET['searchTerm']

The settings in the SQL and Variables fields should now look like this:

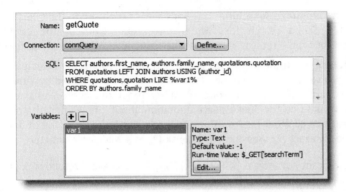

5. Click OK to close the Recordset dialog box, save the page, and load it into a browser. The quotations contain a lot of seasonal references, so enter summer or winter in the Search for field. You should see a list of quotations that contain the search term.

6. Searches with the % wildcard aren't limited to single words. Try entering just x in the Search for field. You should see a quotation from Winston Churchill that contains the word "except."

7. You can also search for a phrase. Enter red, red rose, and click the Search button. You should see the following result:

Note that the phrase must be exact and must not be enclosed in quotes.

Check your code, if necessary, against find_quote_02.php in examples/ch17.

This type of wildcard search works fine for even quite large databases. I use it on a database that contains more than 14,000 records, and the search results are normally displayed in one or two seconds. If you need to do a lot of text searches, you might consider FULLTEXT indexing, which offers a more sophisticated range of text search options.

Using a FULLTEXT index

Creating a FULLTEXT index on the column(s) you want to search does away with the need for wildcard characters. You can use FULLTEXT searches in a number of ways, but the following are the most useful:

- **Natural language searching**: This finds all words passed to the query as a runtime variable. So, a search for "winter discontent" (without the quotes) in the quotations table returns all records that contain either "winter" or "discontent."

- **Searching in Boolean mode**: This lets the user refine the search by preceding required words with a plus sign (+) and words to be excluded by a minus sign (–). So, a search for "+winter +discontent" (without the quotes) in the quotations table would find the Shakespeare quotation about "the winter of our discontent" but exclude all other records. Boolean mode also permits the use of double quotes to specify exact phrases and the asterisk (*) as a wildcard character.

These are significant advantages to FULLTEXT, but it does have the following limitations:

- Only MyISAM tables support FULLTEXT indexes. You cannot add a FULLTEXT index to InnoDB tables. So, you need to choose between maintaining referential integrity with foreign key constraints and FULLTEXT searching.

- Only CHAR, VARCHAR, and TEXT columns can be included in a FULLTEXT index.

- Words that occur in more than 50 percent of the records are ignored.

- Words that contain fewer than four characters are ignored.

- More than 500 common words, such as "the," "also," and "always," are designated as *stopwords* that are always ignored, even if preceded with a plus sign in Boolean mode. See http://dev.mysql.com/doc/refman/5.0/en/fulltext-stopwords.html for the full list of stopwords.

- Only full words are matched unless the wildcard asterisk is used in a Boolean search.

- Boolean mode does not work in MySQL 3.23.

- A FULLTEXT index can be created to search multiple columns simultaneously. However, all columns *must* be in the same table.

The syntax for a FULLTEXT search is different from a wildcard search with LIKE. The WHERE clause for a natural language search looks like this:

```
WHERE MATCH (columnName) AGAINST ('searchTerm')
```

For a Boolean search, it looks like this:

```
WHERE MATCH (columnName) AGAINST ('searchTerm' IN BOOLEAN MODE)
```

You can test FULLTEXT searching with find_quote_03.php and find_quote_04.php in examples/ch17. The SQL query in find_quote_03.php performs a natural language search and looks like this:

```
SELECT authors.first_name, authors.family_name, quotations.quotation
FROM quotations LEFT JOIN authors USING (author_id)
WHERE MATCH (quotations.quotation) AGAINST (var1)
ORDER BY authors.family_name
```

The query in find_quote_04.php searches in Boolean mode and looks like this:

```
SELECT authors.first_name, authors.family_name, quotations.quotation
FROM quotations LEFT JOIN authors USING (author_id)
WHERE MATCH (quotations.quotation) AGAINST (var1 IN BOOLEAN MODE)
ORDER BY authors.family_name
```

Since these are text searches, it goes without saying that the Type of the runtime variable must always be set to Text.

Before you can use the example files, you need to add a FULLTEXT index to the quotations table. If you used the InnoDB version of the quotations table, you also need to remove the foreign key constraints and convert it to MyISAM first. Detailed instructions on how to do this were given in Chapter 16.

Adding a FULLTEXT index

Adding a FULLTEXT index to a MyISAM table in phpMyAdmin is as simple as clicking a button.

1. If it's not already open, launch phpMyAdmin, and display the quotations table structure in the main frame.

2. Click the Fulltext icon in the quotation row, as shown in Figure 17-10.

	Field	Type	Collation	Attributes	Null	Default	Extra	Action						
☐	**quote_id**	int(10)		UNSIGNED	No		auto_increment	▤	✎	✕	▦	U	▨	T
☐	**author_id**	int(10)		UNSIGNED	Yes	*NULL*		▤	✎	✕	▦	U	▨	T
☐	**quotation**	varchar(255)	latin1_swedish_ci		No			▤	✎	✕	▦	U	▨	T
↑	Check All / Uncheck All		With selected:	▤		✎	✕	▦	U	▨	T			

Figure 17-10. You can apply a FULLTEXT index easily in phpMyAdmin.

As you can see from Figure 17-10, the Fulltext icon is grayed out for quote_id and author_id, because they're not capable of taking a FULLTEXT index. If the icon is also grayed out for quotation, it probably means that the table is still using the InnoDB storage engine. You must convert the table to MyISAM first.

That's all there is to adding a FULLTEXT index.

A FULLTEXT index is best suited to very large text databases. When building the database, it's recommended that you add the index *after* the data has been imported.

Working with multiple-column indexes

A multiple-column FULLTEXT index allows you to search several columns simultaneously. To create a multiple-column index in phpMyAdmin, select the checkbox alongside each column name in the table structure grid, and click the Fulltext icon at the bottom of the grid.

To create a SQL query for a multiple-column FULLTEXT index, list the column names separated by commas in the parentheses after MATCH like this:

```
WHERE MATCH (column1, column2, column3) AGAINST ('searchTerm')
```

The index must include all columns listed. You cannot create a FULLTEXT index for each column and list them in a MATCH definition. You need to create a separate index for each combination of columns that you want to use in searches.

See http://dev.mysql.com/doc/refman/5.0/en/fulltext-search.html to learn more about FULLTEXT searches.

Searching for values stored in a SET column

You can search for values in a SET column in two ways: you can use a wildcard character search or use the MySQL function, FIND_IN_SET().

The FIND_IN_SET() function takes two arguments: a string containing the value you're searching for and the SET you want to search. Use the following query to find all records containing "Windows" in the os_poll table used at the beginning of this chapter:

```
SELECT os_poll.operating_system
FROM os_poll
WHERE FIND_IN_SET('Windows', os_poll.operating_system)
```

The difference between using FIND_IN_SET() and a wildcard search is that the former finds only an exact match. Using "Win%" in a wildcard search finds everything beginning with "Win." Wildcards are not accepted in FIND_IN_SET().

Counting records

In Chapter 14, I warned you to resist the temptation to renumber primary keys to keep track of how many records you have in a table. To count the number of records, just use this simple query:

```
SELECT COUNT(*) FROM tableName
```

There must be no gap between COUNT and the opening parenthesis.

You can also combine this with a WHERE clause like this:

```
SELECT COUNT(*) FROM tableName WHERE price > 10
SELECT COUNT(*) FROM tableName WHERE first_name = 'John'
```

With SELECT COUNT(*), it's a good idea to use an alias (see Chapter 16) like this:

```
SELECT COUNT(*) AS num_authors FROM authors
```

You can then access the result as num_authors from the Bindings panel. If you don't use an alias, Dreamweaver displays COUNT(*) in the Bindings panel, but when you insert the value in Design view, you see a gold PHP shield instead of a dynamic text object. It works, but the ability to see dynamic text objects makes it easier to understand what's in your page.

The code for this example is in Recordset (countAuthors) in count.php in examples/ch17. There are gaps in the author_id sequence, so the result is 39.

Counting records in a SET column

To count the number of times a value is recorded in a SET column, you can use COUNT(*) with a WHERE clause and FIND_IN_SET() like this:

```
SELECT COUNT(*) AS windows
FROM os_poll
WHERE FIND_IN_SET('Windows', operating_system)
```

However, the problem with this is that you need to create a separate recordset for each value. The way to count all values with a single query involves using the MySQL IF() function. The function works in a similar way to the PHP conditional (ternary) operator. It takes three arguments: the condition you want to test, the value to assign if the test equates to true, and the value to assign if the test equates to false. Unlike the PHP operator, the arguments are separated by commas, so the basic syntax looks like this:

```
IF(condition, true, false)
```

The expression to check whether a particular record contains "Windows" in a SET column looks like this:

```
IF(FIND_IN_SET('Windows', operating_system), 1, NULL)
```

If the record contains "Windows," the IF() function returns 1, which can be interpreted as true. If it doesn't contain "Windows," the value returned is NULL.

So, to get the results of the online poll in os_poll from the beginning of this chapter, you need to build a SQL query that looks like this:

```
SELECT COUNT(IF(FIND_IN_SET('Windows', operating_system), 1, NULL)) ➥
AS windows,
COUNT(IF(FIND_IN_SET('Mac', operating_system), 1, NULL)) AS mac,
COUNT(IF(FIND_IN_SET('Linux', operating_system), 1, NULL)) AS linux
FROM os_poll
```

It looks complicated, but once you break it down into individual sections, it's quite straightforward. You can see the code in count_set.php in examples/ch17.

Eliminating duplicates from a recordset

SQL uses the keyword DISTINCT to eliminate duplicates from a SELECT query. You simply insert DISTINCT immediately after SELECT. The authors table has three Johns and two Williams. The following query results in John and William being listed only once:

```
SELECT DISTINCT first_name FROM authors
```

You can combine this with the COUNT() function to find out the number of distinct records. The query looks like this:

```
SELECT COUNT(DISTINCT first_name) AS num_names FROM authors
```

The code for this example is in Recordset (countUnique) in count.php in examples/ch17. The result for Recordset (countAuthors) is 39 and for Recordset (countUnique) is 33.

Hang on a moment . . . If you eliminate the two duplicate Johns and one duplicate William, the result should be 36. The discrepancy comes from the fact that the first_name column permits NULL values. Three records are NULL. COUNT(DISTINCT) ignores NULL values, making 33 the correct result.

Building complex searches

Often, I get asked how to build more complex searches, for example with a form that has four input fields, all of which are optional. The answer lies in building the SQL query through PHP conditional logic. You begin by creating a recordset without WHERE or ORDER BY clauses and then add the conditions, building up the query piece by piece. The first part can be created in the Recordset dialog box, but the rest needs to be constructed manually.

The file, find_quote_05.php in examples/ch17, has three text input fields: first_name, family_name, and quotation, all of which are optional. The first two fields are designed to search for an exact match, but the final field uses a wildcard match. The following code shows how the query has been built using conditional statements:

```php
// default value for runtime variable
$var1_getQuote = "-1";
if (isset($_GET['quotation'])) {
  $var1_getQuote = $_GET['quotation'];
}
// select database
mysql_select_db($database_connQuery, $connQuery);
// This is the basic query without WHERE or ORDER BY
$query_getQuote = sprintf("SELECT quotations.quotation, ➡
authors.first_name, authors.family_name FROM quotations ➡
LEFT JOIN authors USING (author_id)");
// Set a variable for the WHERE clause
$where = false;
```

```php
// If the first field contains a value, add a WHERE clause
if (isset($_GET['first_name']) && !empty($_GET['first_name'])) {
  $query_getQuote .= sprintf(" WHERE authors.first_name = %s", ➥
GetSQLValueString($_GET['first_name'], "text"));
  // A WHERE clause exists, so set the variable to true
  $where = true;
}
// If the second field contains a value, add it to the query
if (isset($_GET['family_name']) && !empty($_GET['family_name'])) {
  // Add WHERE or AND depending on value of $where
  if ($where) {
    $query_getQuote .= ' AND ';
  } else {
    $query_getQuote .= ' WHERE ';
    $where = true;
  }
  $query_getQuote .= sprintf(" authors.family_name = %s", ➥
GetSQLValueString($_GET['family_name'], "text"));
}
// If the third field contains a value, add it to the query
if (isset($_GET['quotation']) && !empty($_GET['quotation'])) {
  if ($where) {
    $query_getQuote .= ' AND ';
  } else {
    $query_getQuote .= ' WHERE ';
    $where = true;
  }
  $query_getQuote .= sprintf(" quotations.quotation LIKE %s", ➥
GetSQLValueString("%" . $var1_getQuote . "%", "text"));
}
// Finally, add the ORDER BY clause
$query_getQuote .= " ORDER BY authors.family_name";
$getQuote = mysql_query($query_getQuote, $connQuery) or ➥
die(mysql_error());
```

It looks like a lot of code, but the structure is very simple. It begins with the basic query and then uses a series of conditional statements and the combined concatenation operator (.=) to add the WHERE clause. Because all fields are optional, you need a Boolean variable to track whether the WHERE keyword has already been added. If $where is false, you add WHERE to the existing query and set $where to true, so any further additions will use AND instead. Finally, you add the ORDER BY clause.

Each part of the WHERE clause uses sprintf() and GetSQLValueString() to prepare the $_GET variables to be inserted safely into the query. Because GetSQLValueString() is a Dreamweaver function, and not part of core PHP, you must remember to include its definition in your script. The easiest way to do this is to build the first part of the query using the Recordset dialog box, which inserts it automatically into the page. Alternatively, just save a copy of the function in your Snippets panel (see "Saving frequently used code as a snippet" in Chapter 11). Remember to use %s as the placeholder for each variable in the first argument passed to sprintf(). Study the code for the third field carefully to see how to add the wildcard characters for a search based on partial text input.

Enhancing the display of search results

Let's turn now to a couple of techniques that can improve the look and usability of search results: displaying the number of results and, if there are a lot of them, where you are in the list; and giving table rows alternating colors to make the results easier to read.

Displaying the number of search results

The big search engines, such as Google or Yahoo!, always tell you how many records matched your criteria. You could use COUNT() to do the same, but Dreamweaver's Recordset Navigation Status data object makes it child's play.

Using the Recordset Navigation Status data object

You can do this with any page that contains a recordset, but I'll use quote_list.php from the previous chapter because it contains 50 results displayed over several pages. You can use your own file from workfiles/ch16 or copy quote_list_start.php from examples/ch17.

1. Open the page in the Document window, position the insertion point at the end of the page heading, and press Enter/Return to insert a new paragraph above the table that displays the recordset.

2. Select Recordset Navigation Status on the Data tab of the Insert bar, as shown in Figure 17-11. Alternatively, select Insert ➤ Data Objects ➤ Display Record Count ➤ Recordset Navigation Status.

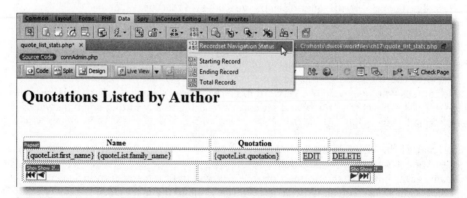

Figure 17-11. Inserting a Recordset Navigation Status data object is done in a couple of clicks.

3. The dialog box has only one option: to choose the recordset you want to use. There's only one on this page, so just click OK. Dreamweaver inserts a mixture of static and dynamic text to display the numbers of the first and last records currently being displayed, plus the total number of records in the recordset.

4. Save the page, and test it in a browser. As you move back and forth through the recordset, the numbers of the currently displayed records change dynamically, as shown in Figure 17-12.

17

Quotations Listed by Author

Records 31 to 45 of 50

Name	Quotation		
Dorothy Parker	There's a hell of a distance between wise-cracking and wit. Wit has truth in it; wise-cracking is simply callisthenics with words.	EDIT	DELETE
JB Priestley	The first fall of snow is not only an event, but it is a magical event. You go to bed in one kind of world and wake up to find yourself in another quite different...	EDIT	DELETE

Figure 17-12. Displaying the current position within a long list of database results makes your site more user-friendly.

Check your code, if necessary, against quote_list_stats.php in examples/ch17.

You can edit the static text surrounding the dynamic text object to customize the display. As you can see in Figure 17-11, the starting record, ending record, and total records numbers can be inserted independently. These independent options can also be accessed from the Display Record Count submenu of the Server Behaviors panel.

Creating striped table rows

Viewing a long list of similar items on a computer screen can be tiring on the eyes, so it's often useful to give alternate rows a background color. This is very easy with a little bit of simple math and PHP. If you divide any number by 2, the remainder is always 1 or 0. Since PHP treats 1 as true and 0 as false (see "The truth according to PHP" in Chapter 10), all you need is a counter; increment it by 1 each time a new table row is added, and use the modulo operator (%) to divide it by 2. The modulo operator returns the remainder of a division, so this produces 1 (true) or 0 (false) every alternate row, which you can use to control the CSS class for a different background color.

Using modulo to create stripes in alternate rows

This exercise uses the same page as in the preceding exercise. It involves locating the code for the repeat region and adding two short blocks of PHP to add the counter and insert the class in every alternate row. You also need to define the class that controls the background color.

1. In the Server Behaviors panel, select Repeat Region (quoteList). This highlights the repeat region, making it easy to find in Code view. The first section looks like this:

```
106        <th scope="col"> </th>
107        </tr>
108 ⊟    <?php do { ?>
109        <tr>
110          <td><?php echo $row_quoteList['first_name']; ?> <?php echo $row_quoteList['family_name']; ?></td>
```

The code shown on line 108 is the start of a do . . . while loop that iterates through the quoteList recordset to display the list of quotations (see Chapter 10 for details of loops).

2. Amend the code like this (new code is shown in bold):

```php
</tr>
<?php $counter = 0; // initialize counter outside loop ?>
<?php do { ?>
  <tr <?php if ($counter++ % 2) {echo 'class="hilite"';} ?>>
    <td><?php echo $row_quoteList['first_name']; ?>
```

The first new block of code initializes the counter outside the loop, while the second increments the counter by 1 inside the loop and uses modulo to create a Boolean (true/false) test to insert the hilite class in alternate rows. I have used separate blocks to avoid breaking Dreamweaver's Repeat Region server behavior code.

The increment operator (++) performs the current calculation and then adds 1 to the variable. So, the first time through the loop $counter is 0. This leaves a remainder of 0 (false), so the hilite class isn't inserted into the <tr> tag. The next time, the calculation produces a remainder of 1 (true), and so on, until the loop comes to an end.

3. Define the hilite class with the background color of your choice. Save the page, and view it in a browser. Voilà, stripes (see Figure 17-13). You can check your code against quote_list_stripes.php in examples/ch17.

Alfred, Lord Tennyson	In the spring a young man's fancy lightly turns to thoughts of love	EDIT	DELETE
Mark Twain	Familiarity breeds contempt — and children.	EDIT	DELETE
Mark Twain	Good breeding consists in concealing how much we think of ourselves and how little we think of the other person.	EDIT	DELETE
Mark Twain	Man is the only animal that blushes. Or needs to.	EDIT	DELETE
François Villon	Mais où sont les neiges d'antan? (But where are the snows of yesteryear?)	EDIT	DELETE

Figure 17-13. Alternately colored rows improve the readability of search results.

Some developers use slightly more complex code to insert a different class in odd-numbered rows, too. This isn't necessary. By utilizing the cascade in your CSS, you can set a default background color for the table and override it with the hilite class like this:

```css
#striped tr, #striped td {background-color: #EEE;}
#striped tr.hilite, #striped tr.hilite td {background-color: #E8F2F8;}
```

These rules will produce alternate pale gray and pale blue stripes in a table with an ID called striped. If you want to use the same effect in more than one table, change striped from an ID to a class.

To get rid of the vertical gaps between cells, set cellpadding to 0, or use border-collapse: collapse in a style rule that applies to the table.

Displaying line breaks in text

HTML ignores whitespace in code, collapsing multiple spaces and newline characters to a single space. As a result, text retrieved from a database is displayed onscreen as a continuous solid block, even if it contains newline characters. To get around this problem, PHP has a handy function called nl2br(), which converts newline characters to HTML <br /> tags.

To display line breaks in text retrieved from a recordset, double-click the dynamic text object in the Server Behaviors panel—it's listed as Dynamic Text (*recordsetName.fieldName*)—to open the Dynamic Text dialog box, and select Convert – New Lines to BRs from the Format menu. This wraps the dynamic text object in nl2br(). Alternatively, add the function manually in Code view like this:

```php
<?php echo nl2br($row_recordsetName['fieldName']); ?>
```

Reusing a recordset

It's sometimes useful to use the same recordset more than once on a page, but you might get a bit of a shock if you try to do so. A practical example will help explain the problem—and the solution.

Rewinding a recordset for reuse

The following exercise shows what happens when you attempt to reuse a recordset after displaying its contents in a repeat region. To gain access to the data, you need to reset the MySQL result resource. If you just want to look at the finished code, it's in rewind_04.php in examples/ch17.

1. Copy rewind_01.php from examples/ch17 to workfiles/ch17, and open it in the Document window. The page has been laid out like this:

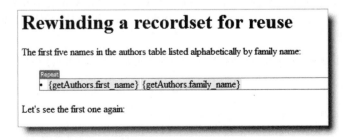

> # Rewinding a recordset for reuse
>
> The first five names in the authors table listed alphabetically by family name:
>
> Repeat
> • {getAuthors.first_name} {getAuthors.family_name}
>
> Let's see the first one again:

The getAuthors recordset retrieves the first five authors alphabetically by family name and displays them in a repeat region as an unordered list.

2. Test the page by clicking the Live View button in the Document toolbar or by loading the page into a browser. You should see the first five names displayed in the unordered list. Nothing will be displayed after the paragraph that reads "Let's display the first one again:" because there's no dynamic text object there yet.

3. Open the Bindings panel, and insert dynamic text objects for first_name and family_name at the bottom of the page, as shown here:

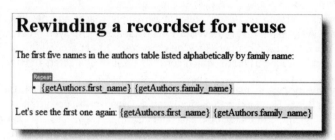

Rewinding a recordset for reuse

The first five names in the authors table listed alphabetically by family name:

Repeat
- {getAuthors.first_name} {getAuthors.family_name}

Let's see the first one again: {getAuthors.first_name} {getAuthors.family_name}

4. Test the page again. There should be no difference from what you saw in step 2. Check your code against rewind_02.php in examples/ch17, if you need to make sure.

So, why do the dynamic text objects no longer work? The answer, as always, lies in the code. A repeat region is simply a PHP do . . . while loop. In Code view, the repeat region that creates the unordered list to display the recordset looks like this:

```
51   <?php do { ?>
52     <li><?php echo $row_getAuthors['first_name']; ?> <?php echo $row_getAuthors['family_name']; ?></li>
53     <?php } while ($row_getAuthors = mysql_fetch_assoc($getAuthors)); ?>
```

In pseudo-code, the PHP code is doing this:

```
do {
    display the first_name and family_name fields in an <li> element
} while (records are still left in the recordset)
```

As the loop progresses, the recordset (or to be more precise, the MySQL result resource) keeps track of its current position by moving an internal pointer. With each iteration, the pointer moves to the next record, and when it gets to the last record, the do . . . while loop comes to a halt. That's why you can't display anything else from the recordset. You have reached the end of the line. But a recordset is just like a fishing line. You can rewind it and use it again.

To rewind a MySQL result resource, you use the mysql_data_seek() function like this:

```
mysql_data_seek(resultResource, 0);
```

This resets the pointer and moves it back to the first record.

In Dreamweaver, the MySQL result resource is stored in a variable that has the same name as your recordset. To reuse a recordset, you also need to prime the variable that holds the current record. The name of this variable is made up of $row_ followed by the recordset name. You prime the variable with the first record like this:

```
$row_recordsetName = mysql_fetch_assoc($recordsetName);
```

Unfortunately, Dreamweaver doesn't let you apply a repeat region to the same record more than once, so you need to code it manually. Let's fix the code in our example page.

17

5. Insert the code highlighted in bold after the do . . . while loop:

```
<?php } while ($row_getAuthors = mysql_fetch_assoc($getAuthors)); ?>
</ul>
<?php mysql_data_seek($getAuthors, 0);
$row_getAuthors = mysql_fetch_assoc($getAuthors); ?>
<p>Let's see the first one again . . .
```

The name of the recordset is getAuthors, so the variables for the recordset and the current record become $getAuthors and $row_getAuthors, respectively.

6. Test the page again. This time, the name of the first author should be displayed again at the bottom of the page (you can check your code against rewind_03.php).

7. You rarely want to use a recordset in exactly the same way, so let's use a table this time and see how to insert the repeat region code manually.

In Design view, position your cursor at the end of the paragraph that displays the name of the first author again. Insert a table with two columns and two rows, and put some column headings in the first row and dynamic text objects for first_name and family_name in the second row, so the page now looks like this:

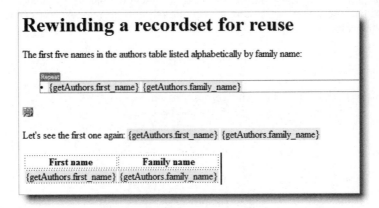

8. Click inside the second table row, and select the entire row by clicking the <tr> tag in the Tag selector at the bottom of the Document window. Although you can't use the Repeat Region server behavior again, this highlights the section of code that you want to repeat. This makes it easier to see where to insert the repeat region code.

9. Switch to Code view, copy the highlighted sections of code from the original repeat region, and paste them into the positions indicated in Figure 17-14.

```
51    <?php do { ?>
          <li><?php echo $row_getAuthors['first_name']; ?> <?php echo $row_getAuthors['family_name']; ?></li>
53        <?php } while ($row_getAuthors = mysql_fetch_assoc($getAuthors)); ?>
54    </ul>
55    <?php mysql_data_seek($getAuthors, 0);
56    $row_getAuthors = mysql_fetch_assoc($getAuthors); ?>
57    <p>Let's see the first one again: <?php echo $row_getAuthors['first_name']; ?> <?php echo $row_getAuthors[
      'family_name']; ?></p>
58    <table width="200">
59      <tr>
60        <th scope="col">First name</th>
61        <th scope="col">Family name</th>
62      </tr>
63      <tr>
64        <td><?php echo $row_getAuthors['first_name']; ?></td>
65        <td><?php echo $row_getAuthors['family_name']; ?></td>
66      </tr>
67    </table>
```

Figure 17-14. Creating a repeat region manually involves copying two short PHP code blocks.

10. Save the page, and test it again. The table should now display the names of the first five authors. Check your code, if necessary, against `rewind_04.php` in `examples/ch17`.

Understanding how a repeat region works

Note that the first name (Woody Allen) is displayed three times: in the original repeat region, in the paragraph after the rewind code, and in the manually coded repeat region. This is because the do . . . while loop doesn't move to the next row of the recordset until the end of the loop.

The code that controls the repeat region is highlighted on lines 51 and 53 of Figure 17-14. In effect, what it does is this:

```
<?php do { // start the repeat region ?>
  Display the contents of the current record
<?php } while (retrieve and store the next record); ?>
```

The code inside the parentheses following while looks like this:

```
$row_getAuthors = mysql_fetch_assoc($getAuthors)
```

It's exactly the same as the code on line 54 of Figure 17-6, which is used to prime the variable that holds the current record. The mysql_fetch_assoc() function retrieves the next available record from a MySQL query result as an associative array (see Chapter 10 for an explanation of associative arrays) and moves the internal pointer to the next record. The array is stored in $row_getAuthors. The name of each column is used as the array key, so $row_getAuthors['first_name'] contains the first_name field of the current record and $row_getAuthors['family_name'] contains the family_name field. You can use these values as often as you like until the next iteration of the loop, when the next record replaces all the values in the array.

Many books and online tutorials use a for or a while loop and place this code at the beginning of the loop. Dreamweaver takes a slightly different approach by retrieving the first record outside the loop and getting each subsequent record at the end of the loop. Either approach is perfectly acceptable. The only reason you need to be aware of this is in case you want to incorporate code from another source. Mixing two styles of coding without understanding how they work might result in records being skipped as the conflicting styles iterate through a set of database results.

Formatting dates and time

Let's turn now to the thorny subject of dates. The calendars of most countries now agree on the current year, month, and date (at least for international purposes—some countries have different calendars for domestic use). What they don't agree on is the order of the component parts. In the United States, it's month, date, year. In Europe, it's date, month, year. And in China and Japan, it's year, month, date.

To avoid this confusion, MySQL stores dates and time in the ISO-approved order of largest unit (year) first, followed by the next largest (month), and so on, down to the smallest (second). In all versions of MySQL, dates are stored in the format YYYY-MM-DD, and times as HH:MM:SS. This inevitably leads to the question, "But how can I store dates in the American (or European) style?" The simple answer is, "You can't. Or as Star Trek fans might put it: resistance is futile."

PHP, on the other hand, takes a completely different approach. It calculates dates as the number of seconds elapsed since 00:00 UTC (Coordinated Universal Time, previously known as GMT or Greenwich mean time) on January 1, 1970—a point in time commonly referred to as the **Unix epoch** (http://en.wikipedia.org/wiki/Unix_epoch) and used as the basis for date and time calculations in many computing languages.

As a result, you need to deal with at least three systems for handling dates: the human system, MySQL, and PHP. The remaining sections of this chapter offer advice on how to navigate through this labyrinth.

Storing the current date and time in MySQL

As I explained in Chapter 14, MySQL has several column types that store dates and times, the most important of which are DATE, DATETIME, and TIMESTAMP. As the name suggests, DATE stores only the year, month, and date; the other two store both the date and the time. Since it's easy to extract just the date part, this might narrow down your choices to just DATETIME and TIMESTAMP. In MySQL 4.1 and above, both store the date and time in the same format. For example, 10:08 a.m. on September 2, 2008, is stored like this:

```
2008-09-02 10:08:00
```

Versions prior to MySQL 4.1 use the same format for a DATETIME column but store the same date and time in a TIMESTAMP column without any punctuation—in other words, like this:

20080902100800

Although this is less human-readable than the current format, it makes no difference, because the functions used for formatting dates and times work identically with either format.

So, what's the difference between DATETIME and TIMESTAMP? It can be summarized as follows:

- DATETIME: This stores any combination of date and time between New Year's Day in the year 1000 to New Year's Eve in the year 9999. The date must be inserted explicitly. If no time is specified, MySQL automatically sets the time element to 00:00:00. If an invalid date is specified, MySQL silently changes it to 0000-00-00 00:00:00.
- TIMESTAMP: The main purpose of this column type is to store the current date and time automatically. However, only one TIMESTAMP column in a table can have this automatic behavior. By default, the first TIMESTAMP column in a table records the current date and time when a record is inserted and updates the date and time whenever the value of at least one other column is changed.

To simplify it even further: use DATETIME when you want to record a specific date, and use TIMESTAMP when you want to record the current date and time.

The problem with simple rules is that life is rarely simple. Sometimes, you might want to store specific dates but have the ability to use the current date and time. The answer is to use the MySQL function NOW(). Unfortunately, Dreamweaver doesn't have the ability to incorporate MySQL functions as values for Insert Record and Update Record server behaviors. You need to adjust the code manually.

Another scenario is where you want to keep track of when a record is updated without losing the time of its original creation. In this case, the answer is to use two TIMESTAMP columns. Since only one TIMESTAMP column can have automatic properties, use the first one to keep track of when the record is updated, and prime the second column with NOW(). If nothing is entered in either column when a record is updated, the first TIMESTAMP column automatically updates to the new date and time, and the second one retains the time of original creation.

> *Since the second TIMESTAMP column is being used to store a static date and time, you might wonder why not use a DATETIME column instead. It's simply a question of efficiency. A TIMESTAMP column requires only half the storage space of a DATETIME one.*

Both scenarios involve using NOW() to insert the value in a MySQL column, so let's see how it's done.

Using NOW() with the Insert Record server behavior

The following exercise shows you how to adapt the code generated by a Dreamweaver Insert Record server behavior to pass a MySQL function, such as NOW(), as the value to be inserted in a column. It takes advantage of an undocumented aspect of Dreamweaver's GetSQLValueString() function.

1. Open phpMyAdmin, and select the dwcs4 database.

2. Create a new table called date_test with five columns (fields). Use the settings in Table 17-1 to define the table.

Table 17-1. Settings for the date_test table

Field	Type	Length/Values	Attributes	Index	A_I
pk	INT		UNSIGNED	PRIMARY	Yes
updated	TIMESTAMP				
created	TIMESTAMP				
fixed_date	DATETIME				
message	VARCHAR	100			

When you save the table definition, the structure should look like this in phpMyAdmin:

Field	Type	Collation	Attributes	Null	Default	Extra
pk	int(10)		UNSIGNED	No		auto_increment
updated	timestamp		on update CURRENT_TIMESTAMP	No	CURRENT_TIMESTAMP	
created	timestamp			No	0000-00-00 00:00:00	
fixed_date	datetime			No		
message	varchar(100)	latin1_swedish_ci		No		

Note that MySQL 5.0 and higher displays the automatic properties of the updated column, because it's the first TIMESTAMP column in the table. The same automatic properties apply even if you're using an older version of MySQL, but they're not displayed in phpMyAdmin.

3. Copy current_date_start.php from examples/ch17 to workfiles/ch17, and save it as current_date.php. The page contains a form with two text fields, one for a message and the other to enter a date, as shown in the following screenshot:

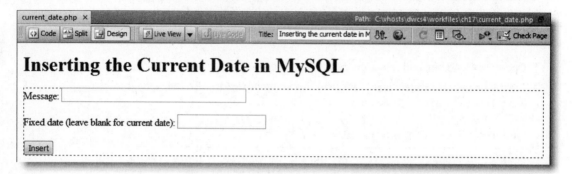

4. Click anywhere inside the form, and insert a hidden field. In the Property inspector, name the hidden field created, and give it the value NOW(), as shown here:

5. Apply an Insert Record server behavior. When you select the date_test table, the settings should look like this:

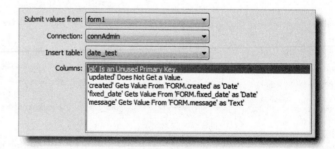

Let's examine these values. Unused Primary Key is fine, because the pk column was set to increment automatically. Does Not Get a Value is also fine for the updated column, because the first TIMESTAMP column is initialized automatically with the current date and time.

The created and fixed_date columns are listed as getting dates. This looks quite promising, but don't be lulled into a false sense of security. Dreamweaver handles a date in the same way as text, surrounding it with quotes, but NOW() is a function and must not be enclosed in quotes. So, these two columns will need to be fixed manually once the server behavior has been applied.

Finally, the message column looks OK, because it's getting its value from the form as text.

6. Click OK to apply the Insert Record server behavior, and then switch to Code view to locate the code generated by Dreamweaver. The section that builds the INSERT query is shown in Figure 17-15.

```
39   if ((isset($_POST["MM_insert"])) && ($_POST["MM_insert"] == "form1")) {
40     $insertSQL = sprintf("INSERT INTO date_test (created, fixed_date, message) VALUES (%s, %s, %s)",
41                          GetSQLValueString($_POST['created'], "date"),
42                          GetSQLValueString($_POST['fixed_date'], "date"),
43                          GetSQLValueString($_POST['message'], "text"));
```

Figure 17-15. You need to edit the Insert Record server behavior code to use NOW() as the value for a date column.

7. The created column gets its value from the hidden field that you created in step 4. However, passing that value to the GetSQLValueString() function as a date data type results in MySQL attempting to insert NOW() as a string. This is invalid for a date column, so you end up with 0000-00-00 00:00:00 instead of the current date and time.

Fortunately, the GetSQLValueString() function accepts two optional arguments for you to incorporate user-defined values in a SQL query. Amend the code shown on line 41 of Figure 17-15 like this:

GetSQLValueString($_POST['created'], **"defined"**, **'NOW()'**),

This tells GetSQLValueString() to incorporate NOW() into the query without any quotes, so it is used correctly as a function. Don't be confused by the quotes around NOW() when you pass it as an argument to GetSQLValueString(). It's what happens inside the function that matters. GetSQLValueString() prepares values for incorporation into a SQL query by removing magic quotes, escaping characters that cause problems with database queries, and adding quotes where required. Using "defined" as the second argument lets you pass a MySQL function safely as the third argument.

8. The code created by Dreamweaver for the fixed_date column is OK as long as the user inserts a date. However, the form in current_date.php instructs the user to leave the field blank to insert the current date. This suggests that you need a conditional statement. Indeed, you do, but that's taken care of inside GetSQLValueString().

As I said earlier, the function accepts two optional arguments. The first optional argument sets the value if the submitted variable contains a value. The second optional argument is used if the submitted variable is empty. So, this is how you edit the code shown on line 42 of Figure 17-15:

GetSQLValueString($_POST['fixed_date'], **"defined"**, ➡
  GetSQLValueString($_POST['fixed_date'], **"date")**, **'NOW()'**),

At first glance, this looks bizarre, but let's analyze what's happening here. The first argument to GetSQLValueString() is $_POST['fixed_date']. This is the value submitted from the form field. The second argument is "defined". This tells GetSQLValueString() to use the third argument if the form field contains a value or to use the fourth argument if the form field is empty. Let's deal with the fourth argument first, because it's straightforward. The fourth argument is 'NOW()', so the SQL query will use NOW() as a function if the form field is left blank.

Now, let's return to the third argument, which is used if the form field isn't blank. If you look at it on its own, it's exactly the same as the original code on line 42 of Figure 17-15. In other words, if the form field contains a value, it's passed to GetSQLValueString() and treated as a date.

9. Save current_date.php, and load it into a browser.

10. The only purpose of the message field is to give you something to update and identify each record. Enter some text, and leave the fixed_date field empty. Click the Insert button. If nothing is wrong with your code, the form should submit the values and remain onscreen with empty fields.

11. Submit the form twice more, once with a date in MySQL format (YYYY-MM-DD) and the other time with a date in American (MM/DD/YYYY) or European (DD/MM/YYYY) format.

12. Click the Browse tab in phpMyAdmin to view the contents of the date_test table. You should see something similar to Figure 17-16.

pk	updated	created	fixed_date	message
1	2008-09-02 14:40:52	2008-09-02 14:40:52	2008-09-02 14:40:52	Fixed date is blank
2	2008-09-02 14:41:04	2008-09-02 14:41:04	2008-08-08 00:00:00	Fixed date has a value
3	2008-09-02 14:41:16	2008-09-02 14:41:16	0000-00-00 00:00:00	Fixed date in US format

Figure 17-16. The fields are correctly populated with the date and time, except when an invalid format is used.

As Figure 17-16 shows, the date and time are the same in all three columns in the first record. The first two columns are the same in the second record, but the fixed_date column has recorded the date (2008-08-08) I entered in MySQL format. However, when I entered 12/25/2008 in the final record, fixed_date was set to 0000-00-00 00:00:00. By the way, this has nothing to do with using forward slashes—MySQL accepts a wide range of separators, which it converts silently to dashes. The problem lies with year, month, and date being in the wrong order. The only solution is to format dates correctly before attempting to store them in MySQL. We'll look at that next.

You can check your code, if necessary, against current_date.php in examples/ch17.

Storing other dates in MySQL

A very simple way to handle dates in user input is to use the YUI Calendar widget (see Chapter 8) or the Spry validation text field widget (see Chapter 9) to enforce a particular format. So if you're in an enclosed environment, such as an intranet, where you can guarantee compliance—and that JavaScript won't be disabled—this might be your solution.

However, getting Internet users to adhere to rules is rather like herding cats. It's far safer to ensure accurate date input by providing separate fields for month, day of the month, and year, and then to use PHP to verify and format the input.

In the examples/ch17 folder of the download files, you will find a page called fixed_date_start.php. When you load it into a browser, it displays a drop-down menu preset to the current month, together with two text fields for the date and year, as shown in Figure 17-17. The Max Chars settings for the text fields have been set to 2 and 4, respectively, to limit the range of mistakes that can be made.

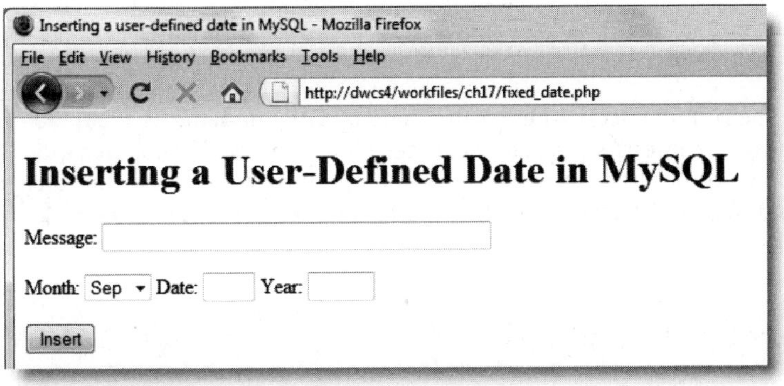

Figure 17-17. Providing separate fields for the date parts is the most reliable way of inserting dates accurately.

The drop-down menu for the month is created in two parts. The first section of code goes in a PHP block above the DOCTYPE declaration and consists of an array of the names of the months, plus the PHP getdate() function. This is how it looks:

```
$months = array('Jan', 'Feb', 'Mar', 'Apr', 'May', 'Jun', 'Jul', 'Aug', ➥
'Sep', 'Oct', 'Nov', 'Dec');
$now = getdate();
```

The getdate() function produces an associative array that contains a number of useful date parts, such as the year, weekday name, and so on. When used without an argument like this, getdate() returns information about the current date, so you can find the number of the current month in $now['mon'] and use it to preset the drop-down menu. You can find a full list of the array elements returned by getdate() at http://docs.php.net/manual/en/function.getdate.php.

The code for the drop-down menu looks like this:

```
<label for="select">Month:</label>
<select name="month" id="month">
<?php for ($i=1;$i<=12;$i++) { ?>
  <option value="<?php echo $i < 10 ? '0'.$i : $i; ?>"
  <?php if ($i == $now['mon']) {
    echo ' selected="selected"'; } ?>><?php echo $months[$i-1]; ?>
  </option>
  <?php } ?>
</select>
```

This uses a for loop to populate the menu's <option> tags. Although counters normally begin at 0, I have set the initial value of $i to 1, because I want to use it for the value of the month.

The second line highlighted in bold uses the conditional operator (see Chapter 10) to test whether $i is less than 10. If it is, a leading zero is added to the number; otherwise, it is left alone. Another way of writing it would be to use this:

```
if ($i < 10) {
  echo '0'.$i;
} else {
  echo $i;
}
```

The third line of PHP checks whether the value of $i is the same as $now['mon']. If it is, the following line inserts selected="selected" into the opening <option> tag. The final part of the script displays the name of the month by drawing it from the $months array. Because indexed arrays begin at 0, you need to subtract 1 from the value of $i to get the right month.

> *I have not created similar drop-down menus for the day and year because PHP is a server-side language. Although you could create a script to display the correct number of days for the month, you would have to reload the page every time the month was changed. You could create an intelligent date input system with JavaScript, but that makes the dangerous assumption that all users will have JavaScript enabled.*

To validate the input from the month, date, and year input fields and format them ready for MySQL, I have created the following function:

```
function formatMySQLDate($month, $day, $year, &$error) {
  $mysqlFormat = null;
  $m = $month;
  $d = trim($day);
  $y = trim($year);
  if (empty($d) || empty($y)) {
    $error = 'Please fill in all fields';
  } elseif (!is_numeric($d) || !is_numeric($y)) {
    $error = 'Please use numbers only';
  } elseif (($d <1 || $d > 31) || ($y < 1000 || $y > 9999)) {
    $error = 'Please use numbers within the correct range';
  } elseif (!checkdate($m,$d,$y)) {
    $error = 'You have used an invalid date';
  } else {
    $d = $d < 10 ? '0'.$d : $d;
    $mysqlFormat = "'$y-$m-$d'";
  }
  return $mysqlFormat;
}
```

The formatMySQLDate() function is one of the snippets you installed in the PHP-DWCS4 folder of the Snippets panel in Chapter 11. It takes four arguments: the month, date, and year values submitted by the form, and a variable to hold any error messages. The fourth argument should be an empty string ready to capture any error message.

In the function definition, the fourth argument is preceded by an ampersand (&). This is the same technique I used in the isSuspect() function in Chapter 11. Normally, passing a variable to a function simply uses a copy of its value; anything that happens in the function has no effect on the variable's original value. However, preceding the argument by & in the function definition passes the actual value to the function, so any changes inside the function are reflected in the main script. This is a technique known as **passing by reference** because it passes a reference to the actual value, rather than a copy.

Let's take a quick look at what happens inside the formatMySQLDate() function. It begins by setting a variable called $mysqlFormat to null. This will be used as the value the function returns, so it will remain null if any errors are found. You don't need to perform any checks on the value of the month, because the drop-down menu has generated it. So, after trimming any whitespace from around the date and year, they are subjected to the first three checks: to see whether they are empty, not numeric, or out of range. You have met the empty() function before. The second check uses is_numeric(), which is basically self-explanatory. It takes advantage of PHP's loose typing. In strict terms of datatypes, the content of a text field is always a string, but is_numeric() also returns true if a string contains a number, such as '5'. (No, it's not clever enough to recognize 'five' as a number.) The third test looks for numbers within acceptable ranges. It looks like this:

```
elseif (($d <1 || $d > 31) || ($y < 1000 || $y > 9999)) {
```

The values set for the day (1–31) are immediately understandable, even though they don't apply to every month. The range for years (1000–9999) is dictated by the legal range for MySQL. I suggest that you use a narrower range, more in line with the requirements of the application you're building. In the unlikely event that you need a year out of that range, you must choose a different column type to store the data. MySQL was not designed to handle stardates from *Star Trek: The Next Generation*!

By using a series of elseif clauses, this code stops testing as soon as it meets the first mistake. If the input has survived the first three tests, it's then subjected to the PHP function checkdate(), which really puts a date through the mill. It's smart enough to know the difference between February 29 in a leap year and an ordinary year.

Finally, if the input has passed all these tests, it's rebuilt in the correct format for insertion into MySQL. The first line of the final else clause uses the ternary operator, as described earlier, to add a leading zero to the day of the month if necessary. The function returns the date wrapped in single quotes, so it can be inserted directly into a SQL query. If an error is found, the function returns null, and the error message can be retrieved from the variable passed as the fourth argument to formatMySQLDate().

Now that you have seen what the formatMySQLDate() function does, let's incorporate it into a page to insert a user-defined date into MySQL.

Inserting a user-defined date into MySQL

The following exercise uses the `formatMySQLDate()` function to validate and format a date ready for insertion into MySQL. It uses the date_test table that was created for the preceding exercise.

1. Copy `fixed_date_start.php` from examples/ch17, and save it in workfiles/ch17 as `fixed_date.php`. The file is based on current_date.php from the previous exercise, so it contains a hidden field called created to set the current date for the second TIMESTAMP column.

2. Apply an Insert Record server behavior. The names of the fields for the date parts no longer match the fixed_date column in the date_test table, so you need to select fixed_date in the Insert Record dialog box, and select one of the date part fields from the Value drop-down menu, as shown in Figure 17-18.

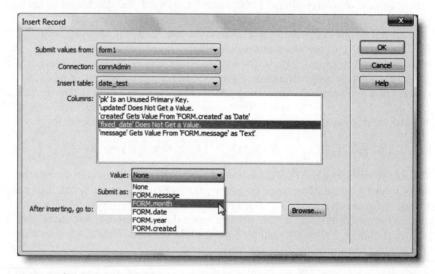

Figure 17-18. You need to select one of the date part fields to match the database column.

3. The other settings should be fine, so click OK to apply the Insert Record server behavior.

4. Locate the Insert Record server behavior code in Code view, and insert the following code at the point indicated in Figure 17-19:

```php
// initialize string for error message
$error = '';
if (array_key_exists('insert', $_POST)) {
  // formatMySQLDate definition goes here

  // format the date parts
  $mysqlDate = formatMySQLDate($_POST['month'], $_POST['date'], ➥
$_POST['year'], $error);
}
if (!$error) {
```

Insert code here →

```
34  $editFormAction = $_SERVER['PHP_SELF'];
35  if (isset($_SERVER['QUERY_STRING'])) {
36    $editFormAction .= "?" . htmlentities($_SERVER['QUERY_STRING']);
37  }
38
39  if ((isset($_POST["MM_insert"])) && ($_POST["MM_insert"] == "form1")) {
40    $insertSQL = sprintf("INSERT INTO date_test (created, fixed_date, message) VALUES (%s, %s, %s)",
41                         GetSQLValueString($_POST['created'], "date"),
42                         GetSQLValueString($_POST['month'], "date"),
43                         GetSQLValueString($_POST['message'], "text"));
44
45    mysql_select_db($database_connAdmin, $connAdmin);
46    $Result1 = mysql_query($insertSQL, $connAdmin) or die(mysql_error());
47  }
48
49  $months = array('Jan', 'Feb', 'Mar', 'Apr', 'May', 'Jun', 'Jul', 'Aug', 'Sep', 'Oct', 'Nov', 'Dec');
```

Figure 17-19. The code to format the date needs to go before the INSERT query.

The new code begins by initializing an empty string to hold any error message generated by the formatMySQLDate() function. A conditional statement then checks whether the insert form has been submitted. If it has, you need to define the formatMySQLDate() function and then pass the date parts and the $error variable to it.

If the date parts constitute a valid date, $error will remain an empty string, so the second conditional statement will equate to false, letting the Insert Record server behavior go ahead.

5. Tidy up the code you have just inserted by inserting the formatMySQLDate() function definition from the PHP-DWCS4 folder of the Snippets panel (it's called Format date for MySQL). Also add a closing curly brace for the second conditional statement just after the Insert Record server behavior code (line 48 in Figure 17-19, although the line number will have increased to about 74).

6. The next task is to edit the code that inserts the values into the SQL query. The code shown on line 41 of Figure 17-19 should look like this:

```
GetSQLValueString($_POST['created'], "defined", 'NOW()'),
```

This is the same edit as in the previous exercise, so it needs no explanation.

7. The line that inserts the user-defined date is on line 42 of Figure 17-19. It needs to be edited like this:

```
GetSQLValueString($_POST['month'], "defined", $mysqlDate),
```

The insert code won't run if an error has been detected by formatMySQLDate(), so you know that $mysqlDate must contain a valid date in MySQL format. The date is already formatted with quotes, so it can be inserted directly into the SQL query.

8. The final change you need to make is to add a warning if the INSERT query didn't run. Add the following code between the page heading and insert form:

```php
<?php
if (isset($error)) {
  echo "<p>$error</p>";
}
?>
```

9. Save fixed_date.php, and load it into a browser. Test it by adding a message and selecting a date. Then check that it has been inserted correctly into the date_test table. Also try an invalid date, such as Feb 29, 2007. You should see an error message, and nothing will be inserted into the database.

You can check your code, if necessary, against fixed_date.php in examples/ch17.

These exercises have dealt only with the Insert Record server behavior, but you use the same techniques to handle dates in the Update Record server behavior.

Now that you have stored dates correctly in MySQL, how do you make them look acceptable to visitors to your site? Many developers who have already dabbled with PHP attempt to use the PHP date() function (covered later in the chapter) to format the date. However, the date() function expects a timestamp based on the number of seconds since the beginning of 1970; a MySQL timestamp is incompatible. Although it's perfectly possible to use PHP to format the date, it's much more efficient to get MySQL to do all the work for you, as explained in the next section.

Using DATE_FORMAT() to output user-friendly dates

MySQL has a wide range of date and time functions. The one that concerns us here is DATE_FORMAT(), which does exactly what its name suggests. The syntax for DATE_FORMAT() is as follows:

DATE_FORMAT(*date, format*)

Normally, *date* is the name of the table column that you want to format, and *format* is a string that tells MySQL which format to use. You build the format string from specifiers. Table 17-2 lists those most commonly used.

Table 17-2. Frequently used MySQL date format specifiers

Period	Specifier	Description	Example
Year	%Y	Four-digit format	2007
	%y	Two-digit format	07
Month	%M	Full name	January, September
	%b	Abbreviated name, three letters	Jan, Sep
	%m	Number, with leading zero	01, 09
	%c	Number, no leading zero	1, 9
Day of month	%d	With leading zero	01, 25
	%e	No leading zero	1, 25
	%D	With English text suffix	1st, 25th

Period	Specifier	Description	Example
Weekday name	%W	Full text	Monday, Thursday
	%a	Abbreviated name, three letters	Mon, Thu
Hour	%H	24-hour clock, with leading zero	01, 23
	%k	24-hour clock, no leading zero	1, 23
	%h	12-hour clock, with leading zero	01, 11
	%l (lowercase "L")	12-hour clock, no leading zero	1, 11
Minute	%i	With leading zero	05, 25
Second	%S	With leading zero	08, 45
AM/PM	%p		

The specifiers can be combined with ordinary text or punctuation in the format string. As always, when using a function in a SQL query, there must be no space between the function name and the opening parenthesis. It's also a good idea to assign the result to an alias using the AS keyword (see Chapter 16). Referring to Table 17-2, you can now format the date in the submitted column of the feedback table in a variety of ways. To present the date in a common U.S. style and retain the name of the original column, use the following:

```
DATE_FORMAT(created, '%c/%e/%Y') AS created
```

To format the same date in European style, reverse the first two specifiers like this:

```
DATE_FORMAT(created, '%e/%c/%Y') AS created
```

You can now format the dates in the date_test table in a way that's easier to read.

Formatting the date and time in the feedback table

The following exercise shows you how to use DATE_FORMAT() to transform the dates stored in the date_test table. The same technique applies to any date or time column. By using different aliases, you can extract different parts of the date or time to use in a variety of ways in your web pages.

1. Create a PHP page called display_dates.php in workfiles/ch17.
2. Open the Recordset dialog box in Advanced mode. Call the recordset getDates, and expand the date_test table in the Database items field at the bottom of the dialog box.

3. Select fixed_date, and click the SELECT button. This creates a query in the SQL field like this:

```
SELECT date_test.fixed_date
FROM date_test
```

4. To keep things simple, I'm going to work with this one column. Amend the query to this:

```
SELECT date_test.fixed_date,
DATE_FORMAT(date_test.fixed_date, '%b %e, %Y') AS us_format,
DATE_FORMAT(date_test.fixed_date, '%e %b %Y') AS eu_format
FROM date_test
```

5. Click the Test button to make sure everything is working correctly. The dates should now be formatted as shown in Figure 17-20.

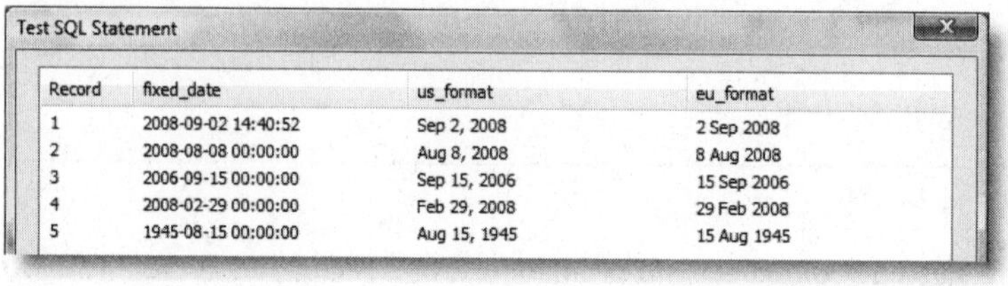

Record	fixed_date	us_format	eu_format
1	2008-09-02 14:40:52	Sep 2, 2008	2 Sep 2008
2	2008-08-08 00:00:00	Aug 8, 2008	8 Aug 2008
3	2006-09-15 00:00:00	Sep 15, 2006	15 Sep 2006
4	2008-02-29 00:00:00	Feb 29, 2008	29 Feb 2008
5	1945-08-15 00:00:00	Aug 15, 1945	15 Aug 1945

Figure 17-20. A combination of DATE_FORMAT() and aliases gives you the same data in three formats.

If Dreamweaver displays a MySQL error message instead, check that you have not left any space between DATE_FORMAT and the opening parenthesis of the function. Although some computer languages allow you to leave a space, MySQL doesn't. Also, make sure that the format string is enclosed in matching *single* quotes. Although single and double quotes are equally acceptable in SQL (and in the test panel), double quotes cause a parse error in Dreamweaver's PHP code when you run the page normally.

6. Close the test panel. I'll leave you to experiment with DATE_FORMAT(). The version of display_dates.php in examples/ch17 displays the three formats in a table.

This gives you just a brief glimpse of MySQL date functions. Others allow you to perform useful calculations, such as working out people's ages from their birthdates, calculating the difference between two dates, and adding to or subtracting from dates. You can find details of all MySQL date and time functions, together with examples at http://dev.mysql.com/doc/refman/5.0/en/date-and-time-functions.html.

Working with dates in PHP

PHP handles dates in a very different way from MySQL that's not as easy to visualize in everyday terms. Whereas MySQL timestamps are based on the human calendar, it's impossible for anyone—except, perhaps, a mathematical genius—to read the date from a PHP timestamp, as this example shows:

```
1220350080  // Unix timestamp for 10:08:00 UTC on September 2, 2008
```

As mentioned earlier, this seemingly arbitrary figure is the number of seconds since the beginning of 1970. Except when referring to the current time, all dates in PHP need to be converted to a Unix timestamp. After performing any calculations, you format the result in a more human-readable way by using the date() or strftime() function, which I'll describe shortly. But first, let's take a look at time zones and Unix timestamps.

Setting the correct time zone

The internal workings of the PHP date and time functions were revised in PHP 5.1 and require a time zone to be defined. Normally, this should be done by setting the value of date.timezone in php.ini; but if your hosting company forgets to do so, or you want to use a different time zone, you need to set it yourself. You can do this in three different ways.

The simplest way is to add the following at the beginning of any script that uses date or time functions:

```
ini_set('date.timezone', 'timezone');
```

You can find a full list of valid time zones at http://docs.php.net/manual/en/timezones.php. The correct setting for where I live is this:

```
ini_set('date.timezone', 'Europe/London');
```

ini_set() fails silently if your server doesn't support the date.timezone setting. As long as you use a valid PHP time zone, your scripts will automatically use this setting whenever your server is upgraded.

A slightly longer way is to add this (with the appropriate time zone) before using date and time functions:

```
if (function_exists('date_default_timezone_set')) {
  date_default_timezone_set('Europe/London');
}
```

If your remote server runs Apache, you may be able to set a default time zone for your entire site by putting the following in an .htaccess file in the site root (use the correct time zone for your location):

```
php_value date.timezone 'Europe/London'
```

This works only if Apache has been set up to allow .htaccess to override default settings.

Creating a Unix timestamp

PHP offers two main ways of creating a Unix timestamp. The first uses mktime() and is based on the actual date and time; the other attempts to parse any English date or time expression with strtotime().

The mktime() function takes six arguments as follows:

```
mktime(hour, minutes, seconds, month, date, year)
```

All arguments are optional. If a value is omitted, it is set to the current date and time. However, you can't skip arguments; as soon as you leave one out, all remaining ones must also be omitted. Consequently, if you are interested only in the date, you need to set the first three arguments to 0 (midnight) like this:

```
$Xmas2008 = mktime(0, 0, 0, 12, 25, 2008);
```

The strtotime() function attempts to parse dates from American English but holds some unpleasant surprises. The following expressions produce the correct timestamp for Christmas day 2008:

```
$Xmas2008 = strtotime('12/25/2008');
$Xmas2008 = strtotime('2008-12-25');
```

However, replacing the slashes with hyphens in the first example, as follows, produces a false result:

```
$notXmas = strtotime('12-25-2008'); // produces Jan 1, 1970 timestamp
```

To avoid such problems, it's best to use the name of the month, either spelled out in full or just the first three letters, and to place the year at the end of the string.

The real value of strtotime(), however, lies in its ability to add or subtract from dates by parsing simple time-related expressions. For instance, strtotime() understands all these expressions:

```
strtotime('tomorrow');
strtotime('yesterday');
strtotime('last Monday');
strtotime('next Thursday');
strtotime('-3 weeks');
strtotime('+1 week 2 days');
```

> Be careful when using next in a strtotime() expression. In versions prior to PHP 4.4, it is incorrectly interpreted as +2, instead of +1.

The previous examples calculate the timestamp based on the current date and time. However, you can supply a specific timestamp as a second, optional argument to strtotime(). This means you can add or subtract from a particular date. The following example calculates the timestamp for January 6, 2009:

```
$Xmas2008 = mktime(0, 0, 0, 12, 25, 2008);
$twelfthNight = strtotime('+12 days', $Xmas2008);
```

If you ever need to generate a Unix timestamp from a date-type column in MySQL, you can use the UNIX_TIMESTAMP() function in a SELECT statement like this:

```
SELECT UNIX_TIMESTAMP(submitted) AS PHPtimestamp FROM feedback
```

Formatting dates in PHP

PHP offers two functions that format dates: date(), which displays the names of weekdays and months in English only, and strftime(), which uses the server's locale. So, if the server's locale is set to Spanish, date() displays Saturday, but strftime() displays sábado. Both functions take as their first, required argument a string that indicates the format in which you want to display the date. A second, optional argument specifies the timestamp, but if it's omitted, the current date and time are assumed.

There are a lot of format characters. Some are easy to remember, but many seem to have no obvious reasoning behind them. You can find a full list at http://docs.php.net/manual/en/function.date.php and http://docs.php.net/manual/en/function.strftime.php. Table 17-3 lists the most useful.

Table 17-3. The main format characters used in the date() and strftime() functions

Unit	date()	strftime()	Description	Example
Day	d	%d	Day of the month with leading zero	01 through 31
	j	%e*	Day of the month without leading zero	1 through 31
	S		English ordinal suffix for day of the month	st, nd, rd, or th
	D	%a	First three letters of day name	Sun, Tue
	l (lowercase "L")	%A	Full name of day	Sunday, Tuesday
Month	m	%m	Number of month with leading zero	01 through 12
	n		Number of month without leading zero	1 through 12
	M	%b	First three letters of month name	Jan, Jul
	F	%B	Full name of month	January, July
Year	Y	%Y	Year displayed as four digits	2007
	y	%y	Year displayed as two digits	07
Hour	g		Hour in 12-hour format without leading zero	1 through 12
	h	%I	Hour in 12-hour format with leading zero	01 through 12
	G		Hour in 24-hour format without leading zero	0 through 23
	H	%H	Hour in 24-hour format with leading zero	01 through 23
Minutes	i	%M	Minutes with leading zero if necessary	00 through 59
Seconds	s	%S	Seconds with leading zero if necessary	00 through 59
AM/PM	a	%p	Lowercase	am
AM/PM	A		Uppercase	PM

Note: %e is not supported on Windows.

You can combine these format characters with punctuation to display the current date in your web pages according to your own preferences. For instance, the following code (in dates.php in examples/ch17) produces output similar to that shown in Figure 17-21.

```
<p>American style: <?php echo date('l, F jS, Y'); ?></p>
<p>European style: <?php echo date('l, jS F Y'); ?></p>
```

Figure 17-21. The PHP date() function formats the current date or a Unix timestamp in various styles.

Chapter review

As I said at the outset of this chapter, building SQL queries is a vast subject. The more you learn, the more you realize just how much more there is to know. Even when working with a single table, you can fine-tune your searches by using MySQL functions and aliases. So, it's important to break out of the confines of the Recordset dialog box in Simple mode and learn how to build queries that extract the information that you want—and in the format you want. When you have a moment to spare, visit http://dev.mysql.com/doc/refman/ 5.0/en/functions.html, and take a look at the impressive range of functions that you can use in MySQL queries. The most useful categories are the string and date and time functions. This chapter has shown you how to format the date with MySQL functions, but there are many more, including functions that calculate the difference between two dates and functions that add or subtract any time period to or from a date. The online documentation has lots of examples showing how to use the functions. Experiment with them and take your SQL skills to a new level.

The next chapter takes a break from working with MySQL and shows you how to use the Dreamweaver XSL Transformation server behavior to extract information from online news feeds and other XML documents.

Extensible Markup Language (XML) is probably one of the most hyped and least understood aspects of web development. XML has the simple objective of storing data in a format that both humans and computers can easily understand. It's not a database, and it's not a programming language. It's a highly structured way of presenting data. Because it uses tags like HTML, XML looks very familiar to web developers. However, there is no master list of tags or attributes, and although XML frequently contains data intended for display on the Web, it provides no way of displaying it.

That's where programs like Dreamweaver come in. The XSL Transformation server behavior processes raw XML and incorporates it in a web page, using a combination of PHP and Extensible Stylesheet Language Transformations (XSLT), a language for transforming XML into HTML.

In this chapter, you'll learn about the following:

- What XML and XSLT do
- Determining whether your host supports XSLT within PHP
- Drawing data from a live news feed into your site
- Experimenting with the XPath Expression Builder

A quick guide to XML and XSLT

XML became a W3C standard in February 1998, and XSLT followed almost two years later, in November 1999. Because of the "Stylesheet" in its name, the role of XSLT is often described as being to format XML documents in a similar way to CSS. However, there is no real similarity. The real strength of XSLT lies in its ability to manipulate data, sorting and filtering it in much the same way as SQL does with a database. Unfortunately, it's not an easy language to learn, but the XSL Transformation server behavior in Dreamweaver eases the process considerably.

Before delving into the mysteries of XSLT, let's take a look at the structure of an XML document.

What an XML document looks like

XML is closely related to HTML, so it looks reassuringly familiar, but there are two fundamental differences between them:

- HTML has a fixed range of tags and attributes. In XML, you create your own.
- HTML tags are concerned with the structure of a page (<head>, <body>, <p>, <table>, and so on), whereas XML tags normally describe the data they contain (for instance, the following example uses <Book> to store details of individual books).

The following is a simple example of an XML document:

```
<?xml version="1.0" ?>
<BookList>
  <Book ISBN="978-1-4302-1610-0">
    <Title>The Essential Guide to Dreamweaver CS4 with CSS, Ajax, ➥
      and PHP</Title>
    <Authors>
      <Author>David Powers</Author>
    </Authors>
    <Publisher>friends of ED</Publisher>
    <ListPrice>49.99</ListPrice>
  </Book>
  <Book ISBN="978-1-4302-1606-3">
    <Title>HTML and CSS Web Standards Solutions: A Web Standardista's ➥
      Approach</Title>
    <Authors>
      <Author>Christopher Murphy</Author>
      <Author>Nicklas Persson</Author>
    </Authors>
    <Publisher>friends of ED</Publisher>
    <ListPrice>39.99</ListPrice>
  </Book>
</BookList>
```

The first line is the **XML declaration**, often also referred to as the **XML prolog**, which tells browsers and processors that it's an XML document. The XML declaration is recommended but not required. However, if you do include it, the XML declaration *must* be the first thing in the document. The W3C recommends using XML 1.0 unless you need the highly specialized features of XML 1.1 (http://www.w3.org/TR/2004/REC-xml11-20040204/#sec-xml11). The XML declaration can also contain an encoding attribute. If this attribute is omitted, as in the previous example, XML parsers automatically use Unicode (UTF-8 or UTF-16).

As you can see from the example document, the tags give no indication as to how the document is intended to look. In fact, it's normally recommended that they shouldn't, because XML is intended primarily to store data in a hierarchical structure according to meaning and without any reference to presentation. Unless you are working in a large collaborative project, which needs to use a standardized vocabulary, you can make up your own tags, as I have done here. They can be made up not only of alphanumeric characters but also accented characters, Greek, Cyrillic, Chinese, and Japanese—in fact, any valid Unicode character. However, they cannot include any whitespace or punctuation other than the hyphen (-), underscore (_), and period (.), and they cannot begin with xml in any combination of uppercase or lowercase letters.

The goals of XML include being human-legible, and terseness is considered of minimal importance. So, instead of using <Pub>, which could mean publisher, publication date, or somewhere to get a drink, I have been specific and used <Publisher>. The most important thing about an XML document is that it must be **well formed**. The main rules of what constitutes a well-formed document are as follows:

- There can be only one root element.
- Every start tag must have a matching closing tag.
- Empty elements can omit the closing tag, but, if they do so, must have a forward slash before the closing angle bracket (/>).
- Elements must be properly nested.
- Attribute values must be in quotes.
- In the content of an element or attribute value, < and & must be replaced by < and &, respectively.

An empty element is one that doesn't have any content, although it can have attributes that point to content stored elsewhere. To borrow a couple of examples from XHTML, which is HTML 4.01 reformulated to adhere to XML rules, <img> and <br> are empty elements. The src attribute of the <img> tag points to the location of the image, but the tag itself is empty. The <br> tag simply creates a line break, so never has any content. To comply with XML rules, they can be written as <img></img> and
</br> or use the shorthand <img/> and <br/>. To avoid problems with older browsers, a space is normally inserted before the closing forward slash in XHTML, but this is *not* a requirement of XML.

Since XML is concerned only with the storage of data, and not its presentation, it's also possible to have empty elements that contain all their data in the tag's attributes. For example, this is a perfectly valid way to store details of movies in XML:

```
<?xml version="1.0" ?>
<movies>
  <movie title="Atonement" duration="123"/>
  <movie title="La Vie en Rose" duration="140"/>
</movies>
```

If you look at both examples, you will see they have only one root element: <BookList> or <movies>. All other elements are nested inside the root element, and the nesting follows an orderly pattern. In the first example, even when a book has only one author, the <Author> tag is still nested inside <Authors>, and the value of the ISBN attribute is always in quotes. While these strict rules make XML more time-consuming to write, the predictability of a well-formed document makes it a lot easier to process. As you will see shortly, when you define an XML source, Dreamweaver instantly builds a diagrammatic representation of the document structure that enables you to manipulate its content with XSLT.

Using HTML entities in XML

Among the conditions of being well-formed is the need to replace < and & with the HTML entities < and & in the content of an element or attribute value. This often leads to the misconception that XML supports the full range of HTML entities, such as é

(for é). It doesn't. XML understands only the following five entities: < (<), & (&), > (>), " ("), and ' (').

When creating an XML document in an accented language, such as Spanish, French, or German, you should use accented characters in the same way as in ordinary text. A key principle of XML is that it should be human-readable. You can use other HTML entities in XML, but they will not be automatically rendered as their text equivalent. The XSL Transformation server behavior defines the most frequently used HTML entities so they render correctly. If your XML source contains other HTML entities, you can add your own definitions to the XSL page, as described in "Understanding how XSLT is structured" later in the chapter.

> *A good starting place to learn more about XML is the XML FAQ, edited by Peter Flynn,*
> *at* http://xml.silmaril.ie.

Using XSLT to display XML

There are two ways of using XSLT: client-side and server-side. With client-side XSLT, you create an XSL page and link it to the XML document just like linking a CSS style sheet to an ordinary web page. The job of interpreting the XSLT instructions is then left up to the visitor's browser. Most modern browsers are now capable of handling client-side XSLT, but support is by no means universal. This lack of universal support means you can use it only in controlled environments, such as an intranet, where you know that everyone is using a compatible browser.

Another drawback of client-side XSLT is that the XSL and XML documents must both reside in the same folder on the web server. So, if you want to display the contents of a news feed from another site, you must first download the XML feed and store it locally.

To get round these problems, you can use PHP to process the XSLT on the server. This converts the XML into HTML before it's sent from the server, providing your visitors with exactly the same page regardless of which browser they're using. Moreover, with server-side transformation, you can pull the XML feed from any publicly available source on the Internet.

As I mentioned earlier, XSLT is a difficult language, but Dreamweaver automatically builds the XSL page for you. All you need to do is embed the XSL fragment in a PHP page. We'll take a look at XSLT code in "Understanding how XSLT is structured" later in the chapter, but first let's see it in action.

Checking your server's support for XSLT

PHP 4 and PHP 5 handle XSLT completely differently, but Dreamweaver's XSL Transformation server behavior has been designed to work seamlessly with both by automatically detecting the version of PHP running on your server. However, XSLT isn't enabled by default, so you need to check that it is supported.

Create a page containing the following single-line script, and upload it to your remote server to display details of the server's PHP configuration:

```
<?php phpinfo(); ?>
```

Check for the value of allow_url_fopen in the PHP Core section close to the top of the page. It must be set to On, as shown in the following screenshot:

Configuration

PHP Core

Directive	Local Value	Master Value
allow_call_time_pass_reference	Off	Off
allow_url_fopen	On	On
allow_url_include	Off	Off
always_populate_raw_post_data	Off	Off
arg_separator.input	&	&
ʳ.output		&

Scroll almost to the bottom of the page, and look for a section similar to that shown in the following screenshot:

xsl

XSL	enabled
libxslt Version	1.1.17
libxslt compiled against libxml Version	2.6.26
EXSLT	enabled
libexslt Version	0.8.13

This shows what you are likely to see on a server running PHP 5 if it has been configured to handle XSLT. The configuration details will look slightly different on a PHP 4 installation. Instead of xsl, it should say xslt, but it should be in the same position just above the Additional Modules section, close to the bottom of the page. The difference in name reflects the functions they use. Although the XSL Transformation server behavior works with PHP 4, you should seriously consider moving to a PHP 5 server as soon as possible. All support for PHP 4 ended in August 2008.

If you can't find either xsl or xslt, contact your host, and ask for the server to be upgraded. If hosts realize there is a genuine demand for new features, they are likely to respond, or risk losing business. If your host doesn't support XSLT, you can build the pages in the rest of this chapter and test them on your local computer, but you won't be able to upload them to your website.

The XSL Transformation server behavior requires both settings to be enabled. Unfortunately, many hosting companies turn off allow_url_fopen. With older versions of

PHP, this was an understandable security measure. Improved security in PHP 5 makes this no longer necessary—another reason to move to PHP 5 if you're still stuck with PHP 4.

Pulling in an RSS news feed

You can use the XSL Transformation server behavior with any XML file, but one of its most useful applications is working with a live news feed. For this book, I have chosen one of the feeds from BBC Online primarily because it offers very good news coverage. The feed is also very easy to work with, and the BBC welcomes its use on websites, subject to certain simple terms and conditions. You can find the full details at http://news.bbc.co.uk/ 2/hi/help/rss/4498287.stm, but the main conditions are as follows:

- You cannot use the BBC logo on your site.
- You must provide a link back to the original story on the BBC website.
- You must attribute the source, using a specified formula, such as "From BBC News."
- You are not allowed to edit or alter the content in any way.
- You cannot use the content on sites that promote pornography, hatred, terrorism, or any illegal activity.

Of course, another reason for choosing the BBC is sentimental. I worked in BBC News for nearly 30 years, both as a correspondent and as an editor. I remember sitting in a basement in Marylebone High Street more than a decade ago talking to Mike Smartt about the Internet's potential for news. In spite of skepticism all around, he was convinced it was the way of the future. I knew he was right, but without Mike's vision and drive as the first editor of BBC Online, it wouldn't have become the force that it is today.

To see all RSS feeds available from BBC News, go to http://news.bbc.co.uk/2/hi/help/3223484.stm. There are nearly 20 specialist news feeds, ranging from world news, health,   science, and business to British news and entertainment. If you prefer news with an American flavor, try the *New York Times* (http://www.nytimes.com/services/xml/ rss/index.html) or CNN (http://www.cnn.com/services/rss). In fact, you can get RSS feeds wherever you see the orange RSS or XML logos shown alongside. Much RSS content is copyright protected, so always make sure you study the terms of use carefully.

RSS is one of those sets of initials that no one can agree on what they really stand for. Some say it means Really Simple Syndication. Others say it's Rich Site Summary. Yet others insist that it stands for RDF Site Summary, and that RDF is the Resource Description Framework. They're all equally valid; the important thing is that RSS feeds all conform to the rules of XML, so they're ideal for handling with the Dreamweaver XSL Transformation server behavior.

Figure 18-1 shows what the news feed looks like when it's incorporated into the sidebar of the "Stroll Along the Thames" page that has been used in several chapters throughout this book.

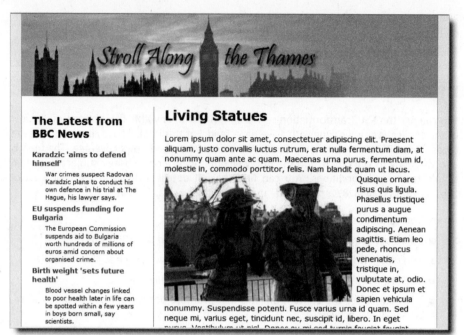

Figure 18-1.
Live news headlines from an external news feed can add constantly changing interest to a site.

How Dreamweaver handles server-side XSLT

When a visitor requests the page shown in Figure 18-1, it looks and works in exactly the same way as any other web page. However, what goes on in the background is considerably more complex.

The XSL Transformation server behavior relies on two external files, as follows:

- **MM_XSLTransform.class.php**: Dreamweaver creates this file automatically and stores it in the MM_XSLTransform subfolder of the includes folder. If you don't already have an includes folder, Dreamweaver creates it. This file is similar to the Spry JavaScript libraries in that it contains all the PHP code needed to process XSLT and XML. It's also responsible for importing the XML source. All you need to do is remember to upload this file to your remote server when deploying your site.

- An XSL file that contains details of the XML source and how you want to display the data it contains. Dreamweaver calls this an **XSLT fragment**.

You create the XSLT fragment using the same drag-and-drop interface as for all dynamic data. Instead of PHP code, everything in the XSLT fragment uses XSLT syntax. The great thing from the developer's point of view is that you don't need to know any XSLT syntax for it to work. Of course, if you *do* know XSLT syntax, you can get the XSL Transformation server behavior to do a great deal more.

Figure 18-2 shows a simplified outline of what happens when a visitor to a site requests a page that includes code generated by the XSL Transformation server behavior.

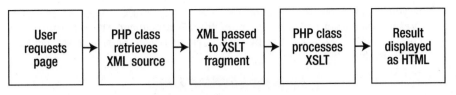

Figure 18-2.
How the XSL
Transformation
server behavior
communicates with
an XML data source

Using XSLT to access the XML source data

Using the XSL Transformation server behavior is a two-stage process, as follows:

1. Create an XSLT fragment to access the XML source, and extract the data that you want.

2. Embed the XSLT fragment in a PHP page.

The following instructions use the BBC Online world news feed. The principles behind displaying any XML source are the same, but I suggest you use the same feed until you are comfortable with the process, because some of the concepts might be unfamiliar.

Creating the XSLT fragment

Because you are working with a live feed, you need to be connected to the Internet for several steps during the following section.

1. From the Dreamweaver File menu, choose New. In the New Document dialog box, select Blank Page, and XSLT (Fragment) as Page Type. Click Create.

> *You must use* XSLT (Fragment) *in the* New Document *dialog box. Do not use* XSLT (Entire page) *in the Dreamweaver welcome screen or the* New Document *dialog box. The option for* XSLT (Entire page) *is used only for client-side XSLT. For a tutorial on client-side XSLT, visit* http://www.adobe.com/devnet/dreamweaver/ articles/display_xml_data.html.

2. Dreamweaver immediately presents you with the Locate XML Source dialog box shown here. It offers two options: to work with a local XML file or to work with a remote one on the Internet. Select the radio button labeled Attach a remote file on the Internet, and insert the following URL: http://newsrss.bbc.co.uk/rss/ newsonline_world_edition/front_page/rss.xml. Click OK.

3. If you don't know the URL of the XML file, clicking Cancel doesn't stop Dreamweaver from creating a page for the XSLT fragment. You can reopen the Locate XML Source dialog box by clicking either Source or XML in the Bindings panel, as shown here:

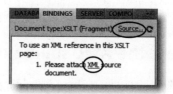

4. As long as you are connected to the Internet, Dreamweaver will contact the BBC Online site and populate the Bindings panel with a document tree like that shown in Figure 18-3. This shows you the structure (Dreamweaver uses the technical term, **schema**) of the XML document sent by the RSS feed.

5. Before working with the XML data, save the page as bbc_feed.xsl in workfiles/ch18. On Windows, Dreamweaver will automatically add the .xsl on the end of the file name, even if you delete it in the Save As dialog box.

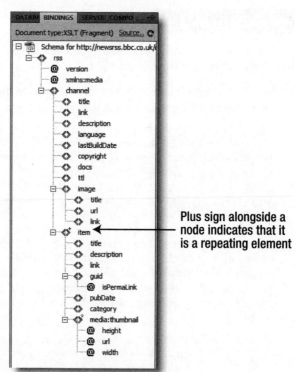

Figure 18-3.
Dreamweaver builds a tree (or schema) of the XML source in the Bindings panel.

Plus sign alongside a node indicates that it is a repeating element

Take a good look at Figure 18-3 or the actual schema in your own Bindings panel. You'll see that it's like a family tree. The angle brackets (<>) represent the different **element nodes** of the source document, with the name shown alongside. The top level or **root element** of the XML document is rss. As you go up and down the structure, nodes share a **parent-child relationship**. Go up a level to reach the parent; go down a level to reach the child or children. This genealogical terminology also extends to nodes on the same level, which are called **siblings**. So, item is a child of channel and a sibling to image. Dreamweaver builds this diagrammatic hierarchy to make it easier for you to identify the elements you want to manipulate, and XSLT uses it as a sort of road map to perform the transformation.

Attributes that appear within XML tags are designated by @. So at the top of Figure 18-3, you can see that rss has two attributes: version and xmlns:media. The channel and image nodes contain child nodes that describe the feed. The news comes further down: in the eighth element node from the bottom labeled item.

The important thing to note about item is that it has a tiny plus sign to the upper right of the angle brackets. This indicates that it's a repeating element.

Branching off item are seven child nodes: title, description, link, guid (with an attribute isPermaLink), pubDate, category, and media:thumbnail The ones we are interested in are title, which contains the headline; description, which contains a summary of the news story; and link, the URL to the full story.

6. Make sure you're in Design view, select title from the item node in the Bindings panel, and drag it into the page.

> *It's very easy to go wrong when selecting nodes, because several share the same name. There are three nodes each called* title *and* link, *and there are two called* description. *All the nodes that you need to select are children of the* item *repeating node.*

7. You should now see a dynamic placeholder inside the page. The placeholder indicates the path to title within the hierarchy of the XML document. Select the placeholder and select Heading 3 from the Format drop-down menu in the HTML view of the Property inspector. The page should now look like the screenshot alongside.

8. Click to the right of the dynamic placeholder, and press Enter/Return to insert a new paragraph. Highlight description in the item node, and drag it into the paragraph that you have just created. You should now have a similar dynamic placeholder for {rss/channel/item/description}.

9. The news feed contains a large number of news items, so you need to apply a repeat region to it. The simplest way to do this would have been to put the news feed into a table or surround each item with a <div>, but either solution results in unnecessary code. Open Split view, and click inside Code view to highlight all the

code from the opening <h3> tag to the closing </p> tag, as shown in the following screenshot:

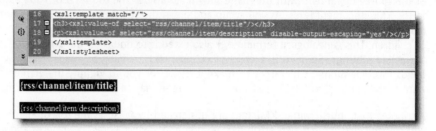

Don't worry about the meaning of the code. It's simply the XSLT way of inserting dynamic data in the same way as PHP does with echo and a variable. Just make sure that the opening and closing HTML tags are properly selected.

10. Look at the Insert bar. You'll see a new XSLT tab has appeared. It's displayed only when the current document is an XSL file. Select the XSLT tab, and click the Repeat Region button as shown here. Alternatively, use the menu option: Insert ➤ XSLT Objects ➤ Repeat Region.

11. This brings up a completely different dialog box from the one you used with the PHP server behavior. It's the XPath Expression Builder.

XPath is the W3C standard that describes how to identify parts of an XML document. In many ways, it's very similar to ordinary file paths and URLs, but it has many more options (http://www.w3.org/TR/xpath), including functions. The XPath Expression Builder incorporates a lot of these functions and builds an XPath with the correct syntax for you.

All you need to do is highlight the parent node of the elements that you want to repeat—in other words, item. In the XPath Expression Builder (Repeat Region) dialog box, scroll down to the bottom of the section labeled Select node to repeat over, and select item. Dreamweaver inserts rss/channel/item into the Expression field at the bottom. Click OK.

12. When the XPath Expression Builder closes, the dynamic placeholders will have changed to just the node names. This is because the XPath expression created in the previous step tells the underlying XSLT code where to find them. There will also be a gray border around the placeholders with a tab labeled xsl:for-each at the top-left corner, as shown alongside, indicating that this is now a repeat region.

13. Save bbc_feed.xsl, and press F12/Opt+F12 to view the page in a browser. If you are connected to the Internet, you should see something like Figure 18-4, except with the very latest headlines, not something from all those months ago when I was writing this book.

Look in the browser address bar, and you'll see that Dreamweaver is using a temporary file, even if you have set your preferences not to use temporary files. You can't use an XSLT fragment in a browser on its own, and you can't use Live view, but Dreamweaver processes it internally so you can check that everything is working as expected before embedding it into a PHP file.

You can check your code against bbc_feed_01.xsl in examples/ch18.

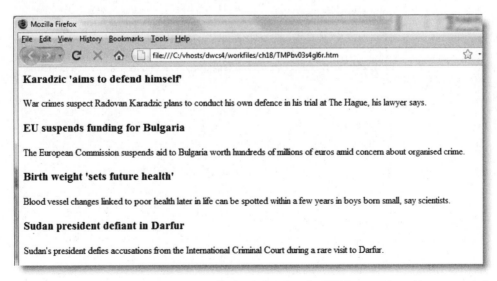

Figure 18-4. Dreamweaver uses a temporary file to confirm that the XSLT fragment is working as expected.

> *When testing XSLT fragments, you might see the temporary files listed in the Dreamweaver Files panel. This is nothing to worry about. Dreamweaver automatically clears them up.*

As part of the BBC conditions of use, you must either provide a link back to the complete story or insert a link to the part of the BBC site from which the feed was drawn. Since the XML source contains a link node (see the schema in Figure 18-3), it's easy to provide a link to each story by converting its headline into a link.

Converting the headlines into links

Continue working with the XSLT fragment from the previous exercise. Alternatively, use bbc_feed_01.xsl in examples/ch18.

1. In Design view, select the title dynamic placeholder, and click the Browse for File icon to the right of the Link field in the HTML view of the Property inspector.

2. When the Select File dialog box opens, choose Data sources as the option for Select file from. (It's a radio button at the top of the dialog box in Windows but an ordinary button at the bottom of the dialog box in the Mac version.) Scroll down inside the area labeled Select node to display, and select link, as shown in the following screenshot. Leave the other options at their default settings, and click OK.

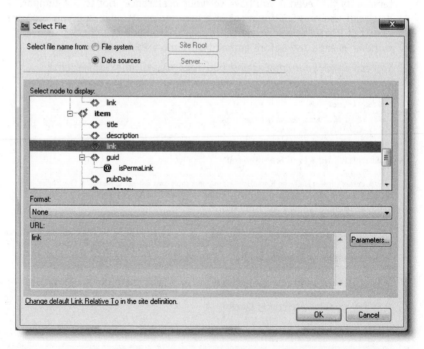

3. Look in the Link field in the Property inspector. It should contain {link}, indicating that it will draw its value from the link node in the XML source.

4. Save bbc_feed.xsl, and press F12/Opt+F12 to test it again. This time, the headlines should have been converted to links. Click one of them to check that it takes you to the relevant story on the BBC website.

   You can check your code against bbc_feed_02.xsl in examples/ch18.

The BBC news feed normally contains 20 or more items. Unlike the Repeat Region server behavior, the XPath Expression Builder (Repeat Region) dialog box has no option to limit the number of items displayed. Instead, you need to use an XSLT conditional region, as shown in the following exercise.

Restricting the number of items in an XSLT repeat region

Continue working with the XSLT fragment from the previous exercise. Alternatively, use bbc_feed_02.xsl in examples/ch18. The following instructions show you how to limit the page to displaying the first five items.

1. Open Split view, and click in Code view to select all the code from the opening <h3> tag to the closing </p> tag in the same way as in step 10 in "Creating an XSLT fragment." Then click the Conditional Region button in the XSLT tab of the Insert bar, as shown in the following screenshot (or select Insert ➤ XSLT Objects ➤ Conditional Region):

2. The Conditional Region dialog box contains just one field, Test. Enter the following code, and click OK:

   ```
   position() <= 5
   ```

   XSLT uses the position() function to determine a node's position in the XML hierarchy. Unlike PHP or JavaScript, it begins counting at 1, so you need to use <= 5 to display the first five items.

3. Save bbc_feed.xsl, and press F12/Opt+F12 to test it again. This time, just the first five items should be displayed. You can check your code against bbc_feed_03.xsl.

Dreamweaver places another gray border around the dynamic placeholders in Design view, with an xsl:if tab at the top-left corner. Confusingly, Dreamweaver positions the xsl:if tab above the repeat region's xsl:for-each tab, giving the incorrect impression that the repeat region is nested inside the conditional one. In Figure 18-5, the conditional region has been selected by clicking the xsl:if gray tab. As you can see, lines 18–21 are highlighted in the underlying code. The code that controls the repeat region is on line 17, and the closing tag of the repeat region is on line 22. If in doubt about the order of code, check the Tag selector at the bottom of the Document window, because it always displays the correct hierarchy of parent and child tags.

```
17  <xsl:for-each select="rss/channel/item">
18    <xsl:if test="position() &lt;= 5">
19      <h3><a href="{link}"><xsl:value-of select="title"/></a></h3>
20      <p><xsl:value-of select="description" disable-output-escaping="yes"/></p>
21    </xsl:if>
22  </xsl:for-each>
```

Figure 18-5. XSLT uses <xsl:if> tags to create a simple conditional region.

As you can see on line 18 of Figure 18-5, Dreamweaver has converted the less-than operator from < to <. XSLT follows the rules of XML and cannot use < within the test attribute value. Although it looks strange, it's the way that XSLT expects it. More important, it works!

Displaying the news feed in a web page

Now that you have got the XSLT fragment to display the items that you want, it's time to embed the XSLT into a PHP page. To save time, I have created a copy of the "Stroll Along the Thames" page with a <div> called news in the sidebar. The style sheet contains a small number of extra rules to adjust the font size, margins, padding, and colors of the news <div>. The rules use basic CSS, so I'll leave you to study the style sheet yourself and just concentrate on the mechanics of embedding the XSLT fragment into the page.

Embedding the XSLT fragment in a dynamic page

You can't use the XSLT fragment on its own; you need to serve it through a dynamic page so that the PHP server behavior can perform the necessary server-side transformation.

1. Copy stroll_xsl_start.php and stroll_xsl.css from examples/ch18 to workfiles/ch18, and rename stroll_xsl_start.php as stroll_xsl.php.

2. Open Split view, and highlight the placeholder text in the news <div>. Make sure that only the placeholder text is selected, and press Delete. The insertion point should be between the opening and closing <div> tags.

3. Click the XSL Transform button in the Data tab of the Insert bar, as shown in the next screenshot. Alternatively, select Insert ➤ Data Objects ➤ XSL Transformation.

4. In the XSL Transformation dialog box that opens, click the top Browse button, and navigate to bbc_feed.xsl. When you click OK in the Select XSLT File dialog box, Dreamweaver automatically populates the XML URI field. This is the address of the BBC RSS feed, which Dreamweaver gets from the XSLT fragment. You don't need to bother with XSLT parameters, so click OK. XSLT parameters are explained later in the chapter.

5. Your page should now look like Figure 18-6. Although it looks as though the XSLT fragment has just been included in the page in the same way as a PHP include file, the underlying code is completely different. Notice that the embedded version displays the repeat region and conditional region tabs superimposed on each other.

Figure 18-6. The XSLT fragment embedded in a PHP page

6. Save stroll_xsl.php, and test the page by clicking the Live View button in the Document toolbar. (Although it won't work with an XSLT fragment on its own, you can use it after embedding the fragment in a dynamic page.) It should now look like Figure 18-1.

Compare your code, if necessary, with stroll_xsl.php in examples/ch18.

When deploying on the Internet a page that contains an embedded XSLT fragment, don't forget to upload the XSL page and the PHP class that does all the hard work: MM_XSLTransform.class.php, which is located in includes/MM_XSLTransform.

If instead of the latest news headlines, you see an MM_XSL Transform error message, it means that your remote server doesn't have the necessary support for XSLT. Pressure your hosting company to provide support, or move to one that does. As noted earlier, another problem might be that your hosting company has turned off allow_url_fopen. In that case, urge Adobe to upgrade the XSL Transformation server behavior by submitting a feature request to http://www.adobe.com/cfusion/mmform/index.cfm?name=wishform. You can use the same address to submit bug reports to Adobe.

Talking of bugs, there's one in the XSL Transformation server behavior, but it's easy to fix.

Fixing a bug in the XSL Transformation server behavior

When you use the XSL Transformation server behavior in a page deployed on a PHP 5 server, the server behavior precedes the generated output with an XML declaration. As I mentioned at the beginning of the chapter, the XML declaration is not required, but if it is used, it must be the first thing in the page. However, if you run stroll_xsl.php on a PHP 5 server and view the source code in the browser, you'll see that the XML declaration is embedded at the point you applied the server behavior, as shown in the following screenshot:

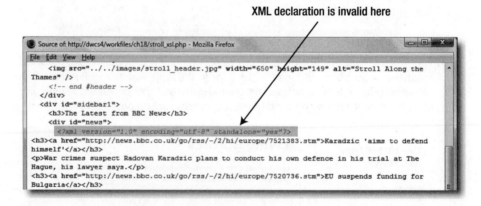

This creates invalid code. Fortunately, it's very easy to fix. The code that does all the hard work in the XSL Transformation server behavior is stored in an external file called MM_XSLTransform.class.php, which is located in the includes/MM_XSLTransform folder of your site. By changing just two lines of code in this file, you can eliminate the bug not just on the current page but on any page in the site that uses this server behavior. The following instructions show you how.

These instructions apply only to using the XSL Transformation server behavior on a PHP 5 server. I have not done any testing on PHP 4, because PHP 4 reached the end of official support in August 2008.

1. Open `MM_XSLTransform.class.php` in the includes/MM_XSLTransform folder. Check that the version number on line 2 is 0.6.3. If the number is different, check this book's page on the friends of ED website (http://friendsofed.com/book.html?isbn=9781430216100) to see whether any updates or corrections have been issued.

2. Save a copy of `MM_XSLTransform.class.php` as `MM_XSLTransform.class_orig.php`. This is your backup in case anything goes wrong. Close the backup file.

3. Switch to Code view, right-click, and select Functions from the context menu. As shown in Figure 18-7, this displays a list of all functions in the page. The one you want is called `transformDocument_domxml5` right at the bottom of the list. Click this to be taken to the first line of the function definition.

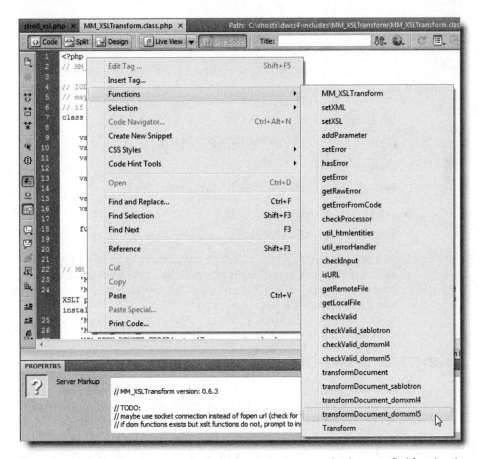

Figure 18-7. The Functions menu on the Code view context menu makes it easy to find functions in a long file.

4. The full listing of the `transformDocument_domxml5()` function looks like this:

```
386   function transformDocument_domxml5(&$xml, &$xsl, &$params) {
387       $magic_quotes_runtime_orig = get_magic_quotes_runtime();
388       set_magic_quotes_runtime(0);
389       $xmlDom = new DOMDocument;
390       $xslDom = new DOMDocument;
391       $xmlDom->loadXML($xml);
392       $xslDom->loadXML($xsl);
393       $proc = new XSLTProcessor;
394       foreach ($params as $key => $value) {
395           $proc->setParameter('', $key, $value);
396       }
397       $old_error_reporting = error_reporting(E_ALL);
398       $old_error_handler = set_error_handler(array(&$this, 'util_errorHandler'));
399       $proc->importStyleSheet($xslDom);
400       $result = $proc->transformToDoc($xmlDom);
401       restore_error_handler();
402       error_reporting($old_error_reporting);
403       if ($this->hasError()) {
404           $myError = $this->getErrorFromCode('MM_TRANSFORMATION_ERROR');
405           $myError .= $this->getRawError();
406           $myError .= $this->getErrorFromCode('MM_TRANSFORM_D5_ERROR', array($this->xslname));
407           $myError .= $this->util_htmlentities($xsl);
408           $this->setError($myError);
409           set_magic_quotes_runtime($magic_quotes_runtime_orig);
410           return;
411       }
412       $output = $result->saveXML();
413       set_magic_quotes_runtime($magic_quotes_runtime_orig);
414       return $output;
415   }
```

The code on line 400 looks like this:

```
$result = $proc->transformToDoc($xmlDom);
```

Change it to this:

```
$output = $proc->transformToXML($xmlDom);
```

5. Delete the following code (it's line 412):

```
$output = $result->saveXML();
```

6. Save `MM_XSLTransform.class.php`. That's all there is to it! Test `stroll_xsl.php` again to make sure everything is still working correctly. If you check the source code in your browser, you'll see that the XML declaration is no longer there, and your page will now validate.

Being a bit more adventurous with XSLT

Up to now, I have deliberately avoided discussing most of the code that's being generated. There's actually very little of it in the XSLT fragment and PHP page, because all the processing is done by an external PHP class. What's more, the code in the XSLT fragment is very different from what you've been working with in previous chapters. In the remaining pages of this chapter, I'd like to show you just a few of the things you can do if you decide to experiment with XSLT and XPath. Instead of using a live news feed as the XML source,

I've prepared an XML document that contains details of the friends of ED and Apress catalog. (The appendix shows you how to generate XML from your own data in MySQL.)

Setting up a local XML source

Getting XML data from a local source involves nothing more complicated than telling Dreamweaver where to find it. You will find a copy of booklist.xml in the examples/ch18 folder, and you can access it directly from there. Open it, and take a look at its structure. The root element is called BookList, and it contains ten elements each called Book, which look like this:

```
<Book ISBN="978-1-4302-1610-0">
  <Title>The Essential Guide to Dreamweaver CS4 with CSS, Ajax, ➥
and PHP</Title>
  <Authors>
    <Author>David Powers</Author>
  </Authors>
  <Publisher>friends of ED</Publisher>
  <ListPrice>49.99</ListPrice>
</Book>
```

Each Book element or node has an attribute called ISBN and four child elements: Title, Authors, Publisher, and ListPrice. In turn, Authors can have one or more child elements called Author.

The following series of exercises shows you how to access the XML structure for use in a web page.

> Each exercise builds upon the previous one. The finished code for each exercise is in examples/ch18.

Displaying the node tree (schema) of booklist.xml

Before you can do anything with the XML data, you need to create an XSLT fragment and display the node tree or schema.

1. Choose File ➤ New ➤ Blank Page ➤ XSLT (Fragment).
2. In the Locate XML Source dialog box, choose the default option (Attach a local file on my computer or local area network), and click the Browse button to navigate to booklist.xml in examples/ch18.

   Notice that the dialog box you use to locate the XML file is called Locate Source XML for XSL Template. Although XSL templates are very different from Dreamweaver templates, the idea is the same: an XSL template defines the basic pattern that will be applied to all the data passed to it.

   After locating booklist.xml, click OK (or Choose on a Mac). Click OK to close the Locate XML Source dialog box.

825

3. This attaches `booklist.xml` to the XSLT fragment and displays the structure of the document in the Bindings panel, as shown in Figure 18-8. Although the document tree is much shorter than the BBC RSS feed, it contains two repeating nodes: Book and Author. Moreover, Author is a grandchild of Book. In other words, you have a repeating region within a repeating region. Each book can have more than one author, so this makes handling this XML document more complex than the BBC feed.

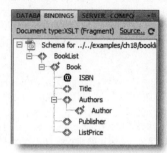

Figure 18-8.
The node tree (schema)
of booklist.xml

4. Save the XSLT fragment as `books1.xsl` in `workfiles/ch18`.

Displaying the book list in a table

Since the purpose is to show you a few of the things you can do with XSLT in Dreamweaver, I don't plan on styling the content. The data in the book list is best displayed in a table, so that's what I'll use.

1. Switch to Design view, and insert a table in `books1.xsl`. The table should have two rows and five columns. Set Table width to 90 percent and Cell padding to 4, leaving both Border thickness and Cell spacing blank. Set Header to Top, and click OK.

2. Give the first row the following headings: Title, Author(s), Publisher, ISBN, and Price.

3. Drag the Title node from the Bindings panel, and drop it in the second row so that the dynamic placeholder sits beneath the Title heading in the first row. Do the same for Publisher, ISBN, and ListPrice, dropping them in the appropriate cells in the second row. What should you do about the Author(s) cell? You want to show the names of all the authors, so you probably think you should use the Author node. Illogical though it may seem, drag the parent node, Authors, *not* the child node.

4. Click anywhere in the second row, and then select <tr> in the Tag selector to highlight the entire table row.

5. In the XSLT tab of the Insert bar, click the Repeat Region button, and select the Book node in the XPath Expression Builder (Repeat Region) dialog box. Click OK. Your page should now look like this:

Title	Author(s)	Publisher	ISBN	Price
{Title}	{Authors}	{Publisher}	{@ISBN}	{ListPrice}

90% (679)

6. Save books1.xsl, and press F12/Opt+F12 to view the XSLT fragment in a browser. Surprise, surprise . . . all the authors' names are listed. To understand why, you need to dive into the mysteries of XSLT syntax.

Understanding how XSLT is structured

Now's the time to look at an XSLT fragment in detail in Code view. The first line of books1.xsl looks like this:

```
<?xml version="1.0" encoding="utf-8"?> ➥
<!-- DWXMLSource="../../examples/ch18/booklist.xml" -->
```

The first part is the XML declaration. As I mentioned earlier, using the XML declaration is not mandatory, but if used, it must always be the first thing in the document. By default, Dreamweaver inserts the encoding attribute using the same value as in your Dreamweaver preferences. If your XML source uses a different encoding, you should change the setting for your XSLT fragment and any dynamic page that you intend to embed it in. Do this by choosing Page Properties from the Modify menu. In the Page Properties dialog box, select the Title/Encoding category, and set Encoding to the appropriate value.

The second part of the first line is an XML comment (the same format as HTML is used), where Dreamweaver stores the location of the XML source.

The next ten lines define common HTML entities. As mentioned earlier, only five entities are predefined in XML, so Dreamweaver anticipates the need for others that are likely to occur in XML feeds. You can also define others, if necessary.

Defining new entities

If you discover that your XSLT fragments are having problems with unrecognized entities, add a new definition on a new line within this section, using the same format. For example, if you want to add the entity for lowercase *e* acute (é), add this line:

```
<!ENTITY eacute   "&#233;">
```

In other words, remove the leading & and trailing semicolon from the HTML entity, and put the character entity equivalent in quotes. You can find a full list of HTML entities and their character entity equivalents at http://www.w3.org/TR/html4/sgml/entities.html.

Embedding HTML in XSLT

The rest of the code in the page is a mixture of XSLT and HTML. The two fit together in a very similar way to PHP and HTML. The XSLT processor handles anything in an XSLT tag (they all begin with <xsl:), and it treats anything outside as literal text. I have reproduced here the main XSLT code from books1.xsl and highlighted some key points in bold:

```
<xsl:stylesheet version="1.0" xmlns:xsl="http://www.w3.org/1999/ ➥
XSL/Transform">
<xsl:output method="html" encoding="utf-8"/>
```

```
<xsl:template match="/">
<table width="80%" cellpadding="4">
  <tr>
    <th scope="col">Title</th>
    <th scope="col">Author(s)</th>
    <th scope="col">Publisher</th>
    <th scope="col">ISBN</th>
    <th scope="col">Price</th>
  </tr>
  <xsl:for-each select="BookList/Book">
    <tr>
      <td><xsl:value-of select="Title"/></td>
      <td><xsl:value-of select="Authors"/></td>
      <td><xsl:value-of select="Publisher"/></td>
      <td><xsl:value-of select="@ISBN"/></td>
      <td><xsl:value-of select="ListPrice"/></td>
    </tr>
  </xsl:for-each>
</table>
</xsl:template>
</xsl:stylesheet>
```

The first line that I have highlighted creates an XSLT template. XSLT templates match a certain part of the XML source (which is why the attribute is called match). The closing
</xsl:template> tag is on the second line from the bottom, so all the code in between is
part of the template. The value of match is /, which is the XPath way of indicating the document root. In other words, this set of XSLT instructions will be applied to the whole of the
XML source, rather than just a specific part of it.

The next highlighted line uses <xsl:for-each>. As you can probably guess, this is the way
that XSLT creates a loop or repeat region. The value of select is BookList/Book, so the
loop applies to every Book node or element in the XML document. As the loop goes
through each Book node, the <xsl:value-of> instruction gets the selected value. When it
gets to the Authors node, it also loops through the child nodes. That's why you see all the
author's names displayed in the table, even though you haven't selected the Author node
in your XSLT fragment.

Accessing nested repeating elements

In some respects, the way that XSLT loops through the child nodes is quite useful, but
there are no commas between the authors' names. You need a way of getting to the
Author nodes and manipulating them. This is where things get interesting or fiendishly
complicated, depending on your point of view. I'll try to keep things as simple as possible.
Once you understand what's happening, it's a lot simpler than it may seem on your first
attempt.

Accessing the Author elements directly

This uses the same XSLT fragment as in the previous exercise. Save `books1.xsl` as `books2.xsl` before continuing, and then work with the new version.

1. Switch back to Design view, if necessary, and select the {Authors} placeholder in the second row of the table; then press Delete. The second cell of the second row should now be empty.

2. Select the Author repeating node in the Bindings panel, and drag and drop it into the empty cell. Instead of inserting an Author dynamic placeholder, as you might expect, Dreamweaver inserts an XSLT repeat region with a text placeholder, as shown here:

3. Highlight the words Content goes here, and press Delete. Make sure you remove only the text and not the gray tab labeled xsl:for-each. Don't click anywhere in the document, because the cursor *must* remain inside the repeat region.

4. In the XSLT tab of the Insert bar, click the Dynamic Text button (or choose Insert ➤ XSLT Objects ➤ Dynamic Text). This opens the XPath Expression Builder. Select Author. It may appear as though Dreamweaver hasn't created anything in the Expression field, but look a bit closer. There's a single period (.) there, which is the XPath way of saying "current node." Click OK.

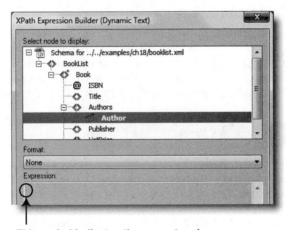

This period indicates the current node

5. You should now have a current-node dynamic placeholder inside the repeat region.

6. Save `books2.xsl`, and press F12/Opt+F12 to view the output in a browser. The authors' names are there, but the result looks worse—there's no space between them any more. Switch back to Dreamweaver, where you'll put it right.

18

7. Select the current-node dynamic placeholder that you created in step 5. Open Split view. You will see the following line highlighted in the underlying code:

```
<xsl:value-of select="."/>
```

8. Click inside Code view, and add the following code on a new line underneath. I've shown the preceding and following lines to help you get the right location.

```
<xsl:value-of select="."/>
<xsl:text>, </xsl:text>
</xsl:for-each></td>
```

When you start typing, Dreamweaver code hints will display the available XSLT tags. To save typing, you can scroll down to xsl:text and press Enter/Return. Automatic code completion will also insert the correct closing tag after you type </.

This inserts a comma followed by a space after the name of each author. You could just type the comma, but to get the space, you need to wrap it in the <xsl:text> tags.

9. Save books2.xsl, and view it in a browser. This is progress, but you don't want a comma after the last name. To deal with that, you need to use a conditional region.

Creating conditional regions

When working with an XSLT fragment, there are two options on the XSLT tab of the Insert bar (and XSLT Objects submenu of the Insert menu) for creating a conditional region—Conditional Region and Multiple Conditional Region. We'll take a closer look at both of them. First, a simple conditional expression.

Testing a single condition

You used a simple conditional expression in "Restricting the number of items in an XSLT repeat region" earlier in the chapter. As Figure 18-5 shows, the code inserted by Dreamweaver is very similar in structure to a PHP if statement. In the same way as a pair of curly braces, the <xsl:if> tags surround the code you want to display only if the condition is met. The condition is specified as the test attribute in the opening <xsl:if> tag.

Removing the final comma from authors' names

This builds on the XSLT fragment from the previous exercise and shows you how to get rid of the comma following the name of the last author. Save books2.xsl as books3.xsl, and work on the new document.

1. Open Split view, and highlight the line that you inserted in step 8 of the previous exercise. Alternatively, click the xsl:text tab in Design view. Click the Conditional Region button in the XSLT tab of the Insert bar.

2. Earlier in the chapter, you used the position() function to select the first five elements in the item node. Another intuitively named function, last(), determines whether an element is the last one in the current node. You don't want the comma

to be displayed if the author's name is the last one, so type position() != last() in the Test field of the Conditional Region dialog box. != has the same meaning as in PHP.

3. Save books3.xsl, and view it in a browser. The final comma is no longer displayed, so single author's names appear on their own, but the names of multiple authors are nicely formatted as a comma-separated list.

If you look in Code view, you'll see that the <xsl:text> tags that insert the comma and space have been surrounded by <xsl:if> tags like this:

```
<xsl:if test="position() != last()">
  <xsl:text>, </xsl:text>
</xsl:if>
```

Testing alternative conditions

Although there's a comma between each of the author's names when there are more than one, it would be more natural to replace the comma with "and" or "&" before the last name. The logic behind how you do this is simple. Instead of placing the comma *after* each author's name, create a conditional statement that decides whether to put a comma or "and" *before* the name. In pseudo-code this becomes:

```
if (position is greater than 1 AND position is not last) {
  insert a comma before the name
} else if (position is greater than 1 AND position is last) {
  insert "and" before the name
}
```

The if . . . else structure is exactly what you would use in PHP, but the XSLT syntax is a little more complex. XSLT wraps the whole conditional block in <xsl:choose> tags; <xsl:when> equates to if; and <xsl:otherwise> equates to else. Dreamweaver takes care of inserting the correct tags when you select Multiple Conditional Region from the XSLT tab of the Insert bar or from the XSLT Objects submenu of the Insert menu.

Inserting "and" before the final author's name

Save books3.xsl as books4.xsl, and continue working with the new file. In this exercise, you'll use a multiple conditional region to replace the final comma in a list of authors' names with "and."

1. Things are beginning to look rather crowded in the table cell that contains the dynamic placeholders for the authors' names. You need to click the xsl:if tab indicated by the arrow in the screenshot alongside.

   You will know that you have selected it correctly if the Property inspector displays the test expression for the conditional region as shown here (this is also how you would edit it).

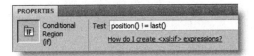

> *If you have difficulty selecting the tab, use the Zoom tool (it looks like a magnifying glass) at the bottom right of the Document window. When you select the Zoom tool, click on the area that you want to magnify until it's big enough to work with. Then choose the Select tool (an arrow). To zoom out, select the Zoom tool again and hold down Alt/Opt while clicking.*

2. Open Split view. The conditional region that you inserted in the preceding exercise should be highlighted. Since the syntax for a multiple conditional region is completely different, press Delete to remove the highlighted code.

3. In Code view, your cursor will be just below `<xsl:value-of select="."/>`. This is what XSLT uses to display the name of each author. This time, the comma needs to go in front of the author's name, so insert it as `<xsl:text>` on a new line above, like this:

```
<td><xsl:for-each select="Authors/Author">
  <xsl:text>, </xsl:text>
  <xsl:value-of select="."/>
```

4. Highlight the line you have just inserted, and click the Multiple Conditional Region button on the XSLT tab of the Insert bar, as shown in the following screenshot:

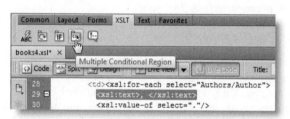

5. Type the following in the Test field of the Multiple Conditional Region dialog box:

```
position() > 1 and position() != last()
```

This will show the comma and space if the element is neither first nor last. Click OK.

6. If you thought the table cell was crowded before, just look at it now! Dreamweaver inserts Content goes here as a placeholder inside `<xsl:otherwise>`. This is where you are expected to create a default value if all tests fail. However, you don't want a default for this conditional region, so highlight Content goes here, and delete it. Keep Split view open to make sure you don't delete any XSLT tags.

7. To create the second condition, you need to position your cursor inside Code view immediately before the opening `<xsl:otherwise>` tag. Then click the Conditional Region button on the XSLT tab of the Insert bar. Make sure you click the one for a single condition (marked with IF), and *not* the icon for a multiple condition.

8. Type the following in the Test field of the Conditional Region dialog box, and then click OK:

```
position() > 1 and position() = last()
```

You'll use this test to insert "and" surrounded by a space on either side before the last author's name. It's necessary to check that the position is greater than 1, because you don't want "and" to appear before the names of single authors. Also notice that XSLT uses a single equal sign to test for equality.

9. There's now a severe overcrowding problem in the table cell, as Dreamweaver inserts another Content goes here to indicate where to insert what will be displayed when the test evaluates to true. It's easier to work in Code view at this stage, so click inside Code view, and replace Content goes here with the following:

```
<xsl:text> and </xsl:text>
```

> As you're typing, you'll notice that the greater-than sign you added in step 8 has been replaced by >. This is because > indicates the end of a tag, so XSLT conditional expressions use the HTML entity instead. XSLT also requires quotes in expressions. Dreamweaver handles all the necessary conversions automatically if you use the appropriate dialog boxes.

10. Save books4.xsl, and view it in a browser. You should see commas between names, with "and" separating the final two.

11. Change `<xsl:text> and </xsl:text>` to `<xsl:text> & </xsl:text>`, and view the page again. It won't work. You get the following error:

SAXParseException: Expected entity name for reference (books4.xsl, line 34, column 27)

This is because & is used by XML-related languages, such as XSLT, to designate an entity. Replace & with &, and all will be well.

Sorting elements

XSLT has many powerful features, including the ability to sort nodes, so they appear in a different order from the original XML source. Dreamweaver doesn't generate the code for you automatically, but it's very easy to do by hand.

Sorting the book list by title and publisher

Save books4.xsl as books5.xsl, and continue working with the new document. This exercise shows you how to sort the books first by title and then by publisher and title.

1. In Code view, locate the following line (it should be around line 25):

```
<xsl:for-each select="BookList/Book">
```

2. Insert a new line immediately below, and add the code shown in bold:

```
<xsl:for-each select="BookList/Book">
<xsl:sort select="Title"/>
```

3. Save the page, and view it in a browser. The value of select determines which node is used to sort the document. The list is now sorted by the books' titles.

   You can use multiple sort conditions by adding similar tags in the order of priority that you want to give each element.

4. To sort by publisher and then by title, use the following:

```
<xsl:for-each select="BookList/Book">
<xsl:sort select="Publisher"/>
<xsl:sort select="Title"/>
```

5. Test the page again. All the Apress books appear first, sorted in alphabetical order according to title, followed by the friends of ED books similarly sorted.

6. But, hey, this is a friends of ED book. Surely the order should be reversed. No problem. Just add an order attribute to the `<xsl:sort>` tag like this:

```
<xsl:sort select="Publisher" order="descending"/>
```

   Note that, as you type the code, Dreamweaver displays code hints for XSLT, showing you the available options.

7. All is now right with the world: the friends of ED books are listed first. Like PHP, *XSLT is case-sensitive*, so make sure you use the correct case for the node names.

Formatting elements

You may have noticed that there's a drop-down menu labeled Format in the middle of the XPath Expression Builder. This allows you to apply 22 preset formats to the content of a node. Most of them deal with formatting numbers or currency.

Formatting the book prices

Save books5.xsl as books6.xsl, and continue working with the new file. This exercise shows you how to format the book prices using the dollar and other currency symbols.

1. In Design view, select the ListPrice dynamic placeholder in the second row of the table, and click the Dynamic Text button in the XSLT tab of the Insert bar. This opens the XPath Expression Builder.

2. Make sure that ListPrice is selected in the field labeled Select node to display, activate the Format drop-down menu, and select Currency – Leading 0, 2 Decimal Places. The Expression field displays the XPath function that will be inserted in the underlying code: format-number(ListPrice, '$#0.00'). Click OK.

3. Save books6.xsl, and view it in a browser. Nothing is different—the prices don't have any currency symbol. This is because the parser used by Dreamweaver can't process all XSLT functions.

4. Create a PHP page called books.php. The only reason you need this page is to embed the XSLT fragment, but it's best to insert some ordinary text. Otherwise, you won't be able to click inside the Document window after the fragment has been embedded. Type a heading, such as Good Books. Move the cursor out of the heading, and select the XSL Transformation button on the Data tab of the Insert bar.

5. In the XSL Transformation dialog box, click the top Browse button, and select books6.xsl as the XSLT file. Click OK (or Choose on a Mac) to close both dialog boxes.

6. Save books.php, and test it in Live view or a browser. The currency symbols now appear correctly.

At the bottom of the Format drop-down menu in the XPath Expression Builder is an option to edit the format list. Ideally, this should be the place to create a custom currency format for sterling or euros. Unfortunately, Dreamweaver converts both the £ and € symbols to their HTML equivalents, which not only prevents them being displayed in the final page but also prevents you from using the XPath Expression Builder to edit any element to which you apply the format. The solution, fortunately, is very simple: apply one of the standard currency formats and edit it manually in Code view.

Change this:

```
format-number(ListPrice, '$#0.00')
```

to this (for pounds sterling):

```
format-number(ListPrice, '£#0.00')
```

or this (for euros):

```
format-number(ListPrice, '€#0.00')
```

You may wonder why the actual symbol is used instead of an entity. It's because the second argument to format-number() is a string literal. If you use an entity, it will be ignored.

Displaying output selectively

There are two ways of displaying output that meets certain criteria. One is to use an XPath filter. The other is to use a parameter. Let's take a quick look at both of them.

Filtering nodes with XPath

The XPath Expression Builder has an option that lets you build filters to display XML data selectively. The filters work in a very similar way to a WHERE clause in a SQL query, so you should have little difficulty understanding how they work.

Selecting books by price

Save books6.xsl as books7.xsl, and continue working with the new file. This exercise shows you how to select books cheaper than or equal to a specified price.

1. Select the repeat region for the second table row by clicking the xsl:for-each tab above the {Title} dynamic placeholder. You can tell that you have selected it correctly by checking the Property inspector, which should look like this:

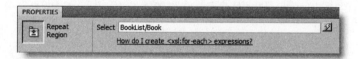

2. Click the lightning bolt icon to the right of the Select field in the Property inspector to open the XPath Expression Builder (Repeat Region) dialog box.

3. Click the triangle to the side of Build Filter in the middle of the XPath Expression Builder to expand the filter builder.

4. Click the plus button at the top of the Build Filter area. Click in the Where field to activate the drop-down menu that contains a list of all nodes. Select ListPrice.

5. Click in the Operator field, and choose <= (less than or equal to).

6. Click in the Value field, and type 40. Click anywhere inside the dialog box to remove the focus from the Value field. The Build Filter area should now look like this:

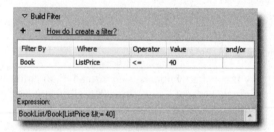

The Expression field below the Build Filter area shows you the XPath expression that Dreamweaver will insert into the XSLT code.

7. Click OK. Save books7.xsl, and view the page in a browser. Wow, computer books are getting expensive! Instead of the previous ten books, you should now see just four—all priced $40 or less. One of them is my *PHP Object-Oriented Solutions*. Grab it—it's a bargain.

Selecting books by price and publisher

As you can see from the preceding screenshot, the Build Filter area has an and/or option. This exercise shows you how to filter XML data using more than one condition. Save books7.xsl as books8.xsl, and continue working with the new file.

1. Repeat steps 1 and 2 of the previous exercise to open the XPath Expression Builder. Expand the Build Filter area if it's not already open.

2. Click in the and/or field, and select and from the drop-down menu.

3. Click the plus button at the top left of the Build Filter area to add another filter.

4. Click the Where field and select Publisher.

5. Leave Operator at the default =.

6. Click the Value field and type 'Apress'—it *must* be in quotes (single or double: it doesn't matter). The Build Filter area should now look like this.

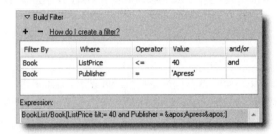

7. Click OK, save the page, and view it in a browser. You will now see just one title listed.

Look at the Expression field and the underlying code, and you will see that Dreamweaver has converted the quotes and the less-than operator to HTML entities, saving you a lot of effort with building XPath expressions. Remember to use the normal characters in the dialog boxes so that Dreamweaver can convert them correctly. It's also vital to remember that strings entered in the Value field must always be in quotes.

Using XSLT parameters to filter data

The other way of selecting output is by passing one or more parameters from the PHP page to the XSLT fragment. This is much more interactive, because the decision about what to display is dynamically generated, unlike filters, which are hard-coded into the XSLT instructions.

Creating a default parameter to select the publisher

Before using a parameter to change the content dynamically, you need to create a default parameter inside the XSLT fragment. Save books8.xsl as books9.xsl, and continue working with the new page.

1. Insert an XSLT parameter after the opening `<xsl:output>` tag (around line 15) like this:

```
<xsl:output method="html" encoding="utf-8"/>
<xsl:param name="pub" select="'friends of ED'"/>
<xsl:template match="/">
```

The `<xsl:param>` tag takes two attributes: name, which is self-explanatory, and select, which sets the parameter value. Note that there are two sets of quotes around friends of ED. The double quotes surround the value of select, which is a string and must itself be enclosed in quotes. To avoid a clash, single quotes are used for the inner pair.

By declaring the parameter immediately after the `<xsl:output>` tag, you make it global in scope—in other words, available throughout the XSLT script.

2. Switch to Design view, select the xsl:for-each tab that controls the repeat region for the entire table row, and click the lighting bolt icon in the Property inspector to open the XPath Expression Builder. You should see the same two filters as in step 6 of the last exercise.

3. Highlight the first filter (based on ListPrice), and click the minus button to remove it.

4. Click inside the Value field of the remaining filter to reveal a drop-down menu. You should now see your XSLT parameter listed with a dollar sign in front of it. Select $pub in place of 'Apress', as shown in the following screenshot:

The Expression field should now read BookList/Book[Publisher = $pub]. Click OK.

5. Save books9.xsl, and view it in a browser. Only friends of ED books should be listed.

Once you have defined a default parameter, you can use it to change the content of an XSLT fragment dynamically when it's embedded in a PHP page.

Sending a parameter from a PHP page

This simple exercise demonstrates how you can toggle between displaying books published by Apress and friends of ED, using a jump menu to send the parameter to the XSLT fragment through a URL query string.

1. Create a new PHP page called books_param.php.

2. From the Insert menu, select Form ➤ Jump Menu.

3. In the Insert Jump Menu dialog box, insert Apress in the Text field, and insert ?pub=Apress in the field labeled When selected, go to URL. This will add the name and value of the parameter to a query string that will be added to the URL when the page reloads.

4. Click the plus button to add a second menu item. Insert friends of ED in the Text field and ?pub=friends of ED for When selected, go to URL. Leave the other options in the dialog box unchanged. When you have finished, it should look like this:

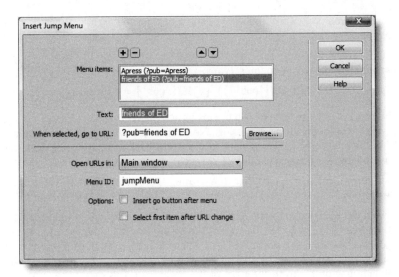

18

5. Click OK to insert the jump menu, and then select the menu object in Design view. In the Property inspector, change the name of the menu to pub. You also need the menu to display the currently selected value. Apart from the first time the page loads, this comes from the value of pub in the URL query string. Before clicking the Dynamic button in the Property inspector, you need to create a URL variable for Dreamweaver to use.

6. Open the Bindings panel, click the plus button, and select URL variable. Type pub in the Name field, and click OK.

7. Make sure the menu item is still selected in Design view, and click the Dynamic button in the Property inspector. When the Dynamic List/Menu dialog box opens, click the lightning bolt icon alongside the field labeled Select value equal to.

8. Expand the URL tree in the Dynamic Data dialog box, select pub, and click OK. Also click OK in the Dynamic List/Menu dialog box to close it.

9. Unfortunately, the code created by Dreamweaver needs tweaking slightly. Open Code view or Split view. The jump menu code should look like this:

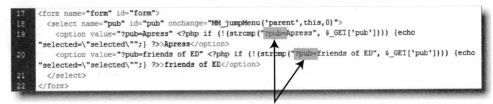

Delete the two highlighted sections

10. Delete the two sections indicated in the preceding screenshot by removing ?pub= from the PHP code. This is necessary because $_GET['pub'] contains just the value of the pub variable, not the whole query string. Be careful to remove the correct sections—you still want the full query string in the value attribute of each `<option>` tag.

11. `$_GET['pub']` won't be set when the page first loads, so add the following code immediately above the opening `<form>` tag:

```php
<?php if (!isset($_GET['pub'])) {$_GET['pub'] = 'Apress';} ?>
```

This sets the default value of pub to Apress and prevents any error from being generated if the query string is missing. I've deliberately chosen the opposite default from the one in the XSLT fragment to show how passing a parameter from outside takes precedence over the value of select in `<xsl:param>`.

12. Position your cursor just after the closing `</form>` tag, and switch back to Design view.

13. Embed the XSLT fragment by clicking the XSL Transformation button in the Data tab of the Insert bar. In the XSL Transformation dialog box, click the top Browse button, and select books9.xsl as the XSLT file. Then click the plus button alongside XSLT parameters. Type pub in the Name field of the Add Parameter dialog box, and click the lightning bolt icon to the right of the Value field. This opens the Dynamic Data dialog box, where you should select pub from the URL tree.

14. When you click OK to close the Dynamic Data dialog box, the Default value field is no longer grayed out in the Add Parameter dialog box. This is where you can insert a default value to be passed to the XSLT fragment. However, it's not necessary because you created a default value in the `<xsl:param>` tag in the previous exercise.

15. When you click OK to close the Add Parameter dialog box, you'll see the pub parameter listed, as shown in the following screenshot. An Edit button has been added in case you need to make any changes. Click OK to close the XSL Transformation dialog box.

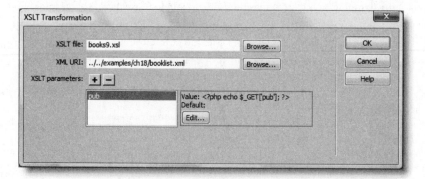

16. Save books_param.php, and press F12/Opt+F12 to view it in a browser. It should look like Figure 18-9 (I have added a few minimal style rules to make it look a little more presentable). Even though the default parameter in the XSLT fragment was set to friends of ED, the parameter sent from the PHP page takes precedence.

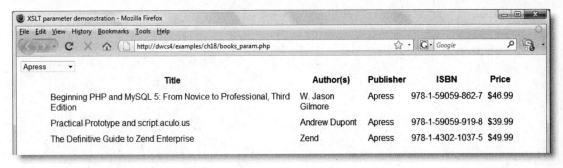

Figure 18-9. The contents of the XML document have been sorted, formatted, and displayed selectively through a combination of XSLT and PHP.

17. Select friends of ED from the jump menu, and the display will change, showing only foED books.

Chapter review

This has been only a brief introduction to working with XSLT. It's a massive and complex subject, but I think Dreamweaver has done a good job of making it more accessible to nonexperts. However, in spite of its power, XSLT has failed to take the web development community by storm. Although lack of browser support for client-side XSLT has played some part in holding it back, I think the main reason probably lies in the fact that XSLT on its own doesn't style the output. It manipulates data in a similar way to PHP, and since most XML is generated dynamically from a database, developers prefer to go straight to the source and use more familiar server-side technologies. The nonintuitive syntax is also a major put off for many developers.

In the next chapter, we'll look at handling XML with Spry, Adobe's implementation of Ajax. The Dreamweaver interface for handling Spry data sets has changed considerably since it was first introduced in Dreamweaver CS3. In addition to XML, Spry data sets can now be generated from an HTML source.

Select gallery: England ▾

Thumbnail	Caption
	Buckingham Palace and St James's Park
	A typical English country garden in Oxford
	Dancing round the daisies at Capel Manor
	Leaden skies over the Dome in London

The ability to manipulate data without the need to reload the web page lies at the very heart of Ajax. Done well, it can greatly improve the user experience: pages updated seamlessly without the need to wait for all content to reload. However, the reality often leaves much to be desired. The biggest failing lies in pages that rely wholly on Ajax to load their content, leaving nothing for search engines to index. The implementation of Spry data sets in the previous version of Dreamweaver fell down badly on this score. If you disabled JavaScript in your browser and visited a photo gallery that drew its content from a Spry data set, you were greeted by a page of meaningless code. In Dreamweaver CS3, Spry was capable of consuming data only from XML documents, so it was impractical to point visitors and search engines to alternative content without building two completely separate pages.

In response to criticism, Adobe has radically changed how you work with Spry data sets. Spry can now extract data from tables and other HTML structures, in addition to XML. Of course, you still need to create the HTML page that the data set uses, but this can be done very quickly if the content is drawn from a database with a recordset and repeat region. The advantages of using an HTML page as the data source are twofold: you're using a familiar technology, so development should be faster; moreover, the HTML data source remains in the underlying code, thereby providing content for search engines to index, as well as for anyone visiting your site with JavaScript disabled. Building the Spry data set and a lot of its associated HTML is now handled by a sophisticated wizard.

So, what is a Spry data set? Basically, it's the same as a recordset. However, instead of displaying all the results in the page when it loads, Spry retains most of the data in the browser's memory. When you click a link or activate a menu, it uses DOM manipulation to replace the existing content with the relevant data stored in memory. It's a useful technique for displaying details of upcoming events, product information, or a photo gallery. The data is loaded at the same time as the page is created, but you can set a timer mechanism to update the data set periodically. However, sending asynchronous requests for new data is not supported through the Dreamweaver interface.

In this chapter, you'll learn about the following:

- Displaying images using details drawn from a database or a Spry data set
- Creating a Spry data set from HTML and XML data sources
- Displaying data in a sortable table
- Using a Spry detail region to display related information
- Distinguishing the different types of Spry repeat regions
- Building a Spry online photo gallery

You don't need a deep knowledge of JavaScript to use Spry data sets. In fact, you don't need any knowledge at all. Nevertheless, you'll get more out of working with Spry if you know what the code looks like and what it's for. So, this chapter also invites you to dive into Code view to see what's going on under the hood.

> For security reasons, browsers do not permit Spry and other Ajax frameworks to create data sets from a data source located on a different domain. To get around this restriction, use the XSLT server behavior, as described in the previous chapter, or access the data source through a proxy script (see the appendix for details of how to create a proxy script).

Creating a Spry data set from HTML

To create a Spry data set, you need a data source that presents information in a structured manner. One obvious place to find such a data source is a database. However, you can't create a Spry data set directly from a recordset; you first need to lay out the data in an HTML structure, such as a table. Although this sounds like a disadvantage, it's actually a good thing, because the underlying data structure remains in the page for the benefit of search engines and anyone browsing with JavaScript disabled. However, if JavaScript is enabled in the visitor's browser, Spry manipulates the DOM, hiding the original HTML structure and presenting the contents of the data set dynamically, for example, as a sortable table or master-detail set.

For the exercises in this chapter, I have created a database table called ch19_gallery, which contains details of a series of photos of England and Japan. The photos are included in images/gallery in the download files for this book. You'll use this database table and photos to experiment with Spry data sets and eventually build the photo gallery shown in Figure 19-1.

Figure 19-1. The gallery uses a combination of JavaScript and PHP to change images without reloading the page.

Generating the HTML source

You can use any HTML structure to populate a Spry data set, as long as it presents data in a predictable manner. An existing table or list created in a static web page will do, but it's far more efficient to use a recordset. Not only is the data in an organized structure, but also the HTML structure is automatically updated whenever changes are made to the database table. To speed things up, I have created a SQL file to create the ch19_gallery table and populate it with data. So, let's create the table and generate the HTML source for the Spry data sets that will be used for the gallery.

Creating the database table

The following instructions show you how to load the ch19_gallery table into the dwcs4 database:

1. Load phpMyAdmin into your browser, and select the dwcs4 database.
2. Select the Import tab, and click the Browse button to navigate to ch19_gallery.sql in the extras folder of the download files for this book. If you're using MySQL 4.0, choose ch19_gallery40.sql instead.
3. Click Go to import the SQL, which will create the ch19_gallery table and populate it with data.
4. Select the ch19_gallery table in the navigation frame on the left side of phpMyAdmin. The first few records should look like Figure 19-2.

photo_id	filename	category	width	height	caption	description
1	basin.jpg	JPN	350	237	Water basin at Ryoanji temple, Kyoto	<p>Most visitors to Ryoanji Temple go to see just …
2	buck_palace.jpg	ENG	400	300	Buckingham Palace and St James's Park	<p>St James's Park is my favourite among all the p…
3	countrygarden.jpg	ENG	374	283	A typical English country garden in Oxford	<p>The quintessential English country garden is a …
4	daisydance.jpg	ENG	243	273	Dancing round the daisies at Capel Manor	<p>Capel Manor, just to the North of London, has 1…

Figure 19-2. The ch19_gallery table contains details of photos of England and Japan.

Each record contains the file name, dimensions, caption, and description of a photograph, plus the category to which it belongs: JPN for Japan and ENG for England.

Generating the HTML tables

The HTML data source that will be used for the Spry data sets will display the gallery images and thumbnails in plain tables. This exercise shows you how to bind the file names and dimensions of the images to <img> tags through the Bindings panel.

1. In Dreamweaver, create a new PHP page, and save it as gallery_eng.php in workfiles/ch19. Give the page the title Photo gallery: England.

2. Open the Recordset dialog box in Simple mode. Name the first recordset getENGphotos, use connQuery as the connection, and select the ch19_gallery table.

3. In the Columns field, select the Selected radio button, hold down the Ctrl/Cmd key, and select all the columns except photo_id and category.

4. You want the recordset to contain only those records that belong to the ENG category, so select category from the Filter drop-down menu. Leave the drop-down menu alongside on the default equal sign. Then select Entered Value from the left drop-down menu in the next row. This lets you specify the desired value in the field alongside. So, type ENG in that field. The values entered in the Recordset dialog box should look like this:

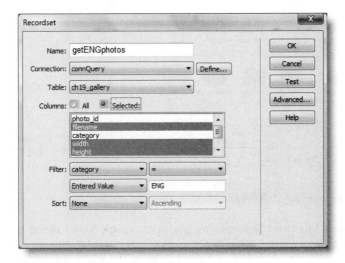

19

5. Insert a table with two rows and four columns. Make the table 100-percent wide, and insert table headers in the first row like this:

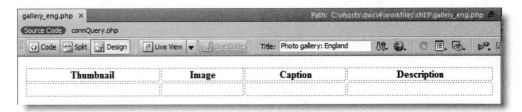

6. The recordset contains the file names of photos in the images/gallery folder. Smaller thumbnail images have the same names as their larger equivalents and are stored in images/gallery/thumbs. To display the images, you need to bind the data in the recordsets to <img> tags. This is done through a combination of the Select Image Source dialog box and the Bindings panel.

Position your cursor inside the first cell of the second row, and click the Image button on the Insert bar. Alternatively, select Insert ➤ Image, or press Ctrl+Alt+I/Opt+Cmd+I.

7. In the Select Image Source dialog box, navigate to the `images/gallery/thumbs` folder, select the value in the URL field, and cut it to your clipboard. Then select the Data sources radio button at the top of the dialog box, as shown in the following illustration. (In the Mac version of Dreamweaver, Data sources is a regular button located at the bottom of the dialog box.)

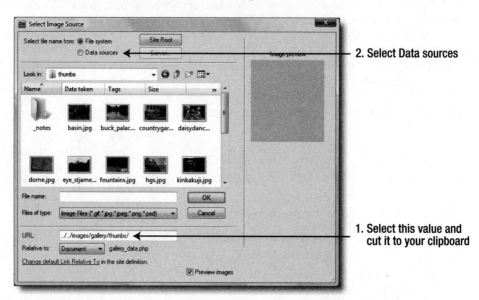

2. Select Data sources

1. Select this value and cut it to your clipboard

8. When you select Data sources, the Select Image Source dialog box displays the recordsets and any other dynamic data sources available to the page. Expand the getENGphotos recordset, and select filename. This inserts the necessary PHP code in the URL field. However, you need to add the path to the thumbs folder, so position your cursor in front of the PHP code, and paste the value from your clipboard, as shown in the following illustration. Then click OK (Choose on a Mac) to close the dialog box.

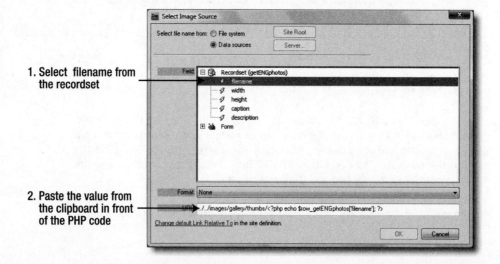

1. Select filename from the recordset

2. Paste the value from the clipboard in front of the PHP code

9. In the Image Tag Accessibility Attributes dialog box, activate the Alternate text drop-down menu to select <empty>, and click OK.

10. You now have a dynamic image placeholder in the first cell of the table. With the placeholder still selected, enter 80 in the field labeled W and 54 in the field labeled H in the Property inspector. This sets the width and height of the image. All the thumbnails are the same size, so you can insert explicit values.

11. Next, you need to create dynamic placeholders for the main images. Since the main images and thumbnails use the same file names, repeat steps 6–9, only this time your cursor should be in the second cell, and in step 7, navigate to the images/gallery folder.

12. The main images are different sizes, so you need to bind the width and height from the recordset. You can also use the caption as the alternate text.

   To do this, open the Bindings panel, and expand Recordset (getENGphotos). With the dynamic image placeholder still selected in the second cell, select width from the getENGphotos recordset. Then activate the Bind to drop-down menu at the bottom of the Bindings panel, select img.width, and click the Bind button, as shown in Figure 19-3. This inserts PHP code in the image's width attribute so that it uses the correct value from the recordset.

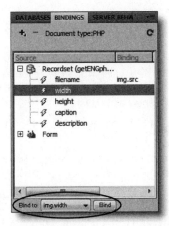

Figure 19-3.
Use the Bindings panel to apply dynamic values to attributes of the selected tag.

13. Repeat step 12, binding height from the recordset to img.height, and caption to img.alt.

14. Insert dynamic text placeholders for the caption and description columns in the third and fourth cells. Your page should now look like this:

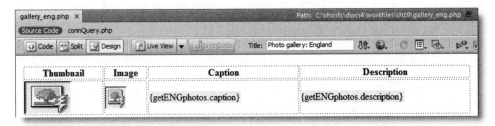

15. Save gallery_eng.php, and click the Live View button to check that the data is being displayed correctly, as shown in Figure 19-4.

Figure 19-4. The raw data is contained in an unstyled table.

16. If everything is OK, deactivate Live view, click inside the second row of the table, and select <tr> in the Tag selector at the bottom of the Document window. Apply a Repeat Region server behavior to display all records.

17. Select the whole table, and give it an ID by typing ENGdata into the field on the left side of the Property inspector.

18. Save gallery_eng.php, and test it in a browser. You should see a table with eight records displaying similar content to that shown in Figure 19-4.

19. Create another page called gallery_jpn.php. It should be identical to gallery_eng.php, except it should display the Japanese photos. In step 4, call the recordset getJPNphotos, and enter JPN in the field alongside Entered Value. In step 17, use JPNdata as the ID for the table.

20. Check your code, if necessary, against gallery_eng.php and gallery_jpn.php in examples/ch19.

Now that your data is in a predictable structure, you can use the Spry Data Set wizard.

Using the Spry Data Set wizard

The way you create a Spry data set has been completely rethought in Dreamweaver CS4. The Spry XML Data Set and Spry Table buttons and menu commands have been replaced by a single option, Spry Data Set, which launches a wizard that takes you through the process of creating the data set in a visual and intuitive manner. It also creates the basic HTML and CSS to display the data set in a variety of formats.

To use the Spry Data Set wizard, the data source must be in one of the following formats:

- **HTML table**: The table must have an ID. Data can be stored in either rows or columns. The wizard regards each table as a **data container**.
- **HTML elements**: The wizard can extract data stored in any HTML elements. The parent element (or data container) must have an ID, and the category or column that each child element belongs to needs to be clearly identifiable. This is usually done by assigning a class. For example, instead of building the tables in gallery_eng.php and gallery_jpn.php, you could put the same information in paragraphs and identify the thumbnails, images, captions, and descriptions with class names. This is probably the most cumbersome way of creating a data container.
- **XML**: You can use a static XML document or one generated dynamically from a database.

The wizard takes you through three steps, as follows:

1. Selection of the data source
2. Data configuration
3. HTML layout

You can omit the final step if you don't want Dreamweaver to create HTML to display the data set. The first two steps are identical for every data set. The final step offers a number of different options. Let's start by walking through the wizard to create a Spry data set and display it in a table.

Displaying a data set in a Spry table

The final step of the Spry Data Set wizard has options for setting classes on alternate rows of a Spry table. So, before diving into creating a Spry table, you need to do a little planning and decide how you want the table to look. The following options are available for setting CSS classes:

- Odd row class: This sets the styles for odd-numbered rows.
- Even row class: This sets the styles for even-numbered rows.
- Hover class: This determines how you want a row to look when the mouse hovers over it.
- Select class: This styles the currently selected row.

All these classes are optional, and you can set them later in Code view, but it's easier to create skeleton style rules first. I have created some simple styles in spry_table.css, which you can find in examples/ch19. The rules look like this:

```
body {
  color:#000;
  background-color:#FFF;
  font-family:Verdana, Arial, Helvetica, sans-serif;
}
```

19

```
th, td {
  padding:3px 10px;
}
th {
  cursor:pointer;
}
.odd {
  background-color:#EEE;
}
.even {
  background-color:#E8F2F8;
}
.hover {
  cursor:pointer;
  background-color:#B4C6DB;
}
.selected {
  color:#FFF;
  background-color:#999;
}
#details, #spryTable {
  float:left;
  font-size:85%;
}
#spryTable {
  width:350px;
}
#details {
  width:450px;
  margin:15px 0 0 30px;
}
dl {
  width:600px;
  font-size:85%;
}
```

The odd rows will have a light gray background, and the even rows will have a light blue one. Spry tables are interactive but don't use <a> tags, so you need to change the cursor explicitly to look like a hand when the mouse pointer passes over a table row. Spry applies the setting for Hover class only over table rows, so you must create a separate rule to change the cursor for table headers. The color I have chosen for table rows when the mouse passes over them is dark blue, with white text on a dark gray background for the selected row.

Figure 19-5 shows the simple Spry table and detail region that you'll build in the next couple of exercises. Clicking the Thumbnail or Caption column header reorders the rows according to which column you clicked. The main image and description are displayed in a Spry detail region floating alongside the table and are automatically updated depending on the currently selected row—all without the need to refresh the page.

Figure 19-5. A Spry table can be sorted and display related information in a detail region without reloading the page.

Creating a sortable table

This exercise shows you how to create a Spry sortable table to display selected columns from a data set. The instructions form the basis for creating any Spry data set. They assume you created the ch19_gallery table and gallery_eng.php in the previous exercises. If you don't have a copy of gallery_eng.php, use gallery_eng.php in examples/ch19.

1. Save gallery_eng.php as spry_table.php in workfiles/ch19, and attach spry_table.css in the examples/ch19 folder (attaching a style sheet was covered in Chapter 4).

2. Click the Spry Data Set button in the Spry tab of the Insert bar, as shown in the following screenshot, or choose Insert ➤ Spry ➤ Spry Data Set.

3. This launches the Spry Data Set wizard (see Figure 19-6). When it first loads, the wizard looks like a vast empty space. For it to spring to life, you need to specify the data source in the fields at the top of the dialog box.

As shown in the preceding screenshot, there are five options:

- Select Data Type: The drop-down menu offers a choice of HTML and XML. This always defaults to HTML.

- Data Set Name: Dreamweaver automatically populates this with ds1, ds2, and so on. As with recordsets, it's better to choose a more descriptive name. The value inserted here is used as a JavaScript variable, so it must not begin with a number, and it cannot contain any spaces, hyphens, or other punctuation apart from the underscore(_).

- Detect: This is displayed only when Select Data Type is set to HTML. It determines the HTML structures that the wizard uses to detect the data source. The default is Tables. The other options are Divs, Lists, and Custom.

- Specify Data File: Use the Browse button to navigate to the file that contains the data source. This can be either an external file or the current file.

- Design time feed: This option caters for the situation where the actual data file is generated dynamically and not available on the development computer. Clicking this link displays a dialog box where you can specify a static file that contains dummy data in the same format as the actual data file.

Enter dsPhotos in the Data Set Name field, and use the Browse button to select the current file, spry_table.php. The Data Selection field of the wizard should display the image of Buckingham Palace and St James's Park, together with its thumbnail, caption, and description.

4. To select the data to be used in the data set, you need to select a data container, in other words, the table you created earlier. There are two ways of doing this. Either you can click the yellow right-facing arrow at the top-left of the data container in the Data Selection field or you can select its name from the Data Containers drop-down menu at the top-right of the Data Selection field. Use either method to select the ENGdata table.

The wizard should now look like Figure 9-6. The Data Selection field shows a visual representation of the data set, while the Data Preview field shows the raw data.

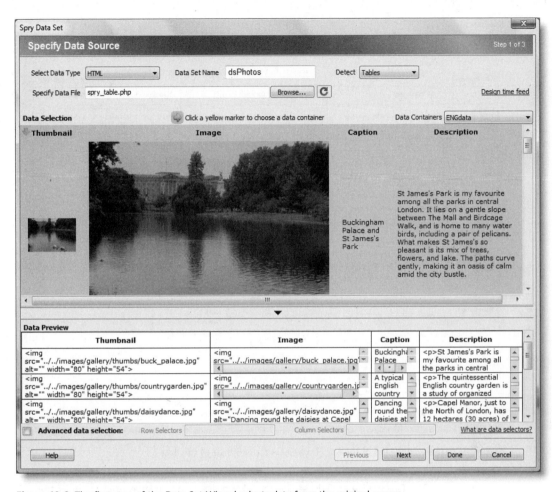

Figure 19-6. The first step of the Data Set Wizard selects data from the original source.

> *The* Advanced data selection *checkbox at the bottom left of the wizard is used only when you use other HTML structures to define the data container. Selecting the checkbox enables the* Row Selectors *and* Column Selectors *fields, where you list the HTML elements and class names that identify the rows and columns of the data set.*

5. Click Next to move to the next step in the wizard (see Figure 19-7). This is where you configure the data.

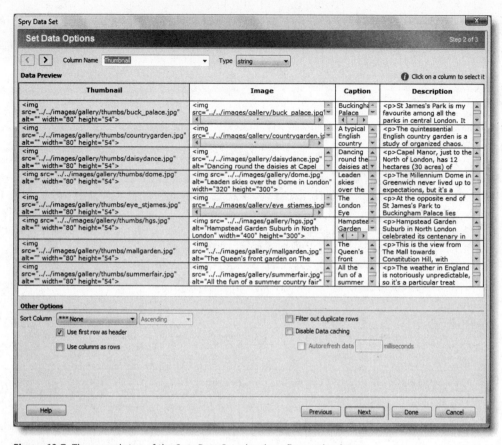

Figure 19-7. The second step of the Spry Data Set wizard configures the data.

The Column Name field at the top of the dialog box displays the name of the column currently selected in the Data Preview field. By default, Dreamweaver uses the names in the first table row. However, if the first row contains data instead of header names, deselect the checkbox labeled Use first row as header at the bottom left of the dialog box. This changes the column names to column0, column1, and so on. You can edit these generic names in the Column Name field. Names taken from the data table itself cannot be edited.

The Type drop-down menu alongside the Column Name field sets the data type. By default, everything is treated as a string. To change the data type, select the column by clicking it in the Data Preview field, or use the left and right arrows to the left of the Column Name field. The available options are string, number, date, and html. The first three affect the sort order of the column. The final one, html, should be used for data that includes HTML tags. If you fail to do so, the HTML tags will be displayed in the web page rather than be used to structure the data.

Most of the options in the Other Options section are self-explanatory. You can select one of the columns to sort the data in ascending or descending order, change the orientation of the data by selecting Use columns as rows, and filter out any duplicate rows.

The final option, Disable Data caching, makes the web page more responsive to changes in the original data. By default, the data set remains in the browser's cache and isn't updated when changes are made to the data source. If you select this checkbox, you need to enter in the Autorefresh data field how frequently the web page should check the original data source. The value needs to be expressed in milliseconds, so entering 60000 in this field would check the original data source once a minute.

There is no option to exclude specific columns from the final data set, although it's up to you which columns to display in the web page. However, it's inefficient to include large amounts of redundant data in a data set, so you should take this into account when designing the original data container and include only data that you want to use.

6. Select the Description column by clicking it in the Data Preview field, set the Type drop-down menu to html, and then click Next to move to the final step of the wizard, which is shown in Figure 19-8.

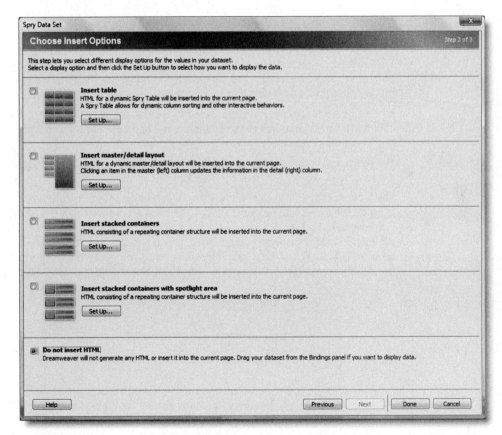

Figure 19-8. The final step of the Spry Data Set wizard lets you display the data in a variety of formats.

7. The final step has four display options, as well as the option not to insert any HTML. For this exercise, select the Insert table radio button, and then click the Set Up button alongside the illustration of a table.

8. This opens the Spry Data Set – Insert Table dialog box, as shown here:

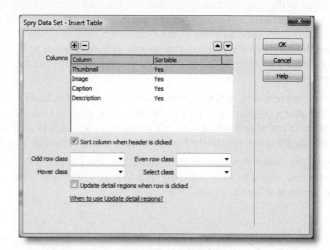

The layout and functionality of the dialog box should be immediately familiar from other parts of Dreamweaver. You can remove a column by selecting it and clicking the minus button; and if you change your mind, restore it using the plus button.

By default, each column is sortable when its header is clicked. If you don't want a column to be sortable, select the column name and deselect the checkbox at the bottom of the Columns area.

The remaining options set the CSS classes discussed earlier and let you update one or more detail regions when a row is clicked.

The table in Figure 19-5 displays just the Thumbnail and Caption columns, so highlight the other two and delete them. Set the class drop-down menus to match the classes in spry_table.css (you might need to select the class name twice, because the menus appear to be temperamental), and select the checkbox labeled Update detail regions when row is clicked. This will be used to display the main image and description for each row in the table. The dialog box should now look like this:

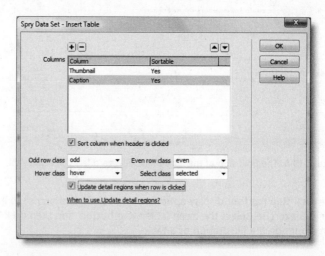

9. Click OK to close the dialog box. This takes you back to the Spry Data Set wizard. If you're unsure about any of the settings, click Previous to return to the earlier steps of the wizard, and make any changes. Otherwise, click Done to close the wizard and create the Spry data set and its associated Spry table.

10. Save spry_table.php, and click OK to copy the Spry dependent files to your Spry assets folder. The page should now look like Figure 19-9. As you can see, a new table has been added, similar to the one built from the PHP recordset.

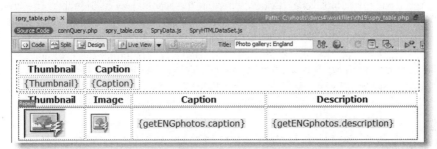

Figure 19-9. In Design view, a Spry table gives no real indication of what it will look like in a browser.

11. Click the Live View button to see what the page will look like in a browser. It should look similar to Figure 19-5 minus the image and description. We'll add them in a moment, but first test the page by running the mouse over the rows and clicking the column headers to sort the data. The important thing to notice is that only the thumbnails and captions are displayed; the unstyled HTML table being used as the data source has been removed from the DOM.

12. Deactivate Live view, and press F12/Opt+F12 to view the page in a browser. As long as JavaScript is enabled, it should look the same. Right-click to select the option to view the page's source code. The original HTML data source is still there, so the page remains accessible to search engines and anyone viewing it with JavaScript disabled. The code generated by Dreamweaver uses the data in the HTML table to populate the Spry table, and then hides the HTML table.

Check your code, if necessary, against spry_table_01.php in examples/ch19.

> *Live view processes only the current page through the testing server, so you can use it to view the output of a Spry data set only if the data source is in the same page. If you want to use Live view to test a Spry data set that uses a dynamically generated data source in an external page, load the page that generates the data source into a browser, and save it as a static HTML file. Use the static file for testing, and then switch back to the dynamic data source when deploying the site on the Internet.*

Displaying related data in a Spry detail region

A Spry table is basically a repeat region applied to a single table row. However, instead of using PHP to generate the other rows on the web server, it uses JavaScript to manipulate the DOM inside the browser. An advantage of doing this is that Spry can respond to mouse events, such as moving over an element or clicking a table cell. By creating a Spry detail region, you can change its contents in response to such events. Adding a detail region is very easy, as you'll see in the following exercise.

859

Adding an updatable detail region

This exercise builds on the preceding one by adding a Spry detail region to display the main image and description when you click the related table row. Continue using the same page, or copy spry_table_01.php from examples/ch19, and save it in workfiles/ch19 as spry_table.php.

1. In spry_table.php, click anywhere in the second row of the table. The <div> and <tr> tags in the Tag selector at the bottom of the Document window are highlighted in orange, indicating that they contain Spry data set code.

2. Select the <div> tag, right-click, and select Set ID from the context menu. Set the ID to spryTable. This is one of the style rules defined in spry_table.css. It floats the <div> left and sets its width to 350 pixels.

3. With the <div> still selected, press the right arrow key once to move the insertion point outside the <div>.

4. To display the description, you need to create a Spry detail region. Click the Spry Region button on the Spry tab of the Insert bar, as shown in the following screenshot, or select Insert ➤ Spry ➤ Spry Region.

5. This opens the Insert Spry Region dialog box, as shown here:

The options let you choose a <div> or <span> as the container. Most of the time, you'll want to use a <div>, unless you want the region to appear inline. You also have the choice of Region or Detail Region. The link at the bottom of the dialog box opens the Dreamweaver help files to explain the difference. Basically, a Spry region is used to display multiple elements from a data set, such as a table. A Spry detail region gives you access to the currently selected element within the data set. In this case, you're going to display the main image and description of whichever thumbnail or caption the user clicks in the table.

The remaining options in the dialog box let you choose the data set if there's more than one on the page and whether to wrap the region around the current selection or to replace it. Since nothing is currently selected in spry_table.php, the Wrap selection and Replace selection options are grayed out.

Use the settings shown in the preceding screenshot, and click OK.

6. Dreamweaver inserts the Spry region with placeholder text, as shown here:

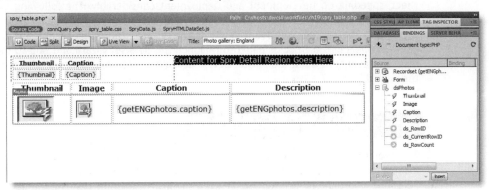

7. Open the Bindings panel. As you can see from the preceding screenshot, dynamic objects for Spry data set values are listed in the same way as for a recordset or in an XSLT fragment. At the bottom of the list are three Spry data objects that can be used to get access to the row ID, current row ID, and row count.

The data objects that you're interested in at the moment are Image and Description. Select Image, and use it to replace the placeholder text in the Spry detail region. You can either drag and drop it or use the Insert button at the bottom of the Bindings panel.

8. With the Image dynamic placeholder still selected, select Paragraph from the Format drop-down menu in the HTML view of the Property inspector.

9. The data in the Description column is already formatted in paragraphs, so you need to move the insertion point outside the closing </p> tag but remain inside the Spry detail region <div>. So, select <p> in the Tag selector, and press your right arrow key once. Then insert Description from the Bindings panel.

10. You now need to apply an ID to the Spry detail region <div>. Select <div> in the Tag selector, right-click, and select details from Set ID in the context menu.

11. The page should now look like this (if you have a small monitor, the details <div> might be forced down below the <div> that contains the Spry table):

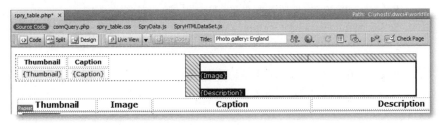

In Design view, it still looks very unimpressive, but when you save the page and test it in a browser, it should look like Figure 19-5 and be fully interactive.

You can check your code against spry_table_02.php in examples/ch19.

Creating a master-detail set in a single operation

Adding a Spry detail region to a table, as you have just done, creates a master-detail set. However, one of the other options in the final step of the Spry Data Set wizard also creates a master-detail set in a single operation. What's more, it comes with its own style sheet, speeding up development and deployment considerably. The following exercise describes how to set up the options for a master-detail set. Since you already have a data set in spry_table.php, you could delete the Spry table and detail region, and double-click dsPhotos in the Bindings panel to relaunch the data set wizard and skip to the final step. However, let's build the master-detail set from scratch to practice all three steps of the wizard.

Setting the options for a master-detail set

This exercise guides you through the Spry Data Set wizard to create a master-detail set in a single operation. Since the first two steps of the wizard were described in detail in the "Creating a sortable table" exercise, I'll keep the instructions for defining the data source brief and concentrate on the final step. This exercise assumes you have created the ch19_gallery table and gallery_jpn.php, as described earlier in the chapter.

1. Save gallery_jpn.php as master_detail.php in workfiles/ch19.

2. In master_detail.php, launch the Spry Data Set wizard from the Spry tab of the Insert bar or the Insert menu.

3. In the first step of the wizard dialog box, use the following settings:

   - Select Data Type: HTML
   - Data Set Name: dsPhotos
   - Detect: Tables
   - Specify Data File: master_detail.php
   - Data Containers: JPNdata

   Just to introduce a little variety, I have chosen JPNdata as the source for the data set. The fact that I have used the same name as before for the data set, dsPhotos, doesn't matter. The data set is being used in a different page, so there is no conflict. As you'll see later in this chapter, you can use Spry to change the data source dynamically.

4. Click Next to move to the second step of the data set wizard.

5. Select the Description column, and set the value of Type to html. Leave the other options at their default settings, and click Next to move to the final step of the wizard.

6. Select the Insert master/detail layout radio button, and click the Set Up button alongside to open the following dialog box:

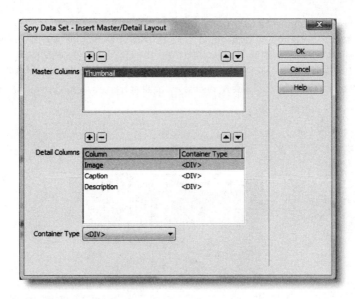

The Master Columns field determines which columns you want to display as a click-able list on the left of the page. For this exercise, you're going to use the Caption column. However, at least one column must always be selected in the Master Columns field, so you can't delete Thumbnail without first adding Caption.

7. Click the plus button above the Master Columns field, select Caption from the Add Columns dialog box that opens, and click OK. This adds Caption to the Master Columns field.

8. You can now safely select Thumbnail in the Master Columns field, and click the minus button to remove it.

9. The Detail Columns field determines what to display in a box on the right side of the page when one of the items is clicked in the list on the left of the page. Since Caption is used in the Master Columns list, select Caption in the Detail Columns field, and click the minus button to remove it.

10. This leaves Image and Description in the Detail Columns field. You can select how the content will be displayed by selecting a value from the Container Type drop-down menu at the bottom of the dialog box. The available options are <DIV>, <P>, <SPAN>, and <H1> through <H6>.

    Select Image, and set the value of Container Type to <P>.

11. The Description column is already formatted as HTML, so set its Container Type to <DIV>.

12. Click OK to close the Spry Data Set – Insert Master/Detail Layout dialog box, and then click Done to close the wizard.

13. Save master_detail.php, and click OK when prompted to copy the dependent files to your Spry assets folder.

14. Press F12/Opt+F12 to test the page in a browser. There you have a simple, but elegantly designed master-detail set, as shown in Figure 19-10. As before, Spry removes the original HTML table from the DOM, but it remains in the underlying HTML code for search engines and anyone with JavaScript disabled to access.

You can check your code, if necessary, against `master_detail.php` in examples/ch19.

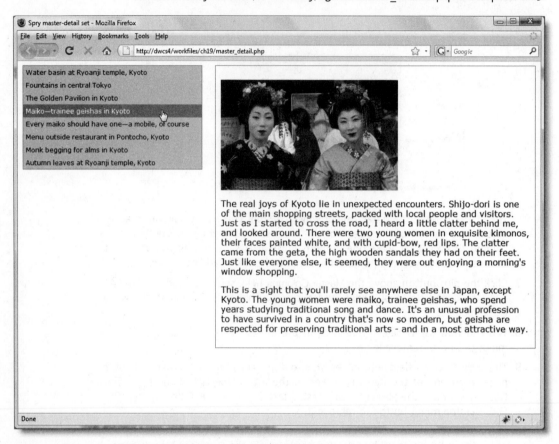

Figure 19-10. The Spry Data Set wizard creates a master-detail set in just a few minutes.

Displaying a data set as a list

Dreamweaver can create four types of lists from a Spry data set: unordered (<ul>), ordered (<ol>), definition (<dl>), and drop-down menus (<select>). The way you create them is similar to a detail region by selecting a button in the Spry tab of the Insert bar or using an option on the Insert ➤ Spry menu. In other words, the data set must already exist. A list must be inside a Spry region, which either you can create first or you can leave it up to Dreamweaver to wrap the list in a Spry region when you have finished.

Unordered and ordered lists have only two options: the data set and the name of the column that you want to display. Definition lists and drop-down menus have an extra option because both have a label and value for each item in the list. I'll show you how to create a drop-down menu when building the photo gallery later, but let's look briefly at creating a Spry definition list. To avoid the need to go through the Spry Data Set wizard again, let's adapt spry_table.php from earlier in the chapter.

Creating a Spry definition list

This exercise shows you how to display the Caption and Description columns of the dsPhotos data set as a Spry definition list. The result won't look very elegant, but the purpose is simply to demonstrate how to create a list with Spry. Use spry_table_02.php in examples/ch19 if you don't have your own copy of the file.

1. In spry_table.php, delete the Spry table and detail region, but leave the original HTML table intact. This leaves you with the Spry data set definition and all the external files still attached.

2. Save the page as spry_list.php.

3. Click the Spry Repeat List button in the Spry tab of the Insert bar, as shown in the following screenshot, or select Insert ➤ Spry ➤ Spry Repeat List.

4. This opens the Spry Repeat List dialog box, as shown here:

The Container tag drop-down menu contains the following four options:

- **UL (Unordered List)**: This creates an unordered list using `<ul>` tags and populates the `<li>` tags with the values stored in the column selected as Display column. Only one column can be selected.

- **OL (Ordered List)**: This creates an ordered (numbered) list using `<ol>` tags. In other respects, it's identical to the previous option.

- **DL (Definition List)**: This creates a definition list using `<dl>` tags. When you select this option, the Display column option is replaced by DT Column and DD Column, which let you choose what to display in the `<dt>` and `<dd>` tags.

- SELECT (Drop-down List): **This creates a drop-down menu using** `<select>` **tags.** When you select this option, a Value column option is added at the bottom of the dialog box. Display column determines the value displayed in the drop-down, and Value column sets the value attribute of each `<option>` tag. You'll see this in operation when building the Spry gallery later in the chapter.

Whichever option you choose for Container tag, **the** Spry Data Set **option selects the** data set to be used. There's only one data set on the current page, so it's selected by default.

5. Select DL (Definition List) for Container tag, set DT column to Caption, and set DD column to Description. This will display the information as a definition list. Click OK to save the settings, and click Yes when Dreamweaver asks whether you want to insert a Spry region. The page should now look like this in Split view:

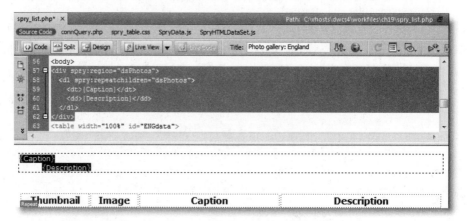

As you can see from the preceding screenshot, Dreamweaver has inserted a `<div>` on lines 57–62, and set the `spry:region` property to dsPhotos, the name of the data set to use.

The opening tag of the definition list on line 58 contains the `spry:repeatchildren` property, which is also set to dsPhotos. This tells the browser to loop through the dsPhotos data set for each child element of the `<dl>` tag—in other words, the `<dt>` and `<dd>` tags.

Lines 59–60 insert {Caption} and {Description} data objects in the `<dt>` and `<dd>` tags, respectively.

Dreamweaver does all this coding for you automatically, so you don't need to bother about it unless you want to start using Spry in more sophisticated ways.

> *Sometimes, Dreamweaver fails to prompt you to add a Spry region when you click* OK *to close the* Insert Spry Repeat List *dialog box. If this happens, select the definition list, and click the* Spry Region *button on the* Insert *bar, or select* Insert ➤ Spry ➤ Spry Region. *Set* Container *to* DIV, Type *to* Region, Spry Data Set *to the same data set as the definition list uses, and select the option to wrap the current selection.*

6. Save spry_list.php, and press F12/Opt+F12 to view the page in a browser. It should look like Figure 19-11.

You can check your code, if necessary, against spry_list.php in examples/ch19.

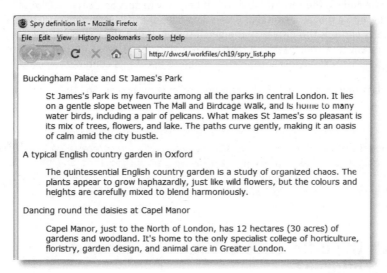

Figure 19-11. The contents of the Spry data set are now displayed as a definition list.

Understanding the Spry data code

I don't intend to go into great detail about how the code works. The whole idea of the Spry Data Set wizard is to make it easy to use Ajax without needing to become a JavaScript guru, but it does help to recognize the code and have a basic understanding of what it's for.

The table and detail region in spry_table.php use remarkably little code, as you can see from the following listing (all the Spry code is highlighted in bold):

```
<div id="spryTable" spry:region="dsPhotos">
  <table>
    <tr>
      <th spry:sort="Thumbnail">Thumbnail</th>
      <th spry:sort="Caption">Caption</th>
    </tr>
    <tr spry:repeat="dsPhotos" spry:setrow="dsPhotos" spry:odd= ➥
"odd" spry:even="even" spry:hover="hover" spry:select="selected">
      <td>{Thumbnail}</td>
      <td>{Caption}</td>
    </tr>
  </table>
</div>
<div id="details" spry:detailregion="dsPhotos">
<p>{Image}</p>{Description}
</div>
```

Even if you don't know how it works, the Spry syntax is easy to follow. Everything begins with spry: followed by the name of a property and its value. The property names are all very intuitive: region, sort, repeat, and so on.

Take the code in the second table row. It begins with spry:repeat="dsPhotos". This turns the row into a repeat region that draws data from the dsPhotos data set. The spry:setrow property controls the display in the detail region. When the row is clicked, Spry sets it as the current row, which sends a message—or triggers an event, to use the correct terminology—that tells any dsPhotos detail region to update its contents.

The data objects that hold the contents are in curly braces. So, {Description} tells the browser to display the current description.

> *If you forget to set one of the classes in a Spry table, you can easily edit the repeat row by adding* spry:odd, spry:even, spry:hover, *or* spry:select *and the name of the class. Dreamweaver code hints speed up the process by displaying the available options after you type* spry: *in Code view.*

What's the difference between repeat and repeatchildren?

If you're interested in taking Spry further, look more closely at the code in the Spry table and the Spry definition list. Both use Spry repeat regions, but there's a subtle difference between them.

The repeat region in the table is defined in the <tr> tag of the second row like this:

```
<tr spry:repeat="dsPhotos" spry:setrow="dsPhotos" spry:odd="odd" ➥
spry:even="even" spry:hover="hover" spry:select="selected">
  <td>{file}</td>
  <td>{caption}</td>
</tr>
```

The repeat region in the definition list is defined like this:

```
<dl spry:repeatchildren="dsPhotos">
  <dt>{Caption}</dt>
  <dd>{Description}</dd>
</dl>
```

In the table, the spry:repeat property repeats an element and all of its content for each row in the data set. In other words, it repeats the table row (<tr>) and its two cells (<td>) for each row in the dsPhotos data set. This results in the creation of eight table rows.

In the definition list, on the other hand, spry:repeatchildren repeats all the children of a given element for each row in a data set. The property is defined in the <dl> tag, which has two children: <dt> and <dd>. As a result, Spry creates *one* definition list with a <dt> and <dd> pair for every row in the dsPhoto data set.

So, the difference can be summarized as follows:

- spry:repeat repeats the element in which it is declared.
- spry:repeatchildren doesn't repeat the element itself but does repeat its children.

Because Spry manipulates the content in the browser window without creating any underlying source code for you to inspect, it can sometimes be difficult to grasp the difference between what's happening. For example, if you change the code in the <dl> tag from spry:repeatchildren to spry:repeat, the output seems to be identical. However, if you create a style rule to add a visible border around a definition list, the difference becomes obvious. With spry:repeatchildren, there's a single border around the list, but with spry:repeat, you get a border around each list item (see Figure 19-12). In other words, the <dl> element is also repeated, so you end up with eight definition lists instead of one.

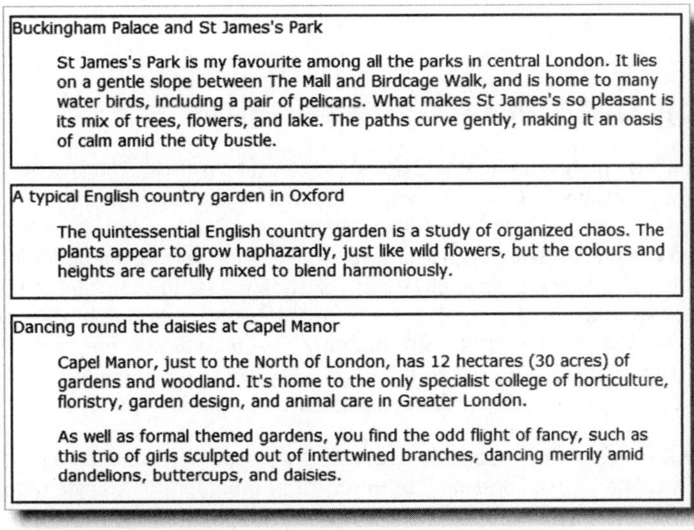

Figure 19-12. Using spry:repeat with the <dl> tag creates a separate definition list for each row of the data set.

This might tempt you to remove the Spry property from the <dl> tag and use spry:repeat directly on the <dt> and <dd> elements like this:

```
<dl>
  <dt spry:repeat="dsPhotos">{file}</dt>
  <dd spry:repeat="dsPhotos">{caption}</dd>
</dl>
```

Figure 19-13 shows what happens—all the <dt> elements are repeated first, followed by all the <dd> elements.

Buckingham Palace and St James's Park
A typical English country garden in Oxford
Dancing round the daisies at Capel Manor
Leaden skies over the Dome in London
The London Eye keeps watch over the Foreign Office
Hampstead Garden Suburb in North London
The Queen's front garden on The Mall in London
All the fun of a summer country fair

St James's Park is my favourite among all the parks in central London. It lies on a gentle slope between The Mall and Birdcage Walk, and is home to many water birds, including a pair of pelicans. What makes St James's so pleasant is its mix of trees, flowers, and lake. The paths curve gently, making it an oasis of calm amid the city bustle.

The quintessential English country garden is a study of organized chaos. The plants appear to grow haphazardly, just like wild flowers, but the colours and heights are carefully mixed to blend harmoniously.

Figure 19-13. Using the wrong type of Spry repeat region brings unwanted results.

You get equally undesirable results if you use spry:repeatchildren in the <tr> tag of the table. Instead of eight table rows with two table cells each, you get one table row with 16 table cells.

Switching data sets dynamically

The pages you have built so far in this chapter use two data sources, ENGdata and JPNdata. Rather than display them in separate pages, let's switch between them using a Spry select list. This uses an HTML <select> element to create a drop-down menu. The <option> tags are populated automatically by a Spry data set, in the same way as the definition list that you built in the "Displaying a data set as a list" section earlier in the chapter. However, it has the added advantage that you can use it to dispatch information that other Spry components can respond to. As a result, you'll not only be able to display the main images and descriptions without needing to reload the page, but you'll also be able to switch between the two sets of photos without reloading, making a smooth user experience.

To save time, I have created a page (gallery_select_start.php in examples/ch19) that builds an HTML data source containing both sets of photographs in a single table, with an extra column for the category to which each photo belongs. The page is laid out the same way as spry_table.php earlier in the chapter with the thumbnails and captions in a Spry table on the left and the image and description in a Spry detail region on the right. Below that are two tables that act as the HTML data containers. The first one has an ID called photos; it acts as the data container for the gallery. The second table is called galleries. This will be used as the data container for the drop-down menu; the left column identifies the categories, and the right one shows the values that will be displayed in the menu.

Filtering a Spry data set

Spry data sets support two types of filters: destructive and nondestructive. A **destructive filter** removes elements permanently from a data set. For example, if you use a destructive filter to remove the Japanese photos from the data set, the only way to gain access to the Japanese photos is to rebuild the data set. A **nondestructive filter**, on the other hand, removes the elements temporarily, so this is the type of filter you need to switch between the two sets.

You create both types of filters the same way by defining a function that determines whether to reject or include a row in the filtered set. The function takes three arguments: the data set, the current row, and the row number. If the data in the row conforms to your filter criteria, the function must return the row. Otherwise, it must return null.

To apply the filter, you pass the name of the filter function to the data set's `filterData()` method for a destructive filter or to its `filter()` method for a nondestructive filter.

Filtering the photo data set

The following exercise shows you how to apply a nondestructive filter to the dsPhotos data set in gallery_select_start.php.

1. Open gallery_select_start.php in examples/ch19, and save it as gallery_select.php in workfiles/ch19. When Dreamweaver asks whether you want to update the links, click No. You can close gallery_select_start.php, because you don't need it any more.

2. Press F12/Opt+F12 to launch gallery_select.php in a browser to make sure that it's working correctly.

   If the browser displays a message saying it failed to retrieve the data set, locate the following line of code (it should be on or around line 50):

   ```
   var dsPhotos = new Spry.Data.HTMLDataSet(../../examples/ch19/null, ➡
   "photos");
   ```

   Change it to this:

   ```
   var dsPhotos = new Spry.Data.HTMLDataSet(null, "photos");
   ```

   When the data container is in the same page as the data set, the first argument to HTMLDataSet() should be null. Dreamweaver tries to add the path in front of null if you tell it to update links or if you move the file within the Files panel.

3. Once you have confirmed that gallery_select.php is working correctly, you can build the filter. The code that creates the dsPhotos data set looks like this (it begins around line 50):

   ```
   var dsPhotos = new Spry.Data.HTMLDataSet(null, "photos");
   dsPhotos.setColumnType("Description", "html");
   ```

   JavaScript lets you define your own properties for objects, so let's give dsPhotos a gallery property with a default value of 'JPN'. Add the following code to the existing script block:

   ```
   var dsPhotos = new Spry.Data.HTMLDataSet(null, "photos");
   dsPhotos.setColumnType("Description", "html");
   dsPhotos.gallery = 'JPN';
   ```

4. Now define the filter function. Add the following code immediately after the line in the preceding step:

```
function chooseSet(dataSet, row, rowNumber)
{
  if (row['Category'] == dsPhotos.gallery) {
    return row;
  }
  return null;
}
```

As explained earlier, the filter function takes three arguments; it returns rows that match the filter criteria, and it returns null for nonmatching rows. The conditional statement checks whether the value of Category in the current row is the same as dsPhotos.gallery. If it is, the row is returned. Otherwise, the filter function returns null. You don't need an else clause because return immediately brings the function to an end. The function never reaches return null if the condition equates to true.

5. Finally, apply the filter nondestructively by passing the name of the function to the data set's filter() method. The full code looks like this:

```
var dsPhotos = new Spry.Data.HTMLDataSet(null, "photos");
dsPhotos.setColumnType("Description", "html");
dsPhotos.gallery = 'JPN';
function chooseSet(dataSet, row, rowNumber)
{
  if (row['Category'] == dsPhotos.gallery) {
    return row;
  }
  return null;
}
dsPhotos.filter(chooseSet);
```

6. Save gallery_select.php, and test it in a browser. Only the photos of Japan should be displayed. The photos of England have been filtered out of the data set, but they're not displayed in the data container either.

7. Change the default value of dsPhotos.gallery in the third line of code to 'ENG'. Save the page, and view it again. This time, only the photos of England should be displayed. The next task is to make the switch dynamic with a Spry select list, which you'll build in the next section.

Check your code, if necessary, with gallery_select_01.php in examples/ch19.

Creating a Spry select list

Creating a Spry select list uses the same technique as described earlier in the chapter in "Displaying a data set as a list." It involves the following three steps:

1. Create the data set that will be used in the Spry select list.

2. Insert a Spry region bound to the data set.

3. Insert a Spry repeat list, and set the options for a Spry select list.

The data container for the Spry select list already exists in gallery_select.php, so you're ready to start.

Creating the Spry data set for the select list

Because you're going to use the data set to populate a select list, you don't want the Spry Data Set wizard to create any HTML. However, the galleries table in gallery_select.php doesn't have any headings, so you need to assign your own. Continue working with gallery_select.php from the preceding exercise. Alternatively, use gallery_select_01.php in examples/ch19 (do *not* update the links when prompted by Dreamweaver).

1. Open gallery_select.php, and launch the Spry Data Set wizard.

2. In the first step of the wizard, use the following settings:
   - Select Data Type: HTML
   - Data Set Name: dsGalleries
   - Detect: Tables
   - Specify Data File: gallery_select.php
   - Data Containers: galleries

   The Data Preview field should look like this:

Data Preview	
ENG	**England**
JPN	Japan

3. Click Next to move to the second step of the wizard.

4. Currently, the first row of the table in gallery_select.php is being used as headers for the data set columns, so deselect the checkbox labeled Use first row as header. This changes the display in the Data Preview field by adding column0 and column1 at the head of the two columns. You can leave the generic names, but it makes the data set a lot easier to use if you assign more meaningful names.

5. Select column0, and type source in the Column Name field.

6. Select column1, type label in the Column Name field, and press Enter/Return to effect the change. The Data Preview field should now look like this:

7. You don't need any HTML created, so just click Done to close the wizard.

   You can check your code, if necessary, against gallery_select_02.php in examples/ch19.

You won't see any change in gallery_select.php in Design view, but the dsGalleries data set is now listed in the Bindings panel, and the data set definition has been added to the <head> of the page.

Now that the data set has been created, you can insert the Spry select list.

Using a Spry select list to change page content

Unlike a normal <select> element, when you insert a Spry select list into a page, Dreamweaver doesn't prompt you to insert <form> tags at the same time. This is because you can use Spry to respond to changes in the selected option without the need to submit a form. All that's necessary is to add an onchange event handler to the select list. This dispatches details of the selected item to other Spry elements, updating the page in the same way as clicking a row in a Spry table. I'll explain how it works in more detail when you add the onchange event handler. But first, let's insert the Spry select list.

Inserting a Spry select list to display the photo galleries

These instructions show you how to add a Spry select list to gallery_select.php to display the details of the available photo galleries. It draws its data from the dsGalleries data set that you created in the preceding exercise. Continue working with the same page as before. Alternatively, use gallery_select_02.php in examples/ch19.

1. In Design view, select the spryTable <div>, and press your left arrow key to move the insertion point to the top of the page. If you check in Split view, the insertion point should be between the opening <body> tag and the opening tag of the <div>.

2. Click the Spry Region button on the Insert bar, or select Insert ➤ Spry ➤ Spry Region.

3. In the Insert Spry Region dialog box, use the following settings, and then click OK:

   ■ Container: DIV

   ■ Type: Region

   ■ Spry Data Set: dsGalleries

   This creates a Spry region and primes it to use the correct data set for the select list.

4. The <div> created by the Insert Spry Region dialog box contains placeholder text. Leave this selected, and insert the Spry select list by clicking the Spry Repeat List button on the Spry tab of the Insert bar or by selecting Insert ➤ Spry ➤ Spry Repeat List.

5. In the Insert Spry Repeat List dialog box, use the following settings, and then click OK:

This draws the data from the dsGalleries data set and uses the label column to determine the text shown by each option and the source column to set the option's value attribute.

6. The placeholder text should have been replaced by a select menu element. Change the name of the menu element in the Property inspector from the default value, select, to selectGallery.

7. Let's add a label to the select menu. Press your left arrow key to move the insertion point in front of the menu element. Then click the Label button in the Forms tab of the Insert bar, as shown in the following screenshot. Alternatively, select Insert ➤ Form ➤ Label.

This opens Split view with the insertion point between two <label> tags. Type Select gallery followed by a colon and a space. Then edit the opening <label> tag to add the for attribute, and set its value to selectGallery. Click back in Design view, or press F5 to view the change. The page should now look like this:

8. Save gallery_select.php, and test it in a browser. In most browsers, the drop-down menu should display England by default. However, Internet Explorer doesn't play ball and displays the last item instead—in other words, Japan.

9. To fix the problem in Internet Explorer, you need to use the Spry equivalent of a conditional statement. You indicate a condition by adding the spry:choose attribute to the parent element—in this case, the <select> tag, which you need to amend like this:

```
<select name="selectGallery" id="selectGallery" ➥
spry:repeatchildren="dsGalleries" spry:choose="spry:choose">
```

10. Internally, a Spry data set is like a database recordset, and each row has an ID called ds_RowID, rather like a database primary key. Spry keeps track of the currently selected row through another property called ds_CurrentRowID. When the data set is first created, ds_CurrentRowID is set to the first row. So, to display the first <option> element correctly, you need to check whether ds_RowID and

ds_CurrentRowID are the same. If they are, you want to add selected="selected" to the <option> tag.

To create a condition in Spry, you use the spry:when attribute. Amend the <option> tag like this:

```
<option value="{source}" spry:when="{ds_CurrentRowID} == {ds_RowID}" ➥
selected="selected">{label}</option>
```

11. Although this adds selected="selected" to the <option> tag when the two IDs are equal, it has the undesired side effect of preventing any other <option> tags from displaying. So, you need to add another <option> tag to display the remaining values. This uses the spry:default attribute like this:

```
<option value="{source}" spry:default="spry:default">{label}</option>
```

12. The completed <select> list looks like this:

```
<select name="selectGallery" id="selectGallery" ➥
  spry:repeatchildren="dsGalleries" spry:choose="spry:choose">
  <option value="{source}" spry:when="{ds_CurrentRowID} == {ds_RowID}" ➥
    selected="selected">{label}</option>
  <option value="{source}" spry:default="spry:default">{label}</option>
</select>
```

13. If you test the page in Internet Explorer, the correct item should now display when the page first loads. It also works correctly in other modern browsers. However, nothing happens yet if you select Japan. You'll fix that next. But first, check your code, if necessary against gallery_select_03.php in examples/ch19.

The Spry select list works like a normal <select> element. The value of label in the each row of the data set is displayed as text in a drop-down menu, and the value of source is stored in the value attribute of the corresponding <option> tag. To display the correct set of photos, you need to change the value of dsPhotos.gallery whenever an option is selected in the drop-down menu. You do this by creating a function that resets and refilters the dsPhotos data set and by attaching the function to the onchange attribute of the <select> menu, as shown in the next exercise.

Wiring up the Spry select list

The following instructions show you how to reset the data set that contains details of the photos to be displayed. Continue working with gallery_select.php. Alternatively, use gallery_select_03.php in examples/ch19. All the work needs to be done in the underlying code, so roll up your sleeves and switch to Code view.

1. Amend the <select> tag to pass the value of the currently selected item in the drop-down menu to an event handler called changeSet() like this:

```
<select name="selectGallery" id="selectGallery" ➥
spry:repeatchildren="dsGalleries" spry:choose="spry:choose" ➥
onchange="changeSet(this.value)">
```

By passing this.value as the argument, changeSet() obtains ENG or JPN from the <option> tag. You now need to define changeSet().

2. Scroll up to the section in the <head> of the page where the two Spry data sets are defined. It looks like this:

```
50   var dsPhotos = new Spry.Data.HTMLDataSet(null, "photos");
51   dsPhotos.setColumnType("Description", "html");
52   dsPhotos.gallery = 'ENG';
53   function chooseSet(dataSet, row, rowNumber)
54   {
55       if (row['Category'] == dsPhotos.gallery) {
56           return row;
57       }
58       return null;
59   }
60   dsPhotos.filter(chooseSet);
61   var dsGalleries = new Spry.Data.HTMLDataSet(null, "galleries", {firstRowAsHeaders: false, columnNames: [
     'source', 'label']});
```

3. It's not important where you define changeSet() within this code block, but to keep things grouped together logically, insert some space after the code shown on line 60 of the preceding screenshot, and enter the following code:

```
function changeSet(set)
{
  dsPhotos.gallery = set;
  dsPhotos.filter(chooseSet);
}
```

This takes the value passed to the function and assigns it to dsPhotos.gallery. So, if Japan is chosen from the drop-down menu, dsPhotos.gallery is reset to 'JPN'. The next line applies chooseSet() as a nondestructive filter in the same way as when the page first loads. Since chooseSet() filters the data set according to the value of dsPhotos.gallery, this refilters dsPhotos and selects only the Japanese photos.

4. Save gallery_select.php, and test the page in a browser. When you select Japan from the drop-down menu, the thumbnails and their associated captions should change. However, the image and description in the Spry detail region don't update until you click one of the thumbnails or captions. This is because the changeSet() event handler doesn't broadcast the change to the detail region. You need to reset the data set's current row number to 0 and then loop through each row until you find the first one that belongs to the filtered set.

5. Amend changeSet() like this:

```
function changeSet(set)
{
  dsPhotos.gallery = set;
  dsPhotos.filter(chooseSet);
  dsPhotos.setCurrentRowNumber(0);
  var rows = dsPhotos.getData();
  for (var i = 0; i < rows.length; i++) {
    if (rows[i]['Category'] == set) {
```

```
        dsPhotos.setCurrentRowNumber(i);
        break;
      }
    }
  }
```

The first line of new code resets the current row number of the dsPhotos data set to 0. The next line uses the getData() method to store the data set temporarily in a variable called rows. The loop then iterates through each row, checking the value of the Category column and incrementing i by one each time. As soon as it finds a value that equals the value passed to changeSet(), it sets the data set's current row number to i and brings the loop to an end with break.

6. Save gallery_select.php, and load it into a browser. Select Japan from the drop-down menu, and the new gallery is displayed without needing to reload the page, as shown in Figure 19-14. Check your code, if necessary, against gallery_select_04.php in examples/ch19.

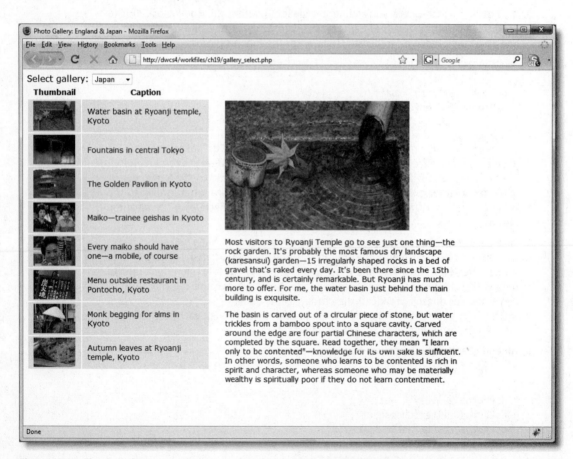

Figure 19-14. The drop-down menu displays a new gallery without reloading the page.

Creating a Spry data set from XML

As I mentioned at the beginning of the chapter, originally Spry data sets could be created only from XML. Although Adobe now encourages the use of an HTML data source in preference to XML, you can still use an XML source. You build a data set from XML through the Spry Data Set wizard in very much the same way as with an HTML data source, but there are some important differences, so this section gives a brief outline of the process. It uses an XML document called england.xml, which contains details of the eight photos of England used in the preceding exercises.

The structure of england.xml looks like this:

```
<?xml version="1.0" encoding="utf-8"?>
<gallery>
  <photo>
    <file width="400" height="300">buck_palace.jpg</file>
    <caption>Buckingham Palace and St James's Park</caption>
    <description><![CDATA[<p>St James's Park . . .
</p>]]></description>
  </photo>
  <photo>
    <file width="374" height="283">countrygarden.jpg</file>
    <caption>A typical English country garden in Oxford</caption>
    <description><![CDATA[<p>The . . .</p>]]></description>
  </photo>
</gallery>
```

In other words, the details of each photo are in a top-level repeating node called <photo>. The file name is in a child node called <file>, which stores the image dimensions as attributes. Two other child nodes, called <caption> and <description>, contain the remaining details of the photo. The <description> node uses a CDATA section, which permits the use of HTML tags inside an XML text node.

Using the Spry Data Set wizard with an XML document

The structure of england.xml is similar to the HTML table you created as a data source in gallery_eng.php, but it contains no image tags, so the resulting Spry data set will need to store the file name and the image dimensions separately.

The following instructions show you how to create a Spry data set from an XML document and then incorporate it in a master-detail set to display images by binding data to the attributes of HTML tags. Since the Spry Data Set wizard was covered in detail earlier in the chapter, I'll concentrate on the differences of working with an XML data source.

1. Create a new page called spry_xml.php in workfiles/ch19. (You can also use an .html file name extension, because no PHP is involved in this process.)

2. Launch the Spry Data Set wizard from the Spry tab of the Insert bar or the Insert menu.

3. In the first step of the wizard, select XML from the Select Data Type drop-down menu. As soon as you do so, the Detect drop-down menu disappears, and the Data Selection field changes to Row element.

4. Change Data Set Name to dsPhotos, and use the Browse button to set the Specify Data File field to use examples/ch19/england.xml. This populates the Row element field with a diagrammatic representation of the XML hierarchy in the same way as the Bindings panel does when you create an XSLT fragment (see Chapter 18).

5. In the same way as with an XSLT fragment, you need to select the repeating node, which is indicated by a small plus icon alongside a pair of angle brackets. Select photo in the Row element field. This now populates the Data Preview field with rows and columns representing the data set. The first step of the wizard should now look like Figure 19-15.

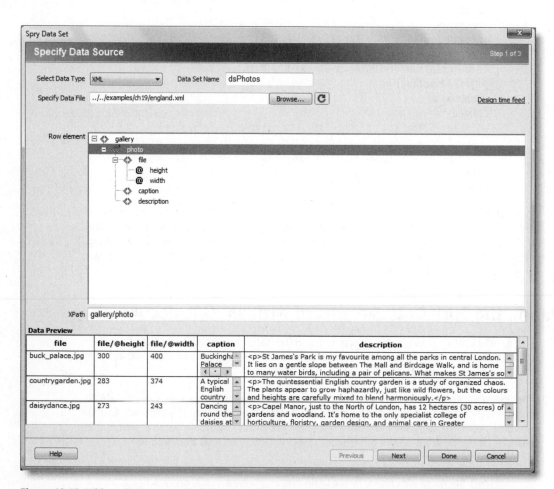

Figure 19-15. With an XML source, the first step of the data set wizard closely resembles working with an XSLT fragment.

Notice that the dimensions of the image are displayed as file/@height and file/@width, indicating that they are attributes of the <file> node. Only the file names are shown, not the actual images, because the XML data source is text only.

6. Click Next to move to the second step of the wizard. As you can see in Figure 19-16, it's almost identical to the second step for an HTML source. You can't change the column names, and the options not to use the first row as headers and switch rows to columns are not relevant to XML. The other options are the same.

7. Set Type to number for file/@height and file/@width; and for description, set Type to html. Then click Next to move to the final step of the wizard.

8. The final step is identical to when you use an HTML data source. Select the Insert master/detail layout radio button, and then click the Set Up button alongside.

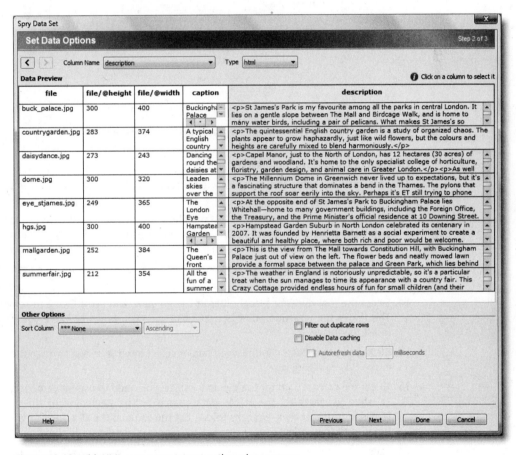

Figure 19-16. With XML, you cannot rename the column names.

9. I explained how the Spry Data Set – Insert Master/Detail Layout dialog box works in the "Setting the options for a master-detail set" exercise earlier in the chapter, so I won't go into the details again. Use the following settings, and then click OK.

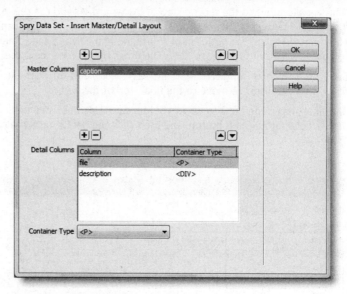

10. Click Done to close the wizard.

11. Save spry_xml.php, and click OK when prompted to copy dependent files to your Spry assets folder.

12. Because the XML data source is a static file, you can use Live view to see the output. It should look similar to Figure 19-10, only the file name is displayed instead of an image. You need to insert the image yourself and bind the Spry data to it.

13. Turn off Live view. It's best to work in Split view so you can see what's happening in the underlying code.

14. Select the {file} dynamic placeholder in Design view, and press Delete to remove it. This leaves the insertion point between the <p> tags, which is where you want to insert the image.

15. Click the Images button in the Insert bar, or select Insert ➤ Image to open the Select Image Source dialog box.

16. To get the correct path for the dynamic image, you need to use the same technique as when you created the HTML data source at the beginning of this chapter. Navigate to the images/gallery folder, cut the value in the URL field to your clipboard, and then select Data sources in the Select Image Source dialog box.

17. Select file from the dsPhotos data set, and paste the path back in front of the dynamic placeholder, as shown here:

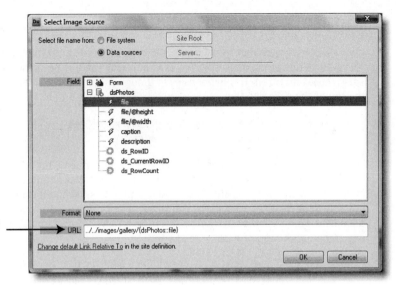

Paste the path to the gallery folder here

18. Click OK to close the Select Image Source dialog box, and set the alternate text to <empty> when prompted.

Notice that the code inserted in Code view uses {file} instead of {dsPhotos::file}. This is because it's in a dsPhotos detail region. The prefix isn't required when the data set is the same as that for the detail region.

19. Finally, you need to bind file/@height to img.height, file/@width to img.width, and caption to img.alt through the Bindings panel in the same way as you did for the HTML image at the beginning of the chapter. The code for the image tag should end up looking like this in Split view:

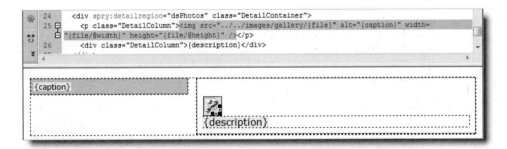

20. Save spry_xml.php, and test it in Live view or a browser. It should look the same as Figure 19-10, except it uses the photos of England.

You can check your code, if necessary, against spry_xml.php in examples/ch19.

This example uses a static XML document. However, you can also generate the XML data source dynamically with PHP. Details of how to do so are in the appendix.

Validating pages that use Spry

If you submit a page that uses Spry to the W3C validator at http://validator.w3.org/, you get a series of errors saying, for example, that there is no attribute spry:region or spry:repeatchildren. This happens even though Dreamweaver amends the <html> tag at the top of the page like this:

```
<html xmlns="http://www.w3.org/1999/xhtml" ➥
xmlns:spry="http://ns.adobe.com/spry">
```

The code highlighted in bold declares spry as a **namespace**. This tells the browser not to confuse anything prefixed with spry: with standard HTML attributes or custom attributes from other namespaces, such as other Ajax frameworks. While this prevents conflicts, it's not sufficient for W3C validation. You need to tell the validator where to find the Spry document type definition (DTD) by inserting an ENTITY declararation into the DOCTYPE declaration at the top of each page like this:

```
<!DOCTYPE html PUBLIC "-//W3C//DTD XHTML 1.0 Transitional//EN" ➥
 "http://www.w3.org/TR/xhtml1/DTD/xhtml1-transitional.dtd"
[
<!ENTITY % SPRY SYSTEM "http://www.adobe.com/dtd/spry.dtd">
%SPRY;
]>
<html xmlns="http://www.w3.org/1999/xhtml" ➥
xmlns:spry="http://ns.adobe.com/spry">
```

So, why doesn't Dreamweaver add the necessary code? Figure 19-17 shows why. Internet Explorer, Firefox, and Safari all fail to understand the <!ENTITY> declaration and display %SPRY;]> at the top of the page if you include it (see http://labs.adobe.com/technologies/spry/articles/validation/validating_spry.html).

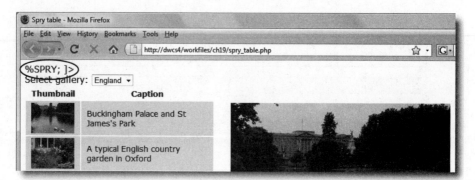

Figure 19-17. Most leading browsers can't cope with the code needed to ensure that Spry validates.

If W3C validation is a mandatory requirement for your website, you have two options: don't use Spry, or remove the Spry markup from the page with Dreamweaver CS4's new JavaScript Extractor.

The JavaScript Extractor was covered in Chapter 8, but let's put it to practical use converting the gallery you have worked on throughout this chapter.

Converting the Spry gallery to use unobtrusive JavaScript

This brief exercise shows you how to extract the Spry markup from `gallery_select.php` so that the page validates against W3C standards. Continue using the same file as in previous exercises. Alternatively, use `gallery_select_04.php` in exercises/ch19 as your starting point.

1. With `gallery_select.php` open in the Document window, select Commands ➤ Externalize JavaScript.

2. Because the page has a `.php` file name extension, Dreamweaver displays a warning that it's not recommended to run the command on pages with server-side code and asks whether you want to proceed anyway. The warning is there because the JavaScript Extractor might not be able to identify the right elements to extract if server-side code, such as PHP, and HTML are mixed within the body of the page. That's not the case here, so it's safe to go ahead. Click Yes.

3. In the Externalize JavaScript dialog box, select Externalize JavaScript and attach unobtrusively. As shown in Figure 19-18, Dreamweaver displays a list of all the JavaScript elements that will be removed. You want to remove all of them, so leave everything selected, and click OK.

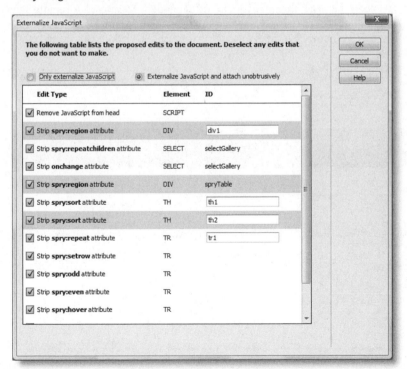

Figure 19-18. The JavaScript Extractor identifies all the JavaScript elements and Spry markup in the page.

885

4. Dreamweaver displays a report of what it has done, as shown in the screenshot alongside.

   The important information is at the bottom of the report: the names of two external JavaScript files that need to be uploaded with the page. The first one, SpryDOMUtils.js, will be saved to your Spry assets folder. The second one, gallery_select.js, contains the unobtrusive JavaScript code, and it will be created in the same folder as the original page.

5. Click OK to dismiss the report, and save the page. If this is the first time you have used the JavaScript Extractor in a site, you will see a message telling you that SpryDOMUtils.js is being copied to your Spry assets folder. Click OK to dismiss the message.

6. Test the page in a browser to make sure it still works as before. You can check your code, if necessary, against gallery_select_05.php and gallery_select.js in examples/ch19.

7. Upload the page, together with all its dependent files, to your remote server, and submit its URL to the W3C validator at http://validator.w3.org/. As Figure 19-19 shows, you now have a Spry gallery that passes validation with flying colors.

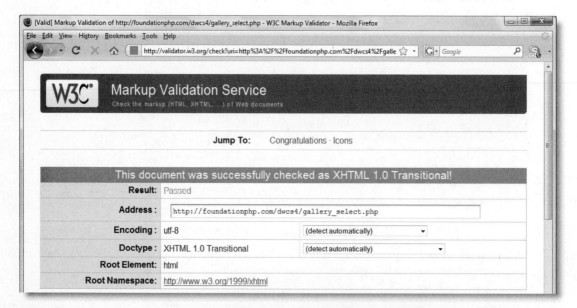

Figure 19-19. Attaching the Spry markup with unobtrusive JavaScript produces a valid page.

Chapter review

The changes to the way Dreamweaver CS4 handles Spry data sets make them much easier to use, particularly with an HTML data source. By locating the data source in the same page and manipulating the DOM to redisplay it, Spry data sets now provide indexable content for search engines, as well as maintaining accessibility for the small minority of people who browse the Web with JavaScript disabled.

The pages used in the examples in this chapter contain only Spry data sets. In a real-world application, this is likely to be impractical, except perhaps for an image gallery. Important content should always be embedded in the main part of the page, where it's immediately accessible to everyone. Spry and other JavaScript techniques should be used to enhance user experience, but they shouldn't be used as the sole means of delivering content. So, if you use an XML data source for a Spry data set, you should always remember to provide a link to an alternative page that contains the same basic information.

Your journey through Dreamweaver CS4, CSS, JavaScript, and PHP is almost at an end. In the final chapter, I'll deal with important maintenance issues concerned with MySQL backups and how to deploy your web masterpieces on a live website.

19

You've built your site and created your database, and now it's time to go live. If you have structured your Dreamweaver site as an exact copy of the site you intend to deploy on the Internet, going live is a pretty straightforward process. Assuming you have defined your remote server as described in Chapter 2, you can deploy your web pages a number of ways through the Dreamweaver interface. Probably the most common way to do so is through the Files panel. Select the file(s) you want to upload, and click the Put button. You can also upload the current page by pressing Ctrl+Shift+U/Shift+Cmd+U, or selecting Put from the File management menu on the Document toolbar (see Figure 1-25 in Chapter 1). You can even right-click files in the Results panel and select Put from the context menu. However, Dreamweaver is not capable of uploading the content of a MySQL database; and there are several other issues with deploying a site that sometimes cause confusion, so this chapter tries to clear up any doubts you might have.

In this chapter, you'll learn about the following:

- Deciding which files to upload
- Preventing development assets from being uploaded
- Exporting a MySQL database to a SQL file
- Using a SQL file to transfer a MySQL database to another server
- Adapting connection files to work with your live MySQL server

Uploading your web pages

The key to uploading your website successfully lies in registering the details of your remote server correctly in the Dreamweaver Site Definition dialog box, as described in Chapter 2. Dreamweaver considers the site root to be whatever value you entered in the Host directory field of the Remote Info category (see Figure 2-6); and it uploads files using the same folder hierarchy as in the Files panel. Usually, there is no need to create new folders on the remote site; Dreamweaver does it automatically when you upload the contents of the folder.

The following sections describe how to upload files to a remote server. However, apart from designating individual files and folders to be excluded from batch uploading—a technique Dreamweaver calls **cloaking**, the same techniques apply equally to downloading files. To download, use the Get button instead of the Put button.

Uploading a whole site

The easiest way to upload a whole site is to select the site's root folder in the Files panel, and click the Put button, as shown in the following screenshot:

Before it goes ahead, Dreamweaver displays an alert asking you to confirm this operation. If you click OK, it takes you at your word and uploads everything within the site. However, be warned that Dreamweaver's FTP engine is unlikely to win any Olympic gold medals. I find it adequate for most site maintenance, but it can be excruciatingly slow if you have a lot of files. For example, a typical WordPress blog (http://wordpress.org/) contains more than 750 files in 175 folders. Although Dreamweaver uploads the files in the background, you cannot switch the Files panel to work on a different site until the upload process has completed. There's also no way to resume the upload if the connection is dropped. When uploading a site of this size, I find it much faster to use a third-party FTP program, such as FileZilla, a free open source program for Windows, Mac, and Linux (http://filezilla-project.org), or CuteFTP, a commercial program for Windows and Mac (http://www.cuteftp.com/products/ftp_clients.aspx).

For a few dozen files, uploading the whole site through Dreamweaver is no problem, but you should still restrict the files that are transferred by cloaking anything that's not required on the remote server.

Cloaking files not required on the remote server

Cloaking prevents files from being uploaded to your remote server when uploading the entire site or using Dreamweaver's site synchronization feature (described later in this chapter). You can cloak files in two ways: you can apply cloaking automatically to all files that have a particular file name extension, or you can designate individual files or folders.

To enable automatic cloaking for specific file name extensions, open the Site Definition dialog box, and select the Cloaking category (see Figure 20-1). The quick and easy way to do this is by right-clicking any file or folder in the Files panel and then selecting Cloaking ➤ Settings from the context menu.

Figure 20-1.
You can enable automatic cloaking of specified file types through the Site Definition dialog box.

To designate the types of files to be cloaked, select the checkbox labeled Cloak files ending with. This enables the text field below, where you enter all the file name extensions that you want to exclude when uploading or synchronizing the site. As you can see in Figure 20-1, .fla and .psd are already listed. These are Flash and Photoshop work files that store all the layers, symbols, and other information about a Flash movie or image. Neither should ever be deployed on a website.

Sites created with earlier versions of Dreamweaver and migrated to Dreamweaver CS4 list .png instead of .psd. This is the file name extension for work files created by Fireworks. However, it is also the file name extension for images stored in the Portable Networks Graphic (http://www.libpng.org/pub/png/) format supported by all modern browsers. So if your site uses .png images, you might want to remove .png from the list.

There should be a single space between each file name extension, and the extension itself should begin with a period. So, for example, if you want to exclude saved queries for Find and Replace (.dwr files) and Dreamweaver extensions (.mxp files), you need to edit the list as shown in the screenshot alongside:

> *Templates (as distinct from child pages created from a template) should never be uploaded to the remote server. If you use templates, add .dwt and .dwt.php to this list.*

When you click OK to save the changes, Dreamweaver displays an alert telling you that it needs to rebuild the site cache. Click OK again, and after the site cache has been rebuilt, files belonging to the specified types are displayed in the Files panel with a red diagonal stripe through the icon alongside the file name, as shown in Figure 20-2. Rebuilding the cache can take a long time on a large site, so this is not an option you should change frequently. It's best done when you first define the site.

Figure 20-2.
A red diagonal stripe through the icon alongside a file or folder indicates it has been cloaked.

To cloak individual files or folders, right-click the file or folder in the Files panel, and select Cloaking ➤ Cloak from the context menu.

Cloaking excludes files and folders when you select the entire site to be uploaded or when synchronizing the site. However, you can override cloaking temporarily by selecting cloaked files or folders and clicking the Put button.

To turn off cloaking for individual files and folders, right-click the file(s) or folder(s) in the Files panel, and select Cloaking ➤ Uncloak. However, you cannot use this method to uncloak files that have been cloaked automatically through their file name extension. Automatic cloaking is an all-or-nothing option: all files that use the same extension are affected. Equally, selecting Cloaking ➤ Uncloak All from the context menu in the Files panel is a blanket operation; it uncloaks every file in the site.

Synchronizing a site

By default, Dreamweaver maintains information about the local and remote versions of the site to enable them to be synchronized. To synchronize a site, select Site ➤ Synchronize Sitewide. Alternatively, select Synchronize from the context menu in the Files panel. This opens the Synchronize Files dialog box, as shown here:

The Synchronize drop-down menu has the following two options, both of which are self-explanatory:

- Entire '*Sitename*' Site
- Selected Local Files Only

The Direction drop-down menu has the following three options:

- Put newer files to remote: This updates the remote site with files that have been changed in Dreamweaver.
- Get newer files from remote: This updates your local version with files that have been updated on the remote server. Normally, this applies only if more than one person is responsible for managing the site or if you use more than one computer to maintain a site.
- Get and Put newer files: This looks for the latest versions on both the remote server and your local version and transfers them accordingly.

The options offered by the checkbox at the bottom of the Synchronize Files dialog box depend on your choice for Direction. When putting newer files to the remote server, select the checkbox to delete files that don't exist in your local version. When getting newer files from the remote server, select the checkbox to delete local files that don't exist on the remote server. The checkbox is grayed out if you set Direction to Get and Put newer files. Although deleting files sounds potentially dangerous, you get a chance to review Dreamweaver's decision for each file before committing yourself.

After making your selections in the Synchronize Files dialog box, click the Preview button. Dreamweaver connects to the remote server and checks the status of the remote files. This can take some time, depending on the size of the site. When Dreamweaver has gathered the synchronization information, it displays the Synchronize dialog box (see Figure 20-3). This lists all the files that are out of sync. The buttons at the bottom left of the dialog box give you the opportunity to override Dreamweaver's proposed actions or resolve issues that Dreamweaver can't handle. The dialog box is resizable to make it easier to read messages in the Status field. The Compare button requires a third-party file comparison utility to be set up in the File Compare category of the Preferences panel, as described in Chapter 2.

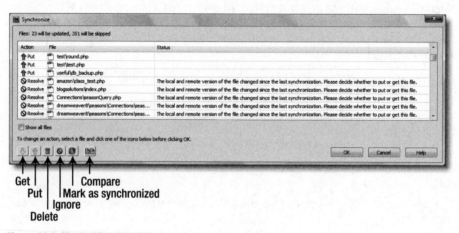

Figure 20-3. The Synchronize dialog box gives you the opportunity to override Dreamweaver's decisions.

After making any changes to the proposed operations, click OK, and sit back while Dreamweaver carries out your instructions. You can click the Hide button on the Background File Activity dialog box and continue working in Dreamweaver. However, you cannot switch to another site until the transfer has completed.

The file synchronization feature creates a file called dwsync.xml for each folder in your site. This XML file contains details of the local and remote timestamps of each file in the folder, and it is stored in a hidden folder called _notes (see http://www.adobe.com/go/ kb400972 for a detailed explanation). For the system to work accurately, both your local computer and remote server need to create accurate timestamps. Problems inevitably arise if your computer clock is out of sync with the one on the remote server.

The greatest weakness of file synchronization affects everyone in countries that observe daylight saving time. Twice a year, when the clocks change, Dreamweaver displays inaccurate warnings that you're about to replace a newer file on the remote server. This happens even when you use normal Put *operations, because Dreamweaver checks the information in* dwsync.xml *each time a file is transferred. If in doubt, use File Compare, as described in Chapter 2.*

You can find synchronization information about an individual file by right-clicking the file name in the Files panel and selecting Display Synchronize Information from the context menu. This displays a panel of information similar to that shown in Figure 20-4.

Figure 20-4. You can display synchronization information for an individual file.

Selecting recently modified files

If you find synchronization unreliable or too time-consuming, the Files panel has a little known feature that selects recently modified files. To access this feature, open the Files panel options menu by clicking the top-right of the panel, as shown in the following screenshot:

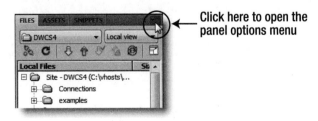

Click here to open the panel options menu

In the panel options menu, select Edit ➤ Select Recently Modified. Alternatively, right-click any file or folder in the Files panel, and select Select ➤ Recently Modified from the context menu. This opens the dialog box shown in Figure 20-5. After setting your selection criteria, click OK. Dreamweaver selects all matching files in the Files panel, which are then ready for you to upload by clicking the Put button, or for you to perform any other batch operation. To select all files created or modified during the current day, select the second radio button, and set both dates to today's date.

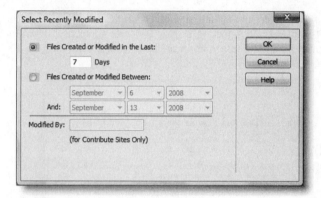

Figure 20-5. You can select files that have been created or modified in recent days or within a specific range of dates.

The Results panel also lets you upload files that have just been modified by a Find and Replace operation. Right-click the file name in the Results panel, and select Put from the context menu.

Viewing the local and remote sites side by side

The drop-down menu at the top right of the Files panel lets you select only one view of your site at a time: Local view, Remote view, Testing server, or Repository view (this last option requires a Subversion repository to be set up in your site definition, as described in Chapter 2). However, it can be useful to display two views side by side. To do so, click the Expand/Collapse button at the top right of the Files panel, as shown here:

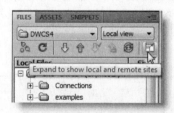

By default, this expands the Files panel to fill the application window, as shown in Figure 20-6. However, if you have converted the Files panel to a floating panel, it remains floating and resizable. In both cases, the local view remains on the right side of the panel, while the left side opens to display the remote view. If no files are displayed in the left panel, Dreamweaver prompts you to connect to the remote server. If you prefer to show the local files on the left, you can reverse the default positions in the Site category of the Preferences panel (Edit ➤ Preferences, or Dreamweaver ➤ Preferences on a Mac).

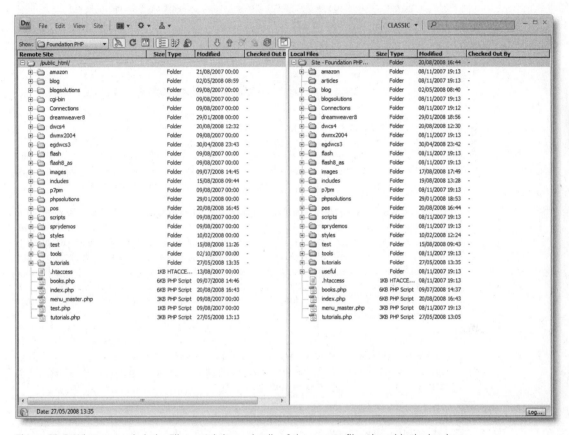

20

Figure 20-6. When expanded, the Files panel shows details of the remote files alongside the local ones.

You can use this expanded view to drag and drop local files into the remote site, and vice versa, but it's a tricky process because you need to drop the files on the target folder icon. It's easy to miss the correct icon, destroying the file hierarchy of your site. Instead of dragging and dropping, expand the folders to highlight the files you want to transfer, and use the Put and Get buttons to perform the actual transfer.

You can also inspect the testing server and repository view in the expanded Files panel by clicking the buttons to the left of the Get button.

To collapse the Files panel to its normal size, click the same button you used to expand it.

Uploading dependent files

Most web pages have a number of dependent files: style sheets, external JavaScript files, images, and so on. Dreamweaver presents you with the following dialog box whenever you click the Put or Get button, asking whether you want to transfer dependent files at the same time.

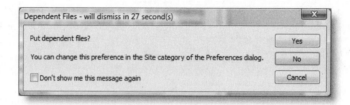

It's important to realize that the default button on this dialog box is No. If you press Enter/Return or do nothing for 30 seconds, the dialog box closes and transfers only the selected file(s). To transfer dependent files, you must click the Yes button before the dialog box closes automatically. If you don't want to be asked each time you perform a transfer operation, select the checkbox labeled Don't show me this message again.

You can change the dependent file options in the Site category in the Preferences panel (Edit ➤ Preferences; Dreamweaver ➤ Preferences on a Mac). Dreamweaver treats dependent files separately for put and get operations, so you can reenable the automatic prompt by selecting the appropriate checkbox in the Preferences panel. You can also change the number of seconds the prompt remains on the screen or prevent it from closing automatically. If you uncheck Select default action after *n* seconds, the Dependent Files dialog box remains onscreen until you click one of the buttons. More importantly, the default button changes from No to Yes.

Deciding whether to let Dreamweaver transfer dependent files automatically is a matter of preference. Experienced developers usually want to know exactly what is being transferred, so they disable the Dependent Files dialog box. If you do likewise, don't forget to upload the following categories of files:

- Images
- External style sheets
- External JavaScript files
- Assets for Spry and other web widgets
- SWF (Flash and Flex) support files in the Scripts folder

One of the most frequently asked questions in Dreamweaver online forums is "Why does my Flash movie, Spry accordion, or some other feature work fine locally but not on my remote server?" The answer is almost invariably that a dependent file hasn't been uploaded. Another explanation is that the file path to the dependent file is incorrect. That's usually because the site has been incorrectly defined.

> *Dreamweaver cannot detect dependent files that are linked dynamically through JavaScript or PHP. You must upload these independently.*

Transferring database tables

MySQL doesn't store your database in a single file that you can simply upload to your website. Even if you find the right files, you're likely to damage them unless the MySQL server is turned off. Anyway, most hosting companies won't permit you to upload the raw files, because it would also involve shutting down their server, causing a great deal of inconvenience for everyone.

Nevertheless, moving a database from one server to another is very easy with a graphic front end to MySQL. I'll show you how to do it with phpMyAdmin, since most hosting companies provide phpMyAdmin as part of their package. If you want to use a different front end, consult the program's documentation. However, for security reasons, most hosting companies do not permit direct connection to the MySQL server, so you normally need to use the host's installation of phpMyAdmin to import the data. Navicat (http://www.navicat.com/) gets around this issue by transferring the data through the web server on port 80.

Transferring a database or database table with phpMyAdmin involves creating a backup **dump** of the data and loading it into the other database. The dump is a text file that contains all the necessary Structured Query Language (SQL) commands to populate an individual table or even an entire database elsewhere.

Creating a backup with phpMyAdmin

These instructions show you how to back up an entire database. You can also back up individual tables in the same way by selecting the tables in step 4.

1. Launch phpMyAdmin, and select the database you want to back up from the list or drop-down menu in the navigation frame.

2. When the database details have loaded into the main frame, select Export from the tabs along the top of the screen, as shown here:

3. The rather fearsome-looking screen shown in Figure 20-7 opens. In spite of all the options, you need to concern yourself with only a few.

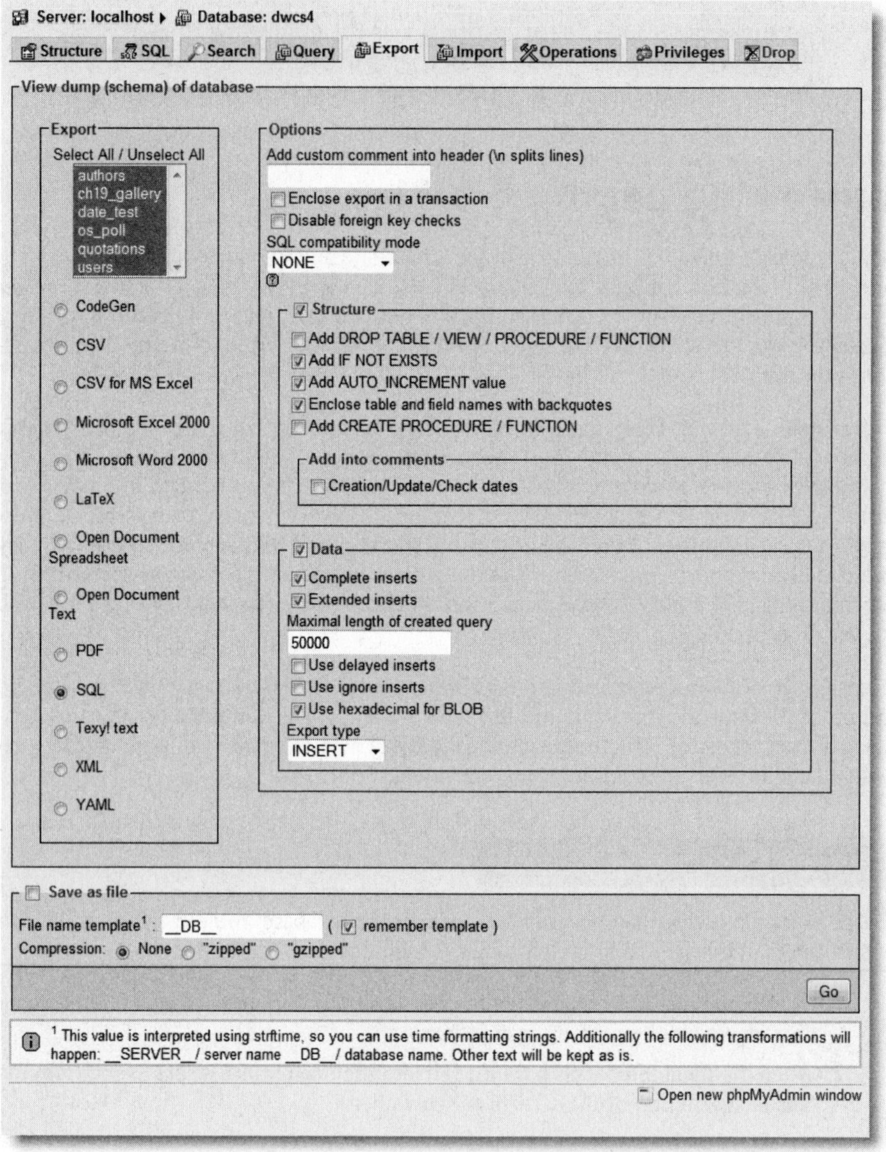

Figure 20-7. phpMyAdmin offers a wide range of choices when exporting data from MySQL.

4. The Export section on the left of the screen lists all the tables in your database. Click Select All, and leave the radio buttons on the default SQL. Alternatively, Ctrl-click/Cmd-click to select the tables you want to export.

5. If the database has *never* been transferred to the other server before, the only option that you need to set on the right side of the screen is the drop-down menu labeled SQL compatibility mode. The setting depends on the version of

MySQL on the other server (only the first two numbers, such as 4.0, 4.1, or 5.0, are important):

- If the other server is running the same version of MySQL, choose NONE.
- If you are transferring between MySQL 4.1 and MySQL 5.0 (in either direction), choose NONE.
- If the other server is running MySQL 4.0, choose MYSQL40.

6. If the database has *already* been transferred on a previous occasion, select Add DROP TABLE / VIEW / PROCEDURE / FUNCTION in the Structure section. The existing contents of each table are dropped and are replaced with the data in the backup file.

7. Put a check mark in the box alongside Save as file at the bottom of the screen. The default setting in File name template is __DB__, which automatically gives the backup file the same name as your database. So, in this case, it will become dwcs4.sql. If you add anything after the final double underscore, phpMyAdmin will add this to the name. For instance, you might want to indicate the date of the backup, so you could add 20090704 for a backup made on July 4, 2009. The file would then be named dwcs420090704.sql.

Loading data from a backup file

Once you have created a .sql file containing the data exported from a database, you can transfer it to another MySQL server using the version of phpMyAdmin on the remote server.

1. If a database of the same name doesn't already exist on the target server, create the database, but don't create any tables.

2. Launch the version of phpMyAdmin used by the target server, and select the database you plan to transfer the data to. Click the Import tab in the main frame (on versions of phpMyAdmin earlier than 2.7.0, click the SQL tab instead).

3. Use the Browse button to locate the SQL file on your local computer, and click Go. That's it!

> *Because phpMyAdmin uses PHP to upload the file, the maximum size of any backup is normally limited to 2MB, which is the default maximum size for any file upload. If you are transferring a very large database, use the phpMyAdmin Export and Import tabs to back up and transfer individual tables. Alternatively, contact your hosting company for advice on transferring your database.*

Configuring the remote MySQL connection

Many hosting companies locate MySQL and the web server on the same computer. Consequently, the host name PHP uses to connect to the database remains localhost. If you set up your local testing environment to use the same database name, user account, and password as your remote server, all you need to do is upload the Connections folder and its contents, and everything should work the same as on your local computer.

However, some hosting companies locate MySQL on a separate computer and give you an IP address or domain name that must be used instead of localhost. Unfortunately, Dreamweaver does not have the option to specify different connection details for local testing and remote deployment. The simplest way to get around this problem is to create different copies of the connection files for the local and remote connection. Once you have uploaded the connection file(s) to your remote server, cloak the local connection file(s) in your Dreamweaver site to prevent accidentally overwriting the remote versions (cloaking was described earlier in this chapter).

Figure 20-8 shows the contents of the connection file for the connAdmin user account used in the examples for this book. As you can see, the file name and the variables used in the file are all based on the name of the user account. The variable names are all self-explanatory.

```php
<?php
# FileName="Connection_php_mysql.htm"
# Type="MYSQL"
# HTTP="true"
$hostname_connAdmin = "localhost";
$database_connAdmin = "dwcs4";
$username_connAdmin = "cs4admin";
$password_connAdmin = "humpty";
$connAdmin = mysql_pconnect($hostname_connAdmin, $username_connAdmin, $password_connAdmin) or trigger_error(
mysql_error(),E_USER_ERROR);
?>
```

Figure 20-8. The MySQL connection file contains the login details for the MySQL user account.

To create a connection file for your remote server, use the following instructions:

1. Save a copy of the connection file as *filename*_local.php.

2. Close the copy, and edit the original connection file, replacing localhost (shown on line 5 of Figure 20-8) with the IP address or domain name of the server where your MySQL account is located (use the MySQL domain name, *not* your own domain name).

3. Make any other changes necessary to the database, username, and password.

4. Save the page, and upload it to your remote server.

5. Delete the local copy of the page you have just uploaded.

6. Rename *filename*_local.php to restore its original name.

7. Right-click the renamed local file, and select Cloaking ➤ Cloak from the context menu.

You now have different versions of the connection file on your local computer and remote server. This enables you to continue testing locally with your local MySQL settings, and the files should work seamlessly with the remote settings when they're uploaded. However, it's important not to select the option to upload dependent files, because this will overwrite the remote connection file, even though it has been cloaked. Cloaking excludes files only when using file synchronization.

> When editing connection files, make sure you don't add any whitespace or newline characters outside the PHP tags, because this will prevent sessions from being created and server behaviors from redirecting to other pages. Also, make sure you don't select Include Unicode Signature (BOM) in the page properties (see "Avoiding the 'headers already sent' error" in Chapter 12).

Chapter review

This brief look at deploying your website on the Internet brings to an end this marathon journey through working with Dreamweaver CS4. I hope you have found it enjoyable and instructive. In spite of the length of this book, I have not been able to cover every aspect of Dreamweaver, CSS, Ajax, and PHP. In the short history of the Internet, the technology of website design has grown at a breathtaking pace—almost as rapid as that of the Internet itself. Dreamweaver will do a lot of the hard work for you, but your success in creating websites that stand out from among the crowd depends on mastering a range of skills, or perhaps combining your own strengths with those of experts in other aspects of web development.

Good luck, but above all have fun.

20

Some of the exercises in Chapters 18 and 19 use static XML documents as a data source. This was done to enable you to concentrate on working with the XML data, without the added complication of generating the XML document. Typing out XML documents is both tedious and usually unnecessary, because XML is principally used as a platform-neutral way of sharing data that is stored in a database. It's much more efficient to generate the XML dynamically using a server-side language, such as PHP. Unfortunately, Dreamweaver doesn't have a server behavior to automate this process. However, it's not difficult to adapt a recordset to generate XML output, which you can serve dynamically or save to a static file.

As mentioned in Chapter 19, security restrictions in browsers prevent Spry and other Ajax frameworks from using XML documents that are hosted on a different domain. However, you can get around this problem by using a proxy script to retrieve the remote XML document.

This appendix extends your ability to work with XML by showing you how to do the following:

- Customize a recordset to generate XML on the fly
- Use a PHP proxy script to retrieve XML from a different domain
- Generate and save a static XML document

Converting a recordset to generate XML

Generating XML from a recordset is very similar to creating any other web page that displays content drawn from a database. The main difference is that you replace all the HTML tags with XML tags. Before getting down to the detail, here's a brief outline of the steps involved:

1. Create a recordset.
2. Build a skeleton of XML tags for the repeating element and its child nodes.
3. Populate the child nodes with dynamic text objects from the recordset.
4. Apply a Repeat Region server behavior to the repeating element.
5. Remove the HTML code from the page.
6. Add the root node tags.
7. Add headers and the XML declaration to tell Dreamweaver and browsers to treat the output as XML.

You build everything like an ordinary web page and remove the DOCTYPE declaration and HTML tags, leaving behind just the code to create the XML feed. However, it's important to leave all the HTML code in the page until you have applied the Repeat Region server behavior. Otherwise, Dreamweaver cannot recognize where to insert the code and refuses to apply the server behavior.

The following instructions show you how to create an XML feed of details of the Japanese images in the ch19_gallery table:

1. Create a new PHP page called `japan_xml.php` in `workfiles/appendix`.

2. Open the Recordset dialog box in Simple mode, and create a recordset called getPhotos. This doesn't need administrative privileges, so use connQuery for Connection, and select ch19_gallery in the Table field.

   You don't need the `photo_id` and `category` columns for the XML output, so select all other columns except those two.

   However, you do want to retrieve only those records where category is set to JPN. Set Filter to category, and leave the second drop-down set to =. Since JPN is a fixed value, select Entered Value from the third drop-down, and type JPN in the field alongside.

   When you have finished, the settings should look like this:

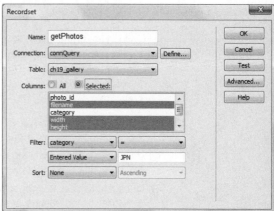

3. Use the Test button to make sure the record-set works, and then click OK to save it.

4. Now build a skeleton for the repeating ele-ment, `<photo>`, and its child nodes. You need just one set of tags, because the repeat region generates the rest. Switch to Code view, and insert the following code between the `<body>` tags:

```
<body>
  <photo>
    <filename></filename>
    <width></width>
    <height></height>
    <caption></caption>
    <description><![CDATA[]]></description>
  </photo>
</body>
```

The `<description>` node contains HTML, so I have added opening and closing CDATA tags inside the node tags (CDATA sections instruct XML parsers to treat their content as plain character data). When building your own XML, create a similar skeleton using the node names of your choice.

As you're typing, you'll notice that Dreamweaver code hints recognize your custom XML tags, making it easier to complete the closing tags.

> *You need to insert the XML skeleton between the `<body>` tags in order to use the Repeat Region server behavior.*

5. Now populate the child nodes with dynamic text objects from the recordset. Position the insertion point between the opening and closing `<filename>` tags.

A

6. Open the Bindings panel, expand the recordset, select filename, and click the Insert button. This inserts a dynamic text object inside the <filename> child node.

7. Repeat steps 5 and 6 with the other child node tags, positioning the insertion point between the CDATA tags for the <description> node. The XML skeleton should now look like this:

```
<photo>
    <filename><?php echo $row_getPhotos['filename']; ?></filename>
    <width><?php echo $row_getPhotos['width']; ?></width>
    <height><?php echo $row_getPhotos['height']; ?></height>
    <caption><?php echo $row_getPhotos['caption']; ?></caption>
    <description><![CDATA[<?php echo $row_getPhotos['description']; ?> ➡
]]></description>
</photo>
```

8. Select the XML skeleton from the opening <photo> tag to the closing </photo> one, and apply a Repeat Region server behavior (use the Server Behaviors panel, the Data tab of the Insert bar, or the Insert ➤ Data Objects submenu). In the Repeat Region dialog box, select Show All Records.

9. Once the Repeat Region server behavior has been applied, you can get rid of the unwanted HTML. Select everything from the opening tag of the DOCTYPE declaration to the opening PHP tag at the start of the repeat region that you have just created, as shown in the following screenshot:

10. Delete the selected code, and replace it with the opening tag of the XML root node like this:

```
$totalRows_getPhotos = mysql_num_rows($getPhotos);
?>
<gallery>
<?php do { ?>
```

11. Scroll down and replace the closing </body> and </html> tags with the closing tag of the XML root node (</gallery>).

12. The last change you need to make is to insert headers and the XML declaration to tell Dreamweaver and browsers to treat the output as XML. Without them, they treat it as plain text. The headers go just before the closing PHP tag shown on line 39 of the preceding screenshot, like this:

```
$totalRows_getPhotos = mysql_num_rows($getPhotos);
// Send the headers
header('Content-type: text/xml');
header('Pragma: public');
header('Cache-control: private');
header('Expires: -1');
// Add the XML declaration
echo '<?xml version="1.0" encoding="utf-8"?>';
?>
<gallery>
```

> Forgetting the headers is a common cause of problems when generating XML on the fly. Since you're using a file with a .php extension, the web server doesn't know that it's meant to treat the output as XML without sending the Content-type header. The remaining three headers are optional but are designed to prevent the XML output from being cached. The XML declaration isn't strictly necessary, but it's usual to include it. I have used echo to insert the XML declaration to avoid conflicts with servers that permit the short opening PHP tag (<?).

A

13. Save japan_xml.php, and test the page in a browser. It should look the same as Figure A-1. You can compare your code with japan_xml.php in examples/appendix.

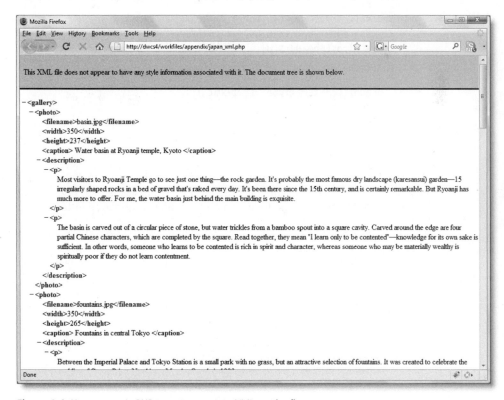

Figure A-1. You can use a PHP page to generate XML on the fly.

Not only is generating XML dynamically like this a lot easier than typing out everything laboriously in an XML document, but it also has the advantage that the XML data source is automatically updated each time you make any changes to the records in the database.

Using a proxy script to fetch a remote feed

Security restrictions in browsers prevent Spry and other Ajax frameworks from accessing an XML source that's hosted on a different domain from the web page. To get around this restriction, you need to use a **proxy script**. This retrieves the data from the remote server and mirrors it locally, making it appear that the data and the web page come from the same domain.

How you do this depends on the configuration of your server. Display the server's configuration details by uploading a page that contains the single command <?php phpinfo(); ?> and then displaying it in a browser. Check the value of allow_url_fopen in the PHP Core section at the top of the page. If it's On, this allows you to open remote files directly, so a few lines of code will do the trick. The following example, which you can find in proxy.php in examples/appendix, acts as a proxy for the friends of ED RSS feed:

```php
<?php
$url = 'http://friendsofed.com/news.php';
// Get remote headers
$headers = get_headers($url);
// Make sure the first header includes 'OK'
if (stripos($headers[0], 'OK')) {
  $remote = file_get_contents($url);
  // Send an XML header and display the feed
  header('Content-Type: text/xml');
  echo $remote;
} else {
  echo "Cannot open remote file at $url";
}?>
```

This script checks that the remote feed is available and stores it in a variable called $remote. The two lines highlighted in bold create an XML header and output the content of $remote. If the feed can't be found, an error message is displayed instead.

If your hosting company doesn't allow you to open remote files directly, it might have provided an alternative through the cURL (Client URL Library) extension. You can tell whether cURL is available by displaying the output of phpinfo(). If you can see a listing similar to the following screenshot, cURL is enabled:

curl	
cURL support	enabled
cURL Information	libcurl/7.16.0 OpenSSL/0.9.8e zlib/1.2.3

The cURL extension lets you communicate with many different types of servers with a large number of protocols. The following script, which is in curl.php in examples/appendix, does the same as proxy.php, using a cURL session to retrieve the friends of ED RSS feed:

```php
<?php
$url = 'http://friendsofed.com/news.php';
// Open the cURL session
if ($session = curl_init($url)) {
  // Block HTTP headers, and get XML only
  curl_setopt($session, CURLOPT_HEADER, false);
  curl_setopt($session, CURLOPT_RETURNTRANSFER, true);
  // Get the remote feed
  $remote = curl_exec($session);
  // Close the cURL session
  curl_close($session);
  // Check that the feed was retrieved successfully
  if ($remote) {
    // Send an XML header and display the feed
    header('Content-Type: text/xml');
    echo $remote;
  } else {
    echo "No content found at $url";
  }
} else {
  echo "Cannot initialize session";
}
?>
```

Again, the content of the feed is stored in a variable called $remote. If the cURL session succeeds, the lines highlighted in bold output an XML header and the content of $remote. For more details about cURL, visit http://docs.php.net/manual/en/ref.curl.php.

In both files, all you need to do to fetch a different feed is replace the value of $url with a different address.

If you're using PHP 5.2 or higher, there's a custom PHP class in my book *PHP Object-Oriented Solutions* (friends of ED, ISBN: 978-1-4302-1011-5) that automatically selects the most efficient method of retrieving a remote file so you don't need to worry about arbitrary changes in your hosting company's security settings.

> *When using a remote XML or RSS feed, remember to check ownership of copyright and any restrictions on reuse of material contained in the feed. Using copyrighted material without permission could land you a hefty legal bill.*

Using a static XML document as a cache

A potential problem with XML generated on the fly from a database or through a proxy script is that slow network connections will slow down the response. Even worse, the dynamic source may be unavailable. So, you might want to consider generating a static XML document and using that instead. This is particularly appropriate if the XML content is unlikely to change very often or if you have a site with very heavy traffic. Instead of putting repeated strain on the database server, for example, the static document acts as a cache, which is faster and more efficient.

The principle behind creating a static document from a dynamic source is very simple: capture the XML output in a PHP variable and use PHP file system functions to write the document to your site or local hard disk. Before you can do this, you need to make sure that the web server has permission to write to the target folder.

Setting permission for PHP to write files

Most hosting companies use Linux servers, which impose strict rules about the ownership of files and directories. Writing a file creates a new version of the file on the server, so the user needs all three privileges—read, write, and execute. However, in most cases, PHP doesn't run in *your* name, but as the web server—usually nobody or apache. Unless your hosting company has configured PHP to run in your own name, you need to give global access (chmod 777) to every directory to which you want to be able to write files. Since 777 is the least secure setting, you need to adopt a cautious approach. Begin by testing the scripts in this section with a setting of 700. If that doesn't work, try 770, and use 777 only as a last resort.

Windows servers use a different system of setting permissions. Consult your hosting company if you have problems writing files.

When testing locally, there are usually no permissions issues on Windows.

However, on Mac OS X, you need to change the permissions of any folder that you want PHP to be able to write to like this:

1. Select the folder in Finder, and press Cmd+I or choose File ➤ Get Info.
2. In the Ownership & Permissions section at the bottom of the Info window, click the triangle alongside Details to reveal the permissions for all users.
3. Change the setting for Others from Read only to Read & Write, and close the Info window. The folder is now writable.

Using PHP to write to a file

Writing to a file with PHP isn't difficult, but it involves three steps, as follows:

1. Create a resource handler to open the file.
2. Write the contents to the file.
3. Close the file.

Each step uses an intuitively named function: fopen(), fwrite(), and fclose(). Unfortunately, fopen() has a bewildering range of options that prepare the file for reading and writing in different ways. If you're interested in the details, study the PHP online manual at http://docs.php.net/manual/en/function.fopen.php or read Chapter 7 of my book *PHP Solutions: Dynamic Web Design Made Easy* (friends of ED, ISBN-13: 978-1-59059-731-6).

The option that I'm going to use overwrites any existing content in the file. This is ideal for creating a static XML document from a dynamic source. All you need to do is run the script each time you update the contents of your database, and the XML document is automatically updated. I have wrapped the script in a custom function, so you can use it in conjunction with any script that you want to write the contents of a variable to an external file.

The function, complete with inline comments, follows (if you installed the snippets extension in Chapter 11, it's in Write to file in the PHP-DWCS4 folder of the Snippets panel):

```php
// function to overwrite content in a file
function writeToFile($content, $targetFile) {
  // open the file ready for writing
  if (!$file = fopen($targetFile, 'w')) {
    echo "Cannot create $targetFile";
    exit;
  }
  // write the content to the file
  if (fwrite($file,$content) === false) {
    echo "Cannot write to $targetFile";
    exit;
  }
  echo "Success: content updated in $targetFile";
  // close the file
  fclose($file);
}
```

The writeToFile() function takes two arguments, as follows:

- The content that you want to write to the file
- The name of the target file

To create an XML document from a remote source, include the writeToFile() definition. Then delete the following lines from proxy.php or curl.php in the previous section (they are highlighted in bold in the full listings):

```php
header('Content-Type: text/xml');
echo $remote;
```

Replace them with a call to the writeToFile() function like this:

```php
$xmlfile = 'foed.xml';
writeToFile($remote, $xmlfile);
```

This creates a file called foed.xml that contains the latest version of the friends of ED RSS feed. If there's any problem with creating the file, an appropriate error message is displayed instead.

To create a static XML document from an XML source generated dynamically using the technique described in the "Converting a recordset to generate XML" section, you need to adapt proxy.php.

The script in proxy.php uses the file_get_contents() function to retrieve the XML from a remote source. If you try to use this on a local file, such as japan_xml.php, instead of the XML, you get the PHP script that generates the XML. So, instead of using the file name, you need to use the full URL so that the file is processed by the web server.

The script looks like this (it's in local_proxy_write.php in examples/appendix):

```php
<?php
$url = 'http://dwcs4/workfiles/appendix/japan_xml.php';
// Get remote headers
$headers = get_headers($url);
// Make sure the first header includes 'OK'
if (stripos($headers[0], 'OK')) {
  $xml = file_get_contents($url);
  // Set the name of the file to write the XML to
  $xmlfile = 'japan_proxy.xml';
  // function to overwrite content in a file
  function writeToFile($content, $targetFile) {
  // open the file ready for writing
  if (!$file = fopen($targetFile, 'w')) {
    echo "Cannot create $targetFile";
    exit;
  }
  // write the content to the file
  if (fwrite($file,$content) === false) {
    echo "Cannot write to $targetFile";
    exit;
  }
  echo "Success: content updated in $targetFile";
  // close the file
  fclose($file);
  }
  // Write to the file
  writeToFile($xml, $xmlfile);
} else {
  echo "Cannot open file at $url";
}
?>
```

This gets the XML generated by japan_xml.php (the file that created XML from a record-set earlier in this appendix) and writes it to a file called japan_proxy.xml. To use this script with another page that generates XML on the fly, just change the values of $url and $xmlfile.

To find the correct value for $url, open in the Document window the page that generates the XML source, and press F12/Opt+F12 to view the XML output in the browser. Select the URL in the browser address bar, and paste it into local_proxy_write.php. This won't work if you have set your Dreamweaver preferences to use a temporary file for Preview in Browser (see Chapter 2 for details of how to change the setting).

> Although I designed the writeToFile() function to write an XML source to file, it is completely generic. It writes any string stored in the first argument to the file named in the second argument.

INDEX

Numbers and symbols

A

XML for Flash
Sas Jacobs

1-59059-543-2 $39.99 [US]

Foundation
Actionscript Animation
Making Things Move!
Keith Peters

1-59059-518-1 $39.99 [US]

Foundation
Flash 8
Sham Bhangal and Kristian Besley

1-59059-542-4 $36.99 [US]

Foundation
ASP.NET 2.0 for Flash
Ryan Moore

1-59059-517-3 $39.99 [US]

Foundation
Flash 8 Video
Tom Green
Jordan Chilcott

1-59059-651-X $44.99 [US]

EXPERIENCE THE
DESIGNER TO DESIGNER™
DIFFERENCE

Foundation
Flash Applications for Mobile Devices
Zhifeng Leggett
Weyers de Boer
Scott Janousek

1-59059-558-0 $49.99 [US]

New Masters of Flash
Volume 3

1-59059-314-6 $59.99 [US]

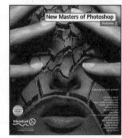
New Masters of Photoshop
Volume 2

1-59059-315-4 $59.99 [US]

Object-Oriented ActionScript for Flash 8
PETER ELST and TODD YARD

1-59059-619-6 $44.99 [US]

Extending Flash MX 2004
Complete Guide and Reference to JavaScript Flash
Keith Peters and Todd Yard

1-59059-304-9 $49.99 [US]

Apache Essentials
Install, Configure, Maintain

1-59059-355-3 $24.99 [US]

Macromedia
Dreamweaver MX 2004
Design, Projects
Rachel Andrew
Craig Grannell
Allan Kent
Christopher Schmitt

1-59059-409-6 $39.99 [US]

TOM GREEN and TIAGO DIAS
From
After Effects to Flash
Poetry in Motion Graphics

1-59059-748-6 $49.99 [US]

AdvancED
ActionScript Components
Mastering the Flash Component Architecture

1-59059-593-9 $49.99 [US]

AdvancED
Flash Interface Design
MICHAEL KEMPER
DAVID SCHULTZ
BRIAN MONNONE

1-59059-555-6 $44.99 [US]

DOM Scripting
Web Design with JavaScript and the Document Object Model

Jeremy Keith

1-59059-533-5 $34.99 [US]

FOREWORD BY MOLLY E. HOLZSCHLAG
Web Accessibility
Web Standards and Regulatory Compliance

1-59059-638-2 $49.99 [US]

HTML Mastery
Semantics, Standards, and Styling

Paul Haine

1-59059-765-6 $34.99 [US]

Blog Design Solutions

1-59059-581-5 $39.99 [US]

CSS Mastery
Advanced Web Standards Solutions

ANDY BUDD
with Cameron Moll & Simon Collison

1-59059-614-5 $34.99 [US]

Flash Application Design Solutions
The Flash Usability Handbook

KA WAI CHEUNG
and CRAIG BRYANT

1-59059-594-7 $39.99 [US]

WEB STANDARDS SOLUTIONS
The Markup and Style Handbook

1-59059-381-2 $34.99 [US]

PODCAST SOLUTIONS
The Complete Guide to Podcasting

BY MICHAEL W GEOGHEGAN
and DAN KLASS

1-59059-554-8 $24.99 [US]

friendsofed.com/forums

Join the friends of ED forums to find out more about our books, discover useful technology tips and tricks, or get a helping hand on a challenging project. *Designer to Designer*™ is what it's all about—our community sharing ideas and inspiring each other. In the friends of ED forums, you'll find a wide range of topics to discuss, so look around, find a forum, and dive right in!

- **Books and Information**

  Chat about friends of ED books, gossip about the community, or even tell us some bad jokes!

- **Flash**

  Discuss design issues, ActionScript, dynamic content, and video and sound.

- **Web Design**

  From front-end frustrations to back-end blight, share your problems and your knowledge here.

- **Site Check**

  Show off your work or get new ideas.

- **Digital Imagery**

  Create eye candy with Photoshop, Fireworks, Illustrator, and FreeHand.

- **ArchivED**

  Browse through an archive of old questions and answers.

HOW TO PARTICIPATE

Go to the friends of ED forums at **www.friendsofed.com/forums**.

Visit **www.friendsofed.com** to get the latest on our books, find out what's going on in the community, and discover some of the slickest sites online today!

friendsof
DESIGNER TO DESIGNER™
an Apress® company